American Students

American Students

A Selected Bibliography on Student Activism and Related Topics

Philip G. Altbach
University of Wisconsin – Madison

David H. Kelly
Indiana University

Introductory Essay by
Philip G. Altbach

Lexington Books
D.C. Heath and Company
Lexington, Massachusetts
Toronto   London

Library of Congress Cataloging in Publication Data

Altbach, Philip G
  American students.

  Published in 1967 under title: A select bibliography on students,
politics, and higher education; and in 1968 under title: Student politics
and higher education in the United States; a select bibliography.
  1. College students—United States—Political activity—Bibliography.
I. Kelly, David H., joint author. II. Title.
Z5814.S86A55   1973   016.3781'98'1   73-7992
ISBN 0-669-85100-0

Published simultaneously in Canada.

Printed in the United States of America.

International Standard Book Number: 0-669-85100-0

Library of Congress Catalog Card Number: 73-7992

Contents

Acknowledgments   xi

Preface   xiii

Student Activism and Academic Research:
Action and Reaction, *Philip G. Altbach*   1

Notes on Research and Sources   2
Theoretical and Comparative Perspectives   8
General Commentary   12
Historical Aspects   13
Sociological and Psychological Variables   15
Research and Commentary on Student Organizations and Movements   23
The New Left: Its Origins, Development, and Decline   38
The Youth Subculture   51
Other Aspects of Student Activism   53
Conclusion   56

Notes   61

The Bibliography   89

Chapter 1
Students and Student Activism   91

A. General Material   91
B. Theoretical Material   96
C. Historical Variables   100
D. Comparative Perspectives   102
E. Sociological and Psychological Aspects of Student Activism   105
    1. *Studies on the meaning of youth in America*   105
    2. *Sociological considerations of student involvement*   108
        a. Institutional correlates of student activism   112
        b. Personal background and values of activists   113
        c. Student leadership   117
    3. *Psychological considerations of student activism*   119
        a. Psychological background of college life and student activism   119
        b. Student attitudes and values: general   123
        c. Student attitudes toward politics   132

      d. Student attitudes toward minority groups, civil rights, and liberties   136
      e. Student attitudes toward war and international affairs   139
      f. Student alienation   141
      g. Generational conflict   143
F. Student Organizations and Movements   148
    1. *Antiwar student activity*   148
    2. *The student power movement*   153
    3. *Conservative student organizations and activities*   164
    4. *The liberal student movement*   166
      a. U.S. National Student Association (USNSA)   166
      b. The Peace Corps and the American student   169
    5. *Student religious organizations and movements*   171
G. Single Campus or Issue Campaigns   174
    1. *The Berkeley Student Revolt: 1964 and its aftermath*   174
    2. *Columbia University crisis: Spring 1968*   183
    3. *Kent State: Spring 1970*   188
    4. *Jackson State: Spring 1970*   189
    5. *Cambodia protest—miscellaneous reactions*   190
    6. *Chicago demonstration: 1968 and aftermath*   190
    7. *San Francisco State College protests*   191
    8. *Cornell University protest*   193
    9. *Activism at the University of Wisconsin*   194
    10. *Protests at Harvard University*   195
    11. *Protests at California colleges other than University of California (Berkeley) and San Francisco State College*   197
    12. *Activism at the University of Chicago*   198
    13. *ROTC*   199
    14. *Civil liberties activism*   200
    15. *Miscellaneous and single campus student activities*   200
H. Radical Student Politics and Youth Activities   203
    1. *Student Left: 1910 to 1920*   203
    2. *Student Left: 1920 to 1930*   204
    3. *Student Left: 1930 to 1940*   205
    4. *Student Left: 1940 to 1950*   209
    5. *Student Left: 1950 to 1960*   210
    6. *Student Left: 1960 to 1970*   211
    7. *Student Left: 1970-*   219
    8. *Students for a Democratic Society (SDS)*   220
    9. *Weatherman*   223
    10. *Ideological aspects of radical student politics*   225
I. Reactions to the Student Revolt of the 1960s   231

1.	*Sympathetic comment and analysis of the New Left*	231
2.	*Comment and analysis of the New Left*	233
3.	*Conservative commentary*	253
4.	*Political reaction and opinion on activism*	257
5.	*Official reports on dissent and activism*	258
6.	*Autobiographical accounts*	260

J. The Counterculture   261
1. *Counterculture–The Beats*   261
2. *Counterculture of the 1960s and 1970s*   262
K. Effects of Activism on and in the University   269
1. *Civil liberties and academic freedom: general*   269
2. *Student rights*   284
3. *Legal aspects of student activism and discipline*   280
4. *The crisis of the American university: pre-1960*   288
5. *The crisis of the American university: 1960-*   289
6. *Faculty and student activism*   295
7. *University reform*   299
8. *Administrative response to activism*   303
9. *Politics of higher education*   305
10. *Police on campus*   306

Chapter 2
Minority Students in American Higher Education   309

A. Black Students in Higher Education   309
1. *Black students: demographic trends*   309
2. *Higher education for black students*   310
3. *Black students: general materials*   313
4. *Historical materials on black students*   316
5. *Psychological study of black students*   317
6. *Black colleges and their students*   319
B. Black Student Activism   322
1. *Civil rights movement: pre-1965*   322
2. *Civil rights movement: post-1965*   329
3. *Mississippi summer project*   332
4. *Black student movements on campus*   333
5. *Black studies*   337
C. Ethnic and Religious Groups in Higher Education   339
1. *Ethnic students: general materials*   339
2. *Jews in higher education*   341
3. *Catholics in higher education*   343
D. Women in American Higher Education   344

1. *Demographic data, personal background, and status of women students* — 344
2. *Philosophy and structure of higher education for women* — 345
3. *Women in college: general material* — 348
   a. Psychological aspects and attitudes of college women — 352
   b. Sexual and personal liberty of college women — 358
   c. Women's movement on campus and women in the student left — 359
4. *Women and graduate schools* — 361
5. *Education and career patterns of college women* — 362

Chapter 3
Students and Student Life in America — 367

A. Who Are the Students? — 367
  1. *Socioeconomic and statistical studies of the general student body* — 367
  2. *The student body at varying types of institutions* — 376
  3. *Student's background and the choice of academic field* — 380
  4. *Why students get into college* — 384
    a. The college admission system — 384
    b. Reform of college admission: the open door — 385
B. Aspects of Student Life: General and Historical — 386
  1. *Before 1900* — 386
  2. *1900 to 1930* — 388
  3. *1930 to 1950* — 30-
  4. *1950 to 1960* — 392
  5. *1960-* — 306
C. The Student and Academic Life — 403
  1. *Relationship to faculty* — 403
    a. The impact of teachers on students and general studies — 403
    b. The teaching aspect — 407
    c. Student evaluation of faculty — 409
    d. Teachers or researchers: the question of faculty role — 410
  2. *Student Achievement: general considerations* — 412
    a. Prediction and quantified correlates of achievement — 417
    b. Achievement in specific fields and junior colleges — 419
    c. Psychological aspects of achievement—motivation and creativity — 422
    d. Sociological aspects of achievement — 423
    e. Underachievement in college — 426
    f. The gifted student — 427
  3. *Adjustment to college and problems of the course through college* — 428

    4. *Educational philosophy and curriculum patterns:*
       relevance and change   432
    5. *The changing classroom and institutional innovation*   435
    6. *Grading*   441
    7. *Student cheating*   442
D. General Social and Psychological Aspects of Student Life   444
    1. *Student subcultures*   444
    2. *The idea of college environment*   447
    3. *The influence of student peer groups*   453
    4. *The residential pattern of students*   457
    5. *Sex on the campus*   460
    6. *Married students*   466
    7. *The study of student attitudes*   468
       a. Student attitudes toward education and educational
          goals   468
       b. Student attitudes toward job orientation   470
       c. Student attitudes toward religion   476
       d. Students' attitudes (miscellaneous)   480
       e. Attitude change in students   482
       f. Persistence of attitudes   490
E. Nonactivist Campus Activities   491
    1. *The role of the fraternity and sorority*   491
    2. *The student press*   495
    3. *Other campus activities*   496
F. The Problems of Students   499
    1. *Drugs on campus*   500
    2. *Dropping out of the university*   504
    3. *Students who change schools*   512
    4. *The role of counseling in higher education*   513
    5. *Student financial problems and employment*   518
    6. *Job market for college graduates*   520
G. Graduate Students: General Material   521
    1. *Students in professional schools*   531
    2. *The graduate student as teacher*   534

Chapter 4
Bibliographies   535

About the Authors   539

Acknowledgments

This volume was made possible by a grant from the National Endowment for the Humanities. Additional support was provided by the Exxon Educational Foundation through a matching grant to the National Endowment for the Humanities. The University of Wisconsin-Madison School of Education also provided some assistance. In particular, the encouragement and help of Mr. Armen Tashdinian of the NEH and Dean Donald McCarty of the University of Wisconsin's School of Education are appreciated.

This bibliography would have been much more difficult to prepare without the cooperation and assistance of researchers in the field. We are particularly indebted to Professors Kenneth Feldman of the State University of New York at Stony Brook, Kenneth Keniston of Yale University, and Seymour Martin Lipset of Harvard. The contributions of Professor Lipset, the United Ministries in Higher Education, and the Hazen Foundation to the publication of the first (1968) edition of the bibliography were also important. Dagmar Schultz was very helpful in the collection of data and Jan Sauer also assisted in the research. Judy Chow supervised the typing of the volume.

To those scholars whose relevant and useful work we have inadvertently left out of this bibliography, we apologize.

Philip G. Altbach
David H. Kelly

Madison, Wisconsin
February, 1973

xi

Preface

This bibliography has a dual focus. While it is primarily concerned with presenting a comprehensive listing of available materials on student activism in American higher education, we have also tried to provide a more selective guide to literature on other aspects of American students such as student attitudes, educational reform, minority group students, and a range of other topics. We have tried to provide a comprehensive and complete bibliography in the area of student political activism—although there is no question that some relevant publications have escaped us. We make no such claim for the material on other aspects of student life. Indeed, in these sections, we have tried to list materials which will have general relevance.

The organization of the bibliography is basically simple, and no attempts to set up complex taxonomic schemes have been made. Listings are arranged in various categories and subcategories which provide a logical framework to the specific bibliographic references. While no comprehensive effort has been made to provide cross-references, especially significant materials which fall into more than one category have been listed in each relevant section of the bibliography. Nevertheless, the reader is urged to scan all relevant subject areas to locate material. The categories are listed in the Table of Contents for easier reference and an attempt has been made to place closely related categories together in the body of the bibliography. Within each section, books are listed first, in alphabetical order, followed by articles. Doctoral dissertations are listed with books.

In an area which is expanding very rapidly, a bibliography such as this one will be dated very quickly. Nevertheless, it is hoped that the reader will find some material of interest, and will be stimulated to search further. This is a selected bibliography. Some published material which was considered of only peripheral interest has been excluded, and books and articles of special importance are starred (*). While this bibliography is not annotated, the reader is referred to the introductory essay, which provides a guide to some of the most useful writings concerning student activism and short descriptions of some of those materials. Unpublished material has been excluded from this bibliography, despite the fact that some of the best work on American students has appeared in mimeographed or privately circulated papers. Material from defunct and extremely ephemeral student journals has, in some cases, also been excluded because it was felt that such material would be unavailable even to the most careful scholar. We have, on the other hand, tried to include material on students from journals which may not normally find their way into academic libraries.

Doctoral theses and dissertations have been included, since such materials are generally available from University Microfilms and other sources. Master's theses and papers have not been included. In sum, we have tried to provide as accurate and complete a guide to the literature on American students as possible, including materials which are likely to be available to the academic community.

The bibliographer's chronic problem of when to stop adding new entries has been solved, as it must be to go to press, arbitrarily. Nothing published after November of 1972 is included here, although we have tried to present as much contemporary material as possible. No cutoff date was applied to older references if they seemed pertinent to contemporary social science, and some listings go back as far as the late nineteenth century. Nevertheless, the great bulk of the included writings were produced within the past fifteen years, indicating the recent growth of the field. Most dramatically, the publications of the 1969–1972 period show particularly impressive growth and, to some extent, an increase in quality. As noted, materials related directly to activism on campus are most adequately covered, due largely to the research experience of the director of the project. Materials in sociology, history, and political science, as well as the writings of activist organizations and leaders, are covered particularly well, while some of the psychological literature, for example, has received less thorough attention.[a] Selected materials concerning general problems of American higher education which reflect on student activism are listed in this bibliography, but no major effort has been made to provide a complete bibliography on aspects of the crisis in American higher education.

This bibliography is a revised version of a publication first issued in 1968 (Philip G. Altbach, *Student Politics and Higher Education in the United States: A Select Bibliography,* [Cambridge, Mass.: Harvard Center for International Affairs, 1968]. This bibliography, which not only updates the 1968 edition but expands substantially on its scope, includes more than 9,000 separate listings. It is therefore clear that the literature related to student activism and to students generally has expanded, and is still in the process of growth. Readers interested in student activism outside the United States are referred to Philip G. Altbach, *A Select Bibliography on Students, Politics, and Higher Education* (revised edition) (Cambridge, Mass.: Harvard Center for International Affairs, 1970).

[a.] Readers concerned with psychological aspects of American students are referred particularly to Theodore Newcomb and Kenneth Feldman, *The Impact of College on Students,* (San Francisco: Jossey-Bass, 1968), 2 volumes.

American Students

American Students

Student Activism and Academic Research:
Action and Reaction [1]

Philip G. Altbach

The 1960s might well be called the era of student revolutions in Western nations. The United States, with only a minor tradition of student activism, joined a host of other nations which have seen disruption of academic institutions and sometimes major political disturbances by university students. While it is by no means clear that student activism and unrest will be a permanent part of the political equation in the United States, there is no question that university students have achieved a position of unparalleled importance in the United States. The attention given to them by the mass media, academic and government officials, and scholars is an indication of this new position of importance.

An analysis of the literature concerning students and student activism can tell us much about the nature of student problems and concerns and also about those who are writing about students and those who are sponsoring research concerning student activism. It is the purpose of this essay to point to some of the directions of research about American students and particularly concerning student activism in recent years and to evaluate some of this research. One cannot separate the research from the researchers, however, and some attention will be given to the nature and sponsorship of research on students. Our concern here is mainly with analysis of activism—the bibliography is most complete on this topic. But the bibliography also highlights relevant research on other aspects of student life—sociological studies relating to student social class, racial minorities in the universities, curriculum reform, and many other topics. Even on the relatively limited topic of student activism it is not possible to provide a complete analysis of the literature. The scope of materials has grown so much in the late sixties that a full discussion of all relevant studies and analyses is an almost impossible task. Thus, this essay deals with broad categories and only with what are considered the most important works in the various topical areas.

Student activism and student life in general have become important issues in American society. Events such as the Berkeley student revolt of 1964—the first of the major uprisings in the United States (and certainly the most analyzed, with more than 200 references listed in this bibliography)—major disruptions at such universities as Harvard, Wisconsin, Chicago, Columbia, and, of course, Kent State and Jackson State, have proved that students have the power to cause significant damage to major institutions of higher learning. Students have also participated in broader political struggles with some effect; student participation in Eugene McCarthy's presidential bid in 1968 helped to force

1

Lyndon Johnson to step down, and students have been key participants in the antiwar movement, from the teach-ins of the mid-sixties to the major public reaction against the Cambodian invasion of 1970.

American students have also become an important element in the population, in part because there are so many of them, and they are crucial to an increasingly technological society. The student population in universities has grown from about 3.5 million in 1960 to about 7 million in 1971. The percentage of the age group attending some form of postsecondary education in the United States has grown to 41 percent. [2] Thus, the university, along with its faculty and students, has moved to the center of society and naturally attracts much public attention, and increasing analysis as well. Society depends on the universities to provide needed research as well as to train highly skilled manpower. It is obvious that serious disruption of the academic system constitutes a threat to society.

Notes on Research and Sources

As noted above, research on student activism is largely a product of the past decade, and has grown particularly since the Berkeley student revolt of 1964. Aside from the fact that American students were not especially prominent in activist movements and proved no threat to either university or society prior to the sixties, there are a number of other, perhaps more general reasons, why student activism has been studied seriously only in recent times;

1. Student movements have been politically important and visible to the broader society for only a relatively short period of time. During the 1930s, when the student movement was very active on many campuses, available research talent was more concerned with the labor movement and the other major social forces at work during the depression.
2. Student movements, often quite transitory in nature, left fewer records than did adult organizations, and student generations change so quickly that detailed research is often a difficult undertaking.
3. The major studies of revolutionary movements and events were often written by individuals sympathetic to the movements from a historical point of view. To stress the role of youth and students, as contrasted with forces such as social classes or religious groups, would seem in a sense to underemphasize the seriousness and significance of social transformations. It would turn them into Children's Crusades.
4. The Marxist theory of social change had a considerable influence on interpretations of revolutions and political movements. From the standard Marxist perspective, intellectuals and students were not independent social forces. Rather they were viewed as vacillating, unreliable, petty bourgeois elements likely to shift with the prevailing ideological winds.

5. The American university, in general, has been only recently subjected to scientific research. Academics have been busy for a number of decades studying other aspects of American society, but their own institutions have been relatively unresearched. This is as true for students as for other elements of the university.

As is clear from the listings in this bibliography, all this is changing. Based largely on the dramatic events in American universities in the past decade, much research and analysis has been undertaken, and funds have become available for this purpose as well.

The most fruitful source for research and information concerning student activism is the periodical literature, particularly in the years before 1960, when books on students were relatively rare. Journals of all kinds have featured articles and reports on student activism, and at least one new journal has been established which focuses entirely on youth and student issues. This journal, *Youth and Society*, published by the Youth Studies Center at the University of Southern California, was founded in 1969 and has featured many articles relating to student activism and student affairs generally. Other professional journals in the field of higher education have also provided detailed coverage of student activism from a variety of perspectives. The *Journal of Higher Education, Liberal Education*, the *Journal of the National Association of Student Personnel Administrators*, the *Journal of the National Association of Women Deans and Counselors* are among those which have traditionally devoted substantial attention to student problems from a range of perspectives. Three new journals, *Change*, the *Chronicle of Higher Education*, and *Higher Education*, also provide useful data and analysis. *Minerva*, the *Comparative Education Review*, and the (London) *Times Higher Education Supplement* provide continuing analyses from a comparative and non-American context.

General education journals also provide continuing analysis of student related issues. This was particularly true during the dramatic period of the late sixties, but to an extent continues in today's less active milieu. Such organs as *School and Society, Sociology of Education, Teachers College Record, Phi Delta Kappan*, and others feature occasional articles concerning college students and activism. While this bibliography provides perhaps the most comprehensive listing of materials concerning students currently available, there are a number of other bibliographical sources also available. Perhaps the best source is *College Student Personnel Abstracts*, a quarterly publication which lists relevant articles and books and provides annotations. An annual bibliography prepared by the American Association for Higher Education is also valuable, as are Lewis Mayhew's annual volumes, *The Literature of Higher Education*. [3] Standard bibliographical sources are also useful, but on a rather selective basis. Such reference tools as *The Reader's Guide to Periodical Literature, Humanities and Social Science Index, Public Affairs Information Index, Education Index, Psychological*

Abstracts, Sociological Abstracts, and other specialized serial listings are also valuable. Such bibliographical sources by no means exhaust the journals which feature commentary and analysis on students, but will provide a valuable source.

The popular press has featured in recent years substantial analysis and commentary, and while the number of articles on the topic appearing in the seventies seems to have declined along with the leveling off of activism on campus, such journals are nevertheless good sources for data. The *New York Times* has provided coverage of most nationally prominent activist movements, although it has been much more thorough in its coverage of demonstrations in New York and Boston than of activism in other parts of the country. Mass circulation magazines such as *Life, Look* and *The Saturday Evening Post* have carried stories on students, usually emphasizing the violent nature of confrontations and other dramatic elements of student activism. [4] Both *Harper's* [5] and *Atlantic* [6] have devoted special issues to student problems and have provided continuing coverage of activism. *Time* [7] and *Newsweek* [8] have also devoted substantial attention to students and youth, and have devoted several cover stories to the topic. Several of the quarterlies have given substantial attention to student activism. *Daedalus* [9] has been particularly concerned with university and student questions in the past few years. *The Public Interest* [10] also devoted a special issue to students and has had a continuing interest, from a generally critical viewpoint, in student activism and university affairs. The liberal weeklies and monthlies—journals such as *The Nation, Saturday Review, New Republic, New Leader, Commentary,* and others—have featured articles with some analytical focus, and have often printed perceptive analyses of student activism. The more radical journals also have devoted substantial attention to student activism, although this has tapered off considerably in the past few years. The perspective of these journals has in general been favorable toward the activist movement, but some, such as *Dissent,* have been quite critical of some elements of the New Left. Among the journals which have devoted attention to student activism in recent years are *The Guardian, New Politics, Dissent, Political Affairs, Partisan Review, Liberation,* and others.

A number of journals have emerged from the student movement and from the university in recent years, and these have been very interested in and concerned with student activism and politics. Being closer to the scene and also more directly involved with activism, they have devoted substantial attention to student politics and have featured many very useful articles. These journals range in political orientation from the conservative *New Individualist Review,* a thoughtful quarterly from Chicago, to the (now defunct) SDS-affiliated periodical, *New Left Notes.* The *Activist* and *Motive* reflect a left-liberal viewpoint generally. *New University Thought,* founded by radical graduate students at the University of Chicago in the early sixties and now defunct, *Studies on the Left,* a Marxist-oriented journal published by graduate students at Wisconsin, and its more recent counterpart, *Socialist Revolution,* are examples of the high-quality discourse taking place among student radicals during the sixties. *Radical America,* one of the few student-edited serious journals still published, is also in this class. *Leviathan* was an effort of SDS students and alumni to move beyond the campus with radical journalism which, after several years of publication in the late sixties, failed. [11] One should not omit the underground press, an extremely powerful force on campus, from this discussion either, since this unprecedented element of journalism had a profound influence on many activists and has featured much discussion of student activism. [12] College student newspapers have also been a source of information concerning activism, and are an invaluable source when considering local campus events. Many student newspapers, particularly on the more active and militant campuses, are liberal or radical in nature and provide a sympathetic perspective on student activism. Without question, the range of student journals, from religiously-oriented publications such as the Methodist *Motive,* and the YMCA's *Intercollegian* (both now defunct), to the conservative Young Americans for Freedom *New Guard* and the various radical journals are a primary and very important source of comment, analysis, and data on students and student activism.

The major academic journals have also featured articles concerning students, and have been particularly concerned with this subject since the mid-sixties. General university-oriented journals such as *Daedalus, Science, The Public Interest,* and *The American Scholar* have become increasingly concerned with educational problems. The more specialized disciplinary journals, particularly in the social sciences, have also been concerned with students and educational problems. Examples are the *American Sociological Review,* the *American Journal of Sociology, Transaction* (Society), *American Behavioral Scientist, Psychology Today, Journal of Social Issues,* [13] *Social Problems,* and others. Most of the articles in these journals have dealt with specific studies based on data collected by individual faculty members.

In addition to journal articles, the number of books on students and student activism has grown dramatically in recent years. Many of the most relevant volumes will be discussed in this essay and are listed in the bibliography, but many recent books deal with student activism in peripheral ways or are related to activism but do not discuss it directly. An example of this type of book is William O'Neill's *Coming Apart,* which features a discussion of the role of student activism in the decade as well as a discussion of other elements of the culture of the sixties. [14] Ronald Berman's *America in the Sixties* provides a similar analysis, but from a more conservative perspective. [15] Thus, the increase in the number of books directly concerning student activism, on higher education generally, and on related topics which discuss students has been impressive, and these books provide a new source of data and analysis. [16]

In addition to the publications and journals cited above, there are several institutes and centers which have been particularly active in research on student activism. As of this writing, some of these are no longer functioning, but they produced a substantial number of studies during their periods of activity. The Institute for the Study of Human Problems at Stanford University, directed by Professor Joseph Katz, has been engaged in psychological research on student activists and more generally on university problems. The Comparative National Development Project, which functioned until 1971, directed by Professor S.M. Lipset at Harvard University, was concerned primarily with student activism overseas, although some work on American students was also produced. [17] Professor Richard Flacks, while he was on the faculty of the University of Chicago, directed a research project on Youth and Social Change, and his studies of the social origins of student protesters have emerged from this project. [18] The Center for Research and Development in Higher Education at the University of California at Berkeley has been engaged in research on broader problems of higher education, including student protest, and the Higher Education Research Group at Educational Testing Service, chaired by Dr. Richard Peterson, has conducted studies of student activism as well. The U.S. National Student Association has long been interested in aspects of student activism and educational reform and its Center for Educational Reform and its publiclation *Ed Centric* have been particularly active in this area. In addition, such organizations as the American Council on Education have sponsored research in areas of student politics. The recently established ERIC Clearinghouse in Higher Education in Washington, D.C. has provided a valuable agency for collecting relevant research studies in all aspects of higher education. Thus, various agencies and research projects have been engaged in continuing research on aspects of student activism. Most of these projects have been funded by government agencies or foundations and many are no longer in existence due in part to the decline in interest in student activism by both funding agencies and the scholarly community.

A final, and quite important, source of both data and interpretation on student activism are the many reports and official documents prepared by government agencies at the state and federal levels and occasionally by private foundations and organizations on this topic. During the late sixties, when the student problem was a matter of major public concern, a number of official investigatory bodies were established to provide guidelines to do something about student activism. The reports issued as a result of these efforts are both valuable research and interpretative tools themselves, and they are also useful guides to the thinking of segments of the establishment at the time. For both the researchers and the interested observer, these reports provide a valuable tool well worth consultation.

The most important single report issued during this period was that of the President's Commission on Campus Unrest, which was appointed in the aftermath of the Kent State violence. This report, the recommendations of which were completely ignored by the Nixon administration, is a particularly useful, generally honest, and dispassionate analysis of the student movement of the sixties and its results. [19] Another federally-sponsored investigation of campus unrest can be found in one of the volumes issued by the Commission on the Causes and Prevention of Violence, originally appointed in the aftermath of President Kennedy's assassination. [20] The section on student activism is a generally accurate compilation of research findings and largely liberal interpretation of the available research. An early report on various aspects of American student life was sponsored by the Hazen Foundation and deals not only with student activism, but with educational reform, *in loco parentis,* and other matters. [21] If major universities had followed some of the Hazen recommendations soon after the report was published, perhaps some of the edge might have been taken off the student unrest of the late sixties. With the financial support of the Ford Foundation and with unofficial backing of the U.S. Department of Health, Education and Welfare, Frank Newman of Stanford University chaired a committee whose report received a good deal of publicity when it was issued in 1971. [22] The Newman report strongly criticized universities for their unwillingness to engage in meaningful reforms on the one hand and for having no guidelines for dealing with student dissent on the other.

A number of agencies concerned with higher education have issued reports dealing with student dissent. The Carnegie Commission on Higher Education's report on dissent in the university has been quite influential although it came too late to have much impact on institutional response to the activism of the New Left. [23] Like most of the other reports, it stresses university reform, sensitivity to the specific demands of students, and a policy of firmness with disruptive activism. The American Council on Education's commission on campus tensions, which was chaired by Sol Linowitz, follows the general guidelines of the reports already mentioned, although in some respects it is a bit more conservative. [24] The National Association of State Universities and Land Grant Colleges also issued a report on campus tensions, as did the American Bar Association. [25] The A.B.A.'s report, not surprisingly, stresses legal questions and considers that the maintenance of order on campus is an important element in the equation. [26] Many states have also issued reports on student activism. One of the best of these was the report issued by the state of New York. [27]

A brief note concerning the funding of research concerning student activism and the general orientation of most researchers in the field is also relevant here, since this field is, by its very nature, highly political and subject to the interpretation of individual scholars and analysts. Most of the funded research studies which have been undertaken concerning student activism have been aimed at understanding a "problem" which had to be dealt with by authorities, whether government or academic. This is particularly true, of course, for the various government commissions, but it is also the case in some of the studies undertaken by universities and education agencies such as the American Council on Education or the Carnegie Commission on Higher Education. While an accurate figure is unavailable concerning the amount of money spent during the 1960s on research on student activism, it is likely that the amount is more than $1 million.

And while it is possible that government agencies or the large private foundations would fund projects which take a critical stance toward the mainstream of American academic life, such situations are generally rare. [28]

The growth in the literature on student activism was due, in large part, to the university crisis of the 1960s, and the fact that both those with responsibility for higher education and some segments of the public at large were very much concerned with the direction of the universities and with student activism. It is very difficult to generalize about the orientation of the writing concerning student activism. Without question, almost all political and academic viewpoints are adequately represented in the literature. The writings of Tom Hayden, Abbie Hoffman, and others reflect the extreme left of the spectrum, while Sidney Hook and others have a conservative view of the situation. The mainstream of writing on this topic is, however, probably in the liberal tradition, reflecting the orientation of American social science and the campus intellectual climate generally. For it has been social scientists who have written most about student activism, and their interpretations have had the widest acceptance in the literature. And within this general ideological framework, it is possible to discern a shift toward a more critical stance as the student movement became more militant and focused some of its attacks on the university itself. Thus, as the academic community was threatened by activism, it became more critical of those involved in the student movement.

It is not the purpose of this discussion to taint one group of analysts of student activism with a particular label or to imply that research funded by foundations or government agencies is necessarily completely biased and therefore useless. It is, however, important to keep in mind the purposes of those writing about student activism and the sources of their funding and data if a useful perspective is to be possible. It is hoped that the reader will keep this critical orientation in mind in any analysis of the literature.

Theoretical and Comparative Perspectives

The United States is by no means the only country to have developed a volatile student movement in recent years. Indeed, American student activism is not among the most important movements in terms of its impact on the university or society or in terms of massive student participation. It is not possible here to provide a complete discussion of the literature on student activism outside the United States, but some discussion of the general comparative literature will provide some useful perspectives for analysts of the American scene. [29] It is generally the case that student movements in advanced industrial societies have not succeeded in directly influencing societal affairs as have student movements in the developing areas. While student movements have been active from time to time in Western Europe, they have not had much impact on the political system. France in 1968 was somewhat an exception in this regard. [30]

Students in developing countries have toppled governments and caused major political unrest and upheaval. They are taken seriously by governments and are often considered important parts of the political system. The prospects for students' achieving such a position in the industrialized countries seems fairly remote, and in recent years, they have been able to achieve a position of any political importance only when other elements of the society have, for various reasons, abdicated their political roles. For example, the existence of the Grand Coalition in West Germany, which combined the two major opposition parties in the late 1960s helped the student movement to gain credibility and importance as an extraparliamentary opposition. Similarly, the unparalleled power of Charles DeGaulle was in part responsible for the success of the May Movement of 1968. And in the United States, it was the student activist movement which articulated opposition to the Vietnam War and succeeded in mobilizing public opinion. Without student participation, it is unlikely that the antiwar movement would have been as effective as it was. Nevertheless, it seems that only under these rather special circumstances are students able to assume a key political role in the advanced nations.

A brief and partial enumeration of some of the reasons why students are such a key element in developing nations will provide some useful contrasts to the United States and explain, in part, the lack of effective student power in America:

1. Students are in many countries considered an incipient élite which, because it will assume the reins of government, is considered to be important and is listened to.
2. Students constitute a tiny proportion of their age cohort, and they are, therefore, more important as individuals to their societies than in countries with very large student populations.
3. Students are often concentrated on a single campus located in the capital city, or in a few universities, and they are, therefore, easier to organize and mobilize for demonstrations and other activities.
4. There are often long traditions of student political activism, in many countries dating from successful student participation in national liberation struggles, and student activism is seen as a legitimate undertaking by both students and the wider society.
5. Students often come from the upper strata of society and are, therefore, often protected from severe punishment by their social class backgrounds and family influence.

These and other factors make it possible for students in many countries to engage in widespread and sometimes successful political action. Many of these variables are not evident in the advanced industrial nations of Europe and North America, therefore making successful student participation in national and international politics more difficult. This is not to say that such participation is impossible, as the events of May 1968 in France indicate.

Despite the massive analytic attention given to student activism in recent years, there is no adequate theoretical framework for the analysis of student activism. A number of writers have posited theories, but none of these are adequate to explain activism in comparative terms, or even in terms of most countries. There is certainly no agreement among scholars working in the area, regardless of political or methodological persuasion, concerning an appropriate framework. Perhaps the most well-known theory of student activism is that posited by Lewis Feuer, in this book *The Conflict of Generations*. [31] Feuer explains all student activism in terms of the conflict of generations and particularly the psychological notion of the animosity between fathers and sons. While Feuer marshalls much evidence, on a rather selective basis, from many societies, his overall analysis is unconvincing. Other writers have also dealt with general theories of student activism, and it is worthwhile for those concerned with American student movements to consult such theoretical writings. Books and articles by Seymour Martin Lipset, [32] Philip G. Altbach, [33] E. Wight Bakke and Mary S. Bakke, [34] Ian Weinberg and Kenneth Walker, [35] Edward Shils, [36] Frank Pinner, [37] and others deal with generalizations and hypotheses concerning student activism in various historical and geographical situations. Christian Bay and John and Martha Rowntree present some interesting hypotheses which are useful in analysing the American scene. [38, 39]

Social scientists have generalized about youth and students in various contexts, and these analyses are also useful in trying to understand American student activism. The writings of S.N. Eisenstadt, [40] Karl Mannheim, [41] and Erik Erikson [42] are particularly important in this regard. Anthropologists George Pettitt and Margaret Mead have also written perceptively about youth and students. [43, 44]

A number of writers provide insights into the theoretical basis of student activism while concentrating primarily on American students. Among the most useful of these writers are Kenneth Keniston, [45] William McIntyre, [46] Michael Miles, [47] S.M. Lipset, [48] and Richard Flacks. [49]

As has been noted, there is a large literature concerning student activism outside the United States. These works will be of use primarily as comparative views for the study of American student activism. Donald Emmerson's edited volume deals with a number of developing countries, [50] and S.M. Lipset's *Student Politics* provides analysis of both advanced and developing areas, [51] as does S.M. Lipset and P.G. Altbach's edited book, *Students in Revolt*. [52] Alexander Cockburn and Robin Blackburn's collection of essays provides a fairly radical perspective on student activism. [53] Julian Nagel's edited volume provides a British perspective on international student activism, [54] and Stephen Spender provides a sympathetic yet analytic discussion of student activism, focusing on Europe and the United States. [55] Countries such as France have received a great deal of analysis from commentators while others, including most of the developing world, have not.

While it is still impossible to draw a clear set of hypotheses concerning comparative student activism, a number of questions are raised in many studies which make it possible to discern some of the major concerns and questions raised by the literature:

1. What are the campus conditions which tend to involve students in various countries in political activity?
2. What are the historical circumstances under which students are likely to be politically involved?
3. Who are the activists? What are their social class background, fields of academic concentration, vocational interest, political ideologies, etc.?
4. What have the responses to student activism been in differing circumstances, and what have the results of activism been in different countries?

Researchers have not in general dealt with a fifth point which seems to this observer to be an important one:

5. What are the political and educational programs of activist movements and organizations? What implications do these programs have for the university and for society generally?

It has not been possible here to delineate all of the perspectives and theoretical and comparative concerns of those concerned with the study of student activism, but a number of key issues have been indicated here. It is clear that much work has to be done if there is to be adequate theoretical understanding of student activism. The task, indeed, may be impossible, and researchers may have to limit themselves to analyzing particular countries or even particular periods in the development of student activism. It is also clear that the phenomenon is not an isolated one, but is directly related to other aspects of society and to developments in the university. A comparative analysis makes this point particularly clear, since it is often possible to explain student activism in different contexts by a careful analysis of the extra-university issues in that particular society. And while the researcher must be aware of variables, it is also important to examine the programs and policies of the activist movement as well. If this bibliography makes it easier to deal with the many variables in a constructive manner, then it will have more than succeeded in its purpose.

General Commentary

In this section, and in more specific ways in the following sections, some of the key literature on aspects of student activism will be discussed. The main purpose of this discussion is to point to some of the most salient studies and analyses available and to place this literature in some coherent context. It is not possible to present a complete analysis of the literature here, and there are wide gaps in the coverage provided in this essay. There is hardly a commentator on the American social scene who has not written on student activism, nor a major American magazine which has not published a special issue on students. One of the first major commentators to deal seriously with American students was David Riesman, who has written a number of articles analyzing student activism from a generally sympathetic and always stimulating viewpoint. [56] Seymour Martin Lipset and Philip G. Altbach attempted to place research on student activism in a coherent framework several years ago, and although this analysis is now somewhat out of date, it remains useful. [57] S.M. Lipset's *Rebellion in the University* presents one of the most comprehensive accounts of student activism in the United States, [58] dealing with historical aspects as well as current sociological surveys and studies.

A number of the anthologies of essays on students and what is called the university crisis present reasonably coherent analyses of the state of student activism and higher education. Julian Foster and Durward Long's edited volume *Protest! Student Activism in America* provides both a survey of current analysis and some useful case studies as well. [59] Immanuel Wallerstein and Paul Starr's two-volume *University Crisis Reader* is probably the best single collection dealing with all of the ramifications of the events of the sixties, from student activism to other academic issues. [60] Among the other useful anthologies are those edited by Philip G. Altbach and Robert S. Laufer, [61] Howard Becker, [62] Edward Sampson and Harold Korn, [63] James McEvoy and Abraham Miller, [64] and Christopher Katope and Paul Zolbrod. [65] Irving Howe, and Daniel Bell and Irving Kristol have edited anthologies which take a somewhat more critical view of the New Left than the books cited above. [66, 67] John and Susan Erlich have edited a collection which is quite favorable to the New Left and includes selections from the more radical writings on student activism. [68]

Several individually authored volumes provide useful overviews of American student activism. Nathan Glazer writes from a fairly critical stance, but as a moderate radical. [69] Michael Miles, a supporter of the activist movement, attempts to place it in the context of American society in the sixties. [70] Gil Green writes from the perspective of the American Communist Party, [71] and Sidney Hook, as a conservative. [72] Kenneth Keniston, one of the most influential writers on the topic, has collected some of his writings on students in an excellent discussion of many of the aspects of the crisis of the sixties. [73] These are but a few of the many volumes written in recent years in efforts to explain what proved a particularly complicated and surprising series of events on the American campus. It is perhaps significant that the student revolt of the sixties was as perplexing to radical analysts as to more conservative critics.

A number of studies of the nature and scope of student activism in the sixties have been undertaken. E.G. Williamson and John Cowan provide data on the political climate on American university campuses based on a servey of university administrators. [74] Richard Peterson uses similar techniques in his excellent analyses of student activism in the United States. [75] The Urban Research Corporation has also prepared several useful surveys of the scope of student protest. [76]

Much of the now quite substantial literature on the university crisis is directly related to student activism, and it is important for the serious analyst of student activism to understand the nature of the changes which have been taking place in American higher education. A classic in this area is Clark Kerr's *The Uses of the University*, [77] a volume which succinctly outlines the development of the postwar university. Harold Taylor's *Students Without Teachers* looks at the university and student activism from a more radical perspective than does Kerr. [78] Eric Ashby and Joseph Ben-David have each written short volumes which deal with the state of American higher education from the perspectives of foreign observers. [79, 80] The edited volume by David Riesman and Verne Stadtman offers specific analyses of seventeen of the nation's most volatile campuses, with emphasis on student activism in many of these analyses. [81] Robert Nisbet offers a stimulating though fairly conservative view of the crisis of the American university and places at least some of the blame for the deterioration of teaching on the immense and largely unplanned stress on research and outside funding. [82] The essays in Carlos Krutybosch and Sheldon Messinger's edited volume also point to many of the changes which have taken place in American higher education. [83] These are but a few of the books and articles which have appeared since the mid-sixties concerning the university crisis and the role of students in this crisis. It is perhaps worth noting that some of the literature which is now appearing takes a rather different tone than materials published as late as 1970, since other elements of crisis made themselves felt in the seventies—such things as severe financial stringencies, falling undergraduate enrollments, and unprecedented difficulties in finding jobs for new Ph.D.'s. What can be called the problem of student activism seems to have abated somewhat, although few observers are willing to predict for how long.

Historical Aspects

The history of American student activism has, in general, been overlooked in recent research, although some historical writing has been done. There is also a small tradition of historical writing concerning student politics and social concern. In addition, there has been some research and substantial commentary concerning the general nature of student life and campus affairs which helps to provide some perspective to the study of student activism. (See section IIIB, 1 to 5). The two most comprehensive discussions of student activism with stress on politics have been done by Philip G. Altbach, [84] who mainly discusses the organizational history of student activism in the United States from 1900 to 1960, and by Seymour Martin Lipset, [85] who deals with the history of student activism in his general discussion of student politics. He places greatest stress on the historical changes in student attitudes over time. As early as 1901, Henry D. Sheldon wrote about student life in America, and discussed the various types of student organization in universities at the time. [86] C.F. Thwing dealt with similar issues in several books. [87] Not very surprisingly, very little of this early research was devoted to political activism, which was very limited at the time. Early writings concerning American students were, by and large, limited to descriptive considerations of student life, and there was little empirical research concerning political activities or any aspects of student attitudes. Student political activism was sporadic before 1910 and it was difficult for scholars to devote much attention to this aspect of student life in the absence of any organizations. In addition, few felt that student activism was an important research topic. Student religious movements were important in the 1880–1940 period, and they received some attention, most notably from Clarence Shedd. [88]

The first major American radical student organization, the Intercollegiate Socialist Society, which was organized in 1905 and maintained itself, under various names, for four decades, has received little attention from historians. [89] The ISS journal, the *Intercollegiate Socialist,* is also a valuable source of organizational history. The thirties saw the rise of the first mass student movement in American history, and this period has received some analytic attention. Hal Draper's memoir of his participation in the politics of the period is particularly valuable, [90] as is George Rawick's Ph.D. dissertation. [91] James Wechsler, another alumnus of the period, has written a contemporary account. [92] Patti Peterson has written about the antiwar movement of the thirties. [93] Chapters in works by Lewis Feuer and by Norman Cantor also provide data and interpretation on the student movement of the thirties. [94, 95] Despite these books, however, it is fair to say that the first major American student movement needs substantially more analysis.

More recent student activism also lacks comprehensive analysis. Portions of the volumes by Philip G. Altbach and by Seymour Martin Lipset deal with the fifties and early sixties, [96, 97] but a comprehensive analysis of student activism in the fifties, in many ways the formative period for the New Left, remains to be done. Andre Schiffrin has written a memoir of this period, [98] and some of the student journals of the early sixties such as *New University Thought* and *Studies on the Left* have relevant commentary. The U.S. National Student Association, one of the most important student groups of that period, has re-

ceived some attention. Martin McLaughlin's doctoral dissertation deals with the
early period of the NSA [99] and the volume by Philip G. Altbach and Norman
Uphoff focuses on some of the NSA's international activities. [100] James
O'Brien makes some reference to the late fifties in his research which, however,
is focused mainly on the New Left. [101] Massimo Teodori's monumental volume
on the development of the New Left also deals in small part with the fifties, but
this period has thus far escaped seriously analytic attention. [102] Discussions
of the state of the campus in the fifties was provided in annual collections of
articles in the *Nation*. [103] The gist of these comments was that the campus
was fairly quiet politically. There has been a good deal more historical analysis
and commentary on the New Left, and this will be discussed later in this essay.

Sociological and Psychological Variables

Sociologists and psychologists have been among the most active observers of
student activism, and a number of publications have appeared analyzing American college students from these perspectives. The available literature ranges from
theoretical discussions of the role of students in society by men such as Bruno
Bettelheim and Lewis Feuer to data-based studies of various kinds. [104] Social
scientists have approached the study of student activism and university students
generally from a wide variety of methodological perspectives. They have also had
a range of political views, which to some extent affect research on students.
Funding agencies often have fairly specific concerns when they provide money
for research projects, and the social scientists who direct such research projects
must naturally take these concerns into account. Psychologists and psychiatrists
are often interested in broader issues of student activism because of their direct
involvement with students through university psychiatric services and counseling
programs. A few sociologists, themselves former activists, have been interested in
aspects of student activism from a sympathetic perspective, while others, perhaps
a larger number, take a more "professional" stance in their work.

It is often impossible to clearly delineate the discipline of a particular work.
Kenneth Keniston, for example, has written perceptively on aspects of student
activism from an essentially psychological perspective, although his observations
have sociological as well as psychological relevance. [105] Keniston's analyses are
based on depth interviews with small numbers of activists and, as a psychologist,
he has delved into some of the motivations of activists as well as commenting on
their political activities. A number of writers have tried to analyze the generation
gap from a range of perspectives since this issue attracted public attention. A
cross-cultural consideration by sociologists, historians, and others can be found
in the *Journal of Contemporary History*. [106] Karl Mannheim and S.N. Eisenstadt provide some of the most useful theoretical understandings of generational
conflict, [107, 108] and writers like Robert S. Laufer, [109] Vern L. Bengtson,

[110] Robert Lifton, [111] and Philip Slater [112] all present cogent analyses of aspects of the conflict of generations. Lewis Feuer presents his own analysis of generational conflict, unconvincing to this writer but nevertheless an important aspect of the literature. [113] William Braden, a journalist, deals with generational conflict in his thoughtful book, *Age of Aquarius,* [114] and Margaret Mead also perceptively discusses the generation gap. [115] Charles Reich, in his much-quoted volume, deals with generational differences, but his analysis has left many commentators unimpressed because of its overall superficiality. [116]

The psychological literature on students and student activism is probably the greatest in extent of any of the social science disciplines largely because psychologists have been using students for studies of attitudes and other variables since at least the 1920s. Much of the early research has little to do with student activism, but it does permit scholars to make some comparative comments concerning changes in student attitudes over time. Philip Jacob gives a good summary of most of the studies of the impact of college which were done before 1958. [117] Much of the more recent literature is of direct interest to an understanding of student activism. Traditional psychological literature on students focuses on questions such as adjustment of students to college, the impact of the college environment, social and academic interaction among students, achievement and motivation, psychological problems of students related to a range of issues such as sex, peer conflicts, and similar topics. Without question, the most thorough recent volume on psychology of college students, with a major focus on the impact of college on the student, is Theodore Newcomb and Kenneth Feldman's 1968 classic. [118] Kenneth Feldman has recently edited a volume which presents a well-rounded psychological perspective on many aspects of student life and of the institutional relations between students and university. [119]

Other writers have also been interested in the psychological issues related to American students. Erik Erikson is particularly valuable in this respect. [120] Samuel Bellman and Kaoru Yamamoto have edited volumes which are useful in any overall consideration of students and politics from the psychological perspective. [121, 122] Some of the articles in Lawrence Dennis and Joseph Kauffman's edited volume also deals with psychological issues. [123] Arthur W. Chickering's well-known volume, *Education and Identity,* provides a general consideration of the psychological aspects of student life. [124] Michael Wertheimer has also edited a volume which deals with general aspects of student psychological problems, with a stress on issues related to student activism. [125] Most of the general volumes, particularly those which are edited collections, provide a good deal of duplication in their treatment of such issues of student stress, alienation, adjustment, and other factors.

There are also a number of more specific psychological studies dealing with particular aspects of student attitudes and activism. Joseph Katz and his colleagues at the Institute for the Study of Human Problems at Stanford University have made major contributions in this area. [126] Graham Blaine and Charles

MacArthur, [127] and Robert Coles, [128] all of Harvard University, have also investigated some of the psychological problems of college students in an age of affluence, with stress on activism.

The most complete psychoanalytic consideration of student activism can be found in Robert Liebert's volume, *Radical and Militant Youth,* a case study of students who participated in the Columbia University demonstration of 1968. [129] Joshua Fishman and Frederic Solomon have done pioneering research on student participation in social action movements from a psychological perspective, and have done research on participants in the civil rights movement. [130] Kenneth Keniston's research also deals with the psychological aspects of student activism. [131] Related literature on other aspects of student activism is quite extensive in the psychological journals. This is particularly true since 1965. Among the more interesting articles are those by Jesse Geller and Gary Howard, [132] D.G. Jensen, et al., [133] and Alice Gold, et al. [134]

Among the most numerous kinds of research studies concerning students are on attitudes. Some of these studies, particularly those conducted in the past few years, relate directly to activism, but most do not and are only of indirect interest to student politics. In addition, studies of student attitudes have a long history, a few dating back to the early years of the twentieth century. Professors have often used students as their subjects in research on attitudes and this is the way in which the literature grew large prior to any interest in activism. There are at least 300 separate references in this bibliography to studies of student attitudes, ranging from research on occupational attitudes of students, to studies of attitudes toward education, politics, and activism. (See section IE3 for materials relating to attitudes.) S.M. Lipset, in his various writings, makes substantial use of student attitude surveys, and his writings are a useful summary of relevant research. [135]

In this discussion, only the most relevant studies relating in some way to activism are discussed; much of the other literature, while quite interesting, is of peripheral interest. One of the best recent studies of student attitudes relating to a wide range of subjects was prepared by the Daniel Yankelovich organization. It is entitled *The Changing Values on Campus.* [136] One of the early volumes dealing with student attitudes was *Student Attitudes* by Daniel Katz and Floyd Allport. [137] In the fifties, the most important volume dealing with student attitudes and values was that of Rose Goldsen et al. [138] The major polling organizations have been particularly concerned with student attitudes on a range of subjects, particularly since 1964. The results of polls by the Louis Harris organization, Roper, and Gallup, among others, can be found in newspapers and journals such as *Time* and *Newsweek.* [139] Charles Havice has collected some of the more relevant recent writings, [140] and Mary Lystad has also collected some useful data. [141] Norman Zinberg, a psychiatrist, has dealt with attitudes toward political commitment. [142] Charles Bolton and Kenneth Kammeyer deal with a range of student attitudes, some of which relate to politics. [143]

Student attitudes toward politics have been discussed by a number of writers. One of the earliest volumes dealing with this topic is by E. Nelson and was published in 1938. [144] A.W. Astin has discussed student attitudes toward campus protest. [145] Victor Gelineau and David Kantor have also discussed student attitudes and protest. [146] A number of student political attitudes have been conducted in the context of the various student crises of recent years. Among the more significant of such studies are those by Henry Finney and by Hanen Selvin and Warren Hagstrom, [147, 148] which deal with the Berkeley crisis of 1964. Robert Somers also deals with Berkeley from a different perspective. [149] Marshall Meyer has written about Harvard students in crisis and Morgan and Judith Lyons have discussed student attitudes during crisis at the University of Wisconsin. [150, 151] Other discussions of student reactions and attitudes toward crisis have also appeared.

The number of articles concerning student political attitudes is quite large, and many of the more general discussions of aspects of activism often deal with attitudes in a substantive manner. Kenneth Keniston's recent bibliography on empirical studies of student activism provides a fairly complete discussion of attitudes studies as well as other empirical materials. [152]

The broader sociological literature concerning students, particularly that written since 1964, provides many insights into activism and many of the studies deal directly with activism and the many variables related to it. Many of the edited collections on students contain the writings of the major sociological commentators on student activism. S.M. Lipset, Richard Flacks, Richard Peterson, Alexander W. Astin, and a few other scholars are cited repeatedly in the literature and their writings are quite influential. S.M. Lipset and P.G. Altbach's article "Student Politics and Higher Education in the United States" summarizes much of the important sociological literature up to 1966. [153] Sociologists have examined such variables as social class and religious backgrounds of activists and nonactivists, differences in academic orientation and performance among activists and nonactivists, aspects of generational conflict, institutional variables regarding student activism and other elements of activism. Some of the most cogent general discussion of student activism and the crisis of the university in general terms has come from sociologists such as David Riesman and Christopher Jencks, [154] Martin Trow, [155] and others. Sociologists, however, have often tended to examine their own variables as if they were the only factors impinging on student activism, and thus fail to present a coherent picture of a particular event or of a general phenomenon.

There are a number of general books that have a major sociological emphasis which deal with student activism. Among the more useful anthologies focusing on sociological variables are those by Philip G. Altbach and Robert S. Laufer, [156] Howard Becker, [157] Shirley and John Clark, [158] Julian Foster and Durward Long, [159] Edward Sampson and Howard Korn, [160] and Thomas J. Cottle. [161] Richard Flacks has written a general volume which focuses on sociological variables, [162] and Kenneth Keniston's recent collection of essays provides both sociological and psychological insights. [163] S.M. Lipset, in his recent volume, also makes use of sociological as well as historical and psychological data in his analyses. [164] Most of this general sociological analysis agrees that student activists tend to come from more affluent segments of the population, that the parents of activists tend themselves to be liberal, that there is not a profound generational conflict involved in the motivations of activists, and that activists tend to be among the better students in terms of academic measurements. Interpretations of the importance of activist movements and of their role on campus differ greatly among sociological analysts, but there does seem to be a general consensus concerning social class, religious, and other variables concerning the activists themselves. Most of the sociological material is based on various kinds of surveys of students, although some analysts use interviews or other means for obtaining data.

To take one issue of concern to sociologists—the family background of activists—one can note a number of relevant studies relating directly to this issue. Research done by Richard Braungart, [165] Riley Dunlap, [166] David Westby and Richard Braungart, [167] and by Richard Flacks, [168] all shed light on family variables. While there are variations in the results and in interpretations given to them, most analysts agree on the general directions which have been outlined above concerning the social class and family situations of most student activists. Some recent data, however, indicate that as the student movement grew, the social class base of the movement broadened somewhat. [169]

Other sociological studies have examined other aspects of student activism. Jan Hajda has dealt with alienation among student intellectuals, [170] an important factor leading to political activism. Kenneth Keniston has also dealt with alienated students in several of his writings. [171] A number of writers have tried to deal with the complicated sociological issue of student subcultures and their impact on activism. [172] Richard Peterson's discussion is one of the most useful in that he delineates a number of kinds of campus subcultures. [173] It is clear that these subcultures help to shape the political and social environment of a campus and are, therefore, of crucial importance in understanding the nature and scope of student activism. Martin Trow has also done some valuable work in defining some aspects of student subcultures. [174] On an international scale, Frank Pinner has noted the differentation between various types of students in the context of Western European higher education. [175]

A number of reports on the scope of student activism have been completed by sociologists and other social scientists in efforts to pinpoint just where student activism occurs and trying to discuss some of the implications of these occurrences. Alexander Astin, [176] Richard Peterson, [177] and the Urban Research Corporation [178] have prepared the most useful of these reports. It is perhaps significant that this kind of research was done in the late sixties, when student activism was at a high level, and it has tapered off in the past few years. These studies generalize about the issues which motivated student dissent and the kinds of institutions which have seen the most disruption and demonstrations.

Sociologists have also been concerned with a range of other issues related to student activism. Helen Astin, for example, has written about the self perceptions of student activists, [179] while Jean Block et al. have written about socialization of student activists. [180] Leonard Baird has summarized some of the literature on the nature of protesting students, [181] and A.W. Astin and A.E. Bayer have written of the kinds of institutions which have activist movements and the institutional consequences of activism. [182] Richard Braungart has combined political science and sociology in his consideration of right- and left-wing students. [183] Braungart has also written analyses of the SDS and YAF, the two most important radical and conservative student groups of the sixties, and has sought to explain their differing bases of support. [184]

The question of generational conflict has been a key concern of many social scientists, and has been considered a key explanatory variable for student activism. The literature on generations extends beyond concern with college and university students. We are concerned here mainly with dealing with students, and with some of the most significant theoretical studies. It is clear that no consensus has been reached among analysts concerning the nature of generational conflict or its role in stimulating student activism. And much of the recent writing on this topic has been speculative. Nevertheless, it is an area of research which clearly has some relevance to a consideration of student activism, and one which has been deemed relevant by researchers in recent years.

Writers like Lewis Feuer have attributed the entire motivation of student activism to generational conflict. [185] Other writers have emphasized the importance of generational differences in the modern student activist movement. And it is true that one of the hallmarks of the New Left is its independence from adult political organizations and parties. There was relatively little support for the activist movement among older radicals and liberals, in contrast to earlier periods of student activism. The generational experiences of the student activist generation, according to some writers, was a key element in their political orientation and attitudes, and this experience was qualitatively different than previous periods. This general notion is developed by such writers as Robert Laufer and Philip Slater. [186, 187] The impact of the Vietnam War on young people, according to some analysts, was very great, and the fact that the war lasted for more than ten years intensified this impact.

Generational conflict also does not directly affect the university situation in all cases, and not all of the literature is directly relevant to higher educational contexts. Yet, the concept of generational conflict is an important one in understanding the nature of the student movement of the sixties, and it has certainly received much attention from commentators. At least some of the commentary dealing with generational conflict comes from analysts of student activism who take a very conservative position on the whole question. Lewis Feuer is perhaps the best known exponent of this position, [188] although psychoanalyst Bruno Bettelheim also stresses generational conflict as an aspect of student revolt in his various writings on the subject. [189] Other writers, including S.M. Lipset and Kenneth Keniston, [190, 191] do not place much stress on generational conflict as an aspect of student activism and, indeed, point out that activists and their parents are rather close in terms of their political orientations and that overt hostility is not generally present in these family situations. Nevertheless, generational questions are a key element of the debate on student activism in the United States.

The literature on generational conflict spans the range of orientations and approaches. Several survey studies of youth and students have been conducted which shed light on this question. A study prepared by Daniel Yankelovich for the Columbia Broadcasting System indicates that there are many differences between the older generation and the present generation of college and university students. [192] A study by M.P. Strommen and his colleagues also sheds light on this issue. [193] G.C. Kinloch has conducted a study on conflicts between college freshmen and their parents, [194] and S.M. Lipset and E. Rabb have analyzed survey data and have concluded that the generation gap is somewhat exaggerated. [195] Samuel Lubell has also analyzed the generation gap in an article in the *Public Interest*. [196] Lubell's data indicate that a major part of the generation gap may be caused by changing occupational structures and the discontinuities engendered by it. Russell Middleton and Snell Putney's early study of generational differences and political beliefs is a pioneering one. [197]

The general analyses of generational problems which have been mentioned earlier in this essay, particularly those of Margaret Mead, [198] George Pettitt, [199] Charles Reich, [200] and a volume edited by Gene Stanford, [201] are all of use in understanding generational differences. Sociologist Bennett Berger deals with generational lengths in his essay. [202] Robert J. Lifton, a psychologist, has commented perceptively on generational problems, [203] and takes the position that new and unprecedented historical experiences have had a profound impact on the current generation of students and youth generally. S.N. Eisenstadt has written generally about generational conflict among students and posits the view that the conflict is related to a more generalized rejection of the values of the dominant (adult) society. [204] Lewis Feuer has provided a more specific exposition of his general theories in an article on Jewish students and generational conflict. [205]

One of the most astute commentators on generational conflict is Vern Bengtson. His survey of the literature on generation problems is an excellent discussion of the available material, and he has also written on generational conflicts among the young with a perspective of a study of elderly people. [206] P. Abrams, in the *Journal of Contemporary History*, has written a very useful general commentary on generational conflict in industrial societies. [207] Ted Goertzel, a sociologist, has criticized some of the prevalent themes on generational conflict in his recent article. [208] J. Adelson's article, [209] along with such commentators as S.M. Lipset, agrees that the generational conflict hypothesis has been exaggerated in much of the literature. Edgar Z. Friedenberg has been a prolific writer on generational questions. [210] His views are in general sympathetic to the radical movement. He has stressed the legitimate causes that young people are upset with the adult society, and traces much of the generational conflict which he sees in society to the social problems which are quite evident and to the alienation of youth with these problems and the unprecedented challenges of a postindustrial society. Robert Laufer's analysis, [211] which is based on interviews of students, follows this general explanatory emphasis, as does Gerald Rosenfeld's case study of Berkeley students during the Free Speech Movement. [212] Paul Lauter and Florence Howe have written a book which deals only in part with generational conflict, but is a most useful overall analysis of the problems of young people in modern society. [213] Their viewpoint is quite sympathetic to young radicals, and nonstudents as well as students are considered.

The literature on generational conflict falls into several general categories. Some writers feel that much of student activism can be explained by the desire of young people, and particularly those young people from relatively privileged families, to revolt against parental authority without much reference to the social or political questions which may be the immediate levers of protest. Others feel that generational revolt is a more generalized alienation of growing numbers of young people from the ethos and policies of the society at large, which may translate as the adult generation. Some analysts feel that the entire question of generational conflict has been greatly exaggerated in the literature on student protest and that the real causes for activism lie in other factors—political, educational, ideological. The empirical base for much of the writing on generational conflict is rather weak, and theorizing on the basis of psychological or psychoanalytic generalization has some problems in terms of its application to the student activists of the sixties. Nevertheless, the generational literature has become an important aspect of commentary on student activism since the early sixties—it was earlier cited only rarely by analysts of student movement—and remains an important theme in the literature. It is clear that if this element of analysis is to be fully useful as an analytic tool, more work will have to be done on the subject.

This discussion of some of the sociological and psychological material relating to student activism is obviously incomplete. This bibliography lists at least 500 books and articles which relate to sociological and psychological variables concerning students, with many of those dealing directly with activism and aspects of student politics. The literature in this area, particularly on the psychological side, is relatively old, although the concern of social scientists with student politics and activism is fairly new. The amount of material of a generally high quality on activist-related topics has grown very impressively in the past five years. This essay has not dealt with doctoral dissertations, which are an important source of sociological data and analysis on student activism. This indicates that there has been much interest among advanced graduate students in activist-related research. Thus, social scientific interest in activism has become an important field of inquiry in recent years. Indeed, the sociology of higher education and of students has become a minor subfield within sociology in recent years. Certainly the attention given to higher education and students in journals such as *Sociology of Education,* as well as in the "mainstream" sociological journals, is an indication of this growing interest and concern. It is likely that research and writing on students particularly will taper off somewhat if the activist thrust on campuses continues at a low level. But concern has shifted somewhat from students to faculty, administrators, and other elements of the academic community and it is likely that social scientists will continue to shed valuable light on the nature and problems of American higher education.

There is relatively little one can say about the direction and ideology of social science research on students, since it spans a range of methodological and political interests. The bulk of the research, particularly the large number of studies related to student attitudes, is based on surveys and questionnaires. The methodological sophistication of analysis of such surveys has increased impressively in recent years, as has the scope of the surveys themselves. The recent student survey conducted by the American Council on Education for the Carnegie Commission on Higher Education and not yet available in published form included a sample of more than 100,000 college and university students. Some writers have tried to apply more theoretical perspectives to their analyses of students, and a few have attempted to set up typologies of student attitudes and other elements of activism. Few of these, however, have been very convincing. The political perspectives of social scientists differ substantially, of course, but most take a liberal view of student involvement in politics. In the early years of the sixties, many social scientists supported student civil rights activity, but as the student movement became more militant and attacked the universities, many faculty analysts became more critical. While most of the research attempts to be objective in nature, the perspective of the researcher cannot but have a role in the results and interpretations of the research. A few social scientists, such as Richard Flacks, have fairly consistently supported the activist movement and some others, such as Daniel Bell and Irving Kristol, have been almost uniformly critical. But most fall somewhere in the middle with a stress on the critical side in the late sixties.

Research and Commentary on Student Organizations and Movements

In this section, a number of the key specific issues and events related to student activism will be discussed, with an effort to provide commentary on some of the key resources in each of these areas. It is not possible to discuss in any detail all relevant aspects of activism—the bibliography is divided into more than 100 categories—but it is our purpose here to deal with some of the more important aspects in which substantial research has been done.

a. The Major Student Movements: Peace, Religious, Civil Rights

Student political activism in the United States has been concerned over the years with a number of broad social concerns. The most notable of these are peace (anitwar) questions, civil rights (race), religious social action, and to a lesser extent, civil liberties. At times, these concerns are articulated in single-issue organizations such as the Student Peace Union. Ad hoc groups formed to conduct a particular demonstration or protest are another means of expressing political concern. Broader organizations dealing with a range of sociopolitical concerns, such as the SDS or the YMCA, have also been common on the campus. This general direction of American student activism is discussed by Philip G. Altbach. [214]

One of the earliest expressions of student social concern came from the religious student organizations, the first of which was the YM-YWCA movement, which became important on campus in the 1890s. There is no good historical account of the social action aspects of student Christian organizations, which extend from the Y movement to the various Protestant (and to a lesser extent the Jewish and Catholic) denominational groups. Clarence Shedd, in his various books, has provided the most adequate discussion available to date, [215] but it is clear that substantially more research is needed on this topic. More recently, articles in *Motive* magazine, a liberal student-edited Methodist publication, and in such journals as the *Intercollegian,* the organ of the National Student Council of YMCAs, have featured analysis of student Christian social action. But, in general, analysis from both historical and social scientific bases on the religious student movement is lacking. One of the few studies of the attitudes of religious attitudes can be found in a recent doctoral dissertation by Douglas Gurak, which analyzes participants in the University Christian Movement, a recently dissolved federation of Protestant campus religious organizations. [216] A radical Catholic perspective on student activism can be found in the volume by Francis Carling. [217]

One of the continuing concerns of student activism, particularly in times of political quiet on campus, has been the issue of civil liberties and academic free-dom. Indeed, it was the civil liberties issue which first aroused student concern after the political quiet of the 1950s. Again, civil liberties has received only very little attention from analysts. One of the few commentaries on this question, written from the perspective of the early sixties at Berkeley, is the volume by

David Horowitz. [218] Several collections of documents also focus on the civil liberties activism which took place in the San Francisco area in 1960–61. [219] General student attitudes toward academic freedom and civil liberties are more adequately discussed in the literature.

The first student organizations to emerge from the apathy of the fifties were peace groups, concerned largely with nuclear testing and related questions concerning the arms race. P.G. Altbach devoted substantial attention to antiwar activism in historical context. [220] James Wechsler, in his volume on the student movement of the thirties, devotes substantial attention to antiwar activism, which was one of the key issues at that time. [221] Patti Peterson also deals with some of the historical elements of student peace activism in America. [222] More recently, the origins of the Student Peace Union are discussed by Alan Brick, [223] and the teach-in movement is analyzed by Louis Menashe and Ronald Radosh. [224] Irving Louis Horowitz provides an overall analysis of the strategy and tactics of the antiwar movement. [225] Relevant documents and position papers from the various student antiwar groups are provided in Massimo Teodori's invaluable collection on the New Left, [226] and in Paul Jacobs and Saul Landau's edited volume on the *New Radicals*. [227] A listing of relevant student peace groups active in 1961 is available in *New University Thought*. [228]

While the student antiwar movement has received some analytic attention, it too has by and large been neglected by researchers. This is particularly dramatic because war-peace issues have been among the most important concerns of the largely middle-class American student community since the 1920s, and were the issues which sparked the massive student activism of the thirties.

The civil rights movement became the most important focus of student activism after the decline of the peace movement around 1963 and succeeded in attracting unprecedented student support (since the 1930s at least), and touched an important element in the society at large. The early sit-in and nonviolent civil rights activities, particularly in the South, brought a sense of national urgency to the issue of race relations and had an impact in terms of national legislation and public opinion. The fact that the early civil rights groups, and most notably the Student Nonviolent Coordinating Committee (SNCC) were unsuccessful in their own terms—racial discrimination did not end in either North or South, and institutional racism in many areas of American life continued despite the student movement—had an important impact on radicalizing the student movement and paved the way for the advent of Black Power as a political ideology. Research on the civil rights movement, too, is limited, although this aspect of student activism has received at least some analytic attention from a variety of viewpoints.

The first major study of the student civil rights movement is Howard Zinn's excellent volume on SNCC, [229] which is basically historical in orientation. Pat Watters deals with a somewhat later period in SNCC's development. [230] Jacob Fishman and Fredric Solomon have dealt perceptively with some of the psychological factors involved in civil rights activity on campus, [231] while John Orbell has dealt with some of the sociological variables in an excellent study of the Southern sit-in students. [232] More recently, the writings of Anthony Orum has written perhaps the best sociological study of black student protest. [233] His volume also covers some historical aspects of the early civil rights and black student movements. Anthony and Amy Orum have focused further sociological attention on the civil rights movement. [234] The Orums found, for example, that poorer black college students participated in civil rights activities as frequently as their wealthier counterparts at black schools. Robert Coles, one of the most perceptive of observers of modern youth, has written about student activists in the South during the early period of the civil rights movement. [235] Coles' comments focus on the experience of protest, personality factors, and the impact of political activism on individuals. More ideological and tactical considerations in the civil rights movement are considered in such publications as the *National Guardian,* the *Activist, New South,* and others. The number of articles dealing with detailed aspects of the civil rights movement on campus is quite large in such publications, since civil rights was a key preoccupation on campus from 1963 until 1966, and strong interest in race relations and in black power has continued to the present. The *Movement,* a West-coast SNCC-oriented newspaper, is a particularly good source. Its pages not only give factual information about civil rights activities, but it chronicles the change in the civil rights movement from a multiracial orientation and an emphasis on integration as a goal to a stress on black power and the move off-campus. Later, the publications of the Black Panther party also reflect currents and trends in the black movement.

The number of articles on the early period of the Student Nonviolent Coordinating Committee is quite large and many provide excellent insights. Anne Braden, [236] a veteran civil rights worker, wrote a useful overview of the movement in the *Monthly Review* and Charles Jones has analyzed SNCC, [237] as has Tom Hayden. [238] These articles approach the movement from a very sympathetic viewpoint. Hayden is particularly interested in pressing the civil rights movement to take up issues of poor people and to deemphasize its campus orientation. Michael Walzer and John Ehle have perceptively described some of the key elements of the Southern civil rights movement on the basis of first-hand observations. [239, 240] E.J. Shoben and Philip Werdell, [241] as well as Staughton Lynd and Roberta Yancy [242] have written of the southern civil rights movement in the mid-sixties as well. Donald Mathews and James Prothro have written an overview of the role of black students in the protest movement in an article which brings together material from a number of sources. [243] Several other contributions to the volume edited by James McEvoy and Abraham Miller provide useful perspectives on the change from integration to Black Power in the civil rights movement. [244] Michael Aiken, N.J. Demerath, and Gerald Marwell provide an analysis of white participants in the southern civil rights movement. [245]

The post-1966 period of the civil rights movement and the growth and development of the black student movement on campus has received less analytic attention and is probably a more complex phenomena than the earlier "integrationist" phase of the movement. Some of the more relevant materials concerning the transformation of the civil rights movement to the black student movement, and the resulting exclusion of white students from the struggle, will be discussed here. In addition, material relating to the growth of black power on campus and to the black studies efforts of the late 1960s will also be presented. (Materials on this topic can be found in Section IIB of the bibliography.) Durward Long has written an analysis of the scope of black protest activities, and his article provides some insights into the nature of black student protest with a stress on the post-1967 period. [246] Perhaps the best short documentation concerning the civil rights and Black Power student movements can be found in Massimo Teodori's volume, [247] Gene Roberts' article on the transition of SNCC into a Black Power organization helps place some of the key issues and events in a useful perspective. [248] Harold Jacobs analyzes some of the ideological questions related to black power and the student movement. [249]

A recent overview of the black student movement can be found in the President's Commission on Campus Unrest. [250] This volume also provides a detailed description and analysis of the tragedy at Jackson State College in 1970. [251] These discussions are, for the most part, fair and balanced and provide the reader with an overview of a complicated topic as well as detailed descriptions of specific incidents. Journals like the *Black Panther* also provide continuing coverage of black student activities from a radical perspective. Several books have been written on specific cases of black student unrest. Probably the best known of these is Harry Edwards' volume, which is written from the perspective of a black activist. [252] Jack Nelson and Jack Bass, two journalists, have written perceptively on another protest situation. [253] Earl Anthony's volume, also written from a black radical perspective, deals with a California black student struggle. [254] Finally, two white professors have edited a volume dealing with Cornell University's black crisis, a situation which caused the resignation of the university's president as well as national attention. [255] The Urban Research Corporation's report on Cornell also sheds light on the dynamic of black student protest and some of its causes. [256]

A large number of journal articles have dealt with incidents of black student protest. A *Newsweek* survey summarized some of the most important protest incidents among black students, [257] and S.F. McDowell et al. have focused on Howard University, probably the most important black university in the country. [258] Most of the available articles cover local incidents and are of only limited value in terms of a broader perspective on the subject.

Some thoughtful analysis has emerged concerning the development of black studies programs at many universities. This development, which was stimulated by the black student movement of the late 1960s, and was clearly a child of the student revolt of the 1960s, has reached major proportions with the establishment of black studies programs at many universities. While the administrative and curricular aspects of the black studies movement is beyond the scope of this essay, it is nevertheless of substantial importance in understanding the recent university crisis and is an important offshoot of student activism. The most useful single volume dealing with many aspects of black studies movement is John Blassingame's edited book. [259] Henry Rosovsky's discussion of the creation of a black studies program at Harvard and John Bunzel's critical analysis of black studies at San Francisco State College present more conservative discussions from the perspectives of white academics. [260, 261] A survey in the *Black Scholar* also provides data on the scope of black student revolt and its impact on black studies programs. [262]

Despite these analyses, it is clear that much research needs to be done on the black studies movement and the black student movement generally. There is, for example, no overall discussion of the historical and ideological background of the black student movement. Part of the problem is that white social scientists have been unable (or perhaps unwilling) to write in detail about the movement, particularly since whites have been excluded from it, and the relatively few black social scientists have often been too busy with their own involvement in the movement to write dispassionately about it.

b. The Women's Movement

It is perhaps significant that our discussion of the black student movement should be followed by a discussion of the women's movement on campus, since this element of student activism is the other major social movement of minorities in American higher education. It is, of course, impossible to deal here with the varied aspects of the women's liberation movement in the United States, and it is clear that the campus women's movement is only a part of the broader movement. Yet, it is fair to say that a significant part of the women's movement started on campus in the sense that it began with women disenchanted with their treatment in the male-dominated New Left. Marge Piercy, and Kathy McAffee and Myrna Wood deal with the relationship of the women's movement and the broader radical movement. [263, 264] Gail P. Kelly has also discussed this question. [265] Edith H. Altbach deals with the relationship of the New Left and the women's movement in several of her writings. [266] While writers differ on the nature of the relationship of the women's movement to the New Left in particular and the campus generally, there is general agreement that the academic world has been an important focus for the women's movement, at least in the late 1960s.

The lack of serious and thorough analysis of the women's movement on campus is surprising, particularly given the growing numbers of recent books concerning women. This dearth of analysis is perhaps due in part to the fact that an independent campus-based women's movement of national scope has not emerged. Most women's activism on campus has been local in nature, and is often linked to other organizations, such as the National Organization for Women. The best overall anthology concerning the women's movement remains Robin Morgan's *Sisterhood is Powerful,* which deals with the campus situation and the ideological aspects of women's liberation to some extent. [267] A more journalistic account can be found in the volume by Judith Hole and Ellen Levine, who devote some attention to the campus and to the women's movement generally, [268]

Particular attention is given to the campus in Janet Lever and Pepper Schwartz's volume, which focuses on women at Yale. [269] Joanne Evans Gardner has written broadly of the campus women's movement, [270] as have Caroline Bird and Kate Millet, [271, 272] both well-known analysts and ideologues of the women's movement. One of the major, and quite recent thrusts, of the women's movement has been legal and other action to achieve equality in higher education at various levels. A recent *U.S. News and World Report* article summarizes some of the efforts in this direction. [273]

Despite this sporadic commentary and analysis, there is no full-scale study of the women's movement focusing on the universities, nor of the impact of the academic context for the growth of women's literation in the 1960s. Clearly, the women's movement is one of the key thrusts of a significant segment of student activism, and has clear implications for all of American higher education. From the viewpoint of both the women's movement itself and from that of the universities which must deal with increasingly militant demands for equity from academic women—both faculty and students—sustained research is called for.

c. Student Power

One of the issues which attracted a great deal of attention among students during the middle and late 1960s can be loosely defined as student power. This set of concerns related to the control by students over various aspects of their institutions and their own lives as students. Part of the thrust was a mostly successful but gradual relaxation of *in loco parentis* requirements at most major universities. Another, somewhat more political thrust was an effort to gain more control by students over curriculum, institutional governance, and related matters. For a short period, student power was a key organizing tool of the SDS, and groups like the National Student Association have taken a consistent interest in this issue. Probably the best collection of relevant materials on student power, from the perspective of advocates, is Edward Schwartz's edited volume. [274] Rick Kean's volume stresses both educational reform and student power, again from a fairly radical perspective. [275] The NSA's journal, *EdCentric* deals systematically with educational reform and student power. [276] Other directly relevant aspects of the student power question deal with the role and function of student governments and the appropriate role of students in the academic governance process. Some of these matters are discussed in the available literature.

The role of student power as a tactic of the activist movement is covered not only in the Schwartz volume, but documents are provided in Massimo Teodori's book, particularly in the section entitled "The Radicalization of the Movement: Student Power." [277] Carl Davidson, one of the key SDS theorists, discusses tactical aspects of the student power question in his chapter in the volume edited by Immanuel Wallerstein and Paul Starr. [278] George Anastaplo discusses some of the philosophic aspects of student power. [279] Another consideration of the role of the New Left in the context of American higher education can be found in Carl Davidson's pamphlet. [280] Davidson emphasizes student power as one of the means of achieving power in at least one area of American society—the university. It is important to emphasize that while student power was an element of New Left tactics for the academic year of 1968, it was soon superceded by other issues, such as the Vietnam War.

The National Student Association has had a long standing concern with student power. Part of this interest was expressed in efforts to strengthen student governments, the NSA main constituency. Eliot Friedson's edited volume deals with the role and tactics of student government. [281] The NSA's *Student Government Bulletin,* published during the 1950s, also focused on these issues. Broader aspects of student participation in academic affairs are found in Harry Lunn's book and in Neal Johnson's edited volume. [282, 283] Both of these individuals were connected with the NSA.

Many academic and other observers of the university scene have written about student power and generally on the role of students in university affairs. Irving Louis Horowitz and William Friedland's volume deals in some detail with student power and the factors which influence student control over institutions of higher education. [284] Harold Hodgkinson's monograph discusses some of the relevant institutional considerations, [285] as does the report of the American Council on Education. [286] Earl McGrath's volume is one of few sources which is based on a research study and which generally supports the concept of student participation in governance. [287] Two articles, by Robert Shaffer and Stanford Cazier, [288, 289] in the volume edited by Julian Foster and Durward Long, provide very useful analyses of student government and student power generally. A symposium in the *American Journal of Comparative Law* considers student power from legal and other perspectives in a useful compilation of articles. [290] J. Jameson and R.M. Hessler present some perspectives on student power, [291] and J.P. Kramer deals with the issue in fairly general consideration. [292]

Writings by students of both liberal and radical persuasions take a fairly militant position on the subject, demanding substantial student participation in university governance and a complete end to any vestiges of *in loco parentis.* Curiously, few American students have looked to Latin American or to European models of student participation in university affairs, or to European student unions for guidance in formulating demands or perspectives. [293] Most nonstudent analysts of student power have been concerned with devising ways of involving students in the mainstream of university governance, but in generally token roles. Most agree that students should have some voice in their academic institutions—a remarkable shift in the past few years—but the consensus among academics is that this voice should be fairly unimportant in terms of the total institution and in many areas it should be advisory only. Some efforts have been made to involve students in the academic committee structure, but by and large these efforts have not been particularly effective. And since the New Left has placed less emphasis on student involvement, administrators and others have been moving more slowly to implement reform proposals. Nevertheless, the area of student power has been widely discussed in the literature and is one of the continuing concerns of at least a part of the politically aware student community.

d. Conservative Student Activism

Right-wing political activism has not been in the forefront of commentary on campus activism in recent years, but it is nevertheless an important aspect of the student movement, and moreover provides a useful comparison with other elements of student activism. The student right reached its height of popularity around 1962, and is not particularly important at the present time. The major organization of the student right, the Young Americans for Freedom (YAF), was founded in 1960 and its journal, *New Guard,* provides coverage of conservative campus activities. Lawrence Schiff has provided the most detailed sociological and psychological insights into the student conservative movement. [294] The Opinion Research Corporation provides some additional research on the nature of campus conservatism. [295] Other reports on the campus conservative movement can be found in *Time,* [296] and in articles by Ron Dorfman, [297] Alan Elms, [298] and Steven V. Roberts. [299] Journals such as the *National Review* cover student conservative movements from a sympathetic viewpoint. Most of the commentary on the conservative movement has been critical, since most commentators of the student scene are liberals. This is particularly true of the social sciences, the source of most commentary on student activism.

Some conservatives have written about the right-wing student movement, and their writings generally provide some useful information. Edward Cain's *They'd Rather Be Right* and M. Stanton Evan's *Revolt on the Campus* provide favorable and perhaps somewhat exaggerated accounts of the accomplishments of the campus conservative movement. [300, 301] More recently Jerome Tuccille has written about the campus movement in a sympathetic vein. [302] Publications issued by the Young Americans for Freedom also provide data on the campus conservative movement.

For the most part, there has been very little objective research concerning student conservatives. One of the few analysts to compare left and right activists is Richard Braungart, whose two articles deal with family backgrounds, attitudes, and other aspects of leaders of both the YAF and the radical SDS. [303] Despite lavish financing and fairly large memberships (YAF has claimed more than 20,000 members, although this figure is probably exaggerated), the campus conservative groups have not make a major impact on student politics in the United States. They were unable to take over the liberal National Student Association, one of their cherished aims, although they did convince many student governments to withdraw from the NSA. And, perhaps most important, they were unable to greatly influence the student culture of the sixties, which was almost totally dominated by liberal and radical currents. The campus conservative movement, despite much money and fairly large numbers of members, has been unable to exert much influence. The overwhelmingly liberal attitudes of college students, according to the opinion polls, mitigates against conservative impact on campus. But even in the fifties, when the numbers of conservatives on campus was greater, articulate conservative student organizations did not emerge. In any case, the campus conservative movement has not been fully examined by social scientists and others, and is certainly a fruitful avenue for research.

e. The U.S. National Student Association and the International Involvement of American Students

One of the largest postwar student organizations concerned with politics and social action is the U.S. National Student Association (NSA), a federation of student governments are several hundred American colleges and universities with some 1,500,000 affiliated members. NSA achieved international fame in 1967 when its previously clandestine links with the Central Intelligence Agency were revealed and it was discovered that a large proportion of the NSA's budget came indirectly from the CIA. [304] The incident aroused a good deal of discussion and debate and almost led to the collapse of the organization. Despite the nature of this incident and the fact that NSA was financed for more than a decade by the CIA (this financing was mainly, although not exclusively devoted to the international aspects of NSA's programs) the NSA was an active force on the campus, and during the "silent fifties" was probably the most important liberal force in the student community. NSA was concerned from an early date with civil liberties on campus, with educational reform, and was one of the first national organizations to become involved in the civil rights movement. Yet, NSA was never a radical organization and always remained firmly within the ranks of the liberal movement. Despite the fact that the NSA was, and remains in 1972, the largest politically-oriented student organization in the United

States, its importance on the campus should not be exaggerated. Most of its affiliated members have little to do with the organization, and it has only a small impact on campus events or on the student movement. It played a very small role in the student movement of the sixties and in the antiwar movement. Its base is local campus student governments, and these agencies themselves are usually removed from the active political culture of the campus.

There is no detailed study of the NSA available, and the need for such a study still exists. Martin McLaughlin has covered the very early period in NSA's history, from 1946 until 1948, in his dissertation. [305] Other historical summaries have been written by Robert Kernish and Peter T. Jones. [306, 307] The Jones study is mainly concerned with the NSA's role in international affairs, but it also deals with domestic matters. Philip G. Altbach and Norman Uphoff focus to some extent on the NSA in their volume on international student politics. [308]

The contemporary NSA has received some attention as well, although relatively little is known about its activities. Eliot Friedson edited a book on student government leaders which has some relevance to the NSA as well. [309] Ralph Keyes has written a general analysis of NSA in the sixties and the problems of basing a major student organization on campus student governments. [310] Lawrence Landry pointed to the role of the NSA in the fifties, [311] while Debbie Meier also deals with this period from a much more critical perspective. [312] Ron Dorfman et al. discussed efforts of conservative student groups to take over the NSA, [313] and Young Americans for Freedom have published a highly critical report on NSA. [314] The literature concerning the NSA is inadequate, and one would hope particularly to have additional data on the political role of the NSA during the fifties, its role in the civil rights movement, and other aspects. The NSA has been a key training ground for more "establishment" student activists of a liberal mold, and many of its alumni have been active, for example, in Eugene McCarthy's and George McGovern's presidential bids and in similar kinds of liberal political efforts. The NSA, it seems, has produced relatively few activists of the militant variety.

f. Campus Case Studies: Berkeley and Others

One of the most active areas for research and writing on student activism since 1964 has been the analysis and description of student unrest on specific campuses around the nation. While most occurences of student activism have received little more than coverage in the local press of the particular area, a few examples of campus activism have received widespread national publicity and also much analytic attention. It is certainly not possible to discuss all of the campuses which have received serious analytic attention—there are probably close to 400 books and articles listed in this bibliography concerning individual campus agitation, not including newspaper coverage. In general, the institutions which have received analytic attention have been those at which activism has been dramatic and sustained, amd also where research-oriented professors have been stimulated to write books and articles.

The first major outbreak of militant student activism on the scale large enough to disrupt academic functions and attract national publicity was the Berkeley student revolt of 1964—perhaps the "classic" example of student militancy. In part because it was first and in part because of the prestige of the Berkeley campus, Berkeley attracted widespread national publicity. It also stimulated researchers and others—at Berkeley and around the nation—to write about the events and their significance. The crisis involved large sections of the Berkeley faculty, who immediately turned to their pens in order to explicate their views. And despite the fact that other incidents of student unrest have occurred since 1964—some with more violence than was seen at Berkeley—the University of California still has the largest number of studies and commentary available concerning its trials and tribulations since 1964. This bibliography lists some 150 books, articles, and doctoral dissertations concerning Berkeley. (See Section IG1).

The first volume to appear concerning the 1964 Berkeley events, a collection of source materials and commentary edited by S.M. Lipset and S.S. Wolin, remains the best collection available. [315] It was soon joined by another anthology edited by Michael Miller and Susan Gilmore, [316] which takes a somewhat more liberal viewpoint than the Lipset-Wolin volume. Hal Draper, [317] an intellectual mentor of the radical movement, wrote a volume about the Berkeley events from a radical pro-student viewpoint. Lewis Feuer, then a Berkeley professor and one of the most conservative commentators on the Berkeley events, has written several accounts and analyses of the events. [318] Without question, the most thorough and analytic account of the 1964 Berkeley crisis was written by Max Heirich, who has brought sociological analysis to bear on most of the aspects of the crisis in a dispassionate way. [319] Heirich's volume will remain the classic study of the event, and is a model for further research. Another excellent study, also prepared originally as a doctoral dissertation, is C. Michael Otten's volume which places the 1964 crisis in the context of student-university relations throughout the University of California's history. [320].

It is not possible to present the range of studies and commentary which has appeared concerning Berkeley. William Watts and David Whittaker have written a number of articles which focus sociological evidence on the Berkeley situation, and these provide a useful perspective for analysis. [321] Joseph Gusfield, [322] John Seeley, [323] and others have attempted to place Berkeley in the context of American higher education. One of the most useful general commentaries on Berkeley is that of Sheldon Wolin and John Schaar. [324] Wolin and Schaar discuss Berkeley in the context of the crisis of American higher education and claim that Berkeley's problems are typical of much of higher education. Terry Lunsford, in his study, discusses some of the research implications of the 1964 Berkeley crisis. [325] Elinor Langer's articles in *Science* over an extended period of time also provide a thoughtful analysis of California's problems. [326] Gerald Rosenfeld has used the Berkeley crisis to discuss the problem of generational revolt. [327]

The various Berkeley crises also produced a number of volumes concerning university reform. Some of these studies deal completely with the University of California, but most are of wider relevance. The most comprehensive is Caleb Foote and Associates' volume on university reform. [328] Joseph Tussman's volume describes an experiment in curricular reform and organization at Berkeley, [329] and Martin Trow deals with some of the educational implications of the Berkeley events. [330] In a sense, Berkeley provided a "model" both for other incidents of student activism and also for research and commentary on particular events on other campuses. There is no doubt that analysts have dealt with numerous aspects of the Berkeley crisis of 1964 and the other later crises which have taken place at Berkeley and which have received national attention. Even today, Berkeley remains almost synonymous with student activism.

Berkeley is by no means the only campus to be affected by student dissent in the United States, and other institutions and situations have received much attention as well, although no single university even approaches the massive amount of published work done about Berkeley. The Columbia University crisis of 1968 received national attention in the mass media and also substantial analytical attention. The most complete volume on the Columbia crisis is that by Jerry Avorn et al. [331] An official report on the events also provides useful information and analysis. [332] A radical perspective is provided in Joanne Grant's edited volume and James Simon Kunen has written a widely cited autobiographical essay concerning his own participation, as an undergraduate student, in the confrontation. [333, 334] Robert Liebert's psychoanalytic analysis of the participants in the confrontation sheds some light on the impact of violent protest on students who are active in these activities. [335] At least one general book dealing with the problems of the American university emerged from the Columbia crisis, that of Immanuel Wallerstein. [336] Wallerstein, a political scientist, writes cogently of the broader implications of events like those at Columbia, and notes the complex relations between students, universities, and government, the impact of the Vietnam War, and other elements of crisis.

A number of insightful articles have also appeared on the Columbia crisis which shed additional light on the events. The interpretation of many of these articles differ substantially, and a small sampling of the more useful contributions are listed here. C. Auger, A.H. Barton, and R. Maurice have written persuasively of the relationship between the crisis and the proposals of the student radicals. [337] A.H. Barton has reported on attitudes of students and others during the crisis, [338] and Dankwart Rustow and others have presented a varied analysis of the crisis. [339] Steve Halliwell, an active radical during the crisis, has presented the SDS position on the crisis in his chapter in Priscilla Long's *New Left* reader. [340] Richard Greenman, [341] a faculty radical at Columbia presents a sympathetic analysis of the crisis.

Other university crises have also been analyzed in some detail. Events at Harvard in 1969 in four particularly useful volumes were published. Lawrence Eichel and his colleagues from the *Harvard Crimson* provide an overall description and analysis of the events from a reasonably objective viewpoint. [342] Steven Kelman provides a more polemical analysis from the viewpoint of a critical socialist-oriented student. [343] Kelman feels that while many of the issues which concerned the students were legitimate, the demonstrations were manipulated by a small group of radicals, who were indirectly helped by the reaction of the university's administrators. Richard Zorza, another Harvard undergraduate, discusses the events of the confrontation from the viewpoint of a generally sympathetic student follower. [344] The Urban Research Corporation has provided an outside evaluation of the Harvard confrontation which is useful as a nonpartisan analysis of the events. [345] S.M. Lipset is currently working on a volume tracing student protest at Harvard during the past three centuries, and will place the dramatic confrontation of 1969 in historical context.

San Francisco State College is one of the few "nonprestigious" schools to receive a substantial amount of analytic attention from commentators. SF State's crisis was a long one, beginning in 1968 and continuing until the installation of S.I. Hayakawa as president in 1970. As the San Francisco situation involved a militant faculty union as well as student activism, and as the school is located in a large urban area and is a commuter school not usually subject to mass protest, it is an interesting case study. The two best interpretative studies of San Francisco State are those and Robert Smith et al. and by Arlene Kaplan Daniels et al. [346, 347] Both volumes are thoughtful and useful in analyzing other campus situations. The Smith book is written from the perspective of liberal administrators caught in the middle of a crisis, while the Daniels volume presents the perspective of the radical faculty members involved in the militant American Federation of Teachers local on the campus. William Orrick, Jr., [348] has provided a reasonably objective description of the crisis, while Dikran Karagueuzian, [349] and William Barlow and Peter Shapiro have written about the crisis from the perspective of actively involved students. [350] Barlow and Shapiro are committed radicals, while Karagueuzian was editor of the student newspaper and a liberal. These two books provide some interesting contrasts. Finally, Leo Litwak and Herbert Wilner, [351] both SF faculty members with strong social consciences, write movingly in an autobiographical style of the reaction of faculty to the crisis. In addition to these volumes, there are a number of articles which deal with the SF State situation from a variety of perspectives. While San Francisco State College has probably received less social science analysis than the other institutions, most of the levels of activists in the crisis have been analyzed by active participants. Administrators, faculty, and students from differing perspectives have all provided their own viewpoints.

One of the most dramatic and tragic incidents of student activism during the sixties was the Kent State crisis, in which five students were killed in the aftermath of the American invasion of Cambodia in 1970. While the total number of analyses of Kent State is much less than for Berkeley or even San Francisco State, a number of useful books and articles have been written. Certainly the most popular account of the crisis is James Michener's book. [352] A number of other analyses, however, provide more accurate if somewhat less exciting material concerning the crisis and its aftermath. Joe Eszterhas and Michael Roberts have written what is probably the best overall analysis of the situation [353] and Ottavio Casale and Louis Paskoff provide relevant documents as well as analysis in their book. [354] The President's Commission on Campus Unrest also has published a thorough and dispassionate report of the events. [355] Finally, I.F. Stone has sifted through documentary materials for his account of the events, which stress the legal materials presented to various tribunals. [356] The events at Jackson State College in Mississippi, which also resulted in death for several students and massive campus violence, have received much less analytic attention. The two main sources of analysis are reports by the President's Commission on Campus Unrest and by the Southern Regional Council. [357, 358] The materials on both Kent and Jackson State emphasize the specific events of the crisis, and there is little analysis of the broader campus or social conditions which led to the crises. Michener in this volume, does try to create a sense of the nature of Kent State University, and points out that it was a far different institution than Berkeley, Harvard, or even San Francisco State College, the kinds of schools which had traditionally seen major student activist movements. Kent State was a relatively low-prestige institution which had seen relatively little unrest and had a student population usually apolitical. It was the combination of a conservative environment with a dramatic upsurge in militancy among students because of the Cambodian invasion that led to the tragedy.

Without doubt, the most dramatic series of student demonstrations in American history resulted from the Cambodia-Kent State events, and many universities were closed down for extended periods and some suffered major property damage. Hundreds of thousands of students were involved in activist demonstrations and many were arrested. Several analyses of these events have appeared. Richard Peterson and John Bilorusky have provided a broad national overview of reaction to the events and a case study of a single campus—the University of California at Berkeley. [359] The Urban Research Corporation also compiled a report of the events which they described as the "first national student strike in US history." [360]

Other schools and incidents of activism have also received serious analytic attention, although not to the extent of the institutions and events described above. Stanford and Cornell are cited in Irving Louis Horowitz and William Friedland's book, which also deals with more general aspects of student activism and university crisis. [361] Cushing Strout and David Grossvogel's edited volume also deals in detail with the Cornell crisis, [362] and a number of articles deal with the 1971 academic freedom situation at Stanford University, [363] in which a professor of English was fired for his political views and activities. The University of Wisconsin at Madison, one of the nation's more active campuses, has received attention in the volume edited by Philip G. Altbach, Robert S. Laufer, and Shiela McVey. [364] Several case studies appear in Julian Foster and Durward Long's volume, [365] and David Riesman and Verne Stadtman's [366] recent volume provides case studies of some seventeen universities and colleges which have been under stress because of student activism and other matters in the past decade. Immanuel Wallerstein and Paul Starr's valuable anthology also has a number of analyses of particular campuses, [367] and includes documents from many universities. Local and national publications, such as *Time, Newsweek,* and to some extent the *New York Times,* provide continuing coverage of campus unrest, and topical higher education periodicals such as *Change* and the *Chronicle of Higher Education* also provide continuing coverage, often in substantial detail.

There is relatively little that can be said about the great number of institutional case studies which are cited here—and the many more which are not cited. Many are of high quality, and for a few institutions, such as Berkeley, Harvard, and Columbia, there is sufficient detailed information and analysis to provide a quite detailed understanding of the crises. With a few exceptions, most of the writing represents the particular viewpoints of participants or direct observers in the events, and therefore dispassionate analysis is relatively rare. Few institutions have been subjected to full-scale analysis of all of the aspects—administrative as well as student—that contributed to the crises and to the unrest. The response of administrators and often of law enforcement officials has a great deal to do with the nature of student activism on a campus, and such elements have, by and large, received less attention than student activists in the case study literature. What is more, most American universities and colleges, even those which have seen student unrest and demonstrations during the sixties, have not been analyzed. The bulk of the writing concerns the prestigious universities and little attention has been given—with the exceptions of Kent State, San Francisco State, and a few others—of institutions with less prestige and national prominence. It is important to understand student activism and the political dynamic at such schools as well as at Berkeley and Harvard.

The New Left: Its Origins, Development, and Decline

Without question, the most important development in student activism in the United States, at least since the 1930s, was the New Left. While the student movement of the sixties, which has loosely been called the New Left because of its contrasting elements from previous radical movements, failed to bring about massive social change in America, it had a profound impact on campus and at least some impact on American society generally. It is not possible here to discuss the major factors contributing to the rise of the student movement in the sixties or the characteristics of the movement, some of the key elements can be mentioned and the main writings discussed. The literature seems to agree on the following generalizations concerning the New Left of the sixties:

1. Without question, the New Left was the most important development on the campus since the student movement of the thirties in terms of numbers of participants, level of organization, and impact on both university and society.

2. The New Left differs from the "Old Left" in a number of ways. It by and large broke its ties to adult political parties and organization, developed to some extent its own ideologies, and no longer depended on the issues which had motivated the small radical movement for several decades. In other words, the New Left had the seeds of an indigenous radical movement with relatively broad support.

3. The New Left was issue-oriented, and its efforts to create a mass ideologically based student movement failed. Its major thrust came from the Vietnam War, although many of its supporters and almost all of its leadership had a deep distrust of the general direction of American society, and of American capitalism.

4. The New Left was perhaps the first student movement in American history which turned on the universities as arenas of attack and criticism. For the first time, student radicals saw the universities as active enemies which had to be fought.

5. The bulk of support for the New Left came from middle-class college and university students, and efforts to expand both the social base of the movement and its scope to nonuniversity settings failed, although at the height of the movement there was growing support from students at nonprestigous schools and from growing numbers of working class students.

6. The most notable success of the New Left was to dramatize the issue of the Vietnam War and to bring it into the consciousness of American public opinion. Students played a role in first raising the war as a political issue, and later in forcing Lyndon Johnson not to run for the presidency, and finally in making the war unpopular among a growing proportion of the population.

7. The complexity of effectively functioning in the American political system, internal ideological splits, a perceived failure to bring about massive social change, and increasingly radical tactics all combined to bring the main thrust of the New Left to an end by late 1970. Indeed, the split in the SDS

in 1969 effectively destroyed the most important single organization of the period, and it was only the spontaneous activism of the Cambodia-Kent State reaction that saw a temporary rebirth of the movement.

These are but a few generalizations which emerge from many of the writings on the New Left. It is clear that the New Left come out of the tradition of radical activism on campus, although it displays important differences as well. It will, inevitably, have an impact on the next phase of activism on American campuses.

There has been much writing about the New Left, by analysts, by friends and enemies of the movement, and by journalists and others. For a short period, the New Left was one of the major issues in the mass media and for a short time was considered as the major problem facing the United States by the American public, according to the Gallup Poll. It is clearly impossible to discuss the mass of material which has been written about the New Left. Several key areas will get most attention here: the writings and programmatic statements of the movement itself, since many analysts have ignored what the movement was saying about itself and to the society at large; analyses of the history and development of the New Left; and relevant commentary and analysis of the New Left by outsiders.

a. The New Left Views Itself

While there is a pronounced lack of consensus about what the New Left means (I have defined it rather broadly as the radical student movement which emerged in the early sixties and which lasted roughly until the Cambodia crisis of 1970), there is a vast bulk of materials seeking to define it and to develop a coherent ideological and tactical position. Much of the discussion of the radical movements occured in the journals of the movement itself. Of particular value in this regard is the SDS's newspaper *New Left Notes,* which appeared fairly regularly from 1966 until 1969, when several different versions of the paper were published by rival groups for a short period. The *National Guardian,* a radical weekly which was "captured" by young New Left journalists in 1968 and later split when an even more radical group sought to change the editorial policy of the paper and ended by starting their own *Liberated Guardian,* also provided both coverage of student activities and featured extended discussions of ideological and tactical concerns. The underground press, particularly during its fairly political period in the late sixties, also provided coverage of New Left activities and debates. None of these sources are cataloged in this essay or in the bibliography which follows, but they are nevertheless key sources for any serious researcher. In addition, pamphlets issued by Students for a Democratic Society, Southern Students Organizing Committee, and other New Left groups, provide a valuable source of analysis and discussion. Such materials are, unfortunately, not readily available.. Finally, student journals such as *Radical America,* which was for a time loosely affiliated to SDS, the *Activist, Leviathan, Socialist Revolution,* and the *Youth Socialist,* the publication of the Trotskyist Young Socialist Alliance, are particularly important sources.

New Left sympathizers have written a number of books seeking to explain the movement and to create a coherent ideological position. Without question, the most comprehensive and useful collection of New Left writings, which includes materials on cultural as well as political topics, is Mitchell Goodman's *The Movement Toward a New America.* [368] An earlier collection which has excerpts from the key SDS ideological position, the Port Huron Statement, is Mitchell Cohen and Dennis Hale's volume. [369] Arthur Lothstein has brought together some of the most coherent writings of New Left theorists, [370] while Priscilla Long has edited a more general reader with a New Left orientation. [371] Carl Oglesby has been one of the most prolific New Left writers, [372] and was a former president of SDS. His article in *Liberation,* and his early volume written with Dennis Schaull provide useful perspectives.

One of the more popular statements of student alienation, which had wide circulation among undergraduates is Jerry Farber's *Student as Nigger,* which summarizes some of the feelings of radical students during the late sixties. [373] A short collection of essays published by the *New Republic* discusses some of the perspectives of some of the early leaders of the New Left, [374] while James O'Brien discusses some of the historical development of the New Left's most insightful historian and coherently discusses both the development of movements and organizations and the ideological and tactical trends which were evident during the period from 1965 to 1969. [375] Tariq Ali's reader provides a link between the American New Left and some of the writings from European student movements, [376] and Paul Breines has edited a volume on the thought of Herbert Marcuse, [377] one of the New Left's most influential mentors. While Marcuse's writings have all been significant for New Left leaders (it is likely that the rank and file absorbed Marcuse through the writings of more popular figures), his books *Eros and Civilization, One Dimensional Man,* and his essay "Repressive Tolerance" have been particularly influential. [378]

Other anthologies of New Left writings have also appeared, and these are of some use in obtaining an overview of ideological currents. William Slate has edited a modest volume, [379] and Terrence Cook and P. Morgan's edited volume deals with the concept of "participatory democracy," [380] an ideology which sought to replace the formal organizational forms of the old left with new, more personal, means of decision-making in smaller groups. Participatory democracy did not function very well, and was particularly unworkable when strong ideological differences developed among SDS leaders. [381] Carl Oglesby's reader provides additional ideological perspectives, [382] as does the volume edited by John and Susan Erlich. [383]

A number of writers have also tried to place the New Left in ideological perspective. Greg Calvert and Carol Nieman have written a volume putting forth their own ideological view. [384] Richard Flacks, [385] among others, was responsible for the development of the concept of the "new working class"—an effort to place the student movement in the forefront of social change in America by postulating that the emerging technocratic middle classes were in the vanguard of change. Herbert Gintis has also written on this theme. [386] A selection of New Left writings can be found in M. Teodori's excellent edited volume. [387] Further documentary material can be found in Paul Jacobs and Saul Landau's early volume on the New Left. [388]

While not directly relating to understanding formal ideological patterns of the New Left, several autobiographical volumes have appeared by radical leaders which provide a more qualitative view of some of the motivations for participation in student activism. These volumes are by no means a sample of student opinion, but do reflect the thinking and feeling of some active students. Without question, the best known autobiographical statement concerning the New Left is the book by James Simon Kunen, which was even made into a motion picture. [389] Richard Zorza's account of his experiences during the Harvard confrontation of 1969 is similar to Kunen's volume in that it focuses on a single campus. [390] Paul Cowan's book describes his own political metamorphosis as a student in the mid-sixties and his experiences in the Peace Corps, [391] while Raymond Mungo provides a description of his work with the Liberation News Service, the factional disputes of the radical movement, and his eventual renunciation of politics. [392] Thomas Powers' biographical account of Diana Oughton, [393] a Weatherman activist and terrorist in the late sixties, gives a picture of the most extreme elements of the radical student movement at the time, while Dotson Rader's semi-autobiographical novel describes a somewhat earlier period in the student movement. [394] Donald Reeves, a black activist, describes his experiences as a high school organizer in New York City in the late sixties and the interplay between black power and other elements in the student movement. [395] Clancy Sigal provides some historical perspective in his novel, which focuses partly on student life and politics in the fifties. [396] Finally, Kate Haracz's journal of her experiences as an undergraduate at Michigan State University provides a feeling for the alienation felt by many students in the late sixties. [397]

While these biographical and autobiographical statements provide few common themes and yield few generalizations, they are examples of the thinking of some of the more articulate activists and concerned students of the period. Almost without exception, these volumes reflect a profound dissatisfaction with many of the basic tenets of modern American society. And the materials which were written in the late sixties reflect this disillusionment and disgust more dramatically than earlier materials. The students writing these statements differ in their political orientations, class backgrounds, and approaches to their topics. Some, such as Raymond Mungo, took the hippie route of withdrawal from politics altogether, while others, such as Diana Oughton, became terrorists. Paul

Cowen, in one of the most thoughtful statements of the group, reflects the growing dissatisfaction and disillusionment of a liberal turned radical in the context of America in the late sixties.

In general, these materials do not present a totally coherent approach to politics or to the student movement. Yet, the programmatic statements and commentaries of the New Left do present an effort to create a new ideological synthesis of the American experience. Without question, this effort was not entirely successful, and at least part of the reason for the decline of the New Left as an organized political movement is that there was no community of beliefs concerning ideology and tactics. The documents do reflect an increasing disillusionment with American capitalism over time. The relative moderation of the Port Huron Statement is contrasted dramatically with some of the articles in *Leviathan* or of the Weathermen. [398] Growing tactical radicalization became obvious when the student movement failed by more moderate means to have any impact on the Vietnam War and other pressing social issues.

The student movement of the sixties presented, in many ways, a distorted picture of American reality, and failed to create an ideological basis for understanding American society. While attacking the university for its complicity with the American Establishment, the New Left did not present a viable approach to university reform. [399] Its programs, in sum, were by and large negative statements about a society in trouble, but little was offered in the way of a positive program. And even in areas where the New Left made a contribution, such as the development of the theory of "participatory democracy," the practice of these programs was often not particularly successful. On the other hand, the activist movement of the sixties functioned in a particularly difficult period. The stresses of the Vietnam War were particularly great, and much energy was spent on trying to bring the war to an end. And it is certainly true that making major changes in American society is a difficult process even under the best of circumstances. The New Left did make an effort to break from the ideological confines of earlier radical movements, and did succeed in building the most effective student movement in American history. And unlike the student movement of the thirties, the New Left campus movement was wholly independent of adult organizations and parties, and was often built in opposition to older radical groups. Without question, it is important to carefully examine the perspectives and ideological positions of the New Left in any effort to examine and analyze the campus scene during the sixties. And the New Left has provided an ample collection of materials on which to base such an analysis.

b. The History and Development of the New Left

In this section, some of the major analytic writings concerning the student movement of the sixties are discussed. This section is intended as a guide for understanding the nature and development of the movement, and commentaries concerning campus activism will be presented in the following section. The history of the student movement of the sixties still remains to be written in a clear and thorough manner. Yet, there is no question but that this period in the development of American student activism has received more attention from scholars, participants, and others than any other period and thus it is possible to obtain a fairly thorough understanding of the campus during the sixties. Many of the writings cited in previous sections will be useful in this section as well.

As has been noted, some of the best sources for the continuing development of the New Left and its various organizations are radical journals, particularly those published by the student movement. *New Left Notes,* the SDS periodical, provides continuing coverage of SDS and other New Left activity. The *Young Socialist* has coverage of the growth and development of the Young Socialist Alliance, and magazines like *New Politics,* the *Independent Socialist, Leviathan,* and others provide both news and commentary on organizations and ideological currents. The most careful historian of the New Left is James O'Brien, [400] who is currently completing his book on this subject. Earlier periods of New Left history are covered in the volumes by S.M. Lipset and by Philip G. Altbach. [401, 402] Alan Adelson has written a volume specifically on the Students for a Democratic Society, [403] which provides both a historical account and commentary on its later development. This volume is particularly useful for its discussion of the later, more factionalized period of SDS' history. Jack Newfield's sympathetic account deals with the pre-1966 period of the New Left and is quite valuable. [404] Richard Peterson's booklet deals with the scope of radical student activism and is useful in providing information concerning the nature of protests. [405] Massimo Teodori's edited volume is a key resource for the early history of the SDS and other New Left movements, [406] and provides a coherent documentary analysis of the various currents in the radical student movement. Paul Jacobs and Saul Landau, provide both commentary and documentary sources on the early period of the New Left. [407]

In addition to these volumes, a large number of articles are relevant to an understanding of the history and development of the New Left. Alexander W. Astin's analysis of the scope of student protest supplements Richard Peterson's research on this topic. [408] Carl Davidson's article deals with campus organizing during the 1968 period of SDS's campus emphasis. [409] Penina Glazer has written perceptively of the "style of protest" and politics of the New Left, [410] and Stoughton Lynd has dealt with both historical developments and ideological matters. [411]

The Students for a Democratic Society (SDS) was the major New Left organization to emerge in the sixties and, because of this fact, became a focus for much of the analysis given to the movement as a whole. The SDS was, as is clear from this essay, only a part of the total movement and to a substantial extent it did not provide coherent leadership to the campus movement although it did succeed on a number of occasions in coordinating campus political sentiment. Nevertheless, it is a symbol of the student movement of the sixties, and in reality reflected many of the currents going on among radical students at the time. The SDS is a difficult organization to analyze, since its central leadership for much of the sixties was not very strong and its own image was one of a coordinating agency rather than a provider of clear ideological and tactical direction. During its later period, many splits and ideological disputes within the organization weakened it as a campus-based movement and also present problems in analyzing it.

The writings of James O'Brien and Alan Adelson provide the most adequate description and analysis of the SDS over time currently available. [412, 413] A number of documents prepared by the Senate Internal Security Committee and the House Committee on Internal Security and published by the Government Printing Office provide commentary on various aspects of the SDS and other elements of the New Left. [414] While this material provides some useful facts concerning particular aspects of student activism, the analysis is very biased and some of the reporting inaccurate, uninformed, or simply malicious. Material from right-wing propaganda sources as well as more accurate reports are indiscriminately used. The investigative reports on the SDS do provide some analysis of the activities of the SDS on various campuses, and as such constitute useful information. Early SDS activities were covered in detail, and generally quite favorably in the liberal journals. Articles by Richard Blumenthal and James Jacobs in the *Nation* are typical of such reporting. [415, 416] Several articles in *Liberation* provide a deeper description and analysis of SDS activities and ideologies. In this regard, articles by Norm Fruchter and Richard Rothstein are particularly valuable. [417, 418] Both articles deal with the internal conflicts and ideological concerns of the organization in its later period.

Richard Rothstein has written of one of the early thrusts of SDS, its efforts to organize within working-class and other communities, in his *Radical America* article. [419] Peter Wiley also comments on this aspect of SDS's development. [420] Tom Hayden, in his various writings, exemplifies some of the thinking of the SDS on various questions, as well as describing some of his own concerns. Hayden's long-term activities in Newark and his involvement in community organizing there are part of this thrust in the SDS. [421] The latter period of SDS history, a period that was marked by increasing radicalization, alienation from the mainstream of American society, and finally factional disputes and splits, is covered most adequately in Harold Jacob's edited volume. [422] Continuing coverage in the pages of *New Left Notes* and other movement journals is also a good source of commentary. A recent collection of the statements of the most radical of the factions, the Weathermen, can be found in their recent publication. [423] Steven Kelman, in several of his articles, describes some of the disputes within the SDS from a critical viewpoint. [424] Perhaps the best readily available collection of documents concerning the factionalization of SDS can be found in I. Wallerstein and P. Starr's edited volumes. [425] James Weinstein, [426] a socialist theoretician, has analyzed the Weatherman and its ideological position in an article in *Socialist Revolution,* and Michael Parker has written on other aspects of SDS ideological strife. [427] Another critical article on SDS politics from a radical perspective is by Paula Reimer. [428] Irving Howe, a socialist commentator on current politics, provides perhaps the most thorough although quite critical examinations of the ideological shifts of the SDS. [429]

The basis for a reasonably complete understanding of the major organization of the New Left, the SDS is available in the publications listed in this section, and in newspaper and radical journal sources. Clearly, there is a need to collate this material into a full analysis of one of the most important student organizations in the history of the American student movement. Other elements of the student movement of the sixties are less well understood. The causes for the growth and analysis of the role of groups like the Young Socialist Alliance, the International Socialists, and other ideologically sophisticated and active campus organizations need to be undertaken. The Black Power period of the civil rights movement and the broader black student movement has received only slight attention from analysts, and detailed analysis of the antiwar movement still needs to be done. The problem with much of the activist movement of the sixties is that it was on an ad hoc and relatively unorganized basis, and few continuing or regional student groups developed which are convenient to follow. The reason for the focus on the SDS in the mass media during the sixties is in part due to the fact that there were few identifiable leaders of the student movement. This fact alone is important in understanding the dynamic of the movement and its tactical and ideological thrusts.

c. Commentary and Analysis on the New Left

The amount of commentary on the New Left, from every conceivable viewpoint, is impressive. For a short period during 1968–1970, when the New Left was one of the most controversial issues in American society, there was a large market for books, journal articles, television specials, and other discussion of the New Left. Much of the commentary is of little use in gaining a broader perspective and much is of a purely topical nature. Yet, some of the volumes of material will be of lasting interest to those concerned with understanding the New Left particularly and student activism in America generally. In this section, a small portion of the most valuable commentary and analysis on the student movement of the sixties will be briefly discussed. The perspectives represented in these materials vary from extreme conservative to radical, but most of the more enlightened analysis comes from those with a liberal or moderately radical viewpoint. The conservatives tend to impose generalizations of "Communist con-

spiracies" on their analyses of the student movement, which clearly are not valid during this period, while the more militant activists, with a few exceptions, wrote little and much of their work is more of a propagandistic than analytic nature.

There are a number of key volumes which provide a wide range of commentary and analysis on student unrest. Nathan Glazer's book is quite critical of many of the trends of the student movement of the sixties, [430] but is written from a left-liberal perspective and is generally thoughtful. Alexander Klein, [431] in his edited volume, includes short articles from a wide range of viewpoints on all aspects of the student revolt and is useful as a sourcebook of opinions of such noted commentators as Spiro Agnew and Susan Sontag. George Thayer has several chapters on student activism and the New Left is his liberally-oriented book, [432] and Kenneth and Patricia Dolbeare include a chapter on the New Left in their volume on American ideologies. [433] Some of the more perceptive general volumes on student activism include some of the best commentaries on the student movement of the sixties, and these constitute key sources. On the conservative side, Lewis Feuer's volume is a useful statement of one viewpoint, [434] while Michael Miles makes a convincing case based on more radical views. [435] S.M. Lipset, [436] in his various writings, provides a critical but thoughtful analysis of the New Left and the student movement, often in comparative perspective. Kenneth Keniston's generally favorable views toward student activism are best expounded in his recent volume of collected essays. [437] He includes articles of general analysis as well as psychologically-oriented materials.

A number of analyses have appeared which have a very sympathetic view toward the New Left, most of which are written by radicals. The exact perspective of these materials differs, of course, and some radical analysts became less sympathetic toward the movement as it entered its more adventuristic phase. Todd Gitlin, [438] an early SDS officer and radical analyst, wrote an early evaluation of the New Left in his short pamphlet. Mitchell Goodman's classic book of readings on the radical culture of the sixties has a number of commentaries on student activism, [439] all from a sympathetic viewpoint. Priscilla Long's edited volume also includes a number of thoughtful essays, all from a New Left perspective. [440] Charles Reich, in his well-known volume, analyzes the student movement of the sixties in the context of American society. [441]

A number of fairly early analyses deal with student activism in the early sixties and seek to analyze trends occuring at the time. Paul Booth and Lee Webb, both SDS activists, have dealt with some of the ideological questions facing the student movement, pointing out the necessity for the student protest movement to develop a coherent ideological perspective. [442] This theme was an often repeated one among ideologically concerned activists in the mid-sixties, when the SDS and other New Left groups were trying to shift from a campus-orientation based on ad hoc protest to a wider movement with a coherent perspective on social change and politics.

Hal Draper wrote a favorable analysis of student activism in order to counter some of the criticisms from liberal commentators, [443] and Ronald Aronson analyzed some of the criticisms of the New Left from a pro-radical viewpoint. [444] These articles are characterized by their faith that the New Left was in the process of developing a new ideological synthesis and was, for a number of reasons, worthy of radical support. Daniel Aaron brought together a number of generally radical views in his symposium on the New Left. [445] More recently, Norman Birnbaum and Marjorie Childers have written a coherent and thoughtful account of the New Left in their essay in Julian Nagel's *Student Power*. [446] Richard Flacks' *Playboy* interview covered many aspects of New Left politics, as have his other articles. Flacks is, without question, one of the most thoughtful analysts of the New Left and has fairly consistently taken a favorable view. [447] Perhaps significantly, Flacks has been least sympathetic with the more "adventuristic" current of the New Left of the late sixties. Flacks, and others such as Barbara and Al Haber, [448] and Staughton Lynd, [449] sought to create an organization for alumni of the student movement. For a while, the focus of these efforts was around the Movement for a Democratic Society and the New University Conference. Publications such as the NUC's newsletter and the *Radicals in the Professions Newsletter* tried to coordinate national efforts. The NUC formally disbanded in 1972 and the MDS had been dissolved previously. These efforts were based on the notion of the "new working class" and the concept that professionals were the most likely group in the society to become involved in radical political action. Neither the NUC, which during its heyday in 1968–1969 had several thousand members and very active campus groups, some of which were important elements of the New Left in their areas, on more than a score of campuses, nor the other efforts to organize post-campus radicals have received any serious attention.

Herbert Gans, [450] a sympathetic sociologist, wrote of the possible sectarianism in the student movement in 1965, but still maintained a favorable view. Julius Jacobson and Jack Newfield, [451, 452] both nonstudent radical commentators, have written generally sympathetic defenses of the New Left aimed against liberal critics of the student movement.

Radical commentaries on the New Left have little in common except perhaps for a polemical desire to refute the arguments of liberals and others who have been critical of the movement. There is no discernible line of argument which recurs in this literature, except perhaps for the view that it is important for the radical movement to establish new roots and ideologies, and that the New Left is at least trying to achieve this goal and is worthy of support. These commentators also agree that since the New Left is the only viable social movement flourishing in the United States (in the late sixties), it must be supported.

By and large the mainstream of commentary and analysis of the New Left is written from a liberal political viewpoint, although there is some conservative commentary as well. The liberal analysis generally took a favorable stance in the early sixties, but when the SDS split from its adult sponsors, the League for Industrial Democracy, in 1968 and began to turn increasingly toward the left in both ideology and tactics, most of the liberal analysts became more critical. This current can be seen in the writings of Irving Howe, [453] one of the most astute of the liberal commentators on student activism, and in Nathan Glazer's volume. [454] But as with the radical analysts, there is no clear ideological position of stance which characterizes the liberal approach to student activism.

Patrick Gleeson, [455] in his edited book, provides a range of viewpoints analyzing the student movement, while Roger Rapoport and Lawrence Kirshbaum have written a fairly sympathetic book on general aspects of the student movement. [456] The President's Commission on Campus Unrest featured some discussion of the New Left and some of its causes, and treats the subject in a fairly unbiased manner. [457] Paul Hollander's article deals with some of the underlying political questions of the New Left, [458] and argues that the movement has not developed a really coherent ideology. Carl Landauer's analysis of the New Left focuses on criticisms of its failure to examine economic issues, its lack of a coherent ideology, and other matters. [459] Robert A. Nisbet, [460] a sociologist, also offers a critical analysis of the New Left and the student movement generally. James Brann, [461] concentrated on analyzing why large numbers of students become sympathetic with the New Left, and Armand Mauss discusses some of the differences between the old and the new left. [462] A special issue of the *Journal of Social Issues* concentrates in the old left-New Left conflict and contrast. [463] Staughton Lynd's analysis of the New Left was written from the perspective of an "old leftist" in substantial sympathy with the movement. [464] Tom Kahn takes a much more critical stance in his article, and stresses the ideological shortcomings and incipient antidemocratic trends in the New Left. [465] Kahn, a democratic socialist, takes a view which is typical of many democratic socialists. This view is critical of the ideological direction of the New Left, its stress on the developing areas, and its strident anti-American tone. Irving Howe's volume presents a very good example of this current of commentary on the New Left. [466]

Clark Kerr, [467] one of the major commentators on American higher education, has had relatively little to say about student unrest. One of his articles is reprinted in Julian Foster and Durward Long's volume. Kerr's comments are rather general and somewhat critical of the direction of the student movement. Joseph Katz and Nevitt Stanford, [468] both perceptive commentators on students, have discussed their analysis of the causes of student unrest in the *Saturday Review*. James Lynch has also written about the causes of student unrest. [469]

Although the materials cited above are by no means uniformly favorable toward the New Left and student unrest, they are for the most part reasonably dispassionate in their analyses. There is also a body of literature which is quite critical of the student movement and which are written from a conservative political stance. Professor Sidney Hook, the well-known philosopher, has been one of the most consistent and articulate conservative critics of campus unrest. [470] He has been particularly concerned about the "politicization of the campus," a theme which runs through much of the conservative literature on student unrest, and is a major concern of many liberals as well. The best overall conservative treatment of the New Left is a volume edited by William P. Gerberding and Duane Smith. [471] Although some of the critics included in this volume are liberal, most are political conservative, and one of the main themes of the volume is the "protection" of the university from political unrest and destruction by the student left. Robert Brustein, [472] Dean of the Yale Drama School, has written a scathing attack on the student left which stresses the lack of substance in much of what the student left tried to do. The editors of *U.S. News and World Report* prepared a volume which purports to be a report on New Left activities but is mostly a criticism of the student movement. [473] John Coyne, Jr.'s humorous volume entitled *The Kumquat Statement* is an attack on the "romantic" politics of such authors as James Simon Kunen, [474] author of the *Strawberry Statement*. The Free Society Association, [475] a conservative organization, published a report on the student left from a conservative viewpoint. At least two "exposes" of radical student activism have been published. These are by William T. Divale and by Philip Abbott Luce. [476, 477] Both of these books were written from the perspective of young "infiltrators" of the New Left who present a lurid picture of the operation of the student movement. E. Merrill Root wrote a critique of liberal and radical movements on campus in 1955, [478] and William Shinto has brought this critique up to date. [479] The Young Americans for Freedom published a study of campus unrest aimed at refuting some of the liberal assumptions of the President's Commission on Campus Unrest. [480]

A large number of articles have also appeared from a conservative perspective. Student journals such as the Young Americans for Freedom's *New Guard* and the *Intercollegiate Review,* a thoughtful quarterly published by the conservative Intercollegiate Society of Individualists, have given substantial attention to the New Left. General conservative publications such as the *National Review, Modern Age* and others have also devoted attention to the student movement. M. Drachkovitch, [481] a political scientist, has written critically of the New Left. Andrew Greeley, [482] a sociologist, has been a consistent critic of the New Left and the student movement generally and has been particularly concerned with the politicization of the university. S.I. Hayakawa, [483] until recently president of San Francisco State University and himself involved in the dramatic events on that campus, has been one of the most popular spokesmen in opposition to the New Left. While his writings have covered most of the key issues concerning student activism, he is more noted for his dramatic style than cogent analysis. Irving Kristol had also been a persistent and articulate critic of the New Left, but from a more liberal point of view. [484] Kristol's concerns have centered around the politicization of the university, the lack of articulate ideology of the New Left, and their generally nihilistic position.

There is little that binds the commentary on student activism and the New Left in any coherent shape. Every political viewpoint finds expression, as do a range of methodological approaches. Some of the literature is of high intellectual quality, while other material is not particularly thoughtful. Some of the commentary remains relevant and useful, while much of it is of little use in trying to obtain a broader perspective on student activism in the United States. This section has attempted to provide a few of the more useful sources from a range of viewpoints and perspectives.

The Youth Subculture

One of the very interesting aspects of the student movement of the sixties was the rise of what has been called a counterculture composed largely of young people and based to a substantial extent in and around universities. Much attention has been given to this counterculture and its implications for the broader society. Such phenomena as the spreading use of drugs among young people, a rejection of much of the ethic of the American Establishment, large numbers of dropouts from the universities, the development of youth ghettos, and, of course, the stress on generational conflict as an element of growing up in America are all parts of what is clearly a new aspect of the campus scene. The student activist movements of previous years developed no explicit youth culture and relatively few activists were as alienated from the broader society than at least a portion of the current generation of student activists seems to be.

It is a mistake, of course, to overemphasize the importance to American society of the counterculture, as some writers have been prone to do. Charles Reich, for example, has posited the unlikely situation of the values of the counterculture eventually taking over the broader society. The proportion of students self-consciously participating in the counterculture is small, as is the proportion actively involved in student politics. Yet, it seems that elements of the counterculture and its values have permeated many elements of campus life in the sixties and seventies. The prevalence of rock music, the use of drugs, and styles of dress of the counterculture are all important indicators of its impact.

Much of the literature on the counterculture does not directly concern student activism, but since a large portion of the counterculture has roots on campus and its impact is perhaps greatest in university communities, it is important to understand this element of modern America when seeking to understand the student movement. One of the most influential analyses of the counterculture, indeed the book in which the term counterculture was coined, is Theodore Roszak's *The Making of a Counter Culture.* [485] Joseph Berke's edited volume provides a range of material on the counterculture, most of it from a sympathetic perspective. [486] Berke's volume is unique in that both American and European writings are included. William Braden's thoughtful book also deals with the counterculture as well as with student activism directly. [487] Ross V. Speck, a psychiatrist, has written a thoughtful volume stressing the emergence of drugs as an important element of the counterculture and centering on a detailed investigation of several communes. [488] Keith Melville has written perceptively on the theories behind the commune movement, [489] and Ron Roberts has written an account of the commune movement on the basis of visits to a number of them. [490] Sherri Cavan's insightful sociological account of the San Francisco hippie movement of 1967–1968 provides a detailed analysis of a particular community, [491] and Lewis Yablonsky's broader sociological investigation of the counterculture and the hippies provides an excellent overview of the total movement and its implications. [492] Several collections of articles from the underground press, an offshoot of both the counterculture and the student movement, have appeared, and these provide a selection of materials which relate to the concerns of the movement at specific points in time. Among these collections are those edited by Jerry Hopkins and by Jesse Kornbluth. [493, 494] Another general volume on the counterculture which stresses its campus base is J. Simmons and Barry Winograd's book on the California scene. [495] The editors of *Ramparts,* a journal which has paid a good deal of attention to the counterculture, have edited a volume bringing together some of the materials from that journal. [496]

A number of articles have perceptively analyzed the counterculture as well. Sociologist M.J. Yinger wrote an early analysis of the nature of the counterculture, [497] while Bennett M. Berger, [498] a keen student of alternative life styles, has speculated on hippie morality. A number of commentators have been quite critical of various aspects of the counterculture and of hippies. Roger Starr and Michael Lerner have written generally critical articles focusing on different aspects of the counterculture. [499, 500] Sociologist Jesse Pitts has emphasized the generational style of the counterculture and is quite critical of many of its norms. [501] Gilbert Geis has also analyzed aspects of the style of the counterculture. [502] Andrew Greeley has written perceptively of the religious significance of the counterculture, [503] and has also made some critical remarks on the general nature of the movement.

Other writers have written more approvingly of the movement. Stewart Hall's essay on the hippies certified them as an important American social movement, [504] and is a valuable contribution in placing the hippies in the context of American social change. Michael Brown has written of the problems which the hippie movement has had surviving in a hostile intellectual and physical environment. [505] Gerald Dworkin also writes about the hippies as an aspect of American social change, [506] and R. Serge Denisoff and M.H. Levine have written about the counterculture from the perspective of its music. [507] John Berks has provided an excellent guide to the underground press, [508] certainly one of the most important aspects of the counterculture and its major means of national communication. Finally, Robert Denhardt and H. David Allen have analyzed youth responses to cultural change. [509] One of the most reliable guides to events in the counterculture is the journal *Rolling Stone.* This bi-weekly newspaper covers both political and cultural affairs.

Many consider that drugs are a key element of the counterculture, and there has been a good deal of writing concerning drugs on campus in general and some analysis of the role of drugs in student activism. [510] It should be remembered that the beginnings of the drug culture, among the middle classes at least, started on campus, and the psychedelic drugs like LSD had their most important impact in university communities. Richard Blum et al. have written in detail about the campus drug culture and drugs in general. [511] A number of books of a rather general and journalistic nature dealing with students and drugs have been published. Richard Goldstein's volume, [512] published in 1966, is one of the first of these books. James Carey and Helen Nowlis have also written on this subject. [513, 514] The booklet edited by C. Hollander for the National Students Association deals with campus drug use from a variety of perspectives. [515] Princeton University has also examined student drug use and has produced a useful report, focusing mainly on psychedelic drugs. [516] Howard Becker's article on the campus drug scene focuses on means of ending the rising number of tension producing "busts" for drug possession at universities. [517] Kenneth Keniston has also written on the question of drugs on campus. [518]

While not all of the analyses mentioned here have been of direct relevance to the student movement, the links between student activism and the counterculture are quite strong. As noted, much of the support for countercultural institutions, such as the underground press, come from the campus, and with the exception of rural communes, hippies and other countercultural elements tend to congregate near universities. While there is no adequate data available, it is very likely that there is a good deal of migration of individuals between the counterculture and the campus.

Other Aspects of Student Activism

a. Legal Aspects of Student Activism,
Discipline, and Academic Freedom

The legal aspects of student life have received substantial attention in recent years, particularly since authorities have had to deal with students in terms of law enforcement agencies, court cases and other means. Students, too, have taken to the courts on several occasions to press their case and achieve change. As a result of these pressures, a substantial literature concerning student discipline and the rights and responsibilities of students has appeared.

A number of scholars and organizations such as the American Civil Liberties Union have been concerned with the question of student rights and freedom, and several reports have been issued on this topic. The ACLU's 1970 report summarizes aspects of the academic freedom and civil liberties of students. [519] The National Student Association has taken a strong interest in various aspects of student rights. Roland Liebert's volumes deal with various aspects of student rights, [520] and Neal Johnson's edited volume on *in loco parentis* sheds light on this controversial issue. [521] O.W. Knorr and W.J. Minter's edited volume presents one of the most useful discussions, from a range of viewpoints concerning student and faculty rights and responsibilities. [522] Michael Nussbaum's book is aimed primarily at giving students an idea of their rights and the means to protect them, but it is also a useful summary of relevant literature. [523] Louis Vaccaro and James T. Covert, Jr. and E.G. Williamson and John Cowan have provided excellent summaries of student freedom of expression and guides to policy on these matters. [524, 525]

There has been a good deal of legal writing in the area of student rights and freedoms as well. Michael T. Johnson has written on the constitutional rights of students and Philip Moneypenny's writings on these topics cover a range of issues. [526, 527] William Van Alstyne has written on this topic from a lawyer's viewpoint as well. [528]

Student discipline has also received a good deal of attention from both lawyers and educators. The amount of attention has increased substantially since the major disruptions on campus in the sixties, and the legal literature is now quite extensive. For the first time, administrators and others concerned with student discipline seem to have a reasonably firm background in factual material for student discipline issues. The political and ethical problems concerned with this question remain, of course, and these are not easily solved by reference to legal precedent. Volumes by M.M. Chambers, [529] and by Thomas Brady and Laverne Snoxell [530] focus attention on student discipline problems and their legal ramifications. The University of Georgia's Institute of Higher Education has prepared a volume dealing with legal aspects of student discipline, [531] and Grace Holme's edited volume provides additional data and interpretation on legal aspects of student discipline. [532] A series of articles in various law journals deal with student disciplinary procedures and the legal ramifications of such procedures. William Van Alstyne's writings on this subject are among the best available, and he has devoted much attention to student discipline in recent years. [533] Ira Heyman, William Beaney, and Sol Jacobson have also written perceptively on this topic from various legal points of view, but also with a general focus on the broader policy-related issues of discipline and due process for students. [534, 535, 536] More technical considerations of this topic also abound in the legal literature and many of these references can be found in the bibliography. (See Section IK3.)

The literature on students rights and student discipline, while largely dominated by lawyers and legal experts, provides some useful broader perspectives for the consideration of student activism and campus life generally. This literature indicates that universities are, after all, parts of a broader social and legal system and that both students and administrators are constrained by outside legal and other forces. And since increasingly both students and administrators have taken to the courts for redress of grievances or to achieve disciplinary ends, the legal literature has taken on new importance.

b. The Faculty and Student Activism

Conservative commentators have for a long time postulated that the predominantly liberal faculty had a major role in fomenting student unrest. Student activists, on the other hand, have increasingly looked on the faculty as a conservative force on campus and as an enemy. To some extent, both of these views are probably correct. But it is difficult to discover just what role the faculty has played since very little serious analysis of the faculty's role in the campus unrest of the sixties, or for that matter earlier periods, has been conducted. Research on faculty and on the academic profession generally is of recent origins, and thus it is not surprising that there is relatively little information on this aspect of student activism. [537] Particularly surprising is the lack of reportage or serious analysis on that relatively small group of radical faculty which did play an important role in the unrest of the sixties. As mentioned, there are almost no data on the most important organization of radical faculty members, the New University Conference, and the case studies of activism make relatively few references to the faculty role. It seems to be generally true that the faculty played little direct role in the activism of the sixties, and were particularly uninvolved in the more militant phases of the student movement in the late sixties. Yet, as S.M. Lipset and others point out, [538] student unrest on many campuses caused major conflicts within faculties, often along liberal-conservative lines and that administrators not only had to face hostile students but a divided and often indecisive faculty.

Robert Boruch, [539] has reported on a range of faculty involvement in protest activities in what remains the most thorough consideration of this issue. Arlene Kaplan Daniels et al. discuss the faculty role at a single institution, San Francisco State College, in the unrest of the late sixties in their book. [540] Alan E. Bayer has focused on the faculty role in student unrest in a recent article, but finds little actual faculty involvement in protest demonstrations, [541] Stephen Cole and H. Adamsons have written about the determinants of faculty support for student demonstrations and find in general that the social sciences tend to be more pro-student than the other disciplines. [542] This finding is also confirmed in some of the research by E.C. Ladd and S.M. Lipset. [543]

Faculty attitudes toward politics and student activism have received some attention in the literature. David Armor et al. have examined faculty attitudes toward the Vietnam War, [544] and the writings of S.M. Lipset and E.C. Ladd, Jr., based on the findings of the Carnegie Commission on Higher Education questionnaire of faculty provide much data on faculty opinions concerning higher education, politics, and student-related issues as well. The Lipset-Ladd data as well as a number of other studies, indicate that academics have not supported militant activism although they are often ambivalent about the role of students in politics and often sympathetic with the antiwar views of the students. [545] Differences according to discipline and institution are quite significant in this data. The experiences of faculty radicals are considered in several articles. Jim Green writes of the problems of radical historians and Norman Birnbaum is concerned with the New University Conference. [546, 547] Robert S. Laufer writes of generational differences among faculty and their contribution to radicalism, [548] and Richard Robbins has written rather critically of the radical faculty. [549] D. Rabinowitz and Irving Kristol have also written critically of radical faculty and their support for student causes. [550, 551] Erwin Knoll, a journalist, and historian Andrew Hacker have written articles on the radicalization of faculty in the sixties. [552, 553] These two earlier articles stress the dissent from the Vietnam War and also rejection among some younger faculty of the role of models of their elders and a rejection of some of the norms of scholarly life. Two of the most useful articles on faculty involvement in student dissent are those by William Morgan, [554] who deals with faculty efforts to mediate disputes, and J. Victor Baldridge, [555] who sees faculty political involvement in the context of the political dimension of the university itself. Finally, John Spiegel deals with professorial reactions to campus protest in his *Transaction* article. [556]

Conclusion

The amount of research and writing on student activism which has occurred in the past decade is impressive, and it is now possible to say that there is a basic literature on the general aspects of American students and particularly on elements of the activist movement. Much of the material which is included in this bibliography, and a very large body of data which has been excluded, is of little relevance in obtaining a disciplined view of student activism of related issues. This material is purely reportorial in nature and yields few insights. Yet, solid research has been done, and an adequate data base in many areas of this topic is available. The list of topics which need basic research, which was evident in the first edition of this bibliography, published in 1968, is somewhat shorter now. Clearly, a great deal of valuable research has been done.

Students, of course, are a particularly difficult group on which to do research, and some of the problems with the available data stem from the subjects of the research. Not the least of these problems is the ephemeral nature of most student organizations, and particularly of their leaders. A student generation, after all, lasts perhaps four years, and unlike many of the developing countries, there is no tradition of the "permanent student" in the United States. Students are, in addition, notoriously fickle politically. Issues which motivate student protest change from month to month, causing shifts in organizations and leadership. The rapid disappearance of the New Left following the bifurcation of the SDS and Richard Nixon's election as president in 1968 is perhaps indicative of how quickly a seemingly stable and important student movement can collapse. By the same token, the massive and generally spontaneous protests which occurred after the Cambodian invasion are an indication that an activist movement can resurrect itself if the proper social conditions are present.

It is often difficult to analyze just what aspects of student activism are most important to the campus community. At least some of the analysis which the New Left was subjected to might have better been aimed at less dramatic but perhaps more representative aspects of the student community. While it is clear that all activism is a phenomenon of a minority—usually a small minority—of the student population, this does not make activist organizations and movements any less important. Indeed, like the situation in many developing countries, American student activists may act as a conscience and voice for their generation, speaking for the majority of students who are seemingly apathetic but who can be mobilized on dramatic occasions. Student activism follows definite geographic and disciplinary lines—there is more campus political consciousness at the larger, more prestigious, universities of the North and West than at institutions in the South, denominational colleges, and smaller state universities. Furthermore, a large proportion of the activists are concentrated in the social sciences and humanities. As a result of these ecological and disciplinary factors, the institutions and disciplines which have less activism have been virtually ignored by researchers—and yet these institutions have occasionally flared up and are certainly of key importance to the university system as a whole. The outbreak of violence at Kent State University, typical of the nonactive campuses, was quite unexpected. The literature on student activism has suggested some of these generalizations. Certainly, more hypotheses are possible and desirable.

There are still major gaps in the research available on student activism and related questions. It is hoped that this essay might point to some of the areas which need additional research and might stimulate scholars and others concerned with this field to undertake relevant research projects. Without question, the research boom of the late sixties has to some extent passed, but there is still a need for research. The universities and their problems remain, and student activism has been a recurring theme in twentieth century America. In addition to the need for additional research, there is also a need for those concerned with student activism and students generally, to take a greater interest in the research which has been conducted. It is always surprising that protagonists on both sides, as well as academic planners, have often ignored studies and commentary which might have been relevant in dealing with specific problems.

The following areas need particular attention from scholars:

1. Elements of the history of American student activism. Some periods have been dealt with rather thoroughly—particularly the sixties. Others have received some attention, such as the thirties. But the twenties and the fifties still need to be much more fully researched.

2. The campus Black Power and civil rights movements, and more broadly, problems of black students. While the activist segment of the black movement has received some analytical attention, additional research needs to be done, and the problems of the growing minority of black students in American colleges and universities need much research—and of course solutions as well.

3. The student right. Although some research has been done on this aspect of American student politics, a great deal more should be undertaken in order to obtain a clear picture of this element of student activism.

4. Student religious groups. This area of student activism has received only the most cursory of analysis despite the fact that it involves thousands of highly motivated students. The role of the campus ministry also needs additional research. The recent religious revival of 1971 needs further analysis as well.

5. Moderate student organizations, such as the U.S. National Student Association, the Young Democrats and Republicans, and similar groups have received very little attention from researchers.

6. The dynamic of Institutional response to activism needs additional attention. Some research on individual universities under stress has been undertaken, but more research on the ways in which administratives, faculty, and others in responsible institutional positions react to crisis will be valuable.

7. Theoretical analysis concerning aspects of student activism in the United States and in comparative context are needed. Some analysts have generalized about the generic nature of student activism, but by and large these explanations are not very convincing. Clearly, there is more work needed in this area so that it might be possible to understand the phenomenon in more generalized ways.

8. The ideologies and programs of activist movements and organizations have received some attention from analysts. In order to understand better the dynamic of student protest, it is necessary to understand the programs which have been stressed by activist organizations and movement. Many commentators have avoided looking seriously at the demands raised by the student movement.

9. The women's movement and in general the problems and situation of women in American universities. This element of the activist movements became particularly important in the past few years.

These are only a few of the crucial areas which need additional research. The newness of the field in terms of research and the fact that student activism has involved some of the critical areas of academic life has worked against substantive research. It is hoped that the urgency of some of the issues involved, and the continuing need for a deeper understanding of the dynamics of higher education in America, will help to stimulate needed research and reflection.

The study of student activism is clearly not a separate discipline, and as yet is not even a subfield such as the sociology of education or science. It is, perhaps, a sub-subfield within the sociology or history of education, although the research in the area has been highly multidisciplinary and it is critically important to keep this emphasis. In part as a result of the multidisciplinary nature of the field and the rapid recent growth of interest in it, there has been almost no coordination of research and it is often difficult to locate relevant information. The ERIC Clearinghouse on Higher Education, some of the publications of the Center for Research and Development in Higher Education at the University of California at Berkeley, [557] a recent bibliography of empirical research on students by Kenneth Keniston, [558] and a few other bibliographies have helped to improve the situation.

It seems clear that research in this field will continue to improve both in quality and quantity. There has, however, clearly been a peak, at least for the foreseeable future, in the amount of research being conducted and the amount of money available for research on students. The study of student activism and student life generally is not an esoteric subject for irrelevant academics, but is a matter of major concern to university administrators, faculty members, and perhaps in the long run to government officials. As the universities continue to expand, to attract larger, more heterogenous, and to some extent more sophisticated student populations, and to become increasingly important in American cultural and political life, student activism will continue to be an issue, although probably not of the intensity that it was during the late sixties. What is more, the whole field of higher education, which has in a few years expanded as a field of study and research within education and the social sciences, will continue to grow. Research on higher education generally will expand with both a policy orientation and in the "pure" sense. Departments and centers concerned with higher education have developed at a number of universities, and these will generate research for doctoral dissertations and faculty and student projects of various kinds. And research on students will be an important element in this growing interest in and institutionalization of studies on higher education.

The New Left of the 1960s proved not to be a permanent phenomenon on the campus, and the level of activism substantially abated in the early 1970s. Such a development was not surprising, since student activism has ebbed and flowed in American history. Issues come and go—the Vietnam War, civil rights and civil liberties, and others all flourished as matters of campus concern during the sixties—and it is difficult to predict what might be the next focus of student activism. Or student concern may move in entirely new directions, such as concern with ecology, interest in occult religion or other things. But that American students will from time to time be concerned with social issues and that the changing patterns of student interests and orientations will be of importance to both the campus and the society generally is clear.

Notes

1. This essay is a revised and expanded version of the introduction to the original (1968) edition of this bibliography.
2. These statistics are taken from Seymour E. Harris, *A Statistical Portrait of Higher Education* (New York: McGraw-Hill, 1972). This volume, a product of the Carnegie Commission on Higher Education, is without question the best source of all kinds of statistical information concerning American higher education.
3. Lewis Mayhew, *The Literature of Higher Education, 1972* (San Francisco: Jossey-Bass, 1972). A volume was also prepared in 1971.
4. For an example of typical reporting in student activism, see Richard Armstrong, "The Explosive Revival of the Far Left," *Saturday Evening Post* 238 (May 1965): 27–32.
5. See *Harper's* 231 (October 1961): 121–82, for a special issue on the college scene.
6. See the *Atlantic* 216 (November 1965): 108–160, for a consideration of the troubled campus.
7. "'Man of the Year' Twenty-five and Under," *Time* 89 (January 6, 1967): 18–23.
8. "Students Protest," *Newsweek* (May 6, 1968): 40–53.
9. *Daedalus* has been particularly concerned with student questions during the sixties, and published at least four major special issues on this and related topics. See "Youth: Change and Challenge," *Daedalus* 91 (Winter 1962); "Students and Politics," *Daedalus* 97 (Winter 1968); "Rights and Responsibilities: The University's Dilemma," *Daedalus* 99 (Summer 1970); "The Embattled University," *Daedalus* 99 (Winter 1970).
10. See *The Public Interest* (Fall 1968), special issue on student activism and the university crisis.
11. One of the best collections which includes much political commentary from the underground press as well as other journals is Mitchell Goodman, *The Movement Toward a New America* (New York: Knopf, 1970).
12. Because of the generally ephemeral nature of the underground press and its unmanageable scope, this bibliography has not listed articles from these publications. For a discussion of the underground press, see R. Glessing, *The Underground Press in America* (Bloomington, Indiana: Indiana University Press, 1971).
13. The *Journal of Social Issues* has devoted two special issues to student activism, and these are among the best collections of scholarly articles available. These are "Stirrings Out of Apathy: Student Activism and the

62

Decade of Protest," *Journal of Social Issues* 23 (July 1967): 1–140; "The New Left and the Old," *Journal of Social Issues* 27, 1 (1971): 1–206.

14. William O'Neill, *Coming Apart: An Informal History of America in the Sixties* (Chicago: Quadrangle, 1971).

15. Ronald Berman, *America in the Sixties: An Intellectual History* (New York: Harper, 1968).

16. A new firm, Jossey Bass Publishers, of San Francisco, has published many of the more perceptive books on higher education, including several on students and student activism. The appearance of a publisher specializing almost completely in higher education is an indication of the growth of the field.

17. The Comparative National Development Project was responsible for the production of a number of volumes on student activism. Among them are S.M. Lipset, ed., *Student Politics* (New York: Basic Books, 1967); S.M. Lipset and P.G. Altbach, eds., *Students in Revolt* (Boston: Beacon Press, 1970); Arthur Liebman et al., *Latin American Students* (Cambridge, Mass.: Harvard University Press, 1972); Richard Walter, *Students and Politics in Argentina* (New York: Basic Books, 1968); P.G. Altbach, ed., *Turmoil and Transition: Higher Education and Student Politics in India* (New York: Basic Books, 1968) and others.

18. Richard Flacks, "The Liberated Generation: An Exploration of the Roots of Student Protest," *Journal of Social Issues* 23 (July 1967): 52–75.

19. *Report of the President's Commission on Campus Unrest* (New York: Arno Press, 1970). Many states have also investigated student unrest, with varying degrees of objectivity. Among those states which have issued officially sponsored reports on student activism are New York, Illinois, Pennsylvania, Michigan, and Washington.

20. "Student Protest," in Jerome Skolnick, *The Politics of Protest* (Report to the National Commission on the Causes and Prevention of Violence) (New York: Bantam, 1969), pp. 81–124.

21. Committee on the Student in Higher Education, *Report on the Student in Higher Education* (New Haven, Conn.: Hazen Foundation, 1968).

22. Frank Newman et al., *Report on Higher Education: Report to the Secretary of Health, Education and Welfare* (Washington, D.C.: Government Printing Office, 1971).

23. Carnegie Commission on Higher Education, *Dissent and Disruption: Proposals for Consideration by the Campus* (New York: McGraw-Hill, 1971).

24. Sol Linowitz, *Campus Tensions: Analysis and Recommendations* (Washington, D.C.: American Council on Education, 1970).

25. *Constructive Changes to Ease Campus Tensions* (Washington, D.C.: National Association of State Universities and Land Grant Colleges, 1970).

26. American Bar Association, Commission on Campus Governance and Student Dissent, *Report* (Chicago: American Bar Association, 1970).

27. Temporary Commission to Study the Causes of Campus Unrest, *The Academy in Turmoil: First Report* (Albany, New York: State of New York, 1970).

28. At least one such critical volume funded by a foundation source is Roger Rapaport and Lawrence Kirshbaum, *Is the Library Burning?* (New York:

Random House, 1969). Some of the work of Richard Flacks, a sociologist who has been generally sympathetic to the New Left, was also funded by foundation sources.

29. For a bibliography dealing with non-American aspects of student activism, see Philip G. Altbach, *A Select Bibliography on Students, Politics and Higher Education* (revised edition) (Cambridge, Mass.: Harvard Center for International Affairs, 1970).

30. For an overall discussion of European student activism, see John. and Barbara Ehrenreich, *Long March, Short Spring* (New York: Monthly Review Press, 1970). See also the various writings of Frank Pinner, including his "Students—A Marginal Elite in Politics," in P.G. Altbach and R.S. Laufer, eds., *The New Pilgrims* (New York: McKay, 1972), pp. 281–96; "Western European Student Movements Through Changing Times," in S.M. Lipset and P.G. Altbach, eds., *Students in Revolt* (Boston: Beacon Press, 1970), pp. 60–95; "Student Trade Unionism in France, Belgium and Holland," *Sociology of Education* 37 (Spring 1964): 1–23. The literature on France and the "events" of May 1968 is also very extensive. See particularly Alain Touraine, *The May Movement: Revolt and Reform* (New York: Random House, 1971); and Alain Schnapp and Pierre Vidal-Naquet, *The French Student Uprising: An Analytical Documentary* (Boston: Beacon Press, 1971).

31. Lewis Feuer, *The Conflict of Generations: The Character and Significance of Student Movements* (New York: Basic Books, 1968).

32. Seymour Martin Lipset, "Students and Politics in Comparative Perspective," in S.M. Lipset and P.G. Altbach, eds., *op. cit.,* pp. xv–xxxiv, note No. 17.

33. Philip G. Altbach, "Students and Politics," in S.M. Lipset, ed., *Student Politics,* pp. 74–93, *op. cit.,* note No. 17.

34. E. Wright Bakke and Mary S. Bakke, *Campus Challenge: Student Activism in Perspective* (Hamden, Conn.: Archon Books, 1971).

35. Ian Weinberg and Kenneth Walker, "Student Politics and Political Systems: Toward a Typology," *American Journal of Sociology* 75 (July 1969): 77–96.

36. Edward Shils, "Dreams of Plentitude, Nightmares of Scarcity," in S.M. Lipset and P.G. Altbach and S.M. Lipset, eds., *op. cit.,* pp. 1–34, note No. 17.

37. Frank Pinner, "Students—A Marginal Elite in Politics," in P.G. Altbach and R.S. Laufer, *op. cit.,* pp. 281–96, note No. 30.

38. Christian Bay, "Political and Apolitical Students: Facts in Search of a Theory," *Journal of Social Issues* 23 (July 1967): 76–91.

39. John and Martha Rowntree, "The Political Economy of Youth," *Our Generation* 6 (May–July 1968): 155–90.

40. S.N. Eisenstadt, *From Generation to Generation,* (Glencoe, Ill.: Free Press, 1956); and S.N. Eisenstadt, "Generational Conflict and Intellectual Antinomianism," in P.G. Altbach and R.S. Laufer, eds., *op. cit.,* pp. 139–54, note No. 30; S.N. Eisenstadt, "Changing Patterns of Youth Protest in Different Stages of Development of Modern Societies," *Youth and Society* 1 (December 1969): 135–49.

41. Karl Mannheim, "The Problem of Generations," in P.G. Altbach and R.S. Laufer, eds., *op. cit.,* pp. 101–138, note No. 30.

42. Erik Erikson, "Reflections on the Dissent of Contemporary Youth,"

Daedalus 99 (Winter 1970): 154–76; and Erik Erikson, "Youth: Fidelity and Diversity," *Daedalus* 91 (Winter 1962): 5–28.

43. George Pettitt, *Prisoners of Culture* (New York: Scribners, 1970).

44. Margaret Mead, *Culture and Committment* (Garden City, N.Y.: Doubleday, 1970).

45. Kenneth Keniston, *Youth and Dissent* (New York: Harcourt Brace Jovanovich, 1971).

46. William McIntyre, "Student Movements," *Editorial Research Reports* 2 (1957): 913–29.

47. Michael Miles, *The Radical Probe: The Logic of Student Rebellion* (New York: Atheneum, 1971).

48. S.M. Lipset, *Rebellion in the University* (Boston: Little Brown, 1972).

49. Richard Flacks, *Youth and Social Change* (Chicago: Markham, 1972).

50. Donald Emmerson, ed., *Students and Politics in Developing Nations* (New York: Praeger, 1967).

51. S.M. Lipset, ed., *Student Politics, op. cit.,* note No. 17.

52. S.M. Lipset and P.G. Altbach, eds., *op. cit.,* note No. 17.

53. A. Cockburn and R. Blackburn, eds., *Student Power* (Baltimore, Md.: Penguin Books, 1969).

54. Julian Nagel, ed., *Student Power* (London: Merlin Press, 1969).

55. Stephen Spender, *The Year of the Young Rebels* (New York: Vintage, 1969).

56. David Riesman, "The Found Generation," *American Scholar* 25 (Autumn 1956): 421–35; "The College Student in an Age of Organization," *Chicago Review* 12 (Autumn 1958): 50–68; "The Uncommited Generation," *Encounter* 15 (November 1966): 25–30, among other articles. Comments on students and student activism can also be found in Christopher Jencks and David Riesman, *The Academic Revolution* (Garden City, N.Y.: Doubleday, 1968). This volume remains one of the best overall analyses of the current state of American higher education.

57. Seymour Martin Lipset and Philip G. Altbach, "Student Politics and Higher Education in the United States," in S.M. Lipset, ed., *Student Politics, op. cit.,* pp. 199–252, note No. 17.

58. S.M. Lipset, *Rebellion in the University, op. cit.,* note No. 48.

59. Julian Foster and Durward Long, eds., *Protest!: Student Activism in America* (New York: Morrow, 1970).

60. Immanuel Wallerstein and Paul Starr, eds., *The University Crisis Reader* (New York: Random House, 1971), 2 volumes.

61. Philip G. Altbach and Robert S. Laufer, eds., *op. cit.,* note No. 30.

62. Howard Becker, ed., *Campus Power Struggle* (Chicago: Aldine, 1970).

63. Edward Sampson and Harold Korn, eds., *Student Activism and Protest* (San Francisco: Jossey-Bass, 1970).

64. James McEvoy and Abraham Miller, eds., *Black Power and Student Rebellion* (Belmont, Calif.: Wadsworth, 1969).

65. Christopher Katope and Paul Zolbrod, eds., *Beyond Berkeley: A Sourcebook in Student Values* (Cleveland: World, 1966).

66. Irving Howe, ed., *Beyond the New Left* (New York: McCall, 1970).

67. Daniel Bell and Irving Kristol, eds., *Confrontation: The Student Rebellion and the University* (New York: Basic Books, 1969). This volume stems from a special issue of the *Public Interest*.

68. John and Susan Erlich, eds., *Student Power, Participation and Revolution* (New York: Association Press, 1970).

69. Nathan Glazer, *Remembering the Answers: Essays on the American Student Revolt* (New York: Basic Books, 1970).

70. Michael W. Miles, *The Radical Probe: The Logic of Student Rebellion* (New York: Atheneum, 1971).

71. Gil Green, *The New Radicalism: Anarchist or Marxist?* (New York: International Publishers, 1971).

72. Sidney Hook, *Academic Freedom and Academic Anarchy* (New York: Cowles, 1970).

73. Kenneth Keniston, *Youth and Dissent: The Rise of a New Opposition* (New York: Harcourt Brace Jovanovich, 1971).

74. E.G. Williamson and John Cowan, *The American Student's Freedom of Expression* (Minneapolis, Minn.: University of Minnesota Press, 1966).

75. Richard E. Peterson, *The Scope of Organized Student Protest in 1964-65* (Princeton, N.J.: Educational Testing Service, 1966). A similar volume was prepared for 1966-67. See also Richard Peterson and John Bilorusky, *May, 1960: The Campus Aftermath of Cambodia and Kent State* (New York: McGraw-Hill, 1971).

76. Urban Research Corporation, *Student Protests, 1969: Summary* (Chicago: Urban Research Corporation, 1970).

77. Clark Kerr, *The Uses of the University* (New York: Harper, 1963).

78. Harold Taylor, *Students Without Teachers: The Crisis in the University* (New York: McGraw-Hill, 1969).

79. Eric Ashby, *Any Person, Any Study: An Essay on Higher Education in the United States* (New York: McGraw-Hill, 1971).

80. Joseph Ben-David, *American Higher Education: Directions Old and New* (New York: McGraw-Hill, 1972).

81. David Riesman and Verne Stadtman, eds., *Academic Transformation* (New York: McGraw-Hill, 1973).

82. Robert Nisbet, *The Degradation of the Academic Dogma* (New York: Basic Books, 1971).

83. Carlos Krutybosch and Sheldon Messinger, eds., *The State of the University; Authority and Change* (Beverly Hills, Calif.: Sage Publications, 1970).

84. Philip G. Altbach, *Student Politics in America* (New York: McGraw-Hill, forthcoming).

85. Seymour Martin Lipset, *Rebellion in the University, op. cit.,* note No. 48. See also S.M. Lipset, "Student Opposition in the United States," *Government and Opposition* 1 (April 1966): 351-74.

86. Henry D. Sheldon, *Student Life and Customs* (New York: Appleton, 1901).

87. C.F. Thwing, *The American College in American Life* (New York: Putnam's Sons, 1897).

88. Clarence P. Shedd, *Two Centuries of Student Christian Movements: Their Origin and Intercollegiate Life* (New York: Association Press, 1934). See

also Owen Pence, *The YMCA and Social Need* (New York: Association Press, 1939).

89. Harold Lewack, *Campus Rebels: A Brief History of the Student League for Industrial Democracy* (New York: Student League for Industrial Democracy, 1953). P.G. Altbach, *op. cit.*, note No. 84 also deals with this organization in some detail, as does S.M. Lipset, *Rebellion . . ., op. cit.*, note No. 48.

90. Hal Draper, "The Student Movement in the Thirties: A Political History," in R.J. Simon, ed., *As We Saw The Thirties* (Urbana, Ill.: University of Illinois Press, 1967): 151–89.

91. George Rawick, "The New Deal and Youth," Ph.D. dissertation, Department of History, University of Wisconsin, 1957.

92. James Wechsler, *Revolt on the Campus* (New York: Covici-Friede, 1935).

93. Patti Peterson, "Student Organizations and the Anti-War Movement in America, 1900–1960," *American Studies* 13 (Spring 1972): 131–48.

94. Lewis S. Feuer, *op. cit.*, note No. 31.

95. Norman Cantor, *The Age of Protest: Dissent and Rebellion in the Twentieth Century* (New York: Hawthorn, 1969).

96. Philip G. Altbach, *op. cit.*, note No. 84.

97. Seymour Martin Lipset, *op. cit.*, note No. 48.

98. Andre Schffrin, "The Student Movement of the 1950's: A Personal Reminiscence," *Radical America* 2 (May-June 1968): 26–40.

99. Martin McLaughlin, *Political Processes in American National Student Organizations* (Ann Arbor, Mich.: Edwards Brothers, 1948).

100. Philip G. Altbach and Norman Uphoff, *The Student Internationals* (Metuchen, N.J.: Scarecrow Press, 1973).

101. James O'Brien, "The Development of a New Left in the United States, 1960–1965," Ph.D. dissertation, Department of History, University of Wisconsin, 1971. See also James O'Brien, *History of the New Left, 1960–1968* (Boston: New England Free Press, 1969).

102. Massimo Teodori, ed., *The New Left: A Documentary History* (Indianapolis, Indiana: Bobbs-Merrill, 1969).

103. "The Careful Young Men: Symposium," *Nation* 184 (March 9, 1957): 199–214. See also George Rawick, "The American Student: A Profile," *Dissent* 1 (1954): 393–98.

104. Bruno Bettelheim, "College Student Rebellion: Explanations and Answers," *Phi Delta Kappan* 50 (May 1969): 511–14. See also "The Problem of Generations," in E. Erikson, ed., *Youth: Challenge and Change* (New York: Basic Books, 1963), pp. 64–93, and Lewis Feuer, *op. cit.*, note No. 31.

105. Kenneth Keniston, *op. cit.;* Kenneth Keniston, *The Young Radicals* (New York: Harcourt Brace 1968); Kenneth Keniston, *The Uncommitted: Alienated Youth in American Society* (New York: Harcourt Brace, 1960) presents an earlier perspective on student alienation. Keniston also deals with activism in his article, "The Sources of Student Dissent," *Journal of Social Issues* 23 (July 1967): 108–137.

106. "Generations in Conflict," *Journal of Contemporary History* 5, (No. 2, 1970): 3–190.

107. Karl Mannheim, *op. cit.*, note No. 41.

108. S.N. Eisenstadt, *op. cit.,* note No. 40 and S.N. Eisenstadt, *op. cit.,* note No. 40.

109. Robert S. Laufer, "Sources of Generational Consciousness and Conflict," in P.G. Altbach and R.S. Laufer, eds., *op. cit.,* pp. 218–37, note No. 30.

110. Vern L. Bengtson, "The Generation Gap: A Review and Typology and Social-Psychological Perspectives," in *ibid.,* pp. 195–217. Bengtson's article is a particularly good discussion of the literature in this field.

111. Robert J. Lifton, "The New History," in *ibid.,* pp. 182–194.

112. Philip Slater, *"The Pursuit of Loneliness* (Boston: Beacon Press, 1970). Slater's book is one of the best analyses available.

113. Lewis Feuer, *op. cit.,* note No. 31.

114. William Braden, *Age of Aquarius* (Chicago: Quadrangle, 1970).

115. Margaret Mead, *op. cit.,* note No. 44.

116. Charles Reich, *The Greening of America* (New York: Random House, 1970).

117. Philip Jacob, *Changing Values in College: An Exploratory Study of the Impact of College Teaching* (New York: Harper, 1957).

118. Theodore Newcomb and Kenneth A. Feldman, *The Impact of College on Students* (San Francisco: Jossey-Bass, 1968), 2 volumes. This bibliography depended on this volume for references on psychological issues.

119. Kenneth A. Feldman, ed., *College and Student: Selected Readings in the Social Psychology of Higher Education* (New York: Pergamon Press, 1972).

120. Erik Erikson, ed., *The Challenge of Youth* (Garden City, N.Y.: Doubleday Anchor, 1965). See also Erik Erikson, *Childhood and Society* (New York: Norton, 1950).

121. Kaoru Yamamoto, ed., *The College Student and His Culture: An Analysis* (Boston: Houghton Mifflin, 1968).

122. Samuel Bellman, ed., *The College Experience* (San Francisco: Chandler 1962).

123. Lawrence Dennis and Joseph Kauffman, eds., *The College and the Student* (Washington, D.C.: American Council on Education, 1966).

124. Arthur W. Chickering, *Education and Identity* (San Francisco: Jossey-Bass, 1969).

125. Michael Wertheimer, ed., *Confrontation: Psychology and the Problems of Today* (Glenview, Ill.: Scotts Foresman, 1970).

126. Joseph Katz, ed., *No Time for Youth* (San Francisco: Jossey-Bass, 1968).

127. Graham Blaine and Charles MacArthur, *Emotional Problems of the Student* (Garden City, N.Y.: Doubleday, 1966).

128. Robert Coles, "Psychiatric Observations on Students Demonstrating for Peace," *American Journal of Orthopsychiatry* 37 (January 1967): 107–111, and Robert Coles, "Social Struggle and Weariness," *Psychiatry* 27 (November 1964): 305–315.

129. Robert Liebert, *Radical and Militant Youth: A Psychoanalytic Inquiry* (New York: Praeger, 1970).

130. Joshua Fishman and Frederic Solomon, "Youth and Social Action, An Introduction," *Journal of Social Issues* 20 (October 1964): 1–29; Joshua Fishman and Frederic Solomon, "The Psychosocial Meaning of NonVio-

68

lence in Student Civil Rights Activity," *Psychiatry* 27 (May 1964): 91–99. Joshua Fishman and Frederic Solomon, "Youth and Peace: A Psychosocial Study of Student Peace Demonstrators in Washington, D.C.," *Journal of Social Issues* 20 (October 1964): 54–74, and other articles.

131. See particularly Kenneth Keniston, *Young Radicals, op. cit.*

132. Jesse Geller and Gary Howard, "Some Sociophysical Characteristics of Student Political Activists," *Journal of Applied Social Psychology* 2 (April-June 1972): 114–37.

133. D.G. Jensen, B.B. Winborn, and W.D. Martinson, "Characteristics Associated With Campus Socio-Political Action Leadership," *Journal of Counseling Psychology* 15 (November 1968): 552–62.

134. Alice Gold, Lucy Friedman and Richard Christie, "The Anatomy of Revolutionists," *Journal of Applied Social Psychology* 1 (January 1971): 26–43.

135. See particularly S.M. Lipset, *Rebellion in the University, op. cit.*, note No. 48, and S.M. Lipset and P.G. Altbach, "Student Politics and Higher Education in the United States," *op. cit.*, note No. 57. See also S.M. Lipset and E.C. Ladd, Jr., "The Political Future of Activist Generations," in P.G. Altbach and R.S. Laufer, eds., *op. cit.*, pp. 63–84, note No. 30.

136. Daniel Yankelovich, Inc., *The Changing Values on Campus: Political and Personal Attitudes of Today's College Students* (New York: Pocket Books, 1972).

137. Daniel Katz and Floyd Allport, *Student Attitudes* (Syracuse, N.Y.: Craftsman Press, 1931).

138. Rose Goldsen, Morris Rosenberg, Robin Williams, Jr., and Edward Suchman, *What College Students Think* (Princeton, N.J.: Van Nostrand, 1960).

139. See particularly "Campus '65: The College Generation Looks at Itself," *Newsweek* 65 (March 22, 1965): 43–48; and "The U.S. Campus Mood, '71: A Newsweek Poll," *Newsweek* (February 22, 1971), pp. 61. Many other such poll results have also appeared in *Time* and *Newsweek* among other journals.

140. Charles Havice, ed., *Campus Values: Some Considerations for Collegians* (New York: Scribners, 1968). This volume deals with aspects of student values other than opinions and attitudes.

141. Mary Lystad, ed., *As They See It: Changing Values of College Youth* (Cambridge, Mass.: Schenkman, 1972).

142. Norman Zinberg, "A Return to Commitment," *Antioch Review* 26 (Fall 1966): 332–44.

143. Charles Bolton and Kenneth Kammeyer, *The University Student: A Study of Student Behavior and Values* (New Haven, Conn.: College and University Press, 1967).

144. E. Nelson, *Radicalism-Conservatism in Student Attitudes* (Columbus, Ohio: Ohio State University Press, 1938).

145. A.W. Astin, *Some Effects of Campus Protests on Student Attitudes* (Washington, D.C.: American Council on Education, 1970).

146. Victor Gelineau and David Kantor, "Pro-social Commitment Among College Students," *Journal of Social Issues* 20 (October 1964): 112–30.

147. Henry Finney, "Political Liberalism at Berkeley: An Application of

Perspectives from the New Student Left," *Journal of Social Issues* 27, 1 (1971): 35–62.

148. Hanen Selvin and Warren Hagstrom, "Determinants of Support for Civil Liberties," in S.M. Lipset and S. Wolin, eds., *The Berkeley Student Revolt* (Garden City, N.Y.: Doubleday, 1965), pp. 494–518.

149. Robert Somers, "The Mainsprings of the Rebellion: A Survey of Berkeley Students in November, 1964," in S.M. Lipset and S. Wolin, eds., *op. cit.*, pp. 530–58, note No. 148.

150. Marshall Meyer, "Harvard Students in the Midst of Crisis," *Sociology of Education* 44 (Summer 1971): 245–69.

151. Morgan and Judith Lyons, "Black Student Power," in P.G. Altbach, R.S. Laufer and S. McVey, eds., *Academic Supermarkets* (San Francisco: Jossey-Bass, 1971), pp. 303–321.

152. Kenneth Keniston, *Radicals and Militants: An Annotated Bibliography of Empirical Research on Campus Unrest* (Lexington, Mass.: Heath Lexington, 1973).

153. S.M. Lipset and P.G. Altbach, "Student Politics and Higher Education in the United States," *op. cit.*, note No. 57.

154. Christopher Jencks and David Riesman, *op. cit.*, note No. 56.

155. Martin Trow, "Reflections on the Transition from Mass to Universal Higher Education," *Daedalus* 99 (Winter 1970): 1–42.

156. Philip G. Altbach and Robert S. Laufer, eds., *op. cit.*, note No. 30.

157. Howard Becker, ed., *op. cit.*, note No. 62.

158. Shirley and John Clark, eds., *Youth in Modern Society* (New York: Holt, Rinehart and Winston, 1972).

159. Julian Foster and Durward Long, eds., *op. cit.*, note No. 59.

160. Edward Sampson and Howard Korn, eds., *op. cit.*, note No. 63.

161. Thomas J. Cottle, ed., *The Prospect of Youth: Contexts for Sociological Inquiry* (Boston: Little, Brown, 1972).

162. Richard Flacks, *Youth and Social Change, op. cit.*, note No. 49.

163. Kenneth Keniston, *Youth and Dissent, op. cit.*, note No. 45.

164. S.M. Lipset, *Rebellion in the University, op. cit.*, note No. 48.

165. Richard Braungart, "Family Status, Socialization, and Student Politics: A Multivariable Analysis," *American Journal of Sociology* 77 (July 1971): 108–130.

166. Riley Dunlap, "Radical and Conservative Student Activists: A Comparison of Family Backgrounds," *Pacific Sociological Review* 13 (Summer 1970).

167. David Westby and Richard Braungart, "Class and Politics in the Family Backgrounds of Student Political Activists," *American Sociological Review* 31 (October 1966): 690–92.

168. Richard Flacks, "The Liberated Generation: An Exploration of the Roots of Student Protest," *Journal of Social Issues* 23 (July 1967): 52–75.

169. Milton Mankoff and Richard Flacks, "The Changing Social Base of the American Student Movement," in P.G. Altbach and R.S. Laufer, eds., *op. cit.*, pp. 63–84, note No. 30.

170. Jan Hajda, "Alienation and Integration of Student Intellectuals," *American Sociological Review* 26 (October 1961): 758–76.

171. Kenneth Keniston, "Psychology of Alienated Students," in Chad Gordon

and Kenneth Gergen, eds., *The Self in Social Interaction* (New York: Wiley, 1968), pp. 405–415. See also Kenneth Keniston, *The Uncommitted: Alienated Youth in American Society, op. cit.,* note No. 105.

172. For further discussion of student subcultures and the impact of the general university situation, see Section IIID1.

173. Richard Peterson, "The Student Left in American Higher Education," *Daedalus* 97 (Winter 1968): 293–317.

174. Martin Trow, "The Campus Viewed as Culture," in H.T. Sprague, ed., *Research on College Students* (Boulder, Colo.: Western Interstate Commission for Higher Education, 1960); and Martin Trow, "Student Subcultures and Administrative Action," in R. Sutherland et al., eds., *Personality Factors on the College Campus* (Austin, Texas: Hogg Foundation, 1962).

175. Frank Pinner, "Tradition and Transgression," *Daedalus* 97 (Winter 1968): 137–55.

176. Alexander W. Astin, *Campus Unrest, 1969–70* (Washington, D.C.: American Council on Education, 1970); A.W. Astin, "Campus Disruption, 1968–1969," in F.F. Korten, S.W. Cook, and J.I. Lacey, eds., *Psychology and the Problems of Society* (Washington, D.C.: American Psychological Association, 1970), A.W. Astin and R. Boruch, *A National Study of Student Unrest* (Washington, D.C.: American Council on Education, 1969).

177. Richard Peterson, *The Scope of Organized Student Unrest, op. cit.,* note No. 75.

178. Urban Research Corporation, *op. cit.,* note No. 76.

179. Helen S. Astin, "Self Perceptions of Student Activists," *Journal of College Student Personnel* 12 (July 1971): 263–70.

180. Jean Block et al., "Socialization Correlates of Student Activists," *Journal of Social Issues* 25 (Autumn 1969): 143–77.

181. Leonard Baird, "Who Protests: A Study of Student Activists," in Julian Foster and Durward Long, eds., *op. cit.,* pp. 123–33, note No. 59.

182. A.W. Astin and A.E. Bayer, "Antecedents and Consequents of Disruptive Campus Protests," *Measurement and Evaluation in Guidance* 4 (April 1971): 18–30.

183. Richard Braungart, "Status Politics and Student Politics: An Analysis of Left- and Right-Wing Student Activists," *Youth and Society* 3 (December 1971): 195–210.

184. Richard Braungart, "SDS and YAF: A Comparison of Two Student Radical Groups in the Mid-1960's" *Youth and Society* 2 (Summer 1971): 441–58.

185. Lewis Feuer, *The Conflict of Generations, op. cit.,* note No. 31.

186. Robert Laufer, "Sources of Generational Consciousness and Conflict," in P.G. Altbach and R.S. Laufer, eds., *op. cit.,* pp. 218–237, note No. 30.

187. Philip Slater, *The Pursuit of Loneliness, op. cit.,* note No. 112.

188. Lewis Feuer, *op. cit.,* note No. 31.

189. For a summary of Bettelheim's thinking on student unrest, see the interview with him in Thomas Braden, *op. cit.,* pp. 59–82, note No. 114.

190. S.M. Lipset, *Rebellion in the University, op. cit.,* note No. 48.

191. Kenneth Keniston, *Youth and Dissent, op. cit.,* note No. 45.

192. Columbia Broadcasting System, *Generations Apart: A Study of the Generation Gap* (New York: Columbia Broadcasting System, 1969).

193. M.P. Strommen, M. Brekke, R. Underwager, and L.A. Johnson, *A Study of Generations* (Minneapolis, Minn.: Augsburg Publishing Co., 1972).

194. G.C. Kinloch, "Parent-Youth Conflict at Home: An Investigation Among College Freshmen," *American Journal of Orthopsychiatry* 40 (July 1970): 658–64.

195. S.M. Lipset and E. Rabb, "Non Generation Gap," *Commentary* 50 (August 1970): 35–39.

196. Samuel Lubell, "That Generation Gap," *Public Interest* 13 (Fall 1968): 52–60.

197. Russell Middleton and Snell Putney, "Student Rebellion Against Parental Political Beliefs," *Social Forces* 41 (May 1963): 377–83.

198. Margaret Mead, *op. cit.,* note No. 44.

199. George Pettitt, *op. cit.,* note No. 43.

200. Charles Reich, *op. cit.,* note No. 116. See also Philip Nobile, ed., *The Con III Controversy, The Critics Look at the Greening of America* (New York: Pocket Books, 1971) for a discussion of various views of Reich's controversial book.

201. Gene Stanford, ed., *Generation Rap: An Anthology About Youth and the Establishment* (New York: Dell, 1971).

202. Bennett Berger, "How Long is a Generation," in B.M. Berger, *Looking for America* (Englewood Cliffs, N.J.: Prentice Hall, 1971), pp. 13–20.

203. Robert J. Lifton, "The New History," in P.G. Altbach and R.S. Laufer, eds., *op. cit.,* pp. 182–95, note No. 30.

204. S.N. Eisenstadt, "Generational Conflict and Intellectual Antinomianism," in P.G. Altbach and R.S. Laufer, eds., *op. cit.,* pp. 139–54, note No. 30.

205. Lewis Feuer, "Jewish Students as Bearers of Generational Conflict," *Midstream* 16 (April 1970): 58–64.

206. Vern Bengtson, "The Generation Gap," in P.G. Altbach and R.S. Laufer, eds., *op. cit.,* pp. 195–217, note No. 30. Vern Bengtson, "Inter-Age Perceptions and the Generation Gap," *The Gerontologist* 11 (Winter 1971): 85–89; Vern Bengtson "Generational Difference and the Developmental Stake," *Aging and Human Development* 2 (1971): 249–60.

207. P. Abrams, "Rites de Passage: The Conflict of Generations in Industrial Society," *Journal of Contemporary History* 5, 1 (1970): 175–80.

208. Ted Goertzel, "Generational Conflict and Social Change," *Youth and Society* 3 (March 1972): 327–52.

209. J. Adelson, "What Generation Gap?" *New York Times Magazine* (January 18, 1970), pp. 10ff.

210. Edgar Z. Friedenberg, "Current Patterns of Generational Conflict," *Journal of Social Issues* 25 (April 1969): 21–38; Edgar Z. Friedenberg, "The Re-

72

volt Against Democracy," *Change* 1 (May-June 1969): 11–17; Edgar Z. Friedenberg, "Generation Gap," *Annals of the American Academy of Political and Social Science* 382 (March 1969): 32–42.

211. Robert Laufer, "Sources of Generational Consciousness and Conflict," *op. cit.,* note No. 30.

212. Gerald Rosenfeld, "Generational Revolt and the Free Speech Movement," *Liberation* 10 (December 1965): 13–17.

213. Paul Lauter and Florence Howe, *The Conspiracy of the Young* (New York: World, 1970).

214. Philip G. Altbach, *Student Politics in America, op. cit.,* note No. 84.

215. Clarence Shedd, *op. cit.,* note No. 88.

216. Douglas Gurak, "The University Christian Movement: The Political Socialization of Religious Activists," Ph.D. dissertation, Department of Sociology, University of Wisconsin, 1973.

217. Francis Carling, *Move Over: Students, Politics, Religion* (New York: Sheed and Ward, 1969).

218. David Horowitz, *Student* (New York: Ballantine Books, 1962).

219. "Documents: The Beginning of the Movement: Peace Protest and Civil Liberties," in M. Teodori, ed., *The New Left: A Documentary History* (Indianapolis, Indiana: Bobbs-Merrill, 1969), pp. 120–27. See also "The San Francisco Affair," in A.T. Anderson and B.D. Biggs, eds., *A Focus on Rebellion* (San Francisco: Chandler, 1962), pp. 3–93.

220. P.G. Altbach, *op. cit.,* note No. 84.

221. James Wechsler, *Revolt on the Campus, op. cit.,* note No. 92.

222. Patti Peterson, *op. cit.,* note No. 93.

223. Alan Brick, "Peace Moves on the Campus," *Fellowship* 25 (September 1, 1959): 8–12.

224. Louis Menashe and Ronald Radosh, eds., *Teach-Ins, USA: Reports, Opinions, Documents* (New York: Praeger, 1967).

225. Irving Louis Horowitz, *The Struggle is the Message: The Organization and Ideology of the Anti-War Movement* (Berkeley, California: Glendessary Press, 1970).

226. Massimo Teodori, ed., *op. cit.,* pp. 297–317, 240–70, note No. 219.

227. Paul Jacobs and Saul Landau, eds., *The New Radicals* (New York: Vintage, 1966), pp. 249–66.

228. New University Thought Peace Research Committee, "Student Peace Groups," *New University Thought* 1 (Spring 1961): 75–80.

229. Howard Zinn, SNCC, *The New Abolitionists* (Boston: Beacon Press, 1964).

230. Pat Watters, *Encounter With the Future* (Atlanta: Southern Regional Council, 1965).

231. Jacob Fishman and Fredric Solomon, "The Psychosocial Meaning of Nonviolence in Student Civil Rights Activity," *Psychiatry* 27 (May 1964): 91–99; Jacob Fishman and Fredric Solomon, "Youth and Social Change:

Perspectives on the Sit-In Movement," *American Journal of Orthopsychiatry* 33 (1963): 872–82; Jacob Fishman and Fredric Solomon, "Youth and Social Action: Action and Identity Formation in the First Student Sit-in Demonstration," *Journal of Social Issues* 20 (April 1964): 36–45.

232. John Orbell, "Protest Participation Among Southern Negro College Students," *American Political Science Review* 61 (June 1967): 446–56.

233. Anthony Orum, *Black Students in Protest: A Study of the Origins of the Black Student Movement* (Washington, D.C.: American Sociological Association, 1972).

234. Anthony Orum, "Patterns of Protest: The Politics of Black Youth in the Sixties," in A. Orum, ed., *The Seeds of Politics: Youth and Politics in America* (Englewood Cliffs, N.J.: Prentice Hall, 1972), pp. 271–82; Anthony and Amy Orum, "The Class and Status Bases of Negro Student Protest," *Social Science Quarterly* 49 (December 1968): 521–33.

235. Robert Coles, "Serpents and Doves: Nonviolent Youth in the South," in Erik Erikson, ed., *The Challenge of Youth, op. cit.*, pp. 223–59, note No. 42.

236. Anne Braden, "The Southern Freedom Movement in Perspective," *Monthly Review* 17 (August-September 1965): 1–13.

237. Charles Jones, "SNCC: Non-Violence and Revolution," *New University Thought* 3 (September-October 1963): 8–19.

238. Tom Hayden, "SNCC: The Qualities of Protest," *Studies on the Left* 5 (Winter 1965): 113–24.

239. Michael Walzer, "A Cup of Coffee and a Seat," *Dissent* 7 (Spring 1960): 111–20.

240. John Ehle, *The Free Men* (New York: Harper and Row, 1965).

241. E.J. Shoben and Philip Werdell, "SDS and SNCC: Profiles of Two Student Organizations," *School and Society* 96 (October 26, 1968): 365–72.

242. Staughton Lynd and Roberta Yancy, "Southern Negro Students," *Dissent* 11 (Summer 1964): 39–45.

243. Donald Mathews and James Prothero, "Negro Students and the Protest Movement," in J. McEvoy and A. Miller, eds., *op. cit.*, pp. 379–417, note No. 64.

244. See particularly the chapters by Stokley Carmichael and Charles Hamilton, and by Melvin Posey and by Nathan Hare in *ibid*, note No. 64.

245. Michael Aiken, N.J. Demerath, and Gerald Marwell, *Dynamics of Idealism* (San Francisco: Jossey-Bass, 1971).

246. Durward Long, "Black Protest," in Julian Foster and Durward Long, eds., *op. cit.*, pp. 459–82.

247. "Documents: The Radicalization of the Movement: Black Power," in M. Teodori, ed., *op. cit.*, pp. 271–96.

248. Gene Roberts, "From 'Freedom High' to 'Black Power': The Story of SNICK," *New York Times Magazine* (September 25, 1966), pp. 27–30ff.

249. Harold Jacobs, "SNCC and Black Power," *International Socialist Journal* 4 (August 1967): 647–72.

74

250. President's Commission on Campus Unrest, *op. cit.*, pp. 91–116, note No. 19.
251. *Ibid.*, pp. 411–65.
252. Harry Edwards, *Black Students* (New York: Free Press, 1970).
253. Jack Nelson and Jack Bass, *The Orangeburg Massacre* (New York: World, 1970).
254. Earl Anthony, *The Time of the Furnaces: A Case Study of Black Student Revolt* (New York: Dial Press, 1971).
255. Cushing Strout and David Grossvogel, eds., *Divided We Stand: Reflections on the Crisis at Cornell* (Garden City, N.Y.: Doubleday, 1970).
256. Urban Research Corporation, *Guns on Campus: Student Protest at Cornell* (Chicago: Urban Research Corporation, 1970).
257. "Black Mood on Campus: Symposium," *Newsweek* 73 (February 10, 1969): 53–59.
258. S.F. McDowell, G. Lowe, Jr., and D.A. Dockett, "Howard University's Student Protest Movement," *Public Opinion Quarterly* 34 (Fall 1970): 383–88.
259. John Blassingame, ed., *New Perspectives on Black Studies* (Urbana, Ill.: University of Illinois Press, 1971).
260. Henry Rosovsky, "Black Studies at Harvard: Personal Reflections Concerning Recent Events," *American Scholar* 38 (Autumn 1969): 562–72.
261. John Bunzel, "Black Studies at San Francisco State," *Public Interest* (Fall 1968): 22–38.
262. "Student Strikes, 1968–1969," *Black Scholar* 1 (January-February 1970): 65–75.
263. Marge Piercy, "The Grand Coolie Damn," in Robin Morgan, ed., *Sisterhood is Powerful* (New York: Vintage Books, 1970), pp. 421–37.
264. Kathy McAffee and Myrna Wood, "Bread and Roses," in Edith H. Altbach, ed., *From Feminism to Liberation* (Cambridge, Mass.: Schenkman, 1971), pp. 21–38.
265. Gail P. Kelly, "Women's Liberation and the New Left," in *ibid.*, pp. 39–46, note No. 264.
266. Edith H. Altbach, "Notes on a Movement," in *ibid.*, pp. 1–18, and Edith H. Altbach, *Women in American Society* (Lexington, Mass.: D.C. Heath, 1973, in press.)
267. Robin Morgan, ed., *op. cit.*, note No. 263.
268. Judith Hole and Ellen Levine, *Rebirth of Feminism* (New York: Quadrangle, 1971).
269. Janet Lever and Pepper Schwartz, *Women at Yale: Liberating A College Campus* (Indianapolis, Indiana: Bobbs-Merrill, 1971).
270. Joanne Evans Gardner, "The Feminist Movement," in G. Kerry Smith, ed., *The Troubled Campus* (San Francisco: Jossey-Bass, 1970), pp. 46–53.
271. Caroline Bird, "Women's Lib and the Women's Colleges," *Change* 4 (April 1972): 60–65.
272. Kate Millet, "Libbies, Smithies, Vassarites," *Change* 2 (September, October 1970): 42–50.
273. A. Pifer, "Newest Campus Crusade: Equal Rights for Women," *U.S. News and World Report* 71 (December 13, 1971): 79–82.

274. Edward Schwartz, ed., *Student Power* (Washington, D.C.: U.S. National Student Association, 1969).

275. Rick Kean, *Change: Thought From the Educational Reform Movement* (Washington, D.C.: U.S. National Student Association, 1970).

276. See Sections I F 2 and III D of the bibliography for further analysis of both student power and the relationship of students with their academic and social environment on campus.

277. Massimo Teodori, ed., *op. cit.,* pp. 318–47, note No. 102.

278. Carl Davidson, "The Praxis of Student Power: Strategy and Tactics," in I. Wallerstein and P. Starr, eds., *op. cit.,* (Vol. 2), pp. 108–124, note No. 60.

279. George Anastaplo, "Daring of Moderation: Student Power and the Melian Dialogue," *School Review* 78 (August 1970): 451–81.

280. Carl Davidson, *The New Radicals and the Multiversity* (Chicago: Students for a Democratic Society, 1968).

281. Eliot Friedson, ed., *Student Government, Student Leaders and the American College* (Philadelphia, Pa.: U.S. National Student Association, 1955).

282. Harry Lunn, Jr., *The Student's Role in College Policy Making* (Washington, D.C.: American Council on Education, 1957).

283. Neal Johnson, ed., *Student-Faculty-Administration Relations and the Role of Students in Policy Formation* (Philadelphia, Pa.: U.S. National Student Association, 1962).

284. Irving Louis Horowitz and William Friedland, *The Knowledge Factory: Student Power and Academic Politics in America* (Chicago: Aldine, 1970).

285. Harold Hodgkinson, *Student Participation in Campus Governance* (Berkeley, Calif.: Center for Research and Development in Higher Education, University of California, 1969).

286. American Council on Education, *Student's Role in College Policy Making* (Washington, D.C.: American Council on Education, 1957).

287. Earl McGrath, *Should Students Share the Power? A Study of Their Role in College and University Governance* (Philadelphia, Pa.: Temple University Press, 1970).

288. Robert Shaffer, "Student Government: Sandbox or Soapbox?" in Julian Foster and Durward Long, eds., *op. cit.,* pp. 497–505, note No. 59.

289. Stanford Cazier, "Student Power and *In Loco Parentis,*" in *ibid.,* pp. 506–530.

290. "Student Power in University Affairs: A Symposium," *American Journal of Comparative Law* 17, 3 (1969): 331–417.

291. J. Jameson and R.M. Hessler, "Natives are Restless: The Ethos and Mythos of Student Power," *Human Organization* 29 (Summer 1970): 81–94.

292. J.P. Kramer, "What Student Power Means," *New York Times Magazine* (May 16, 1968), pp. 32–33 ff.

293. For an excellent article on the concept of student trade unions in Europe, see Frank Pinner, "Student Trade Unionism in France, Belgium, and Holland," *op. cit.,* note No. 30. See also A. Belden Fields, *Student Politics in France* (New York: Basic Books, 1970).

294. Lawrence Schiff, "Dynamic Young Fogies: Rebels on the Right," *Transaction* 3 (November 1966): 30–36, Lawrence Schiff, "The Obedient Rebels: A Study of College Conversions to Conservatism," *Journal of Social Issues*

20 (October 1964): 74–96. See also Lawrence Schiff, "The Conservative Movement on American College Campuses," Ph.D. dissertation, Harvard University, 1964.

295. Opinion Research Corporation, *Conservatism on the Campus* (Princeton, N.J.: Opinion Research Corporation, 1962).

296. "Campus Conservatives," *Time* 127 (February 10, 1961): 34–37.

297. Ron Dorfman, et al., "The Right at NSA," *New University Thought* 2 (Autumn 1961): 25–32.

298. Alan Elms, "The Conservative Ripple," *Nation* 192 (May 27, 1961): 458–60, 468.

299. Steven V. Roberts, "Image on the Right," *Nation* 194 (May 19, 1962): 440–42.

300. Edward Cain, *They'd Rather Be Right: Youth and Conservatism* (New York: Macmillan, 1963).

301. M. Stanton Evans, *Revolt on the Campus* (Chicago: Regency, 1961).

302. Jerome Tuccille, *It Usually Begins With Ayn Rand* (New York: Stein and Day, 1971).

303. Richard Braungart, "Status Politics and Student Politics," *op. cit.*, note No. 183, and Richard Braungart, "SDS and YAF: A Comparison of Two Student Radical Groups," *op. cit.*, note No. 184.

304. The original expose of the NSA-CIA links appeared in *Ramparts*. See Sol Stern, "NSA:CIA," *Ramparts* 5 (March 1967): 29–38. The direct commentary on the incident is quite extensive. See, for example, "The CIA and the Students," *Time* 89 (February 24, 1967): 13–17; Philip G. Altbach, "CIA Spies or Deserving Students," *Christian Century* 84 (March 15, 1967): 352–54; Robert McDonal, "NSA/CIA: The Kiddies and their Playmates," *Transition* No. 31 (June-July, 1967): 14–19; Betty Gannett, "The CIA-Weapon of the Cold War," *Political Affairs* 46 (May 1967): 19–31.

305. Martin McLaughlin, *Political Processes in American National Student Organizations* (Ann Arbor, Michigan: Edward Brothers, 1948). See also Martin McLaughlin, "Spotlight on Students," *Catholic World* 166 (November 1947): 130–37.

306. Robert Kernish, *The History of the U.S.N.S.A.* (Washington, D.C.: U.S. National Student Association, 1965).

307. Peter T. Jones, *The History of the United States National Student Association Relations with the International Union of Students, 1945–1956* (Philadelphia, Pa.: Foreign Policy Research Institute, 1956).

308. Philip G. Altbach and Norman Uphoff, *op. cit.*, note No. 100.

309. Eliot Friedson, ed., *Student Government, Student Leaders, and The American College* (Philadelphia, Pa.: U.S. National Student Association, 1955).

310. Ralph Keyes, "What Makes NSA Run?", *Change* 2 (March-April 1970): 33–38.

311. Lawrence Landry, "NSA: Student Voice of the Silent Generation," *New University Thought* 1 (Spring 1960): 88–95.

312. Debbie Meier, "Careerism on the Campus: Two Faces of Conformity," *Anvil* 7 (Spring-Summer 1956): 9–12.

313. Ron Dorfman, Paul Levy, and Richard Merbaum, "The Right at NSA," *New University Thought* 2 (Autumn 1961): 25–32;

314. Young Americans for Freedom, *A Report on the U.S. National Student Association* (Washington, D.C.: Young Americans for Freedom, 1963).

315. S.M. Lipset and S.S. Wolin, eds., *op. cit.*, note No. 148.

316. Michael Miller and Susan Gilmore, eds., *Revolution at Berkeley* (New York: Dell, 1965).

317. Hal Draper, *Berkeley: The New Student Revolt* (New York: Grove Press, 1965).

318. Lewis Feuer, *The Conflict of Generations, op. cit.*, pp. 436–500; Lewis Feuer, "Rebellion at Berkeley," *New Leader* 47 (December 21, 1964): 3–12; Lewis Feuer, "Pornopolitics and the University," *New Leader* 48 (April 1965): 14–19; Lewis Feuer, "The Decline of Freedom at Berkeley," *Atlantic* 218 (August 1966): 78–82.

319. Max Heirich, *The Spiral of Conflict: Berkeley, 1964* (New York: Columbia University Press, 1964).

320. C. Michael Otten, *University Authority and the Student: The Berkeley Experience* (Berkeley and Los Angeles: University of California Press, 1970).

321. William Watts and David Whittaker, "Free Speech Advocates at Berkeley," *Journal of Applied Behavioral Science* 2 (January-March 1966): 41–62; William Watts and David Whittaker, "Some Sociological Differences Between Highly Committed Members of the Free Speech Movement and the Student Population at Berkeley," *Journal of Applied Behavioral Science* 1 (January-March 1965); and David Whittaker and William Watts, "Personal Characteristics of a Nonconformist Youth Subculture: A Study of the Berkeley Non-student," *Journal of Social Issues* 25 (April 1969): 65–89.

322. Joseph Gusfield, "Beyond Berkeley: High Noon on Campus," *Transaction* 2 (March-April, 1965): 3–11.

323. John Seeley, "The 'Berkeley Issue' In Time and Place," in H. Adelman and D. Lee, eds., *The University Game* (Toronto: Anansi, 1968), pp. 137–46.

324. Sheldon Wolin and John Schaar, *The Berkeley Rebellion and Beyond* (New York: Vintage, 1970).

325. Terry F. Lunsford, *The Free Speech Crisis at the University of California: Some Issues for Social and Legal Research* (Berkeley: Center for Research and Development in Higher Education, 1965).

326. Elinor Langer, "Crisis at Berkeley: Second Front," *Science* 148 (April 16, 1965): 346–49; Elinor Langer, "Crisis at Berkeley: The Civil War," *Science* 148 (April 9, 1965): 198–202; Elinor Langer, "Berkeley Scene, 1966: Politics and Potshots," *Science* 152 (May 20, 1966): 1037–41, and others.

327. Gerald Rosenfeld, *op. cit.*, note No. 212.

328. Caleb Foote and Associates, *The Culture of the University: Governance and Education* (San Francisco: Jossey-Bass, 1968).

329. Joseph Tussman, *Experiment at Berkeley* (New York: Oxford University Press, 1969).

330. Martin Trow, "Conceptions of the University: The Case of Berkeley," *American Behavioral Scientist* 11 (May-June 1968): 14–21.

78

331. Jerry Avorn, et al., eds., *Up Against the Ivy Wall: A History of the Columbia Crisis* (New York: Atheneum, 1968).

332. Archibald Cox et al., *Crisis at Columbia* (New York: Vintage Books, 1968).

333. Joanne Grant, ed., *Confrontation on Campus: The Columbia Pattern for the New Protest* (New York: Signet Books, 1969).

334. James Simon Kunen, *The Strawberry Statement: Notes of a College Revolutionary* (New York: Random House, 1969).

335. Robert Liebert, *op. cit.*, note No. 129.

336. Immanuel Wallerstein, *University in Turmoil: The Politics of Change* (New York: Atheneum, 1969).

337. C. Auger, A.H. Barton, and R. Maurice, "The Nature of the Student Movement and Radical Proposals for Change at Columbia University," *The Human Factor* 9 (Fall 1969): 18–40.

338. A.H. Barton, "Columbia Crisis: Campus, Vietnam, and the Ghetto," *Public Opinion Quarterly* 32 (Fall 1968): 333–51.

339. Dankwart Rustow, Mark Jacobs, Steven V. Roberts, and Amitai Etzioni, "Columbia in Turmoil: Four Articles," *New Leader* 51 (May 20, 1968): 5–19.

340. Steve Halliwell, "Columbia: An Explanation," in P. Long, ed., *The New Left, op. cit.*, pp. 200–215.

341. Richard Greenman, "The Columbia Rebellion," *New Politics* 6 (Summer 1967): 4–12.

342. Lawrence Eichel et al., eds., *The Harvard Strike* (Boston: Houghton Mifflin, 1970).

343. Steven Kelman, *Push Comes to Shove: The Escalation of Student Protest* (Boston: Houghton Mifflin, 1970).

344. Richard Zorza, *The Right To Say 'We': The Adventures of a Young Englishman at Harvard and in the Youth Movement* (New York: Praeger, 1970).

345. Urban Research Corporation, *Harvard's Student Strike: The Politics of Mass Mobilization* (Chicago: Urban Research Corporation, 1970).

346. Robert Smith, Richard Axen, and DeVere Pentony, *By Any Means Necessary: The Revolutionary Struggle at San Francisco State* (San Francisco: Jossey-Bass, 1970). See also DeVere Pentony, Robert Smith, and Richard Axen, *Unfinished Rebellions* (San Francisco: Jossey-Bass, 1971).

347. Arlene Kaplan Daniels et al., *Academics On the Line* (San Francisco: Jossey-Bass, 1970).

348. William Orrick, Jr., *College in Crisis* (Nashville, Tenn.: Aurora Publishers, 1970). This volume was originally prepared for the Commission on Violence.

349. Dikran Karagueuzian, *Blow It Up! The Black Student Revolt At San Francisco State and the Emergence of Dr. Hayakawa* (Boston: Gambit, 1972).

350. William Barlow and Peter Shapiro, *An End to Silence: The San Francisco State Student Movement in the 60s* (New York: Pegasus, 1971).

351. Leo Litwak and Herbert Wilner, *College Days in Earthquake Country: A Personal Record* (New York: Random House, 1971).

352. James Michener, *Kent State: What Happened and Why* (New York: Random House, 1971).

353. Joe Eszterhas and Michael Roberts, *Thirteen Seconds: Confrontation at Kent State* (New York: Dodd, Mead, 1970).

354. Ottavio Casale and Louis Paskoff, eds., *The Kent Affair: Documents and Interpretations* (Boston: Houghton Mifflin, 1971).

355. President's Commission on Campus Unrest, "Kent State," in *Report of the President's Commission on Campus Unrest, op. cit.,* pp. 233–90, note No. 19.

356. I.F. Stone, *The Killings at Kent State: How Murder Went Unpunished* (New York: New York Review Books, 1970).

357. President's Commission on Campus Unrest, "Jackson State," in *Report of the President's Commission on Campus Unrest, op. cit.,* pp. 411–65, note No. 19.

358. Southern Regional Council, *Augusta, Georgia and Jackson State University: Southern Episodes in a National Tragedy: Special Report* (Atlanta, Ga.: Southern Regional Council, 1970).

359. Richard Peterson and John Bilorusky, *May, 1970: The Campus Aftermath of Cambodia and Kent State* (New York: McGraw-Hill, 1971). This volume was prepared for the Carnegie Commission on Higher Education.

360. Urban Research Corporation, *On Strike! A Report on the First National Student Strike in U.S. History* (Chicago: Urban Research Corporation, 1970).

361. Irving Louis Horowitz and William Friedland, *The Knowledge Factory: Student Power and Academic Politics in America* (Chicago: Aldine, 1970).

362. Cushing Strout and David Grossvogel, eds., *op. cit.,* note No. 255.

363. H. Bruce Franklin, "The Real Issues in My Case," *Change* 4 (June 1972): 31–40; Nathan Glazer, "Why a Faculty Cannot Afford a Franklin," *Change* 4 (June 1972): 40–44; J.V. Baldridge and James Stam, "The Dynamics of Conflict on Campus: A Study of the Stanford 'April Third' Movement," in J.V. Baldridge, ed., *Academic Governance* (Berkeley, Calif.: McCutcheon, 1971), pp. 556–79.

364. Philip G. Altbach, Robert S. Laufer, and Shiela McVey, eds., *Academic Supermarkets* (San Francisco: Jossey-Bass, 1971).

365. Julian Foster and Durward Long, eds., *op. cit.,* note No. 59.

366. David Riesman and Verne Stadtman, eds., *op. cit.,* note No. 81.

367. Immanuel Wallerstein and Paul Starr, eds., *op. cit.,* note No. 60.

368. Mitchell Goodman, ed., *op. cit.*

369. Mitchell Cohen and Dennis Hale, eds., *The New Student Left* (Boston: Beacon Press, 1966).

370. Arthur Lothstein, ed., *All We Are Saying . . . The Philosophy of the New Left* (New York: Putnam, 1970).

371. Priscilla Long, ed., *op. cit.,* note No. 340.

372. Carl Oglesby, "Notes on a Decade Ready for the Dustbin," *Liberation* 14 (August-September 1969): 5–19. See also Carl Oglesby and Dennis Schaull, *Containment and Change* (New York: Macmillan, 1967).

373. Jerry Farber, *The Student as Nigger* (North Hollywood, Calif.: Contact Books, 1969).

374. New Republic, *Thoughts of the Young Radicals* (Washington, D.C.: The New Republic, 1966).

375. See James O'Brien, "The Development of the New Left," in P.G. Altbach and R.S. Laufer, eds., *op. cit.,* pp. 32–45. See also James O'Brien, *A History of the New Left* (Boston: New England Free Press, 1969); and James

O'Brien, *The Development of a New Left in the United States, op. cit.*

376. Tariq Ali, ed., *The New Revolutionaries: A Handbook of the International Radical Left* (New York: Murrow, 1969).

377. Paul Breines, ed., *Critical Interruptions: New Left Perspectives on Herbert Marcuse* (New York: Herder and Herder, 1970).

378. Herbert Marcuse, *Eros and Civilization* (New York: Vintage Books, 1962); Herbert Marcuse, *One Dimensional Man* (Boston: Beacon Press, 1964); and Herbert Marcuse, "Repressive Tolerance," in R.P. Wolff, B. Moore, Jr., and H. Marcuse, *A Critique of Pure Tolerance* (Boston: Beacon Press, 1965), pp. 81–118.

379. William Slate, ed., *Power to the People: New Left Writings* (New York: Tower, 1970).

380. Terrence Cook and P. Morgan, eds., *Participatory Democracy* (San Francisco: Canfield Press, 1971).

381. For further discussion of participatory democracy, see John Cammett, "Socialism and Participatory Democracy," in G. Fischer, ed., *Revival of American Socialism* (New York: Oxford University Press, 1971), pp. 41–62; Richard Flacks, "On the Use of Participatory Democracy," *Dissent* 13 (November 1966): 701–709.

382. Carl Oglesby, ed., *The New Left Reader* (New York: Grove Press, 1969).

383. John and Susan Erlich, eds., *op. cit.,* note No. 68.

384. Greg Calvert and Carol Nieman, *A Disrupted History: The New Left and the New Capitalism* (New York: Random House, 1971).

385. Richard Flacks, "The Revolt of the Young Intelligentsia: Revolutionary Class Consciousness in Post Scarcity America," in R. Aya and N. Miller, eds., *Revolution Reconsidered* (New York: Free Press, 1971); Richard Flacks, "On the New Working Class and Strategies for Social Change," in P.G. Altbach and R.S. Laufer, eds., *op. cit.,* pp. 101–138.

386. Herbert Gintis, "The New Working Class and Revolutionary Youth," *Socialist Revolution* 1 (May-June 1970): 13–43.

387. M. Teodori, ed., *op. cit.,* note No. 102.

388. Paul Jacobs and Saul Landau, eds., *op. cit.,* note No. 227.

389. James Simon Kunen, *op. cit.,* note No. 334.

390. Richard Zorza, *op. cit.,* note No. 344.

391. Paul Cowan, *The Making of an UnAmerican* (New York: Viking, 1967).

392. Raymond Mungo, *Famous Long Ago: My Life and Hard Times with the Liberation News Service* (Boston: Beacon Press, 1970).

393. Thomas Powers, *Diana: The Making of a Terrorist* (Boston: Houghton Mifflin, 1970).

394. Dotson Rader, *I Ain't Marchin Anymore* (New York: McKay, 1969).

395. Donald Reeves, *Notes of a Processed Brother* (New York: Pantheon, 1972).

396. Clancy Sigal, *Going Home* (Boston: Houghton Mifflin, 1962).

397. Kate Haracz, "The Education of Kate Haracz: Journal of an Undergraduate," *Change* 2 (May-June 1972): 12–26.

398. Harold Jacobs, ed., *Weatherman* (San Francisco: Ramparts Press, 1970). This volume provides the best analysis and commentary of this trend of the radical student movement.

399. Carl Davidson, *The New Radicals and the Multiversity* (Chicago: Students for a Democratic Society, 1968).

400. James O'Brien, "The Development of the New Left," in P.G. Altbach and R. Laufer, eds., *op. cit.*; James O'Brien, *History of the New Left, op. cit.,* and others.

401. S.M. Lipset, *Rebellion in the University, op. cit.,* note No. 48.

402. Philip G. Altbach, *Student Politics in America, op. cit.,* note No. 84.

403. Alan Adelson, *SDS* (New York: Scribners, 1971). See also K. Sale, *S.D.S.* (New York: Random House, 1973).

404. Jack Newfield, *A Prophetic Minority* (New York: New American Library, 1966).

405. Richard Peterson, *The Scope of Organized Student Protest, op. cit.,* note No. 75.

406. Massimo Teodori, ed., *op. cit.,* note No. 102.

407. Paul Jacobs and Saul Landau, eds., *op. cit.,* note No. 227.

408. Alexander Astin, "New Evidence on Campus Unrest, 1969–1970," *Educational Record* 52 (Winter 1971): 41–46; and A.E. Bayer and Alexander Astin, "Campus Disruption During 1968–1969," *American Council on Education Research Reports* 3, 3 (1969): 46 pp.

409. Carl Davidson, "Campaigning on the Campus," in A. Cockburn and R. Blackburn, eds., *Student Power* (Baltimore, Md.: Penguin Books, 1969), pp. 327–66.

410. Penina M. Glazer, "The New Left," *Journal of Higher Education* 38 (March 1967): 119–30.

411. Staughton Lynd, "Towards a History of the New Left," in P. Long, ed., *op. cit.,* pp. 1–14, note No. 340.

412. James O'Brien, *op. cit.,* note No. 400.

413. Alan Adelson, *op. cit.,* note No. 403.

414. See particularly *The New Left* (Memorandum prepared for the Subcommittee to Investigate the Administration of the Internal Security Act) (Washington, D.C.: Government Printing Office, 1968); *Investigation of Students for a Democratic Society,* (Hearings Before the Committee on Internal Security, House of Representatives) (Washington, D.C.: Government Printing Office, 1969). The SDS investigations are covered in a number of volumes, most of which deal with SDS activities on specific college campuses.

415. Richard Blumenthal, "S.D.S.: Protest is Not Enough," *Nation* 204 (May 22, 1967): 656–60.

416. James Jacobs, "SDS: Between Reform and Revolution," *Nation* 206 (June 10, 1968): 753–56.

417. Norm Fruthter, "SDS: In and Out of Context," *Liberation* 16 (February 1972): 19–33.

418. Richard Rothstein, "Representative Democracy in SDS," *Liberation* 16 (February 1972): 10–18.

419. Richard Rothstein, "ERAP: Revolution of the Organizers," *Radical America* 2 (March-April 1968): 1–18. See also Andrew Kopkind, "Of, By, and for the Poor: The New Generation of Student Organizers," *New Republic* 152 (June 19, 1965): 15–19.

420. Peter Wiley, "Hazard: Socialism and Community Organizing," *Radical America* 2 (January-February 1968): 25–37.

421. Tom Hayden and Carl Wittman, *An Interracial Movement of the Poor?*

(New York: Students for a Democratic Society, 1965); Tom Hayden, *Rebellion in Newark* (New York: Vintage, 1967); Tom Hayden, *Rebellion and Repression* (New York: Meridan Books, 1969).

422. Harold Jacobs, *op. cit.*, note No. 398.

423. *Outlaws of Amerika: Communiques from the Weather Underground* (New York: Liberated Guardian Collective, 1971).

424. Steven Kelman, "The Feud Among the Radicals," *Harpers* 232 (June 1966): 67–72; Steven Kelman, "S.D.S.: The Troubled Voice of the New Left," *New Leader* 47 (September 27, 1965): 8–14.

425. "The Splintering of SDS," in I. Wallerstein and P. Starr, eds., *op. cit.,* pp. 257–320, note No. 60.

426. James Weinstein, "Weatherman," *Socialist Revolution* 1 (January-February 1970): 129–43.

427. Michael Parker, "SDS: Copping Out of American Life," *New Politics* 7 (Fall 1968): 45–50.

428. Paula Reimer, "SDS: An Experiment in Pragmatism Fails," *New Politics* 7 (Fall 1968): 51–57.

429. Irving Howe, "New Styles in Leftism," *Dissent* 12 (Summer 1965): 295–323. See also Irving Howe, *Beyond the New Left* (New York: McCall, 1970). This volume provides a general analysis from a critical perspective of the SDS and the New Left.

430. Nathan Glazer, *op. cit.*, note No. 69.

431. Alexander Klein, ed., *Natural Enemies? Youth and the Clash of Generations* (New York: Lippincott, 1970).

432. George Thayer, *The Further Shores of Politics* (New York: Simon and Schuster, 1967).

433. Kenneth and Patricia Dolbeare, *American Ideologies* (Chicago: Markham, 1971), pp. 145–84.

434. Lewis Feuer, *op. cit.* See also Lewis Feuer, "The Student Left in the USA," *Survey* No. 62 (January 1967): 90–103.

435. Michael Miles, *op. cit.*, note No. 70.

436. S.M. Lipset, *Rebellion in the University, op. cit.,* note No. 48; S.M. Lipset and P.G. Altbach, "Student Politics and Higher Education in the United States, *op. cit.;* S.M. Lipset, "Students and Politics in Comparative Perspective," in S.M. Lipset and P.G. Altbach, eds., *op. cit.,* note No. 30.

437. Kenneth Keniston, *Youth and Dissent, op. cit.,* note No. 45.

438. Todd Gitlin, *The Politics and Vision of the New Left* (San Francisco: Bay Area Radical Education Project, 1968).

439. Mitchell Goodman, ed., *op. cit.,* note No. 11.

440. Pricilla Long, ed., *op. cit.,* note No. 340.

441. Charles Reich, *op. cit.,* note No. 116.

442. Paul Booth and Lee Webb, "From Protest to Radical Politics," *Our Generation* 3-4 (May 1966): 78–89.

443. Hal Draper, "In Defense of the 'New Radicals'," *New Politics* 4 (Summer 1965): 5–28.

444. Ronald Aronson, "The Movement and its Critics," *Studies on the Left* 6 (January-February 1966): 3–19.

445. Daniel Aaron et al., "Confrontation: The Old Left and the New," *American Scholar* 36 (Autumn 1967): 567–89.

446. Norman Birnbaum and Marjorie Childers, "The American Movement," in J. Nagel ed., *Student Power* (London: Merlin Press, 1969), pp. 125–41.

447. Richard Flacks, "Roots of Radicalism," *Playboy* 18 (April 1971): 107–108; Richard Flacks, "On the New Working Class and Strategies for Social Change," in P.G. Altbach and R.S. Laufer, *op. cit.,* pp. 85–100; Milton Mankoff and Richard Flacks, "The Changing Social Base of the American Student Movement," *ibid,* pp. 46–62; Richard Flacks, *Youth and Social Change, op. cit.*

448. Barbara and Al Haber, *Getting By With a Little Help From Our Friends* (Boston: New England Free Press, 1968).

449. Staughton Lynd, "A Program for Post-Campus Radicals," *Liberation* 14 (August-September 1969): 44–46.

450. Herbert Gans, "The New Radicalism: Sect of Action Movement? *Studies on the Left* 5 (Summer 1965): 126–40. See also Herbert Gans, "A Rational Approach to Radicalism," *Studies on the Left* 6 (January-February 1966): 37–47.

451. Julius Jacobson, "In Defense of the Young," *New Politics* 8 (Spring 1970): 4–13.

452. Jack Newfield, "In Defense of Student Radicals," in Gary and James Weaver, eds., *The University and Revolution* (Englewood Cliffs, N.J.: Prentice-Hall, 1969), pp. 43–55. The Weaver and Weaver volume also has a number of other commentaries, from several different viewpoints, on student activism in the sixties. S.M. Lipset's and Russell Kirk's chapters provide quite different perspectives on the student movement of the sixties.

453. Irving Howe, ed., *Beyond the New Left, op. cit.,* note No. 66.

454. Nathan Glazer, *op. cit.,* note No. 69.

455. Patrick Gleeson, ed., *Essays on the Student Movement* (Columbus, Ohio: Charles Merrill, 1970).

456. Roger Rapoport and Lawrence Kirshbaum, *op. cit.,* note No. 28.

457. Report of the President's Commission on Campus Unrest, *op. cit.,* note No. 19, Chapters 1 and 2.

458. Paul Hollander, "How Political is the Student Revolution?" *Youth and Society* 3 (December 1971): 138–58.

459. Carl Landauer, "The Student Revolt," *Yale Review* 60 (December 1970): 175–85.

460. Robert A. Nisbet, "Who Killed the Student Movement?" *Encounter* 34 (February 1970): 10–18.

461. James Brann, "The Straight Kids Lose Faith," *Change* 2 (November-December 1970): 66–71.

462. Armand Mauss, "The Jost Promise of Reconciliation: New Left vs. Old Left," *Journal of Social Issues* 27, 1 (1971): 1–20.

463. "The Old Left and the New," *Journal of Social Issues* 27, 1 (1971), (Special Issue).

464. Staughton Lynd, "The New Left," *Annals of the American Academy of Political and Social Science* 382 (March 1969): 64–72.

465. Tom Kahn, "The Problem of the New Left," *Commentary* 42 (July 1966): 30–38.

466. Irving Howe, ed., *op. cit., note* No. 66.

467. Clark Kerr, "Student Dissent and Confrontation Politics," in Julian Foster and Durward Long, eds., *op. cit.,* pp. 3–10, note No. 59.

468. Joseph Katz and Nevitt Sanford, "Causes of the Student Revolution," *Saturday Review* (December 18, 1965), pp. 64–66, 76–77.

469. James Lynch, "Disorder, Power, and the Students," *Virginia Quarterly Review* 43 (Winter 1967): 36–52.

470. Sidney Hook, *Academic Freedom and Academic Anarchy, op. cit.;* and Sidney Hook, ed., *In Defense of Academic Freedom* (New York: Pegasus, 1971).

471. William Gerberding and Duane Smith, eds., *The Radical Left; The Abuse of Discontent* (Boston: Houghton Mifflin, 1970).

472. Robert Brustein, *Revolution as Theater: Notes on the New Radical Style* (New York: Liveright, 1971).

473. U.S. News and World Report, *Communism and the New Left: What They're Up To Now* (Washington, D.C.: U.S. News and World Report, 1969).

474. John Coyne, Jr., *The Kumquat Statement* (New York: Cowles, 1970).

475. Free Society Association, *The New Student Left* (Washington, D.C.: Free Society Association, 1965).

476. William T. Divale, *I Lived Inside the Campus Revolution* (New York: Cowles, 1970).

477. Philip Abbott Luce, *The New Left* (New York: McKay, 1966).

478. E. Merrill Root, *Collectivism on the Campus: The Battle for the Mind in American Colleges* (New York: Devin Adair, 1955).

479. William Shinto, *The Drama of Student Revolt* (Valley Forge, Pa.: Judson Press, 1970).

480. Young Americans for Freedom University Research Committee, *A Faculty-Student Inquiry into the Causes of Campus Disorders* (Washington, D.C.: Young Americans for Freedom, 1970).

481. M. Drachkovitch, "The New Left in the United States: A Critical Appraisal," *Western Politics* 1 (Spring 1966): 3–21.

482. Andrew M. Greeley, "The End of the Movement," *Change* 4 (April 1972): 42–47.

483. S.I. Hayakawa, "Protests, Pigs, and Power Politics," *Liberal Education* 56 (March 1970): 17–21. See also S.I. Hayakawa, "Gangsters Cash in on Student Revolt: Interview," *U.S. News and World Report* 66 (February 24, 1969): 38–41.

484. Irving Kristol, "What's Bugging the Students?" *Atlantic* 216 (November 1965): 108–111. See also Daniel Bell and Irving Kristol, eds., *op. cit.,* note No. 67.

485. Theodore Roszak, *The Making of a Counter Culture: Reflections on the Technocratic Society and Its Youthful Opposition* (Garden City, N.Y.: Doubleday, 1969).

486. Joseph Berke, ed., *Counter Culture* (London: Peter Owen, 1969).

487. William Braden, *op. cit.,* note No. 114.

488. Ross V. Speck, *The New Families: Youth, Communes, and the Politics of Drugs* (New York: Basic Books, 1972).

489. Keith Melville, *Communes in the Counter-Culture: Origins, Theories* (New York: Murrow, 1972).

490. Ron E. Roberts, *The New Communes: Coming Together in America* (Englewood Cliffs, N.J.: Prentice Hall, 1971).

491. Sherri Cavan, *Hippies of the Haight* (St. Louis, Mo.: New Critics Press, 1971).

492. Lewis Yablonsky, *The Hippie Trip* (New York: Pegasus, 1968).

493. Jerry Hopkins, ed., *The Hippie Papers: Notes from the Underground Press* (New York: New American Library, 1968).

494. Jesse Kornbluth, ed., *Notes from the New Underground* (New York: Viking, 1968).

495. J. Simmons and Barry Winograd, *Its Happening: A Portrait of the Youth Scene Today* (Santa Barbara, California: Marc-Laird, 1966).

496. Editors of Ramparts, eds., *Conversations with the New Reality: Readings in the Cultural Revolution* (San Francisco: Canfield Press, 1972).

497. M.J. Yinger, "Contraculture and Subculture," *American Sociological Review* 25 (October 1960): 625–35.

498. Bennett M. Berger, "Hippie Morality: More Old than New," *Transaction* 5 (December 1967): 19–26.

499. Roger Starr, "The Counter-Culture and Its Apologists," *Commentary* 50 (December 1970): 46–54.

500. Michael Lerner, "Where To?" *Change* 3 (September 1971): 26–34.

501. Jesse Pitts, "The Hippies as Contrameritocracy," *Dissent* 16 (July-August 1969): 326–38.

502. Gilbert Geis, "Hypes, Hippies, and Hypocrites," *Youth and Society* 1 (June 1970): 365–79.

503. Andrew Greeley, "Implications for the Sociology of Religion of Occult Behavior in the Youth Culture." *Youth and Society* 2 (December 1970): 131–40.

504. Stewart Hall, "The Hippies: An American Movement," in J. Nagel, ed., *op. cit.,* pp. 170–202.

505. Michael Brown, "The Condemnation and Persecution of the Hippies," *Transaction* 6 (September 1969): 33–46.

506. Gerald Dworkin, "The Hippies: Permanent Revolution," *Dissent* 16 (March-April 1969): 180–83.

507. R. Serge Denisoff and M.H. Devine, "Generations and Counter Culture: A Study in the Ideology of Music," *Youth and Society* 2 (September 1970): 33–58.

508. John Berks, "The Underground Press: A Special Report," *Rolling Stone* No. 43 (October 4, 1969): 11–32.

509. Robert Denhardt and H. David Allen, "Youth Responses to Cultural Incongruities," *Youth and Society* 3 (December 1971): 237–55.

510. The bibliography has a lengthy section concerning drugs and students, although most of the listings have little direct relevance to student activism. See section III F 1.

511. Richard Blum et al., *Students and Drugs* (San Francisco: Jossey-Bass, 1969); Richard Blum and Associates, *Horatio Alger's Children: The Role of the Family in the Origin and Prevention Drug Risk* (San Francisco: Jossey-Bass, 1972).

512. Richard Goldstein, *1 in 7: Drugs on Campus* (New York: Walker, 1966).

513. Richard Carey, *The College Drug Scene* (Englewood Cliffs, N.J.: Prentice Hall, 1968).

514. Helen Nowlis, *Drugs on the College Campus* (Garden City, N.Y.: Doubleday, 1969).

515. C. Hollander, ed., *Background Papers on Student Drug Involvement* (Washington, D.C.: U.S. National Student Association, 1967).

516. Student Committee on Mental Health, *Psychedelics and the College Student* (Princeton, N.J.: Princeton University Press, 1967).

517. Howard Becker, "Ending Campus Drug Incidents," in H. Becker, ed., *Campus Power Struggle* (Chicago: Aldine, 1970), pp. 137-52.

518. Kenneth Keniston, "Heads and Seekers: Drugs on Campus, Counter Cultures, and American Society," *American Scholar* 38 (Winter 1968-1969): 97-112.

519. American Civil Liberties Union, *Academic Freedom and Civil Liberties of Students in Colleges and Universities* (New York: ACLU, 1970).

520. Roland Liebert, *Problems in Student Rights and Freedoms* (Washington, D.C.: U.S. National Student Association, 1966).

521. Neal Johnson, ed., *In Loco Parentis* (Philadelphia, Pa.: U.S. National Student Association, 1962).

522. O.W. Knorr and W.J. Minter, eds., *Order and Freedom on the Campus: The Rights and Responsibilities of Faculty and Students* (Boulder, Colo.: Western Interstate Commission for Higher Education, 1965).

523. Michael Nussbaum, *Student Legal Rights: What They Are and How to Protect Them* (New York: Harper and Row, 1970).

524. Louis Vaccaro and James T. Covert, eds., *Student Freedom in American Higher Education* (New York: Teachers College Press, 1969).

525. E.G. Williamson and John Cowan, *op. cit.,* note No. 74.

526. Michael T. Johnson, "The Constitutional Rights of College Students," *Texas Law Review* 42 (February 1964): 344-63.

527. Philip Moneypenny, "Toward a Standard for Student Academic Freedom," *Law and Contemporary Problems* 28 (Summer 1963): 625-35.

528. William Van Alstyne, "Student Rights and University Authority," *The College Counsel* 2 (1967): 44-67.

529. M.M. Chambers, *The Colleges and the Courts: The Developing Law Student and the College* (Danville, Ill.: Interstate, 1972).

530. Thomas Brady and Laverne Snoxell, *Student Discipline in Higher Education* (Washington, D.C.: American College Personnell Association, 1968).

531. Institute of Higher Education, University of Georgia, *The Legal Aspects of Student Discipline in Higher Education* (Athens, Ga.: Institute of Higher Education, University of Georgia, 1970).

532. Grace Holmes, ed., *Student Protest and the Law* (Ann Arbor, Michigan: Institute for Continuing Legal Education, University of Michigan, 1969).

533. For a general summary of Van Alstyne's work, see William Van Alstyne, "Student Activism, the Law and the Courts," in Julian Foster and Durward Long, eds., *op. cit.*, pp. 531–53. See also William Van Alstyne, "Student Academic Freedom and the Rule Making Powers of Public Universities: Some Constitutional Considerations," *Law in Transition Quarterly* 2 (Winter 1965): 1–34; William Van Alstyne, "The Judicial Trend Toward Student Academic Freedom," *University of Florida Law Review* 20 (1968): 290–306.

534. Ira Heyman, "Some Thoughts on University Disciplinary Proceedings," *California Law Review* 54 (March 1966): 73–87.

535. William Beaney, "Students, Higher Education and the Law," *Denver Law Journal* 45, 4 (1968): 511–44.

536. Sol Jacobson, "The Expulsion of Students and Due Process of Law," *Journal of Higher Education* 34 (May 1963): 250–55.

537. For more detailed references concerning the role of faculty in student activism and other faculty matters, see Section I K 6.

538. S.M. Lipset, "The Politics of Academia," in D.C. Nichol, ed., *Perspectives on Campus Tensions* (Washington, D.C.: American Council on Education, 1970), pp. 85–118.

539. Robert F. Boruch, *Varieties of Faculty Involvement in Campus Unrest* (Washington, D.C.: American Council on Education, 1969).

540. Arlene Kaplan Daniels, et al., *op. cit.*, note No. 347.

541. Alan E. Bayer, "The Faculty Role in Campus Unrest," *Change* 3 (Winter 1971–72): 10–13ff.

542. Stephen Cole and H. Adamsons, "Determinants of Faculty Support for Student Demonstrations," *Sociology of Education* 42 (Fall 1969): 315–29. See also Stephen Cole and H. Adamsons, "Professional Status and Faculty Support for Student Demonstrations," *Public Opinion Quarterly* 34 (Fall 1970): 389–94.

543. E.C. Ladd, Jr. and S.M. Lipset, "American Social Scientists and the Growth of Campus Political Activism in the 1960's," *Social Science Information* 10, 2 (1971): 105–120.

544. David Armor et al., "Professors! Attitudes Toward the Vietnam War," *Public Opinion Quarterly* 31, 2 (1967): 159–75.

545. S.M. Lipset and E.C. Ladd, Jr., ". . . And What Professors Think," *Psychology Today* 4 (November 1970): 49–52; E.C. Ladd, Jr., and S.M. Lipset, "The Politics of American Political Scientists," *PS* 4 (Spring 1971): 135–44; S.M. Lipset and E.C. Ladd, Jr., "The Divided Professoriate," *Change* 3 (May–June 1971): 54–60.

546. Jim Green, "Intellectuals and Activism: The Dilemma of the Radical Historian," *Activist* 11, 28 (1970): 3–6.

547. Norman Birnbaum, "Dilemmas of Resistence: New Universities Conference," *Nation* 206 (April 22, 1968): 535–38.

548. Robert S. Laufer, "Sources of Generational Conflict Among Faculty," *Youth and Society* 3 (June 1972): 477–90.

549. Richard Robbins, "Up Against the Statler-Hilton Wall," *Dissent* 17 (March-April 1970): 162–70.

550. D. Rabinowitz, "Radicalized Professor: A Portrait," *Commentary* 50 (July 1970): 62–64.

551. Irving Kristol, "Malcontent Professors," *Fortune* 76 (December 1967): 229–30.

552. Erwin Knoll, "Revolt of the Professors," *Saturday Review* 48 (June 1965): 60–61ff.

553. Andrew Hacker, "The Rebelling Young Scholars," *Commentary* 30 (November 1960): 404–412.

554. William Morgan, Faculty Mediation in Campus Conflict," in Julian Foster and Durward Long, eds., *op. cit.*, pp. 365–82, note No. 59.

555. J. Victor Baldridge, "Faculty Activism and Influence Patterns in the University," in J.V. Baldridge, ed., *Academic Governance* (Berkeley, Calif.: McCutcheon, 1971), pp. 293–313.

556. John Spiegel, "Campus Conflict and Professorial Egos," *Transaction* 6 (October 1969): 41–50.

557. See particularly JB Lon Hefferlin et al., *Inventory of Current Research on Postsecondary Education, 1972* (Berkeley, Calif.: Center for Research and Development in Higher Education, 1972).

558. Kenneth Keniston, *op. cit.*, note No. 45.

The Bibliography

1

Students and Student Activism

A. GENERAL MATERIAL

Abeles, Elvin. THE STUDENT AND THE UNIVERSITY: A BACK-
GROUND BOOK ON THE CAMPUS REVOLT. New York: Parents
Magazine Press, 1969.

Adelman, Clifford. GENERATIONS: A COLLAGE ON YOUTHCULT.
New York: Praeger, 1972.

Aldridge, John W. IN THE COUNTRY OF THE YOUNG. New York:
Harper's Magazine Press, 1970.

*Altbach, Philip G. and Robert S. Laufer, eds. THE NEW PILGRIMS:
YOUTH PROTEST IN TRANSITION. New York: McKay, 1972.

Anderson, Walt, ed. THE AGE OF PROTEST. Pacific Palisades, California:
Goodyear, 1969.

Baird, Leonard. A STUDY OF STUDENT ACTIVISM. Iowa City, Iowa:
American College Testing Program, 1969.

Bander, Edward J., ed. TURMOIL ON THE CAMPUS. New York:
H. W. Wilson, 1970.

*Becker, Howard, ed. CAMPUS POWER STRUGGLE. Chicago: Aldine,
1970.

*Bell, Daniel and Irving Kristol, eds. CONFRONTATION: THE STU-
DENTS REBELLION AND THE UNIVERSITIES. New York: Basic Books,
1969.

Berger, Bennett M. LOOKING FOR AMERICA: ESSAYS ON YOUTH,
SUBURBIA, AND OTHER AMERICAN OBSESSIONS. Englewood Cliffs,
New Jersey: Prentice-Hall, 1971.

Blaine, Graham B., jr. YOUTH AND THE HAZARDS OF AFFLUENCE;
THE HIGH SCHOOL AND COLLEGE YEARS. New York: Harper and Row,
1966.

Braden, William. AGE OF AQUARIUS. Chicago: Quadrangle, 1970.

Brickman, William and Stanley Lehrer, eds. CONFLICT AND CHANGE
ON THE CAMPUS: THE RESPONSE TO STUDENT HYPERACTIVISM.
New York: School and Society Books, 1970.

Brown, Michael. THE POLITICS AND ANTI-POLITICS OF THE YOUNG.
Beverly Hills, California: Glencoe Press, 1969.

Buchanan, Garth and Joan Brackett. SUMMARY RESULTS OF THE
SURVEY FOR THE PRESIDENT'S COMMISSION ON CAMPUS UNREST.
Washington: The Urban Institute, 1970.

Buchner, Andrew J., ed. THE NEW AMERICAN REVOLUTION: MORAL,
STUDENT AND THEOLOGICAL. St. Louis: Lutheran Academy for Scholarship, 1968.

91

Butz, O., ed. TO MAKE A DIFFERENCE: A STUDENT LOOK AT AMERICA. New York: Harper & Row, 1967.

Butz, O., ed. UNSILENT GENERATION: AN ANONYMOUS SYMPOSIUM IN WHICH ELEVEN COLLEGE SENIORS LOOK AT THEMSELVES. New York: Rinehart, 1958.

Cantelon, John E. COLLEGE EDUCATION AND THE CAMPUS REVOLUTION. Philadelphia: Westminister Press, 1969.

Clark, Shirley and John, eds. YOUTH IN MODERN SOCIETY. New York: Holt Rinehart and Winston, 1972.

*Cockburn, Alexander and Robin Blackburn, eds. STUDENT POWER. Baltimore: Penguin Books, 1969.

Cottle, Thomas. TIME'S CHILDREN: IMPRESSIONS OF YOUTH. Boston: Little Brown, 1971.

Dietze, Gottfried. YOUTH, UNIVERSITY AND DEMOCRACY. Baltimore: Johns Hopkins Press, 1970.

Douglas, Jack D. YOUTH IN TURMOIL. Chevy Chase, Maryland: National Institute of Mental Health, 1970.

Douglass, R. Bruce, ed. REFLECTIONS ON PROTEST. Richmond, Virginia: John Knox Press, 1967.

Ellsworth, Frank L. and Martha A. Burns. STUDENT ACTIVISM IN AMERICAN HIGHER EDUCATION. Washington: American College Personnel Association, 1970.

*Erlich, John and Susan, eds. STUDENT POWER, PARTICIPATION AND REVOLUTION. New York: Association Press, 1971.

THE ESTABLISHMENT MEETS STUDENTS: A UNIQUE CONFERENCE ON CAMPUS TURMOIL. Lawrenceville, Illinois: Ad-ventures, 1970.

Etzioni, Amitai. DEMONSTRATION DEMOCRACY. New York: Gordon and Breach, 1970.

Foley, James A. and Robert K. Foley. THE COLLEGE SCENE. New York: Cowles Book, 1969.

Footlick, J. K. THE COLLEGE SCENE NOW. Princeton, New Jersey: Newsbook Division, The National Observer, 1967.

*Foster, Julian and Durwood Long, eds. PROTEST! STUDENT ACTIVISM IN AMERICA. New York: Morrow, 1969.

Friedman, Maurice S. THE MODERN PROMETHEAN: A DIALOGUE WITH TODAY'S YOUTH. Wallingford, Pennsylvania: Pendle Hill, 1969.

*Glazer, Nathan. REMEMBERING THE ANSWERS: ESSAYS ON THE AMERICAN STUDENT REVOLT. New York: Basic Books, 1970.

Gleeson, Patrick, ed. ESSAYS ON THE STUDENT MOVEMENT. Columbus, Ohio: Merrill, 1970.

*Goodman, Mitchell, ed. THE MOVEMENT TOWARD A NEW AMERICA: THE BEGINNING OF A LONG REVOLUTION. Philadelphia, Pennsylvania: Pilgrim Press, 1970.

Grant, Joanne. CONFRONTATION ON CAMPUS: THE COLUMBIA PATTERN FOR THE NEW PROTEST. New York: Signet Books, 1969.

Hart, Richard L. and J. G. Saylor, eds. STUDENT UNREST: THREAT OR PROMISE? Washington: Association for Supervision and Curriculum Development, 1970.

Heckman, D. M. "World Views and Students Who Take Risks for Ethical Conviction." Unpublished Ph. D. dissertation, Graduate Theological Union, Berkeley, California.

Heist, Paul. INTELLECT AND COMMITMENT: THE FACES OF DISCONTENT. Berkeley: University of California, Center for the Study of Higher Education, 1965.

Howe, Irving, ed. BEYOND THE NEW LEFT. New York: McCall, 1970.

Howe, Irving, ed. STUDENT ACTIVISM. Indianapolis, Indiana: Bobbs Merrill, 1967.

Katz, Joseph, et al. NO TIME FOR YOUTH. San Francisco: Jossey-Bass, 1968.

Kean, Rick, ed. RUMORS OF CHANGE. Washington, D.C.: U.S. National Student Association, 1970.

Kleemann, Susanne. URSACHEN AND FORMEN DER AMERIKANISCHEN STUDENTENOPPOSITION. Frankfurt, West Germany: Suhrkamp, 1971.

Knorr, O. W. and W. J. Minter, eds. ORDER AND FREEDOM ON THE CAMPUS: THE RIGHTS AND RESPONSIBILITIES OF FACULTY AND STUDENTS. Boulder, Colorado: Western Interstate Commission for Higher Education, 1965.

Knott, Paul D., ed. STUDENT ACTIVISM. Dubuque, Iowa: W. C. Brown, 1971.

*Lauter, Paul and Florence Howe. THE CONSPIRACY OF THE YOUNG. New York: World, 1970.

Levitt, Morton and Ben Rubenstein, eds. YOUTH AND SOCIAL CHANGE. Detroit: Wayne State University Press, 1972.

*Lipset, Seymour Martin. REBELLION IN THE UNIVERSITY. Boston: Little Brown, 1971.

Lombardi, John. STUDENT ACTIVISM IN JUNIOR COLLEGES: AN ADMINISTRATOR'S VIEW. Washington, D.C.: American Association of Junior Colleges, 1969.

Lystad, Mary. AS THEY SEE IT. Cambridge, Massachusetts: Schenkman, 1973.

Mallery, David. FERMENT ON THE CAMPUS; AN ENCOUNTER WITH THE NEW COLLEGE GENERATION. New York: Harper & Row, 1966.

Manners, Elizabeth. THE VULNERABLE GENERATION. New York: McCann and Geoghegan, 1971.

*Massialas, Byron, ed. POLITICAL YOUTH: TRADITIONAL SCHOOLS: NATIONAL AND INTERNATIONAL PERSPECTIVES. Englewood Cliffs, New Jersey: Prentice Hall, 1972.

*Michael, Donald N. THE NEXT GENERATION, THE PROSPECTS AHEAD FOR THE YOUTH OF TODAY AND TOMORROW. New York: Vintage, 1965.

Nye, Russel, Ray Browne and Michael Marsden, eds. CRISES ON CAMPUS. Bowling Green, Ohio: Bowling Green State University Press, 1971.

Orum, Anthony M., ed. THE SEEDS OF POLITICS: YOUTH AND POLITICS IN AMERICA. Englewood Cliffs, New Jersey: Prentice-Hall, 1972.

*Otten, C. Michael. UNIVERSITY AUTHORITY AND THE STUDENT:

THE BERKELEY EXPERIENCE. Berkeley: University of California Press, 1970.

*Pettitt, George Albert. PRISONERS OF CULTURE. New York: Scribner, 1970.

Rapoport, Roger and Laurence J. Kirshbaum. IS THE LIBRARY BURN-ING? New York: Random House, 1969.

Reaske, Christopher Russell and Robert F. Wilson, jr., eds. STUDENT VOICES ON POLITICAL ACTION, CULTURE, AND THE UNIVERSITY. New York: Random House, 1971.

Rogan, Ronald L. CAMPUS APOCALYPSE; THE STUDENT SEARCH TODAY. New York: Seabury, 1969.

Saffen, Wayne. YOUTH TODAY. Philadelphia: Fortress Press, 1971.

*Skolnick, J. H., ed. THE POLITICS OF PROTEST. New York: Ballantine, 1969.

"Student Discontent on the American Campus," POLITICS 1970, Number 1 (1970), (special issue), 1-140.

THE STUDENT REVOLUTION—A SPECIAL REPORT. (Number 60). Princeton: Gallup Opinion Index, 1970.

*STUDENTS AND SOCIETY: REPORT ON A CONFERENCE. Santa Barbara, California: Center for the Study of Democratic Institutions, 1967.

*Teodori, M., ed. THE NEW LEFT: A DOCUMENTARY HISTORY. . Indianapolis, Indiana: Bobbs-Merrill, 1970.

Walton, George H. THE WASTED GENERATION. Philadelphia, Pennsylvania: Chilton Books, 1965.

*Weaver, Gary R. and James H. Weaver. eds. THE UNIVERSITY AND REVOLUTION. Englewood Cliffs, New Jersey: Prentice Hall, 1969.

YOUTH IN TURMOIL. New York: Time-Life Books, 1969.

Adelson, J. "Inventing the Young," COMMENTARY, 51 (May, 1971), 43-48.

Altbach, Philip G. "The Future of the American Student Movement," LIBERAL EDUCATION, 52 (October, 1966), 313-324.

Altbach, Philip. "The Quiet Campus," NEW LEADER, 46 (August 5, 1963), 12-14.

Bazelon, David. "Notes on the New Youth," CHANGE, 3 (May–June, 1971), 44-48.

Blank, Blanch Davis. "Bureaucracy or Democracy: Which is the Enemy in Campus Confrontations?" AAUP BULLETIN, 55 (June, 1969), 257-266.

Brock, William III. " 'Gut' Issues of Campus Unrest," COLLEGE AND UNIVERSITY JOURNAL, 8 (Fall, 1969), 45-48.

Brooks, Thomas R. "Voice of the New Campus 'Underclass'," NEW YORK TIMES MAGAZINE, (November 7, 1965), 25-27+.

Brown, Donald, Chairman. "Social Changes and the College Student: A Symposium," EDUCATIONAL RECORD, 41 (October, 1960), 329-358.

Brzezinski, Zbigniew. "The American Transition," NEW REPUBLIC, 157 (December 23, 1967), 18-21.

Capouya, Emile. "On Living with the Young," MODERN OCCASIONS, 1 (Fall, 1971), 602–610.

Casey, T. J. "Student Unrest: Roots and Solutions," LIBERAL EDUCATION, 55 (May, 1969), 244–254.

de Jouvenel, Bertrand. "Academic Youth and Social Revolution," in John Caffrey, ed. THE FUTURE ACADEMIC COMMUNITY: CONTINUITY AND CHANGE. Washington, D.C.: American Council on Education, 1969, 150–158.

Dobbins, C. G. "Potentialities of New Things," NATIONAL ASSOCIATION OF WOMEN DEANS AND COUNSELORS JOURNAL, 32 (Summer, 1969), 155–161.

Erikson, Erik. "Youth Today and in the Year 2,000," in Alexander Klein, ed. NATURAL ENEMIES? YOUTH AND THE CLASH OF GENERATIONS. New York: Lippincott, 1969, 522–532.

Freedman, J. L. "Parents It's Not all Your Fault, But . . . " JOURNAL OF POLITICS, 31 (August, 1969), 812–817.

Goldsen, Rose K., et al. "Political Apathy, Economic Conservatism," in Bartlett H. Stoodley, ed. SOCIETY AND SELF. New York: Free Press of Glencoe, 1962, 253–278.

Gusfield, Joseph. "Beyond Berkeley: High Noon on Campus," TRANSACTION, 2 (March–April, 1965), 3–7.

Herbert, T. Walter, jr. "The Student Protest Movement," THEOLOGY TODAY, 24 (January, 1968), 464–472.

*Hollander, Paul. "How Political Is the Student Revolution?" YOUTH AND SOCIETY, 3 (December, 1971), 138–158.

Holzner, Burkart. "Institutional Change, Social Stratification, and the Direction of Youth Movements," JOURNAL OF EDUCATIONAL SOCIOLOGY, 36 (October, 1962), 49–56.

Jameson, J. and R. Hessler. "The Natives are Restless: The Ethos and Mythos of Student Power," HUMAN ORGANIZATION, 29 (Summer, 1970), 81–94.

Katz, Joseph and Sanford Nevitt. "Causes of the Student Revolution," SATURDAY REVIEW, (December 18, 1965), 64–66, 76–77.

*Keniston, Kenneth. "The Faces in the Lecture Room," in Robert Morison, ed. THE CONTEMPORARY UNIVERSITY: USA. Boston: Houghton Mifflin, 1966, 315–349.

Keniston, K. "What's Bugging the Students," EDUCATIONAL RECORD, 51 (Spring, 1970), 116–129.

Kon, I. S. "Student Revolt and the 'Generation Conflict' Theory," DEMOCRATIC EDUCATION, (Prague), (Number 1, 1972), 3–13.

*Landauer, Carl. "The Student Revolt, YALE REVIEW, 60 (December, 1970), 175–185.

Lekachman, Robert. "Between Apostles and Technicians: Mind-Blowing and Problem-Solving," DISSENT, 18 (April, 1971), 128–140.

*Lipset, S. M. "Student Opposition in the United States," GOVERNMENT AND OPPOSITION, 1 (April, 1966), 351–374.

Lipset, S. M. "Youth and Politics," in R. K. Merton and R. Nisbet, ed.

CONTEMPORARY SOCIAL PROBLEMS. New York: Harcourt Brace Jovanovich, 1971, 743–791.

Lipset, S. M. and P. G. Altbach. "Student Politics and Higher Education in the United States," COMPARATIVE EDUCATION REVIEW, 10 (June, 1966), 320–349.

*Lipset, S. M. and Philip Altbach. "Student Politics and Higher Education in the United States," in S. M. Lipset, ed. STUDENT POLITICS. New York: Basic Books, 1967, 198–252.

Littell, Franklin. "Students in Search of 'Soul'," in W. Brickman and S. Lehrer, eds. CONFLICT AND CHANGE ON THE CAMPUS: THE RESPONSE TO STUDENT HYPERACTIVISM. New York: School and Society Books, 1970, 190–203.

*Matza, David. "Subterranean Traditions of Youth," ANNALS OF THE AMERICAN ACADEMY OF POLITICAL AND SOCIAL SCIENCE, 338 (November, 1961), 102–118.

Mauss, Armand L. "On Being Strangled by the Stars and Stripes," JOURNAL OF SOCIAL FORCES, 27 (1971), 183–202.

Mayhew, Lewis. "Changing the Balance of Power," SATURDAY REVIEW, (August 17, 1968), 480–481, 489–492.

Myerhoff, Barbara G. "The Revolution as a Trip: Symbol and Paradox," ANNALS OF THE AMERICAN ACADEMY OF POLITICAL AND SOCIAL SCIENCE, 395 (May, 1971), 105–116.

Rush, Gary B. "The Radicalization of Middle Class Youth," INTERNATIONAL SOCIAL SCIENCE JOURNAL, 24 (Number 2, 1972), 312–325.

Shoben, E. J., jr. "Toward Remedies for Restlessness: Issues in Student Unrest," LIBERAL EDUCATION, 54 (May, 1968), 221–230.

*Skolnick, J. "Student Protest," AAUP BULLETIN, 55 (September, 1969), 309–326.

Snow, R. J. "The Political Involvement of Students: Where Freedom Begins and Ends," in L. Vaccaro and J. Covert, eds. STUDENT FREEDOM IN AMERICAN HIGHER EDUCATION. New York: Teachers College Press, 1969, 85–104.

"Students: From the New Youth to the 'Forgotten Man'," in S. Lehrer, eds. LEADERS, TEACHERS, AND LEARNERS IN ACADEME. New York: School and Society Books, 1972, Part 5.

Taylor, E. K. and A. C. Wolfe. "Political Behavior," in S. Withey, ed. A DEGREE AND WHAT ELSE? New York: McGraw-Hill, 1972, 111–126.

Toch, Hans. "Who Left the Bomb in Mistress Murphy's Chowder? A Comment on Violent Youth," YOUTH AND SOCIETY, 2 (March, 1971), 367–377.

Wilson, Everett K. "Our Privileged Pariahs," ANTIOCH REVIEW, 26 (Fall, 1966), 318–331.

B. THEORETICAL MATERIAL

*Bakke, E. Wight and Mary Bakke. CAMPUS CHALLENGE: STUDENT ACTIVISM IN PERSPECTIVE. Hamden, Connecticut: Archon Books, 1971.

Cottle, Thomas J. PROSPECTS OF YOUTH: CONTEXTS FOR SOCIO-
LOGICAL INQUIRY. Boston: Little Brown, 1972

*Eisenstadt, S.N. FROM GENERATION TO GENERATION, Glencoe,
Illinois: Free Press, 1956.

*Erikson, Erik H., ed. YOUTH: CHANGE AND CHALLENGE. New
York: Basic Books, 1963.

*Feldman, Kenneth, ed. COLLEGE AND STUDENT: SELECTED READ-
INGS IN THE SOCIAL PSYCHOLOGY OF HIGHER EDUCATION. New
York: Pergamon, 1972.

*Feuer, Lewis S. THE CONFLICT OF GENERATIONS: THE CHARACTER
AND SIGNIFICANCE OF STUDENT MOVEMENTS. New York: Basic Books,
1969.

*Flacks, Richard. YOUTH AND SOCIAL CHANGE. Chicago: Markham,
1971.

Friedenberg, Edgar Z. COMING OF AGE IN AMERICA. New York: Vintage, 1967.

*Friedenberg, Edgar Z. THE VANISHING ADOLESCENT. Boston: Beacon,
1959.

Habermas, Jurgen. TOWARD A RATIONAL SOCIETY: STUDENT PRO-
TEST, SCIENCE AND POLITICS. Boston: Beacon, 1970.

Hyman, Sidney. YOUTH IN POLITICS: EXPECTATIONS AND REALI-
TIES. New York: Basic Books, 1972.

Keniston, Kenneth. THE UNCOMMITTED: ALIENATED YOUTH IN
AMERICAN SOCIETY. New York: Harcourt Brace and World, 1965.

*Keniston, Kenneth. THE YOUNG RADICALS: NOTES ON COM-
MITTED YOUTH. New York: Harcourt, Brace and World, 1968.

*Keniston, Kenneth. YOUTH AND DISSENT: THE RISE OF A NEW OPPO-
SITION. New York: Harcourt Brace Jovanovich, 1971.

Kerpelman, Larry C. ACTIVISTS AND NONACTIVISTS: A PSYCHOL-
OGICAL STUDY OF AMERICAN COLLEGE STUDENTS. New York: Behavioral Publications, 1972.

*Lipset, Seymour Martin. REBELLION IN THE UNIVERSITY. Boston:
Little Brown, 1972.

*Mead, Margaret. CULTURE AND COMMITMENT; A STUDY OF THE GEN-
ERATION GAP. Garden City, New York: Doubleday, 1970.

*Miles, Michael W. THE RADICAL PROBE: THE LOGIC OF STUDENT RE-
BELLION. New York: Atheneum, 1971.

Musgrove, F. YOUTH AND SOCIAL ORDER. London: Routledge and
Kegan Paul, 1964.

Reich, Charles. THE GREENING OF AMERICA. New York: Random
House, 1970.

*Roszak, T. THE MAKING OF A COUNTER CULTURE, REFLECTIONS
ON THE TECHNOCRATIC SOCIETY AND ITS YOUTHFUL OPPOSITION.
New York: Doubleday, 1969.

*Sampson, Edward E., Harold A. Korn, et al. STUDENT ACTIVISM AND
PROTEST. San Francisco: Jossey-Bass, 1970.

Scott, Marvin B. and Stanford M. Lyman. THE REVOLT OF THE STU-
DENTS. Columbus, Ohio: Charles Merrill, 1972.

*Slater, Phillip. THE PURSUIT OF LONELINESS: AMERICAN CULTURE AT THE BREAKING POINT. Boston: Beacon Press, 1970.

*Smelser, Neil J. THEORY OF COLLECTIVE BEHAVIOR. New York: Free Press of Glencoe, 1963.

Toch, Hans. THE SOCIAL PSYCHOLOGY OF SOCIAL MOVEMENTS. Indianapolis: Bobbs Merrill, 1965.

Allerbeck, Klaus. "Some Structural Conditions for Youth and Student Movements," INTERNATIONAL SOCIAL SCIENCE JOURNAL, 24 (Number 2, 1972), 257–270.

*Altbach, Philip G. "Students and Politics," COMPARATIVE EDUCATION REVIEW, 10 (June, 1966), 175–187.

*Bakke, Wight E. "Roots and Soil of Student Activism," COMPARATIVE EDUCATION REVIEW, 10 (June, 1966), 163–174.

*Bay, Christian. "Political and Apolitical Students: Facts in Search of Theory," JOURNAL OF SOCIAL ISSUES, 23 (July, 1967), 76–91.

Bay, Christian. "Student Political Activism," OUR GENERATION, 5 (June, 1967), 50–74.

Berger, Bennett M. "How Long is a Generation?" in B. M. Berger, ed. LOOKING FOR AMERICA. Englewood Cliffs, New Jersey: Prentice Hall, 1971, 13–20.

Coser, L.A., ed. "Collective Violence and Civil Conflict," JOURNAL OF SOCIAL ISSUES, 28 (Number 1, 1972), 1–212.

Easton, David and Robert D. Hess. "Youth and the Political System," in Seymour M. Lipset and Leo Lowenthal, eds. CULTURE AND SOCIAL CHARACTER. New York: Free Press, 1961, 226–251.

Eisenstadt, S. N. "Archetypal Pattern of Youth," in Erik Erikson, ed. YOUTH: CHANGE AND CHALLENGE. New York: Basic Books, 1963, 24–42.

Eisenstadt, S. N. "Changing Patterns of Youth Protest in Different Stages of Development of Modern Societies," YOUTH AND SOCIETY, 1 (December, 1969), 135–148.

*Erickson, Eric H. "Reflections on the Dissent of Contemporary Youth," DAEDALUS, 99 (Winter, 1970), 154–176.

Erikson, Erik. "Youth: Fidelity and Diversity," DAEDALUS, 91 (Winter, 1962), 5–28.

Feuer, Lewis. "The Sources and Traits of Student Movements," in A. Orum, ed. THE SEEDS OF POLITICS. Englewood Cliffs, New Jersey: Prentice Hall, 1972, 365–385.

Foster, Julian. "Student Protest: What Is Known, What Is Said," in Julian Foster and Durward Long, eds. PROTEST! STUDENT ACTIVISM IN AMERICA. New York: William Morrow, 1970, 27–58.

Gussner, Robert. "Youth: Deauthorization and the New Individualism," YOUTH AND SOCIETY, 4 (September, 1972), 103–125.

Keniston, Kenneth. "Moral Development, Youthful Activism, and Modern Society," YOUTH AND SOCIETY, 1 (September, 1969), 110–126.

Keniston, Kenneth. "Notes on Young Radicals," CHANGE, 1 (November–December, 1969), 25–33.

*Keniston, Kenneth. "The Sources of Student Dissent," JOURNAL OF SOCIAL ISSUES, 23 (July, 1967), 108–135.

Keniston, K. "Student Activism, Moral Development and Mortality," AMERICAN JOURNAL OF ORTHOPSYCHIATRY, 40 (July, 1970), 577–592.

*Keniston, Kenneth. "Why Students Become Radicals," JOURNAL OF AMERICAN COLLEGE HEALTH ASSOCIATION, 17 (December, 1968), 107–118.

*Keniston, Kenneth. "Youth as a Stage of Life," AMERICAN SCHOLAR, 49 (Fall, 1970), 631–654.

Keniston, Kenneth. "Youth, Change and Violence," AMERICAN SCHOLAR, 37 (Spring, 1968), 227–245.

Kerpelman, Larry. "Student Political Activism and Ideology: Comparative Characteristics of Activists and Non-Activists," JOURNAL OF COUNSELING PSYCHOLOGY, 16 (January, 1969), 8–13.

*Laqueur, Walter. "Reflections on Youth Movements," COMMENTARY, 47 (June, 1969) 33–42.

Lipset, Seymour Martin. "Perspective on Student Protest," TEACHING AND LEARNING, (1971), 25–30.

Maccoby, Eleanor E., Richard Mathews and Anton Morton. "Youth and Political Change," PUBLIC OPINION QUARTERLY, 18 (Spring, 1954), 23–39.

*McIntyre, William. "Student Movements," EDITORIAL RESEARCH RE-PORTS, 2 (December 11, 1957), 913–929.

*Mannheim, Karl. "The Problem of Generations," in P. G. Altbach, and R. S. Laufer, eds. THE NEW PILGRIMS. New York: McKay, 1972, 101–139.

Mannheim, Karl. "The Problem of Youth in Modern Society," in K. Mannheim, ed. DIAGNOSIS OF OUR TIME. New York: Oxford, 1944, 31–53.

*Matza, David. "Rebellious Youth: 1969," YOUTH AND SOCIETY, 1 (June, 1970), 455–472.

Matza, David. "Subterranean Traditions of Youth," ANNALS OF THE AMERICAN ACADEMY OF POLITICAL AND SOCIAL SCIENCE, 338 (November, 1961), 102–118.

Myerhoff, Barbara. "New Styles of Humanism: American Youth," YOUTH AND SOCIETY, 1 (December, 1969), 151–178.

Naegele, Kaspar, "Youth and Society: Some Observations," in Erik Erikson, ed. YOUTH: CHANGE AND CHALLENGE. New York: Basic Books, 1963, 43–63.

Neugarten, Bernice. "The Old and the Young in Modern Societies," AMERICAN BEHAVIORAL SCIENTIST, 14 (September, 1970), 13–24.

Parsons, Talcott. "Youth in the Context of American Society," DAEDALUS, 91 (Winter, 1962), 97–123.

*Pinner, F. A. "Students a Marginal Elite in Politics," ANNALS OF THE AMERICAN ACADEMY OF POLITICAL AND SOCIAL SCIENCE, 395 (May, 1971), 127–138.

*Rowntree, John and Margaret. "The Political Economy of Youth," OUR GENERATION, 6 (May–July, 1968), 155–190.

Sampson, Edward E., ed. "Stirrings out of Apathy: Student Activism and the Decade of Protest," JOURNAL OF SOCIAL ISSUES, 23 (July, 1967), 1–139.

*Sampson, Edward E. "Student Activism and the Decade of Protest," JOURNAL OF SOCIAL ISSUES, 23 (July, 1967), 1–33.

Tygart, Clarence E. and Norman Holt. "Examining the Weinberg and Walker Typology of Student Activists," AMERICAN JOURNAL OF SOCIOLOGY, 77 (March, 1972), 957–966.

*Weinberg, I. and K. N. Walker. "Student Politics and Political Systems: Toward a Typology," AMERICAN JOURNAL OF SOCIOLOGY, 75 (July, 1969), 77–96.

Zygulski, Kazimierz. "Sociological Approaches to the Culture of Youth," INTERNATIONAL SOCIAL SCIENCE JOURNAL, 24 (Number 2, 1972), 366–376.

C. HISTORICAL VARIABLES

*Altbach, Philip G. STUDENT POLITICS IN AMERICA. New York: McGraw-Hill, 1974.

Aries, P. CENTURIES OF CHILDHOOD. New York: Random House, 1962.

Bacciocco, Edward, jr. "The New Left from 1956–1969: A Study of Community, Reform, and Revolution." Unpublished Ph.D. dissertation, University of Colorado, Department of Political Science, 1971.

Berman, Ronald. AMERICA IN THE SIXTIES: AN INTELLECTUAL HISTORY. New York: Harper, 1970.

Butterfield, Herbert. THE DISCONTINUITIES BETWEEN THE GENERATIONS IN HISTORY. Cambridge, England: Cambridge University Press, 1972.

Cantor, Norman F. THE AGE OF PROTEST: DISSENT AND REBELLION IN THE TWENTIETH CENTURY. New York: Hawthorn Book, 1969.

Esler, Anthony. BOMBS, BEARDS, AND BARRICADES: 150 YEARS OF YOUTH IN REVOLT. New York: Stein and Day, 1971.

Kempton, Murray. PART OF OUR TIME. New York: Simon and Schuster, 1955.

*Lipset, S. M. REBELLION IN THE UNIVERSITY. Boston: Little Brown, 1972.

O'Neill, William L. COMING APART: AN INFORMAL HISTORY OF AMERICA IN THE 1960'S. Chicago: Quadrangle Books, 1971.

Rosenbrier, Gilbert Miloslav. "An Historical Analysis of Student Unrest." Unpublished Ed. D. dissertation, Boston University, School of Education, 1971.

Stanton, Charles M. "Student Activism on Three California Campuses During the Years 1930–1940 and 1955–1965." Unpublished Ph. D. dissertation, Stanford University, 1967.

Swirski, Barbara. "American Student Political Activity in the Thirties and Sixties: An Analysis of War Protest at Harvard and Wisconsin." Unpublished M.A. dissertation, Michigan State University, Department of Sociology, 1971.

Swirski, Shlomo. "Changes in the Structure of Relations Between Groups and the Emergence of Political Movements: The Student Movement at Harvard and Wisconsin, 1930–1969." Unpublished Ph. D. dissertation, Michigan State University, Department of Political Science, 1971.

Weisenberg, Mira. THE L. I. D.: FIFTY YEARS OF DEMOCRATIC EDU-
CATION 1905–1955. New York: League for Industrial Democracy, 1955.

Yorberg, Betty. UTOPIA AND REALITY: A COLLECTIVE PORTRAIT
OF AMERICAN SOCIALISTS. New York: Columbia University Press, 1969.

*Altbach, Philip G. "A History of the American Peace Movement,"
FELLOWSHIP, 31 (January, March, July, and September, 1965), 22–27,
28–32, 25–29, 28–32.

*Altbach, P. G. and P. Peterson. "Before Berkeley: Historical Perspective
on American Student Activism," ANNALS OF THE AMERICAN ACADEMY OF
POLITICAL AND SOCIAL SCIENCE, 395 (May, 1971), 1–14.

Aron, Raymond. "Student Rebellion: Vision of the Future or Echo from
the Past?" POLITICAL SCIENCE QUARTERLY, 84 (June, 1969), 289–310.

Breitman, George. "The Current Radicalization Compared with Those of
the Past," INTERNATIONAL SOCIALIST REVIEW, 31 (October, 1970),
7–9+.

Bronowski, J. "Protest, Past and Present," AMERICAN SCHOLAR, 38
(Autumn, 1969), 535–546.

Coleman, T. C. III. "American Culture and the College Generation," MID-
WEST QUARTERLY, 11 (October, 1969), 53–63.

Cowley, W. H. "Student Unrest in Perspective," in W. Brickman and S.
Lehrer, ed. CONFLICT AND CHANGE ON THE CAMPUS. New York: School
and Society Books, 1970, 105–112.

Ebersole, Mark C. "The Rise and Fall of Student Generations," LIBERAL
EDUCATION, 51 (October, 1965), 413–418.

Fairchild, James H. "J. H. Fairchild on the Antislavery Commitment of
Oberlin, 1833–1834," in R. Hofstadter and W. Smith, eds. AMERICAN HIGHER
EDUCATION: A DOCUMENTARY HISTORY, VOLUME I. Chicago: Univer-
sity of Chicago Press, 1961.

Gauss, C. "Why Students Riot," COLLIERS, 87 (January 31, 1931),
22–23+.

Glicksberg, C. I. "Communism on the Campus," HARVARD EDUCA-
TIONAL REVIEW, 26 (Summer, 1956), 276–285.

Griffith, D. W. "Capitalists, Colleges, and Communism," CATHOLIC
WORLD, 143 (September, 1936), 702–705.

"History of College Student Unrest," SCHOOL AND SOCIETY, 94
(February 5, 1966), 56.

*Lipset, S. M. "Student Opposition in the United States," GOVERNMENT
AND OPPOSITION, 1 (April, 1966), 351–374.

*Lipset, S. M. and Everett Ladd, jr. "College Generations—from the 1930's
to the 1960's," PUBLIC INTEREST, (Fall, 1971), 99–113.

Lynd, Staughton. "Towards a History of the New Left," in P. Long, ed.
THE NEW LEFT. Boston: Porter Sargent, 1969, 1–13.

Mangano, R. M. and A. L. Casebeer. "Alarming Parallels in Student Anti-
War Activism of the Thirties and Sixties," NATIONAL ASSOCIATION OF STU-
DENT PERSONNEL ADMINISTRATORS JOURNAL, 9 (October, 1971),
119–126.

Mann, Georg. "Two Lefts: A Look Across the Generation Gap," SOUTH ATLANTIC QUARTERLY, 69 (Autumn, 1970), 431–445.

O'Brien, James. "Beyond Reminiscence: The New Left in History," RADICAL AMERICA, 6 (July–August, 1972), 11–48.

*Oglesby, Carl. "Notes on a Decade Ready for the Dustbin," LIBERATION, 14 (August–September, 1969), 5–19.

Peterson, Patti. "Student Organizations and the Antiwar Movement in America, 1900–1960," AMERICAN STUDIES, 13 (Spring, 1972), 131–148.

Reinhold, Meyer. "The Generation Gap in Antiquity," PROCEEDINGS OF THE AMERICAN PHILOSOPHICAL SOCIETY, 114 (October, 1970), 347–365.

Rusk, D. "From the Class of '31 to the Class of '51," NEW YORK TIMES MAGAZINE, (June 3, 1951), 17+.

Spivak, Robert. "Growth of an American Youth Movement, 1905–1941," AMERICAN SCHOLAR, 10 (Summer, 1941), 352–361.

Sturtevant, Julian. "Antislavery sentiment at Illinois College, 1837," in R. Hofstadter and W. Smith, eds. AMERICAN HIGHER EDUCATION: A DOCUMENTARY HISTORY, VOLUME I. Chicago: The University of Chicago Press, 1961, 419–433.

Unger, I. "New Left and American History: Some Recent Trends in United States Historiography," AMERICAN HISTORICAL REVIEW, 72 (July, 1967), 1237–1246.

D. COMPARATIVE PERSPECTIVES

*Archer, Margaret, ed. STUDENTS, UNIVERSITY AND SOCIETY: A COMPARATIVE SOCIOLOGICAL REVIEW. New York: Crane-Russak, 1972.

Brickman, William W. and Stanley Lehrer, eds. CONFLICT AND CHANGE ON THE CAMPUS: THE RESPONSE TO STUDENT HYPERACTIVISM. New York: School and Society Books, 1970.

Buckman, Peter. THE LIMITS OF PROTEST. Indianapolis: Bobbs-Merrill, 1970.

Califano, Joseph A., jr. THE STUDENT REVOLUTION: A GLOBAL CONFRONTATION. New York: Norton, 1970.

Crick, Bernard and William Robson, eds. PROTEST AND DISCONTENT. Harmondsworth: Penguin, 1971.

Crouch, Colin. THE STUDENT REVOLUTION. London: Bodley Head, 1970.

De Jouvenal, Bertrand. ACADEMIC YOUTH AND SOCIAL REVOLUTION. Washington, D. C.: American Council on Education, 1969.

Eckstein, George G. USA: DIE NEUE LINKE AM ENDE? Munich: Hauser, 1970.

Esler, Anthony. BOMBS, BEARDS, AND BARRICADES: 150 YEARS OF YOUTH IN REVOLT. New York: Stein and Day, 1971.

Habermas, Jurgen. TOWARD A RATIONAL SOCIETY: STUDENT PROTEST SCIENCE AND POLITICS. Boston: Beacon Press, 1970.

Harris, Janet, ed. STUDENTS IN REVOLT. New York: McGraw-Hill, 1970.

Hope, Marjorie. YOUTH AGAINST THE WORLD. Boston: Little Brown, 1970.

*Lipset, Seymour Martin, ed. STUDENT POLITICS. New York: Basic Books, 1967.

*Lipset, S. M. and Philip Altbach, eds. STUDENTS IN REVOLT. Boston: Houghton Mifflin, 1969.

*McGuigan, Gerald P., ed. STUDENT PROTEST. Methuen, 1968.

Mandel, Ernest, et al. REVOLUTIONARY STUDENT MOVEMENTS: THEORY AND PRACTICE. New York: Merit, 1970.

*Nagel, Julius, ed. STUDENT POWER. London: Merlin Press, 1969.

Spender, Stephen. THE YEAR OF THE YOUNG REBELS. New York: Random House, 1969.

Adorno, T. W. "Of Barricades and Ivory Towers: An Interview," ENCOUNTER, 33 (September, 1969), 63–69.

Altbach, Philip G. "Students and International Affairs," in Bruce Douglass, ed. REFLECTIONS ON PROTEST. Richmond, Virginia: John Knox Press, 1967, 71–84.

Baker–White, J. "Students in Revolt: The Revolutionaries," 20TH CENTURY, 177 (Third, 1968), 17–18+.

Beloff, M. "Politics of Student Revolt," POLITICAL STUDIES, 17 (1969), 514–517.

Bettelheim, Bruno. "The Anatomy of Academic Discontent," CHANGE, 1 (May–June, 1969), 18–26.

Blewett, John, S. J. "Student Movements: East Asian and American Patterns," in L. Vaccaro and J. T. Covert, eds. FREEDOM IN AMERICAN HIGHER EDUCATION. New York: Teachers' College Press, 1969, 155–165.

Bottomore, T. B. "Students Observed," UNIVERSITIES QUARTERLY, 22 (September, 1968), 425–433.

Bousquet, J. "Student Revolt," INTERNATIONAL SOCIAL SCIENCE JOURNAL, 21 (Number 1, 1969), 135–148.

Brammer, Lawrence M. "The Student Rebel in the University," JOURNAL OF HIGHER EDUCATION, 38 (May, 1967), 257–262.

Brogan, D. W. "The Student Revolt," ENCOUNTER, 31 (July, 1968), 20–25.

Clerc, J. P. and C. Debbasch. "Student Participation in University Governance," WESTERN EUROPEAN EDUCATION, 3 (Winter, 1971–1972), 349–354.

Cranston, Maurice. "Neocommunism and the Student Revolts," STUDIES IN COMPARATIVE COMMUNISM, 1 (July/October, 1968), 4–55.

Crick, B. "The Proper Limits of Student Influence," in D. Martin, ed. ANARCHY AND CULTURE–THE PROBLEM OF THE CONTEMPORARY UNIVERSITY. New York: Columbia University Press, 1969, 155–171.

Duster, Troy. "Student Interests, Student Power, and the Swedish Experience," AMERICAN BEHAVIORAL SCIENTIST, 11 (May–June, 1968), 21–33.

104

Elder, H. "Dissent and Participation," CONVERGENCE, 4 (Number 2, 1971), 74–79.

Falk, K. I. "Revolution at Home and Abroad: Parallels between Germany and U. S.," VITAL SPEECHES, 37 (November 1, 1970), 58–61.

Frye, Northrop. "The University and Personal Life: Student Anarchism and the Educational Conflict" in W. R. Niblett, ed. HIGHER EDUCATION: DEMAND AND RESPONSE. London: Tavistock Publications, 1969, 35–51.

Gellner, E. "The Panther and the Dove: Reflections on Rebelliousness and its Milieu," D. Martin, ed. ANARCHY AND CULTURE: THE PROBLEMS OF THE CONTEMPORARY UNIVERSITY. New York: Columbia University Press, 1969.

Halleck, Seymour L. "Hypotheses of Student Unrest," in Julian Foster and Durward Long, eds. PROTEST! STUDENT ACTIVISM IN AMERICA. New York: Morrow, 1970, 105–122.

Halleck, Seymour. "Twelve Hypotheses of Student Unrest," in G. Kerry Smith, ed. STRESS AND CAMPUS RESPONSE. San Francisco: Jossey-Bass, 1968, 115–133.

Halleck, Seymour L. "Why Students Protest: a Psychiatrist's View," in G. F. McGuigan, ed. STUDENT PROTEST. Toronto: Methuen, 1968, 223–235.

Huntley, James Robert. "Student Unrest in Europe and America: Some Implications for Western Society," RES PUBLICA, 12 (Number 2, 1970), 171–184.

Jupp, James. "The Discontent of Youth," POLITICAL QUARTERLY, 40 (October/December, 1969), 411–418.

Kohak, Erazim. "Being Young in a Postindustrial Society," DISSENT, 18 (February, 1971), 30–41.

Lipset, Seymour M. "American Student Activism in Comparative Perspective," AMERICAN PSYCHOLOGIST, 25 (August, 1970), 675–693.

Lipset, Seymour Martin. "The Possible Effects of Student Activism on International Politics," in S. M. Lipset, and P. G. Altbach, eds. STUDENTS IN REVOLT. Boston: Houghton Mifflin, 1969, 495–524.

*Lipset, Seymour Martin. "Students and Politics in Comparative Perspective," DAEDALUS, 97 (Winter, 1968), 1–28.

Lowenthal, Richard, Lewis Coser, and Irving Howe, "The Worldwide Revolt of the Young," DISSENT, 16 (May–June, 1969), 214–225.

Martinelli, Alberto and Alessandro Cavelli. "Towards a Conceptual Framework for the Comparative Analysis of Student Movements," INTERNATIONAL SOCIAL SCIENCE JOURNAL, 24 (Number 2, 1972), 301–311.

Meyer, John M. and Richard Rubinson. "Structural Determinants of Student Political Activity: A Comparative Interpretation," SOCIOLOGY OF EDUCATION, 45 (Winter, 1972), 23–46.

Moller, Herbert. "Youth as a Force in the Modern World," COMPARATIVE STUDIES IN SOCIETY AND HISTORY, 10 (April, 1968), 237–260.

Mott, J., and N. Goldie. "Social Characteristics of Militant and Anti-Militant Students; Great Britain," UNIVERSITIES QUARTERLY, 26 (Winter, 1971), 28–40.

*Pinner, Frank. "Students—A Marginal Elite in Politics," in P. G. Altbach and R. S. Laufer, eds. THE NEW PILGRIMS. New York: McKay, 1972, 281-296.

Renner, R. R. "Student Unrest in U. S. and Latin American Universities," SCHOOL AND SOCIEITY, 93 (Summer, 1965), 294-297.

Shils, Edward. "Dreams of Plenitude, Nightmares of Scarcity," in Seymour Lipset and Philip Altbach, eds. STUDENTS IN REVOLT. Boston: Houghton Mifflin, 1969, 1-31.

Shils, E. "Plenitude and Scarcity," ENCOUNTER, 32 (May, 1969), 37-48+.

Soares, Glaucio. "The Active Few: A Study of Ideology and Participation," COMPARATIVE EDUCATION REVIEW, 10 (June, 1966), 205-220.

E. SOCIOLOGICAL AND PSYCHOLOGICAL ASPECTS OF STUDENT ACTIVISM

E.1. Studies on the Meaning of Youth in America

Adams, James F, ed. UNDERSTANDING ADOLESCENCE: CURRENT DEVELOPMENTS IN ADOLESCENT PSYCHOLOGY. Boston: Allyn and Bacon, 1968.

Blos, Peter. ON ADOLESCENCE: A PSYCHOANALYTIC INTERPRETA-TION. Glencoe, Illinois: Free Press, 1962.

Douvan, E, and J. Adelson. THE ADOLESCENT EXPERIENCE. New York: Wiley, 1966.

Douvan, Elizabeth and S. B. Withey. A STUDY OF ADOLESCENT BOYS. Ann Arbor: Survey Research Center, University of Michigan, 1955.

Erikson, Erik H, ed. THE CHALLENGE OF YOUTH. Garden City, New York: Doubleday, 1965.

*Erikson, Erik. CHILDHOOD AND SOCIETY, New York: W. W. Norton, 1963.

Frey, Sherman H, ed. ADOLESCENT BEHAVIOR IN SCHOOL: DETERMI-NANT AND OUTCOMES. Chicago: Rand McNally, 1970.

Gillespie, J. M. and G. W. Allport. YOUTH'S OUTLOOK ON THE FUTURE. New York: Doubleday, 1955.

Ginsberg, Eli, ed. VALUES AND IDEALS OF AMERICAN YOUTH. New York Columbia University Press, 1960.

Goldburgh, S. G. THE EXPERIENCE OF ADOLESCENCE. Cambridge, Massachusetts: Schenkman, 1965.

Goodman, Paul. GROWING UP ABSURD; PROBLEMS OF YOUTH IN THE ORGANIZED SYSTEM. New York: Random House, 1960.

Gottlieb, D. and C. E. Ramsey. THE AMERICAN ADOLESCENT. Homewood, Illinois: Dorsey, 1964.

Gottlieb, David, ed. YOUTH IN CONTEMPORARY SOCIETY. Beverly Hills, California: Sage, 1972.

Gottlieb, David, John Reeves, and Warren D. Tenhouten. THE EMERGENCE OF YOUTH SOCIEITES: A CROSS CULTURAL APPROACH. New York: Free Press, 1966.

106

Greenstein, Fred I. CHILDREN AND POLITICS. New Haven: Yale University Press, 1965.

Kandel, Denise and Gerald Lesser. YOUTH IN TWO WORLDS. San Francisco: Jossey-Bass, 1972.

Landis, Paul. ADOLESCENCE AND YOUTH, New York: McGraw-Hill, 1957.

Lupton, Kieth D, ed. THE STUDENT IN SOCIETY. Totowa, New Jersey: Littlefield, Adams, 1969.

Mays, John Barrow. THE YOUNG PRETENDERS: A STUDY OF TEEN-AGE CULTURE IN CONTEMPORARY SOCIETY. New York: Schocken, 1969.

Moore, Allen J. THE YOUNG ADULT GENERATION. Nashville: Abington, 1969.

Porterfield, Austin L. THE NOW GENERATION: SOCIAL PROBLEMS OF YOUTH AS RELATED TO IMAGES OF SELF, FAMILY AND SOCIETY. Fort Worth, Texas: Texas Christian University Press, 1971.

Rapson, R., ed. THE CULT OF YOUTH IN MIDDLE CLASS AMERICA. Lexington, Massachusetts: D. C. Heath, 1971.

Remmers, H. H. and D. H. Radler. THE AMERICAN TEENAGER. Indianapolis, Indiana: Bobbs-Merrill, 1957.

Rogers, D. THE PSYCHOLOGY OF ADOLESCENCE. New York: Appleton Century-Crofts, 1968.

Sebald, H. ADOLESCENCE. New York: Appleton-Century-Crofts, 1968.

Sherif, Muzafer and Carolyn W. Sherif, eds. PROBLEMS OF YOUTH: TRANSITION TO ADULTHOOD IN A CHANGING WORLD. Chicago: Aldine, 1965.

"American Youth: Its Outlook Is Changing the World: Symposium," FORTUNE, 79 (January, 1969), 59–60 and 66–116+.

Ball, Donald W. "Covert Political Rebellion as Ressentiment," SOCIAL FORCES, 43 (October, 1964).

Banks, L. "View through Youthful Eyes," FORTUNE, 81 (April, 1970), 76–77+.

Bazelon, David. "Notes on the New Youth," CHANGE, 3 (May-June, 1971), 44–47.

Berger, Bennett M. "Adolescence and Beyond," SOCIAL PROBLEMS, 10 Spring, 1963), 394–408.

Berger, B. M. "New Stage of American Man Almost Endless Adolescence," NEW YORK TIMES MAGAZINE, (November 2, 1969) 32–33+.

Berger, Bennett. "On the Youthfulness of Youth Cultures," SOCIAL RESEARCH, 30 (Autumn, 1963), 319–342

Bettelheim, B. "Obsolete Youth: Towards a Psychograph of Adolescent Rebellion, "ENCOUNTER, 23 (September, 1969), 29–42.

Cohen, Barry. "Toward Understanding our Youth Culture," YOUTH AND SOCIETY, 3 (June, 1972), 441–457.

Davis, Kingsley. "Adolescence and the Social Structure," ANNALS OF THE AMERICAN ACADEMY OF POLITICAL AND SOCIAL SCIENCE, 225 (November, 1944), 8–16.

Denhardt, Robert and Allen, H. David. "Youth Responses to Cultural Incongruities," YOUTH AND SOCIETY, 3 (December, 1971), 237–247.

Denney, Reuel. "American Youth Today: A Bigger Cost, A Wider Screen," in Erik Erikson, ed. YOUTH: CHANGE AND CHALLANGE. New York, Basic Books 1963.

Douvan, Elizabeth and Adelson, Joseph. The Adolescent Experience and Identity in Wertheimer, Michael, ed. CONFRONTATION: PSYCHOLOGY AND THE PROBLEMS OF TODAY. Glenview, Illinois: Scott Foresman, 1970. 24–27.

Haan, Norma, Smith M. Brewster and Block Jeanne. "The Moral Reasoning of Young Adults: Political-Social Behavior, Family Background and Personality Correlates," JOURNAL OF PERSONALITY AND SOCIAL PSYCHOLOGY, 10 (November, 1969), 183–201.

Jahoda, Marie and Neil Warren. "Myths of Youth," SOCIOLOGY OF EDUCATION, 38 (Winter, 1965), 138–149.

Kahn, Tom. "American Youth: Which Way Now?" AMERICAN FEDERA-TIONIST, 77 (September, 1970), 1–5.

Keniston, K. "You Have to Grow Up in Scarsdale to Know How Bad Things Really Are," NEW YORK TIMES MAGAZINE (April, 27, 1969), 27–29+.

Mead, Margaret. "Growing Up in America," in Alexander Kelin, ed. NATURAL ENEMIES: YOUTH AND THE CLASH OF GENERATIONS. New York: Lippincott, 1969, 54–61.

Parsons, Talcott "Age and Sex in the Social Structure of the United States," AMERICAN SOCIOLOGICAL REVIEW, 7 (October, 1942), 604–616.

Pileggi, N. "Revolutionaries Who Have To Be Home by 7:30; with Discussion," PHI DELTA KAPPAN, 50 (June, 1969), 560–561.

Polk, K. and Halferty, D.S. "Adolescence, Commitment, and Delinquency," JOURNAL OF RESEARCH IN CRIME AND DELINQUENCY, 3 (July, 1966), 82–96.

Reice, S. "Under Twenty-One: Teens Attitudes on Morals, Movies, Tele-vision, Violence, Parents, Protest and Teen-age Peers," MCCALLS, 95 (October, 1968), 50+.

Schwartz, Barry N. "Youth in the Technological Era," MIDWEST QUAR-TERLY, 10 (Spring, 1969), 215–225.

Sobel, Raymond, "Special Problems of Late Adolescence and the College Years," In Judd Marmor, ed. MODERN PSYCHOANALYSIS: NEW DIRECTIONS AND PERSPECTIVES, New York: Basic Books, 1968, 476–491.

"The Teenagers: A Newsweek Survey if What They're Really Like," NEWSWEEK, 67 (March 21, 1966), 57–75.

Toussing, P. W. Hangloose Identity, or Living Death—The Agonizing Choice of Growing Up Today," ADOLESCENCE, 3 (Fall, 1968), 307–318.

Weiner, Irving. "Perspectives on the Modern Adolescent" PSYCHIATRY, 35 (February, 1972), 20–31.

108

E.2. Sociological Considerations of Student Involvement

American Council on Education, CAMPUS DISRUPTION DURING 1968–1969, Washington, D.C.: Publication Division, American Council on Education, 1969.

Astin, Alexander W. CAMPUS UNREST, 1969–1970. Washington: American Council on Education, 1970.

Astin, A., A. Bayer and R. Boruch, *et al.* A NATIONAL STUDY OF STUDENT UNREST. Washington: American Council on Education, 1969.

Astin, H. S. "The Interview Experience: A Survey of Interviewers Who Participated in the Study of Campus Unrest", BSSR RESEARCH REPORT. Washington, D.C.: Bureau of Social Science Research, 1970.

Bayer, Alan E., Alexander Astin and Robert Boruch, *et al.* SOCIAL ISSUES AND PROTEST ACTIVITY: RECENT STUDENT TRENDS. Washington, D.C.: Office of Research, American Council on Education, 1970.

Bowes, Henry P. "University and College Student Rebellion in Retrospect and Some Sociological Implications". Unpublished Ph.D. dissertation, University of Colorado, 1964.

Condie, James Duane. "A Survey of the Incidence of Inappropriate Behavior of University Students as Related to the Geographical Distance From the Student's Home to the University". Unpublished Ed. D. dissertation, University of Denver, 1969.

Fenske, Robert and James Carmody. CORRELATES OF STUDENT INTEREST IN SOCIAL ISSUES. Iowa City, Iowa: American College Testing Program, 1971.

Finlay, David J. YOUTH AND POLITICS: A MODEL (Report Number 2). Western Behavioral Sciences Institute, 1969.

Haines, Richard Laurence. "A Structural Analysis of Student Radical Activism in the United States". Unpublished Ph.D. dissertation, University of Oregon, 1966.

Hunter, Alfred A. "An Empirical Study of Student Radical Activism". Unpublished Ph.D. dissertation, University of Wisconsin, 1972.

Mock, Kathleen. THE POTENTIAL ACTIVIST AND HIS PERCEPTION OF THE UNIVERSITY. Washington, D.C.: American Psychological Association, 1968.

*Peterson, Richard E. THE SCOPE OF ORGANIZED STUDENT PROTEST IN 1964–65. Princeton, New Jersey: Educational Testing Service, 1966.

*Peterson, Richard E. THE SCOPE OF ORGANIZED STUDENT PROTEST IN 1967–1968. Princeton, New Jersey: Educational Testing Service, 1968.

Quarter, Jack. THE STUDENT MOVEMENT OF THE '60'S: A SOCIAL PSYCHOLOGICAL ANALYSIS. Toronto: Ontario Institute for Studies in Education, 1972.

Urban Institute. SURVEY OF CAMPUS INCIDENTS AS INTERPRETED BY COLLEGE PRESIDENTS, FACULTY CHAIRMEN AND STUDENT BODY PRESIDENTS. Washington, D.C.: The Urban Institute.

*Urban Research Corporation. STUDENT PROTESTS 1969: SUMMARY. Chicago, Illinois: Urban Research Corporation, 1970.

Useem, Michael. "Involvement in a Radical Political Movement and Patterns of Friendship: The Draft Resistance Community". Unpublished Ph.D. dissertation, Harvard University.

YOUTH AND THE ESTABLISHMENT. New York: John D. Rockefeller 3rd Fund, 1971.

Albrecht, Stan. "Political Activity, Issue Salience and Political Socialization," ROCKY MOUNTAIN SOCIAL SCIENCE JOURNAL, 8 (April, 1971), 127-136.

Allen, James G. "Student Mob Behavior: a Sociological Approach to its Prevention", JOURNAL OF COLLEGE STUDENT PERSONNEL 3 (March 1962), 119-125.

Allerbeck, K. R. "Some Structural Conditions for Youth and Student Movements", SOCIAL SCIENCE JOURNAL, 24 (Number 2, 1972), 257-270.

*Austin, Alexander. "Determinants of Student Activism", in Julian Foster and Durward Long, eds. PROTEST! STUDENT ACTIVISM IN AMERICA. New York: William Morrow, 1970, 89-101.

Barbee, D. "K-12; Some Keys to Campus Unrest", JOURNAL OF SECONDARY EDUCATION, 44 (December, 1969), 369-374.

*Bayer, A. E. and A. W. Astin. "Campus Unrest, 1970-1971; Was It Really All that Quiet?" EDUCATIONAL RECORD, 52 (Fall, 1971), 301-313.

*Bayer, Alan E. and Alexander Astin. "Violence and Disruption in the US Campus, 1968-9", EDUCATIONAL RECORD, 50 (Fall, 1969), 337-350.

Bell, L. L. "Status Discrepancy and the Radical Rejection of Nonviolence", SOCIOLOGICAL INQUIRY, 38 (1968), 51-64.

Blume, N. "Political Variables Related to Young Republican and Young Democratic Club Activities", JOURNAL OF COLLEGE STUDENT PERSONNEL, 13 (May, 1972), 239-246.

Bowers, William J. "Trends in College Campus Deviance", COLLEGE STUDENT SURVEY, 5 (Spring, 1971), 20-30.

Clarke, J. W. and J. Egan. "Social and Political Dimensions of Campus Protest Activity," JOURNAL OF POLITICS. 34 (May, 1972), 500-523.

Demerath, N. J., III, Gerald Marwell and Michael T. Aiken et al. "Criteria and Contingencies of Success in a Radical Political Movement," JOURNAL OF SOCIAL FORCES, 27 (Number 1, 1971), 63-80.

Flacks, Richard. "Protest or Conform: Some Social-Psychological Perspectives on Legitimacy," JOURNAL OF APPLIED BEHAVIORAL SCIENCE, 5 (April/May/June, 1969), 127-150.

*Flacks, Richard. "Social and Cultural Meanings of Student Revolt: Some Informal Comparative Observations," SOCIAL PROBLEMS, 17 (Winter 1970), 340-357.

Grafton, Clive L. "The Student in Transition: A Decade of Change," COLLEGE STUDENT SURVEY, 2 (Winter, 1968), 56-59.

Greenstein, Fred I. "College Student Reactions to the Assassination of President Kennedy," in Bradley S. Greenberg and Edwin B. Parker, eds. SOCIAL COMMUNICATION IN CRISIS. Stanford: Stanford University Press, 1965, 220-240.

*Heist, Paul. "Intellect and Commitment: the Faces of Discontent," in

O. W. Knorr and W. J. Minter, eds. ORDER AND FREEDOM ON CAMPUS. Boulder, Colorado: Western Interstate Commission for Higher Education, 1965, 61–70.

Hernandez, Jose. "Campus Violence and Nonrealistic Conflict," YOUTH AND SOCIETY, 4 (December, 1972), 155–168.

Hochbaum, S. M. "The Relation between Group Members' Self-Confidence and their Reactions to Group Pressures to University," AMERICAN SOCIOLOGICAL REVIEW, 19 (December, 1954), 678–687.

Hoffer, C. R. "Youth as an Object of Sociological Study," SOCIOLOGY AND SOCIAL RESEARCH, 20 (May–June, 1936), 417–425.

*Horn, J. L. "Student Dissent and the Values of the University: A Problem of Coexistence," MIDWEST QUARTERLY, 13 (April, 1972), 247–268.

Horn, J. L. and Paul Knott. "Activist Youth of the 1960's: Summary and Prognosis," SCIENCE, 171 (March 12, 1971), 977–985.

Horn, John and Paul Knott. "Student Activists and Student Activism: A Profile and Prognosis," in Paul Knott, ed. STUDENT ACTIVISM. Dubuque, Iowa: W. C. Brown, 1971, 166–185.

Horowitz, Irving L. and Martin Liebowitz. "Social Deviance and Political Marginality," SOCIAL PROBLEMS, 15 (Winter, 1968), 280–296.

Hurst, J. C. and R. N. Hubbell. "Does Vociferation = Validity? Comprehensive Campus Opinion on Activist Issues," JOURNAL OF THE NATIONAL ASSOCIATION OF STUDENT PERSONNEL ADMINISTRATORS, 8 (April, 1971), 109–116.

Ivey, A. E. and W. H. Morrill. "Confrontation, Communication, and Encounter: A Conceptual Framework for Student Development," JOURNAL OF THE NATIONAL ASSOCIATION OF STUDENT PERSONNEL ADMINISTRATORS, 7 (April, 1970), 226–234.

Jansen, D. G. and B. B. Winburn. "Perceptions of a University Environment by Social-Political Action Leaders," PERSONNEL AND GUIDANCE JOURNAL, 47 (November, 1968) 218–222.

Kahn, Roger M. and William Bowers. "The Social Context of the Rank and File Student Activist," SOCIOLOGY OF EDUCATION, 43 (Winter, 1970), 38–55.

Kahn, R. M. and W. J. Bowers. "Social Context of the Rank-and-File Student Activist: A Test with Four Hypotheses," SOCIOLOGY OF EDUCATION, 44 (Summer, 1971), 369–373.

Kelley, H. H. "Two Functions of Reference Groups," in H. Proshansky and B. Seidenberg, eds. BASIC STUDIES IN SOCIAL PSYCHOLOGY. New York: Holt, Rinehart and Winston, 1965, 210–215.

Kirby, D. "Counter-culture Explanation of Student Activism," SOCIAL PROBLEMS, 19 (Fall, 1971), 203–216.

Kornberg, Alan and Mary Brehm. "Ideology, Institutional Identification, and Campus Activism," SOCIAL FORCES, 49 (February, 1969), 445–459.

Levine, D. N. "Sociology Confronts Student Protest," SCHOOL REVIEW, 78 (August, 1970), 529–541.

Long, Durward and Julian Foster. "Levels of Protest," in Julian Foster and

Durward Long, eds. PROTEST! STUDENT ACTIVISM IN AMERICA. New York: William Morrow, 1970.

McPhail, Clark. "Student Walk out: A Fortuitous Examination of Elementary Collective Behavior," SOCIAL PROBLEMS, 16 (Spring, 1969), 441–455.

Meyer, John W. and Richard Robinson. "Structural Determinants of Political Activity: A Comparative Interpretation, "SOCIOLOGY OF EDUCATION, 45 (winter, 1972), 23–46.

Nasater, D. "Note on Contextual Effects and the Political Orientation of University Students," AMERICAN SOCIOLOGICAL REVIEW, 33 (April, 1968), 210–219.

Olsen, Marvin E. "Perceived Legitimacy of Social Protest Actions," SOCIAL PROBLEMS, 15 (Winter, 1968), 297–310.

Peterson, Richard E. and J. A. Centra. "Organized Student Protest and Institutional Functioning," EDUCATION. Princeton, New Jersey: Educational Testing Service, 1968.

Ramsey, R. R., Jr. "Subculture Approach to Academic Behavior," JOURNAL OF EDUCATIONAL SOCIOLOGY, 35 (April, 1962), 355–376.

Richman, A. and H. R. Targ. "Impact of Instruction and External Events on Student Orientations and Opinion Consistency Concerning the Vietnam War," SOCIOLOGY OF EDUCATION, 44 (Spring, 1971), 151–169.

Silvern, Louise and Charles Nakamura. "Powerlessness, Social-Political Action, Social-Political Views: Their Interrelation Among College Students," JOURNAL OF SOCIAL ISSUES, 27 (Number 4, 1971), 137–158.

Smith, R. B. "The Vietnam War and Student Militancy," SOCIAL SCIENCE QUARTERLY, 52 (June, 1971), 133–156.

Spaulding, C. B. "Relative Attachment of Students to Groups and Organizations," SOCIOLOGY AND SOCIAL RESEARCH, 50 (July, 1966), 421–435.

Swanson, G. E. "Agitation in Face-to-Face Contacts: A Study of Personalities of Orators (in Student Organizations at University of Michigan)," PUBLIC OPINION QUARTERLY, 21 (Summer, 1957), 288–294.

Tomeh, A. K. "Patterns of Moral Behavior in Two Social Structures," SOCIOLOGY AND SOCIAL RESEARCH, 55 (January, 1971), 149–160.

Trent, J. W. and J. L. Craise. "Commitment and Conformity in the American College," JOURNAL OF SOCIAL ISSUES, 23 (July, 1967), 34–51.

Varg, Paul A. "Intellectual Climate and Student Unrest," JOURNAL OF HIGHER EDUCATION, 37 (February, 1966), 76–80.

Wainerman, C. H. "Intellect and Dissent: A Survey of Cornell Students," CORNELL JOURNAL OF SOCIAL RELATIONS, 2 (Spring, 1967), 101–122.

Walsh, J. and J. Coburn. "ACE Study on Campus Unrest: Questions for Behavioral Scientists," SCIENCE, 165 (July 11, 1969), 157–161.

Washburn, P. "Some Political Implications of Students' Acquisition of Social Science Information," SOCIAL FORCES, 48 (March, 1970), 373–383.

*Youth and Social Action," JOURNAL OF SOCIAL ISSUES, 20 (October, 1964), entire issue.

Zurcher, L. A., jr. et al. "Hasher: A Study of Role Conflict," SOCIAL FORCES, 44 (June, 1966), 505–514.

E.2.a. Institutional Correlates of Student Activism

Volkwein, James Fredricks. "Relationship of College Student Protest and Participation in Policy-Making to Institutional Characteristics." Unpublished Ph.D. dissertation, Cornell University, 1968.

Astin, Alexander W. "Campus Disruption, 1968–1969: An Analysis of Causal Factors," in F. F. Korten, S. W. Cook, and J. I. Lacey, eds. PSYCHOLOGY AND THE PROBLEMS OF SOCIETY, Washington, D.C.: American Psychological Association, 1970, 377–387.

Astin, Alexander W. "New Evidence on Campus Unrest, 1969–1970," EDUCATIONAL RECORD, 52 (Winter, 1971), 41–46.

*Astin, Alexander W. and Alan E. Bayer, "Antecedents and Consequences of Disruptive Campus Protests," MEASUREMENT AND EVALUATION IN GUIDANCE, 4 (April, 1971), 18–30.

Blau, Peter M. and Ellen L. Slaughter, "Institutional Conditions and Student Demonstrations," SOCIAL PROBLEMS, 18 (1971), 475–487.

Dunlap, Riley, "A Comment on 'Multiversity, University Size, University Quality, and Student Protest,' " AMERICAN SOCIOLOGICAL REVIEW, 35 (June, 1970), 525–528.

*El-Assal, Mohamed, "Multiversity, University Size, University Quality, and Student Protest: An Empirical Study," AMERICAN SOCIOLOGICAL REVIEW, 34 (October, 1969), 702–709.

Hilberry, Conrad. "The Dissident Cause: Antioch Student Culture," in Morton Levitt and Ben Rubenstein, eds. YOUTH AND SOCIAL CHANGE. Detroit: Wayne State University Press, 1972, 160–180.

Hitchcock, James. "Politics and Culture in the University," in Morton Levitt and Ben Rubenstein, eds. YOUTH AND SOCIAL CHANGE. Detroit: Wayne State University Press, 1972, 149–159.

*Hodgkinson, Harold. "Student Protest: An Institutional and National Profile," THE RECORD, 71 (May, 1970), 537–555.

Jones, Milton O. "Student Protest in the Junior College," JUNIOR COLLEGE STUDENT PERSONNEL SERVICES, 2 (January, 1969), 2.

*Keniston, Kenneth and Michael Lerner. "Campus Characteristics and Campus Unrest," ANNALS OF THE AMERICAN ACADEMY OF POLITICAL AND SOCIAL SCIENCE, 396 (May, 1971), 39–53.

Kornberg, Alan and Mary Brehm. "Ideology, Institutional Identity and Campus Activism," SOCIAL FORCES, 49 (March, 1971), 445–459.

Meyer, J. W. and R. Rubinson. "Structural Determinants of Student Political Activity: A Comparative Interpretation," SOCIOLOGY OF EDUCATION, 45 (Winter, 1972), 23–46.

Mock, Kathleen. "The Potential Activist and His Perception of the University," JOURNAL OF APPLIED BEHAVIORAL SCIENCE, 7 (January–February, 1971), 3–13.

Sasajima, Masu, Junius A. Davis, and Richard E. Peterson. "Organized Student Protest and Institutional Climate," AMERICAN EDUCATIONAL RESEARCH JOURNAL, 5 (May, 1968), 291–304.

Shively, Aliza, and Morris LeMay. "Student Activists on a 'Non-Activist' Campus," EXPERIMENTAL PUBLICATION SYSTEM, 10 (February, 1971), 387+.

Shoben, E. Joseph, jr. "The Climate of Protest," in Julian Foster and Durward Long, eds. PROTEST! STUDENT ACTIVISM IN AMERICA New York: William Morrow, 1970, 554–581.

Stern, George G. "Campus Environments and Student Unrest," in G. Kerry Smith, ed. AGONY AND PROMISE; CURRENT ISSUES IN HIGHER EDUCATION 1969, San Francisco: Jossey-Bass, 1969, 123–135.

Stern, George G. "Student Values and Their Relationship to the College Environment," in Hall T. Sprague, ed. RESEARCH ON COLLEGE STUDENTS Boulder, Colorado: Western Interstate Commission for Higher Education, 1960, 67–104.

E.2.b. Personal Background and Values of Activists

Cross Reference: For discussion and comment on some of the findings in the following studies see section on Generational Conflict. (Section IE3g)

Astin, Helen. THEMES AND EVENTS OF CAMPUS UNREST IN 22 COLLEGES AND UNIVERSITIES Washington: Bureau of Social Science Research, 1969.

Braungart, Richard. "Family Status, Socialization, and Student Politics: A Multivariate Analysis." Unpublished Ph.D. dissertation, Pennsylvania State University, 1959.

Dewey, Carlyle. "Political Activism, Ideology and Related Characteristics of Majors in Selected Social Studies." Unpublished Ph.D. dissertation, University of Minnesota, 1972.

Doress, Irvin. "A Study of a Sampling of Boston University Student Activists." Unpublished Ed.D. thesis, Boston University, 1969.

Hoover, Richard Edwin. "A Study of Selected Variables Differentiating Joiners and Non-joiners of a Campus Social Reform Movement at the Florida State University." Unpublished Ph.D. dissertation, Florida State University, 1970.

Kahn, Roger M. "Class, Status Inconsistency and Student Political Activism." Unpublished M.A. thesis, Northeastern University, 1970.

Mankoff, Milton. "The Political Socialization of Radicals and Militants in the Wisconsin Student Movement During the 1960's." Unpublished Ph.D. dissertation, University of Wisconsin, 1970.

Mock, Kathleen R. and Paul Heist. POTENTIAL ACTIVISTS: THE CHARACTERISTICS AND BACKGROUNDS OF A CAPABLE AND CHALLENGING MINORITY. Berkeley, California: Center for Research and Development in Higher Education, University of California, 1969.

Paulus, G. "A Multivariate Analysis Study of Student Activists, Leaders, Student Government Leaders, and Non-Activists." Unpublished Ph.D. dissertation, Michigan State University, 1967.

Schneider, Patricia. "A Study of Members of SDS and YD at Harvard." Unpublished B.A. thesis, Wellesley College, 1966.

Thomas, E. Lamar. "Family Congruence on Political Orientations of Political Active Parents and Their College Age Children." Unpublished Ph.D. dissertation, University of Chicago, 1968.

Wainerman, Catalina H. "Social Factors Differentiating a Nonconforming Student Minority: Structural and Social-Psychological Aspects." Unpublished M.A. thesis, Cornell University, 1966.

Wolitzer, Morton. "An Investigation of the Relationship Between Selected Personality Variables and the Involvement in Social Protest Movements." Unpublished Ph.D. dissertation, New York University, 1969.

*Astin, Alexander W. "Personal and Environmental Determinants of Student Activism," MEASUREMENT AND EVALUATION IN GUIDANCE 1 (Fall, 1968), 149–162.

Astin, H. S. "Self-Perceptions of Student Activists," JOURNAL OF COLLEGE STUDENT PERSONNEL, 12 (July, 1971), 263–270.

Baird, Leonard L. "Who Protests: A Study of Student Activists," in Julian Foster and Durward Long, eds. PROTEST! STUDENT ACTIVISM IN AMERICA. New York: William Morrow, 1970.

Block, Jeanne H., Norma Haan, and M. B. Smith. "Activism and Apathy in Contemporary Adolescents," in J. F. Adams, ed. CONTRIBUTIONS TO THE UNDERSTANDING OF ADOLESCENTS. Boston: Allyn and Bacon, 1968, 198–231.

*Block, Jeanne H. et al. "Socialization Correlates of Student Activism," JOURNAL OF SOCIAL ISSUES, 25 (Autumn, 1969), 143–177.

Bloom, E. and C. E. Kennedy. "Student and His Parents," NATIONAL ASSOCIATION OF WOMEN DEANS AND COUNSELORS JOURNAL, 33 (Spring, 1970), 98–105.

Blume, Norman. "Family and the Socialization of YR and YD Presidents in the Midwest," YOUTH AND SOCIETY, 4 (December, 1972), 177–184.

Blume, Norman. "Young Republican and Young Democratic Clubs in the Midwest: A Study of Variables Related to Club Activity," YOUTH AND SOCIETY, 2 (March, 1971), 355–365.

*Braungart, Richard G. "Family Status, Socialization, and Student Politics: A Multivariate Analysis," AMERICAN JOURNAL OF SOCIOLOGY, 77 (July, 1971), 108–130.

*Braungart, Richard G. "Research Note: Parental Identification and Student Politics," SOCIOLOGY OF EDUCATION, 44 (Fall, 1971), 463–475.

*Braungart, Richard G. "SDS and YAF: A Comparison of Two Student Radical Groups in the Mid-1960's," YOUTH AND SOCIETY, 2 (Summer, 1971), 441–458.

*Braungart, Richard G. "Status Politics and Student Politics: An Analysis of Left- and Right-Wing Student Activists," YOUTH AND SOCIETY, 3 (December, 1971), 195–210.

Brick, Allan R. "Activists on Campus and the Literature They Read," FELLOWSHIP 29 (November 1, 1963), 8+.

Cross, K. P. "Some Correlates of Student Protest," NATIONAL ASSOCIA-
TION OF STUDENT PERSONNEL ADMINISTRATORS JOURNAL, 8 (July,
1970), 38–48.

Dunlap, Riley. "Radical and Conservative Student Activists: A Comparison
of Family Backgrounds," PACIFIC SOCIOLOGICAL REVIEW 13 (Summer,
1970).

Erbe, William. "Social Involvement and Political Activity," AMERICAN
SOCIOLOGICAL REVIEW, 29 (April, 1964), 198–215.

Everson, David H. "The Background of Student Support for Student
Protest Activities in the University," PUBLIC AFFAIRS BULLETIN, 3
(March–April, 1970), 1–7.

*Flacks, Richard. "The Liberated Generation: An Exploration of the Roots
of Student Protest," JOURNAL OF SOCIAL ISSUES, 23 (July, 1967), 52–75.

Flacks, Richard. "Student Activists: Result, Not Revolt," PSYCHOLOGY
TODAY, 1 (October, 1967), 18–24.

*Flacks, Richard. "Who Protests: the Social Bases of the Student Movement,"
Julian Foster and Durward Long, eds. PROTEST! STUDENT ACTIVISM IN
AMERICA. New York: William Morrow, 1970.

*Flacks, Richard. "Young Intelligentsia in Revolt," TRANS-ACTION, 7
(June 1970), 46–55.

Frank, J. D. and E. H. Nash. "Commitment to Peace Work: a Preliminary
Study of Determinants and Sustainers of Behavior Change," AMERICAN
JOURNAL OF ORTHOPSYCHIATRY, 35 (January, 1965), 106–119.

Frank, J. D. and J. Schonfield. "Commitment to Peace Work II: A Closer
Look at Determinants," AMERICAN JOURNAL OF ORTHOPSYCHIATRY, 37
(January, 1967), 112–119.

Freeman, Harvey R. and P. Brubaker. "Personality Characteristics of
Campus Demonstrators Compared to Non-demonstrators," JOURNAL OF
COUNSELING PSYCHOLOGY, 18 (September, 1971), 462–464.

Freeman, J. L. "Parents, It's Not All Your Fault, But . . . ," JOURNAL OF
POLITICS, 31 (August, 1969), 812–817.

Gamson, William A. "Sociology's Children of Affluence," AMERICAN
SOCIOLOGIST, 3 (No. 4, 1968), 286–289.

Gaylin, Ned. "The Family Is Dead—Long Live the Family!" YOUTH AND
SOCIETY, 3 (Fall, 1971), 60–80.

Gelineau, V. A. and D. Kantor. "Pro-social Commitment Among College
Students," JOURNAL OF SOCIAL ISSUES 20 (October, 1964), 112–130.

Geller, Jesse and Gary Howard. "Some Sociophysical Characteristics of
Student Political Activists," JOURNAL OF APPLIED SOCIAL PSYCHOLOGY,
2 (April–June, 1972), 114–137.

Gold, Alice, Lucy Friedman, and Richard Christie. "The Anatomy of
Revolutionists," JOURNAL OF APPLIED SOCIAL PSYCHOLOGY, 1 (January,
1971), 26–43.

Goodman, Paul. "The New Aristocrats," PLAYBOY, 14 (March, 1967),
110-111, 152-159.

Gore, P. M. and J. B. Rotter. "Personality Correlate of Social Action,"
JOURNAL OF PERSONALITY, 31 (March, 1963), 58–64.

Haas, Kurt. "Social Correlates of Hostility in a College Sample," BRITISH

JOURNAL OF SOCIAL AND CLINICAL PSYCHOLOGY, 5 (No. 3, 1966), 200–206.

Hitchcock, J. "Fathers and Sons: The Politics of Youth," REVIEW OF POLITICS, 34 (April, 1972), 158–173.

Hodge, Robert W. and Donald J. Treiman. "Social Participation and Social Status," AMERICAN SOCIOLOGICAL REVIEW 33 (October, 1968), 722–740.

Jansen, D. G., B. B. Winborn, and W. D. Martinson. "Characteristics Associated with Campus Socio-Political Action Leadership," JOURNAL OF COUNSELING PSYCHOLOGY, 15 (November, 1968), 552–562.

Kerpelman, Larry. "Characteristics of Activists and Nonactivists," in Paul Knott, ed. STUDENT ACTIVISM. Dubuque, Iowa: W. C. Brown, 1971, 97–106.

*Kerpelman, Larry. "Student Political Activism and Ideology: Comparative Characteristics of Activists and Non-Activists," JOURNAL OF COUNSELING PSYCHOLOGY, 16 (January, 1969), 8–13.

Kohn, M. "Social Class and the Exercise of Paternal Authority," AMERI-CAN SOCIOLOGICAL REVIEW, 24 (June, 1959), 352–366.

Lacy, Virginia. "Political Knowledge of College Activist Groups: SDS, YAF and YD," JOURNAL OF POLITICS, 33 (August, 1971), 840–845.

Lemay, Morris. "Birth Order and College Misconduct," JOURNAL OF INDIVIDUAL PSYCHOLOGY, 24 (No. 2, 1968), 167–189.

*Lipset, Seymour M. "The Activists: A Profile," THE PUBLIC INTEREST, No. 10 (Fall, 1968), 39–51.

*Mankoff, Milton and Richard Flacks. "Changing Social Base of the Ameri-can Student Movement," ANNALS OF THE AMERICAN ACADEMY OF POLITICAL AND SOCIAL SCIENCE, 395 (May, 1971), 54–67.

Miller, Paul R. "The Chicago Demonstrators: a Study in Identity," BULLE-TIN OF THE ATOMIC SCIENTISTS, 25 (April, 1969), 3–6.

Morse, S. J. and S. Peele. "Study of Participants in an Anti-Vietnam War Demonstration," JOURNAL OF SOCIAL ISSUES, 27 (No. 4, 1971), 113–136.

Munk, Michael. "New Left: Background of the Young Radicals," NATIONAL GUARDIAN (September 18, 1965), 3–4.

Newcomb, Theodore M. "Research on Student Characteristics: Current Approaches," in Lawrence Dennis and Joseph Kauffman, eds. THE AMERICAN COLLEGE AND THE STUDENT. Washington, D.C.: American Council on Education, 1966, 101–116.

Oglesby, Carl. "The Spanked and the Unspanked," SATURDAY REVIEW, 50 (May 20, 1967), 110–111, 125–127.

"Playboy's Student Survey," PLAYBOY, 17 (September, 1970), 182–184+.

Polk, K. "Class, Strain, and Rebellion Among Adolescents," SOCIAL PROBLEMS, 17 (Fall, 1969), 214–224.

Portes, Alejandro. "Political Primativism, Differential Socialization, and Lower Class Leftist Radicalism," AMERICAN SOCIOLOGICAL REVIEW, 36 (October, 1971), 820–835.

Pugh, M. D. et al. "Participation in Anti-War Demonstrations: a Test of Parental Continuity Hypothesis," SOCIOLOGY AND SOCIAL RESEARCH, 56 (October, 1971), 19–28.

Rice, Joy K., Julutte Redding, and Thereza Mettel. "Activist and Establishment Leaders," JOURNAL OF COLLEGE STUDENT PERSONNEL, 12 (September, 1971), 336–339.

Rothchild, J. "Un-silent Generation," NATIONAL REVIEW, 21 (June 17, 1969), 591–594+.

Rush, G. B. "The Radicalization of Middle-Class Youth," INTERNATIONAL SOCIAL SCIENCE JOURNAL, 24 (No. 2, 1972), 312–325.

Rush, G. B. "Status Consistency and Right Wing Extremism," AMERICAN SOCIOLOGICAL REVIEW, 32 (February, 1967), 86–91.

Shimkunas, Algimantas M. and Ronald E. Kime. "Personality Correlates of Student Commitment to Social Action," JOURNAL OF PERSONALITY ASSESSMENT, 35 (December, 1971), 561–568.

Smallenburg, C. and H. Smallenburg. "Who Are the Youthful Rebels? With Study Discussion Program," PTA MAGAZINE, 65 (June, 1971), 10–12, 33.

Thomas, L. Eugene. "Family Correlates of Student Political Activism," DEVELOPMENTAL PSYCHOLOGY, 4 (No. 2, 1971), 206–215.

Tygart, C. and N. Holt. "Examining the Weinberg and Walker Typology of Student Activists," AMERICAN JOURNAL OF SOCIOLOGY, 77 (March, 1972), 957–966.

Tygart, C. and N. Holt. "A Research Note on Student Leftist Political Activism and Family Socio-Economic Status," PACIFIC SOCIOLOGICAL REVIEW, 14 (January, 1971), 121–128.

Useem, M. "Ideological and Interpersonal Change in the Radical Protest Movement," SOCIAL PROBLEMS, 19 (Spring, 1972), 451–469.

Van Loon, Eric. "Who Are the Activists?" AMERICAN EDUCATION, 4 (December, 1967–January 1968), 3–4, 28.

*Watts, William A. and David N. E. Whittaker. "Some Sociological Differences Between Highly Committed Members of the Free Speech Movement and the Student Population at Berkeley," JOURNAL OF APPLIED BEHAVIORAL SCIENCE, 2 (January, 1966), 41–62.

Westby, David and Richard Braungart. "Activists and the History of the Future," in Julian Foster and Durward Long, eds. PROTEST! STUDENT ACTIVISM IN AMERICA. New York: William Morrow, 1970, 158–182.

Westby, David and Richard Braungart. "Class and Politics in the Family Backgrounds of Student Political Activists," AMERICAN SOCIOLOGICAL REVIEW, 31 (October, 1966), 690–692.

Winborn, B. B. and D. G. Jansen. "Personality Characteristics of Campus Social-Political Action Leaders," JOURNAL OF COUNSELING PSYCHOLOGY, 14 (November, 1967), 509–513.

E.2.c. Student Leadership

Allen, James Gregory. "Factors Related to Leadership in a College Residence Hall." Unpublished Ph.D. dissertation, Iowa State University, 1960.

Capelle, Macon Harshaw. "Concurrent Validation of the LEADERSHIP

118

OPINION QUESTIONNAIRE for College Student Leadership." Unpublished Ph.D. dissertation, University of Maryland, 1966.

Cornfeld, Bernard. "Leadership Training in an Oriented Agency." Unpublished M.A. thesis, New York School of Social Work, Columbia University, 1954.

Eichler, G. A. STUDIES IN STUDENT LEADERSHIP, Pennsylvania State College, 1933.

*Friedson, Eliot, ed. STUDENT GOVERNMENT, STUDENT LEADERS, AND THE AMERICAN COLLEGE. Philadelphia, Pennsylvania: U.S. National Student Association, 1955.

Hulet, Richard Earle. "Leadership Behavior in Independent and Fraternity Houses." Unpublished Ph.D. dissertation, University of Illinois, 1958.

Ilma, Viola, ed. YOUTH LEADERSHIP SURVEY. New York: The Editor, 1934.

Jansen, D. G. "Characteristics of Student Leaders." Unpublished Ph.D. dissertation, Indiana University, 1967.

Stillion, Glenn Wayne, "Values, Perceptions, and Characteristics of Student Leaders Compared with the General Student Population at Florida State University." Unpublished Ph.D. dissertation, Florida State University, 1968.

Barnett, C. W. "Validating Campus Leadership," EDUCATIONAL RESEARCH BULLETIN, 30 (March, 1951), 67–73+.

Benezet, L. T. "Student Leadership: Dilemmas of Loyalty," EDUCATIONAL RECORD, 35 (October, 1954), 275–280.

Brademas, J. "Leadership for Freedom in a Changing Society," NATIONAL ASSOCIATION OF STUDENT COUNCILS YEARBOOK, 1965, 29–37.

Chapin, F. Stuart. "Extracurricular Activities of College Students; a Study in College Leadership," SCHOOL AND SOCIETY, 23 (February, 1926), 212–216.

Dubno, Peter. "Leadership, Group Effectiveness, and Speed of Decision," JOURNAL OF SOCIAL PSYCHOLOGY, 65 (April, 1965), 351–360.

Flaherty, Sister M. Rita. "Personality Traits of College Leaders," JOURNAL OF EDUCATIONAL RESEARCH, 60 (April, 1967), 377–378.

Gallo, Philip S. and Charles G. McClintock. "Behavioral, Attitudinal and Perceptual Differences Between Leaders and Non-Leaders in Situations of Group Support and Non-Support," JOURNAL OF SOCIAL PSYCHOLOGY, 56 (February, 1962), 121–134.

Greenleaf, E. A. "Student Leadership in a Program of Co-curricular Activities," PERSONNEL AND GUIDANCE JOURNAL, 35 (January, 1957), 293–297.

Hodges, H. M. "Campus Leaders and Non Leaders," SOCIOLOGY AND SOCIAL RESEARCH, 37 (March, 1953), 251–255.

Hunter, E. C. and A. M. Jordan. "An Analysis of Qualities Associated with Leadership Among College Students," JOURNAL OF EDUCATIONAL PSYCHOLOGY, 30 (October, 1939), 497–509.

*Jansen, David, Bob Winborn and William Martinson. "Characteristics Associated with Campus Social-Political Leadership," JOURNAL OF COUNSELING PSYCHOLOGY, 15 (November, 1968), 552–562.

Jansen, David and Bob Winborn. "Perceptions of a University Environment by Social-Political Action Leaders," PERSONNEL AND GUIDANCE JOURNAL, 47 (November, 1968), 218–222.

Liebert, Roland. "Finding and Developing Student Leaders; New Needs and Old Despair," in G. K. Smith, ed. IN SEARCH OF LEADERS. Washington, D.C.: American Association for Higher Education, 1967, 189–194.

Moore, S. "Leaders are Leavers," JOURNAL OF GENERAL EDUCATION, 20 (January, 1969), 291–296.

Rudolph, F. "What's Become of the Campus Hero?" MADEMOISELLE 56 (December, 1962), 94–95+.

Williamson, E. G. "The Group Origins of Student Leaders," EDUCA-TIONAL PSYCHOLOGY AND MEASUREMENT, 8 (Winter, 1948), 603–612.

Williamson, E. G. "Training Student Leaders," in G. K. Smith, ed. IN SEARCH OF LEADERS. Washington, D.C.: American Association for Higher Education, 1967, 186–189.

Williamson, E. G. and D. Hoyt. "Measured Personality Characteristics of Student Leaders," EDUCATIONAL PSYCHOLOGY AND MEASUREMENT, 12 (Spring, 1952), 65–78.

E.3. Psychological Considerations of Student Activism

E.3.a. Psychological Background of College Life and Student Activism

Brim, Orville G., jr. and Stanton Wheeler. SOCIALIZATION AFTER CHILDHOOD: TWO ESSAYS. New York: John Wiley and Sons, 1967.

*Chickering, Arthur W. EDUCATION AND IDENTITY. San Francisco: Jossey-Bass, 1969.

Child Study Association of America. THE FUNCTION OF REBELLION: IS YOUTH CREATING NEW FAMILY VALUES? New York: Child Study Association, 1969.

Constantinople, A. P. "Some Correlates of Happiness and Unhappiness in College Students." Unpublished Ph.D. dissertation, University of Rochester, 1965.

Cook, Joseph B., Marvin A. Hoss, and Robert Vargas. THE SEARCH FOR INDEPENDENCE: ORIENTATION FOR THE JUNIOR COLLEGE STUDENT. Belmont, California: Brooks-Cole, 1968.

Fawcett, James Thomas. "An Observer-Evaluation Method for the Comparative Study of Modal Personality: A Cross-National Investigation Based Upon Q-Sort Descriptions of Students." Unpublished Ph.D. dissertation, University of California, Berkeley, 1965.

*Feldman, Kenneth, ed. COLLEGE AND STUDENT: SELECTED READINGS IN THE PSYCHOLOGY OF HIGHER EDUCATION. Elmsford, New York: Pergamon Press, 1972.

Friis, Robert Harold. "Achievement Need-Press Discrepancy, Anomie and

120

Unrest Among College Students." Unpublished Ph.D. dissertation, Columbia University, 1969.

Group for the Advancement of Psychiatry. THE COLLEGE EXPERIENCE: A FOCUS FOR PSYCHIATRIC RESEARCH. REPORT NO. 52. New York: Author, 1962.

Hearn, Curry Bunn, jr. "Personality Integration and Person Perception in College Males." Unpublished Ph.D. dissertation, George Peabody College for Teachers, 1967.

Heath, D. H. EXPLORATIONS OF MATURITY: STUDIES OF MATURE AND IMMATURE COLLEGE MEN. New York: Appleton-Century-Crofts, 1965.

Heath, D. H. GROWING UP IN COLLEGE: LIBERAL EDUCATION AND MATURITY. San Francisco: Jossey-Bass, 1968.

Katz, Joseph, ed. GROWTH AND CONSTRAINT IN COLLEGE STUDENTS: A STUDY OF THE VARIETIES OF PSYCHOLOGICAL DEVELOPMENT. Stanford, California: Stanford University, Institute for the Study of Human Problems, 1967.

*Kerpelman, Larry C. ACTIVISTS AND NONACTIVISTS: A PSYCHOLOGICAL STUDY OF AMERICAN COLLEGE STUDENTS. New York: Behavioral Publications, 1972.

Kohlberg, L. STAGES IN THE DEVELOPMENT OF MORAL THOUGHT AND ACTION. New York: Holt, Rinehart and Winston, 1969.

*Liebert, Robert. RADICAL AND MILITANT YOUTH: A PSYCHOANALYTIC INQUIRY. New York: Praeger, 1971.

McLaughlin, B. S. "Identity and Personality: a Study of Self-Perceived Identity in College Students." Unpublished Ph.D. dissertation, Harvard University, 1965.

Maxmen, J. S. "Medical Student Activists." Unpublished Residency thesis, Yale University, 1970.

Newcomb, T. M. PERSONALITY AND SOCIAL CHANGE. New York: Dryden, 1957.

Pierce, R. A. PERSONALITY STYLES OF STUDENT ACTIVISTS. New York: University Health Service, University of Rochester, 1971.

Plant, W. T. and E. W. Minium. DIFFERENTIAL PERSONALITY DEVELOPMENT IN YOUNG ADULTS AS RELATED TO ABILITY. U.S. DEPARTMENT OF HEALTH, EDUCATION AND WELFARE COOPERATION RESEARCH PROJECT NO. S–042. San Jose, California: San Jose State College, 1964.

Sherif, Carolyn W., Muzafer Sherif, and Roger E. Nebergall. ATTITUDE AND ATTITUDE CHANGE. Philadelphia, Pennsylvania: W. B. Saunders, 1965.

Sigel, R., ed. LEARNING ABOUT POLITICS: STUDIES IN POLITICAL SOCIALIZATION. New York: Random House, 1968.

Speigel, J. P. THE GROUP PSYCHOLOGY OF CAMPUS DISORDERS: A TRANSACTIONAL APPROACH. Boston: Brandeis University, Lemberg Center for the Study of Violence.

Whittaker, David and William Watts. PSYCHOLOGICAL NEEDS AND NONCONFORMITY. Berkeley, California: Berkeley Center for Research and Development in Higher Education, 1967.

Wertheimer, Michael, ed. CONFRONTATION: PSYCHOLOGY AND THE PROBLEMS OF TODAY. Glenview, Illinois: Scott Foresman, 1970.

Zweig, F. THE STUDENT IN THE AGE OF ANXIETY. New York: Free Press of Glencoe, 1963.

Alker, Henry A. "A Quasi-Paranoid Feature of Students' Extreme Attitudes Against Colonialism," BEHAVIORAL SCIENCE, 16 (May, 1971), 218–221.

Allport, Gordon. "Uniqueness in Students," in W. D. Weatherford, jr., ed. THE GOALS OF HIGHER EDUCATION. Cambridge, Massachusetts: Harvard University Press, 1960.

Athos, Anthony G. " 'Encountering' Young Talent," JOURNAL OF COLLEGE PLACEMENT, 28 (April–May, 1968), 57–62.

Berdie, Ralph F. "Student Ambivalence and Behavior," in Lawrence Dennis and Joseph Kauffman, eds. THE AMERICAN COLLEGE AND THE STUDENT. Washington, D.C.: American Council on Education, 1966, 359–366.

Berlin, I. N. "From Confrontation to Collaboration," AMERICAN JOURNAL OF ORTHOPSYCHIATRY, 40 (April, 1970), 473–480.

Bettelheim, Bruno. "College Student Rebellion: Explanations and Answers," PHI DELTA KAPPAN, 50 (May, 1969), 511–514.

Bettelheim, Bruno. "Perils of Overexposing Youth to College," EDUCATION DIGEST, 35 (April, 1970), 35–38.

Block, J. N. Haan and M. B. Smith. "Moral Reasoning of Young Adults: Political-Social Behavior, Family Background, and Personality Correlates," JOURNAL OF PERSONALITY AND SOCIAL PSYCHOLOGY, 10 (November, 1968), 183–201.

Bloy, Myron B., jr. "A Spiritual Taxonomy," in H. L. Hodgkinson and M. B. Bloy, eds. IDENTITY CRISIS IN HIGHER EDUCATION. San Francisco: Jossey-Bass, 1971, 162–176.

Bowers, William J. "Trends in College Campus Deviance," COLLEGE STUDENT SURVEY, 5 (Spring, 1971), 20–30.

Butler, Alan C. and Lester Carr. "Purpose in Life Through Social Action," JOURNAL OF SOCIAL PSYCHOLOGY, 74 (April, 1968), 243–250.

Campbell, E. Q. "Adolescent Socialization," in D. A. Goslin, ed. HANDBOOK OF SOCIALIZATION THEORY AND RESEARCH. Chicago: Rand McNally, 1969.

Carroll, Jerome F. Y. "Understanding Student Rebellion," ADOLESCENCE, 4 (Summer, 1969), 163–180.

*Coles, Robert. "Psychiatric Observations on Students Demonstrating for Peace," AMERICAN JOURNAL OF ORTHOPSYCHIATRY, 37 (January, 1967), 107–111.

Coles, Robert. "Social Struggle and Weariness," PSYCHIATRY, 27 (November, 1964), 305–315.

Elder, P. "Social Psychological Model for Improving Communication and Reducing Confrontation on the Campus," NATIONAL ASSOCIATION OF STUDENT PERSONNEL ADMINISTRATORS JOURNAL, 8 (October, 1970), 106–114.

Farnsworth, Dana. "A University Psychiatrist Looks at Campus Protest," PSYCHIATRIC OPINION, (December, 1969), 1–6.

*Hadden, Jeffery K. "The Private Generation: Absolute Priority on the Personal," PSYCHOLOGY TODAY, 3 (October, 1969), 32–35, 68–69.

Hall, M. N. "A Conversation with Kenneth Keniston," PSYCHOLOGY TODAY, 2 (November, 1968), 16–23+.

Heath, Roy. "The Reasonable Adventurer," in Kaoru Yamamoto, ed. THE COLLEGE AND ITS CULTURE: AN ANALYSIS. Boston: Houghton Mifflin, 1968, 345–352.

Hendin, R. "Psychoanalyst Looks at Student Revolutionaries," NEW YORK TIMES MAGAZINE, (January, 1971), 16–17+.

Horowitz, Irving Louis. "The Brave New World of Campus Psychiatry," CHANGE, 2 (January–February, 1970), 47–52.

Jencks, Christopher. "Is It All Dr. Spock's Fault?" NEW YORK TIMES MAGAZINE, (March 3, 1968), 27.

Johnson, David W. and Daniel Neale. "The Effect of Models, Reference Groups, and Social Responsibility Norms Upon Participation in Prosocial Action Activities," JOURNAL OF SOCIAL PSYCHOLOGY, 81 (June, 1970), 87–92.

Jones, E. E. and B. M. Daugherty. "Political Orientation and the Perceptual Effects of Anticipated Interaction," JOURNAL OF ABNORMAL AND SOCIAL PSYCHOLOGY, 59 (November, 1959), 340–349.

*Kelman, Herbert C. "A Social-Psychological Model of Political Legitimacy and Its Relevance to Black and White Student Protest Movements," PSYCHIATRY, 33 (May, 1970), 224–246.

*Keniston, Kenneth. "A Second Look at the Uncommitted," SOCIAL POLICY, 2 (July–August, 1971), 6–19.

Kirtley, Donald and Richard Harkless. "Student Political Activity in Relation to Personal and Social Adjustment," JOURNAL OF PSYCHOLOGY, 75 (1970), 253–256.

Krout, M. H. and R. Sanger. "Personality Development in Radicals," SOCIOMETRY, 2 (1939), 31–46.

*Levitt, Morton and Ben Rubenstein. "The Student Revolt: Totem and Taboo Revisited," PSYCHIATRY 34 (May, 1971), 156–167.

Lunsford, Terry F. "Activism, Privatism, and the Moral Advantage," in G. Kerry Smith, ed. STRESS AND CAMPUS RESPONSE. San Francisco: Jossey-Bass, 1968, 91–98.

Maxmen, J. S. "Medical Student Radicals: Conflict and Resolution," AMERICAN JOURNAL OF PSYCHIATRY, 127 (March, 1971), 131–135.

McCormack, Thelma H. "The Motivation of Radicals," AMERICAN JOURNAL OF SOCIOLOGY, 56 (July, 1950), 17–24.

Madison, Peter. "Dynamics of Development and Constraint, Two Case Studies," in Joseph Katz, et al. NO TIME FOR YOUTH. San Francisco: Jossey-Bass, 1968, 74–160.

Menninger, W. Walter. "Student Demonstrations and Confrontations," MENNINGER QUARTERLY, 23 (1969), 1–14.

Michels, Robert. "Pseudoanalyzing the Student Rebels," PSYCHIATRY AND SOCIAL SCIENCE REVIEW, 3 (May, 1969), 2–5.

Middleton, Russell and Snell Putney. "Political Expression of Adolescent Rebellion," AMERICAN JOURNAL OF SOCIOLOGY, 68 (March, 1963), 527-534.

Mitseherlich, Alexander. "Panel on 'Protest and Revolution,' " INTERNATIONAL JOURNAL OF PSYCHO-ANALYSIS, 51 (May, 1970), 211-218.

Nikelly, Arthur G. "Ethical Issues in Research on Student Protest," AMERICAN PSYCHOLOGIST, 26 (1971), 475-478.

Phillips, D. L. "Deffered Gratification in a College Setting: Some Costs and Gains," SOCIAL PROBLEMS, 13 (Winter, 1966), 333-343.

Pressy, Sidney. "Two Basic Neglected Psycho-Educational Problems," in Ohmer Milton and E. J. Shoben, jr., eds. LEARNING AND THE PROFESSORS. Athens, Ohio: Ohio University Press, 1968, 61-71.

Rose, A. M. "Parental Models for Youth," SOCIOLOGY AND SOCIAL RESEARCH, 40 (September, 1955), 3-9.

*Smith, M. Brewster, Norma Haan, and Jeanne Block. "Social-Psychological Aspects of Student Activism," YOUTH AND SOCIETY, 1 (March, 1970), 261-288.

*Solomon, Fredric and Jacob Fishman. "Youth and Peace: A Psychological Study of Student Peace Demonstrators in Washington, D.C.," JOURNAL OF SOCIAL ISSUES, 20 (October, 1964), 54-74.

Solomon, Fredric and Jacob Fishman. "Youth and Social Action: Action and Identity Formation in the First Student Sit-In Demonstration," JOURNAL OF SOCIAL ISSUES, 20 (April, 1964), 36-45.

Vali-Woh, A. "The Student: A Psychosocial Entity," MENTAL HYGIENE, 51 (January, 1967), 55-68.

Werner, F. H. "Acculturation and Milieu Therapy in Student Transition," in G. D. Spindler, ed. EDUCATION AND CULTURE: ANTHROPOLOGICAL APPROACHES. New York: Holt, 1963, 259-267.

Williamson, E. G. "Today's College Student," MICHIGAN COLLEGE PERSONNEL ASSOCIATION JOURNAL 3 (Spring, 1966).

Willoughby, R. R. "A Sampling of Student Opinion," JOURNAL OF SOCIAL PSYCHOLOGY, 1 (February, 1930), 164-169.

Yankelovich, D. "New Naturalism: Excerpt from the Changing Values on Campus," SATURDAY REVIEW, 55 (April 1, 1972), 32-37.

"Youth and Establishment Collaboration? Yankelovich Survey," CURRENT, 127 (March, 1971), 15-19.

*Zinberg, Norman E. "A Return to Commitment," ANTIOCH REVIEW, 26 (Fall, 1966), 332-344.

E.3.b. Student Attitudes and Values: General

Allwood, M. S. THE NEW GENERATION: STUDIES IN THE ATTITUDES AND BEHAVIOR OF CONTEMPORARY AMERICAN STUDENTS. Mt. Pleasant, Iowa: The New Prairie, 1964.

Bidwell, C. E., ed. THE AMERICAN COLLEGE AND STUDENT PER-

124

SONALITY: A SURVEY OF RESEARCH PROGRESS AND PROBLEMS. New York: Social Science Research Council, 1960.

Bolton, C. D. and K. C. W. Kammeyer. THE UNIVERSITY STUDENT: A STUDY OF STUDENT BEHAVIOR AND VALUES. New Haven, Connecticut: College and University Press, 1967.

Boynton, Paul L. A STUDY OF THE RELATIONSHIP BETWEEN THE INTELLIGENCE AND MORAL JUDGMENTS OF COLLEGE STUDENTS. Nashville, Tennessee: George Peabody College for Teachers, 1929.

Butner, Irma. "Valuations Expressed by College Students Relative to Education, Work, Family Life, and Leisure. A Study Directed to the Normative Base of American Society." Unpublished Ph.D. dissertation, University of Iowa, 1956.

Canning, William M. "A Psycho-Educational Study of a Group of Adult, Non-High School Graduates Matriculating in a College Degree Curriculum." Unpublished Ph.D. dissertation, Northwestern University, 1955.

Casebeer, Arthur. "Student Democrative Values Within Various Administrative Climates of Selected Colleges and Universities." Unpublished Ph.D. dissertation, Oregon State University, 1963.

Claster, B. "College Student Differences in Situations of Authority, Individualism, and Social Dating." Unpublished Ph.D. dissertation, Northwestern University, 1966.

Corey, Fay L. VALUES OF FUTURE TEACHERS: A STUDY OF ATTITUDES TOWARD CONTEMPORARY ISSUES. New York: Bureau of Publications, Teachers College, Columbia University, 1955.

David, Jack, ed. THE DEVELOPMENT OF STUDENT VALUES IN HIGHER EDUCATION. Washington, D.C.: U.S. National Student Association, n.d.

Einhorn, Carl Murray. "The Differences in Social Beliefs Held by Selected Education and Non-Education Seniors at the University of Michigan." Unpublished Ph.D. Dissertation, University of Michigan, 1956.

Gallop International, Inc. GALLOP OPINION INDEX: SPECIAL REPORT ON THE ATTITUDES OF COLLEGE STUDENTS, Report No. 48, Princeton: Gallop International, Inc. 1969.

Gillespie, J. M. and G. W. Allport. YOUTH'S OUTLOOK ON THE FUTURE: A CROSS-NATIONAL STUDY. New York: Doubleday, 1955.

Girling, Paul Alvin. "A Study of Values Held By American Theological Students." Unpublished Ed.D. thesis, Colorado State College, 1968.

*Goldsen, Rose, Morris Rosenberg, Robin Williams, jr., and Edward Suchman. WHAT COLLEGE STUDENTS THINK. Princeton, New Jersey: Van Nostrand, 1960.

Havice, Charles W., ed. CAMPUS VALUES: SOME CONSIDERATIONS FOR COLLEGIANS. New York: Scribner, 1968.

Henderson, D. and P. Northrup. STUDENT ATTITUDE SURVEY I. STUDENT AFFAIRS RESEARCH REPORT 64-3. University Park, Pennsylvania: Office of Student Affairs, Pennsylvania State University, 1964.

Katz, Daniel and Floyd Allport. STUDENT ATTITUDES. Syracuse, New York: Craftsman Press, 1931.

Krick, Blance. "A Study of Certain Values and Attitudes of Students in a Liberal Arts College." Unpublished Ph.D. dissertation, Indiana University, 1963.

Lehmann, Irvin J. and Paul L. Dressel. CRITICAL THINKING, ATTITUDES, AND VALUES IN HIGHER EDUCATION. East Lansing, Michigan: Michigan State University, 1962.

Lehmann, Irvin J. and S. O. Ikenberry. CRITICAL THINKING, ATTITUDES AND VALUES IN HIGHER EDUCATION: A PRELIMINARY REPORT. East Lansing, Michigan: Michigan State University, 1959.

Lloyd-Jones, Esther. SOCIAL COMPETENCE AND COLLEGE STUDENTS. Washington, D.C.: American Council on Education, 1940.

*Lystad, Mary H., ed. AS THEY SEE IT: CHANGING VALUES OF COLLEGE YOUTH. Cambridge, Massachusetts: Schenkman, 1973.

McLeish, John. STUDENTS' ATTITUDES AND COLLEGE ENVIRONMENTS. Cambridge: Cambridge Institute of Education, 1970.

MacNaughton, William S. COMPOSITE VALUE PATTERNS IN NON-CURRICULAR AREAS OF STUDENT LIFE AT DARTMOUTH: AN INTERIM REPORT OF THE CLASS OF 1965: STUDY OF STUDENT ATTITUDES. Hanover: Office of Student Counseling, Dartmouth College, 1963.

Maller, J. B. and E. M. Glaser. THE INTEREST-VALUES INVENTORY FOR HIGH SCHOOL AND COLLEGE STUDENTS AND ADULTS. New York: Bureau of Publications, Teachers College, Columbia University, 1939.

Miller, Norman. "Social Class and Value Differences Among American College Students." Unpublished Ph.D. dissertation, Columbia University, 1958.

Mills, W. W. "MMPI Profile Pattern and Scale Stability Throughout Four Years of College Attendance." Unpublished Ph.D. dissertation, University of Michigan, 1954.

Murphy, Gardner and Rensis Likert. PUBLIC OPINION AND THE INDIVIDUAL; A PSYCHOLOGICAL STUDY OF STUDENT ATTITUDES ON PUBLIC QUESTIONS, WITH A RETEST FIVE YEARS LATER. New York: Harper & Brothers, 1938.

Olson, L. H. STUDENT ATTITUDES INVENTORY. East Lansing, Michigan: Office of Evaluation Studies, Michigan State University, 1964.

Pennsylvania State University, Office of Student Affairs. STUDENT OPINION SURVEY, FALL, 1965. STUDENT AFFAIRS RESEARCH REPORT 66–3. University Park, Pennsylvania: Pennsylvania State University, Office of Student Affairs, 1966.

Peterson, R. E. SOME BIOGRAPHICAL AND ATTITUDINAL CHARACTERISTICS OF ENTERING COLLEGE FRESHMEN: A SUMMARY REPORT OF A QUESTIONNAIRE SURVEY. Research Bulletin R.B. 64–63, Princeton, New Jersey: Educational Testing Service, 1964.

Peterson, R. E. SOME DATA FROM THE COLLEGE STUDENT QUESTIONNAIRES PERTINENT TO THE GENERAL QUESTION OF COLLEGE STUDENT DISCONTENT. Princeton, New Jersey: Educational Testing Service, 1965.

Pfeiffer, Harrison S. "Social Attitudes of Freshmen in Michigan Colleges." Unpublished Ph.D. dissertation, Columbia University, 1951.

Purdue Opinion Panel. YOUTH'S VOCATIONAL PLANS AND ATTI-

TUDES TOWARD SCHOOL: YOUTH'S ATTITUDES TOWARD THE SELEC-
TIVE SERVICE SYSTEM. Lafayette, Indiana: Measurement and Research
Center, Purdue University, November, 1966.

Roper Research Associates. A STUDY OF THE BELIEFS AND ATTI-
TUDES OF MALE COLLEGE SENIORS, FRESHMEN AND ALUMNI. New
Jersey: Standard Oil, 1969.

*Sanford, Nevitt. COLLEGE AND CHARACTER. New York: John Wiley
and Sons, 1964.

Smith, John E. VALUE CONVICTIONS AND HIGHER EDUCATION.
New Haven, Connecticut: Hazen Foundation, 1958.

Spacie, Edwin G. "The Structure of Beliefs Among Selected College
Freshmen." Unpublished Ed.D. thesis, Michigan State University, 1956.

Townsend, Agatha. COLLEGE FRESHMEN SPEAK OUT. New York:
Harper, 1956.

Twomey, A. E. "A Study of Values of a Select Group of Undergraduate
Students." Unpublished Ph.D. dissertation, Colorado State College, 1962.

Vreeland, R. S. "Organizational Structure and Moral Orientations: a Study
of Harvard Houses." Unpublished Ph.D. dissertation, Harvard University, 1963.

Wilson, Thomas P. COLLEGES AND STUDENT VALUES: AN OVER-
VIEW OF EDUCATIONAL AND RESEARCH CONCERNS. New York:
Carnegie Foundation, 1964.

*Yankelovich, Daniel, ed. THE CHANGING VALUES ON CAMPUS:
POLITICAL AND PERSONAL ATTITUDES OF TODAY'S COLLEGE STU-
DENTS. New York: Pocket Books, 1972.

Aceto, Thomas D. "Direct Action on the Campus: An Analysis," JOURNAL
OF THE NATIONAL ASSOCIATION OF STUDENT PERSONNEL ADMINIS-
TRATORS, 6 (October, 1968), 68–74.

Adler, M. J. "This Pre-War Generation," HARPER'S, 181 (October, 1940),
524–534.

Allport, Gordon. "Values and Our Youth," in Esther Lloyd-Jones and
Herman Estrin, eds. THE AMERICAN STUDENT AND HIS COLLEGE.
Boston: Houghton Mifflin, 1967, 347–356.

Althoff, S. A. and E. J. Nussel. "Social Class Trends in the Practices and
Attitudes of College Students Regarding Sex, Smoking, Drinking, and the Use
of Drugs," THE JOURNAL OF SCHOOL HEALTH, 41 (September, 1971),
390–394.

Barkley, K. L. "Development of the Moral Judgment of Students,"
CHARACTER AND PERSONALITY, 10 (December, 1942), 199–212.

Barrett, Laurence. "What the Campus Thinks," NATION, 182 (May 12,
1956), 402–403.

*Bayer, Alan E., Alexander W. Astin and Robert F. Boruch. "College
Students' Attitudes Toward Social Issues: 1967–1970," EDUCATIONAL
RECORD, 52 (Winter, 1971), 52–59.

Bernreuter, Robert G. "The College Student: He is Thinking, Talking,
Acting," PENN STATE ALUMNI NEWS, 52 (July, 1966), 10–14.

Bidwell, C. E. and R. S. Vreeland. "College Education and Moral Orienta-

tion: an Organizational Approach," ADMINISTRATIVE SCIENCE QUAR-
TERLY, 8 (September, 1963), 166–191.

Bittner, J. R. "Student Value Profiles of State and Church-Related
Colleges," COLLEGE STUDENT SURVEY, 2 (Spring, 1968), 1–4.

Blaine, Graham B., jr. "College Students and Moral Values," in Lawrence
Dennis and Joseph Kauffman, eds. THE AMERICAN COLLEGE AND THE
STUDENT, Washington, D.C.: American Council on Education, 1966, 372–376.

Bottrill, J. "The Social Intelligence of Students," JOURNAL OF PSY-
CHOLOGY, 66 (July, 1967), 211–213.

Bradbury, M. "Sex, Success and Sympathy," TWENTIETH CENTURY,
161 (February, 1957), 116–124.

Bushnell, John. "Student Values: a Summary of Research and Future
Problems," in Marjorie Carpenter, ed. THE LARGER LEARNING: TEACHING
VALUES TO COLLEGE STUDENTS. Dubuque, Iowa: William C. Brown, 1960,
45–61.

Callahan, Daniel. "Facts, Values, and Commitments," in H. L. Hodgkinson
and M. B. Bloy, jr., eds. IDENTITY CRISIS IN HIGHER EDUCATION. San
Francisco: Jossey-Bass, 1971, 13–26.

"Campus '65: The College Generation Looks at Itself: A Newsweek
Survey," NEWSWEEK, 65 (March 22, 1965), 43–48+.

Carlson, H. B. "Attitudes of Undergraduate Students," JOURNAL OF
SOCIAL PSYCHOLOGY, 5, 1934, 202–213.

"Changes in Today's College Students," U.S. NEWS AND WORLD
REPORT, 56 (February 17, 1964), 66–71.

Cooley, W. W. "Differences Among College Students," in J. C. Flanagan and
W. W. Cooley, eds. PROJECT TALENT: ONE-YEAR FOLLOW-UP STUDIES,
U.S. Department of Health, Education and Welfare Research Project No. 2333.
Pittsburgh, Pennsylvania: School of Education, University of Pittsburgh, 1966,
131–156.

Cousins, A. N. "Class of '61," SOCIAL EDUCATION, 25 (October, 1961),
276–280.

Dow, S. "Questionnaires for Students," CLASSICAL JOURNAL, 46
(April, 1951), 350–354.

Dow, S. "Some Student Opinions," CLASSICAL JOURNAL, 46 (May,
1951), 404–408+.

Downie, N. M. et al. "Opinions of Syracuse University Students on Some
Widely Discussed Current Issues," EDUCATIONAL AND PSYCHOLOGICAL
MEASUREMENT, 10 (No. 4, 1950), 628–636.

Dudycha, G. J. "The Moral Belief of College Students," INTERNATIONAL
JOURNAL OF ETHICS, 43 (1933), 194–204.

Edgar, E. E. "Values, Social Science, and General Education," JOURNAL
OF GENERAL EDUCATION, 5 (April, 1951), 168–180.

Eisenman, Russell. "Values and Attitudes in Adolescence," in James F.
Adams, ed. UNDERSTANDING ADOLESCENCE: CURRENT DEVELOP-
MENTS IN ADOLESCENT PSYCHOLOGY. Boston: Allyn and Bacon, 1968,
183–197.

Ephron, Nora. "Campus '65: What Our Students Are Really Like," NEW YORK POST MAGAZINE, (November 29–December 10, 1965).

Farnsworth, Dana L. "Attitudes and Values of College Students," in Arthur Kroll, ed. ISSUES IN AMERICAN EDUCATION, New York: Oxford, 1970, 22–42.

Fishman, J. A. "Why Are the Values of College Students Changing?" EDUCATIONAL RECORD, 41 (October, 1960), 342–346.

Garrison, K. C. and M. Mann. "A Study of the Opinions of College Students," JOURNAL OF SOCIAL PSYCHOLOGY, 2 (1931), 168–177.

Gilbert, Eugene. "Tragic Fact: Our Young Voters Don't Care," LOOK, 20 (October 2, 1956), 100–108.

Glicksberg, C. I. "College Students Face the Meaning of Life," ASSOCIATION OF AMERICAN COLLEGES BULLETIN, 43 (October, 1957), 441–455.

*Goertzel, Ted. "Changes in the Values of College Students 1958 to 1970–1971," PACIFIC SOCIOLOGICAL REVIEW, 15 (April, 1972), 235–244.

*Goldsen, Rose K. "High Hopes and Campus Realities," in Lawrence Dennis and Joseph Kauffman, eds. THE AMERICAN COLLEGE AND THE STUDENT. Washington, D.C.: American Council on Education, 1966, 117–122.

Goodson, M. R. *et al.*, eds. "Value-Choices of College Sophomores; a Comparative Study," JOURNAL OF EDUCATION, 144 (December, 1961), 3–31.

Gordon, J. H. "Value Differences Between Freshmen and Seniors at a State University," COLLEGE STUDENT SURVEY, 1 (No. 3, 1967), 69–70, 92.

Grafton, C. L. "The Student in Transition: A Decade of Change," COLLEGE STUDENT SURVEY, 2 (Winter, 1968), 56–59.

Hadden, J. K. "The Private Generation," PSYCHOLOGY, 3 (1969), 32–35, 68–69.

Harris, D. H. "Group Differences in Values Within a University," JOURNAL OF ABNORMAL AND SOCIAL PSYCHOLOGY, 29 (April–June, 1934), 95–102.

Heise, David R. "Norms and Individual Patterns in Student Deviancy," SOCIAL PROBLEMS, 16 (Summer, 1968), 78–92.

*Heist, P. "Diversity in College Student Characteristics," JOURNAL OF EDUCATIONAL SOCIOLOGY, 33 (February, 1960), 279–291.

Hershenson, David B. "Family Religious Background, Secondary Schooling, and Value Orientation of College Students," SOCIOLOGICAL ANALYSIS, 28 (Summer, 1967), 93–96.

Hochreich, Dorothy J. and Julian B. Rotter. "Have College Students Become Less Trusting?" JOURNAL OF PERSONALITY AND SOCIAL PSYCHOLOGY, 15 (July, 1970), 211–214.

*Hoge, Dean R. "College Students' Value Patterns in the 1950's and 1960's," SOCIOLOGY OF EDUCATION, 44 (Spring, 1971), 170–197.

Hunter, E. C. "Attitudes of College Freshmen: 1934–1949," JOURNAL OF PSYCHOLOGY, 31 (April, 1951), 281–296.

Jacob, P. E. "Social Change and Student Values," EDUCATIONAL RECORD, 41 (October, 1960), 338–342.

*Jacob, Philip. "Student Values: 1957," in G. K. Smith, ed. 1945–1970: TWENTY-FIVE YEARS. San Francisco: Jossey-Bass, 1970, 75–84.

Jacob, P. E. "What Will Be the Implications for the Colleges and Universities of the Changing Patterns in Student Values?" CURRENT ISSUES IN HIGHER EDUCATION, (1957), 88–95.

Jent, H. C. "Student Attitudes May Have Undemocratic Roots," EDUCATIONAL FORUM, 30 (January, 1966), 197–204.

Jones, Edward S. "The Opinions of College Students," JOURNAL OF APPLIED PSYCHOLOGY, 10 (December, 1926), 427–436.

Kerver, T. J. "Student Attitude and Opinion at the University of Wisconsin," COLLEGE AND UNIVERSITY JOURNAL, 11 (March, 1972), 23–26.

Klinger, M. R. and J. Veroff. "Cross-Cultural Dimensions Expressed in Moral Values," PERSONNEL AND GUIDANCE JOURNAL, 42 (May, 1964), 899–903.

Klushhohn, C. "Have There Been Discernible Shifts in American Values During the Past Generations?" in E. E. Morison, ed. THE AMERICAN STYLE, New York: Harper, 1958, 145–217.

Knode, J. C. "Attitudes on State University Campuses," AMERICAN SOCIOLOGICAL REVIEW, 8 (December, 1943), 666–673.

Lehmann, I. J. "Critical Thinking Ability, Attitudes, and Values Among College Students," JOURNAL OF TEACHER EDUCATION, 13 (December, 1962), 376–385.

Lehmann, I. J. "Some Socio-Cultural Differences in Attitudes and Values," JOURNAL OF EDUCATIONAL SOCIOLOGY, 36 (September, 1962), 1–9.

Lehmann, I. J. and I. K. Payne. "Exploration of Attitude and Value Changes of College Freshmen," PERSONNEL AND GUIDANCE JOURNAL, 41 (January, 1963), 403–408.

Lerner, Michael. "Respectable Bigotry," AMERICAN SCHOLAR, 38 (Autumn, 1969), 606–617.

Levi, Albert William. "Social Beliefs of College Students," JOURNAL OF HIGHER EDUCATION, 15 (March, 1944), 127–134.

Lewis, L. B. "Two Cultures: Some Empirical Findings," EDUCATIONAL RECORD, 48 (Summer, 1967), 260–267.

Loper, R. J., J. M. Robertson, and E. O. Swanson. "College Freshman MMPI Norms Over a Fourteen-Year Period," JOURNAL OF COLLEGE STUDENT PERSONNEL, 9 (November, 1968), 404–407.

Lundberg, G. A. and V. Beazley. " 'Consciousness of a Kind' in a College Population," SOCIOMETRY, 11 (February–May, 1948), 59–74.

McCann, C. J. and C. Bahn. "The Typical Student—a Study of Perceptions," JOURNAL OF COLLEGE STUDENT PERSONNEL, 9 (March, 1968), 100–104.

McCorquodale, M. K. "What They'll Die For in Houston," HARPER, 223 (October, 1961), 179–182.

McNeely, Dave. "A Wide Variety," NEW YORK TIMES MAGAZINE, (November 19, 1963), 24–25+.

Mayhew, L. B. and W. H. Hill. "Attitude Inventories," JOURNAL OF HIGHER EDUCATION, 21 (October, 1950), 375–379+.

Miller, Harry L. "The Relation of Social Class to Slum School Attitudes Among Education Students in an Urban College," JOURNAL OF TEACHER EDUCATION, 19 (Winter, 1968), 416–425.

Miller, H. and W. Wilson. "Relation of Sexual Behaviors, Values, and Conflict to Avowed Happiness and Personal Adjustment," PSYCHOLOGICAL REPORTS, 23 (December, 1968), 1075–1086.

Mogar, R. E. "Value Orientations of College Students: Preliminary Data and Review of the Literature," PSYCHOLOGICAL REPORTS, 15 (December, 1964), 739–770.

Morgenstern, J. et al. "Campus '65: the College Generation Looks at Itself and the World Around It," TIME, 65 (March 22, 1965), 43–63.

"New Mood of College Students, Results of a National Survey; Opinions of Students and College Presidents," U.S. NEWS AND WORLD REPORT, 72 (June 19, 1972), 28–32+.

*"New Mood On Campus: Survey," NEWSWEEK, 74 (December 29, 1969), 42–45.

*"New Youth Poll: Life-Louis Harris Poll," LIFE, 70 (January 8, 1971), 22–27+.

Olmsted, M. S. "Character and Social Role," AMERICAN JOURNAL OF SOCIOLOGY, 63 (July, 1957), 49–57.

*"Opinion on Campus: Analysis of, and Commentary on Questions and Responses of National Review Poll," NATIONAL REVIEW, 23 (June 15, 1971), 635–650.

"Poll of Student Presidents," COLLEGE MANAGEMENT, 3 (June–August, 1968), 20–27.

Montague, J. B., jr. "Real and Ideal Culture Patterns as Revealed in Students' Responses to Dichotomous Questions," JOURNAL OF EDUCATIONAL PSYCHOLOGY, 24 (November, 1950), 167–176.

Pressey, S. L. "Changes From 1923 to 1943 in the Attitudes of Public School and University Students," JOURNAL OF PSYCHOLOGY, 21 (January, 1946), 173–188.

"Purdue Finds Out What Students Think," JOURNAL OF COLLEGE PLACEMENT, 32 (February, 1972), 68–69+.

Rautman, A. L. "Youth in Search of a Standard," MENTAL HYGIENE, 30 (October, 1946), 597–605.

"Results of a Special Survey of College Students," GALLUP OPINION INDEX, (June, 1970), 10–24.

Rettig, Salomon and Benjamin Pasamanick. "Changes in Moral Values Among College Students: A Factorial Study," AMERICAN SOCIOLOGICAL REVIEW, 24 (December, 1959), 856–863.

Rettig, Salomon and Benjamin Pasamanick. "Changes in Moral Values Over Three Decades, 1929–1958," SOCIAL PROBLEMS, 6 (Spring, 1959), 320–328.

Rettig, Salomon and Benjamin Pasamanick. "Differences in the Structure of Moral Values of Students and Alumni," AMERICAN SOCIOLOGICAL REVIEW, 25 (August, 1960), 550–555.

Rettig, Salomon and Benjamin Pasamanick. "Invariance in Factor Structure of Moral Value Judgments from American and Korean College Students," SOCIOMETRY, 25 (March, 1962), 73–84.

Richards, James M. "Life Goals of American College Freshmen," JOURNAL OF COUNSELING PSYCHOLOGY, 13 (No. 1, 1966), 12–20.

Riesman, David. "Found Generation," AMERICAN SCHOLAR, 25 (Fall, 1956), 262–263.

Riesman, David. "The Jacob Report," AMERICAN SOCIOLOGICAL REVIEW, 23 (December, 1958), 732–738.

*Riesman, David. "The Uncommitted Generation: 'Junior Organization Men' in America," ENCOUNTER, 15 (November, 1960), 25–30.

Robinson, D. W. "Student Values: Methods of Appraisal and Some Implications," LIBERAL EDUCATION, 49 (May, 1963), 226–234.

Rosen, Peter I. "The Myth of Unanimity: Student Opinions on Critical Issues," SOCIOLOGY OF EDUCATION, 37 (Winter, 1963) 129–149.

Rosenberg, M. "Misanthropy and Political Ideology," AMERICAN SOCIOLOGICAL REVIEW, 21 (December, 1956), 690–695.

Sanford, R. N. "Today's College Students Look at Themselves, Their Society and Their Profession; with Discussion" NATIONAL COMMISSION ON TEACHER EDUCATION AND PROFESSIONAL STANDARDS. OFFICIAL REPORT. 1962, 60–77.

Sarachek, Bernard. "Student Views of the 'Establishment'—An Opinion Survey in the Kansas City Area," BUSINESS AND GOVERNMENT REVIEW, 11 (March–April, 1970), 11–16.

Scott, W. A. "Empirical Assessment of Values and Ideologies," AMERICAN SOCIOLOGICAL REVIEW, 30 (June, 1965), 299–310.

Singh, P. N. et al. "A Comparative Study of Selected Attitudes, Values, and Personality Characteristics of American, Chinese, and Indian Students," JOURNAL OF SOCIAL PSYCHOLOGY, 57 (June, 1962), 123–132.

Smith, John E. "Value Convictions and Higher Education," in Kaozu Yamamoto, ed. THE COLLEGE STUDENT AND HIS CULTURE: AN ANALYSIS, Boston: Houghton Mifflin, 1968, 317–325.

Smith, M. B. "Morality and Student Protest," in Michael Werthheimer, ed. CONFRONTATION: PSYCHOLOGY AND THE PROBLEMS OF TODAY. Glenview, Illinois: Scott Foresman, 1970, 28–34.

"Special Feature on Campus Unrest: Representative Sampling of Thinking by Students: Symposium," TODAY'S EDUCATION, 58 (November, 1969), 25–33.

*"Special Report the Attitudes of College Students," GALLUP OPINION INDEX, (June, 1969), 1–48.

*"Special Survey of College Students, May, 1968," GALLUP OPINION INDEX, (July, 1968), 31–40.

Spoerl, D. T. "Values of the Post-War College Student," JOURNAL OF SOCIAL PSYCHOLOGY, 35 (May, 1952), 217–225.

Stern, G. G. "The Measurement of Psychological Characteristics of Students and Learning Environments," HARVARD EDUCATIONAL REVIEW, 33 (Winter, 1963), 5–41.

Stewar, R. G. "Some Attitudes of College Students Toward Certain Aspects of Social, Political and Economic Change," EDUCATIONAL AND PSYCHOLOGICAL MEASUREMENT, 30 (Spring, 1970), 111–118.

"Students and Their Values," JOURNAL OF THE NATIONAL ASSOCIATION OF WOMEN DEANS AND COUNSELORS, 30 (Fall, 1966), 1–45.

Suchman, E. A. "The Values of American College Students," in A. E.

132

Traxler, ed. LONG RANGE PLANNING FOR EDUCATION, Washington, D.C.:
American Council on Education, 1958.

"A Symposium: Values of American College Students," RELIGIOUS
EDUCATION, 55 (January–February, 1960), 15–48.

Telford, C. W. "An Experimental Study of Some Factors Influencing the
Social Attitudes of College Students," JOURNAL OF SOCIAL PSYCHOLOGY,
5 (1934), 421–427.

Thornburg, H. D. "Student Assessment of Contemporary Issues," COL-
LEGE STUDENT SURVEY, 3 (1969), 1–5, 22.

*"The U.S. Campus Mood, '71: A Newsweek Poll," NEWSWEEK, (February
22, 1971), 61.

Vanderpol, J. A. "Student Opinion: Sacred Cow or Booby Trap?"
JOURNAL OF TEACHER EDUCATION, 10 (December, 1959), 401–412.

"Views of Deans and Students," NATIONAL ASSOCIATION OF DEANS
OF WOMEN JOURNAL, 19 (March, 1956), 99–112.

Vreeland, Rebecca and Charles Bidwell. "Classifying University Departments: an Approach to the Analysis of Their Effects on Undergraduates' Values
and Attitudes," SOCIOLOGY OF EDUCATION, 39 (Summer, 1966), 237–254.

Vreeland, Rebecca and Charles Bidwell. "Organizational Effects on Student
Attitudes: A Study of the Harvard Houses," SOCIOLOGY OF EDUCATION, 38
(Spring, 1965), 233–250.

Warnath, C. F. and H. R. Fordyce. "Inventoried Values of Entering
College Freshmen," PERSONNEL AND GUIDANCE JOURNAL, 40 (November,
1961), 277–281.

Webb, Sam C. "Changes in Student Personal Qualities Associated With
Change in Intellectual Abilities," COLLEGE AND UNIVERSITY, 41 (Spring,
1966), 280–289.

"What They Believe: Fortune-Yankelovich Survey," FORTUNE, 79
(January, 1969), 70–71+.

Whittaker, D. and W. A. Watts. "Personality Characteristics Associated
with Activism and Disaffiliation in Today's College-Age Youth," JOURNAL OF
COUNSELING PSYCHOLOGY, 18 (May, 1971), 200–206.

"Why Students Act That Way: A Gallup Study," U.S. NEWS AND WORLD
REPORT, 66 (June 2, 1969), 34–35.

Williams, M. S. "Socio-Economic Analysis of the Functions and Attitude of
Wartime Youths," SOCIAL FORCES, 24 (December, 1945), 200–210.

E.3.c. Student Attitudes Toward Politics

Adams, Larry Dewayne. "College Student Attitudes Toward Protest: Some
Relevant Factors." Unpublished Ph.D. dissertation, Florida State University,
1969.

Astin, A. W. SOME EFFECTS OF CAMPUS PROTESTS ON STUDENT
ATTITUDES. Washington, D.C.: American Council on Education, 1970.

Balch, George Irwin. "Political Trust, Political Involvement, and Orientations
Toward Political Change Among American College Students." Unpublished
Ph.D. dissertation, Indiana University, 1971.

Educational Reviewer, Inc. A SURVEY OF THE POLITICAL AND RELIGIOUS ATTITUDES OF AMERICAN COLLEGE STUDENTS. New York: Educational Reviewer, 1964.

Finney, H. C. "Development and Change of Political Liberalism among Berkeley Undergraduates." Unpublished Ph.D. dissertation, University of California—Berkeley, 1967.

Lyons, Morgan Irving. "Campus Reactions to Student Protest." Unpublished Ph.D. dissertation, University of Wisconsin, 1971.

McGaw, Dickinson Lamb, jr. "The Effects of Socializing Agents on Students' Learning of Political Attitudes." Unpublished Ph.D. dissertation, Indiana University, 1968.

Nelson, E. RADICALISM-CONSERVATIVISM IN STUDENT ATTITUDES. Columbus: Ohio University Press, 1938.

Riffer, Roger. "Determinants of University Students' Political Attitudes and Presidential Preference: A Theoretical Model." Unpublished Ed.D. dissertation, Harvard University, 1970.

Roessler, Richard T. "Political Orientation and Self Structure: A Multiple Hypotheses Study of Middle Non Activism Among College Students." Unpublished Ph.D. dissertation, Claremont Graduate School and University Center, 1971.

Adelson, J. and R. P. O'Neil. "Growth of Political Ideas in Adolescence: the Sense of Community," JOURNAL OF PERSONALITY AND SOCIAL PSYCHOLOGY, (Number 3, 1966), 295–306.

Agger, Robert E., M. N. Goldstein and S. A. Pearl, et al. "Political Cynicism: Meaning and Measurement," JOURNAL OF POLITICS, 23 (August, 1961), 477–506.

Albjerg, M. H. "College Youth Reflect on Democracy," SCHOOL AND SOCIETY, 74 (August 11, 1951), 81–84.

Beck, Paul Allen and M. Kent Jennings. "Lowering the Voting Age: The Case of the Reluctant Electorate," PUBLIC OPINION QUARTERLY, 33 (Fall, 1969), 370–379.

Best, W. H. and C. P. Sohner. "Social Distance Methodology in the Measurement of Political Attitudes," SOCIOLOGY AND SOCIAL RESEARCH, 40 (March, 1956), 266–270.

Breems, E. L., et al. "Changes in Liberalism-Conservatism of College Students Since the Depression," JOURNAL OF SOCIAL PSYCHOLOGY, 14 (1941), 99–107.

Batter, William R. "Reactions of University Audiences to Controversial Speakers," JOURNAL OF COLLEGE STUDENT PERSONNEL, 9 (September, 1968), 291–298.

Centers, Richard. "Children of the New Deal: Social Stratification and Adolescent Attitudes," INTERNATIONAL JOURNAL OF OPINION AND ATTITUDE RESEARCH, (Number 3, 1950), 315–335.

Christenson, Red M. and Patrick J. Carpetta. "The Impact of College on Political Attitudes: A Research Note," SOCIAL SCIENCE QUARTERLY, 44 (September, 1968), 315–320.

Crain, William C. "Young Activists' Conceptions of an Ideal Society," YOUTH AND SOCIETY, 4 (December, 1972), 203–236.

"Current Views of College Students on Politics and Drugs," GALLUP OPINION INDEX, (February, 1972), 1–30.

Douglas, J. "Verbal Image: Student Perceptions of Political Figures," SPEECH MONOGRAPHS, 39 (March, 1972), 1–15.

Drucker, A. J. and H. H. Remmers. "Citizenship Attitudes of Graduated Seniors at Purdue University, U.S. College Graduates and High School Pupils," JOURNAL OF EDUCATIONAL PSYCHOLOGY, 42 (April, 1951), 231–235.

Fay, Paul and Warren Middleton. "Certain Factors Related to Liberal and Conservative Attitudes of College Students: 1, Father's Occupation; Size of Home Town," JOURNAL OF SOCIAL PSYCHOLOGY, 11 (February, 1940), 91–105.

Finlay, David and Douglas Simon. "Self and Nation," YOUTH AND SOCIETY, 3 (June, 1972), 427–440.

Forbes, G. B. and M. Gipson. "Political Attitudes and Opinions, Need for Social Approval, Dogmatism and Anxiety in Negro and White College Students," JOURNAL OF NEGRO EDUCATION, 38 (Winter, 1969), 61–63.

Freehill, M. F. "Democratic College Student," JOURNAL OF EDUCATIONAL PSYCHOLOGY, 46 (December, 1955), 477–487.

Garrison, Karl. "A Comparative Study of the Attitudes of College Students Toward Certain Domestic and World Problems," JOURNAL OF SOCIAL PSYCHOLOGY, 34 (August, 1951), 47–54.

*Gelineau, Victor and David Kantor. "Pro-social Commitment Among College Students," JOURNAL OF SOCIAL ISSUES, 20 (October, 1964), 112–130.

Good, T. L. and D. A. Bates. "Politics and Youth: Attitudes of Young America," CLEARING HOUSE, 43 (March, 1969), 396–400.

Gordon, D. M. "Rebellion in Context: A Student's View of Students," in Robert S. Morison, ed. THE CONTEMPORARY UNIVERSITY: U.S.A. Boston: Houghton-Mifflin, 1966, 292–314.

Gump, P. V. "Anti-Democratic Trends and Student Reaction to President Truman's Dismissal of General MacArthur," JOURNAL OF SOCIAL PSYCHOLOGY, 38 (August, 1953), 131–135.

Gundlach, Ralph. "Confusion Among Undergraduates in Political and Economic Ideas," JOURNAL OF ABNORMAL AND SOCIAL PSYCHOLOGY, 32 (October–December, 1934), 357–367.

Harris, A. J., H. H. Remmers, and C. Ellison. "The Relation Between Liberal and Conservative Attitudes in College Students, and Other Factors," JOURNAL OF SOCIAL PSYCHOLOGY, 3 (August, 1932), 320–335.

Hourtoule, G. O. "Student Apathy: A National Epidemic," COLLEGE AND UNIVERSITY, 37 (Fall, 1961), 45–51.

"Is Student Opinion Swinging Left?" CHRISTIAN CENTURY, 50 (March 22, 1933), 380–381.

Jaros, Dean, Herbert Hirsch and F. Fleron, jr. "The Malevolent Leader: Political Socialization in an American Sub-culture," in A. Orum, ed. THE

SEEDS OF POLITICS, Englewood Cliffs, New Jersey: Prentice Hall, 1972, 195–211.

Kitley, Donald. "Conformity and Prejudice in Authoritarians of Opposing Political Ideologies," JOURNAL OF PSYCHOLOGY, 70 (November, 1968), 199–204.

Lipset, S. M. "Opinion Formation in a Crisis Situation," PUBLIC OPINION QUARTERLY, 17 (Spring, 1953), 20–46.

*Lipset, Seymour M. "Polls and Protests," FOREIGN AFFAIRS, 49 (April, 1971), 548–555.

McClintock, C. and Henry Turner. "The Impact of College Upon Political Knowledge, Participation, and Values," HUMAN RELATIONS, 15 (May, 1962), 163–176.

Mauss, Armand L. "The Reluctant Right: Right-Wing Anti-Communism Among Libertarian University Students," SOCIOLOGY OF EDUCATION, 40 (Winter, 1967), 39–54.

Meier, Harold C. and William Orzen. "Student Legitimations of Campus Activism: Some Survey Findings," SOCIAL PROBLEMS, 19 (1971), 181–191.

Middleton, R. and S. Putney. "Influences of Political Beliefs of American College Students," IL POLITICO. (Italy) 29 (June, 1964), 484–492.

Moore, G. and K. C. Garrison. "Comparative Study of Social and Political Attitudes of College Students," JOURNAL OF ABNORMAL AND SOCIAL PSYCHOLOGY, 27 (July, 1932), 195–208.

Moore, H. T. "Innate Factors in Radicalism and Conservatism," JOURNAL OF ABNORMAL AND SOCIAL PSYCHOLOGY, 20 (October, 1925), 234–244.

Morgan, C. L. and H. H. Remmers. "Liberalism and Conservatism of College Students as Affected by the Depression," SCHOOL AND SOCIETY, 41 (June 8, 1935), 780–784.

Mussen, P. and A. Warren. "Personality and Political Participation," HUMAN RELATIONS, 5 (February, 1952), 65–82.

Nelson, Erland. "Radicalism-Conservatism in Student Attitudes," PSY-CHOLOGICAL MONOGRAPHS, 50 (4, 1938), 1–32.

Nogee, Philip and Murray Levin. "Some Determinants of Political Attitudes Among College Voters," PUBLIC OPINION QUARTERLY, 22 (Winter, 1958–59), 449–463.

Nowicki, Stephen, jr. "Conservatism and Liberalism in College Students," PSYCHOLOGICAL REPORTS, 25 (Number 1, 1969), 252.

Pace, C. R. "What Kind of Citizens Do College Graduates Become?" JOURNAL OF GENERAL EDUCATION, 3 (April, 1949), 197–202.

"Results of Survey of College Students, February, 1971," GALLUP OPINION INDEX, (February, 1971), 1–46.

Rose, Peter. "Student Opinion on the 1956 Presidential Election," PUBLIC OPINION QUARTERLY, 21 (Fall, 1957), 371–376.

Sargent, L. and T. Webb. "Radical Speaker on the University Campus; A Study in Attitude Change," JOURNAL OF COMMUNICATION, 16 (September, 1966), 199–212.

Silvern, L. E. and C. Y. Nakamura. "Powerlessness, Social-Political Action,

Social-Political Views: Their Interrelation Among College Students," JOURNAL OF SOCIAL ISSUES, 27 (Number 4, 1971), 137–157.

Silverson, Randolph. "College Youth and the Cold War: An End to Mirror Images?" YOUTH AND SOCIETY, 3 (June, 1972), 314–326.

Somit, A. *et al.* "Effect of the Introductory Political Science Course on Student Attitudes toward Personal Political Participation," AMERICAN POLITICAL SCIENCE REVIEW, 52 (December, 1958), 1129–1132.

"Student Attitudes to Politics," STUDENT WORLD, 57 (Number 2, 1964), 158–169.

"Survey of the Political and Religious Attitudes of American College Students," NATIONAL REVIEW, 16 (October 8, 1963), 279–302.

Washburn, Philo C. "Cognition and Political Demonstrations: A Pilot Study," SOCIAL SCIENCE QUARTERLY, 51 (December, 1970), 617–627.

E.3.d. Student Attitudes Toward Minority Groups, Civil Rights and Liberties

Himelhoch, Jerome. "The Dynamics of Tolerance. A Study of Social and Psychological Factors in the Development of Ethnic Attitudes Among Certain College Students." Unpublished Ph.D. dissertation, Columbia University, 1952.

O'Rielly, Charles T. "Race Prejudice Among Catholic College Students in the United States and Italy: a Comparative Study of the Role of Religion and Personality in Inter-Group Relations." Unpublished Ph.D. dissertation, University of Notre Dame, 1956.

Sayler, Roland Ivan. "An Exploration of Race Prejudice in College Students and Interracial Contact." Unpublished Ed.D. thesis, University of Washington, 1969.

Stember, C. H. *Education and Attitude Change: The Effect of Schooling on Prejudice Against Minority Groups.* New York: Institute of Human Relations Press, 1961.

Arkoff, A. and G. M. Meredith. "Consistency in Attitudes Toward Civil Liberties," JOURNAL OF SOCIAL PSYCHOLOGY, 70 (December, 1966), 265–274.

Athanasion, R. "Technique Without Mystique: a Study of Authoritarianism in Engineering Students," EDUCATIONAL AND PSYCHOLOGICAL MEASURE-MENT, 28 (Winter, 1968), 1181–1188.

Barker, E. N. "Authoritarianism of the Political Right, Center and Left," JOURNAL OF SOCIAL ISSUES, 19 (April, 1963), 63–74.

Bolton, E. B. "Effect of Knowledge Upon Attitudes Toward the Negro," JOURNAL OF SOCIAL PSYCHOLOGY, 6 (1935), 68–90.

Crotty, William J. "Democratic Norms and the College Student," SOCI-OLOGY OF EDUCATION, 40 (Summer, 1967), 200–218.

Dahmer, C., jr. and E. McGinnies. "Shifting Sentiments Toward Civil Rights in a Southern University," PUBLIC OPINION QUARTERLY, 13 (No. 2, 1949), 241–251.

Eckhardt, Kenneth W. "Religiosity and Civil Rights Militancy," REVIEW OF RELIGIOUS RESEARCH, 11 (Spring, 1970), 197–203.

Eddy, Elizabeth M. "Attitudes Towards Desegregation Among Southern Students on a Northern Campus," JOURNAL OF SOCIAL PSYCHOLOGY, 62 (April, 1964), 285–302.

Engel, Gerald. "Some College Students' Responses Concerning Negroes of Differing Religious Background," JOURNAL OF SOCIAL PSYCHOLOGY, 74 (April, 1968), 275–283.

Farber, M. L. "The Communist Trial: College Student Opinion and Democratic Institutions," PUBLIC OPINION QUARTERLY, 14 (Spring, 1950), 89–92.

Fearing, F. "Structure of Opinion: A Loyalty Oath Poll," PUBLIC OPINION QUARTERLY, 14 (Winter, 1950), 729–743.

Finney, Henry. "Change in Civil Libertarianism Among University Students (Part I): The Development of Political Identity," JOURNAL OF SOCIAL ISSUES, 27 (November 1, 1971), 35–61.

Fox, J. T. "Authoritarianism in the St. Ambrose College Student," RELIGIOUS EDUCATION, 60 (May–June, 1965), 272–276.

Fulton, R. J. "Survey of Student Opinion on the Present National Emergency," HIGH POINTS, 33 (September, 1951), 12–18.

Garrison, K. C. and V. S. Burch. "A Study of Racial Attitudes of College Students," JOURNAL OF SOCIAL PSYCHOLOGY, 4 (May, 1933), 230–235.

Grace, H. A. "Geo-ethnic Preference Inventory: World Cultures and Autistic Thinking," JOURNAL OF EDUCATIONAL PSYCHOLOGY, 42 (April, 1951), 206–214.

Himelhoch, J. "Tolerance and Personality Needs: A Study of the Liberalization of Ethnic Attitudes Among Minority Group College Students," AMERICAN SOCIOLOGICAL REVIEW, 15 (February, 1950), 79–88.

Holt, N. and C. E. Tygart. "Political Tolerance and Higher Education," THE PACIFIC SOCIOLOGICAL REVIEW, 12 (Spring, 1969), 27–33.

Holtzman, J. "Attitudes Toward Integration of Segregated and Integrated Students," INTEGRATED EDUCATION: RACE AND SCHOOLS, 10 (May, 1972), 52–56.

Holtzman, W. H. "Attitudes of College Men Toward Nonsegregation in Texas Schools," PUBLIC OPINION QUARTERLY, 20 (Fall, 1956), 559–569.

House, James S. and Robert D. Fischer. "Authoritarianism, Age and Black Militancy," SOCIOMETRY, 34 (No. 2, 1971), 174–197.

Hyman, H. H. and P. B. Sheatsley. "Trends in Public Opinion on Civil Liberties," JOURNAL OF SOCIAL ISSUES, 9 (No. 3, 1953), 6–16.

Kelly, J. G., Jean Ferson, and W. H. Holtzman. "The Measurement of Attitudes Toward the Negro in the South," JOURNAL OF SOCIAL PSYCHOLOGY, 48 (November, 1958), 305–317.

Laird, D. S. and C. F. Cumbee. "Experiment in Modifying Ethnic Attitudes of College Students," JOURNAL OF EDUCATIONAL SOCIOLOGY, 25 (March, 1952), 401–409.

Lawton, J. H. "Alternative: Student Dialogue Attacks Racism," CATHOLIC EDUCATIONAL REVIEW, 66 (November, 1968), 489–497.

McConnell, T. R. "Differences in Student Attitudes Toward Civil Liberties,"

138

in R. Sutherland, *et al.* PERSONALITY FACTORS ON THE COLLEGE CAMPUS. Austin, Texas: Hogg Foundation for Mental Health, 1962, 29–42.

McGinnies, Elliott. "Attitudes Toward Civil Liberties Among Japanese and American University Students," JOURNAL OF PSYCHOLOGY, 58 (July, 1964), 177–186.

Maykovich, M. K. "Changes in Racial Stereotypes Among College Students," HUMAN RELATIONS, 24 (October, 1971), 371–386.

Muir, Donald E. "The First Years of Desegregation: Patterns of Acceptance of Black Students on a Deep-South Campus, 1963–1969," SOCIAL FORCES, 49 (March, 1971), 371–378.

Musser, Mary Ann. "CSQ Freshman Attitudes Toward Black Political Leaders in the American Society," in Patricia Wright, ed. INSTITUTIONAL RESEARCH AND COMMUNICATION IN HIGHER EDUCATION. PROCEED-INGS OF THE TENTH ANNUAL FORUM ON INSTITUTIONAL RESEARCH. n.p.: Association for Institutional Research, 1970, 276–279.

Noble, Lois A. and R. E. Noble. "A Study of the Attitudes of College Students Toward Civil Rights," JOURNAL OF SOCIAL PSYCHOLOGY, 40 (November, 1954), 289–297.

Pennington, S. and L. E. Mitchell. "Sex Differences in Reactions to Minority Group Status," JOURNAL OF NEGRO EDUCATION, 28 (Winter, 1959), 35–41.

Piedmont, Eugene B. "Changing Racial Attitudes at a Southern University: 1947–1964", JOURNAL OF NEGRO EDUCATION, 36 (Winter, 1961), 32–41.

Plant, W. T. "Changes in Ethnocentrism Associated with a Four-Year College Education," JOURNAL OF EDUCATIONAL PSYCHOLOGY, 49 (June, 1958), 162–165.

Plant, W. T. "Changes in Intolerance and Authoritarianism for Sorority and Nonsorority Women Enrolled in College for Two Years," JOURNAL OF SOCIAL PSYCHOLOGY, 68 (February, 1966), 79–83.

Plant, W. T. "Longitudinal Changes in Intolerance and Authoritarianism for Subjects Differing in Amount of College Education Over Four Years," GENETIC PSYCHOLOGY MONOGRAPHS, 72 (November, 1965), 247-287.

Porterfield, A. L. "Education and Race Attitudes," SOCIOLOGY AND SOCIAL RESEARCH, 21 (July–August, 1937), 538–543.

Proenza, Luis and Bonnie R. Strickland. "A Study of Prejudice in Negro and White College Students," JOURNAL OF SOCIAL PSYCHOLOGY, 67 (December, 1965), 273–281.

Prothro, E. T. and J. A. Jensen. "Group Differences in Ethnic Attitudes of Louisiana College Students," SOCIOLOGY AND SOCIAL RESEARCH, 34 (March, 1950), 252–258.

Prothro, E. T. and O. K. Miles. "Comparison of Ethnic Attitudes of College Students and Middle Class Adults from the Same State," JOURNAL OF SOCIAL PSYCHOLOGY, 36 (August, 1952), 53–58.

Richard, E. S. "Attitudes of College Students in South West Toward Ethnic Groups in the U.S.," SOCIOLOGY AND SOCIAL RESEARCH, 35 (September, 1950), 22–30.

Robin, S. S. and F. Story. "Ideological Consistency of College Students:

The Bill of Rights and Attitudes Towards Minority Groups," SOCIOLOGY AND SOCIAL RESEARCH, 48 (January, 1964), 187–196.

Segal, B. E. and P. K. Thomsen. "Status Orientation and Ethnic Sentiment Among Undergraduates," AMERICAN JOURNAL OF SOCIOLOGY, 71 (July, 1965), 60–67.

*Selvin, Hanan C. and Warren O. Hagstrom. "Determinants of Support for Civil Liberties," BRITISH JOURNAL OF SOCIOLOGY, 11 (March, 1960), 51–73.

Shonbar, R. A. "Student Attitudes Toward Communists: Relation Between Intensity of Attitude and Amount of Information," JOURNAL OF PSYCHOLOGY, 27 (January, 1949), 55–71.

Sims, V. M. and J. R. Patrick. "Attitude Toward the Negro of Northern and Southern College Students," JOURNAL OF SOCIAL PSYCHOLOGY, 7 (May, 1936), 192–204.

Stephenson, C. M. "The Relation Between the Attitudes Toward Negroes of Seniors in a School of Education and Their Major Subject," JOURNAL OF EDUCATIONAL RESEARCH, 49 (September, 1955), 113–121.

Stephenson, C. M. "Relation Between the Attitudes Toward Negroes of White College Students and the College or School in Which They are Registered," JOURNAL OF SOCIAL PSYCHOLOGY, 36 (November, 1952), 197–204.

Struening, Elmer L. "Anti-Democratic Attitudes in Midwest University," in H. H. Remmers, ed. ANTI-DEMOCRATIC ATTITUDES IN THE AMERICAN SCHOOLS. Evanston, Illinois: Northwestern University Press, 1963.

Voss, V. "University of Alabama: How Deep Deep South Students Feel About Integration," MADEMOISELLE, 43 (August, 1956), 310–312+.

Wilner, Daniel and Frank Fearing. "The Structure of Opinion: A 'Loyalty Oath' Poll," PUBLIC OPINION QUARTERLY, 15 (Winter, 1950), 729–744.

E.3.e. Student Attitudes Toward War and International Affairs

Harper, Heber R. WHAT EUROPEAN AND AMERICAN STUDENTS THINK ON INTERNATIONAL PROBLEMS. New York: Teachers College, Columbia University, 1931.

Olmstead, F. THE SIGNIFICANCE OF THE COLLEGE PEACE POLL. New York: War Resisters League, 1940.

U.S. Congress, House of Representatives. STUDENT VIEWS TOWARD UNITED STATES POLICY IN SOUTHEAST ASIA HEARINGS. Ad Hoc Committee of Members of the House of Representatives. 91st Congress, 2nd Session. Washington, D.C.: Government Printing Office, 1970.

Aldous, J. and I. Tallman. "Immediacy of Situation and Conventionality as Influences on Attitudes Toward War," SOCIOLOGY AND SOCIAL RESEARCH, 56 (April, 1972), 356–367.

Blau, P. M. "Orientation of College Students Toward International Relations," AMERICAN JOURNAL OF SOCIOLOGY, 59 (November, 1953), 205–214.

140

*Chesler, Mark and Richard Schmuck. "Student Reactions to the Cuban Crisis and Public Dissent," PUBLIC OPINION QUARTERLY, 28 (Fall, 1964), 467–482.

Connors, J. R., Leonard Burnham, and K. Burnham. "Religion and Opposition to War Among College Students," SOCIOLOGICAL ANALYSIS, 29 (Winter, 1968), 211–219.

Cowdry, R. W. *et al.* "War and Military Obligation: Private Attitudes and Public Actions," JOURNAL OF PERSONALITY, 38 (December, 1970), 525–549.

Cram, Paul P. "Undergraduates and the War," ATLANTIC MONTHLY, 166 (October, 1940), 410–421.

Eckhardt, W. E. and N. Z. Alcock. "Ideology and Personality in War/Peace Attitudes," JOURNAL OF SOCIAL PSYCHOLOGY, 81 (June, 1970), 105–116.

Farnsworth, Paul. "Changes in 'Attitudes Toward War' During the College Years," JOURNAL OF SOCIAL PSYCHOLOGY, 8 (1937), 274–279.

Garai, J. E. "Information of College Students on Current Affairs," JOURNAL OF EDUCATIONAL SOCIOLOGY, 36 (October, 1962), 57–65.

Garrison, K. C. "World Minded Attitudes of College Students in a Southern University," JOURNAL OF SOCIAL PSYCHOLOGY, 54 (June, 1961), 147–153.

Kelman, S. J. "Youth and Foreign Policy," FOREIGN AFFAIRS, 48 (April, 1970), 414–426.

Kirkendall, Lester. "A Study of the Changes, Formation, and Persistence of Attitudes of Pacifism," JOURNAL OF EDUCATIONAL SOCIOLOGY, 2 (December, 1937), 222–228.

Miller, D. C. "Effect of the War Declaration on the National Morale of American College Students," AMERICAN SOCIOLOGICAL REVIEW, 7 (October, 1942), 631–644.

Miller, D. C. "National Morale of American College Students in 1941," AMERICAN SOCIOLOGICAL REVIEW, 7 (April, 1942), 194–213.

"The National Student League War Poll," SCHOOL AND SOCIETY, 39 (April 7, 1934), 433–434.

Pedersen, R. F. "Youth, Change, and Foreign Policy," DEPARTMENT OF STATE BULLETIN, 63 (December 14, 1970), 718–722.

Perrin, N. "College Seniors and the War: Views of Dartmouth Students," NEW YORKER, 44 (July 20, 1968), 56+.

Philbach, C. T. "Student Attitudes Toward War," SOCIOLOGY AND SOCIAL RESEARCH, 20 (January–February, 1936), 248–254.

Porterfield, Austin. "Opinions About War," SOCIOLOGY AND SOCIAL RESEARCH, 22 (January–February, 1938), 252–264.

Putney, Snell and Russel Middleton. "Some Factors Associated With Student Acceptance or Rejection of War," AMERICAN SOCIOLOGICAL REVIEW, 27 (October, 1962), 655–667.

Richman, Alvin and Harry R. Targ. "The Impact of Instruction and External Events on Student Orientations and Opinion Consistency Concerning the Vietnam War," SOCIOLOGY OF EDUCATION, 44 (Spring, 1970), 151–169.

Sawyer, R. M. "Campus and War: a Historical Perspective," PHI DELTA KAPPAN, 49 (May, 1968), 522–524.

Sebald, Hans and R. N. Gallegos, "Voices of War and Peace—What Do They Know?: Attitudes and Knowledge About the War in South East Asia," PACIFIC SOCIOLOGICAL REVIEW, 14 (October, 1971), 487–510.

Sharp, L. and R. Krasnesor. "College Students and Military Service: the Experience of an Earlier Cohort," SOCIOLOGY OF EDUCATION, 41 (Fall, 1968), 390–400.

Smith, John Jeffery. "What One College Thinks Concerning War and Peace," JOURNAL OF APPLIED PSYCHOLOGY, 17 (February, 1933), 17–28.

Sowards, Genevieve. "A Study of the War Attitudes of College Students," JOURNAL OF ABNORMAL AND SOCIAL PSYCHOLOGY, 29 (October–December, 1934), 328–333.

Suchman E. A. *et al.* "Attitudes Toward the Korean War," PUBLIC OPINION QUARTERLY, 17 (No. 2, 1953), 171–184.

*Suchman, E., Robin Williams and Rose K. Goldsen. "Student Reaction to Impending Military Service," AMERICAN SOCIOLOGICAL REVIEW, 18 (June, 1953), 293–304.

Tygart, C. E. "Religiosity and University Student Anti-Vietnam Attitudes: a Negative or Curvilinear Relationship?" SOCIOLOGICAL ANALYSIS, 32 (Summer, 1971), 120–129.

E.3.f. Student Alienation

Gould, Laurence J. "The Alienation Syndrome: Psycho-Social Correlates and Behavioral Consequences." Unpublished Ph.D. dissertation, University of Connecticut, 1965.

Herron, Donald George. "Alienation and Student Orientation in the Contemporary University." Unpublished Ph.D. dissertation, University of Minnesota, 1970.

*Keniston, Kenneth. THE UNCOMMITED: ALIENATED YOUTH IN AMERICAN SOCIETY. New York: Harcourt, Brace & World, 1965.

Rogers, William R. THE ALIENATED STUDENT. Nashville, Tennessee: Division of Higher Education, Board of Education, United Methodist Church, 1969.

Stout, Robert J. "A Study of Alienation of Three Diverse Ohio College Campuses." Unpublished Ph.D. dissertation, Bowling Green State University, Ohio.

Vaughan, Charles Edwin. "An Empirical Study of the Relationship Between Participation in University Extra-Curricular Activities and Student Alienation." Unpublished Ph.D. dissertation, University of Minnesota, 1969.

Whittaker, David Neil Eaton. "Psychological Characteristics of Alienated, Nonconformist, College-Age Youth as Indicated by AVL, OPI, ACL and SVIB-M/W Group Profiles." Unpublished Ph.D. dissertation, University of California at Berkeley, 1967.

Whyte, Donald Richard. "Social Alienation Among College Students." Unpublished Ph.D. dissertation, Cornell University, 1963.

"Alienated vs. Society," SCHOOL AND SOCIETY, 95 (April 15, 1967), 252–268.

Bordin, Edward S. "The Role of Alienation in Identity Formation in College Students," in J. C. Heston and W. B. Frich, eds. COUNSELING FOR THE LIBERAL ARTS CAMPUS: THE ALBION SYMPOSIUM. Yellow Springs, Ohio: Antioch Press, 1968, 8–20.

Brown, W. N. "Alienated Youth," MENTAL HYGIENE, 52 (No. 3, 1968), 330–349.

Burbach, H. J. and M. A. Thompson. "Alienation Among College Freshmen: a Comparison of Puerto Rican, Black, and White Students," JOURNAL OF COLLEGE STUDENT PERSONNEL, 12 (July, 1971), 248–252.

*Feuer, Lewis. "Alienation: The Marxism of Contemporary Student Movements," in Milorad M. Drachkovitch, ed. MARXIST IDEOLOGY IN THE CONTEMPORARY WORLD–ITS APPEALS AND PARADOXES. New York: Praeger, 1966.

Foley, Tom. "The Problem of Alienated Youth," POLITICAL AFFAIRS, 46 (June, 1967), 61–63.

*Hajda, Jan. "Alienation and Integration of Student Intellectuals," AMERICAN SOCIOLOGICAL REVIEW, 26 (October, 1961), 758–776.

Holian, J., jr. "Alienation and Social Awareness Among College Students," SOCIOLOGICAL QUARTERLY, (Winter, 1972), 114–125.

"How Colleges Combat Alienation and Improve Teaching," PHI DELTA KAPPAN, 47 (April, 1966), 410–414.

Kean, R. "Finding People Who Feel Alienated and Alone in Their Best Impulses and Most Honest Perceptions and Telling Them They're Not Crazy," WILSON LIBRARY BULLETIN, 44 (September, 1969), 36–44.

Kelman, S. "These are Three of the Alienated," NEW YORK TIMES MAGAZINE, (October 22, 1967), 38–39+.

*Keniston, Kenneth. "Alienation and the Decline of Utopia," in H. M. Ruitenbeek, ed. VARIETIES OF MODERN SOCIAL THEORY, New York: E. P. Dutton, 1963, 79–117.

*Keniston, Kenneth. "Psychology of Alienated Students," in Chad Gordon and Kenneth Gergen, eds. THE SELF IN SOCIAL INTERACTION. New York: Wiley, 1968, 405–415.

Longton, Stuart. "Demythologizing the Student Revolt," PHI DELTA KAPPAN, 51 (June, 1970), 540–544.

Mann, John. "Alienation, Restlessness, and Violence," CHANGING EDUCATION, 4 (Winter, 1969–1970), 13–15.

Martin, Warren B. "An Answer for Anomie," TEACHERS COLLEGE RECORD, 68 (October, 1966), 21–32.

Menninger, R. "What Troubles our Troubled Youth?" MENTAL HYGIENE, 52 (July, 1968), 323–330.

Messer, Mark. "The Conceptual Importance of Being 'Far Out': Or, The First Humanists, Too, Were Alienated Beyond Redemption," in Morton Levitt and Ben Rubenstein, eds. YOUTH AND SOCIAL CHANGE, Detroit: Wayne State University Press, 1972, 111–115.

Middleton, Russell. "Alienation, Race, and Education," AMERICAN SOCIOLOGICAL REVIEW, 28 (December, 1963), 973–977.

*Oppenheimer, Martin. "The Student Movement as a Response to Alienation," JOURNAL OF HUMAN RELATIONS, 16 (First Quarter, 1968), 1–16.

Powell, W. D. "Alienation Among Resident Students at Selected Institutions," NATIONAL ASSOCIATION OF WOMEN DEANS AND COUNSELORS JOURNAL, 35 (Summer, 1972), 189–192.

Rapport, Victor and Bernard Goldman. "The Lonely Student," in Esther Lloyd-Jones and Herman Estrin, eds. THE AMERICAN STUDENT AND HIS COLLEGE. Boston: Houghton Mifflin, 1967, 120–125.

Riedel, M. "Are Students Disenchanted with Materialism?" CONTEMPORARY EDUCATION, 42 (October, 1970), 8–13.

Thompson, Benjamin. "Student Alienation," in G. K. Smith, ed. THE TROUBLED CAMPUS. San Francisco: Jossey-Bass, 1970, 94–100.

*Watts, William A., Steve Lynch, and David Whittaker. "Alienation and Activism in Today's College Age Youth: Socialization Patterns and Current Family Relationships," JOURNAL OF COUNSELING PSYCHOLOGY, 16 (January, 1969), 1–7.

*Westby, David L. and Richard G. Braungart. "The Alienation of Generations and Status Politics: Alternative Explanations of Student Political Activism," in Roberta S. Sigel, ed. LEARNING ABOUT POLITICS. New York: Random House, 1970, 476–490.

Williamson, E. G. "Alienation of Students: Have We Missed Their Signals?" JOURNAL OF THE NATIONAL ASSOCIATION OF WOMEN DEANS AND COUNSELORS, 30 (Fall, 1966), 27–32.

*Wittermans, Tamme and Irving Kraus. "Structural Marginality and Social Worth," SOCIOLOGY AND SOCIAL RESEARCH, 48 (April, 1964), 348–360.

E.3.g. Generational Conflict

Cross-Reference. Some comment and analysis of this topic is found in the section on Personal Background and Values of Activists.

*Braden, William. AGE OF AQUARIUS. Chicago: Quadrangle, 1970.

Brown, James Patrick and James A. Kearns III. ERA OF CHALLENGE. St. Louis: Herder, 1970.

Columbia Broadcasting System. (Conducted by Daniel Yankelovich). GENERATIONS APART: A STUDY OF THE GENERATION GAP. New York: Columbia Broadcasting System, 1969.

*Feuer, Lewis S. THE CONFLICT OF GENERATIONS: THE CHARACTER AND SIGNIFICANCE OF STUDENT MOVEMENTS. New York: Basic Books, 1969.

Klein, Alexander. NATURAL ENEMIES? YOUTH AND THE CLASH OF GENERATIONS. Philadelphia, Pennsylvania: Lippincott, 1970.

Lorber, Richard and Ernest Fladell. THE GAP. New York: McGraw-Hill, 1968.

*Mead, Margaret. CULTURE AND COMMITMENT: A STUDY OF THE GENERATION GAP. Garden City, New York: American Museum of Natural History, Natural History Press, 1970.

Nobile, Philip, ed. THE CON III CONTROVERSY: THE CRITICS LOOK AT THE GREENING OF AMERICA. New York: Pocket Books, 1971.

Pearson, Gerald H. ADOLESCENCE AND THE CONFLICT OF GENERATIONS: AN INTRODUCTION TO SOME PSYCHOANALYTIC CONTRIBUTIONS TO THE UNDERSTANDING OF ADOLESCENCE. New York: Norton, 1958.

Perlman, Samuel. STUDENTS VERSUS PARENTS: PROBLEMS AND CONFLICTS. Cambridge, Massachusetts: Doyle, 1969.

*Reich, Charles. THE GREENING OF AMERICA. New York: Random House, 1970.

Richardson, Roy Lewis. "Parent-Child Relationships and the Divergent Student." Unpublished Ed.D. thesis, University of Missouri, 1965.

Self, William L. BRIDGING THE GENERATION GAP. Nashville, Tennessee: Broadman Press, 1971.

Stanford, Gene, ed. GENERATION RAP: AN ANTHOLOGY ABOUT YOUTH AND THE ESTABLISHMENT. New York: Dell, 1971.

Strommen, M. P., M. Brekke, R. Underwager, and A. L. Johnson. A STUDY OF GENERATIONS. Minneapolis, Minnesota: Augsburg, 1972.

Troll, Lillian E. "Personality Similarities Between College Students and Their Parents." Unpublished Ph.D. dissertation, University of Chicago.

Van Ree, F. COLLIDING GENERATIONS. Varanasi: Narachetna Prakashan, 1970.

*Abrams, P. "Rites de Passage: The Conflict of Generations in Industrial Society," JOURNAL OF CONTEMPORARY HISTORY, 5 (No. 1, 1970), 175–180.

Adelson, J. "What Generation Gap?" NEW YORK TIMES MAGAZINE, (January 18, 1970), 10+.

Aldous, J. "The Consequences of Intergenerational Continuity," JOURNAL OF MARRIAGE AND THE FAMILY, 26 (No. 5, 1965), 462–468.

Bardis, P. D. "Attitudes Toward the Family Among College Students and Their Parents," SOCIOLOGY AND SOCIAL RESEARCH, 43 (May, 1959), 352–358.

Bazelon, David T. "The Kids and the Cockers," DISSENT, 7 (Autumn, 1965), 484–486.

Beggs, Daniel C. and Henry A. Copeland. "The Student in 1970: Social Issues and the Generation Gap," UNIVERSITY INDEX, (July 16, 1970).

*Bengtson, Vern. "The Generation Gap: A Review and Typology of Social-Psychological Perspective," YOUTH AND SOCIETY, 2 (September, 1970), 7–32.

Bengtson, Vern. "Inter-Age Perceptions and the Generation Gap," THE GERONTOLOGIST, 11 (Winter, 1971), 85–89.

Bengtson, Vern and Joseph Kuypers. "Generational Difference and the Developmental Stake," AGING AND HUMAN DEVELOPMENT, 2 (1971), 249–260.

*Berger, R.M. "How Long Is a Generation," BRITISH JOURNAL OF SOCI-OLOGY, 11 (March, 1960), 10–23.

*Bettelheim, Bruno. "The Problem of Generations," in Erik Erikson, ed. YOUTH: CHANGE AND CHALLENGE. New York: Basic Books, 1963, 64–93.

Brown, R. D. "Relationships of Parental Perceptions of University Life to Their Characterizations of College Sons and Daughters, " EDUCATIONAL AND PSYCHOLOGICAL MEASUREMENT, 32 (Summer, 1972), 365–375.

Chu, Franklin. "The Real Generation Gap," CHANGE, 2 (November–December, 1970), 45–49.

Cross, K. P. "Is There a Generation Gap?" NATIONAL ASSOCIATION OF WOMEN DEANS AND COUNSELORS JOURNAL, 31 (Winter, 1968), 53–56.

Davis, Kingsley. "The Sociology of Parent-Youth Conflict," AMERICAN SOCIOLOGICAL REVIEW, 5 (August, 1940), 523–535.

"Dialogue Between the Generations," HARPER'S, 235 (October, 1967), 45–64.

Drake, J. T. "Some Factors Influencing Students Attitudes Toward Older People," SOCIAL FORCES, 35 (March, 1957), 266–271.

Dumke, Glenn. "Bad Days at Generation Gap," in Gary Weaver and James Weaver, eds. THE UNIVERSITY AND REVOLUTION, Englewood Cliffs, New Jersey: Prentice-Hall, 1969, 121–132.

Duscha, J. "Surprising Report on the Generation Gap," SCIENCE DIGEST, 63 (May, 1968), 67–71.

*Eisenstadt, S. N. "Contemporary Student Rebellions–Intellectual Rebellion and Generational Conflict," ACTA SOCIOLOGICIA, 14 (No. 3, 1971), 169–182.

*Eisenstadt, S. N. "Generational Conflict and Intellectual Antinomianism," ANNALS OF THE AMERICAN ACADEMY OF POLITICAL AND SOCIAL SCIENCE, 395 (May, 1971), 68–79.

Endleman, Robert. "Oedipal Elements in Student Rebellions," PSYCHOANALYTIC REVIEW, 57 (No. 3, 1970), 442–471.

Evoy, J. J. "Dialogue Across the Gap," AMERICA, 120 (March 29, 1969), 356–359.

Feuer, Lewis. "Jewish Students as Bearers of Generational Conflict," MIDSTREAM, 16 (April, 1970), 58–64.

*Friedenburg, E. Z. "Current Patterns of a Generational Conflict," JOURNAL OF SOCIAL ISSUES, 25 (April, 1969), 21–38.

Friedenberg, E. Z. "Generation Gap," ANNALS OF THE AMERICAN ACADEMY OF POLITICAL AND SOCIAL SCIENCE, 382 (March, 1969), 32–42.

Friedenberg, E. Z. "A Polite Encounter Between the Generations," NEW YORK TIMES MAGAZINE, (January 16, 1966), 10+.

Friedenberg, E. Z. "The Revolt Against Democracy," CHANGE, 1 (May-June, 1969), 11–17.

Friedenberg, E. Z. "Social Class Factors in Generational Conflict," in Morton Levitt and Ben Rubenstein, eds. YOUTH AND SOCIAL CHANGE, Detroit: Wayne State University Press, 1972, 47–62.

Goertzel, Ted. "Generational Conflict and Social Change," YOUTH AND SOCIETY, 3 (March, 1972), 327–352.

Haan, Norma. "Moral Redefinition in Families as the Critical Aspect of the Generational Gap, YOUTH AND SOCIETY, 2 (March, 1971), 259–284.

Halleck, S. L. "Generation Gap: A Problem of Values," EDUCATION DIGEST, 34 (January, 1969), 32–35.

Heath, Clark and L. W. Gregory. "Problems of Normal College Students and Their Families," in Theodore Newcomb, ed. THE ADOLESCENT, New York: Dryden Press, 1953, 67–74.

Hentoff, Nat. "Beyond the Generational Gap," LIBERATION, 10 (August, 1965), 11–13.

Herrera, F. "Generation Gap and International Development: Youth Movement," AMERICAS, 22 (April, 1970), 13–20.

Hess, S. "Closing the Generation Gap: Search for a National Policy: Interview," U.S. NEWS AND WORLD REPORT, 68 (February 16, 1970), 56–59.

*Jencks, Christopher and David Riesman. "The War Between the Generations," THE RECORD, 69 (October, 1967), 1–21.

Kempton, Murray. "Growing Old With the New Left," NEW YORK REVIEW OF BOOKS, 8 (January 26, 1967), 28–32.

Kinloch, G. C. "Parent-Youth Conflict at Home: an Investigation Among University Freshmen," AMERICAN JOURNAL OF ORTHOPSYCHIATRY, 40 (July, 1970), 658–664.

Kleinberg, Otto. "Feuer, Freud, and the Fathers," SATURDAY REVIEW, 52 (July 19, 1969), 730–731, 736–737.

Kretzmann, J. P. "Generation Gap," CHRISTIAN CENTURY, 85 (May 8, 1968), 616–619.

*Lambert, T. Allen. "Generations and Change: Toward A Theory of Generations as a Force in Historical Process," YOUTH AND SOCIETY, 4 (September, 1972), 21–46.

Larson, A. "Politics, Social Change and the Conflict of a Generation," MIDWEST QUARTERLY, 11 (January, 1970), 123–137.

*Laufer, Robert S. "Sources of Generational Consciousness and Conflict," ANNALS OF THE AMERICAN ACADEMY OF POLITICAL AND SOCIAL SCIENCE, 395 (May, 1971), 80–94.

Lazerwitz, B. and L. Rowitz. "The Three Generations Hypothesis," AMERICAN JOURNAL OF SOCIOLOGY, 69 (March, 1964), 529–538.

Le Shan, E. J. "What? Americans Hate Kids?" NEW YORK TIMES MAGAZINE, (December 1, 1968), 129–130+.

Levitt, Morris. "Notes on Student Rebellion Against Parental Political Beliefs," SOCIAL FORCES, 43 (March, 1965), 427–430.

Lifton, R. J. "Young and the Old: Notes on a New History: Excerpts from History and Survival," ATLANTIC 224 (September, 1969), 47–54 and (October, 1969), 83–88.

*Lipset, S. M. and E. Raab. "Non-Generation Gap," COMMENTARY, 50 (August, 1970), 35–39.

Lloyd, A. G. "Parent-Youth Conflicts of College Students," SOCIOLOGY AND SOCIAL RESEARCH, 36 (March–April, 1952), 227–230.

Lubell, Samuel. "That 'Generation Gap,' " THE PUBLIC INTEREST, No. 13 (Fall, 1968), 52–60.

*Mannheim, Karl. "The Problem of Generations," in P. G. Altbach and R. S. Laufer, eds. THE NEW PILGRIMS, New York: McKay, 1972, 101–138.

Middleton, Russell and Snell Putney. "Student Rebellion Against Parental Political Beliefs," SOCIAL FORCES, 41 (May, 1963), 377–383.

Noble, J. "Generation Gropiosis," WILSON LIBRARY BULLETIN, 43 (October, 1968), 134–139.

Poirier, Richard. "The War Against the Young," ATLANTIC, (October, 1968), 55–64.

Rafferty, Keith. "Mama, Stay Away From My Door," in Esther Lloyd-Jones and Herman Estrin, eds. THE AMERICAN STUDENT AND HIS COLLEGE, Boston: Houghton Mifflin, 1967, 116–120.

Rapoport, David. "Generations in America," in Bernard Crick and William Robson, eds. PROTEST AND DISCONTENT, Baltimore, Maryland: Penguin Books, 1970, 180–193.

Raushenbush, E. "From Where I Sit; College Students and the Generation Gap," MADEMOISELLE, 66 (January, 1968), 61+.

Reik, L. E. "War of the Generations," NATION, 188 (May 16, 1959), 451–455.

Reinhold, Meyer. "The Generation Gap in Antiquity," PROCEEDINGS OF THE AMERICAN PHILOSOPHICAL SOCIETY, 114 (October, 1970), 347–365.

*Rosenfeld, Gerald. "Generational Revolt and the Free Speech Movement," LIBERATION, 10 (December, 1965), 13–17 and (January, 1966), 15–21, 23.

Rosenhaupt, H. "Bridge at Generation Gap," JOURNAL OF HIGHER EDUCATION, 41 (April, 1970), 256–263.

Simmons, Luiz. "The Real Generation Gap: A Speculation on the Meaning and Implications of the Generation Gap," YOUTH AND SOCIETY, 3 (Fall, 1971), 119–130.

Thomas, L. Eugene. "Political Generation Gap: A Study of Liberal and Non-Activist Students and Their Parents," JOURNAL OF SOCIAL PSYCHOLOGY, 84 (1971), 313–314.

Troll, L. E., B. Neugarten and R. J. Kraines. "Similarities in Values and Other Personality Characteristics in College Students and Their Parents," MERRILL PALMER QUARTERLY, 15 (October, 1969), 323–336.

Tyler, Gus. "Generation Gap or Gap within a Generation?" DISSENT, 18 (April, 1971), 145–154.

Wagoner, Walter. "The Campus and the Generation Gap," in Charles Havice, ed. CAMPUS VALUES, New York: Scribner's 1968, 17–23.

Williams, Eugene I. jr. and Carl D. Williams. "Relationship Between Authoritarian Attitudes of College Students, Estimation of Parents' Attitudes, and Actual Parental Attitudes," JOURNAL OF SOCIAL PSYCHOLOGY, 61 (October, 1963), 43–48.

Zelnik, Reginald E. "Prodigal Fathers and Existential Sons," DISSENT, 13 (May–June, 1966), 285–290.

148

F. STUDENT ORGANIZATIONS AND MOVEMENTS

Cross Reference: This general section lists material of a broad
nature or at a lesser known campus: also see specific campuses
and events in the following general section.

F.1. Anti-War Student Activity

Bowers, Robert E. "The American Peace Movement, 1933–1941," Unpublished Ph.D. dissertation, Department of History, University of Wisconsin,
1949.

Carling, Francis. MOVE OVER: STUDENT POLITICS RELIGION. New
York: Sheed and Ward, 1969.

Ferber, Michael and Staughton Lynd. THE RESISTANCE. Boston:
Beacon, 1971.

Geller, Jesse and Gary Howard. STUDENT ACTIVISM AND THE WAR IN
VIETNAM. Washington, D.C.: American Psychological Association, 1969.

Horowitz, Irving Louis. THE STRUGGLE IS THE MESSAGE: THE
ORGANIZATION AND IDEOLOGY OF THE ANTI-WAR MOVEMENTS.
Berkeley, California: Glendessary Press, 1970.

Hurwitz, Ken. MARCHING TO NOWHERE. New York: Norton, 1971.

Lynd, Alice, ed. WE WON'T GO, PERSONAL ACCOUNTS OF WAR
OBJECTORS. Boston: Beacon Press, 1968.

Menashe, Louis and Ronald Radosh, eds. TEACH-INS: U.S.A.: REPORTS,
OPINIONS, DOCUMENTS. New York: Praeger, 1967.

Swirski, Barbara. "American Student Political Activity in the Thirties and
Sixties: An Analysis of War Protest at Harvard and Wisconsin." Unpublished
M.A. dissertation, Department of Sociology, Michigan State University, 1971.

Thorne, Barrie. "Resisting the Draft: An Ethnography of the Draft
Resistance Movement." Unpublished Ph.D. dissertation, Brandeis University,
1969.

Trytten, Merriam H. STUDENT DEFERMENT IN SELECTIVE SERVICE:
A VITAL FACTOR IN NATIONAL SECURITY. Minneapolis: University of
Minnesota Press, 1952.

U.S. Congress. House. Committee on Internal Security. NEW MOBILI-
ZATION COMMITTEE TO END THE WAR IN VIETNAM. HEARINGS.
91st Congress. 2nd Session. Washington: Government Printing Office, 1970.

U.S. Congress. House. Committee on Internal Security. SUBVERSIVE IN-
VOLVEMENT IN THE ORIGIN, LEADERSHIP, AND ACTIVITIES OF THE
NEW MOBILIZATION COMMITTEE TO END THE WAR IN VIETNAM AND
ITS PREDECESSOR ORGANIZATIONS. STAFF STUDY. Washington:
Government Printing Office, 1970.

U.S. Congress. House. Committee on UnAmerican Activities. COMMUNIST
ORIGIN AND MANIPULATION OF VIETNAM WEEK, APRIL 8–15, 1967.
REPORT. (90th Congress. 1st Session). Washington: Government Printing
Office, 1967.

U.S. Congress. Senate. Committee on the Judiciary. Subcommittee to

Investigate the Administration of the Internal Security Acts and Other Internal Security Laws. THE ANTI-VIETNAM AGITATION AND THE TEACH-IN MOVEMENT: THE PROBLEM OF COMMUNIST INFILTRATION AND EXPLOITATION. Washington: Government Printing Office, 1965.

*Urban Research Corporation. ON STRIKE . . . SHUT IT DOWN. A REPORT ON THE FIRST NATIONAL STUDENT STRIKE IN U.S. HISTORY. Chicago: Urban Research Corporation, 1970.

Wamsley, Gary L. SELECTIVE SERVICE AND A CHANGING AMERICA. Columbus, Ohio: Merrill, 1969.

*Wittner, Lawrence. REBELS AGAINST WAR: THE AMERICAN PEACE MOVEMENT: 1941-1960. New York: Columbia University Press, 1969.

Allen, Devere. "The Peace Movement Moves Left," ANNALS OF THE AMERICAN ACADEMY OF POLITICAL AND SOCIAL SCIENCE, 175 (September, 1934), 150-155.

Altbach, Philip G. "A History of the American Peace Movement," FELLOWSHIP, 31 (January, March, July, September 1965), 22-27, 28-32, 25-29, 28-32.

Altbach, Philip. "Peace Moves on the Campus, MOTIVE, 21 (January, 1961), 36-37.

"Ask Bonus for Future Wars (Veterans of Future Wars)", LITERARY DIGEST, 121 (August 11, 1934), 13.

Backus, Michael E. "Student Deferment and Equal Protection," COLUMBIA SURVEY OF HUMAN RIGHTS LAW, 1 (1967-1968), 68-83.

Barnard, Eunice. "Students Lay a Barrage Against War," NEW YORK TIMES MAGAZINE, (April 29, 1934), 5+.

Boulding, Kenneth. "What the First 'Teach In' Taught Us," DISSENT, 13 (January-February, 1966), 10-15.

Brick, Alan. "Peace Moves on the Campus," FELLOWSHIP, 25 (September 1, 1959), 8-12.

Brown, Sam. "The Politics of Peace," WASHINGTON MONTHLY, 2 August, 1970), 24-46.

Calkins, Ken. "The Student Peace Union," FELLOWSHIP, 26 (March 1, 1960), 5-7.

Campbell, Jeffrey W. "Youth, Religion, and Peace," SOCIALIST REVIEW, 6 (July/August, 1938), 11-13.

Converse, P. and H. Schuman. "Silent Majorities and the Vietnam War," SCIENTIFIC AMERICAN, 222 (June, 1970), 17-26.

Cottin, Jonathan. "Faculty-Student Alliance Seeks to Elect Peace-Oriented Congress," NATIONAL JOURNAL, 2 (August 15, 1969), 1759-1768.

"Day of Dissent: the Impact of the Nation's Vietnam Protest: Moratorium Day," LIFE, 67 (October 24, 1969), 32-41.

Dellinger, Dave. "Escalation in the Peace Movement," LIBERATION, 10 (October, 1965), 20-24.

Deming, Barbara. "The Ordeal of SANE," NATION, 192 (March 11, 1961), 200-205.

Didion, Joan. "Just Folks at a School for Nonviolence," in William O'Neill, ed. AMERICAN SOCIETY SINCE 1945. Chicago: Quadrangle Books, 1969, 184-198.

150

*"Documents: The Beginning of the Movement: Peace Protest and Civil Liberties," in Massimo Teodori, ed. THE NEW LEFT: A DOCUMENTARY HISTORY. Indianapolis: Bobbs-Merrill, 1969, 120–127.

*"Documents: The Radicalization of the Movement: Anti Draft Resistance," in Massimo Teodori, ed. THE NEW LEFT: A DOCUMENTARY HISTORY. Indianapolis: Bobbs-Merrill, 1969, 297–317.

*"Documents: The Radicalization of the Movement: Anti War Protest," in Massimo Teodori, ed. THE NEW LEFT: A DOCUMENTARY HISTORY. Indianapolis, Indiana: Bobbs-Merrill, 1969, 240–270.

*"Documents on 'The Vietnam Anti-War Campaign'," in Paul Jacobs and Saul Landau, eds. THE NEW RADICALS. New York: Vintage, 1966, 249–266.

Dolenar, Louis. "Right or Wrong: A Matter of Pride," in Christopher Reashe and Robert Wilson, jr., eds. STUDENT VOICES/ONE. New York: Random House, 1971, 47–50.

"Doubts about Vietnam: Letter to President Johnson from Student Leaders," NEWSWEEK, 70 (May 2, 1966), 3–4.

"Dow Shalt Not Kill," in Ethel Romm, ed. THE OPEN CONSPIRACY. New York: K. S. Giniger, 1970, 197–208.

"Draft Cometh: Sampling of Graduate Schools Opinion: Symposium," AMERICAN FORUM, 74 (May, 1968), 17–19.

Draper, Harold. "The American Student Union Faces the Student Antiwar Strike," AMERICAN SOCIALIST MONTHLY, 5 (April, 1936), 7–12.

Drescher, Earl. "Diary of a Peace March," POLICE CHIEF, 37 (March, 1970), 16–24.

DuPlessix, F. "Reporter at Large: the Moratorium and the New Mobe," NEW YORKER, 45 (January 3, 1970), 32–40+.

Eisen, Jon and Dennis Hale. "Parades, Peace and Politics," ACTIVIST, 7 (Spring, 1967), 16, 22.

Esty, J. C., jr. "Draft Dodger or Patriot? Dilemma of the College Student," NATION, 188 (January 10, 1959), 27–31.

Flacks, R. "Some Social Implications of the Teach-ins," in L. Menashe and R. Radosh, eds. TEACH-INS U.S.A. New York: Praeger, 1967, 285–287.

Flacks, R. and T. Hayden. "Peace Research, U.S.A.," OUR GENERATION AGAINST NUCLEAR WAR, 3 (Fall, 1964), 55–61.

Flacks, Richard, F. Howe and P. Lauter, et al. "On the Draft," NEW YORK REVIEW OF BOOKS, 8 (April, 1967), 3–5.

Flacks, Richard, P. Lauter and F. Howe, et al. The Draft: Reform versus Resistance," LIBERATION, (January, 1967), 34–39.

Friedman, Paul. "Draft Resistance Movement," POLITICAL AFFAIRS, 47 (April, 1968), 58–61.

Gergen, Mary and Kenneth. "How the War Affects the Campuses," CHANGE, 3 (January–February, 1971), 10–11+.

Gibson, H. and J. E. Thomas. "Selective Service System; Student Certification Reporting, COLLEGE AND UNIVERSITY, 47, (Winter, 1972), 118–124.

Gilbert, James. "The Teach-In: Protest or Cooperation?" STUDIES ON THE LEFT, 5 (Summer, 1965), 73–81.

Ginsberg, Allen. "Berkeley Vietnam Days," LIBERATION, 10 (January, 1966), 42–47.

Goodman, Paul. "We Won't Go," NEW YORK REVIEW OF BOOKS, 8 (May 18, 1967), 17–20.

Goodman, W. "New Mobe (1): Who's Who? What's What?" NEW YORK TIMES MAGAZINE, (November 30, 1969), 25–27+.

Grauman, Lawrence, jr. "The University and the Draft," NEW LEADER, 49 (August 1, 1966), 8–11.

Guttman, A. "Protest against the War in Vietnam," ANNUALS OF THE AMERICAN ACADEMY OF POLITICAL AND SOCIAL SCIENCE, 382 (March, 1969), 56–63.

Haber, William. "Authority without Freedom. The Birth of the Teach-In," MICHIGAN QUARTERLY REVIEW, 7 (Fall, 1968), 262–267.

Hadsell, J. S. "Oakland: How to Lose in Winning; Berkeley Student Sit-In at Induction Center," CHRISTIAN CENTURY, 84 (November 15, 1967), 1476–1478.

Halleck, S. L. "Students and the Draft: A Psychiatrist's Report," PROGRESSIVE, 32 (February, 1968), 26–30.

Hauck, Robb J. and Maude A. Stewart. "College Men and the Draft," JOURNAL OF COLLEGE STUDENT PERSONNEL, 11 (November, 1970), 439–444.

Hayden, Tom. "A Protest Against the Draft and Death of Intellect," in L. Menasche and R. Radosh, eds. TEACH-INS, U.S.A. New York: Praeger, 1967, 334–336.

Heisler, Francis. "The New Conscientious Objector," LIBERATION, 11 (January, 1967), 25–28.

"Hell No, We Won't Go," RAMPARTS, 6 (December, 1967), 28–33.

Hentoff, N. "Them and Us: Are Peace Protest Self-Therapy," in W. Anderson, ed. THE AGE OF PROTEST. Pacific Palisades, California: Goodyear, 1969, 254–261.

Hoppock, R. "Student Reaction to Student Ratings," SCHOOL AND SOCIETY, 76 (November 8, 1952), 293–295.

"Induction of Student Demonstrators," SCHOOL AND SOCIETY, 96 (March 2, 1968), 156–157.

Kimball, Penn T. "The Veterans of Future Wars: Princeton's Greatest Political Movement Started Just 30 Years Ago," PRINCETON MAGAZINE, (April 19, 1966), 12–14.

Kristol I. and A. Hartley. "Teaching In, Speaking Out," ENCOUNTER, 25 (August, 1965), 65–72.

La Farge, O. "Colleges and War," SCRIBNERS, 78 (July, 1925), 13–17.

Langer, E. "Oakland Seven: Organizers of Stop the Draft Week," ATLANTIC, 224 (October, 1969), 76–82.

Lathrop, Peter. "Teach-Ins: New Force or Isolated Phenomenon?" STUDIES ON THE LEFT, 8 (Fall, 1968), 98–107.

Levine, Bruce. "Universities and the War Games," NEW POLITICS, 6 (Summer, 1967), 16–20.

Levitas, M. "2–3, Too Smart to Fight? A Report from the University of Michigan," NEW YORK TIMES MAGAZINE, (April 24, 1966), 27+.

Levitas, M. "Vietnam Comes to Oregon University; Campus Protest Called the Teach-in," NEW YORK TIMES MAGAZINE, (May 9, 1965), 24–25+.

Mack, R. W. "Ideology Versus Intellect: The Vietnamization of the University," SOCIAL PROBLEMS, 18 (Fall, 1970), 137–144.

*McReynolds, David. "Pacifists in Battle," NEW POLITICS, 4 (Summer, 1965), 29–35.

McReynolds, David. "The Resistance," NEW POLITICS, 6 (Winter, 1967), 57–61.

McWilliams, W. C. and D. Hale. "The Vietnam Protest," COMMONWEAL, 83 (December 17, 1965), 333–336.

Martin, P. W. "Trial by Hershey," NATION, 206 (January 29, 1968), 139–143.

Meehan, T. "New Mobe (II): The Kids in Bus Number 28," NEW YORK TIMES MAGAZINE, (November 30, 1969), 28–29+.

Mullaney, A. "Protesting the Draft," in Jonathan Allen, ed. MARCH 4, SCIENTISTS, STUDENT AND SOCIETY, Cambridge, Massachusetts: Massachusetts Institute of Technology Press, 1970, 116–123.

Nasmyth, G. W. "Peace Movement in the Colleges," INDEPENDENT, 68 (February 17, 1910), 362–365.

New University Thought Peace Research Committee. "Student Peace Groups," NEW UNIVERSITY THOUGHT, 1 (Spring, 1961), 75–80.

Oglesby, Carl. "The Teach-Ins: A Student Response," DISSENT, 7 (Autumn, 1965), 478–481.

"Open Letter to Faculty Participants in the Vietnam Day Committee (and Reply by the Vietnam Day Committee), "LIBERATION, 10 (November, 1965), 20–25.

Peck, Sidney. "The Anti-War Movement and Radical Politics," NEW POLITICS, 8 (Winter, 1969), 4–11.

Perrin, N. "Our Far-Flung Correspondents: Dartmouth '70 and the War," NEW YORKER, 46 (July 18, 1970), 53–58.

*Peterson, Patti M. "Student Organizations and the Antiwar Movement in America, 1900–1960, "AMERICAN STUDIES, 13 (Spring, 1972), 131–148.

"Report from the Editors: The March on Washington," STUDIES ON THE LEFT, 5 (Spring, 1965), 61–69.

Saari, John L. "Students Lobby for Peace," INTERCOLLEGIAN, 79 (May, 1962), 3–6.

Scott, J. "Jocks 1, War 0: Athletes Protest United States Southeast Asia Policy," RAMPARTS, 9 (August, 1970), 15–18.

Scott, Joan W. "The Teach-In: a National Movement or the End of an Affair?" STUDIES ON THE LEFT, 5 (Summer, 1965), 82–87.

Sherman, E. F. "Dissenters and Deserters," NEW REPUBLIC, 158 (January 6, 1968), 23–27.

Smith, R. B. "Campus Protests and the Vietnam War," in James F. Short and Marvin E. Wolfgang, eds. COLLECTIVE VIOLENCE. Chicago: Aldine, 1970, 157–167.

Smith, Robert. "The Vietnam War and Student Militancy," SOCIAL SCIENCE QUARTERLY, 52 (June, 1971), 133–156.

Stein, Robert and Carolyn Conners. "The Civil Defense Protests in New York," NEW UNIVERSITY THOUGHT, 1 (Spring, 1961), 81–83.

Strack, Celeste. "The Student Movement Against War," in W. Bower, ed. THE COLLEGE WRITER. New York: Norton, 1935, 121–127.

"Student Revolt and the Anti-War Movement," INDEPENDENT SOCIALIST," Number 3 (December, 1967), 8–15.

"Students and the Draft—A Statement," DISSENT, 15 (May–June, 1968), 193–194, 196.

Students for a Democratic Society. OUR FIGHT IS HERE—ESSAYS ON DRAFT RESISTANCE. Chicago: Students for a Democratic Society, 1968.

Tarr, C. W. "Students and Selective Service," NATIONAL ASSOCIATION OF SECONDARY SCHOOL PRINCIPALS BULLETIN, 55 (May, 1971), 22–27.

Tax, Sol. "War and the Draft," in M. Fried, M. Harris and R. Murphy, eds., WAR. Garden City, New York: Doubleday, 1968, 195–207.

"Vietnam on the Campus," EDUCATIONAL RECORD, 48 (Fall, 1967), 363–368.

Weissman, Steve. "Beyond the Moral Imperative," LIBERATION, 11 August, 1966), 43–48.

Weissman, Steve. "The National Coordinating Committee Convention," LIBERATION, 10 (January, 1966), 48–50.

Wisconsin Draft Resistance Union. "What is Guerrilla Theater, Anyway? (1968)," in John and Susan Erlich, eds. STUDENT POWER, PARTICIPATION AND REVOLUTION. New York: Association Press, 1970, 225–245.

Wolf, Michael. "Struggle of the Toiling Youth for Peace," CLARITY, 1 (Summer, 1940), 2–12.

Zagarell, Michael. "World Student Strike Against Vietnam War and Racism," POLITICAL AFFAIRS, 47 (March, 1968), 20–28.

F.2. The Student Power Movement

Aceto, Thomas D. "Student Participation in Policy-Making and the Use of Direct Action at the Midwest CIC Universities." Unpublished Ph.D. dissertation, Syracuse University, 1967.

American Association for Higher Education. A PRODUCTIVE VOICE FOR STUDENTS: A WORKING PAPER ON CAMPUS GOVERNANCE PREPARED FOR THE NATIONAL SUMMER CONFERENCE FOR ACADEMIC DEANS. July 31, 1967. Washington D.C.: American Association for Higher Education, 1968.

American Association of Colleges for Teacher Education. STUDENT PARTICIPATION IN COLLEGE POLICY DETERMINATION AND ADMINISTRATION. Washington: American Association of Colleges for Teacher Education, 1959.

American Council on Education. STUDENT'S ROLE IN COLLEGE POLICY-MAKING. Washington, D.C.: American Council on Education, 1957.

*Barnhart, Michael William. "Left-wing Student Radicalism and Academic

154

Administration." Unpublished Ph.D. dissertation, University of Washington, 1970, 71-76, 926.

Benovitch, Joseph, *et al*. REPORT OF THE COMMITTEE ON STUDENT INVOLVEMENT IN THE UNIVERSITY. Columbus: Ohio State University, 1969.

Brooks, Gary B. "A Study of the Acceptability and Perceived Effectiveness of Selected Methods of Student Expression to Faculty, Student Leaders and Administrators." Unpublished Ph.D. dissertation, Indiana University, 1967.

Cahill, David. STUDENT GOVERNANCE IN RESIDENCE HALLS. Bloomington: Indiana University, 1967.

Carr, Alden J. STUDENT PARTICIPATION IN COLLEGE POLICY DETERMINATION AND ADMINISTRATOR. Washington, D.C.: American Association of Colleges of Teacher Education, 1959.

Carter, E. S. PLANNING STUDENT'S ROLES IN EMERGING UNIVERSITIES. Washington D.C.: Council of Graduate Schools in the U.S., 1969.

Dungan, Ralph A. and Gordon Klopf. STUDENT LEADERSHIP AND GOVERNMENT IN HIGHER EDUCATION. Madison, Wisconsin: National Student Association, 1948.

Falvey, Frances E. STUDENT PARTICIPATION IN COLLEGE ADMINISTRATION. New York: Columbia University, Teachers College, 1952.

Fenton, John H. and Gail Gleason. STUDENT POWER AT THE UNIVERSITY OF MASSACHUSETTS: A CASE STUDY. Amherst, Mass.: Bureau of Government Research, University of Massachusetts, 1969, 71.

Ferguson, Gerald D., jr. "Student Attitudes Toward Active Participation in College Administration." Unpublished Ph.D. dissertation, Colorado State College, 1970.

Friedson, Eliot, ed. STUDENT GOVERNMENT, STUDENT LEADERS AND THE AMERICAN COLLEGE. Philadelphia, Pennsylvania: U.S. National Student Association, 1955.

Follett, Charles Willard. "Student Participation in the Decision Making Process in Colleges and Universities of Ohio." Unpublished Ph.D. dissertation, Ohio State University, 1969.

Gerth, Donald R. THE ROLE OF STUDENTS IN GOVERNANCE: STUDENT RIGHTS, PRIVILEGES, FREEDOMS, AND RESPONSIBILITIES. Report to Academic Senate of the California State Colleges. Los Angeles: California State Colleges, 1966.

Grant, William. "The Development of Student Government: A History of the Board of Student Representatives of Columbia University, 1892-1925." Unpublished Ph.D. dissertation, Columbia University, 1964.

Hodgkinson, Harold. GOVERNANCE AND FACTIONS—WHO DECIDES WHO DECIDES? Berkeley: Center for Research and Development in Higher Education, University of California, 1968.

Hodgkinson, Harold. STUDENT PARTICIPATION IN CAMPUS GOVERNANCE. Berkeley: Center for Research and Development in Higher Education, University of California, 1969.

Hodgkinson, Harold L. and Richard L. Meeth, eds. POWER AND AUTHORITY. Jossey-Bass, 1971.

Holt, Andrew William. "Student Participation in Decision-making in Academic Affairs." Unpublished Ph.D. dissertation, State University of New York at Buffalo, 1969.

*Horowitz, Irving Louis and William H. Friedland. THE KNOWLEDGE FACTORY: STUDENT POWER AND ACADEMIC POLITICS IN AMERICA. Chicago: Aldine, 1970.

Illinois. University of Illinois. Provost's Committee on the Governance of Students. STUDENT GOVERNANCE AT ILLINOIS. Urbana: University of Illinois, 1966.

Johnston, Neal, ed. STUDENT-FACULTY-ADMINISTRATION RELATIONS AND THE ROLE OF STUDENTS IN POLICY FORMATION. Philadelphia: U.S. National Student Association, 1962.

Joughin, Louis. THE ROLE OF THE STUDENT IN COLLEGE AND UNIVERSITY GOVERNMENT. Washington, D.C.: American Association of University Professors, 1968.

Keeton, Morris. SHARED AUTHORITY OF CAMPUS. Washington: American Association for Higher Education, 1971, 166.

Kerr, William Rolfe. "Student Participation in University Governance and Academic Decision-Making." Unpublished Ph.D. dissertation, University of Utah, 1970.

Kiley, Robert R. RESPONSIBILITY IN STUDENT SELF GOVERNMENT, Philadelphia, Pennsylvania: U.S. National Student Association 1958.

Krisch, Dorothea M., ed. STUDENT WELFARE. Philadelphia: U. S. National Student Association, 1964.

Klopf, Gordon. COLLEGE STUDENT GOVERNMENT. New York: Harper and Brothers, 1960.

Locklin, Ralph and Clifford Stewart. STUDENTS, FACULTY, AND ADMINISTRATOR PERCEPTIONS OF DECISION-MAKING AT FOUR COLLEGES. Washington, D.C.: American Educational Research Association, 1970.

Longshore, K. Wallace and Bernard S. Yudowitz. TOWARDS A DEMOCRATIC CAMPUS: A STUDENT'S MANUAL FOR BETTER HUMAN RELATIONS. Philadelphia: U.S. National Students Association, 1955.

Lunn, Harry H. THE STUDENT'S ROLE IN COLLEGE POLICY-MAKING. Washington, D.C.: American Council on Education, 1957.

McGrath, Earl J. SHOULD STUDENTS SHARE THE POWER? A STUDY OF THEIR ROLE IN COLLEGE AND UNIVERSITY GOVERNANCE. Philadelphia, Pennsylvania: Temple University Press, 1970.

Magrath, C. Peter. STUDENT PARTICIPATION: WHAT HAPPENS WHEN WE TRY IT? Washington: American Council on Education, 1969.

Meehan, Mary, ed. ROLE AND STRUCTURE OF STUDENT GOVERNMENT. Washington: United States National Student Association, 1966.

Milton, Ohmer. SURVEY OF FACULTY VIEWS ON STUDENT PARTICIPATION IN DECISION MAKING. Washington, D.C.: Office of Education, U.S. Department of Health, Education and Welfare, 1968.

Mitau, Theodore G. STUDENT PARTICIPATION IN CAMPUS GOVERNANCE. St. Paul, Minnesota: Minnesota State College Board, 1969.

Morison, Robert S. STUDENTS AND DECISION MAKING. Washington, D.C.: Public Affairs Press, 1970.

Office of Institutional Research, ed. CONSTRUCTIVE CHANGES TO EASE CAMPUS TENSIONS. Washington: National Association of State Universities and Land-Grant Colleges, 1970.

Roark, Eldridge Waldo, jr. "The Nature of Student Participation in University Decision-Making on Campuses Experiencing Various Degrees of Organized Student Protest, and the Extent to Which Student Governments are Utilized as Channels For These Acitvities." Unpublished Ph.D. dissertation, Syracuse University, 1971.

Robinson, Lora and Janet Shoenfeld. STUDENT PARTICIPATION IN ACADEMIC GOVERNANCE. Washington, D.C.: ERIC Clearing House on Higher Education, 1970.

*Schwartz, Edward, ed. STUDENT POWER: PHILOSPHY, PROGRAM, TACTICS. Washington, D.C.: U.S. National Student Association, 1968.

Sexton, Donald G. "Student Participation in Governance in Selected Colleges and Universities," Unpublished Ph.D. dissertation, University of Tennessee, 1968.

Shoben, Edward, jr. STUDENT AND UNIVERSITY GOVERNANCE. Buffalo: State University of New York, 1969.

Sindler, Allan P. A CASE STUDY IN STUDENT-UNIVERSITY RELATIONS. Washington: American Council on Education, 1969.

Spurr, Stephan. THE RELATIVE ROLES OF FACULTY AND STUDENTS IN DECISION-MAKING. Washington, D.C.: Council of Graduate Schools in the U.S., 1969.

STATEMENT ON STUDENT-FACULTY-ADMINISTRATIVE RELATIONSHIPS. Washington, D.C.: National Association of State Universities and Land Grant Colleges, 1969.

STUDENTS' ASPIRATION AND PARTICIPATION. (Final Report on International Conference on Students' Aspirations and Participation of Students in University Management, Oslo, August 4–9, 1969). Oslo: Universitetsforlaget, 1970.

Alexander, Leon J. "Campus Peace Restored Through Student Bargaining," LOS ANGELES BAR BULLETIN, 44 (April, 1969), 253–257.

Alexander, William H. "Rethinking Student Government for Larger Universities," JOURNAL OF HIGHER EDUCATION, 40 (January, 1969), 39–46.

Allen, Lucille, *et al.* "Student Participation in Campus Government," in Ester Lloyd Jones and Margaret R. Smith, eds. STUDENT PERSONNEL WORK AS DEEPER TEACHING. New York: Harper, 1954, 131–151.

*Anastaplo, G. "Daring of Moderation: Student Power and the Melian Dialogue," SCHOOL REVIEW, 78 (August, 1970), 451–481.

Antes, R. "Involving Students in University Governance," NATIONAL ASSOCIATION OF STUDENT PERSONNEL ADMINISTRATORS JOURNAL, 9 (July, 1971), 48–56.

Aron, Henry. "Ronald Reagan and the Student Power Advocates: A

Case of Fraternal Twins," JOURNAL OF HUMAN RELATIONS, 19 (1971), 367–376.

Bacheller, John D. "Students in Governance," in D. R. Gerth, J. Heehn, and Associates, eds. AN INVISIBLE GIANT. San Francisco: Jossey-Bass, 1971, 165–177.

Berman, Deborah. "Evolving Patterns of Democratic Social Control at Brandeis University," JOURNAL OF EDUCATIONAL SOCIOLOGY, 28 (April, 1955), 353–360.

Betts, W. W., jr. "Hermes and Apollo," PEABODY JOURNAL OF EDU-CATION, 48 (October, 1970), 49–55.

Biggs, D. A. and E. G. Williamson. "Conflict Resolution on the Campus: A Case Study," JOURNAL OF COLLEGE STUDENT PERSONNEL, 11 (March, 1970), 97–102.

Bloland, P. A. "A Newer Concept in Student Government," JOURNAL OF HIGHER EDUCATION, 32 (February, 1961), 94–97.

Boren, James. "Cooperative Government at the University of Minnesota," in Mary Meehan, ed. ROLE AND STRUCTURE OF STUDENT GOVERN-MENT, Washington, D.C.: U.S. National Student Association, 1966.

Bowen, H. R. "Governance and Educational Reform," CURRENT IS-SUES IN HIGHER EDUCATION, 24 (1969), 173–186.

Bowles, W. D. "Student Participation in Academic Governance," EDU-CATIONAL RECORD, 49 (Summer, 1968), 257–262.

Brann, James. "National Rally for Student Power," NATION, 205 (December 18, 1967), 658–660.

Brother, Louis. "Role of Student Government in the Student Person-nel Program," EDUCATIONAL AND PSYCHOLOGICAL MEASUREMENT, 10 (Number 3, 1950), 569–576.

Brown, J. A. "Student Power," NATIONAL ASSOCIATION OF WOMEN DEANS AND COUNSELORS JOURNAL, 32 (Spring, 1969), 97–103.

Brunson, May. "Student Involvement in University Governance: Sense or Nonsense?" NATIONAL ASSOCIATION OF WOMEN DEANS AND COUN-SELORS JOURNAL, 32 (Summer, 1969), 169–175.

Bundy, McGeorge. "Faculty Power," in Alexander Klein, ed. NATURAL ENEMIES? YOUTH AND THE CLASH OF GENERATIONS. New York: Lippincott, 1969, 160–171.

Bunzel, John H. and Earl J. McGrath. "Student Participation: No, Yes," HUMANIST, 30 (September–October, 1970), 32–39.

Butler, William R. "Student Involvement in the Decision-Making Pro-cess," JOURNAL OF COLLEGE STUDENT PERSONNEL 7 (November, 1966), 331–335.

Carter, L. J. "U. of California at Santa Cruz: New Deal for Under-graduates?" SCIENCE, 171 (January 15, 1971), 153–157.

Cazier, Stanford. "Student Power and In Loco Parentis," in Julian Foster and Durward Long, eds. PROTEST! STUDENT ACTIVISM IN AMERICA. New York: William Morrow, 1970, 506–530.

Covert, E. Richard. "Student Government: Social and Political Action," in Esther Lloyd-Jones and Herman Estrin, eds. THE AMERICAN STUDENT AND HIS COLLEGE. Boston: Houghton Mifflin, 1967.

Crane, Robert. "Student Governance and the Issue of Student Freedom," in L. Vaccaro and J. T. Covert, eds. STUDENT FREEDOM IN AMERICAN HIGHER EDUCATION. New York: Teachers College Press, 1969, 49–63.

Cutler, Richard L. "The New Role of the Student in the Academic Society," in CURRENT ISSUES IN HIGHER EDUCATION, 1966: HIGHER EDUCATION REFLECTS-ON ITSELF AND ON THE LARGER SOCIETY. Washington: Association for Higher Education, 1966, 154–157.

Davidson, Carl. "The Praxis of Student Power: Strategy and Tactics," in Immanuel Wallerstein and Paul Starr, eds. THE UNIVERSITY CRISIS READER, II. New York: Random House, 1971, 108–124.

Davidson, Carl. "Student Power: Radical View," in Edward Schwartz, ed. STUDENT POWER. Washington: U.S. National Student Association, 1969, 7–11.

Davidson, Carl. "Toward Institutional Resistance," in Immanuel Wallerstein and Paul Starr, eds. THE UNIVERSITY CRISIS READER. II. New York: Random House, 1971, 127–138.

Davis, John and Vann Latham. "A Survey of Practices Concerning Student Membership on Academic Committees," in Hans H. Indorf, ed. POLITICS 1970. Greenville, North Carolina: Political Science Department, East Carolina University, 1970, 121–128.

Dixon, James P. "The Student's Role in Educational Policy," in Lawrence Dennis and Joseph Kauffman, eds. THE AMERICAN COLLEGE AND THE STUDENT. Washington: American Council on Education, 1966, 164–168.

"Documents: The Radicalization of the Movement: Student Power," in Massimo Teodori, ed. THE NEW LEFT: A DOCUMENTARY HISTORY. Indianapolis: Bobbs Merrill, 1969, 318–347.

Doran, Bernadette. "Both Sides Are Talking: IS Anybody Listening? Administrators and Students Are Seeking Viable Methods for and Communicating Their Desires and Demands—And Are Getting a Variety of Responses," COLLEGE AND UNIVERSITY BUSINESS, 50 (February, 1971), 53–58+.

Eckert, R. E. "Participation in University Policy-Making: A Second Look," AAUP BULLETIN, 56 (September, 1970), 308–314.

Eddy, Edward. "The Student Views the College Administrator," in G. K. Smith, ed. IN SEARCH OF LEADERS. Washington, D.C.: American Association for Higher Education, 1967, 195–200.

Eddy, Edward D., jr. "Some Suggestions for Student Involvement in Educational Policy," in Lawrence Dennis and Joseph Kauffman, eds. THE AMERICAN COLLEGE AND THE STUDENT. Washington: American Council on Education, 1966, 169–172.

Falvey, Frances E. "Student Participation in College Administration," in TEACHERS COLLEGE STUDIES IN EDUCATION. New York: Bureau of Publications, Teachers College, Columbia University, 1952.

Fellman, David and Stephan Lieurance. "Faculty Power Versus Student Power: Collision Course?" LIBERAL EDUCATION, 56 (March, 1970), 61–75.

Findlay, J. F. "Student Government, Medieval, Colonial and Modern Style," SCHOOL ACTIVITIES, 2 (April–May, 1940), 315–316+.

Foley, G. A. "Group Work: Getting to Know it Better: Student Committees," SCHOOL REVIEW, 60 (April, 1952), 213–218.

Folger, John. "Student Pressures on Colleges and Universities," CURRENT ISSUES IN HIGHER EDUCATION, (1965), 84–88.

Frankel, Charles. "Student Power: The Rhetoric and the Possibilities," SATURDAY REVIEW, (November 2, 1968), 23–25.

Frankel, Charles, *et al.* "Student Power: A Symposium," HUMANIST, 29 (May–June, 1969), 11–16.

Frick, Ivan E. "Reflections on Participatory Democracy," LIBERAL EDUCATION, 55 (May, 1969), 262–271.

Gallo, Gregory. "Student Government: A Student View," NATIONAL ASSOCIATION OF STUDENT PERSONNEL ADMINISTRATORS JOURNAL, 46 (October, 1964), 12–15.

Garcia-Passalacgua, J. M. "Decisions! The College Administrator and Student Unrest," EDUCATIONAL RECORD, 50 (Fall, 1969), 420–425.

Gardner, David P. "The Power Struggle to Convert the University," EDUCATIONAL RECORD, 50 (Spring, 1969), 113–120.

Golden, Patricia and Ned Rosen. "Student Attitudes Toward Participation in University Administration; An Empirical Study Related to Managerial Prerogatives," JOURNAL OF COLLEGE STUDENT PERSONNEL, 7 (November, 1966), 323–330.

Gould, Samuel B., *et al.* "To What Extent Can Administration Involve Faculty and Student Participation and Still be Efficient?" CURRENT ISSUES IN HIGHER EDUCATION, (1959), 156–171.

"Governing a College: How Much Should Students Have to Say?" COLLEGE MANAGEMENT, (May, 1969), 30–39.

Greene, Theodore P. "John Cotton, Anne Hutchinson, and the Student Power Movement," in G. Kerry Smith, ed. STRESS AND CAMPUS RESPONSE. San Francisco: Jossey-Bass, 1968, 99–105.

Grinnell, Sherman K. "The Informal Action Group: One Way to Collaborate in a University," JOURNAL OF APPLIED BEHAVIORAL SCIENCE, 5 (No. 1, 1969), 75–103.

Hale, Dennis and Peter Miller. "Bureaucracy and Protest at Oberlin," NEWS AND LETTERS, 10 (May, 1965).

Hayden, Tom. "CONTRA in Loco Parentis," DISSENT, 11 (Winter, 1964), 104–107.

Heady, Ferrell. "To What Extent Can Administration Involve Faculty-Student Participation and Still be Efficient," CURRENT ISSUES IN HIGHER EDUCATION, 1959. Washington: National Education Association, 1959, 160–164.

Heff, Charles B. "The Administrative Challenge of the New Student Activism," JOURNAL OF HIGHER EDUCATION, 39 (February, 1968), 69–76.

160

Heffner, Ray. "The Student Voice in Institutional Policy," AGB RE-PORTS, 10 (February, 1968), 3–10.

Hellerich, M. H. "Vital Relationship Between Student Government and Campus Community," COLLEGE AND UNIVERSITY, 35, Number 3 (Spring, 1960), 271–280.

Hodgkinson, Harold L. "Student Participation in Governance," in EDUCATION TASK FORCE PAPERS PREPARED FOR THE WHITE HOUSE CONFERENCE ON YOUTH. Berkeley, California: Center for Research and Development in Higher Education, University of California, 1971, 39–66.

Hodgkinson, Harold. "Students and an Intellectual Community," EDUCATIONAL RECORD, 49 (Fall, 1968), 398–406.

Hoffman, Stanley. "Participation in Perspective?" DAEDALUS, 99 (Winter, 1970), 177–221.

Jameson, J. and R. M. Hessler. "Natives are Restless: The Ethos and Mythos of Student Power," HUMAN ORGANIZATION, 29 (Summer, 1970), 81–94.

Johnston, Robert. "Student Culture and Student Power," in H. L. Hodgkinson and L. R. Meeth, eds. POWER AND AUTHORITY. San Francisco: Jossey-Bass, 1971, 85–98.

Johnstone, D. B. "Student and His Power," JOURNAL OF HIGHER EDUCATION, 40 (March, 1969), 205–218.

Jones, Boisfeuillet. "The Case for Student Power and Campus Democracy—A Contradiction," in Morton Levitt and Ben Rubenstein, eds. YOUTH AND SOCIAL CHANGE. Detroit: Wayne State University Press, 1972, 290–302.

Katz, Joseph. "Participatory Reform Instead of Compliance," JOURNAL OF THE AMERICAN ASSOCIATION OF UNIVERSITY WOMEN, 61 (May, 1968), 166, 185+.

Katz, Joseph and Nevitt Sanford. "The New Student Power and Needed Educational Reforms," PHI DELTA KAPPAN, 47 (April, 1966), 397–401.

Keet n, M. "Disenfranchised on Campus," JOURNAL OF HIGHER EDUCATION, 41 (June, 1970), 421–429.

Kerins, Francis J. "Student Autonomy and Administrative Control," JOURNAL OF HIGHER EDUCATION, 30 (February, 1959), 61–66.

Kerlinger, Fred N. "Student Participation in University Educational Decision Making," TEACHERS COLLEGE RECORD, 70 (October, 1968), 45–51.

Keyes, Ralph. "Student Involvement: the Why and How," NATIONAL ASSOCIATION OF STUDENT PERSONNEL ADMINISTRATORS JOURNAL, 6 (October, 1968), 72–82.

Kinnison, W. A. "New Power Relationships on the Campus; Student and the Non-academic Employee," JOURNAL OF HIGHER EDUCATION, 39 (June, 1968), 309–315.

Kraft, I. "Student Power in American Higher Education," EDUCATIONAL FORUM, 35 (March, 1971), 329–337.

Kramer, J. P. "What Student Power Means," NEW YORK TIMES MAGAZINE, (May 26, 1968), 32–33+.

LaGaipa, J. J. "Student Power and Dogmatism," JOURNAL OF PSY-CHOLOGY, 73 (November, 1969), 201–207.

Levi, Julian. "Legal Aspects of University Governance," EDUCATION-AL RECORD, 50 (Fall, 1969), 405–410.

Levi, Julian. "Student Unrest and the Role of Student Participation in Institutional Government," COLLEGE COUNSEL, 4 (1969), 23–43.

Lewy, G. and S. Rothman. "On Student Power," AAUP BULLETIN, 56 (September, 1970), 279–282; Discussion, 57 (March, 1971), 129–131+.

Logan, John, jr. "A Look at Current College-Student Relationships," in Esther Lloyd-Jones and H. Estrin–THE AMERICAN STUDENT AND HIS COLLEGE. Boston: Houghton Mifflin, 1967, 96–99.

Lunn, H. H., jr. and R. M. Strozier. "How Can Student Participation and Responsibility in Campus Life Be Developed More Effectively?" in CURRENT ISSUES IN HIGHER EDUCATION, 1955, 258–265.

McDonough, John R. "The Role of Students in Governing the University," in Immanuel Wallerstein and Paul Starr, ed. THE UNIVERSITY CRISIS READER, 2. New York: Random House, 1971, 500–506.

McGuire, Edward D. "The Role of the Student in College Policy Making," PERSONNEL AND GUIDANCE JOURNAL, 38 (January, 1960), 378–384.

McHugh, W. F. "Collective Bargaining and the College Student," JOURNAL OF HIGHER EDUCATION, 42 (March, 1971), 175–185.

McMahon, E. E. and C. R. Foster, jr. "The Undergraduate Point of View on Student Participation," SCHOOL AND SOCIETY, 35 (June 4, 1932), 768–770.

McNamara, R. J. "Students and Power: A Fordham Reflection: A Bitter Conflict Has Arisen in Academia Which Can Only Be Resolved Through Structures of Mutural Respect and Active Cooperation Among Students, Faculty and Administration," THOUGHT, 43 (Summer, 1968), 202–210.

*Magrath, C. Peter. "Student Participation: What Happens When We Try It?" in John Caffrey, ed. THE FUTURE ACADEMIC COMMUNITY: CONTINUITY AND CHANGE. Washington: American Council on Education, 1969, 97–118.

Martin, H. L. "Student Representation in the College and University Affairs: a Survey by the Southern Universities Student Government Association," STUDENT GOVERNMENT BULLETIN. 11 (Fall, 1966), 8–16.

Martin, Warren B. "Should Students Rule?" MOTIVE, (1967), 12–17.

Martin, Warren B. "Student Participation in Academic Governance," CURRENT ISSUES IN HIGHER EDUCATION, 1967. Washington: Association for Higher Education, 1967, 173–177.

Martinez, F. R. "California College Student Government Association," JUNIOR COLLEGE JOURNAL, 30 (September, 1959), 29–34.

Muston, Ray. "Concept of Student Participation in Governance Becomes Formalized and More Public as it Gains Momentum," COLLEGE AND UNIVERSITY BUSINESS, 48 (March, 1970).

Nelson, Bryce. "Student Power: Demands for Change at Stony Brook's 'Talk-In,' " SCIENCE, 162 (November 1, 1968), 545–548.

O'Brien, D. J. "Power to the Students," COMMONWEAL, 91 (October 3, 1969), 15–18+.

Oliver, R. "On Pedagogy and Student Power; A Proposal," RECORD, 70 (January, 1969), 374–379.

Orwig, Mel. "The Bureaucracy of the Campus and the Student's Place in It," JOURNAL OF THE NATIONAL ASSOCIATION OF WOMEN DEANS AND COUNSELORS, 31 (Winter, 1968), 80–82.

Parente, William J. "A Student Voice in Academic Policy," in W. Brickman and S. Lehrer, eds. CONFLICT AND CHANGE ON THE CAMPUS. New York: School and Society Books, 1970, 243–246.

Penney, James F. "Variations on a Theme; In Loco Parentis," JOURNAL OF COLLEGE STUDENT PERSONNEL, 8 (January, 1967), 22–25.

Peterson, B. H. "Student Government in Collegiate Institutions," JOURNAL OF HIGHER EDUCATION, 14 (April, 1943), 205–208.

Peterson, Martha. "Student Government: An Administrative View," in The American Student and his College, in Esther Lloyd-Jones and Herman Estrin, eds. THE AMERICAN STUDENT AND HIS COLLEGE. Boston: Houghton Mifflin, 1967, 246–250.

Peterson, Martha. "What Principles Should Govern Decisions When Students Disavow Institutional Policies?" in G. K. Smith, ed. CURRENT ISSUES IN HIGHER EDUCATION, 1964: UNDERGRADUATE EDUCATION. Washington, D.C.: National Education Association, 1964, 91–94.

Pillard, Basil. "Participation by Students in Institutional Government," in John D. Russell, ed. STUDENT PERSONNEL SERVICES IN COLLEGES AND UNIVERSITIES. Chicago: University of Chicago Press, 1941, 234–254.

Powell, R. S., jr. "Student Power and the Student Role in Institutional Governance," LIBERAL EDUCATION, 55 (March, 1969), 24–31.

Reynolds, Robert. "Student Governance," CTA JOURNAL, 66 (March, 1968),

Ryan, W. G., et al. "Students Search for Freedom," MIDDLE STATES ASSOCIATION OF COLLEGES AND SECONDARY SCHOOLS PROCEEDINGS, (1967), 80–92.

Scanlon, K. I. "Student Government in Catholic Colleges for Women in the United States," EDUCATIONAL ADMINISTRATION AND SUPERVISION, 44 (March, 1958), 106–120.

Schwartz, Edward. "Student Power–In Response to the Question," in W. Brickman and S. Lehrer, eds. CONFLICT AND CHANGE ON THE CAMPUS: THE RESPONSE TO STUDENT HYPERACTIVISM. New York: School and Society Books, 1970, 247–258.

Shaffer, J. C. "Students in the Policy Process," JOURNAL OF HIGHER EDUCATION, 41 (Spring, 1970), 341–349.

Shaffer, Robert H. "Student Government: Sandbox or Soapbox?" in Julian Foster and Durward Long, eds. PROTEST! STUDENT ACTIVISM IN AMERICA. New York: William Morrow, 1970, 497–505.

Simmons, J. and P. P. Grande. "Student-Administration War of 1966: The Strategy of Escalation," CATHOLIC EDUCATION REVIEW, 64 (December, 1966), 582–589.

Snyder, L. J. "Campus Conflict and Strategies for Student Administration Bargaining," NATIONAL ASSOCIATION OF WOMEN DEANS AND COUNSELORS, 31 (Spring, 1968), 106–111.

Stahl, K. and E. F. Cheit. "Student Power: Two Views," SEVENTEEN, 27 (August, 1968), 384–386+.

Stern, Peter S. "Stanford's Community of Consent," NATION, 211 (September 7, 1970), 174–178.

Stewart, Irvin. "Student Government as a University President Sees It," ASSOCIATION OF AMERICAN COLLEGES BULLETIN, 36 (March, 1950), 90–97.

"Student Participation in Educational Policy Formation," STUDENT GOVERNMENT BULLETIN, Special Issue, 10 (Winter, 1966).

"Student Response to Authority: Symposium," JOURNAL OF COLLEGE STUDENT PERSONNEL, 11 (March, 1970), 83–102.

"Student Power in America: An Assessment," COLLEGE AND UNIVERSITY BUSINESS, 45 (August, 1968), 32–62.

"Student Power in University Affairs: A Symposium," AMERICAN JOURNAL OF COMPARATIVE LAW, 17 (Number 3, 1969), 331–417.

Sturner, W. F. "University Governance Through The Bicameral Legislature," JOURNAL OF HIGHER EDUCATION, 42 (March, 1971), 219–228.

Taylor, Harold. "The Student as a Responsible Person," HARVARD EDUCATIONAL REVIEW, 19 (Spring, 1949), 67–79.

Tigar, Michael E. "Student Participation in Academic Governance," CURRENT ISSUES IN HIGHER EDUCATION, 1966: HIGHER EDUCATION REFLECTS–ON ITSELF AND ON THE LARGER SOCIETY, (1966), 169–174.

Trueblood, Dennis. "Participation of Student Government in the Student Personnel Program," EDUCATIONAL AND PSYCHOLOGICAL MEASUREMENT, 11 (Winter, 1951), 799–803.

Turner, Fred H. "The Role of the University in Student Government," JOURNAL OF COLLEGE STUDENT PERSONNEL, 1 (March, 1960), 18–24.

Turner, F. "Student Movement as a Force for Educational Change," LIBERAL EDUCATION, 56 (March, 1970), 39–50.

Vaccaro, L. C. "Conflict of Authority in the University," COLLEGE AND UNIVERSITY JOURNAL, 44 (Spring, 1969), 232–239.

Vaccaro, L. C. "Power and Conflict in the University," COLLEGE AND UNIVERSITY, 44 (Fall, 1968), 97–107.

Van Alstyne, William. "The Tentative Emergence of Student Power in the United States," AMERICAN JOURNAL OF COMPARATIVE LAW, 17 (Number 3, 1969), 403–417.

Wallace, Jo Anne. "Behind the Free University Crisis," in Immanuel Wallerstein and Paul Starr, eds. THE UNIVERSITY CRISIS READER, II. New York: Random House, 1971, 235–242.

164

Weeks, D. I. "Student Participation in College Administration," SCHOOL AND SOCIETY, 71 (June 24, 1950), 385–387.

Schwartz, Edward. "What We Want and Why," in Alexander Klein, ed. NATURAL ENEMIES? YOUTH AND THE CLASH OF GENERATIONS. New York: Lippincott, 1969, 153–159.

Williamson, E. G. "What Priority is to be Given to Increasing Student Demands for Participation in the Governance of the College?" CURRENT ISSUES IN HIGHER EDUCATION, (1965).

Wilson, G. G. and A. Weisman. "Keeping Student Participation in Its Place," THEORY INTO PRACTICE, 9 (October, 1970), 248–253.

Wilson, P. A. "Some Thoughts on Student Power," NATIONAL ASSOCI-ATION OF STUDENT PERSONNEL ADMINISTRATORS JOURNAL, 8 (October, 1970), 90–96.

Wise, W. Max. "New Configurations in Governance," in G. Kerry Smith, ed. THE TROUBLED CAMPUS. San Francisco: Jossey-Bass, 1970, 131–137.

Wrenn, Robert L. "The Authority Controversy and Today's Student," PERSONNEL AND GUIDANCE JOURNAL, 46 (June, 1968), 949–953.

Younger, John. "Student Self-Government," JOURNAL OF HIGHER EDUCATION, 2 (April, 1931), 204–206.

Zwicker, Barrie. "Rochdale: The Ultimate Freedom," CHANGE, 1 (November–December, 1969), 37–43.

F.3. Conservative Organizations and Activities

Branden, Nathaniel. WHO IS AYN RAND? New York: Paperback Library, 1964.

Cain, Edward. THEY'D RATHER BE RIGHT: YOUTH AND CONSER-VATISM. New York: Macmillan, 1963.

Evans, Medford Stanton. REVOLT ON THE CAMPUS. Chicago: Regnery, 1961.

Hager, James C., jr. POLITICS, CAMPUS STYLE. Washington: Young Americans for Freedom, 1970.

Huston, Tom C. BUILDING THE FREE SOCIETY. Washington, D.C.: Young Americans Freedom, 1965.

McEvoy, J. RADICALS OR CONSERVATIVES? THE CONTEMPORARY AMERICAN RIGHT. Chicago: Rand McNally, 1971.

*Opinion Research Corporation. CONSERVATISM ON THE COLLEGE CAMPUS. Princeton, New Jersey: Opinion Research Corporation, 1962.

Rosenstone, R. A. A PROTEST FROM THE RIGHT. Beverly Hills, California: Glencoe Press, 1968.

Rush, Gary B. "Status Crystalization and Right-Wing Extremist Atti-tudes." Unpublished Ph.D. dissertation, University of Oregon, 1965.

Schiff, Lawrence J. "The Conservative Movement on American College Campuses." Unpublished Ph.D. dissertation, Harvard University, 1964.

Tuccille, Jerome. IT USUALLY BEGINS WITH AYN RAND. New York: Stein and Day, 1971.

Young Americans for Freedom. University Research Committee. A
FACULTY-STUDENT INQUIRY INTO THE CAUSES OF CAMPUS DIS-
ORDERS AND A REBUTTAL OF THE SCRANTON COMMISSION RE-
PORT. Washington: Young Americans for Freedom, 1970.

Young Americans for Freedom. YOUNG AMERICANS FOR FREEDOM
AND YOU. Washington, D.C.: Young Americans for Freedom, N.D.

Breslow, P. "Students for America: Campus McCarthyism," NATION,
178 (March 20, 1954), 240–241.

Brownfeld, Allan C. "Revolution: The Right," MOTIVE, 24 (December,
1963), 34–37.

Buckley, F. R. "Revolt of the Classes: Today's College Students are
Turning Against the Orthodoxy of Collectivism Which Has Held Sway on Campus Over Two Decades," FREEMAN, (September, 1955), 653–656.

Buckley, T. "Student Moves into the 14th C. D." NEW YORK TIMES
MAGAZINE, (June 21, 1970), 10–11+.

Burnham S. "Twelve Rebels of the Student Right," NEW YORK TIMES
MAGAZINE, (March 9, 1969), 32–33+.

"Campus Conservatives," TIME, 127 (February 10, 1961), 34–37.

"Conservative Students," TIME, 32 (October 24, 1938), 40.

"Conservatives on the Campus," NEWSWEEK, 115 (April 10, 1961), 35.

*Dorfman, Ron, Paul Levy and Richard Merbaum. "The Right at N.S.A."
NEW UNIVERSITY THOUGHT, 2 (Autumn, 1961), 25–32.

Elms, Alan C. "The Conservative Ripple," NATION, 192 (May 27,
1961), 458–460, 468.

Fox, George. "Counterrevolution," in D. Myrus, ed. THE YOUTH CUL-
TURE. Chicago: Playboy Press, 1971, 147–151.

Kempton, Murray. "On Growing Up Absurd," PROGRESSIVE, 25
(May, 1961), 11–14.

"Ku Kluxism at Ohio State University," NEW REPUBLIC, 67 (June 10,
1931), 83–85.

Lerner, Charles. "Students for America: McCarthy's Class of '54',"
NEW FOUNDATIONS, 7 (Spring, 1954), 13–18.

Lulves, John. "Is There a Student Conservatism?" NATIONAL REVIEW,
18 (May 31, 1966), 530–531.

MacKay, A. "The View from the Right Side of the Campus," MANION
FORUM, (August 4, 1968), 1–4.

McMahon, Dennis C. "The National Youth Alliance," AMERICAN MER-
CURY, 105 (Spring, 1969), 61–63.

Madden, J. A. "Young Americans for What?" AMERICA, 108
(January 19, 1963), 83–85.

Novak, R. D. "Campus Conservatives," WALL STREET JOURNAL,
(November 30, 1961 and December 1, 1961), 1+.

O'Connell, James M. "The New Conservatism," NEW INDIVIDUAL-
IST REVIEW, 2 (Spring, 1962), 17–21.

Reichley, A. J. "Young Conservatives at Old Harvard," REPORTER,
12 (June 16, 1955), 12–16.

Riley, P. "Conservatism on the Campus," AMERICAN MERCURY, 84 (April, 1957), 39.

Roberts, Steven V. "Image on the Right," NATION, 194 (May 19, 1962), 440–442.

Rothbard, M. N. "A YAF Conversion," LIBERTARIAN FORUM, (November 15, 1969).

Rothbard, M. N., et al. "Old Right/New Left," LEFT AND RIGHT: A JOURNAL OF LIBERTARIAN THOUGHT, 2 (1966), 3–7.

Rush, Gary B. "Status Consistency and Right Wing Extremism," AMERICAN SOCIOLOGICAL REVIEW, 32 (February, 1967), 86–91.

"Sanity at Pittsburgh," NATIONAL REVIEW, 19 (October 3, 1967), 1056–1058.

Schick, E. B. "Student Conservative Revolution and Faculty/Student Conflict," EDUCATIONAL THEORY, 21 (Winter, 1971), 17–32.

*Schiff, L. F. "Dynamic Young Fogies: Rebels on the Right," TRANS-ACTION, 4 (November, 1966), 30–36.

*Schiff, Lawrence. "The Obedient Rebels¾ A Study of College Conversions to Conservatism," JOURNAL OF SOCIAL ISSUES, 20 (October, 1964), 74–96.

Sisk, J. P. "Conservatism on Campus," COMMONWEAL, 73 (January 27, 1961), 451–454.

Treaster, Joseph. "500 Youths Plan Antiradical Crusade," NEW YORK TIMES, (September 14, 1970), 1, 30.

Wallace, Anna. "Fascism Comes to the Campus: The University of California as a Case in Point," NEW REPUBLIC, 81 (January 9, 1935), 238–241.

Wingfield, William. "The Campus Scare Campaign," NATION, 203 (September 12, 1966), 206–208.

F.4. The Liberal Student Movement

Cross Reference: Some material on liberal student activism can be found in the section, on the student left: 1950–1960, and in the section on personal background and values of activists. (Sections IH5 and IE2b.)

F.4.a. U.S. National Student Association (USNSA)

Altbach, Philip G. and Norman T. Uphoff. THE STUDENT INTERNA-TIONALS. Metuchen, New Jersey: Scarecrow Press, 1973.

Friedson, Eliot, ed. STUDENT GOVERNMENT, STUDENT LEADERS, AND THE AMERICAN COLLEGE. Philadelphia, Pennsylvania: U.S. National Student Association, 1955.

Garvey, Edward. HISTORY AND DEVELOPMENT OF U.S.N.S.A. Philadelphia, Pennsylvania: United States National Student Association, 1963.

Green, Reginald H. RESPONSIBILITY IN STUDENT AFFAIRS. Philadelphia: U.S. National Student Association, 1958.

Handel, Larry, STUDENT WELFARE. Washington: U.S. National Student Association, 1965.

Jones, Peter T. THE HISTORY OF THE UNITED STATES NATIONAL STUDENT ASSOCIATION RELATIONS WITH THE INTERNATIONAL UNION OF STUDENTS 1945–1956. Philadelphia, Pennsylvania: Foreign Policy Research Institute, 1956.

Kernish, Robert. THE HISTORY OF THE U.S.N.S.A. Washington, D.C.: National Student Association, 1965.

McLaughlin, Martin. POLITICAL PROCESSES IN AMERICAN NATIONAL STUDENT ORGANIZATIONS. Ann Arbor, Michigan: Edwards Brothers, 1948.

Makuen, Donald R. "An Analysis of the Concept of Student Responsibility in Higher Education, 1950–1960." Unpublished Ed.D. thesis, Teachers College, Columbia University, 1963.

Meehan, Mary ed. ROLE AND STRUCTURE OF STUDENT GOVERNMENT. Washington, D.C.: U.S. National Student Association, 1966.

Schodde, Stephen C. "Certain Foci of the United States National Student Association and Their Implications for Student Personnel Administration." Unpublished Ed.D. dissertation, Teachers College, Columbia University, 1965.

SUMMARY REPORT, 7TH NATIONAL STUDENT CONGRESS. Philadelphia: U.S. National Student Association, 1954.

U.S. National Student Association. THE AMERICAN STUDENT— PROFILE AND PROMISE: U.S.N.S.A. 1947–1957. Philadelphia: U.S. National Student Association, 1957.

U.S. National Student Association. THE CONGRESS AS A COLLEGE: A REPORT ON THE DELEGATE QUESTIONNAIRE. Washington, D.C.: November, 1966, 12.

Young Americans for Freedom. A REPORT ON THE U.S. NATIONAL STUDENT ASSOCIATION. Washington, D.C.: Young Americans for Freedom, 1963.

Altbach, Philip. "CIA Spies or Deserving Students?" CHRISTIAN CENTURY, 84 (March 15, 1967), 352–354.

Bass, Abraham Z. "A Platform for Citizen-Students," SATURDAY REVIEW, 48 (October 16, 1965), 84.

Bebchick, Leonard. "Training for International Leadership," STUDENT GOVERNMENT BULLETIN AND REPORT, 2 (October, 1953), 27–32.

Birenbaum, W. and D. L. Trueblood. "Meeting, 1951," SCHOOL AND SOCIETY, 74 (December 15, 1951), 377–380.

Boitel, H. J. "Students in Action," AMERICA, 105 (April 8, 1961), 64–67.

Brammer, L. M. and F. P. Kramer. "The CIA-NSA Controversy," JOURNAL OF COLLEGE STUDENT PERSONNEL, 8 (July, 1967), 220–224.

"The CIA and the Students," TIME, 89 (February 24, 1967), 13–17.

168

Dorfman, Ron, Paul Levy and Richard Merbaum. "The Right at NSA," NEW UNIVERSITY THOUGHT, 2 (Autumn, 1961), 25–32.

Farrar, J. C. "American Students Talk It Over," NATION, 164 (January 11, 1947), 45–46.

Farrar, C. "Students Map the Future," NATION, 165 (September 20, 1947), 279–280.

Fisher, S. M. "NSA Congress, 1969," AMERICA, 121 (September 27, 1969), 218–222.

Fitzpatrick, E. A. "Student Bill of Rights of the United States National Student Organization," SCHOOL AND SOCIETY, 68 (August 14, 1948), 97–101.

Gannett, Betty. "The CIA–Weapon of the Cold War," POLITICAL AFFAIRS, 46 (May, 1967), 19–31.

Gitlin, Todd and Bob Ross. "The CIA at College: Into Twilight and Back," VILLAGE VOICE, 12 (July 6, 1967), 15+.

Howe, Irving. "The CIA and the Students," DISSENT, 14 (March–April, 1967), 129–130.

Kean, Rick. "The NSA Congress," MOTIVE, 28 (November, 1967), 4–8.

*Keyes, Ralph, "What Makes NSA Run?" CHANGE, 2 (March–April, 1970), 33–38

Klopf, G. and D. Trueblood. "Evaluation," SCHOOL AND SOCIETY, 74 (August 11, 1951), 85–89.

Kuttner, Robert. "Consensus with a Vengeance: NSA and the CIA," ACTIVIST, 7 (Spring, 1967), 9–10.

Landry, Lawrence. "NSA: Student Voice of the Silent Generation," NEW UNIVERSITY THOUGHT, 1 (Spring, 1960), 88–95.

"Life Goes to a Collegiate Convention," LIFE, 29 (September 18, 1950), 164–166+.

Lynch, M. and G. Klopf. "Report on the 1949 Congress," SCHOOL AND SOCIETY, 70 (December 10, 1949), 374–378.

*McDonald, Robert, "NSA/CIA: The Kiddies and their Playmates," TRANSITION, (Kampala, Uganda), Number 31 (June–July, 1967), 14–19.

McLaughlin, M. "Spotlight on Students," CATHOLIC WORLD, 166 (November, 1947), 130–137.

McWilliams, W. C. "CIA and the Students," COMMONWEAL, 85 (March 3, 1967), 611–614.

Marsh, Lee. "NSA," NEW STUDENT, 1 (November, 1947), 3–9.

Matthews, J. B. "USNSA," AMERICAN MERCURY, 87 (December, 1958), 59–63.

Meier, Debbie. "Careerism on the Campus: Two Faces of Conformity," ANVIL, 7 (Spring–Summer, 1956), 9–12.

"NSA: What it is, What It Should Be," MODERATOR, 3 (Summer, 1964), 10–19.

National Supervisory Board, National Student Association. "The NSA Position on the CIA," NATIONAL ASSOCIATION OF STUDENT PERSONNEL ADMINISTRATORS JOURNAL, 4 (April, 1967), 187–190.

Ridgeway, James. "Patriots on the Campus," NEW REPUBLIC, 156 (March 25, 1967), 12–14.

Riggs, Lawrence. "Report by the National Association of Student Personnel Administrators Representative to the Associated Student Governments of the United States of America," NATIONAL ASSOCIATION OF STUDENT PERSONNEL ADMINISTRATORS JOURNAL, 2 (July, 1964), 17–18.

Schodde, Stephen. "The NSA and Student Government," NATIONAL ASSOCIATION OF STUDENT PERSONNEL ADMINISTRATORS JOURNAL, 46 (October, 1964), 15–18.

Shaw, Marvin. "NSA Was Promises," NEW FOUNDATIONS, 1 (Winter, 1948), 49–54.

Shaw, M. "Student America Convenes," POLITICAL AFFAIRS, 26 (October, 1947), 872–886.

Sollen, R. H. "Report on the National Student Association," SCHOOL AND SOCIETY, 70 (July 9, 1949), 21–23.

Stearns, Richard and Dennis Shaul. "Two Views of the NSA-CIA Crisis By Present and Former NSA Officers," MADEMOISELLE, 65 (August, 1967), 232+.

*Stern, Sol. "NSA:CIA," RAMPARTS, 5 (March, 1967), 29–39.

Stern, Sol. "Short Account of International Student Politics and the Cold War with Particular Reference to the NSA, CIA, etc." RAMPARTS, 7 (January 25, 1969), 87–97.

Triesman, David. "The CIA and Student Politics," in A. Cockburn and R. Blackburn, eds. STUDENT POWER. Baltimore: Penguin Books, 1969, 141–162.

Weinberg, Paul. "Ward Heelers on the Campus," NATION, 190 (June 4, 1960), 489–492.

Werdell, Philip R. "The Underbelly of a Supersecret," MODERATOR, 6 (April, 1967), 10–14.

F.4.b. The Peace Corps and the American Student

Ashabranner, Brent K. A MOMENT IN HISTORY: THE FIRST TEN YEARS OF THE PEACE CORPS. Garden City, New York: Doubleday, 1971.

Cowan, Paul. THE MAKING OF AN UN-AMERICAN: A DIALOGUE WITH EXPERIENCE. New York: Viking Press, 1970.

Fuchs, L. H. 'THOSE PECULIAR AMERICANS': THE PEACE CORPS AND THE AMERICAN NATIONAL CHARACTER. New York: Meredith, 1967.

Groebli, John M. RETURNED PEACE CORPS VOLUNTEERS IN THE EDUCATIONAL SYSTEM OF THE STATE OF NEW YORK. Albany: New York State Education Department, 1965.

Hapgood, David. OF WHAT VALUE IS THE PEACE CORPS? New York: Center for International Studies, New York University, 1968.

Hoopes, Roy. THE PEACE CORPS EXPERIENCE. New York: Potter, 1968.

Luce, Iris, ed. LETTERS FROM THE PEACE CORPS. New York: David McKay, 1964.

McGuire, Edna. THE PEACE CORPS, KINDLERS OF THE SPARK. New York: Macmillan, 1966.

Madow, Pauline, ed. THE PEACE CORPS. New York: H. W. Wilson, 1964.

Powell, Richard. DON QUIXOTE U.S.A. New York: Scribner, 1966.

Stein, Morris I. VOLUNTEERS FOR PEACE. New York: Wiley, 1966.

Textor, Robert, ed. CULTURAL FRONTIERS OF THE PEACE CORPS. Cambridge, Massachusetts: Massachusetts Institute of Technology Press, 1966.

U.S. Peace Corps. BIBLIOGRAPHY OF RESEARCH. Washington: U.S. Peace Corps, 1968.

Windmiller, Marshall. THE PEACE CORPS AND PAX AMERICANA. Washington: Public Affairs Press, 1970.

Zeitlin, Arnold. TO THE PEACE CORPS, WITH LOVE. Garden City, New York: Doubleday, 1965.

Bayley, Edwin. "The View from Inside the Peace Corps," PROGRESSIVE, 25 (September, 1961), 27–30.

Berreman, Gerald D. "The Peace Corps: A Dream Betrayed," NATION, 206 (February 26, 1968), 263–268.

Blatchford, J. H. "Peace Corps: Making It in the Seventies," FOREIGN AFFAIRS, 49 (October, 1970), 122–135.

Calvert, Robert, jr. "The Peace Corps and the Colleges," LIBERAL EDUCATION, 52 (October, 1966), 297–302.

Clark, B. "Fresh Spark Plug for the Peace Corps," READER'S DIGEST, 96 (May, 1970), 20–21+.

"Close Look at the Peace Corps and its Volunteers," U.S. NEWS AND WORLD REPORT, 56 (January 6, 1964), 38–41.

Coleman, Joseph. "Discovery of Commitment," in S. M. Clark and J. Clark, eds. YOUTH IN MODERN SOCIETY, New York: Holt, Rinehart, and Winston, 1972, 304–314.

Fairfield, Roy. "The Peace Corps and the University," JOURNAL OF HIGHER EDUCATION, 30 (April, 1964), 189–201.

Hardberger, Phillip D. "The Men of the Peace Corps: 'Founding Fathers' of a New Order," AMERICAN BAR ASSOCIATION JOURNAL, 52 (February, 1966), 131–134.

Hobbs, Nicholas. "A Psychologist in the Peace Corps," AMERICAN PSYCHOLOGIST, 18 (January, 1963), 47–55.

Iverson, Robert. "The Peace Corps Challenge to Higher Education," in G. K. Smith, ed. IN SEARCH OF LEADERS. Washington, D.C.: American Association for Higher Education, 1967, 201–206.

Kauffman, Joseph. "Youth and the Peace Corps," in Erik Erikson, ed. Youth: CHANGE AND CHALLENGE. New York: Basic Books, 1963, 151–160.

Lunstrum, J. "Mystique of the Peace Corps: A Dilemma," PHI DELTA KAPPAN, 48 (November, 1966), 98–102.

Murphy, J. S. "Peace Corps, Universities and Communism: A Note on Bureaucratic Accomodation," TEACHERS COLLEGE RECORD, 68 (March, 1967), 487–492.

Ottenad, Thomas. "The Peace Corps Wins Its Way," PROGRESSIVE, 26 (August, 1962), 19–23.

Parmer, Norman, J., ed. "The Peace Corps," ANNALS OF THE AMERICAN ACADEMY OF POLITICAL AND SOCIAL SCIENCE, 365 (May, 1966), 1–146.

"Peace Corps Catches Fire in Colleges," LIFE, 50 (March 17, 1961), 34–37.

"The Peace Corps 'Kids'," CONNECT, (December, 1963), 67–79.

Pollock, F. "Peace Corps Returnees," NATION, 205 (July 3, 1967), 15–17.

Pearson, David. "The Peace Corps Volunteer Returns," SATURDAY REVIEW, (October 17, 1964), 5488.

Scovill, J. and J. Starke. "What Ever Happened to the Peace Corps?" SENIOR SCHOLASTIC, 98 (February 15, 1971), 9–15.

Shaffer, H. B. "Domestic Peace Corps," EDITORIAL RESEARCH REPORTS, 2 (April 3, 1963), 249–264.

Shaffer, H. B. "Peace Corps Expansion," EDITORIAL RESEARCH REPORTS, 1 (November 28, 1962), 855–872.

F.5. Student Religious Organizations and Movements

Austin, Slice, ed. EDUCATION AND SOCIAL CHANGE: NOTES FROM THE UCM FILES. New York: University Christian Movement, 1968.

Barkman, Paul, Edward R. Dayton and Edward L. Gruman. CHRISTIAN COLLEGIANS AND FOREIGN MISSIONS. New York: Missions Advanced Research and Communications Center, 1969.

*Carling, Francis. MOVE OVER: STUDENTS, POLITICS, RELIGION, New York: Sheed and Ward, 1969.

Clough, Leonard. INTRODUCING THE UNIVERSITY CHRISTIAN MOVEMENT. New York: UCM, 1967.

Colaianni, James. THE CATHOLIC LEFT. New York: Chilton, 1967.

Commission on Student Work, YMCA. WHAT OF THE FUTURE OF STUDENT YMCA'S? New York: National Council of YMCA's, 1941.

Denise, Paul S. PRIVATISM, ACTIVISM AND THE FUTURE OF THE EXTRA-CURRICULUM. Cambridge, Massachusetts: Student Christian Movement in New England, 1964.

Denise, Paul S. THE PROPHETIC MICROCOSM AND THE PARA-CURRICULUM. Cambridge, Massachusetts: Student Christian Movement in New England, 1965.

Friedlander, Albert, ed. NEVER TRUST A GOD OVER THIRTY: NEW STYLES IN CAMPUS MINISTRY. New York: McGraw-Hill, 1967.

Gurak, Douglas T. "The University Christian Movement: The Political Socialization of Religious Activists." Unpublished Ph.D. dissertation, University of Wisconsin, 1973.

Herriott, F. W. CHRISTIAN YOUTH IN ACTION. New York: Missionary Educational Movement, 1935.

Hopkins, C. Howard. STUDENT RELIGION DURING FIFTY YEARS. New York: Association Press, 1935.

Jondahl, H. L. UNREST ON THE CAMPUS: A CHRISTIAN PERSPECTIVE. New York: Friendship Press, 1970.

Leiffer, Murray H. METHODIST STUDENT WORK AT THE COLLEGES AND UNIVERSITIES OF ARIZONA, CALIFORNIA AND NEVADA. Evanston, Illinois: Garrett Theological Seminary, 1951.

Lucci, York. THE YMCA ON THE CAMPUS. New York: Bureau of Applied Social Research, Columbia University, 1960, (mimeographed).

Minneman, C. E., ed. STUDENTS, RELIGION, AND THE CONTEMPORARY UNIVERSITY. Ypsilanti, Michigan: Eastern Michigan University Press, 1970.

Morgan, William H. STUDENT RELIGION DURING FIFTY YEARS: PROGRAMS AND POLICIES OF THE INTERCOLLEGIATE YMCA. New York: Association Press, 1935.

NEW DIRECTION FOR CAMPUS CHRISTIAN ACTION. New York: National Intercollegiate Christian Council, 1938.

Pearson, Fred. THEY DARE TO HOPE: STUDENT PROTEST AND CHRISTIAN RESPONSE. Grand Rapids, Michigan: Eerdmans, 1969.

Pence, Owen E. THE YMCA AND SOCIAL NEED. New York: Association Press, 1946.

Rosenbrook, Patricia C. "The Application of Discriminant Analysis to a Classification of New Left Involvement among Members of the University Christian Movement." Unpublished M.S. Thesis, University of Wisconsin, 1971.

Shedd, Clarence P. A CENTURY OF CHRISTIAN STUDENT INITIATIVE. New York: Association Press, 1945.

Shedd, Clarence P. THE CHURCH FOLLOWS ITS STUDENTS. New Haven, Connecticut: Yale University Press, 1934.

*Shedd, Clarence P. TWO CENTURIES OF STUDENT CHRISTIAN MOVEMENTS: THEIR ORIGIN AND INTERCOLLEGIATE LIFE. New York: Association Press, 1934.

Underwood, Kenneth, ed. THE CHURCH, THE UNIVERSITY AND SOCIAL POLICY. Middletown, Connecticut: Wesleyan University Press, 1969.

Watson, Goodwin B. YOUTH AFTER CONFLICT. New York: Association Press, 1947.

Altbach, Philip. "The Student and Religious Commitment," in M. Cohen, and D. Hale, eds. THE NEW STUDENT LEFT. Boston: Beacon Press, 1967, 22–26.

Bridston, Keith. "The Student Generation and the Ecumenical Movement," MOTIVE, 26 (October, 1965), 24–28.

Bright, W. R. "Christianity on the Campus," AMERICAN MERCURY, 83 (December, 1956), 137–143.

Campbell, Jeffery W. "Youth, Religion, and Peace," SOCIALIST REVIEW, 6 (July–August, 1938), 11–13.

"Cool Generation and the Church," COMMONWEAL, 87 (October 6, 1967), 11–23 and (November 5, 1967), 152–155.

Demerath, N. J. III and Kenneth Lutterman. "The Student Parishioners: Radical Rhetoric and Traditional Reality," in Kenneth Underwood, ed. THE CHURCH, THE UNIVERSITY AND SOCIAL POLICY. VOLUME II. Middleton, Connecticut: Wesleyan University Press, 1969.

Drake, Ann. "University Christian Movement: Prophet or Priest?" NOTES FROM THE GARAGE DOOR, (1967), 2–9.

Douglass, Bruce. "The Student Christian Movement and Student Politics," in Bruce Douglass, ed. REFLECTIONS ON PROTEST. Richmond, Virginia: John Knox Press, 1967, 13–42.

Eddy, J. P. "Report on Religious Activities at Harvard and Radcliffe," COLLEGE STUDENT SURVEY, 2 (Fall, 1968), 31–34, 37.

Goodman, Paul. "Student Chaplains," NEW REPUBLIC, 156 (January 7, 1967), 29–31.

Grennan, Sister Jacqueline. "The Ecumenical World of Search," in Lawrence Dennis and Joseph Kauffman, eds. THE AMERICAN COLLEGE AND THE STUDENT. Washington: American Council on Education, 1966, 381–384.

Hammond, Phillip E. and Robert E. Mitchell. "Segmentation of Radicalism—the Case of the Protestant Campus Minister," AMERICAN JOURNAL OF SOCIOLOGY, 71 (September, 1965), 133–143.

Harrod, George W. "Religious Activities on Campuses of Colleges and Universities," PERSONNEL AND GUIDANCE JOURNAL, 38 (March, 1960), 555–557.

Howell, Leon. "From NSCF to UCM: In Anticipation of a Movement," MOTIVE, 27 (October, 1966), 4–5.

"Is There to Be a Student Christian Movement?" CHRISTIAN CENTURY, 53 (January 15, 1936), 72–73: Discussion, 53 (February 12, 1936), 267–268.

Langford, T. A. "Campus Turmoil: A Religious Dimension," CHRISTIAN CENTURY, 84 (February 8, 1967), 172–174.

McCabe, Sheridan P. "Religious Commitment and Student Freedom on the Church-Related Campus," in L. Vaccaro and J. Covert, eds. STUDENT FREEDOM IN AMERICAN HIGHER EDUCATION. New York: Teachers College Press, 1969, 115–124.

"New Patterns for Student Religious Groups," NATIONAL ASSOCIATION OF STUDENT PERSONNEL ADMINISTRATORS JOURNAL, 44 (April, 1962), 110–122.

Ober, Charles K. "The Beginnings of the North American Student Movement," STUDENT WORLD, 6 (January, 1913), 10–18.

Olds, Glenn A. "Religious Centers," in Erich Walter, ed. RELIGION AND

174

THE STATE UNIVERSITY. Ann Arbor: The University of Michigan Press, 1958, 226–247.

Peterson, W. H. "Religious Groups on State Campuses," RELIGION IN LIFE, 39 (Spring, 1970), 92–106.

Schrading, Paul. "DEGs" Process '67 and the Future of UCM," NOTES FROM THE GARAGE DOOR, (1967), 69–80.

Shomberg, Steve, Charlotte Weeks and Nell Sale. "The UCM and the Movement," MOTIVE, 30 (October, 1969), 50–59.

Stoltenberg, L. "Campus Religious Organizations," RELIGIOUS EDUCATION, 55 (March, 1960), 83–88.

Walsh, J. L. "Self-Inflicted Death: University Christian Movement," COMMONWEAL, 90 (April 11, 1969), 96–97.

Wilder, A. N. "Christianity and the Campus," NEW REPUBLIC, 139 (December 15, 1958), 13–16.

G. SINGLE CAMPUS OR ISSUE CAMPAIGNS

Cross Reference: Events on specific campuses that did not receive widespread comment or recognition have been listed as part of the general movement or as an issue in the previous section.

G.1. The Berkeley Student Revolt
1964—and Its Aftermath

Aptheker, Bettina, Robert Kaufman and Michael Folsom, *et al*. THE FREE SPEECH MOVEMENT AT BERKELEY: AN HISTORICAL NARRATIVE, San Francisco: W. E. B. DuBois Clubs of America, 1965.

Byrne, Jerome C. THE BYRNE REPORT. Berkeley, California: The Free Student Union of the University of California, N.D.

Cavalli, Allessandro and Alberto Martinelli. GLI STUDENTI AMERICANI DOPO BERKELEY. Torino: G. Einaudi, 1969.

Copeland, Alan and Nikki Arai, eds. PEOPLE'S PARK. New York: Ballantine Books, 1969.

*Draper, Hal. BERKELEY: THE NEW STUDENT REVOLT. New York: Grove Press, 1965.

Draper, Hal, ed. THE FSM PAPERS: UNPUBLISHED DOCUMENTS AND EPHEMERA RELATING TO THE FSM. Berkeley, California: ISC Press, 1968.

Finney, H. C. "Development and Change of Political Liberalism Among Berkeley Undergraduates." Unpublished Ph.D. dissertation, University of California, 1967.

Foote, Caleb, *et al*. THE CULTURE OF THE UNIVERSITY; GOVERNANCE AND EDUCATION. San Francisco: Jossey-Bass, 1968.

Free Speech Movement, Steering Committee. WE WANT A UNIVERSITY. Berkeley, California: Free Speech Movement, 1964.

Gardner, David P. THE CALIFORNIA OATH CONTROVERSY. Berkeley, California: University of California Press, 1967.

Garson, Marvin and Ken Blum. THE REGENTS. Berkeley, California: Independent Socialist Club, 1967.

*Heirich, Max. THE BEGINNING: BERKELEY, 1964. New York: Columbia University Press, 1971.

*Heirich, Max Arthur. "Demonstrations at Berkeley: Collective Behavior During the Free Speech Movement of 1964–1965." Unpublished Ph.D. dissertation, University of California at Berkeley, 1967.

Heirich, Max. THE SPIRAL OF CONFLICT: BERKELEY, 1964. New York: Columbia University Press, 1971.

Horowitz, David. STUDENT: THE POLITICAL ACTIVITIES OF BERKELEY STUDENTS. New York: Ballantine, 1962.

Katope, Christopher and Paul Zolbrod, eds. BEYOND BERKELEY: A SOURCEBOOK IN STUDENT VALUES. Cleveland, Ohio: World, 1966.

*Lipset, S. M. and Sheldon Wolin, eds. THE BERKELEY STUDENT RE-VOLT. Garden City, New York: Anchor Books, 1965.

*Lunsford, Terry. THE FREE SPEECH CRISIS AT THE UNIVERSITY OF CALIFORNIA: SOME ISSUES FOR SOCIAL AND LEGAL RESEARCH. Berkeley: Center for Research and Development in Higher Education, 1965.

*Miller, Michael and Susan Gilmore, eds. REVOLUTION AT BERKELEY. New York: Dell, 1965.

*Otten, C. Michael. UNIVERSITY AUTHORITY AND THE STUDENT: THE BERKELEY EXPERIENCE. Berkeley and Los Angeles: University of California Press, 1970.

THE PEOPLE'S PARK: A REPORT ON A CONFRONTATION AT BERKELEY. Sacramento, California: Office of the Governor, 1969.

Radical Student Union. THE USES OF U.C. BERKELEY: RESEARCH. Berkeley: Radical Student Union, 1969.

Rossman, Michael. THE WEDDING WITHIN THE WAR. Garden City, New York: Doubleday, 1971.

Savio, Mario, *et al.* THE FREE SPEECH MOVEMENT AND THE NE-GRO REVOLUTION. Detroit: News and Letters, 1965.

*Sevilla, Teresa Estelle. "Student Authority: Its Development and Role in the Governance of the University of California at Berkeley." Unpublished Ph.D. dissertation, University of California at Berkeley, 1967.

Stewart, George R. THE YEAR OF THE OATH: THE FIGHT FOR ACADEMIC FREEDOM AT THE UNIVERSITY OF CALIFORNIA. Garden City, New York: Doubleday, 1950.

Third World Liberation Front. STRIKE, 1969. Berkeley: Third World Liberation Front, 1969.

Tussman, Joseph. EXPERIMENT AT BERKELEY. New York: Oxford University Press, 1969.

Warshaw, Steven. THE TROUBLE IN BERKELEY. Berkeley, California: Daiblo Press, 1965.

*Wolin, Sheldon S. and John Schaar. THE BERKELEY REBELLION AND BEYOND. New York: Vintage Books, 1970.

Abrams, Richard M. "The Student Rebellion at Berkeley: An Interpretation," MASSACHUSETTS REVIEW, 6 (Winter–Spring, 1965), 353–365.

"Appendix: Documents in the Free Speech Controversy," CALIFORNIA MONTHLY, (February, 1965), 76–92.

Aptheker, B. "Berkeley's Meddlesome Regents," NOTION, 211 (September 7, 1970), 169–173.

Aptheker, Bettina. "Free Speech Revolt on Berkeley Campus," POLITICAL AFFAIRS, 44 (January, 1965), 53–57.

Aptheker, Bettina. "Revolt on the Berkeley Campus," POLITICAL AFFAIRS, 44 (March, 1965), 10–19.

Armistead, Timothy W. "Police on Campus and the Evolution of Personal Commitments: a Survey of Non-strikers Attitudes during a Berkeley Confrontation," ISSUES IN CRIMINOLOGY, 4 (Fall, 1969), 171–184.

Bauer, O. F. "Student Trust at Berkeley," EDUCATION RESEARCH, 52 (Fall, 1972), 361–367.

"Behind California's Campus Revolt," LOOK, 29 (February 23, 1965), 30–42.

"Berkeley Scene: Change Is the Norm," NEWSWEEK, 76 (November 23, 1970), 86–90.

"Berkeley's Three Big Rallies," OVERLAND, 63 (April, 1914), 336–340.

Berns, Robert S. "The Berkeley Uprisings: A Study of the Conditions of Riotous Behavior," AMERICAN JOURNAL OF PSYCHIATRY, 123 (March, 1967), 1165–1169.

Berry, F., et al. "Terror in a Teapot," NATION, 208 (June 23, 1969), 784–788.

"Besides Berkeley, and Beyond," MODERATOR, 4 (November, 1965), 8–13.

Blumenfeld, Neal. "The Psychology of Berkeley," RAMPARTS, 4 (May, 1965), 13–17.

Boler, J. F. "Behind the Protests at Berkeley," COMMONWEAL, 81 (February 4, 1965), 602–605.

Brienberg, Elizabeth. "On the Free Speech Movement," STUDIES ON THE LEFT, 5 (Spring, 1965), 95–97.

Brown, Rick. "Berkeley: The Limits of Student-Faculty Alliance," LIBERATION, 15 (June, 1970), 13–17.

Burks, John, et al. "The Battle for People's Park," ROLLING STONE, Number 35 (June 14, 1969), 1+.

"California: University of Trial," NEWSWEEK, 76 (November 23, 1970), 83–91+.

Calvin, Trillin. "Letter from Berkeley," NEW YORKER, (March 13, 1965), 57–102.

Cass, James. "What Happened at Berkeley," SATURDAY REVIEW, 48 (January 16, 1965), 47–49.

Chain, S. "Telegraph Avenue in Berkeley: After the Barricades Let the People Decide," RAMPARTS, 7 (August 24, 1968), 22–27.

"Chronology of Events: Three Months of Crisis," CALIFORNIA MONTHLY, (February, 1965), 35–74.

"A Chronology of the Berkeley Rebellion," in Christopher Katope and Paul Zolbrod, eds. BEYOND BERKELEY. Cleveland: World, 1966, 3–7.

"Continuing Crisis at Berkeley," CALIFORNIA MONTHLY, (June, 1965), 52–56.

Cox, C. B. "Berkeley's Angry Young Men," in Christopher Katope and Paul Zolbrod, eds. BEYOND BERKELEY. Cleveland, Ohio: World, 1966, 25–28.

Coyne, J. R., jr. "Positively the Last Word on the People's Park," NATIONAL REVIEW, 21 (October 7, 1969), 1003–1005+.

"Documents on 'The FSM—Revolt against Liberal Bureaucracy,' " in Paul Jacobs and Saul Landau, eds. THE NEW RADICALS. New York: Viking, 1966, 206–248.

*"Documents: The Beginning of the Movement: 'Free Speech,' " in M. Teodori, ed. THE NEW LEFT: A DOCUMENTARY HISTORY. Indianapolis: Bobbs-Merrill, 1969, 150–162.

Draper, H. "California Draws a Blank," NATION, 205 (December 25, 1967), 682–685.

Draper, Hal. "Free Speech and the Political Struggle," INDEPENDENT SOCIALIST, Number 4 (April, 1968), 12–16.

*Draper, Hal. "The Mind of Clark Kerr," NEW POLITICS, 3 (Fall, 1964), 51–61.

Draper, Hal, and Nathan Glazer. "FSM: Freedom Fighters or Misguided Rebels?" NEW POLITICS, 4 (Winter, 1965), 25–51.

Eley, Lynn W. "The University of California at Berkeley: Faculty Participation in the Government of the University," AAUP BULLETIN, 50 (March, 1964), 5–13.

Erlich, Reese. "La Guerre N'est Pas Finie," INTERNATIONAL SOCIALIST JOURNAL, 5 (February, 1968).

Feuer, Lewis. "Berkeley and Beyond," CHANGE, 1 (January–February, 1969), 47–50.

Feuer, Lewis. "The Decline of Freedom at Berkeley," ATLANTIC MONTHLY, 218 (August, 1966), 78–82.

Feuer, Lewis. "Inevitability and Institutes," NEW LEADER, 48 (January 18, 1965), 9–10.

*Feuer, Lewis. "Rebellion at Berkeley: The New Multiversity," NEW LEADER, 47 (December 21, 1964), 3–12.

Feuer, Lewis S. "A Reply," NEW LEADER, 48 (January 4, 1965), 15–17.

Fincher, J. "Balancing Act at Berkeley," LIFE, 61 (December 16, 1966), 45–46+.

*Finney, Henry C. "Political Libertarianism at Berkeley: An Application of Perspectives from the New Student Left," JOURNAL OF SOCIAL ISSUES, 27 (Number 1, 1971), 35–62.

Fitch, Robert E. "Extremism in the Defense of . . . " CHRISTIAN CENTURY, 82 (January 6, 1965), 11–15.

"An F.S.M. Miscellany," GRADUATE STUDENT JOURNAL (Berkeley), 4 (Spring, 1965), 13–20.

Galbraith, John Kenneth. "Berkeley in the Age of Innocence," ATLANTIC, 223 (June, 1969), 62–68.

*Gales, Kathleen. "A Campus Revolution," BRITISH JOURNAL OF SOCIOLOGY, 17 (March, 1966), 1–19.

Garson, Marvin. "Aftermath of the Berkeley Revolt," NEW POLITICS, 5 (Winter, 1966), 35–40.

Ginsberg, Allen. "Berkeley Vietnam Days," LIBERATION, 10 (January, 1966), 42–47.

Glazer, N. "Student Power in Berkeley," UNIVERSITIES QUARTERLY, 22 (September, 1968), 404–424.

*Glazer, N. "What Happened at Berkeley," COMMENTARY, 39 (February, 1965), 39–47.

Gold, H. "I Am a UC Student: Do Not Fold, Bend or Mutilate," SATURDAY EVENING POST, 239 (June 18, 1966), 34–36+.

Goldberg, Harold. "Berkeley," FRONTIER, 16 (January, 1965), 8–12.

Golden, Michael. "The Passionate Style in the New Student Politics," ACTIVIST, 6 (May, 1966), 33–36.

*Goodman, Paul. "Berkeley in February," DISSENT, 12 (Spring, 1965). 161–175.

Goodman, Paul. "Ten Letters on Free Speech," LIBERATION, 10 (March, 1965), 33–38.

*Goodman, Paul. "Thoughts on Berkeley," NEW YORK REVIEW OF BOOKS, 3 (January 14, 1965), 5–7.

Greenberg, D. S. "Berkeley: New Crisis Breaks Out on California Campus," SCIENCE, 154 (December 9, 1966), 1304–1306.

Greene, W. "Where Are the Saviors of Yesteryear?" NEW YORK TIMES MAGAZINE, (July 12, 1970), 6–9+.

Griffith W. "People's Park, 270' v 450' of Confrontation," NEW YORK TIMES MAGAZINE, (June 29, 1969), 5–7+.

*Gusfield, Joseph, "Beyond Berkeley: High Noon on Campus," TRANSACTION, 2 (March–April, 1965), 3–7.

Hack, Lothar. "Am Beispiel Berkeley: Rigider Funktionalismus und neue Unmittelbarkeit," (The Example of Berkeley: Rigid Functionalism and the New Immediacy), NEUE KRITIK, 41 (April, 1967), 36–52.

Hadsell, J. S. "Oakland: How to Lose in Winning; Berkeley Student Sit-ins at Induction Center," CHRISTIAN CENTURY, 84 (November 15, 1967), 1476–1478.

Hagstrom, W. O. and H. Selvin. "Determinants of Support for Civil Liberties," BRITISH JOURNAL OF SOCIOLOGY, 11 (March, 1960), 51–73.

Harrison, G. A. "Berkeley: Does that Banner Still Wave?" NEW REPUBLIC, 151 (December 19, 1964), 7–8.

Heath, G. Louis. "Berkeley Protest: A Mass Movement?" UNIVERSITY COLLEGE QUARTERLY, 15 (November, 1969), 3–9.

Heath, G. L. "Political Extra-Curricula at Uppsula and California," SCHOOL AND SOCIETY, 97 (April, 1969), 223–227.

Heath, G. L. "Student Activism at Berkeley After 1964," in W. Brickman and S. Lehrer, eds. CONFLICT AND CHANGE ON THE CAMPUS: THE

RESPONSE TO STUDENT HYPERACTIVISM. New York: School & Society Books, 1970, 160–169.

Heirich, Max and Sam Kaplan. "Yesterday's Discord," CALIFORNIA MONTHLY, (February, 1965), 20–32, and in Seymour M. Lipset and Sheldon S. Wolin, eds. THE BERKELEY STUDENT REVOLT: FACTS AND INTERPRETATIONS. New York: Doubleday Anchor, 1965, 10–35.

Heisler, Friedy B. "A Psychiatrist Looks Back at Berkeley," PROGRESSIVE, 29 (May, 1965), 33–35.

Heyns, Roger. "Extremes of Action are Polarizing Our Campuses," COLLEGE AND UNIVERSITY BUSINESS, 42 (January, 1967), 45–48.

Holt, J. "Radicalization of a Guest Teacher at Berkeley," NEW YORK TIMES MAGAZINE, (February 22, 1970), 30–31+.

Hook, Sidney. "Second Thoughts on Berkeley," TEACHERS COLLEGE RECORD, 67 (October, 1965), 32–63.

Howe, Irving. "Berkeley and Beyond," NEW REPUBLIC, 152 (May 1, 1965), 14–17.

Jacobs, Paul. "Dr. Feuer's Distortions," NEW LEADER, 48 (January 4, 1965), 9–11.

Kaplan, Marshall and Richard Wedington White. "Birth of a Student Movement," LIBERATION, 5 (June, 1960), 12–13.

Kaplan, Samuel. "The Revolt of an Elite: Sources of the F.S.M. Victory," GRADUATE STUDENT JOURNAL, (Berkeley), 4 (Spring, 1965), 26–30, 75–91, and in Christopher Katope and Paul Zolbrod, ed. BEYOND BERKELEY. New York: World, 1966, 89–116.

Kaufman, Bob. "The Berkeley Liberation Program: Whom does it speak for? Whom does it speak to?" in Immanuel Wallerstein and Paul Starr, eds. THE UNIVERSITY CRISIS READER, II. New York, Random House, 1971, 242–247.

Kerr, Clark. "For the Record," NEW LEADER, 48 (January 18, 1965), 8–9.

Kerr, Clark. "On Berkeley and the Multiversity," NEW YORK REVIEW OF BOOKS, 4 (April 8, 1965), 35–36.

Krause, Peggy. "Berkeley Revisited: Where Social Scientists Fail," PHI DELTA KAPPAN, 47 (April, 1966), 421–423.

Langer, Elinor. "Berkeley Scene, 1966: Politics and Potshots," SCIENCE, 152 (May 20, 1966), 1037–1041.

Langer, Elinor. "Crisis at Berkeley: The Civil War," SCIENCE, 148 (April 9, 1965), 198–202.

Langer, Elinor. "Crisis at Berkeley: The Second Front," SCIENCE, 148 (April 16, 1965), 346–349.

Langer, Elinor. "Oakland Seven: Organizers of Stop the Draft week," ATLANTIC, 224 (October, 1969), 76–82.

Langer, Elinor. "Report from California: The Governor and the University," SCIENCE, (March 10, 1967).

Linde, Hans A. "Campus Law: Berkeley Viewed from Eugene," CALIFORNIA LAW REVIEW, 54 (March, 1966), 40–72.

Lipset, S. M. and P. Seabury. "Lesson of Berkeley," REPORTER, 32 (January 28, 1965), 36–40.

Louisell, David W. "Responding to the December 8th Resolution: Of Politics, Free Speech, and Due Process," CALIFORNIA LAW REVIEW, 54 (March, 1960), 107–118.

Lunsford, T. F. "The Berkeley Case," in O. W. Knorr and W. J. Minter, eds. ORDER AND FREEDOM ON THE CAMPUS: THE RIGHTS AND RESPONSIBILITIES OF FACULTY AND STUDENTS. Boulder, Colorado: Western Interstate Commission for Higher Education, 1965, 41–60.

Lyons, Kit. "Berkeley Student Strike," INDEPENDENT SOCIALIST, Number 1 (January–February, 1967), 20–21.

McGuire, Brian. "Berkeley's Best Student: It Wasn't Worth It," SATURDAY EVENING POST, 241 (September 21, 1968), 27+.

*Marine, Gene. "No Fair: The Students Strike at California," NATION, 199 (December 21, 1964), 482–485.

Marris, Peter. "The Meaning of the Berkeley War," NEW SOCIETY, 14 (July 10, 1969), 47–49.

May, Henry F. "Living with Crisis: A View from Berkeley," AMERICAN SCHOLAR, 38 (Autumn, 1969), 588–605.

May, H. F. "Student Movement: Some Impressions of Berkeley," AMERICAN SCHOLAR, 34 (Summer, 1965), 387–399.

Miles, Michael and Martin Roysher. "The Berkeley Thermidor," NEW REPUBLIC, 158 (March 16, 1968), 17–21.

Miller, Colin. "The Student Revolt," FRONTIER, 16 (April, 1965), 11–20.

*Miller, Michael. "Letter from the Berkeley Underground," ESQUIRE (September, 1965), 85–90.

Miller, Mike. "San Francisco: Freedom House," STUDIES ON THE LEFT, 5 (Winter, 1965), 68–74.

Miller, Mike and Gerry Greenberg. "Slate Summer Conference," LIBERAL DEMOCRAT, (San Francisco), 2 (September, 1961), 11–13.

Nagler, Michael. "Berkeley: The Demonstrations," STUDIES ON THE LEFT, 5 (Winter, 1965), 55–62.

Neilands, J. B. "The Rise of Freedom at Berkeley," FRONTIER, 17 (October, 1966), 5–6.

Nelken, Michael. "My Mind is not Property," GRADUATE STUDENT JOURNAL, (Berkeley), 4 (Spring, 1965), 25–29.

O'Neil, Robert M. "Reflections on the Academic Senate Resolutions," CALIFORNIA LAW REVIEW, 54 (March, 1966), 88–106.

Oppenheimer, Martin. "The Berkeley Revolution," NEW POLITICS, 14 (Summer, 1964), 65–69.

*Otten, C. Michael, "Ruling Out Paternalism: Students and Administrators at Berkeley," AMERICAN BEHAVIORAL SCIENTIST, 11 (May–June, 1968), 28–33.

Paff, Joseph, Bill Cavala and Jerry Berman. "The Student Riots at Berkeley: Dissent in the Multiversity," ACTIVIST, 5 (January, 1965), 15–19.

Parkinson, Thomas. "Peoples Park: Berkeley, May, 1969," in Patrick Gleeson, ed. ESSAYS ON THE STUDENT MOVEMENT. Columbus, Ohio: Merrill, 1970, 109–116.

Peterson, William. "What's Left at Berkeley," COLUMBIA UNIVERSITY FORUM, 8 (Spring, 1965), 39–44, also in Seymour Lipset and Sheldon Wolin, eds. THE BERKELEY STUDENT REVOLT: FACTS AND INTERPRETATIONS. Garden City, New York: Doubleday, 1965, 367–385.

Petras, James. "Berkeley and the New Conservative Backlash," NEW LEFT REVIEW, Number 31 (May–June, 1965), 58–64.

Petras, James. "The Politics of Bureaucracy: Strike for Student Power," LIBERATION, 11 (February, 1967), 21–28.

Petras, J. "Politics of Democracy: The Free Speech of Movement," PHI DELTA KAPPAN, 46 (May, 1965), 465–466.

*Petras, James and Michael Shute. "Berkeley, '65," PARTISAN REVIEW, 32 (Spring, 1965), 314–323.

Pierovich, Andrew. "A Season of Discontent," CALIFORNIA MONTHLY, (February, 1965), 6–19.

"The Pilgrims Progress: God and the Man at Berkeley," ACTIVIST, 5 (May, 1965), 3–4.

Porter, William. "Report from Berkeley," MOTIVE, 25 (April, 1965), 35–38.

Quann, C. J. "Student Unrest, a Double Image," COLLEGE AND UNIVERSITY, 44 (Spring, 1969), 256–262.

Raskin, A. H. "The Berkeley Affair: Mr. Kerr vs. Mr. Savio and Co.," NEW YORK TIMES MAGAZINE, (February 14, 1965), 24–25+.

Raskin, A. H. "Berkeley Five Years Later Is Radicalized, Reorganized, Mesmerized," NEW YORK TIMES MAGAZINE, (January 11, 1970), 28–29+.

Raskin, A. H. "I'm Just Here to Study," NEW YORK TIMES MAGAZINE, (January 30, 1966), 12–14.

Roberts, S. V. "Better Earth: Report on Ecology Action Group, Berkeley California," NEW YORK TIMES MAGAZINE, (March 29, 1970), 8–9+.

Rosenfeld, Gerald. "Generational Revolt and the Free Speech Movement," LIBERATION, 10 (December 1965), 13–17.

*Rossman, Michael. "Breakthrough at Berkeley: The Anatomy of a New Political Style," THE CENTER MAGAZINE, 1 (May, 1968), 40–49.

Rubenstein B. and M. Levitt. "Rebellion and Responsibility," YALE REVIEW, 57 (October, 1967), 16–30.

Savio, Mario. "The Berkeley Student Rebellion of 1964," in Christopher Katope and Paul Zolbrod, eds. BEYOND BERKELEY. Cleveland: World, 1966, 83–89.

Savio, Mario. "An End to History," in Seymour Lipset and Sheldon Wolin, eds. THE BERKELEY STUDENT REVOLT: FACTS AND INTERPRETATIONS, New York: Doubleday, 1965, 216–225.

Savio, Mario, et al. "The 'New Radicals': An Exchange," NEW POLITICS, 4 (Spring, 1965), 13–32.

Savio, Mario. "The Uncertain Future of the Multiversity: A Partisan

Scrutiny of Berkeley's Mucatine Report," HARPER'S 233 (October, 1966), 88–90+.

Scheer, R., *et al.* "Battle of Berkeley," RAMPARTS, 8 (August, 1969), 41–59.

Seabury, Paul. "Student Freedom and the Republic of Scholars: Berlin and Berkeley," COMPARATIVE EDUCATION REVIEW, 10 (June, 1966), 350–358.

Searle, John. "Berkeley and Freedom," ATLANTIC, 218 (October, 1966), 110–111.

"A Season of Discontent," CALIFORNIA MONTHLY, 75 (February, 1965).

Seeley, John R. "The 'Berkeley Issue' in Time and Place," OUR GENERATION, 5 (May, 1967), 24–30, and in Howard Adelman and Dennis Lee, eds. THE UNIVERSITY GAME. Toronto: Anansi, 1968, 137–146.

The Select Committee on Education. "The Berkeley Student," in L. B. Mayhew, ed. HIGHER EDUCATION IN THE REVOLUTIONARY DECADES. Berkeley, California: McCutchan, 1967, 315–340.

Selvin, H. C. and W. O. Hagstrom. "Determinants of Support for Civil Liberties," BRITISH JOURNAL OF SOCIOLOGY, 11 (March, 1960), 51–73.

Selznick, P. "Berkeley," COMMENTARY, 39 (March, 1965), 80–85.

Shoben, E. J., jr. "Berkeley Syndrome," TEACHERS COLLEGE RECORD, 66 (April, 1965), 620–623.

Shute, M. "Berkeley Campus in Revolt," NEW POLITICS, 3 (Fall, 1964), 44–50.

Shute, Michael. "Berkeley: The Fragmented Strike," NEW POLITICS, 8 (Spring, 1970), 22–26.

Shute, Michael. "Student Strike at Berkeley," NEW POLITICS 5 (Spring, 1966), 91–93.

Somers, Robert H. "The Berkeley Campus in the Twilight of the Free Speech Movement: Hope or Futility," in J. McEvoy, and A. Miller, eds. BLACK POWER AND STUDENT REBELLION. Belmont, California: Wadsworth, 1969, 419–439.

Somers, Robert H. "The Mainsprings of the Rebellion: A Survey of Berkeley Students in November, 1964," in S. Lipset, and S. Wolin, eds. THE BERKELEY STUDENT REVOLT. Garden City, New York: Doubleday, 1965, 530–558

Spence, Larry D. "Berkeley: What It Demonstrates," STUDIES ON THE LEFT, 5 (Winter, 1965), 63–68.

Stark, Rodney. "Berkeley: Protest+Police=Riot," in J. McEvoy and A. Miller, eds. BLACK POWER AND STUDENT REBELLION. Belmont, California: Wadsworth, 1969, 167–196.

Starobin, Robert. "Graduate Students and the F.S.M.," GRADUATE STUDENT JOURNAL, (Berkeley), 4 (Spring, 1965), 17–25.

Stern, Sol. "A Deeper Disenchantment: The Anti-Bureaucratic Revolt at Berkeley," LIBERATION, 9 (February, 1965), 15–20.

Styron, D. "FSM: Berkeley Free Speech Movement Battles for Student Rights," YOUNG SOCIALIST MAGAZINE, (March/April, 1965), 12–16.

Swanston, David. "Activism vs. Reaganism: The Meddlers at Berkeley," NATION, 206 (February 5, 1968), 171–174.

Tabler, Ward. "Lessons from Berkeley," HUMANIST, 25 (March-April, 1965), 50–52.

*Trillin, Calvin. "Letter from Berkeley," NEW YORKER, 41 (March 13, 1965), 52–54+.

Trow, M. "Bell, Book and Berkeley," AMERICAN BEHAVIORAL SCIENTIST, 11 (May, 1968), 43–48.

*Trow, Martin. "Conceptions of the University: The Case of Berkeley," AMERICAN BEHAVIORAL SCIENTIST, 11 (May-June, 1968), 14–21, and in S. E. Kruytbosch and S. Messinger, eds. THE STATE OF THE UNIVERSITY, Berkeley: Sage, 1968, 27–44.

Trow, Martin. "Some Lessons from Berkeley," in L. E. Dennis and J. Kauffman, eds. THE COLLEGE AND THE STUDENT. Washington, D.C.: American Council on Education, 1966, 126–130.

"University Review—Highlights of Events and Developments," CALIFORNIA MONTHLY, (April, 1966).

Van der Rym, Sim. "Building a People's Park," in G. K. Smith, ed. THE TROUBLED CAMPUS. San Francisco: Jossey-Bass, 1970, 54–72.

Walsh, J. "Campus Politics: Decentralization Is Pattern at Berkeley, Stanford," SCIENCE, 168 (June 5, 1970), 1187–1190.

Watkins, T. H. "State of Insurrection and Rebellion," AMERICAN WEST, 7 (January, 1970), 42–47.

*Watts, William and David Whittaker. "Free Speech Advocates at Berkeley," JOURNAL OF APPLIED BEHAVIORAL SCIENCE, 2 (January-March, 1966), 41–62.

Weissman, Stephan. "What the Students Want," NEW LEADER, 48 (January 4, 1965), 11–15.

Whittaker, David and William Watts. "Personal Characteristics of a Nonconformist Youth Subculture: A Study of the Berkeley Non Student," JOURNAL OF SOCIAL ISSUES, 25 (April, 1969), 65–89.

Wolin, Sheldon and John Schaar. "Berkeley and the Fate of the Multiversity," NEW YORK REVIEW OF BOOKS, 4 (March 11, 1965), 15–18.

Wolin, Sheldon S. and John H. Schaar. "On Berkeley and the Multiversity," NEW YORK REVIEW OF BOOKS, 4 (April 8, 1965), 36.

Wolin, Sheldon and John Schaar. "Berkeley: The Battle of People's Park," in C. E. Kruythosch and S. L. Messinger, eds. THE STATE OF THE UNIVERSITY: AUTHORITY AND CHANGE. Beverly Hills, California: Sage, 1970, 349–362.

*Wolin, Sheldon S. and John Schaar. "Berkeley and the University Revolution," NEW YORK REVIEW OF BOOKS, 6 (February 9, 1967), 18–24.

G.2. Columbia University Crisis: Spring 1968

Aptheker, Bettina. COLUMBIA INCORPORATED. New York: W. E. B. DuBois Clubs of America, 1968.

*Avorn, Jerry L., *et al.* UP AGAINST THE IVY WALL: A HISTORY OF THE COLUMBIA CRISIS. New York: Atheneum, 1968.

Baker, Michael A., *et al.* POLICE ON CAMPUS: THE MASS POLICE ACTION AT COLUMBIA UNIVERSITY, SPRING 1968. New York: New York Civil Liberties Union, 1968.

Barton, Allen H. THE COLUMBIA CRISIS: CAMPUS, VIETNAM, AND THE GHETTO: A SURVEY OF STUDENT AND FACULTY ATTITUDES AND BEHAVIOR AT COLUMBIA UNIVERSITY. New York: Bureau of Applied Social Research, Columbia University, 1968.

Columbia Strike Coordinating Committee. COLUMBIA LIBERATED. New York, The Committee, 1968.

*Cox, Archibald, *et al.* CRISIS AT COLUMBIA. New York: Vintage Paperbacks, 1968.

Grant, Joanne. CONFRONTATION ON CAMPUS: THE COLUMBIA PATTERN FOR THE NEW PROTEST, New York: Signet Books, 1969.

Kahn, Roger. THE BATTLE FOR MORNINGSIDE HEIGHTS: WHY STUDENTS REBEL. New York: William Morrow, 1970.

Kunen, James Simon. THE STRAWBERRY STATEMENT: NOTES OF A COLLEGE REVOLUTIONARY. New York: Random House, 1969.

*Liebert, Robert. RADICAL AND MILITANT YOUTH: A PSYCHO-ANALYTIC INQUIRY. New York: Praeger, 1971.

North American Congress on Latin America. WHO RULES COLUMBIA? New York: North American Congress on Latin America, 1968.

Raugh, More, *et al.* COLUMBIA AND THE COMMUNITY: POST POLICY AND NEW DIRECTIONS. New York: 1968.

Rosenkranz, Richard. ACROSS THE BARRICADES. Philadelphia: Lippincott, 1971.

Rudd, Mark. COLUMBIA. Chicago: Students for a Democratic Society, 1969.

Andrews, J. R. "Confrontation at Columbia: A Case Study in Coercive Rhetoric," QUARTERLY JOURNAL OF SPEECH, 55 (February, 1969), 9–16.

Auger, C., A. H. Barton and R. I. Maurice. "The Nature of the Student Movement and Radical Proposals for Change at Columbia University," THE HUMAN FACTOR, 9 (Fall, 1969), 18–40.

Barton, A. H. "Columbia Crisis: Campus, Vietnam, and the Ghetto," PUBLIC OPINION QUARTERLY, 32 (Fall, 1968), 333–351.

Beichman, Arnold. "The Battle of Columbia," ENCOUNTER, 31 (July, 1968), 33–39.

Beichman, A. "Letter from Columbia," ENCOUNTER, 32 (May, 1969), 14–25.

Beichman, Arnold. "Where Does Columbia Go From Here?" NEW YORK MAGAZINE, 1 (May 27, 1968), 18–22.

*Bell, Daniel. "Columbia and the New Left," PUBLIC INTEREST, Number 13 (Fall, 1968), 61–81.

Brann, J. W. "Continued at Columbia," COMMONWEAL, 89 (October 4, 1968), 7–8.

Brzezinski, Zbigniew. "Revolution and Counterrevolution (But Not Necessarily about Columbia!)." NEW REPUBLIC, 158 (June 1, 1968), 23–27.

Callahan, D. "Bust Number Two at Columbia," COMMONWEAL, 88 (June 7, 1968), 348–350.

"Columbia at Bay," NEWSWEEK, (May 6, 1968), 40–45.

Columbia Daily Spectator. "The University Politicized," in Immanuel Wallerstein and Paul Starr, eds. THE UNIVERSITY CRISIS READER, II. New York: Random House, 1971, 81–85.

"The Columbia Revolt: The Tension of Alliances," in I. Wallerstein and P. Starr, eds. THE UNIVERSITY CRISIS READER, II. New York: Random House, 1971, 81–85.

Columbia Students for a Democratic Society. "The Columbia Statement" in Immanuel Wallerstein and Paul Starr, eds. THE UNIVERSITY CRISIS READER, II. New York: Random House, 1971, 23–48.

"Crisis at Columbia," FOCUS, 3 (Winter, 1968).

"Debacle at Columbia," AMERICA, 118 (May 18, 1968), 662–663.

"A Dialogue on Classroom Disruption," in Immanuel Wallerstein and Paul Starr, eds. THE UNIVERSITY CRISIS READER, II. New York: Random House, 1971, 57–61.

Donadio, S. "Black Power at Columbia," COMMENTARY, 46 (September, 1968), 67–76.

Donadio, S., et al. "Columbia: Seven Interviews," PARTISAN REVIEW, 35 (Summer, 1968), 354–392.

Dupee, F. W. "The Uprising at Columbia," NEW YORK REVIEW OF BOOKS, 11 (September 26, 1968), 20–38.

Edelson, M. "Farewell Columbia," NATIONAL REVIEW, 20 (May 21, 1968), 498–500.

"The Education of a Radical (1968)," in John and Susan Erlich, eds. STUDENT POWER, PARTICIPATION AND REVOLUTION. New York: Association Press, 1970, 45–49.

Etzioni, A. "Confessions of a Professor Caught in a Revolution," NEW YORK TIMES MAGAZINE, (September 15, 1968), 25–27+.

Fried, Albert. "Night Comes to Columbia," NEW POLITICS, 6 (Summer, 1967), 13–15.

Friedman, Robert. "Columbia," in Janet Harris, ed. STUDENTS IN REVOLT. New York: McGraw-Hill, 1970, 61–80.

Ginsberg, Eli. "Black Power and Student Unrest: Reflections on Columbia University and Harlem," GEORGE WASHINGTON LAW REVIEW, 37 (May, 1969), 835–847.

Ginzberg, E. "Delayed Revolution; Lessons from Columbia and Harvard," JOURNAL OF COLLEGE PLACEMENT, 30 (December, 1969), 38–42.

Gold, Alice, Lucy Friedman and Richard Christie. "The Anatomy of Revolutionists," JOURNAL OF APPLIED SOCIAL PSYCHOLOGY, 1 (January, 1971), 26–43.

Goldman, Bruce. "Crisis at Columbia," MIDSTREAM, 14 (June-July, 1968), 46–56.

Goldstein, Richard. "Insurrection at Columbia: The Groovy Revolution: Fold, Spindle, Mutilate," VILLAGE VOICE, (May 2, 1968), 1+.

Greenman, Richard. "The Columbia Rebellion," NEW POLITICS, 6 (Summer, 1967), 4-12.

Gustaitis, R. "Columbia's Neighbors: the Slums of Academe," REPORTER, 37 (October 5, 1967), 34-38 and (November 2, 1967), 40.

Halliwell, Steve. "Columbia: An Explanation," in Priscilla Long, ed. THE NEW LEFT. Boston: Horizon Books, 1969, 200-215.

*Harris, Marvin. "Big Bust on Morningside Heights," NATION, 206 (June 10, 1968), 757-763.

Haushnecht, Murray. "Sources of Student Rebellion: How Shall We Understand the Columbia Uprising?" DISSENT, 15 (September-October, 1968), 389-395.

Hayden, Tom. "Two, Three, Many Columbias," in Alexander Klein, ed. NATURAL ENEMIES? YOUTH AND THE CLASH OF GENERATIONS. New York: Lippincott, 1969, 135-137.

Hays, S. P. "Right Face, Left Face: The Columbia Strike," POLITICAL SCIENCE QUARTERLY, 84 (June, 1969), 311-327.

Hennesy, M. N. "Hoodlumism at Columbia," TIMES EDUCATIONAL SUPPLEMENT, 2763 (May 3, 1968), 1465.

Hofstadter, R. "Columbia's Ordeal," PHI DELTA KAPPAN, 50 (September, 1968), 15-17.

Hofstadter, Richard. "214th Columbia University Commencement Address: June 4, 1968," AMERICAN SCHOLAR, 37 (Autumn, 1968). 583-589.

"Interview with Mark Rudd," PARTISAN REVIEW, 35 (Summer, 1968), 370-375.

James, Sinon. "Diary of a Revolutionist," NEW YORK, 1 (May 27, 1968), 14-17.

Jennings, Frank. "The Savage Rage of Youth," SATURDAY REVIEW, 51 (June 15, 1968), 65-67+.

Johnson, Jane. "A Student's Account of the Columbia Crisis," in Morton Levitt and Ben Rubenstein, eds. YOUTH AND SOCIAL CHANGE. Detroit: Wayne State University Press, 1972, 225-234.

Keller, G. "Six Weeks that Shook Morningside," COLUMBIA COLLEGE TODAY, 15 (1968), 2-97.

Keniston, K. "Report Analysis: Fact Finding Commission on Columbia Disturbances; Cox Commission," HARVARD EDUCATIONAL REVIEW, 39 (Spring, 1969), 373-379.

Kirk, G. "Message to Alumni, Parents, and other Friends of Columbia," SCHOOL AND SOCIETY, 96 (October 26, 1968), 377-383, and in William Brickman and Stanley Lehrer, eds. CONFLICT AND CHANGE ON THE CAMPUS. New York: School and Society, 1970, 381-393.

Kirk, Grayson. "Youth on the College Campus: Rights of the University," VITAL SPEECHES, 32 (February 1, 1966), 248-252.

Knox, G. H. C. "Notes of a Young Radical: Arts Festival at Columbia University to Benefit Political Prisoners," SATURDAY REVIEW, 53 (August 15, 1970), 48-51+.

Lamott, Kenneth. "From La Jolla to Harlem: Bill McGill Takes Over Columbia's Hot Campus," NEW YORK TIMES MAGAZINE, (August 23, 1970), 26+.

Langer, E. "Columbia University: Still at the Crossroads," SCIENCE, 162 (November 22, 1968), 878–883.

Larner, Jeremy. "They Are Taking My Letters," HARPERS, 237 (October, 1968), 45–51.

*Lusky, Lewis and Mary H. Lusky. "Columbia 1968: The Wound Unhealed," POLITICAL SCIENCE QUARTERLY, 84 (June, 1969), 169–188.

McKay, B., et al. "Some Students Speak: Responses to the Columbia Crisis," THE RECORD, 70 (October, 1968), 57–65.

Mathews, John, "Columbia Sweats It Out," NEW REPUBLIC, 159 (October 5, 1968), 8.

Mead, Margaret. "The Wider Significance of the Columbia Upheaval," COLUMBIA FORUM, 11 (Fall, 1968), 5–8, and in W. Brickman and W. Lehrer, eds. CONFLICT AND CHANGE ON THE CAMPUS. New York: School and Society Books, 1970, 170–177.

Metzger, Walter P. "Authority at Columbia," in Immanuel Wallerstein and Paul Starr, eds. THE UNIVERSITY CRISIS READER, II. New York: Random House, 1971, 329–341.

Meyer, J. C. "What Happened at Columbia and Why," NEW GUARD, (September, 1968), 14–17.

"Mutiny at a Great University: with Reports by Student Journalists," LIFE, 64 (May 10, 1968), 36–48A.

"Protest at Columbia," NEW YORKER, 44 (May 4, 1968), 41–43.

Rader, Dotson. "More About Columbia," NEW REPUBLIC, 158 (June 8, 1968), 23–25.

Rader, D. and C. Anderson. "Rebellion at Columbia," NEW REPUBLIC, 158 (May 11, 1968), 9–10.

Ridgeway, James. "Columbia's Filter," NEW REPUBLIC, 158 (March 2, 1968), 9–10.

Ridgeway, James. "Columbia's Real Estate Ventures," NEW REPUBLIC, 158 (May 18, 1968), 15–19.

Rudd, Mark. "Columbia," in Immanuel Wallerstein and Paul Starr, eds. THE UNIVERSITY CRISIS READER, II. New York: Random House, 1971, 177–194.

Rudd, Mark. "Columbia-Notes on the Spring Rebellion," in Carl Oglesby, ed. THE NEW LEFT READER. New York: Grove Press, 1969, 290–312.

Rudd, Mark. "Events and Issues of the Columbia Revolt," in Gary Weaver and James Weaver, eds. THE UNIVERSITY AND REVOLUTION. Englewood Cliffs, New Jersey: Prentice-Hall, 1969, 133–140.

Rudd, Mark. "Speaking Out: Columbia's Strike Leader," SATURDAY EVENING POST, 241 (September 21, 1968), 26–27+.

Rudd, M. and P. Spike. "We Don't Want to be Educated for the CIA," EVERGREEN REVIEW, 12 (August, 1968), 51–55+.

*Rustow, Dankwart, Mark Jacobs, Steven V. Roberts and Amitai Etzioni, et al. "Columbia in Turmoil: Four Articles," NEW LEADER, 51 (May 20, 1968), 5–19.

Seeley, J. R. "Plantation Politics," PSYCHIATRY AND SOCIAL SCIENCE REVIEW, 2 (July, 1968), 16–18.

"The Siege of Columbia," RAMPARTS, 6 (June 15, 1968), 27–39.

Starr, Paul. "Report Card on Columbia," NEW LEADER, 51 (October 7, 1968), 8–12.

Starr, Roger. "The Case of the Columbia Gym," PUBLIC INTEREST, Number 13 (Fall, 1968), 8–14.

Stretch, Bonnie Barrett. "The Ordeal of Academic Revolt," SATURDAY REVIEW, 51 (June 15, 1968), 61–64+.

Trilling, D, "On the Steps of Low Library: Liberalism and the Revolution of the Young," COMMENTARY, 46 (November, 1968), 29–55.

Trilling, D. "Other Night at Columbia: A Report from the Academy (A beat poetry reading)," PARTISAN REVIEW, 26 (Spring, 1959), 214–230.

Trimberger, Ellen Kay. "Columbia: Dynamics of a Student Revolution," in Howard S. Becker, ed. CAMPUS POWER STRUGGLE. Chicago: Aldine, 1970, 27–56.

*Trimberger, E. K. "Why Rebellion at Columbia Was Inevitable," TRANS-ACTION, 5 (September, 1968), 28–38.

Von Hoffman, N. "Columbia and the Closed Corporation," COMMON-WEAL, 89 (January 31, 1969), 566–569.

Wechsler, James. "Columbia Revisited," PROGRESSIVE, 32 (July, 1968), 23–28.

White, Philip V. "Students and the Politics of Protest," FOCUS, 3 (Winter, 1968).

Wilkinson, B. R. "Columbia Recap: School of Library Service during and after the Spring of 1968," LIBRARY JOURNAL 94 (July, 1969), 2567–2570.

Yost, Carson. "Crisis at Columbia: The University Setting," FOCUS, 3 (Winter, 1968).

G.3. Kent State: Spring 1970

Casale, Ottavio and Louis Paskoff, eds. THE KENT AFFAIR: DOCU-MENTS AND INTERPRETATIONS. Boston: Houghton Mifflin, 1971.

*Eszterhas, Joe and Michael D. Roberts. THIRTEEN SECONDS: CON-FRONTATION AT KENT STATE. New York: Dodd, Mead, 1970.

Kent (State) Chapter of the American Association of University Professors. Special Committee of Inquiry. REPORT. Kent, Ohio: 1969.

*Michener, James Albert. KENT STATE: WHAT HAPPENED AND WHY. New York: Random House, 1971.

*O'Neil, Robert, et al. NO HEROES, NO VILLAINS: NEW PERSPECTIVES ON KENT STATE AND JACKSON STATE. San Francisco: Jossey-Bass, 1972.

*Stone, I. F. THE KILLINGS AT KENT STATE: HOW MURDER WENT UNPUNISHED. New York: New York Review, 1970.

Tompkins, Philip K. and E. Vanden Bout Anderson. COMMUNICATIONS CRISIS AT KENT STATE. New York: Gordon and Beach, 1971.

Warren, Bill, ed. THE MIDDLE OF THE COUNTRY: THE EVENTS OF MAY 4TH AS SEEN BY STUDENTS AND FACULTY AT KENT STATE UNIVERSITY. New York: Avon, 1971.

"Behind the Headlines with a Witness from Kent State: Death of A. Krause," SEVENTEEN, 29 (August, 1970), 156+.

Dante, H. L. "Kent State Tragedy: Lessons for Teachers," SOCIAL EDUCATION, 35 (April, 1971), 356–361.

Eszterhas, Joe. "Ohio Honors Its Dead," ROLLING STONE, Number 84 (June 10, 1971), 14–18.

Furlong, W. B. "Guardsmen's View of the Tragedy at Kent State," NEW YORK TIMES MAGAZINE, (June 21, 1970), 12–13+.

Gallagher, T. "Tragedy at Kent State," GOOD HOUSEKEEPING, 171 (October, 1970), 82–83+.

Hummerstone, R. G. "Fifth Victim at Kent State: D. Kohler," LIFE, 69 (October 16, 1970), 42–45.

Keller, Gordon. "Kent State a Year Later," DISSENT, 18 (April, 1971), 171–173.

"Kent State: Four Deaths at Noon," LIFE, 68 (May 15, 1970), 30–35.

"Kent State One Year Later: On the Long Road Back, U.S. NEWS AND WORLD REPORT, 70 (June 14, 1971), 17–20.

Lewis, Jerry. "The Kent Story," NEW POLITICS, 8 (June, 1970), 44–51.

Lewis, Jerry. "A Study of the Kent State Incident Using Smelser's Theory of Collective Behavior," SOCIOLOGICAL INQUIRY, 42 (Number 2, 1972), 87–96.

Molyneaux, David G. "The Kent State Trials End," ROLLING STONE, Number 100 (January 20, 1972), 14–18.

*President's Commission on Campus Unrest. "Kent State," in REPORT OF PRESIDENT'S COMMISSION ON CAMPUS UNREST. New York: Arno Press, 1970, 233–240.

Rudwick, E. and A. Meier. "The Kent State Affair: Social Control of a Putative Value Oriented Movement," SOCIOLOGICAL INQUIRY, 42 (Number 2, 1972), 81–86.

Sanford, D. "Kent State Gag: Report of the Ohio Special Grand Jury," NEW REPUBLIC, 163 (November 7, 1970), 14–17.

Schrag, P. "After Kent State: the First Hundred Days," SATURDAY REVIEW, 53 (August 29, 1970), 12–15+.

G.4. Jackson State: Spring 1970

*O'Neil, Robert, et al. NO HEROES, NO VILLAINS: NEW PERSPECTIVES ON KENT STATE AND JACKSON STATE. San Francisco: Jossey-Bass, 1972.

Southern Regional Council. AUGUSTA, GEORGIA AND JACKSON STATE UNIVERSITY: SOUTHERN EPISODES IN A NATIONAL TRAGEDY. SPECIAL REPORT. Atlanta: Southern Regional Council, 1970.

Lesher, S. "Jackson State a Year After," NEW YORK TIMES MAGA-ZINE, (March 21, 1971), 24–25+.

*President's Commission on Campus Unrest. "Jackson State," in THE

REPORT OF PRESIDENT'S COMMISSION ON CAMPUS UNREST. New York:
Arno Press, 1970, 411–465.

G.5. Cambodia Protest—Miscellaneous Reactions

Dynes, Russel and E. L. Quarantelli. DISRUPTIONS ON THE CAMPUSES
OF OHIO COLLEGES AND UNIVERSITIES, SPRING 1970. Columbus, Ohio:
Ohio Board of United Ministries in Higher Education, 1970.
   *Peterson, Richard and John Bilorusky. MAY, 1970: THE CAMPUS AFTER-
MATH OF CAMBODIA AND KENT STATE. New York: McGraw-Hill, 1971.
   *Urban Research Corporation. ON STRIKE, SHUT IT DOWN: A REPORT
ON THE FIRST NATIONAL STUDENT STRIKE IN U.S. HISTORY. Chicago:
Urban Research Corporation, 1970.

   "Campus Spring Offensive: Harvard, Columbia, Chicago," NEWSWEEK,
73 (April 28, 1969), 66–69.
   DeMott, Benjamin. "Seven Days in May," CHANGE, 2 (September-October,
1970), 55–68.
   Nissen, Steve. "We Will Win (1970)," in John and Susan Erlich, eds. STU-
DENT POWER, PARTICIPATION AND REVOLUTION. New York: Association
Press, 1970, 247–254.
   Stern, Peter S. "Stanford's Community of Consent," NATION, 211
(September 7, 1970), 174–177.

G.6. Chicago Demonstration: 1968 and Aftermath

Clavir, Judy and John Spitzer, eds. THE CONSPIRACY TRIAL. Indian-
apolis: Bobbs-Merrill, 1970.
   Hayden, Tom. TRIAL. New York: Holt, Rinehart and Winston, 1970.
   Hoffman, Abbie, *et al*. THE CONSPIRACY. New York: Dell, 1969.
   Levine, Mark L., *et al*, eds. THE TALES OF HOFFMAN. New York:
Bantam, 1970.
   Lukas, J. Anthony. THE BARNYARD EPITHET AND OTHER OBSCEN-
ITIES: NOTES ON THE CHICAGO CONSPIRACY TRIAL. New York: Harper
& Row, 1970.
   Mailer, Norman. MIAMI AND THE SIEGE OF CHICAGO: AN INFORMAL
HISTORY OF THE REPUBLICAN AND DEMOCRATIC CONVENTIONS OF
1968. London: Weidenfeld and Nicolson, 1968.
   Myrus, Donald, ed. LAW AND DISORDER: THE CHICAGO CONVEN-
TION AND ITS AFTERMATH. Chicago: D. Myrus, 1968.
   Stein, David Lewis. LIVING THE REVOLUTION: THE YIPPIES IN
CHICAGO. Indianapolis: Bobbs-Merrill, 1969.
   U.S. Congress. House. Committee on Un-American Activities. SUBVER-
SIVE INVOLVEMENT IN DISRUPTION OF 1968 DEMOCRATIC PARTY

AND NATIONAL CONVENTION HEARINGS . . . Ninetieth Congress, 2nd Session. Washington: U.S. Government Printing Office, 1968.

Walker, Daniel. RIGHTS IN CONFLICT: THE VIOLENT CONFRONTATION OF DEMONSTRATORS AND POLICE IN THE PARKS AND STREETS OF CHICAGO DURING THE WEEK OF THE DEMOCRATIC NATIONAL CONVENTION OF 1968. Chicago: 1968.

Chomsky, Noam, Paul Lauter and Florence Howe. "Reflections on a Political Trial," NEW YORK REVIEW, 11 (August 22, 1968), 23–30.

"Decline and Fall of the Democratic Party," RAMPARTS, 7 (September 28, 1968), 19–42.

*Marine, Gene. "Chicago: The Trial of the New Culture," ROLLING STONE, Number 55 (April 2, 1970), 38–57.

*Miller, P. R. "Social Activists and Social Change: The Chicago Demonstrators," AMERICAN JOURNAL OF PSYCHIATRY, 126 (June, 1970), 1752–1759.

Miller, P. R. "Revolutionaries among the Chicago Demonstrators," BULLETIN OF THE ATOMIC SCIENTISTS, 26 (February, 1970), 16–21.

Robinson, John P. "Public Reaction to Political Protest: Chicago 1968," PUBLIC OPINION QUARTERLY, 34 (Spring, 1970), 1–9.

Rosenberg, Bernard. "Chicago: Blood and Disaster," DISSENT, 15 (November-December, 1968), 482–487.

Smith, S. "Corruption Behind the Swinging Clubs: with Conclusions from the Walker Report," LIFE, 65 (December 6, 1968), 34–43.

"Strategy of Confrontation–Excerpts from Report by City of Chicago," in C. R. Hormachea and Marion Hormachea, eds. CONFRONTATION: VIOLENCE AND THE POLICE. Boston: Holbrook Press, 1971, 63–81.

Walker, Daniel. "Rights in Conflict," in C. R. Hormachea and Marion Hormachea, eds. CONFRONTATION: VIOLENCE AND THE POLICE. Boston: Holbrook Press, 1971, 82–93.

Wills, G. "Convention in the Streets: Chicago Fallout," NATIONAL REVIEW, 20 (September 24, 1968), 952–959.

G.7. San Francisco State College Protests

*Barlow, William and Peter Shapiro. AN END TO SILENCE: THE SAN FRANCISCO STATE STUDENT MOVEMENT IN THE 60s. New York: Pegasus, 1971.

Berry, John F. "Student Demonstrations in San Francisco, May 12–14, 1960." Unpublished M.A. dissertation, University of California, 1961.

Boyle, Kay. THE LONG WALK AT SAN FRANCISCO STATE, AND OTHER ESSAYS. New York: Grove Press, 1970.

*Daniels, Arlene Kaplan, et al. ACADEMICS ON THE LINE. San Francisco: Jossey-Bass, 1970.

Finberg, Howard, ed. SAN FRANCISCO STATE COLLEGE CRISIS. San Francisco: Insight, 1969.

Karagueuzian, Dikran. BLOW IT UP!: THE BLACK STUDENT REVOLT AT SAN FRANCISCO STATE AND THE EMERGENCE OF DR. HAYAKAWA. Boston: Gambit, 1971.

Litwak, Leo and Herbert Wilner. COLLEGE DAYS IN EARTHQUAKE COUNTRY: A PERSONAL RECORD. New York: Random House, 1971.

Orrick, William H., jr. COLLEGE IN CRISIS. Nashville, Tennessee: Aurora, 1970.

*Pentony, De Vere, Robert Smith, and Richard Axen. UNFINISHED REBELLIONS. San Francisco: Jossey-Bass, 1971.

Research Organizing Committee. STRIKE AT FRISCO STATE! THE STORY BEHIND IT. San Francisco: Private, 1969.

*Smith, Robert, Richard Axen and DeVere Pentony. BY ANY MEANS NECESSARY: THE REVOLUTIONARY STRUGGLE AT SAN FRANCISCO STATE. San Francisco: Jossey-Bass, 1970.

Smith, Robert. THE SAN FRANCISCO STATE EXPERIENCE: WHAT CAN BE LEARNED FROM IT? Washington, D.C.: American Association for Higher Education, 1969.

*Summerskill, John. PRESIDENT SEVEN. New York: World, 1971.

Alpert, Bernard. "Inside San Francisco State," SAN FRANCISCO BUSINESS, 5 (March, 1969), 18–23.

Anderson, B. "Ordeal at San Francisco State College," LIBRARY JOURNAL, 95 (April 1, 1970), 1275–1280.

Anton, Anatol. "Sheepskin," LEVIATHAN, 1 (March, 1970), 7–11.

Barlow, Bill and Peter Shapiro. "State Sails off the Edge," in P. Gleeson, ed. ESSAYS ON THE STUDENT MOVEMENT. Columbus, Ohio: Merrill, 1970, 49–58.

Bunzel, J. H. "War of the Flea at San Francisco State," NEW YORK TIMES MAGAZINE, (November 9, 1969), 28–29+.

Bunzel, J. H., and L. Litwak. "Battle for a College," LOOK, (May 27, 1969), 61–62+.

Cahn, M. M. "1968–1969 San Francisco State College Crisis: A Minority Report," PHI DELTA KAPPAN, 51 (Summer, 1969), 21–25.

Chrisman, Robert. "Observations on Race and Class at San Francisco State," in J. McEvoy and A. Miller, eds. BLACK POWER AND STUDENT REBELLION. Belmont, California: Wadsworth, 1969, 222–232.

Chrutchfield, Nesbit. "San Francisco State," in Janet Harris, ed. STUDENTS IN REVOLT. New York: McGraw-Hill, 1970, 130–153.

Duerr, Edwin C. "Police on the Campus: Crisis at SFSC," EDUCATIONAL RECORD, 50 (Spring, 1969), 126–130.

Gitlin, Todd. "On The Line at San Francisco State," in J. McEvoy and A. Miller, eds. BLACK POWER AND STUDENT REBELLION. Belmont, California: Wadsworth, 1969, 298–306.

Goldman, Ralph M. "Confrontations at San Francisco State," DISSENT, 16 (March/April, 1969), 167–179.

Goldman, Ralph M. "San Francisco State: The Technology of Confrontationism," in Julian Foster, and Durward Long, eds. PROTEST! STUDENT ACTIVISM IN AMERICA. New York: Morrow, 1970, 271–292.

Halperin, I., *et al*. "Three Inside Views of San Francisco State College," EDUCATIONAL RECORD, 50 (May, 1969), 121–137.

Hare, N. "Two Black Radicals Report on Their Campus Struggles," RAMPARTS, 8 (July, 1969), 54–59.

Kovacevich, George J. "Student Unrest in a Legal Perspective: Focus on San Francisco State College," UNIVERSITY OF SAN FRANCISCO LAW REVIEW, 4 (April, 1970), 255–281.

Langguth, A. J. "San Francisco State," HARPER, 239, (September, 1969), 99–100+.

Litwack, Leo. "We Needed A Revolution," in Immanuel Wallerstein and Paul Starr, eds. THE UNIVERSITY CRISIS READER, II. New York: Random House, 1971, 76–81.

McEvoy, J. and A. Miller. "On Strike, Shut It Down; the Crisis at San Francisco State College," TRANS-ACTION, 6 (March, 1969), 18–23+.

Moellering, L. "Impasse on California's Academic Scene," CHRISTIAN CENTURY, 86 (February 26, 1969), 294–298.

Nicolaus, Martin. "S. F. State: History Takes a Leap," NEW LEFT REVIEW, Number 54 (March-April, 1969), 17–31.

Patler, Louie. "San Francisco State College: An In-depth Historical Analysis (1969)," in John and Susan Erlich, eds. STUDENT POWER, PARTICIPATION AND REVOLUTION. New York: Association Press, 1970, 94–100.

Riesman, D. and C. Jencks. "Case Study in Vignette: San Francisco State College: With Reply by G. S. Dumke," TEACHERS COLLEGE RECORD, 63 (January, 1962), 233–266.

Rosenfeld, L. B. "Confrontation Policies of S. I. Hayakawa: A Case Study in Coercive Semantics," TODAY'S SPEECH, 18 (Spring, 1970), 18–22.

Salk, M. "Styles of Handling Student Demonstrations," BULLETIN OF THE ATOMIC SCIENTISTS, 25 (June, 1969), 36–38.

Shapiro, Peter and Bill Barlow, "San Francisco State," LEVIATHAN, 1 (April, 1969), 4–11.

Shorris, E. "Doctor Hayakawa in Thought and Action," RAMPARTS, 8 (November, 1969), 38–42.

Swanston, D. "How to Wreck a Campus; Violence at San Francisco State College," NATION, 206 (January 8, 1968), 27–31.

*Windmiller, Marshall and John Gerassi. "Trouble at San Francisco State," NEW YORK REVIEW OF BOOKS, 10 (April 11, 1968), 38–45.

G.8. Cornell University Protest

Cohen, Michael. GUNS ON CAMPUS: STUDENT PROTEST AT CORNELL. Chicago: Urban Research Corporation, 1970.

Morison, Robert. STUDENTS AND DECISION MAKING. Washington, D.C.: Public Affairs Press, 1970.

194

REPORT OF THE SPECIAL TRUSTEE COMMITTEE ON CAMPUS UNREST AT CORNELL. Ithaca, New York: Cornell University, 1970.

*Strout, Cushing and D. U. Grossvogel, eds. DIVIDED WE STAND: REFLECTIONS ON THE CRISIS AT CORNELL. Garden City, New York: Doubleday, 1970.

Childs, C. "Guns Come to Cornell," LIFE, 66 (May 2, 1969), 20–27.

Dowd, Douglas. "Cornell's Uptight Spring," NEW POLITICS, (October, 1969), 30–44.

*Friedland, H. W. and H. Edwards. "Confrontation at Cornell," TRANS-ACTION, 6 (June, 1969), 29–36+.

*Horowitz, Irving Louis and William Friedland. "Five Years of Confrontation at Cornell," in I. L. Horowitz and W. Friedland, eds., THE KNOWLEDGE FACTORY. Chicago: Aldine, 1970, 220–280.

"It Can't Happen Here, Can It," NEWSWEEK, 73 (May 5, 1969), 23–30.

Rodman, Howard A. "Black-jack at Cornell: Gambling for Power," NEW LEADER, 52 (May 12, 1969), 12–14.

Sanford, David. "Pot Bust at Cornell," NEW REPUBLIC, 156 (April 15, 1967), 17–20.

Sindler, Allan. "A Case Study in Student-University Relations," in John Caffrey, ed., THE FUTURE ACADEMIC COMMUNITY: CONTINUITY AND CHANGE. Washington, D.C.: American Council on Education, 1969, 119–137.

Tarcov, Nathan. "The Last Four Years at Cornell," PUBLIC INTEREST, 13 (Fall 1968), 122–138.

Thelwell, M. "Two Black Radicals Report on Their Campus Struggles," RAMPARTS, 8 (July, 1969), 47–48+.

G.9. Activism at the University of Wisconsin

*Altbach, P. G., R. S. Laufer and S. McVey, eds. ACADEMIC SUPER-MARKETS. San Francisco: Jossey-Bass, 1971.

Graham, Robert H. "Graduate Student Discontentment, Political Activism, and Academic Reform: A Study of the University of Wisconsin, 1966–1970." Unpublished Ph.D. dissertation, University of Wisconsin, 1972.

Lyons, Morgan. "Campus Reactions to Student Protest." Unpublished Ph.D. dissertation, University of Wisconsin, 1971.

McIntyre, Calvin. "The Influence and Influence Strategies of the Wisconsin Student Association on University Policy Making, 1938–1970." Unpublished Ph.D. dissertation, University of Wisconsin, 1972.

Mankoff, Milton. "The Political Socialization of Radicals and Militants in the Wisconsin Student Movement in the 1960s." Unpublished Ph.D. dissertation, University of Wisconsin, 1970.

Rapoport, Roger and Laurence Kirshbaum. IS THE LIBRARY BURNING? New York: Random House, 1969.

Sklar, Bernard. "Faculty Culture and Community Conflict: An Historical, Political and Sociological Analysis of the October 18, 1967 Dow Demonstration at the University of Wisconsin." Unpublished Ph.D. dissertation, University of Chicago, 1970.

Sellery, George C. SOME FERMENTS AT WISCONSIN, 1901–1947. MEMORIES AND REFLECTIONS. Madison: University of Wisconsin Press, 1960.

*Altbach, Philip G. "The Champagne University in the Beer State: Notes on Wisconsin's Crisis," in D. Riesman and V. Stadtman, eds. ACADEMIC TRANS-FORMATIONS, New York: McGraw-Hill, 1973.

Altbach, Philip G. "Students Confront the Universities," PROGRESSIVE, 31 (December, 1967), 17–19.

Christenson, Arlen. "Collective Bargaining in a University, The University of Wisconsin and the Teaching Assistants Association," WISCONSIN LAW REVIEW, (No. 1, 1971), 210–228.

Feinsinger, Nathan and Eleanor Roe. "The University of Wisconsin, Madison Campus–TAA Dispute of 1969–70: A Case Study," WISCONSIN LAW REVIEW, (No. 1, 1971), 229–74.

*Hamilton, Andrew. "Wisconsin: Teaching Assistants Strike Ends in Contract Signing," SCIENCE, 168 (April 17, 1970), 345–349.

Leinster, C. "Shoveling Out the Work of a Lifetime: a Lab in Wisconsin," LIFE, 69 (September 18, 1970), 38–42.

*Long, Durward. "Wisconsin: Changing Styles of Administrative Response," in J. Foster and D. Long, eds., PROTEST, New York: Morrow, 1970, 246–270.

Nwanko, R. L. Nwafo. "Communication in Campus Crises: A Study of Symbolic Interaction," JOURNALISM QUARTERLY, 48 (Autumn 1971), 438–446.

Ridgeway, James. "On Wisconsin: Faculty and Police vs. Students During Anti-Dow Chemical Demonstrations," NEW REPUBLIC, 157 (November 4, 1967), 8–10.

*Sherman, Frederich and David Loeffler, "Universities, Unions and the Rule of Law: The Teaching Assistants at Wisconsin," WISCONSIN LAW REVIEW, (No. 1, 1971), 187–209.

Zolotow, M. "Bohemia on the Campus: Sex, Poetry, and the Higher Emancipation at Wisconsin," AMERICAN MERCURY, 48 (December 1939), 471–476.

G.10. Protests at Harvard University

*Eichel, Lawrence E., et al. THE HARVARD STRIKE. Boston: Houghton Mifflin, 1970.

*Kelman, Steven. PUSH COMES TO SHOVE: THE ESCALATION OF STUDENT PROTEST. Boston: Houghton Mifflin, 1970.

*Lipset, S. M. and David Riesman. POLITICS AND METITOCRACY IN HARVARD COLLEGE. New York: McGraw-Hill, 1973.

Urban Research Corporation. HARVARD'S STUDENT STRIKES, THE POLITICS OF MASS MOBILIZATION. Chicago: Urban Research Corporation, 1970.

196

Zorza, Richard. THE RIGHT TO SAY WE: THE ADVENTURES OF A
YOUNG ENGLISHMAN AT HARVARD AND IN THE YOUTH MOVEMENT.
New York: Praeger, 1970.

Abrams, Elliott. "Cambridge Patterns," NEW LEADER, 52 (April 28,
1969), 7–12.
"Academic Calm of Centuries Broken by a Rampage," LIFE, 66 (April 25,
1969), 24–35.
Bartley, W. W. 3rd. "Religion at Harvard," NEW REPUBLIC, 138 (April
21, 1958), 10–17.
Caffey, Francis G. "Harvard's Political Preferences Since 1860," HARVARD
GRADUATE'S MAGAZINE, 1 (April, 1893), 407–415.
Confrontation in Harvard Yard," LIFE, 66 (April 25, 1969), 24–36.
*Cottle, Thomas J. "The Voices in Harvard Yard," CHANGE, 1 (July-August,
1969), 25–32.
Ginzberg, E. "Delayed Revolution: Lessons from Columbia and Harvard,"
JOURNAL OF COLLEGE PLACEMENT, 30 (December, 1969), 38–42.
Greenstein, M. Robert. "The McNamara Incident at Harvard," DISSENT,
14 (March/April, 1967), 216–219.
Helms, J. C. "Harvard: the Voice of a Non-striker," in I. Wallerstein and
Paul Starr, eds., THE UNIVERSITY CRISIS READER, II. New York: Random
House, 1971, 324–328
Holroyd, M. "Harvard on My Mind," HARPER, 239 (August 1969), 69–72.
Hutchins, F. G. "Moralists Against Managers," ATLANTIC, 224 (July
1969), 53–56.
Kelman, Steven. "The Contented Revolutionaries," NEW LEADER, 52
(April 28, 1969), 12–14.
Kelman, Steven. "A Freshman Paper on Harvard Freshmen," NEW YORK
TIMES MAGAZINE, (December 11, 1966), 50–53+.
Lekachman, Robert. "Harvard—Feints at Revolution," DISSENT, 16 (July/
August, 1969), 321–325.
Lekachman, Robert. "Springtime at Harvard," NEW LEADER, 52 (April
28, 1969), 3–7.
*Meyer, Marshall. "Harvard Students in the Midst of Crisis," SOCIOLOGY
OF EDUCATION, 44 (Summer, 1971), 245–269.
Porter, Kenneth. "The Oxford-Cap War at Harvard," in Alexander De Conde,
ed. STUDENT ACTIVISM: TOWN AND GOWN IN HISTORICAL PERSPEC-
TIVE. New York: Scribner's, 1971. 273–279.
"The Radical Challenge to Discipline," in I. Wallerstein and P. Starr, eds.,
THE UNIVERSITY CRISIS READER, I. New York: Random House, 1971.
456–478.
Reed, John. "The Harvard Renaissance," HARVARD PROGRESSIVE,
(March, 1939), 8, 10, 22.
Reid, J. "Struggle at Harvard," NORTH AMERICAN REVIEW, 6 (Summer,
1969), 54–58.
Ross, G. "Mr. Leavitt Comes to Harvard," NATION, 205 (December 18,
1967), 654–658.

Rudenstine, Neil. "Letter From Harvard: Dow Shalt Not," DISSENT, 15 (January-February, 1968), 74–77.

Samuelson, Robert J. "War on Campus: What Happened When Dow Recruited at Harvard," SCIENCE, 158 (December 8, 1967), 1289–94.

Sayoe, N. "Upheaval at Harvard," NEW STATESMAN, 77 (May 16, 1969), 685–686.

Thwing, Francis. "Radicalism at Harvard," HARVARD GRADUATES' MAGAZINE, 20 (December 1911).

Waldron, Arthur. "A Quest for Seriousness," NEW LEADER, 52 (April 28, 1969), 14–15.

"What Religion at Harvard?" CHRISTIAN CENTURY, 75 (May 14, 1958), 579–582.

G.11. Protests at California Colleges Other Than University of California (Berkeley) and San Francisco State College

Anthony, Earl. THE TIMES OF THE FURNACES: A CASE STUDY OF BLACK STUDENT REVOLT. New York: Dial, 1971.

Epstein, Cy. HOW TO KILL A COLLEGE: THE FACTUAL STORY OF THE ELEMENTS BEHIND THE STUDENT REVOLUTION AT CALIFORNIA STATE COLLEGE, FULLERTON. Los Angeles, California: Sherbourne Press, 1971.

Potter, Robert A. and James J. Súllivan. THE CAMPUS BY THE SEA WHERE THE BANK BURNED DOWN: A REPORT ON THE DISTURBANCES OF UCSB AND ISLA VISTA, 1968–1970. Santa Barbara, California: Faculty and Clergy Observer's Program, 1970.

Rogers, Frederick Rand. TREASON IN AMERICAN EDUCATION: A CASE HISTORY. New York: Pheiades Publications, 1949.

Seidenbaum, Art. CONFRONTATION ON CAMPUS: STUDENT CHALLENGE IN CALIFORNIA. Los Angeles: Ward Ritchie Press, 1969.

Stanton, Charles M. "Student Activism on Three California Campuses During the Years 1930–1940 and 1955–1965." Unpublished Ph.D. dissertation, Stanford University, 1967.

Bacheller, John D. "Students in Governance," in D. R. Gerth, J. Haehn, and Associates, eds. AN INVISIBLE GIANT. San Francisco: Jossey-Bass, 1971. 165–177.

"Campus Revolt: California's Balance Sheet," ENCOUNTER, 35 (December 1970), 81–89.

Elden, J. M. and D. R. Schweitzer. New Third Party Radicalism: The Case of the California Peace and Freedom Party," WESTERN POLITICAL QUARTERLY, 24 (December 1971), 761–775.

Flacks, Richard and Milton Mankoff. "The Bank-Burning: Santa Barbara," NATION, 210 (March 23, 1970), 337–340.

Franklin, H. Bruce. "The Real Issues of My Case," CHANGE, (June 1972), 310–40.

Glazer, Nathan. "Why a Faculty Cannot Afford a Franklin," CHANGE, 4 (May 1972), 40–44.

Griffith, W. "Isla Vista War: Campus Violence in a Class by Itself," NEW YORK TIMES MAGAZINE, (August 30, 1970), 10–11+.

*Horowitz, Irving Louis and William Friedland. "Sit in at Stanford," in J. McEvoy and A. Miller, eds. BLACK POWER AND STUDENT REBELLION. Belmont, California: Wadsworth, 1969, 122–166.

Lundborg, Louis B. "The Lessons of Isla Vista," JOURNAL OF CALIFORNIA LAW ENFORCEMENT, 5 (October 1970), 61–68.

Mayhew, Lewis B. "Dissent: A Campus View," CHANGE, 4 (June 1972), 45–48.

Myerhoff, Barbara. "The Revolution as a Trip: Symbol and Paradox," in P. G. Altbach and R. S. Laufer, eds. THE NEW PILGRIMS. New York: David McKay, 1972, 251–266.

Nevin, D. "Powerless Students," MCCALLS, 97 (July 1970), 44–45+.

Nevin, D. "Uneasy Peace at Valley State," LIFE, 66 (March 14, 1969), 59–68+.

Poss, Stanley. "Lawn Ordure at Fresno State," NEW POLITICS, 8 (Spring, 1970), 14–22.

Schlatter, R. "California Letters," PARTISIAN REVIEW, 35 (Winter 1968), 110–113.

*Stam, James and J. Victor Baldridge. "The Dynamics of Conflict on Campus: A Study of the Stanford 'April Third Movement,' " in J. V. Baldridge, ed. ACADEMIC GOVERNANCE. Berkeley, California: McCutcheon, 1971. 556–579.

"Stanford Sits In—And Out," ECONOMIST, 227 (June 8, 1968), 23–24+.

Stein, Buddy and David Wellman. "The Scheer Campaign," STUDIES ON THE LEFT, 7 (January/February, 1967), 62–78.

Stern, Peter S. "Stanford's Community of Consent," NATION, 211 (September 7, 1970), 174–177.

Walsh, J. "Confrontation at Stanford: Exit Classified Research," SCIENCE, 164 (May 2, 1969), 534–537.

Widmer, K. "Why the Colleges Blew Up: California State College System," NATION, 208 (February 24, 1969), 237–241.

G.12. Activism at the University of Chicago

Aron, Bill. RADICAL IDEOLOGY ON THE UNIVERSITY OF CHICAGO CAMPUS. Chicago: Community and Family Study Center, University of Chicago, 1970.

Illinois State Seditious Activities Investigation Commission. INVESTIGATION OF THE UNIVERSITY OF CHICAGO AND ROOSEVELT COLLEGE, 1949 SPECIAL REPORT. Springfield, 1949.

Weissberg, C. "Students Against the Rank." Unpublished M.A. thesis. Department of Sociology, University of Chicago, 1969.

Cottle, Thomas J. "Strike Week in Chicago," CHANGE, 2 (July-August, 1970), 19–28.

Light, Donald W., jr. "University of Chicago: Strategies of Protest: Developments in Conflict Theory," in J. McEvoy and A. Miller, eds. BLACK POWER AND STUDENT REBELLION. Belmont, California: Wadsworth, 1969, 74–99.

"The Sit-in: A Chronology," UNIVERSITY OF CHICAGO MAGAZINE, 61 (March-April, 1969), 39–47.

G.13. R.O.T.C.

Association of American Universities. SURVEY REPORT: STATUS OF RESERVE OFFICER TRAINING CORPS PROGRAM AT AAU MEMBER INSTITUTIONS. Washington, D.C.: Association of American Universities, 1970.

Brick, Allen. THE CAMPUS MOVEMENT AGAINST ROTC. Chicago: Student Peace Union, n.d.

Lathrop, Robert L. and Elliot H. Donnels. STUDENT DECISIONS TO ELECT ROTC AFTER ONE OR MORE QUARTERS OF UNIVERSITY ATTENDANCE: A SUPPLEMENTARY STUDY. Minneapolis: Bureau of Institutional Research, University of Minnesota, 1962.

Lathrop, Robert L., et al. STUDENT ATTITUDES TOWARD RESERVE OFFICER TRAINING CORPS PROGRAMS: A SURVEY OF FRESHMEN AT THE UNIVERSITY OF MINNESOTA. Minneapolis: Bureau of Institutional Research, University of Minnesota, 1962.

Lyons, Gene and John Masland. EDUCATION AND MILITARY LEADERSHIP: A STUDY OF THE ROTC. Princeton: Princeton University Press, 1959.

Porter, Jack N. "Student Protest, University Decision-Making, and the Technocratic Society: The Case of ROTC." Unpublished Ph.D. dissertation, Northwestern University, 1971.

U.S. Department of Defense, Special Committee on ROTC. REPORT TO THE SECRETARY OF DEFENSE. Washington, D.C.: Government Printing Office, 1969.

Beavau, K. A. "ROTC Widely Resented," TIMES EDUCATIONAL SUPPLEMENT, 2799 (January 10, 1969), 60.

Boughton, Roland N. "A New-Old Look in Air Force Officer Education," EDUCATIONAL RECORD, 41 (October, 1960), 306–311.

Goertzel, Ted and Acco Hengst. "The Military Socialization of University Students," SOCIAL PROBLEMS, 19 (Fall, 1971) 258–267.

Scott, Joseph W. "ROTC Retreat," TRANSACTION, 6 (September 1969), 47–52.

Wycoff, Theodore. "Required ROTC," JOURNAL OF HIGHER EDUCATION, 36 (March, 1965), 147–153.

200

Zahn, G. "Intruder in Academe: Still an Issue," COMMONWEAL, 89 (November 22, 1968), 279–282.

G.14. Civil Liberties Activism

*Horowitz, David. STUDENT: THE POLITICAL ACTIVITIES OF BERKELEY STUDENTS. New York: Ballantine, 1962.

U.S. Congress House Committee on Un-American Activities. OPERATION ABOLITION: THE CAMPAIGN AGAINST THE HOUSE COMMITTEE ON UN-AMERICAN ACTIVITIES; THE FEDERAL BUREAU OF INVESTIGATION AND THE GOVERNMENT SECURITY PROGRAM BY THE EMERGENCY CIVIL LIBERTIES COMMITTEE AND ITS AFFILIATES. Washington, D.C.: Government Printing Office, 1957.

U.S. Congress House Committee on Un-American Activities. THE COM-MUNIST-LEAD RIOTS AGAINST THE HOUSE COMMITTEE ON UN-AMERICAN ACTIVITIES IN SAN FRANCISCO CALIFORNIA MAY 12–14, 1960 REPORT. Washington D.C.: Government Printing Office, 1960.

Allen, Donna. "HUAC Faces the New Spirit," LIBERATION, 11 (October, 1966), 7–12.

Burnstein, Malcolm. "The Un-American Committee in San Francisco," NEW UNIVERSITY THOUGHT, 1 (Summer, 1960), 9–15.

"Documents: The Beginning of the Movement: Peace Protest and Civil Liberties," in M. Teodori, ed. THE NEW LEFT: A DOCUMENTARY HISTORY. Indianapolis, Indiana: Bobbs-Merrill, 1969, 120–127.

"The San Francisco Affairs," in A.T. Anderson and B. P. Biggs, eds. A FOCUS ON REBELLION. San Francisco: Chandler Publishing Company, 1962, 3–93.

Wakefield, D. "Unamericanism Plays the Colleges," NATION, 192 (January 28, 1961), 74–76.

G.15. Miscellaneous and Single Campus
Student Activities

Allen, Jonathan, ed. MARCH 4: SCIENTISTS, STUDENTS, AND SOCIETY. Cambridge, Mass.: MIT Press, 1970.

Dungan, Ralph A. A REPORT TO THE NEW JERSEY LEGISLATURE CONCERNING THE RECENT EVENTS AND DISTURBANCES AT THE NEWARK AND CAMDEN CAMPUSES OF RUTGERS, THE STATE UNIVER-SITY. Trenton: Department of Higher Education, 1969.

Fenton, J. H. and G. Gleason. STUDENT POWER AT THE UNIVERSITY OF MASSACHUSETTS: A CASE STUDY. Amherst, Mass.: Bureau of Govern-ment Research, University of Massachusetts, 1969.

Hersey, John. LETTER TO THE ALUMNI. New York: Knopf, 1970.

Scimecca, J. and R. Damiano. CRISIS AT ST. JOHN'S: STRIKE AND

REVOLUTION ON THE CATHOLIC CAMPUS. New York: Random House, 1968.

Abram, M. B. "Eleven Days at Brandeis, As Seen from the President's Chair," NEW YORK TIMES MAGAZINE, (February 16, 1969), 28–29+.

Anderson, R. B. "Helping to Solve Community Problems; University of Delaware, Newark," COLLEGE MANAGEMENT, 7 (June 1972), 20–23+.

Braitermau, K. "Story of One Student Uprising: Twenty-one Hours at Oberlin College," MIDSTREAM, 15 (August–September, 1969), 11–28.

Braun, S. "Going the Rounds with a Dow Recruiter," NEW YORK TIMES MAGAZINE, (April 13, 1969), 27–29+.

Brooks, Thomas. "The Bust at Stony Brooks," DISSENT, 15 (September–October, 1968), 396–403.

Carter, L. J. "Duke University: Students Demand a New Deal for Negro Workers," SCIENCE, 160 (May 3, 1968), 513–17.

*Crocker, E. C. and M. LaBarre. "Silent Vigil: A Student Nonviolent Demonstration: Duke University," AMERICAN JOURNAL OF ORTHOPSYCHIATRY, 40 (April 1970), 481–492.

Darby, J. M. "Reflections on the Dayton Situation," AMERICA, 116 (April 29, 1967), 650–652.

Faculty Committee to Investigate the Dow Incident of Indiana University. "Indiana: the Anatomy of Violence," in J. Foster and D. Long, eds. PROTEST! STUDENT ACTIVISM IN AMERICA. New York: William Morrow, 1970, 229–245.

Feinstein, Marvin. "The Campus Upheaval at the City College of New York," RECONSTRUCTIONIST, 35 (July 25, 1969), 14–22.

Feir, Robert E. "Can You Still Call It a University if It's On Strike? Or, Is It One If It's Not? Reflections on the Disruption of 'Normal Activities,' May 1970," HELDERBERG REVIEW, 1 (Fall, 1970), 39–47.

Fleming, T. J. "Hesburgh of Notre Dame: (1) He's Destroying this University: (2) He's Bringing It into the Mainstream of American Life," NEW YORK TIMES MAGAZINE, (May 11, 1969), 56–57+.

Gallagher, M. J. "Carnival Revolution," AMERICA, 122 (March 21, 1970), 295–298.

Gartner, Lloyd P. "Five Demands at City College of New York," MIDSTREAM, 15 (October 1969), 15–35.

Grant, P. A. jr. "Ferment on the Campus: Disputes at St. John's University; University of Dayton; Catholic University of America," CATHOLIC WORLD, 205 (August 1967), 293–297.

Grant, Philip. "New Developments in the Saga of St. John's," CHANGING EDUCATION, 3 (Winter/Spring, 1968), 24–27.

Hamalian, L. and J. V. Hatch. "The City College Rebellion Revisited," CHANGING EDUCATION, 4 (Winter, 1969–1970), 15–21.

Hilberry, Conrad. "Civil Disobedience at Oberlin," EDUCATIONAL RECORD, 49 (Spring, 1968), 133–138.

Hill, E. "Revolution (cont.): At the University of Connecticut," NEW YORK TIMES MAGAZINE, (February 28, 1969), 28–29+.

202

Hoffman, Jerry. "Princeton: Radical Organizing and the IDA Campaign," in J. Foster and D. Long, eds. PROTEST! STUDENT ACTIVISM IN AMERICA. New York: William Morrow & Co., 1970, 306–318.

Huxford, G. "Incident at Monmouth," JOURNAL OF HIGHER EDUCATION, 40 (May 1969), 369–380.

Jones, Billy Mac. "Colorado: Sounds of Student Protest Deftly Muted," in J. Foster and D. Long, eds. PROTEST: STUDENT ACTIVISM IN AMERICA. New York: William Morrow, 1970, 293–305.

Keniston, Kenneth. "May Day Weekend at Yale," NEW LEADER, 53 (June 22, 1970), 10–17.

Kornberg, Allan and Joel Smith. "Duke: It Ain't Over Yet: Activism in a Southern University," in J. McEvoy and A. Miller, eds. BLACK POWER AND STUDENT REBELLION. Belmont, California: Wadsworth, 1969, 100–121.

Liberation News Service. "Seizing the Time at Essex," LEVIATHAN, 1 (March 1970), 16–18.

Lincoln, C. E. "Voices of Fisk '70," NEW YORK TIMES MAGAZINE, (June 7, 1970), 30–31+.

McDowell, Sophia, Gilbert Lowe, jr., and Doris Dockett. "Howard University's Student Protest Movement," PUBLIC OPINION QUARTERLY, 34 (Fall, 1970), 384–388.

Mann, P. A. and I. Iscoe. "Mass Behavior and Community Organizations: Reflections on a Peaceful Demonstration," AMERICAN PSYCHOLOGIST, 26 (January 1971), 108–113.

Murray, William C. "The Bearded Sockless Radical of Moo U., "NEW YORK TIMES MAGAZINE, 25 (April 9, 1967), 128–134.

"Notes and Comment: New York City's Troubled Campuses," NEW YORKER, 45 (May 3, 1969), 27–32.

"Our Colleges and Universities," FOCUS/MIDWEST 7 (January–February, 1969), 8–42.

Pekkanen, J. "Ecology: A Cause Becomes a Mass Movement," LIFE, 68 (January 30, 1970), 3, 22–30.

Rainey, T. B. and B. Swall. "Duke Crisis: It Ain't Over," NORTH AMERICAN REVIEW, 6 (Summer, 1969), 30–33+.

Raushenbush, Esther. "The Climate of Sarah Lawrence College," in L. Murphy and E. Raushenbush, eds. ACHIEVEMENT: THE COLLEGE YEARS. New York: Harpers, 1960, 21–57.

Redford, H. "Profiting from Activism: Merritt College Believes in Broad Policies With Few Rules," JUNIOR COLLEGE JOURNAL, 38 (November 1967), 7–12.

Salloch, R. "Cambridge: March 4, the Movement, and MIT," BULLETIN OF ATOMIC SCIENTISTS, 25 (May 1969), 32–35.

Sanford, David. "Protest at Pennsylvania: A Model for Campus Dissent?" NEW REPUBLIC, 160 (March 15, 1969), 19–21.

Scimecca, J. A. "St. John's: Four Years After," COMMONWEAL, 91 (January 16, 1970), 419+, and (February 13, 1970), 523+.

Shower, John. "Preparation for Dow Day," NATION, 205 (December 18, 1967), 648–651.

Sloat, Warren. "Rutgers–The Soft Sell-out," LIBERATION, 12 (March 1967), 18–20.

Solomon, Eric. "Free Speech at Ohio State," ATLANTIC MONTHLY, 206 (November 1965), 119–124.

Stone, Lawrence. "Princeton: The Nation's Service," NEW YORK REVIEW OF BOOKS, 14 (June 18, 1970), 7–10.

Trillin, C. "U.S. Journal: Iowa: Cornell College, Mount Vernon," NEW YORKER, 44 (April 20, 1968), 170+.

Trillin, C. "U.S. Journal: Oshkosh: Student Demonstration," NEW YORKER, 44 (January 4, 1969), 62–66.

Turner, James S. "Ohio State: Free Speech and Student Power," in J. Foster and D. Long, eds. PROTEST! STUDENT ACTIVISM IN AMERICA. New York: William Morrow, 1970, 345–361.

Urofsky, M. I. "High Noon at Catholic U.," NATION, 205 (October 2, 1967), 303–5.

Weiss, P. "Bomb Crater in the American Dream," NATION, 211 (October 5, 1970), 302–305.

H. RADICAL STUDENT POLITICS AND YOUTH ACTIVITIES

Cross Reference: For comparison to activism also see general section on college life by historical periods. (Sections III B 1–5).

H.1. Student Left: 1900–1920

Deming, Seymour. THE PILLAR OF FIRE: A PROFANE BACCALAUREATE. Boston: Small, Maynard, 1915.

Allen, J. H. "Socialism and the Undergraduate," LIVING AGE, 270 (September 2, 1911), 585–592.

Bartlett, S. C. "College Disturbances," FORUM, 4 (December 1887), 424–31.

Bourne, Randolph. "The Price of Radicalism," NEW REPUBLIC, 6 (March 11, 1916), 161.

Bourne, Randolph. "The Two Generations," ATLANTIC MONTHLY, 107 (May 1911), 590–98.

Cantor, Milton. "The Radical Confrontation with Foreign Policy: War and Revolution, 1914–1920," in A. F. Young, ed. DISSENT: EXPLORATIONS IN THE HISTORY OF AMERICAN RADICALISM. De Kalb: Northern Illinois University Press, 1968, 215–250.

Cockerell, T. D. A. "University in Politics," POPULAR SCIENCE, 79 (August 1911), 160–164.

"College Men and Practical Politics," OUTLOOK, 93 (October 30, 1909), 482–483.

Corbin, D. "Struggle for College Democracy," CENTURY, 87 (November 1913), 80–87.

Davies, M. C. "Berkeley's Three Big Rallies," OVERLAND, 63 (April 1914), 336–340.

"Federation of Students," INDEPENDENT, 75 (September 11, 1913), 601–602.

Henderson, Gerald. "The College and the Radicals," HARVARD GRADUATES' MAGAZINE, 20 (December, 1911), 463–465.

Laidler, Harry W. "The Intercollegiate Socialist Society Convention," INTERCOLLEGIATE SOCIALIST, 4 (February/March, 1916), 12–21.

Laidler, Harry W. "Ten Years of I.S.S. Progress," INTERCOLLEGIATE SOCIALIST, 4 (December/January, 1915–16), 16–22.

Lochner, Louis. "The Cosmopolitan Club Movement," in G. Spiller, ed. PAPERS ON INTER-RACIAL PROBLEMS. London: P. S. King, 1911, 439–443.

Nasmyth, G. W. "Peace Movement in the Colleges," INDEPENDENT, 68 (February 17, 1910), 362–365.

"Socialism in the Colleges," CENTURY, 86 (July, 1913), 468–470.

"Sequel of the Student Revolt," NEW REPUBLIC, 21 (February 25, 1920), 380–382.

H.2. Student Left: 1920–1930

Evans, W. Wainwright and B. B. Lindsey. THE REVOLT OF MODERN YOUTH. New York: Boni and Liveright, 1925.

High, Stanley. THE REVOLT OF YOUTH. New York: Abingdon Press, 1924.

New Republic. THE STUDENTS SPEAK OUT! New York: New Republic, 1929.

Van Waters, Miriam. YOUTH IN CONFLICT. New York: Republic Publishing Co., 1926.

Allen, Devere. "Youth Movements Face the Future," WORLD TOMORROW, 7 (May 1924), 147–152.

Baker, L. H. "The National Student Federation of the United States of America," SCHOOL AND SOCIETY, 26 (August 20, 1927), 237–8.

Black, Henry C. "Socialism in American Colleges," BULLETIN OF THE NATIONAL ASSOCIATION FOR CONSTITUTIONAL GOVERNMENT, 4 (December, 1920), 3–46.

Clark, Evans. "College Youth in a Flippant Revolt," NEW YORK TIMES MAGAZINE, (June 7, 1925), 3+.

Coe, George. "Youth and Peace," SCRIBNERS, 78 (July, 1925), 8–13.

Coolidge, Calvin. "Are the Reds Stalking Our College Women?" DELINEATOR, 98 (June, 1921), 4–5.

Deutsch, Benjamin. "College Students and Politics," SCHOOL AND SOCIETY, 16 (December 16, 1922), 673–680.

"Ferment in the Colleges," NEW REPUBLIC, 30 (May 3, 1922), 266–267.

Fox, Lewis, H. N. MacGraken, and Norman Thomas. "Student Affairs: A Symposium on the New National Federation," NEW STUDENT, 5 (January 6, 1926), 8–10.

"Freedom of Discussion in American Colleges," SOCIALIST REVIEW, 8 (March 1920), 252–255.

Graham, Edward K. "The Hampton Institute Strike of 1927: A Case Study of Student Protest," AMERICAN SCHOLAR, 38 (Autumn, 1969), 668–681.

Hicks, Granville. "No Youth Movement for America," CHRISTIAN CENTURY, 43 (April 8, 1926), 443–444.

Hunter, A. A. "Stirring of Youth," FORUM, 72 (December, 1924), 787–793.

Kehr, Marguerite. "The National Student Federation of America," STUDENT GOVERNMENT BULLETIN, 2 (April, 1954), 20–24.

Liberalism in the Colleges," INDEPENDENT, 107 (October 15, 1921), 57–58.

Mallach, Stanley. "Red Kate O'Hare Comes to Madison: The Politics of Free Speech," WISCONSIN MAGAZINE OF HISTORY, 53 (Spring, 1970), 204–222.

Riggs, G. "Radicalism in Our Colleges," FORUM, 66 (September, 1921), 197–209.

Rothschild, J. "Brass Checks and Michigan," NEW REPUBLIC, 34 (March 7, 1923), 43–45

Santayāna, George. "America's Young Radicals," FORUM, 67 (May, 1922), 371–375.

H.3. Student Left: 1930–1940

Beilke, Reuben. "Student Political Action at the University of Wisconsin 1930–1940." Unpublished M.S. dissertation, University of Wisconsin, 1951.

Draper, Hal, ed. OUT OF THEIR OWN MOUTHS. New York: Young Peoples Socialist League, 1936.

Green, Gil. MAKE YOUR DREAMS COME TRUE: REPORT TO THE 8TH NATIONAL CONVENTION OF THE YOUNG COMMUNIST LEAGUE. New York: Workers Library Publishers, 1937.

Hamilton, Albert. STUDENTS AGAINST WAR. National Council of Methodist Youth and World Peace Commission, 1937.

Ilma, Viola. AND NOW YOUTH. New York: Ballou, 1934.

Lash, Joseph P. THE CAMPUS: FORTRESS OF DEMOCRACY. New York: American Student Union, 1938.

Lash, Joseph P. THE CAMPUS STRIKES AGAINST WAR. New York: Student League for Industrial Democracy, 1935.

Lash, Joseph P. ELEANOR ROOSEVELT, A FRIEND'S MEMOIR. Garden City, New York: Doubleday, 1964.

Lash, Joseph P. TOWARD A 'CLOSED SHOP' ON THE CAMPUS. New York: American Student Union, 1937.

Lash, Joseph P. and James A. Wechsler. WAR OUR HERITAGE. New York: Student League for Industrial Democracy, 1935.

*Lewack, Harold. CAMPUS REBELS: A BRIEF HISTORY OF THE STUDENT LEAGUE FOR INDUSTRIAL DEMOCRACY. New York: Student League for Industrial Democracy, 1953.

Moore, H. H., ed. WE ARE THE BUILDERS OF A NEW WORLD: A SUMMONS TO YOUTH. New York: Association Press, 1934.

Pitkin, Walter B. THE CHANCE OF A LIFETIME: MARCHING ORDERS FOR THE LOST GENERATION. New York: Simon and Schuster, 1934.

A PROGRAM FOR AMERICAN YOUTH. Manifesto and Resolutions of Seventh National Convention, Young Communist League of U.S.A. (June 22–27, 1934).

Rawick, George P. "The New Deal and Youth." Unpublished Ph.D. dissertation, University of Wisconsin, 1957.

REPORT OF FIRST AMERICAN YOUTH CONGRESS. New York: Central Bureau for Young America, 1934.

Sellery, George Clarke. SOME FERMENTS AT WISCONSIN, 1901–1947. Madison, Wisconsin: University of Wisconsin Press, 1960.

STUDENTS IN REVOLT: THE STORY OF THE INTERCOLLEGIATE LEAGUE FOR INDUSTRIAL DEMOCRACY. New York, 1933.

Wechsler, James A. THE AGE OF SUSPICION. New York: Random House, 1953.

*Wechsler, James A. REVOLT ON THE CAMPUS. New York: Covici, Friede, 1935.

Wilkins, Ernest. STUDENTS AGAINST WAR. Oberlin, Ohio: Oberlin College, 1935.

Williams, Marguerita P. YOUTH MOVEMENTS HERE AND ABROAD. New York: Russell Sage, 1936.

"American Students Unite," NATION, 142 (January 8, 1936), 33.

Barnard, Eunice. "Politics Begins to Stir Our Campuses," NEW YORK TIMES MAGAZINE, (January 28, 1934), 4+.

Barnard, Eunice. "Students Lay a Barrage Against War," NEW YORK TIMES MAGAZINE, (April 29, 1934), 5+.

Bedford-Jones, Nancy. "My Father is a Liar!" NEW MASSES, 16 (September 3, 1935), 9–11.

Benziger, M. "Swarthmore Communists," COMMONWEAL, 26 (May 14, 1937), 69–71.

Berchtold, William E. "In Search of a Youth Movement," NEW OUTLOOK, 163 (June, 1934), 46–49.

Bliven, Bruce, jr. "Citizens of Tomorrow," NEW REPUBLIC, 97 (January 11, 1939),

Bliven, Bruce, jr. "The Fifth American Youth Congress," NEW REPUBLIC, 99 (July 19, 1939), 302–303.

Brameld, T. B. "College Students React to Social Issues," SOCIAL FRONTIER, 1 (December, 1934), 21–26.

Broun, Heywood. "Broun's Page," (Veterans of Future Wars) NATION, 142 (April 1, 1936), 417.

Buroker, L. P. "American Youth Subverters; Second American Youth Congress, Detroit," NATIONAL REPUBLIC, 23 (September, 1935), 19–20+ (October, 1935), 23–24.

Campbell, Jeffery W. "Youth, Religion and Peace," SOCIALIST REVIEW, 6 (July–August, 1938),

Draper, Hal. "The American Student Union Faces the Student Anti-War Strike," AMERICAN SOCIALIST MONTHLY, 5 (April, 1936), 7–12.

*Draper, Hal. "The Student Movement of the Thirties: A Political History," in Rita Somon, ed. AS WE SAW THE THIRTIES. Urbana, Illinois: University of Illinois Press, 1967, 151–189.

Draper, Theodore. "America's Youth Rejects Fascism," NEW MASSES, 12 (August 28, 1934), 11–13.

Draper, Theodore. "City College's Rebel Generation," NEW MASSES, 13 (November 27, 1934), 13–15.

Foster, William Z. "Is There an American Youth Movement?" NATIONAL STUDENT MIRROR, 1 (March, 1934), 3–5.

Hamilton, Al and Alvaine Hollister. "Left Jingoism on the Campus," SOCIALIST REVIEW, 6 (January–February, 1938), 9-10, 19.

Harriman, Philip L. "The Student-Faculty Congress," JOURNAL OF HIGHER EDUCATION, 8 (November, 1937), 413–416.

Harway, Maxwell. "People's Front in Diapers," AMERICAN SOCIALIST MONTHLY, 5 (August, 1936), 20–24.

"Is There a Student Movement in America?" NEW REPUBLIC, 81 (January 16, 1935), 264.

Jones, Lucille. "Participation by College Students in School and Community Activities," TEACHERS COLLEGE JOURNAL, 10 (March, 1939), 97–99.

Kimball, Penn. "The Veterans of Future Wars: Princeton's Greatest Political Movement Started 30 Years Ago," PRINCETON MAGAZINE, (April 19, 1966), 12–14.

Lash, Joseph P. "Another View of the American Student Union," AMERICAN SOCIALIST MONTHLY, 5 (May, 1936), 28–31.

Lash, Joseph P. "Do the Thirties Have Anthing to Tell the Sixties?" in STUDENT ADVOCATE New York: Greenwood Reprint Corporation, 1968, 1–3.

Laski, Harold. "Why Don't Your Young Men Care?" HARPER'S 163 (July, 1931), 129–136.

"Laying the Ghost of College Communism," LITERARY DIGEST, 120 (July 27, 1935), 18+.

"Left Jingoism on the Campus," SOCIALIST REVIEW, 6 (January–February, 1938), 9-10+.

Lovett, Robert Morss. "The Congress on War and Fascism," NEW REPUBLIC, 80 (October 17, 1934), 263–264.

McDowell, Arthur G. "The Socialist Youth Movement," AMERICAN SOCIALIST QUARTERLY, 3 (Summer, 1934), 43–50.

Meyers, Robin. "War and Peace on the Campus," SOCIALIST REVIEW, 6 (May–June, 1939), 11–15.

Michelfelder, William F. "Adolescent Red," COMMONWEAL, 23 (January 24, 1936), 357.

Neblett, T. F. "Youth Movements in the U.S.," ANNALS OF THE AMERICAN ACADEMY OF POLITICAL AND SOCIAL SCIENCE, 194 (November, 1937), 141–151.

Norlin, George. "Is Radicalism Rampant on the American Campus?" SCHOOL AND SOCIETY, 45 (January 23, 1937), 120–122.

"Pacifism in the Colleges," LITERARY DIGEST, 115 (May 27, 1933), 17–18.

Rodman, Seldon. "Youth Meets in Washington," NATION, 138 (January 17, 1934), 70–71.

Ross, Carl. "American Youth in the Struggle Against Imperialist War," CLARITY, 1 (April–May, 1940), 8–21.

Seidman, Harold. "The Colleges Renounce War," NATION, 136 (May 17, 1933), 554–555.

Seidman, Harold. "How Radical Are College Students?" AMERICAN SCHOLAR, 4 (Summer, 1935), 326–331.

Soule, George. "The Unfound Generation," NEW REPUBLIC, 79 (July 11, 1934),

Strack, Celeste. "The American Students Unite," NEW MASSES, 18 January 14, 1936), 19–21.

Strack, Celeste. "The Student Movement Against War," in W. Bower, ed. THE COLLEGE WRITER, New York: Norton, 1935, 121–127.

Tyler, August. "The Internationalist Socialist Youth Movement," AMERICAN SOCIALIST MONTHLY, 2 (Winter, 1933), 49–56.

Varney, Harold L. "The Left Kidnaps American Youth," AMERICAN MERCURY, 44 (August, 1938), 391–402.

Wallace, Anna. "Fascism Comes to the Campus: the University of California as a Case in Point," NEW REPUBLIC, 81 (January 9, 1935), 238–241.

Wechsler, J. "Ferment in the Colleges," NEW REPUBLIC, 84 (October 16, 1935), 266–268.

Wechsler, J. "Politics on the Campus," NATION, 149 (December 30, 1939), 732–733.

Wechsler, J. "Revolt on Campus: April 13, 1934–April 12, 1935," in Alexander De Conde, ed. STUDENT ACTIVISM: TOWN AND GOWN IN HISTORICAL PERSPECTIVE. New York: Scribner's, 1971, 280–294.

Wechsler, J. "Student Union Begins," NEW REPUBLIC, 85 (January 15, 1936), 279.

Wechsler, J. "Student Unity at Stake," NEW MASSES, 22 (December 29, 1936), 17–19.

Wecter, Dixon. "Reading, 'Riting, and Revolution," AMERICAN MERCURY, 41 (June, 1937), 192–198.

Weiss, Max. "New Developments in the Youth Movement," CLARITY, 1 (Fall, 1940), 19–35.

"Youth's Economic Problem," AMERICAN SOCIALIST MONTHLY, 5 (June, 1934), 19–22.

H.4. Student Left 1940–1950

Allen, Jo. THE BIG SQUEEZE: CRISIS ON THE CAMPUS. Prague: International Union of Students, 1946.

Judson, L. S. THE STUDENT CONGRESS MOVEMENT. New York: Wilson, 1940.

Lindsay, Mary R., ed. DIRECTORY OF YOUTH ORGANIZATIONS. New York: Federal Security Agency, National Youth Administration for New York City, 1940.

McLaughlin, Martin. "Political Processes in American National Student Organizations," Unpublished Ph.D. dissertation, Notre Dame University, 1948.

U.S. Congress, House of Representatives. Committee on Un-American Activities. INVESTIGATION OF UN-AMERICAN PROPAGANDA ACTIVITIES IN THE UNITED STATES. REPORT ON AMERICAN YOUTH FOR DEMOCRACY. 80th Congress. 1st Session. Washington, D.C.: GPO, 1947.

Bogardus, E. S. "The Campus Cooperative Movement," SOCIOLOGY AND SOCIAL RESEARCH, 28 (March–April, 1944), 296–307.

Des Marais, P. "The Young Progressives of America," NEW LEADER, 31 (August 14, 1948), 5.

Hartwell, D. "Politics on the Campus," COLLIERS, 120 (December 20, 1947), 14–15+.

Kaye, S. R. "Ann Arbor Hysteria," NATION, 151 (September 14, 1940), 215–216.

Laski, H. "Students and Politics," NATION, 163 (December 21, 1946), 727–728.

Meltzer, M. and R. Forrest. "The Students Say 'Twaddle,'" NEW MASSES, 38 (January 14, 1941), 10–11.

Jones, H. Mumford. "Undergraduate and Political Responsibility," AMERICAN SCHOLAR, 17 (October, 1948), 395–407.

"Our Generation," NEW FOUNDATIONS, 1 (Fall, 1947), 7–12.

Ross, Carl. "Unity and the Struggle Against Hitlerism," CLARITY, 2 (Summer, 1941), 41–55.

Ross, Irwin. "College Students and the War," NEW REPUBLIC, 103 (July 15, 1940), 79–80.

Ross, Irwin. "The Student Union and the Future," NEW REPUBLIC, 102 (January 8, 1940), 48–49.

Seymour, C. "War's Impact on the Campus: the Undergraduate Confused but Loyal," NEW YORK TIMES MAGAZINE, (September 29, 1940), 3+.

Shaw, Marvin. "Nov. 2nd and After," NEW FOUNDATIONS, 2 (Winter, 1949), 104–109.

Shaw, M. "The Reawakening of the American Student Movement," POLITICAL AFFAIRS, 26 (February, 1947), 132–143.

Shaw, Marvin. "A Student Crusade for Democratic Education," NEW FOUNDATIONS, 2 (Summer, 1949), 226–230.

Shaw, Marvin. "Toward Student Unity," NEW FOUNDATIONS, 1 (Fall, 1947), 71–74.

Shore, Herbert L. "Iron Heel on the Campus," NEW FOUNDATIONS, 1 (Fall, 1947), 75–83.

Spivak, R. G. "Youth Reorganizes," NATION, 152 (January 18, 1941), 71–73.

Steele, Al. "The Struggle Against Social Democratism in the Youth Movement," CLARITY, 1 (Summer, 1940), 65–82.

Williams, Arthur. "The Campus Rallies for All-Out War," CLARITY, 2 (Winter, 1942), 63–73.

"A Young Communist Meets the Press," AMERICAN MERCURY, 69 (August, 1949), 194–201.

H.5. Student Left: 1950–1960

Bacciocco, Edward, jr. "The New Left From 1956–1969: A Study of Community, Reform and Revolution." Unpublished Ph.D. dissertation, University of Colorado, 1971.

Kramer, Gerry. STUDENTS FOR DEMOCRATIC ACTION, A HISTORY. New York: Students for Democratic Action, 1955.

*Lewack, Harold. CAMPUS REBELS. New York: Student League for Industrial Democracy, 1953.

Townsend, Agathe. COLLEGE FRESHMEN SPEAK OUT. New York: Harper, 1956.

U.S. Congress. House of Representatives. Committee on Un-American Activities. COMMUNIST ACTIVITIES AMONG YOUTH GROUPS, BASED ON TESTIMONY OF HARVEY MATUSOW HEARING. 82nd Congress. 2nd Session, 83rd Congress, 2nd Session. Washington, D.C.: Government Printing Office, 1952–1954.

U.S. Congress. House of Representatives. Committee on Un-American Activities. COMMUNIST METHODS OF INFILTRATION (EDUCATION). HEARINGS. 83rd Congress, 1st–2nd Session, Washington, D.C.: Government Printing Office, 1953–1954.

U.S. Congress, House of Representatives. Committee on Un-American Activities. COMMUNIST PROPAGANDA: STUDENT GROUPS, DISTRIBUTORS, AND PROPAGANDISTS. HEARING. 85th Congress, 2nd. Session. Washington, D.C.: Government Printing Office, 1958.

U.S. Congress. Senate Committee on the Judiciary. COMMUNIST TACTICS IN CONTROLLING YOUTH ORGANIZATIONS. Hearing before the Subcommittee to investigate the administration of the Internal Security Act and other Internal Security Laws. 82nd. Congress. 1st and 2nd. Sessions. Washington, D.C.: Government Printing Office, 1952.

Brick, Alan. "Campus Rebels Find a Cause," NATION, 189 (November 28, 1959), 395–397.

Brick, Alan. "Peace Moves on the Campus," FELLOWSHIP, 25 (September 1, 1959), 8–12.

"Call for Revolt on Campus," AMERICAN MERCURY, 73 (October, 1951), 24–29.

Cantor, Norman F. "From the Beats to the New Left," in Norman Cantor, THE AGE OF PROTEST. New York: Hawthorne Books, 1969, 268–307.

"The Careful Young Men: Tomorrow's Leaders Analyzed by Today's Teachers, Symposium," NATION, 184 (March 9, 1957), 199–214.

Cater, Douglass. "Undergraduate Underground," REPORTER, 10 (March 2, 1954), 31–34.

Dickey, J. S. "Conscience and the Undergraduate," ATLANTIC, 195 (April, 1955), 31.

Emmanuel, Pierre. "Americans as Students," ATLANTIC MONTHLY, 194 (August, 1954), 59–62.

Huitt, R. K. "Learning Politics at the Campus-Roots," NEW YORK TIMES MAGAZINE, (April 20, 1958), 42+.

Hymes, D. H. "Robin Hood Goes to College: Opposition to McCarthyism," NATION, 178 (June 5, 1954), 472.

"Is Apathy on the Way Out?" MADEMOISELLE, 51 (May, 1960), 134–135+.

McIntyre, William. "Student Movements," EDITORIAL RESEARCH REPORTS, 2 (December 11, 1957), 913–929.

Meier, Debbie. "Careerism on the Campus: Two Faces of Conformity," ANVIL, 7 (Spring–Summer, 1956), 9–12.

Meyer, Karl. "Students Speak Up On 'McCarthyism,'" PROGRESSIVE, 15 (October, 1951), 28–29.

Morris, W. W. "Miss Rebel on a Texas Campus," NATION, 182 (March 24, 1956), 232–234.

*Riesman, David. "The Found Generation," AMERICAN SCHOLAR, 25 (Autumn, 1956), 421–435.

*Schiffrin, Andre. "The Student Movement in the 1950s: A Reminiscence," RADICAL AMERICA, 2 (May–June, 1968), 26–40.

Seigel, Kalman. "Colleges Fighting Repressive Forces," NEW YORK TIMES, (May 11, 1953), 29.

Smitheman, Kent A. "Students Are Waking Up," NATION, 177 (August 22, 1952), 140.

Webster, James. "A New Road for Student Socialism," MONTHLY REVIEW, 3 (October, 1951), 175–180.

H.6. Student Left: 1960–1970

*Aitken, Jonathan and Michael Beloff. A SHORT WALK ON THE CAMPUS. New York: Atheneum, 1966.

Albornoz, Orlando. ESTUDIANTES NORTE-AMERICANOS: PERFILES POLITICOS. Caracas: Instituto Societas, 1967.

Albornoz, Orlando, ed. ESTUDIANTES Y POLITICA EN LAS AMERICAS. Caracas: Instituto Societas, 1968.

Anderson, Albert and Bernice P. Biggs, eds. A FOCUS ON REBELLION. San Francisco: Chandler Publishing, 1962.

*Astin, Alexander. CAMPUS UNREST, 1969–1970. Washington, D.C.: American Council on Education, 1970.

THE ATLANTIC, the Editors of. THE TROUBLED CAMPUS. Boston: Little Brown, 1966.

*Becker, Howard, ed. CAMPUS POWER STRUGGLE. Chicago: Aldine, 1970.

*Bell, Daniel and Irving Kristol, eds. CONFRONTATION: THE STUDENT REBELLION AND THE MULTIVERSITY. New York: Basic Books, 1969.

Bernstein, Saul. ALTERNATIVES TO VIOLENCE; ALIENATED YOUTH AND RIOTS, RACE, AND POVERTY. New York: Association Press, 1967.

Carling, Francis. MOVE OVER: STUDENTS, POLITICS, RELIGION. New York: Sheed and Ward, 1969.

Coblentz, Stanton Arthur. THE MILITANT DISSENTERS. South Brunswick: A. S. Barnes, 1970.

Eckstein, George G. USA: DIE NEUE LINKE AM ENDE? Munich: C. Hanser, 1970.

*Ehrenreich, Barbara and John Ehrenreich. LONG MARCH, SHORT SPRING: THE STUDENT UPRISING AT HOME AND ABROAD. New York: Monthly Review Press, 1969.

Fernandez, Benedict J. IN OPPOSITION: IMAGES OF AMERICAN DISSENT IN THE SIXTIES. New York: Da Capo Press, 1968.

Franklin, Bruce, ed. FROM THE MOVEMENT TOWARD REVOLUTION. New York: Van Nostrand Reinhold, 1971.

*Friedman, Michael, ed. THE NEW LEFT OF THE SIXTIES. Berkeley, California: Independent Socialist Press, 1972.

Gaddy, D. THE SCOPE OF ORGANIZED STUDENT PROTEST IN JUNIOR COLLEGES. Washington, D.C.: American Association of Junior Colleges, 1970.

Gish, Arthur G. THE NEW LEFT AND CHRISTIAN RADICALISM. Grand Rapids, Michigan: Eerdmans, 1970.

Gitlin, Todd. STUDENT POLITICAL ACTION: THE VIEW OF A PARTICIPANT. Chicago: Students for a Democratic Society, 1965.

Hanff, Helene. THE MOVERS AND SHAKERS: THE YOUNG ACTIVISTS OF THE SIXTIES. New York: S. G. Phillips, 1970.

*Horowitz, David. STUDENT. New York: Ballantine Books, 1962.

*Jacobs, Paul and Saul Landau. THE NEW RADICALS. New York: Vintage Books, 1966.

Levinson, Sandra and Carol Brightman, eds. VENCEREMOS BRIGADE. New York: Simon and Schuster, 1971.

Long, Durward. THE IMPACT OF ACTIVIST STUDENTS IN CHANGING THE GOVERNANCE AND CULTURE OF THE CAMPUS. Washington, D.C.: American Association for Higher Education, 1970.

Luce, Philip Abbott. THE NEW LEFT. New York: David McKay, 1966.

Mungo, Raymond. FAMOUS LONG AGO: MY LIFE AND HARD TIMES WITH LIBERATION NEWS SERVICE. Boston: Beacon Press, 1970.

THE NEW STUDENT LEFT. Washington, D.C.: The Free Society Association, 1965.

Newfield, Jack. BREAD AND ROSES TOO: REPORTING ABOUT AMERICA. New York: Dutton, 1971.

*Newfield, Jack. A PROPHETIC MINORITY. New York: New American Library, 1966.

*O'Brien, J. HISTORY OF THE NEW LEFT, 1960–1968. Boston: New England Free Press, 1969.

*Peterson, Richard E. THE SCOPE OF STUDENT PROTEST IN 1964–1965. Princeton, New Jersey: Educational Testing Service, 1966.

Rappaport, Margaret Mary. "Perspectives on University Student Activism in America: 1960–1970." Unpublished Ph.D. dissertation, University of Colorado, 1971.

Richmond, Al. CAMPUS REBELS. San Francisco: Pacific Publishing Foundation, 1960.

RIGHT ON! A DOCUMENTARY OF STUDENT PROTEST. New York: Bantam Books, 1970.

Simon, Morris, ed. A WORLD IN TRANSITION: STUDENTS IN ACTION. Philadelphia, Pennsylvania: U.S. National Student Association, 1961.

*Spender, Stephen. THE YEAR OF THE YOUNG REBELS. New York: Random House, 1970.

Stolz, Matthew F. POLITICS OF THE NEW LEFT. Beverly Hills, California: Glencoe Press, 1971.

*Teodori, M., ed. THE NEW LEFT: A DOCUMENTARY HISTORY. New York: Bobbs-Merrill, 1970.

U.S. Congress. Senate. Committee of the Judiciary. Subcommittee to Investigate the Administration of the Internal Security Act and Other Internal Security Laws. COMMUNIST APPEAL TO YOUTH AIDED BY NEW ORGANIZATIONS. 87th Congress. 1st Session. Washington, D.C.: Government Printing Office, 1961.

U.S. Congress. Senate. Committee on the Judiciary. Subcommittee to Investigate the Administration of the Internal Security Act and Other Internal Security Laws. COMMUNIST YOUTH PROGRAM HEARINGS. 89th Congress. 1st Session. Washington, D.C.: Government Printing Office, 1965.

U.S. Congress. Senate. Committee on the Judiciary. Subcommittee to Investigate the Administration of the Internal Security Act and Other Internal Security Laws. COMMUNIST YOUTH PROGRAM. REPORT. 89th Congress. 2nd Session. Washington, D.C.: Government Printing Office, 1966.

U.S. Congress. Senate. Committee on the Judiciary. Subcommittee to Investigate the Administration of the Internal Security Laws. EXTENT OF SUBVERSION IN CAMPUS DISORDERS. Washington,D.C.: Government Printing Office, 1970.

U.S. Congress. Senate. Committee on the Judiciary. Hearing before the Subcommittee to Investigate the Administration of the Internal Security Act and Other Internal Security Laws. FAIR PLAY FOR CUBA COMMITTEE. 87th Congress. 1st Session. Washington, D.C.: Government Printing Office, 1961.

214

U.S. Federal Bureau of Investigation. COMMUNIST TARGET: YOUTH. COMMUNIST INFILTRATION AND AGITATION TACTICS. A report by J. Edgar Hoover, director, illustrating Communist strategy and tactics in the rioting which occurred during the House Committee on Un-American Activities hearings, San Francisco, May 12–14, 1960. Washington, D.C.: Government Printing Office, 1960.

*Urban Research Corporation. STUDENT PROTESTS, 1969: SUMMARY. Chicago: Urban Research Corporation, 1970.

van Wolferen, Karel. STUDENT REVOLUTIONARIES OF THE SIXTIES. The Hague: Interdoc, 1971.

Albuquerque Youth Club. "The Communist New Left," POLITICAL AFFAIRS, 45 (June, 1966), 75–80.

Altbach, Philip G. "Is There a Student Movement?" MOTIVE, 24 (November, 1963), 30–34.

Altbach, Philip G. "The Quiet Campus," NEW LEADER, 46 (August 5, 1963), 12–15.

*"The American Revolution, 1969," ROLLING STONE, Special Issue (April 5, 1969), 1–20.

"The American Student, 1963," FELLOWSHIP, 29 (November 1, 1963), 5, 9, 13, 17+.

Armstrong, Richard. "The Explosive Revival of the Far Left," SATURDAY EVENING POST, 238 (May 8, 1965), 27–32, 34, 39.

Aronson, R. and J. Cowley. "The New Left in the United States," in R. Milliband and J. Saville, eds. THE SOCIALIST REGISTER, 1967. London: Merlin Press, 1967, 73–90.

Astin, Alexander. "Campus Disruption, 1968–1969: an Analysis of Causal Factors," in F. F. Korten, S. W. Cook, and J. I. Lacey, eds. PSYCHOLOGY AND THE PROBLEMS OF SOCIETY. Washington, D.C.: American Psychological Association, 1970, 377–387.

Astin, Alexander. "New Evidence on Campus Unrest, 1969–1970," EDUCATIONAL RECORD, 52 (Winter, 1971), 41–46.

*Bayer, A. E. and A. W. Astin. "Campus Disruption During 1968–1969," AMERICAN COUNCIL ON EDUCATION RESEARCH REPORTS, 4 (No. 3, 1969), 46 pp.

Blumberg, Leonard. "American Student Dissent in the Mid-Sixties," in Ronald E. Barnes, et al, eds. THE AIM OF HIGHER EDUCATION: SOCIAL ADJUSTMENT OR HUMAN LIBERATION? St. Louis: United Campus Christian Fellowship, 1966, 16–23.

Braden, Anne. "The Student Revolt, 1960–1961," MONTHLY REVIEW, 17 (July–August, 1965), 24–34.

Brochier, Jean-Jacques and Bernd Oelgart. "U.S.A.," in Jean-Jacques Brochier and Bernd Oelgart. L'INTERNATIONALE ETUDIANTE. Paris: Julliard, 1968, 233–252.

"Campus Causes: '62: Integration and Survival," NATION, 194 (May 19, 1962), 431–446.

"Campus Mood: Quiet So Far: Student Photographers and Writers Illuminate Their Own Scene," LIFE, 67 (December 12, 1969), 40–46.

"Campus Rebels: Who, Why, What?" NEWSWEEK, 72 (September 30, 1968), 63–68.

"Campus Report No. 41: Rebels With a Hundred Causes," NATION, 192 (May 27, 1961), 451–460+.

"Class of '69: Top Students Protest Right Through Commencement: With Answers from Their Elders," LIFE, 66 (June 20, 1969), 28–33.

Cohen, Marshall. "The New Left As an American Opposition Group: Its History and Prospects for the Future," ACTIVIST, 10 (Spring, 1970), 7–11+.

"Continuing Revolt on Campus," URBAN CRISIS MONITOR, 3 (March 27, 1970), 16–43.

Corry, John. "Spokesman for the New Left," NEW YORK TIMES MAGAZINE, (January 23, 1966), 12–13.

"Cynical Idealists of '68," TIME, 91 (June 7, 1968), 78–83.

Davidson, Carl. "Campaigning on the Campus," in A. Cockburn and R. Blackburn, eds. STUDENT POWER. Baltimore, Maryland: Penguin, 1969, 327–366.

Davis, Rennard C. and Bruce Payne. "Weekend at Oberlin," NATION, 194 (May 19, 1962), 431–432.

Diamond, E. "Class of '69: the Violent Years," NEWSWEEK, 73 (June 23, 1969), 68–73.

Dickinson, William B., jr. "Campus Unrest," EDITORIAL RESEARCH REPORTS, 1 (May 19, 1965), 363–379.

"Discontent and Suppression: a National View," COLLEGE AND UNIVERSITY BUSINESS. 45 (August, 1968), 37–39.

"Documents on Origins and Themes [of the New Left]," in Paul Jacobs and Saul Landau, eds. THE NEW RADICALS. New York: Vintage, 1966, 89–114.

"Documents on 'the Leftovers'—Progressive Labor Party, DuBois Clubs, Young Socialist Alliance, and the Young People's Socialist League," in Paul Jacobs and Saul Landau, eds. THE NEW RADICALS. New York: Vintage, 1966, 181–204.

Dunbar, E., ed. "Campus Mood, Spring '68: Panel Discussions," LOOK, 32 (April 2, 1968), 23–27.

Eddy, Edward. "Scratching the Surface: Campus Unrest in 1968," in W. Brickman and S. Lehrer, eds. CONFLICT AND CHANGE ON THE CAMPUS: THE RESPONSE TO THE STUDENT HYPERACTIVISM. New York: School & Society Books, 1970, 120–125.

Eisen, Jonathan and David Steinberg. "The Student Revolt Against Liberalism," THE ANNALS OF THE AMERICAN ACADEMY OF POLITICAL AND SOCIAL SCIENCE, 382 (March, 1969), 83–94.

Erickson, F. Martin. "Turbulence Among Students: 1964," in G. K. Smith, ed. 1945–1970: TWENTY-FIVE YEARS. San Francisco: Jossey-Bass, 1970, 184–189.

*Feuer, Lewis. "The Student Left in the USA," SURVEY, No. 62 (January, 1967), 90–103.

Feuer, Lewis. "Youth in the Sixties," NEW LEADER, 44 (March 6, 1961), 18–22.

Gitlin, Todd. "The Left in Search of Itself," CHRISTIAN CENTURY, 84 (September 27, 1967), 1230–1236.

Glazer, Nathan. "Student Protest in the U.S.," ECONOMIC AND POLITICAL WEEKLY (Bombay), (March 25, 1967), 601–605.

*Glazer, Penina M. "The New Left," JOURNAL OF HIGHER EDUCATION, 38 (March, 1967), 119–130.

Goodman, W. "They March to Different Drummers," NEW YORK TIMES MAGAZINE, (June 26, 1966), 7+.

Hakman, Nathan. "Old and New Left Activity in the Legal Order: an Interpretation," JOURNAL OF SOCIAL FORCES, 27 (1971), 105–122.

Harrington, Michael. "The New Radicals," COMMONWEAL, 82 (September 3, 1965), 623–627.

Harris, Janet. "America, 1969," in Janet Harris, ed. STUDENTS IN REVOLT. New York: McGraw-Hill, 1970, 154–169.

Heckscher, C. "Children's Crusade: After-the-Battle: Report from Senator McCarthy's Army," COMMONWEAL, 89 (October 4, 1968), 12–14.

Heisler, Bob. "The New Left Undergoing Change," POLITICAL AFFAIRS, 45 (March, 1966), 46–48.

*Howe, Irving. "New Styles in Leftism," DISSENT, 12 (Summer, 1965), 295–323.

"Incredible '68: Year of Dissent," LIFE, 66 (January 10, 1969), 38–45.

Joye, Harlan. "Dixie's New Left," TRANSACTION, 7 (September, 1970), 50–56, 60–62.

Katz, Joseph. "The Activist Revolution of 1964," in Joseph Katz, et al. NO TIME FOR YOUTH. (San Francisco: Jossey-Bass, 1968), 386–415.

*Keniston, Kenneth. "American Students and the 'Political Revival,' " AMERICAN SCHOLAR, 32 (Winter, 1962–1963), 40–65.

Kopkind, Andrew. "Introduction: The Young Radicals," in Andrew Kopkind, ed. THOUGHT OF THE YOUNG RADICALS. New York: The New Republic, 1966, 1–10.

*Kopkind, Andrew. "The Sixties and the Movement," RAMPARTS, 11 (February, 1973), 29–35.

*Kopkind, Andrew. "Radicals on the March," NEW REPUBLIC, 153 (December 11, 1965), 15–18.

Kopkind, Andrew. "They'd Rather Be Left," NEW YORK REVIEW OF BOOKS, 9 (September 28, 1967), 3–5.

Lens, Sidney. "The New Left and the Establishment," LIBERATION, 10 (September, 1965), 7–11.

Lowman, Dean. "The New Student Left," JOURNAL OF NATIONAL ASSOCIATION OF WOMEN DEANS AND COUNSELORS, 31 (Winter, 1968), 57–63.

Lynd, Staughton. "The Movement: A New Beginning," LIBERATION, 14 (May, 1969), 6–20.

Lynd, Staughton. "Towards a History of the New Left," in P. Long, ed. THE NEW LEFT, Boston: Porter Sargent, 1969, 1–14.

McKernan, L. F., ed. "Five College Students Speak Out: Questions and Answers," CATHOLIC WORLD, 204 (January, 1967), 198–204.

Miller, William G. "New Brunswick: Community Action Project,"

Miller, William G. "New Brunswick: Community Action Project," STUDIES ON THE LEFT, 5 (Spring, 1965), 74–78.

Mitzman, Arthur. "The Campus Radical in 1960," DISSENT, 7 (Spring, 1960), 142–148.

"The New Radicals," JOHNS HOPKINS MAGAZINE, 17 (October, 1965), Whole Issue.

"New Voices on Campus," MADEMOISELLE, 61 (August, 1965), 302+.

Newfield, J. A. "The Student Left: Idealism and Action," NATION, 201 (November 8, 1965), 330–333.

Newfield, J. A. "The Student Left: Revolt Without Dogma," NATION, 200 (May 10, 1965), 491–495.

Newman, David. "Return of the Campus Rebel," ESQUIRE, 56 (September, 1961), 14–28.

Obear, Frederick W. "Student Activism in the Sixties," in Julian Foster and Durward Long, eds. PROTEST! STUDENT ACTIVISM IN AMERICA. New York: William Morrow, 1970, 11–26.

O'Brien, David J. "Power to the Students," COMMONWEAL, 91 (October 3, 1969), 15–21.

*O'Brien, J. P. "Development of the New Left: Excerpts from the Development of the New Left in the United States, 1960–1965," ANNALS OF THE AMERICAN ACADEMY OF POLITICAL AND SOCIAL SCIENCE. 395 (May, 1971), 15–25.

O'Brien, J. P. "A History of the New Left, 1960–1968," RADICAL AMERICA, 2 (May–June, September–October, and November–December, 1968), 1–25, 1–22, and 38–43.

*O'Brien, J. P. "The New Left's Early Years," RADICAL AMERICA, 2 (May–June, 1968), 1–25.

*Oglesby, Carl. "Notes on a Decade Ready for the Dustbin," LIBERATION, 14 (August–September, 1969), 5–19.

Oglesby, Carl. "Where is the New Left Going?" THE CENTER MAGAZINE, 3 (December, 1970), 33–34.

Peterson, Richard E. "Organized Student Protest in 1964–1965," JOURNAL OF THE NATIONAL ASSOCIATION OF WOMEN DEANS AND COUNSELORS, 30 (Winter, 1967), 50–56.

*Peterson, Richard E. "The Scope of Organized Student Protest," in Julian Foster and Durward Long, eds. PROTEST! STUDENT ACTIVISM IN AMERICA. New York: William Morrow, 1970, 59–80.

*Peterson, Richard E. "The Student Left in American Higher Education," DAEDALUS, 97 (Winter, 1968), 293–317.

Peterson, Richard E. "The Student Protest Movement: Some Facts, Interpretations, and a Plea," in F. F. Korten, S. W. Cook and J. I. Lacey, eds. PSYCHOLOGY AND THE PROBLEMS OF SOCIETY. Washington, D.C.: American Psychological Association, 1970, 388–394.

218

*Petras, James. "The 'New Left' in the United States," INTERNATIONAL SOCIALIST JOURNAL, 2 (September–December, 1965), 654–666.

Powledge, Fred. "New Fraternity: Student and Crypto-Student Organizations," ESQUIRE, 64 (September, 1965), 88–89+.

President's Commission on Campus Unrest. "Student Protest in the 1960's," in REPORT OF THE PRESIDENT'S COMMISSION ON CAMPUS UNREST. New York: Arno Press, 1970, 17–49.

"Rebels Without Causes," FELLOWSHIP. 30 (November, 1964), 2–8.

"The Revolt on the Campus," in P. Brandes, and T. Walwik, eds. A RESEARCH MANUAL FOR THE PERFORMANCE COURSE IN SPEECH, New York: Harper and Row, 1967, 271–340.

"Revolt Without Dogma," MOTIVE, 26 (October, 1965), 20–24.

Rexroth, Kenneth. "Students Take Over," NATION, 191 (July 2, 1960), 4–9.

Rieff, Philip. "The Mirage of College Politics," HARPERS, 233 (October, 1961), 156–163.

Roberts, Steven V. "The Children's Crusade–What Now?" CHANGE, 1 (January–February, 1969), 19–22.

Roberts, S. and C. McWilliams, jr. "Student Leaders and Campus Apathy," NATION, 193 (September 16, 1961), 155–157.

Rubin, Jerry. "An Emergency Letter to My Brothers and Sisters in the Movement," in Patrick Gleeson, ed. ESSAYS ON THE STUDENT MOVEMENT. Columbus, Ohio: Charles-Merrill, 1970, 59–69.

Shoben, E. Joseph, jr., Philip Werdell, and Durward Long, "Radical Student Organizations," in Julian Foster and Durward Long, eds. PROTEST! STUDENT ACTIVISM IN AMERICA. New York: William Morrow, 1970, 202–222.

Short, Ruth Ann. "The Student Movement Moves," MOTIVE, 22 (November 19, 1962), 8–9.

Smith, R. B. "Campus Protests and the Vietnam War," in J. F. Short and M. Wolfgang, eds. COLLECTIVE VIOLENCE. Chicago: Aldine, 1970, 157–167.

"Special Issue on Student Protests," URBAN CRISIS MONITOR, 3 (June 5, 1970), 2–54.

Strickland, William. "The New Student Left," FREEDOMWAYS, 6 (Fall, 1966), 569–572.

"The Student Left: Idealism and Action," NATION, 201 (November, 1965), 330–333.

"Student Protest," NEWSWEEK, 71 (May 6, 1968), 40–53.

Taylor, Harold. "American Idealism, 1965," SATURDAY REVIEW, 48 (June 26, 1965), 14–17.

Troutman, William F., jr. "The New Student Left: Liberal or Radical? The Case of the Southern Student Organizing Committee," in Hans H. Indorf, ed. POLITICS 1970. Greenville, North Carolina: Political Science Department, East Carolina University, 1970, 83–102.

Wakefield, Dan. "Challenge on the Campus," NATION, 190 (March 26, 1960), 268–269+.

Wallace, Rue, Warren Friedman and Linda Friedman. "The Movement at Work: The Community College Scene," LIBERATION, 14 (October, 1969), 34–37.

"War on Campus," NATION, 205 (December 18, 1967), 645–660.

Werthman, Carl. "The Student Organization of Protest," NEW UNIVERSITY THOUGHT, 1 (Fall, 1960), 15–19.

Winter, David B. and Frederick A. Wiecking. "The New Puritans: Achievement and Power Motives of New Left Radicals," BEHAVIORAL SCIENCE, 16 (November, 1971), 523–530.

Wolfe, Alan. "A Summer Look at the Spring Events," AMERICAN ASSOCIATION OF UNIVERSITY PROFESSORS BULLETIN, 56 (September, 1970), 269–272.

Wynn, David. "Should College Students Demonstrate?" THE INTERCOLLEGIAN, 81 (January–February, 1964), 12–15.

H.7. Student Left: 1970–

THE STATE OF THE STUDENT MOVEMENT–1970. New York: League for Industrial Democracy, 1970.

Adler, Judith. "Far From the Center: Political Activism at a Provincial College," LIBERATION, 15 (January, 1971), 40–46.

"Battle for the Democratic Party," TIME, 100 (July 17, 1972), 10–16.

*Bayer, Alan and Alexander Astin. "Campus Unrest, 1970–1971: Was it Really All That Quiet?" EDUCATIONAL RECORD, 52 (Fall, 1971), 301–313.

Beggs, Daniel C. and Henry A. Copeland. "The Student and Politics: 1970," UNIVERSITY INDEX, (July 16, 1970).

Berki, R. N. "Marcuse and the Crisis of the New Radicalism: From Politics to Religion?" JOURNAL OF POLITICS, 34 (February, 1972), 56–92.

"Blockade News Stirs Violence, Fear, and Inertia," ROLLING STONE, No. 110 (June 8, 1972), 25–28.

Blume, R. A. "Quiet on the Campus," TODAY'S EDUCATION, 61 (May, 1972), 38–40+.

Buhle, Paul. "The Eclipse of the New Left: Some Notes," RADICAL AMERICA, 6 (July–August, 1972), 1–10.

"Campus Turns From Violence," U.S. NEWS AND WORLD REPORT, 71 (October 25, 1971), 40–44.

"College-town Worry: Will 18 to 21 Voters Take Over?" U.S. NEWS AND WORLD REPORT, 71 (September 6, 1971), 38–41.

Dunlap, Riley and Richard Gale. "Politics and Ecology: A Political Profile of Student Eco-Activists," YOUTH AND SOCIETY, 3 (June, 1972), 379–398.

*Flacks, Richard. "The New Left and American Politics After Ten Years," JOURNAL OF SOCIAL FORCES, 27 (1971), 21–34.

Gitlin, Todd. "Towards a New Left," PARTISAN REVIEW, 39 (Summer, 1972), 454–461.

Greely, Andrew M. "The End of the Movement," CHANGE, 4 (April, 1972), 42–47.

Greer, E. "Radicals Sober Up; the New American Movement," NATION, 214 (January 17, 1972), 83–86.

Leggett, J. "Metamorphosis of the Campus Radical," NEW YORK TIMES MAGAZINE, (January 30, 1972), 14–17+.

Murphy, William T., jr. "Student Power in the 1970 Elections: A Preliminary Assessment," PS, 4, (1971), 27–32.

Nachman, L. D. "Movement Seeks a Mass: New Left Crisis," NATION, 212 (January 11, 1971), 39–45.

Neuhaus, R. "Loneliness of the Long Distance Radical," CHRISTIAN CENTURY, 89 (April 26, 1972), 477–481.

Rader, D. "New Revolutionaries," PARTISAN REVIEW, 37 (No. 1, 1970), 59–73.

Schick, E. B. "Campus Ferment and Tranquility 1970–1971," SCHOOL AND SOCIETY, 100 (February, 1972), 93–95.

*"Special Report: Student Activism, 1972," CHRONICLE OF HIGHER EDUCATION, 6 (March 13, 1972), 1–8.

Warren, D. L. "State of Quiet Calamity: Misunderstanding of Campus Situation," COMMONWEAL, 95 (March 3, 1972), 519–523.

H.8. Students for a Democratic Society (S.D.S.)

*Adelson, Alan. S.D.S. New York: Charles Scribner's Sons, 1972.

Davidson, Carl. THE NEW RADICALS IN THE MULTIVERSITY. Chicago: Students for a Democratic Society, 1968.

Haber, R. Alan. STUDENTS AND LABOR. Chicago: Students for a Democratic Society, 1962.

Hayden, Tom. STUDENT SOCIAL ACTION. Chicago: Students for a Democratic Society, 1965.

Hayden, Tom and Carl Wittman. AN INTERRACIAL MOVEMENT OF THE POOR? New York: Students for a Democratic Society, 1965.

Illinois. Crime Investigating Commission. REPORT ON THE SDS RIOTS. OCTOBER 8–11, 1969. CHICAGO, ILLINOIS TO THE ILLINOIS GENERAL ASSEMBLY. Chicago: Illinois Crime Investigating Commission, 1970.

Jacobson, Tom. UNIONS AND THE WORKING STUDENT. New York: Students for a Democratic Society, 1963.

Jones, Richard. THE NEW LEFT: STUDENTS FOR A DEMOCRATIC SOCIETY. Washington, D.C.: U.S. Library of Congress, Legislative Reference Service, 1969.

Louisiana. Legislature. Joint Committee on Un-American Activities. STUDENTS FOR A DEMOCRATIC SOCIETY AND THE NEW LEFT. THEIR DANGER TO THE EDUCATIONAL INSTITUTIONS OF THE STATE OF LOUISIANA. Baton Rouge, Louisiana, 1969.

Luce, P. A. YES S.C., THERE REALLY IS AN SDS. Washington, D.C.: Young Americans for Freedom, n.d.

Pope, Richard. DEMOCRACY AND THE UNIVERSITY. Chicago: Students for a Democratic Society, 1965.

Potter, Paul. THE INTELLECTUAL AS AN AGENT OF SOCIAL CHANGE. Chicago: Students for a Democratic Society, 1963.

Potter, Paul. THE NEW RADICAL ENCOUNTERS WITH THE UNIVERSITY. Chicago: Students for a Democratic Society, n.d.

Students for a Democratic Society. AMERICA AND THE NEW ERA. New York: Students for a Democratic Society, 1963.

*Students for a Democratic Society. THE PORT HURON STATEMENT. New York: Students for a Democratic Society, 1964.

U.S. Congress. House. Committee on Internal Security. INVESTIGATION OF STUDENTS FOR A DEMOCRATIC SOCIETY. HEARINGS. 91st Congress. 1st Session. Washington, D.C.: Government Printing Office, 1969.

Weissman, Stephen and Doug Tuthill. FREEDOM AND THE UNIVERSITY. Chicago: Students for a Democratic Society, 1966.

*Blumenthal, Richard. "S.D.S.: Protest is not Enough," NATION, 204 (May 22, 1967), 656–660.

Bolduc, Charlie. "A Brief History of SDS and the Ideology of the New Left," YOUNG SOCIALIST, 12 (May, 1969), 3–7.

*Brooks, T. R. "Metamorphosis in SDS: The New Left is Showing Its Age," NEW YORK TIMES MAGAZINE, (June 15, 1969), 14+.

Calvert, Greg. "Radical Consciousness and the Liberal Mentality," ACTIVIST, 8 (Fall, 1967), 5–6, 33.

"Chicago: JOIN Project," STUDIES ON THE LEFT, 5 (Summer, 1965), 107–125.

*Clark, George. "Students for a Democratic Society," OUR GENERATION, 3 (May, 1966), 30–39.

*"Documents on Students for a Democratic Society," in Paul Jacobs and Saul Landau, eds. THE NEW RADICALS, New York: Vintage, 1966, 149–180.

*"Documents: the Beginning of the Movement: Community Organization," in Massimo Teodori, ed. THE NEW LEFT: A DOCUMENTARY HISTORY. Indianapolis, Indiana: Bobbs-Merrill, 1969, 128–149.

Dunbar, E. "Vanguard of the Campus Revolt: Students for a Democratic Society," LOOK, 32 (October 1, 1968), 23–29.

Eisen, Jonathan. "Heads You Win, Tails We Lost: A Report on the SDS Convention," ACTIVIST, 6 (March, 1966), 6–8.

Feldman, Paul. "New Winds on the Campus: A Report on the SDS National Conference," DISSENT, 13 (March–April, 1966), 183–189.

Flacks, Richard. "Organizing the Unemployed: The Chicago Project," in D. Hale and M. Cohen, eds. THE NEW STUDENT LEFT. Boston: Beacon Press, 1965, 137–152.

Friedman, Sam and Mike Goldfield. "SDS: Ann Arbor Convention," OUR GENERATION, 5 (September, 1967), 106–109.

*Fruchter, Norm. "SDS: In and Out of Context," LIBERATION, 16 (February, 1972), 19–33.

Goldstein, Richard. "The Weapon of Youth," NEW YORK, 1 (October 14, 1968), 28–31.

Hobbs, Albert H. "The SDS Trip: From Vision to Ego Shriek," INTERCOLLEGIATE REVIEW, 5 (Spring, 1969), 147–157.

Hodes, Jeffery. "New Left in Disarray," NEW LEADER, 50 (September 11, 1967), 6–8.

Hoover, John Edgar. "The SDS and the High Schools," PTA MAGAZINE, 64 (January, 1970), 2–5, and 64 (February, 1970), 8–9.

"How SDS will Stir Up Workers," NATION'S BUSINESS, 57 (July, 1969), 74–79.

*Howe, Irving. "New Styles in 'Leftism,' " DISSENT, 12 (Summer, 1965), 295–323.

*Jacobs, James. "SDS: Between Reform and Revolution," NATION, 206 (June 10, 1968), 753–756.

Kahn, Roger. "Collapse of SDS," ESQUIRE, 72 (October, 1969), 140–144.

Kazin, Michael. "Some Notes on SDS," AMERICAN SCHOLAR, 38 (Autumn, 1969), 644–655.

*Kelman, Steven. "S.D.S.: Troubled Voice of the New Left," NEW LEADER, 47 (September 27, 1965), 8–14.

Kissinger, C. Clark. "Starting in '60: or From SLID to Resistance," NEW LEFT NOTES, (June 10, 1968, June 24, 1968, July 8, 1968).

Kopkind, Andrew. "Of, By, and For the Poor: The New Generation of Student Organizers," NEW REPUBLIC, 152 (June 19, 1965), 15–19.

Max, Steve. "The 1965 SDS Convention: From Port Huron to Maplehurst," VIEWPOINT, 1 (Summer, 1965).

Methvin, E. H. "SDS: Engineers of Campus Chaos," READER'S DIGEST, 93 (October, 1968), 103–108.

Milstein, Thomas. " 'New' vs. 'Left' in the SDS," DISSENT, 15 (September–October, 1968), 447–451.

Nachman, L. D. "Obituary for SDS," NATION, 209 (November 24, 1969), 558–561.

Naison, Mark. "In Defense of SDS," LIBERATION, 14 (August–September, 1969), 31–34.

*Newfield, Jack. "SDS: From Port Huron to La Chinoise," EVERGREEN REVIEW, No. 73 (December, 1969), 15–17, 58–60.

"One, Two, Three . . . Many SDS's: Symposium," RAMPARTS, 8 (September, 1969), 6+.

Parker, Michael. "SDS: Copping Out of American Life," NEW POLITICS, 7 (Fall, 1968), 45–50.

Potter, Paul and Todd Gitlin. "A Report from Students for a Democratic Society," DISSENT, 12 (Spring, 1965), 234–237.

Rader, Dotson. "Princeton Weekend With the SDS," NEW REPUBLIC, 157 (December 9, 1967), 14–16.

Reimer, Paula. "SDS: an Experiment in Pragmatism Fails," NEW POLITICS, 7 (Fall, 1968), 51–57.

Report from the Editors. "The SDS March on Washington," STUDIES ON THE LEFT, 5 (Spring, 1965), 61–70.

"Report on Students for a Democratic Society," OUR GENERATION, 4 (November, 1966), 69–72.

Romm, Ethel. "Blueprint for Revolution," NEW YORK, 1 (October 14, 1968), 20–24.

Rosenbaum, R. "Run, Tommy, Run!" ESQUIRE, 76 (July, 1971), 51–58+.

*Rothstein, R. "ERAP: Revolution of the Organizers," RADICAL AMERICA. 2 (March–April, 1968), 1–18.

Rothstein, R. "Representative Democracy in SDS," LIBERATION, 16 (February, 1972), 10–18.

Rothstein, R. " A Short History of ERAP," OUR GENERATION, 3 (May, 1966), 30–39.

Rubenstein, J. "SDS Against the World," NEW YORK, 1 (October 14, 1968), 24–28.

Schulz, W. "Intelligence Report on Today's New Revolutionaries," READERS' DIGEST, 95 (October, 1969), 121–126.

SDS. "Agenda for a Generation," THE INTERCOLLEGIAN, 80 (October–November, 1962), 9–11.

Sedgwich, Peter. "The Two New Lefts," INTERNATIONAL SOCIALISM, 17 (Summer, 1964), 15–23.

Shoben, E. J., jr. and P. R. Werdell. "SDS and SNCC: Profiles of Two Student Organizations," SCHOOL AND SOCIETY, 96 (October 26, 1968), 365–372.

Smith, Jack A. "Where the Revolution Is At: A Report on the SDS Convention," GUARDIAN, 20 (June 22, 1968), 1, 4–5.

Staff Statement. "Radical Education Project (1966)," in John and Susan Erlich, eds. STUDENT POWER, PARTICIPATION AND REVOLUTION. New York: Association Press, 1970, 152–164.

Three Princeton SDS Members. "Potentialities and Limitations of the Student Movement: 1967–1968," in Immanuel Wallerstein and Paul Starr, eds. THE UNIVERSITY CRISIS READER, II. New York: Random House, 1971, 142–147.

Weinberg, Jack and Jack Gerson. "SDS and the Movement," in M. Friedman, ed., THE NEW LEFT OF THE SIXTIES. Berkeley, California: Independent Socialist Press, 1972, 280–288.

Wiley, Peter. "Hazard: Socialism and Community Organizing," RADICAL AMERICA, 2 (January–February, 1968), 25–37.

H.9. "Weatherman"

Fettamen, Ann. TRASHING. San Francisco: Straight Arrow, 1970.

*Jacobs, Harold, ed. WEATHERMAN. Berkeley, California: Ramparts Press, 1971.

Nuttall, Jeff. BOMB CULTURE. New York: Dial Press, 1969.

OUTLAWS OF AMERIKA: COMMUNIQUES FROM THE WEATHER UNDERGROUND. New York: Liberated Guardian Collective, 1971.

224

*Ashley, Karen, *et al.* " 'You Don't Need a Weatherman to Know Which Way the Wind Blows' (1969)," in John and Susan Erlich, eds. STUDENT POWER, PARTICIPATION AND REVOLUTION. New York: Association Press, 1970, 194–200.

Fleming, K., ed. "We'll Blow Up the World: A Nineteen-Year Old U.S. Terrorist Tells His Story," NEWSWEEK, (October 12, 1970), 49–50+.

Greene, Wade. "The Militants Who Play With Dynamite," NEW YORK TIMES MAGAZINE, (October 25, 1970), 38–40+.

Hoover, J. E. "Morality for Violence; Study of New Left Extremism," CHRISTIANITY TODAY, 16 (April 28, 1972), 8–9+.

Howe, Irving. "Political Terrorism: Hysteria on the Left," NEW YORK TIMES MAGAZINE. (April 12, 1970), 25–27+.

"Ideological Struggle in the American Left," POLITICAL AFFAIRS, 42 (August, 1963), 1–18.

Kelman, Steven. "The Feud Among the Radicals," HARPERS, 232 (June, 1966), 67–72.

Kifner, J. "Vandals in the Mother Country," NEW YORK TIMES MAGAZINE, (January 4, 1970), 14–16+.

Klonsky, Mike. "Toward a Revolutionary Youth Movement," in Immanuel Wallerstein and Paul Starr, eds. THE UNIVERSITY CRISIS READER, II. New York: Random House, 1971, 216–222.

Klonsky, Mike *et al.* "Revolutionary Youth Movement II [RYM II] (1969)," in John and Susan Erlich, eds. STUDENT POWER, PARTICIPATION AND REVOLUTION. New York: Association Press, 1970, 188–194.

Mann, Eric. "The Shield Is Gone," THIS MAGAZINE IS ABOUT SCHOOLS, 5 (Winter, 1971), 7–28.

*Ono, Shin'ya. "You Do Need a Weatherman . . .," LEVIATHAN, 1 (December, 1969), 15–21.

"Revolutionaries: A Guide to Who They Are, What They Want," NEWSWEEK, 75 (May 11, 1970), 34–38.

SDS National Council. "Fight Racism: Build a Worker-Student Alliance; Smash Imperialism," in Immanuel Wallerstein, and Paul Starr, eds. THE UNIVERSITY CRISIS READER, II. New York: Random House, 1971, 221–226.

SDS National Council Resolution. "Toward a Revolutionary Youth Movement (1968)," in John and Susan Erlich, eds. STUDENT POWER, PARTICIPATION AND REVOLUTION. New York: Association Press, 1970, 188–193.

*"The Splintering of SDS," in I. Wallerstein and P. Starr, eds. THE UNIVERSITY CRISIS READER, II. New York: Random House, 1971, 257–320.

"Terrorism on Left," NEWSWEEK, 75 (March 23, 1970), 26–30.

Vinther, Peer. "The Reemergence of Stalin," YOUNG SOCIALIST, 12 (July–August, 1969), 3–7.

Weinstein, James. "Weatherman," SOCIALIST REVOLUTION, 1 (January–February, 1970), 1970, 129–143.

Worthy, W. "Bombs Blast a Message of Hate: With Interview with an Admitted Bomber," LIFE, 68 (March 27, 1970), 24–32 A.

H.10. Ideological Aspects of Radical Student Politics

Ali, Tariq, ed. THE NEW REVOLUTIONARIES: A HANDBOOK OF THE INTERNATIONAL RADICAL LEFT. New York: Morrow, 1969.

Bierman, Arthur Kalmer and James A. Gould, eds. PHILOSOPHY FOR A NEW GENERATION. New York: Macmillan, 1970.

Breines, Paul, ed. CRITICAL INTERRUPTIONS: NEW LEFT PERSPECTIVES ON HERBERT MARCUSE. New York: Herder and Herder, 1970.

Calvert, Greg and Carol Nieman. A DISRUPTED HISTORY: THE NEW LEFT AND THE NEW CAPITALISM. New York: Random House, 1971.

Cook, Terrence and P. Morgan, eds. PARTICIPATORY DEMOCRACY. San Francisco: Canfield Press, 1971.

Cranston, Maurice William, ed. THE NEW LEFT: SIX CRITICAL ESSAYS. New York: Library Press, 1971.

Davidson, Carl. TOWARD A STUDENT SYNDICALIST MOVEMENT. Chicago: Students for a Democratic Society, 1966.

*Farber, Jerry. THE STUDENT AS NIGGER. North Hollywood, California: Contact Books, 1969.

Gretton, John. STUDENTS AND WORKERS. London: Macdonald, 1969.

Hayden, Thomas. REBELLION AND REPRESSION: TESTIMONY BY THOMAS HAYDEN BEFORE THE NATIONAL COMMISSION ON THE CAUSES AND PREVENTION OF VIOLENCE AND THE HOUSE UN-AMERICAN ACTIVITIES COMMITTEE. New York: World, 1969.

Hoffman, Abbie. REVOLUTION FOR THE HELL OF IT. New York: Dial Press, 1968.

Leary, Timothy. POLITICS OF ECSTASY. New York: Putnam, 1968.

*Lothstein, Arthur, ed. "ALL WE ARE SAYING . . ." THE PHILOSOPHY OF THE NEW LEFT. New York: Putnam, 1970.

Mandel, Ernest. THE REVOLUTIONARY STUDENT MOVEMENT: THEORY AND PRACTICE. New York: Young Socialist Alliance, 1969.

*New Republic. THOUGHTS OF THE YOUNG RADICALS. Washington, D.C.: New Republic, 1966.

Oglesby, Carl, ed. THE NEW LEFT READER. New York: Grove, 1969.

Oglesby, Carl and Richard Schaull. CONTAINMENT AND CHANGE. New York: Macmillan, 1967.

Rubin, Jerry. DO IT! SCENARIOS OF THE REVOLUTION. New York: Simon and Schuster, 1970.

Rubin, Jerry. WE ARE EVERYWHERE. New York: Harper and Row, 1971.

Saltonstall, Stephen. TOWARD A STRATEGY OF DISRUPTION: STUDENTS AND SOCIETY. Santa Barbara: Center for the Study of Democratic Institutions, 1967.

Slate, William, ed. POWER TO THE PEOPLE: NEW LEFT WRITINGS. New York: Tower Publications, 1970.

W.E.B. DuBois Clubs of America. NOTES ON A CAMPUS PROGRAM.

San Francisco: W.E.B. DuBois Club, 1966.

Weiss, A. von. THE IDEOLOGICAL FOUNDATIONS OF THE NEW LEFT. Hague: Interdoc, 1968.

Abel, L. "Seven Heros of the New Left," NEW YORK TIMES MAGAZINE, (May 5, 1968), 30–31+.

Altbach, Philip G. "The Need for Leadership and Ideology," NEW UNIVERSITY THOUGHT, 2 (Autumn, 1961), 13–17.

Aronowitz, Stanley. "Does the United States Have a New Working Class?" in G. Fischer, ed. THE REVIVAL OF AMERICAN SOCIALISM. New York: Oxford University Press, 1971, 188–216.

*Birnbaum, N. "Making of a Vanguard," PARTISAN REVIEW, 36 (No. 2, 1969), 220–232.

Blackburn, Robin. "Revolutionary Theory: The New Left and Lenin," LEVIATHAN, 1 (October–November, 1969), 4–11.

Booth, Paul, Richard Rothstein, Staughton Lynd. "Make Love Not War," (3 editorials). LIBERATION, 10 (December, 1965), 23–25.

Breines, Paul. "From Guru to Spectre: Marcuse and the Implosion of the Movement," in Paul Breines, ed. CRITICAL INTERRUPTIONS. New York: Herder and Herder, 1970, 1–21.

Breines, Paul. "Marcuse and the New Left in America," in J. Habermas, ed. ANTWORTEN AUF HERBERT MARCUSE. Frankfurt am Main: Suhrkamp, 1968, 133–151.

Brooks, Thomas. "To the East of the Communist Party," NEW YORK TIMES MAGAZINE, (April 25, 1965), 9+.

Brownfeld, A. C. "Does the New Left Have a Political Philosophy?" SOUTH ATLANTIC QUARTERLY, 71 (Winter, 1972), 40–53.

Buckley, Neil. Participatory Democratic Centralism or . . .," THE MOVEMENT, 4 (May, 1968), 8–9, 13+.

Calvert, Greg. "A Left Wing Alternative," in Immanuel Wallerstein, and Paul Starr, eds. THE UNIVERSITY CRISIS READER, II. New York: Random House, 1971, 247–257.

Cammett, John. "Socialism and Participatory Democracy," in George Fischer, ed. THE REVIVAL OF AMERICAN SOCIALISM. New York: Oxford University Press, 1971, 41–62.

Chomsky, Noam. "Some Tasks for the New Left," LIBERATION, 14 (August–September, 1969), 38–43.

Christie, R., L. N. Friedman, and A. Ross. "The New Left and Its Ideology: an Exploratory Study," PROCEEDINGS OF THE 77TH ANNUAL CONVENTION OF THE AMERICAN PSYCHOLOGICAL ASSOCIATION. (1969), 293–294.

*Davidson, Carl. "Multiversity: Crucible of the New Working Class," in I. Wallerstein, and P. Starr, eds. THE UNIVERSITY CRISIS READER, 1. New York: Random House, 1971, 86–99.

Davidson, Carl. "Toward a Movement of Student Syndicalism," in Edward Schwartz, ed. STUDENT POWER, Washington, D.C.: U.S. National Student Association, 1969, 151–164.

*Denitch, Bogdan. "The New Left and the New Working Class," in J. David Colfax and Jack Roach, eds. RADICAL SOCIOLOGY, New York: Basic Books, 1971, 341–352.

*"Documents: New Left Methodology: Nonexclusionism, Participatory Democracy and Direct Action," in M. Teodori, ed. THE NEW LEFT: A DOCUMENTARY HISTORY. Indianapolis, Indiana: Bobbs-Merrill, 1969, 218–239.

*"Documents on 'Ideology, Communism and Coalition' [the New Left]," in Paul Jacobs and Saul Landau, eds. THE NEW RADICALS. New York: Vintage, 1966, 267–310.

*"Documents: Problems and Perspectives: Alternative Structures," in M. Teodori, ed. THE NEW LEFT: A DOCUMENTARY HISTORY. Indianapolis, Indiana: Bobbs-Merrill, 1969, 385–411.

*"Documents: Problems and Perspectives: In Search of a Class Analysis," in M. Teodori, ed. THE NEW LEFT: A DOCUMENTARY HISTORY. Indianapolis, Indiana: Bobbs-Merrill, 1969, 412–437.

*"Documents: Problems and Perspectives: New Politics," in M. Teodori, ed. THE NEW LEFT: A DOCUMENTARY HISTORY. Indianapolis, Indiana: Bobbs-Merrill, 1969, 438–450.

*"Documents: Problems and Perspectives: New Society," in M. Teodori, ed. THE NEW LEFT: A DOCUMENTARY HISTORY. Indianapolis, Indiana: Bobbs-Merrill, 1969, 376–384.

*"Documents: Problems and Perspectives: What Is to Be Done," in M. Teodori, ed. THE NEW LEFT: A DOCUMENTARY HISTORY. Indianapolis, Indiana: Bobbs-Merrill, 1969, 451–473.

*"Documents: the Emergence of a New Left Position: Analysis and Proposals for American Society," in M. Teodori, ed. THE NEW LEFT: A DOCUMENTARY HISTORY. Indianapolis, Indiana: Bobbs-Merrill, 1969, 163–196.

*"Documents: the Emergence of a New Left Position: The Politics of the Movement: Coalition, Autonomy and Organizational Structures," in M. Teodori, ed. THE NEW LEFT: A DOCUMENTARY HISTORY. Indianapolis, Indiana: Bobbs-Merrill, 1969, 197–217.

Edelman, Irwin. "White Radicals and Black Liberation: the Necessity of Coalition," LIBERATION, 13 (September, 1968), 18–25.

Ehrenreich, John and Barbara. "From Resistance to Revolution," MONTHLY REVIEW, 19 (April, 1968), 1–11.

Ewen, Stuart. "A Revolutionary Strategy," RADICAL AMERICA, 2 (May–June, 1968), 45–57.

Ferrier, Jean-Louis. "Herbert Marcuse Defines His New Left Line," in Harold Jaffe and John Tytell, eds. THE AMERICAN EXPERIENCE: A RADICAL READER. New York: Harper and Row, 1970, 117–138.

Flacks, Richard. "Is the Great Society Just a Barbecue?" in A. Kopkind, ed. THOUGHTS OF THE YOUNG RADICALS. New York: New Republic, 1966, 48–57.

*Flacks, Richard. "On the Uses of Participatory Democracy," DISSENT, 13 (November, 1966), 701–709.

*Flacks, Richard. "The Revolt of the Young Intelligentsia: Revolutionary

Class Consciousness in Post-Scarcity America," in R. Aya and N. Miller, eds. REVOLUTION RECONSIDERED. New York: Free Press, 1971,

Flacks, Richard. "Some Roles for Radicals in America," LIBERATION, 12 (June, 1967), 42–46.

Flacks, Richard. "Strategies for Radical Social Change," SOCIAL POLICY, 1 (April, 1971), 7–14.

Frick, Ivan. "Reflections on Participatory Democracy," LIBERAL EDUCATION, 55 (May, 1969), 262–271.

Fruchter, Norman. "Movement Propaganda and the Culture of the Spectacle," LIBERATION, 16 (May, 1971), 4–17.

Fruchter, Norman and Robert Kramer. "An Approach to Community Organizing Projects," STUDIES ON THE LEFT, 6 (March–April, 1966), 31–61.

*Garson, G. David. "The Ideology of the New Student Left," in J. Foster, and Durward Long, eds. PROTEST! STUDENT ACTIVISM IN AMERICA. New York: Morrow, 1970, 184–201.

Getzels, Jacob W. "On the Transformation of Values: a Decade After Port Huron," SCHOOL REVIEW, 80 (August, 1972), 505–520.

Gintis, Herbert. "The New Working Class and Revolutionary Youth," SOCIALIST REVOLUTION, 1 (May–June, 1970), 13–43.

Gitlin, Todd. "Local Pluralism as Theory and Ideology," STUDIES ON THE LEFT, 5 (Summer, 1965), 21–45.

Gitlin, Todd. "New Left: Old Traps," RAMPARTS, 8 (September, 1969), 20+.

Gitlin, Todd. "Theses for the Radical Movement," LIBERATION, 12 (May–June, 1967), 34–36.

Gleason, Ralph J. "The Power of Non-Politics or the Death of the Square Left," EVERGREEN REVIEW, (September, 1967),

Goodman, Paul. "Black Flag of Anarchism," NEW YORK TIMES MAGAZINE, (July 14, 1968), 10–11+.

Gorden, Fred. "Build the Campus Worker-Student Alliance (1969)," in John and Susan Erlich, eds. STUDENT POWER, PARTICIPATION, AND REVOLUTION. New York: Association Press, 1970, 165–170.

*Grant, George. "A Critique of the New Left," OUR GENERATION, 3 (May, 1966), 46–51.

Greeman, Richard. "A Critical Re-Examination of Herbert Marcuse's Works," NEW POLITICS, 6 (Fall, 1967), 12–23.

Hammerquist, Don. "Alienation and the Marxist Vision," POLITICAL AFFAIRS, 45 (October, 1966), 30–40.

Hayden, Tom. "The Ability to Face What Comes," NEW REPUBLIC, 154 (January 15, 1966), 16–18.

Hayden, Tom. "Community Organizing and the War on Poverty," LIBERATION, 10 (November, 1965), 17–19.

Hayden, Tom. "Rolling Stone Interview, Part 1," ROLLING STONE, No. 120 (October 26, 1972), 36–42.

*Hayden, Tom, et al. "Confrontation: the Old Left and the New," AMERICAN SCHOLAR, 36 (Autumn, 1967), 567–588.

Healey, Dorothy. "How to Build a New Left," POLITICAL AFFAIRS, 46 (July, 1967), 17–23.

Hodges, Donald C. "Old and New Working Classes," RADICAL AMERICA, 5 (January–February, 1971), 11–32.

Horowitz, D. "Hand-Me-Down Marxism and the New Left," RAMPARTS, 8 (September, 1969), 16+.

*Howe, Irving. "New Styles in Leftism," DISSENT, 12 (Summer, 1965), 295–323.

Jacobs, Harold and James Petras. "Populist Students and Corporate Society," INTERNATIONAL SOCIALIST JOURNAL, 4 (February, 1967), 144–172.

Johnson, Dale L. "The Ideology of the Campus Revolution," STUDIES ON THE LEFT, 2 (1961), 73–75.

Kelman, S. "Beyond New Leftism," COMMENTARY, 47 (February, 1969), 67–71.

Lasch, Christopher. "From Culture to Politics," in George Fischer, ed. THE REVIVAL OF AMERICAN SOCIALISM. New York: Oxford University Press, 1971, 217–227.

Lasch, Christopher. "Where Do We Go From Here?" NEW YORK REVIEW OF BOOKS, 11 (October 10, 1968), 4–5.

LeBlanc, Paul. "Leaving the New Left," INTERNATIONAL SOCIALIST REVIEW, 33 (November, 1972), 18–39.

Lens, Sidney. "The Ideology of Profits," LIBERATION, 11 (October, 1966), 23–25, 30.

Lens, Sidney "Theory and the Movement," LIBERATION, 12 (May–June, 1967), 28–32.

Levich, Marvin. "The Ideology of Relevance," in Immanuel Wallerstein and Paul Starr, eds. THE UNIVERSITY CRISIS READER, 1. New York: Random House, 1971, 530–536.

Lynd, Staughton. "The New Radicals and Participatory Democracy," DISSENT, 12 (Summer, 1965), 324–333.

Lynd, Staughton. "A Program for Post-Campus Radicals," LIBERATION, 14 (August–September, 1969), 44–46.

Mann, Eric. "Appraisal and Perspectives," in Immanuel Wallerstein and Paul Starr, eds. THE UNIVERSITY CRISIS READER, II. New York: Random House, 1971, 148–160.

Marcuse, Herbert. "Marcuse Defines His New Left Line," NEW YORK TIMES MAGAZINE, (October 27, 1968), 29–31+.

Marcuse, Herbert. "Repressive Tolerance," in R. P. Wolff, B. Moore, jr. and H. Marcuse. A CRITIQUE OF PURE TOLERANCE. Boston: Beacon Press, 1965, 81–118.

*Mills, C. Wright. "Letter to the New Left," NEW LEFT REVIEW, 5 (September–October, 1960), 18–23.

Mills, C. Wright. "On the New Left," STUDIES ON THE LEFT, 2, (1961), 63–72.

"New Left Theory," in P. Long, ed. THE NEW LEFT. Boston: Porter Sargent, 1969, 14–86.

Nolan, David. "Toward a Student Worker Alliance," NEW POLITICS, 7 (June, 1969), 25–30.

Oglesby, Carl. "Let Us Shape the Future," LIBERATION, 10 (January, 1966), 11–14.

Pachter, Henry. "Marxism and America's New Left," SURVEY, No. 62, (January, 1967), 104–113.

Patsons, Howard L. "Philosophy and the New Left in the U.S. Today," HORIZONS, 10 (Spring, 1968), 26–39.

*Petras, James. "Populist Students and Corporate Society," INTERNA-TIONAL SOCIALIST JOURNAL, 4 (February, 1967), 144–172.

Posey, Melvin. "Toward a More Meaningful Revolution: Ideology in Transition," in J. McEvoy and A. Miller, eds. BLACK POWER AND STUDENT REBELLION. Belmont, California: Wadsworth, 1969, 253–276.

Radosh, Ronald. "American Left, Liberal or Radical?" MONTHLY RE-VIEW, 15 (June, 1963), 113–118.

Radosh, Ronald. "American Radicalism: Liberal or Socialist?" MONTH-LY REVIEW, 15 (February, 1963), 564–574.

"Review of the Month: Problems of the Student Movement," MONTHLY REVIEW, 20 (December, 1968), 1–7.

Rothstein, Rich, et al. "The New Movement and Its Organizational Theory: Responses to 'Wasteland Culture,' " OUR GENERATION, 5 (No. 4, 1968), 52–87.

Scheer, R. "Dialectics of Confrontation," RAMPARTS, 8 (August, 1969), 42–49.

Schneider, Eugene V. "C. Wright Mills and the American Left," MONTH-LY REVIEW, 14 (February, 1963), 553–563.

Schweitzer, David R. and James M. Elden. "New Left as Right: Conver-gent Themes of Political Discontent," JOURNAL OF SOCIAL FORCES, 27 (1971), 141–166.

Sklar, Martin. "On the Proletarian Revolution and the End of Political-Economic Society," RADICAL AMERICA, 3 (May–June, 1969), 1–41.

Sklar, Martin and James Weinstein. "Socialism and the New Left," in J. Weinstein and D. Eakins, eds. FOR A NEW AMERICA, New York: Random House, 1970, 317–327.

Stern, Sol. "The Metaphysics of Rebellion: On Herbert Marcuse," RAMPARTS, 6 (June 29, 1968), 55–60.

Stillman, E. "Marcuse: Prophet of the New Left," HORIZON, 11 (Summer, 1969), 26–31.

"Symposium on New Politics," STUDIES ON THE LEFT, 4 (Summer, 1964), 39–49.

Waelder, Robert. "The Philosophy of the New Left," ACTIVIST, 7 (Winter 1966–1967), 5–6, 32.

*Walzer, Michael, ed. "The Young Radicals: A Symposium," DISSENT, 9 (Spring, 1962), 129–163.

Weaver, James. "The Student as Worker," in Gary Weaver and James

Weaver, eds. THE UNIVERSITY AND REVOLUTION. Englewood Cliffs, New Jersey: Prentice-Hall, 1969.

Webster, James. "A New Road for Student Socialism," MONTHLY REVIEW, 3 (October, 1951), 175–180.

Weinstein, James and Martin Sklar. "Socialism and the New Left," STUDIES ON THE LEFT, 6 (March–April, 1966), 62–70.

Wilkerson, Cathy, et al. "The False Privilege (1968)," in John and Susan Erlich, eds. STUDENT POWER, PARTICIPATION AND REVOLUTION. New York: Association Press, 1970, 67–74.

Zinn, Howard. "The Old Left and the New Emancipation from Dogma," NATION, 202 (April 4, 1966), 385–389.

I. REACTIONS TO THE STUDENT REVOLT OF THE 1960s

I.1. Sympathetic Comment and Analysis of the New Left

Armstrong, Gregory, ed. PROTEST: MAN AGAINST SOCIETY. New York: Bantam Books, 1969.

*Cohen, Mitchell and Dennis Hale, eds. THE NEW STUDENT LEFT: AN ANTHOLOGY. Boston: Beacon Press, 1967.

Gitlin, Todd. THE POLITICS AND VISION OF THE NEW LEFT. San Francisco: Bay Area Radical Education Project, 1968.

*Goodman, Michael, ed. THE MOVEMENT TOWARD A NEW AMERICA: THE BEGINNINGS OF A LONG RESOLUTION: A COLLAGE. Philadelphia, Pilgrim Press, 1970.

*Long, Priscilla, ed. THE NEW LEFT. Boston: Porter Sargent, 1969.

Munk, Michael. THE NEW LEFT. New York: National Guardian, 1965.

*Reich, Charles A. THE GREENING OF AMERICA. New York: Random House, 1970.

Romm, Ethel Grodzins, ed. THE OPEN CONSPIRACY: WHAT AMERICA'S ANGRY GENERATION IS SAYING. Harrisburg, Pennsylvania: Stackpole Books, 1970.

Rossman, Michael. THE WEDDING WITHIN THE WAR. Garden City, New York: Doubleday Anchor Books, 1971.

Von Hoffman, Nicholas. WE ARE THE PEOPLE OUR PARENTS WARNED US AGAINST. Chicago: Quadrangle Books, 1968.

Aaron, Daniel, et al. "Confrontation: The Old Left and the New" AMERICAN SCHOLAR, 36 (Autumn, 1967), 567–589.

Altbach, P. G. "Student Activism and Academic Research: Action and Reaction," in P. G. Altbach, STUDENT POLITICS AND HIGHER EDUCATION IN THE UNITED STATES: A SELECT BIBLIOGRAPHY. St. Louis: United Ministries in Higher Education, 1968, 15–39.

Altbach, Philip, D. Hale and S. Kelman. "The New Left," NEW POLITICS, 4 (Spring, 1965), 91–103.

232

Anthony, Richard and Phil Semas. "The Many Voices of the New Left," NEW REPUBLIC, 158 (June 29, 1968), 12–14.

Aptheker, Bettina. "The Student Rebellion, Part I," POLITICAL AFFAIRS, 48 (March, 1969), 15–24.

Aptheker, Bettina. "The Student Rebellion: Part II," POLITICAL AFFAIRS, 48 (April, 1969), 12–23.

Aronson, James. "Beyond Old and New Left: The Emergence of a Third Force," LIBERATION, 14 (August–September, 1969), 22–25.

Aronson, Ronald. "The Movement and Its Critics," STUDIES ON THE LEFT, 6 (January–February, 1966), 3–19.

Baxandell, Lee. "Issues and Constituency of the New Left," LIBERATION, 11 (April, 1966), 21–26.

Birnbaum, Norman and Marjorie Childers. "The American Movement," in J. Nagel, ed., STUDENT POWER. London: Merlin Press, 1969, 125–141.

Bond, J. "Students Are an Oppressed Class: Interview," in J. Romer, ed. MADEMOISELLE, 68 (February, 1969), 166–167+.

*Booth, Paul and Lee Webb. "From Protest to Radical Politics," OUR GENERATION, 3-4 (May, 1966), 78–89.

Bottomore, T. B. "Blacks and Students: Critics of Society," NATION, Volume 207, (November 25, 1968), 565.

Chomsky, Noam. "The Student Movement," HUMANIST, 30 (September–October, 1970), 19–26.

Davidson, Carl. "New Left in Transition," NATIONAL GUARDIAN, (March 23, March 30, and April 6, 1968).

*Davidson, Carl. "Student Syndicalism," OUR GENERATION, 5 (May, 1967), 102–111.

Dolbeare, Kenneth and Patricia Dolbeare. "The New Left," in K. and P. Dolbeare, AMERICAN IDEOLOGIES. Chicago: Markham, 1971, 145–184.

Draper, Hal. "In Defense of the 'New Radicals,' " NEW POLITICS, 4 (Summer, 1965), 5–28.

Farber, Jerry. "The Student as Nigger," THIS MAGAZINE IS ABOUT SCHOOLS, 2 (Winter, 1966), 107–116.

Flacks, Richard. "Roots of Radicalism," PLAYBOY, 18 (April, 1971), 107–108+.

Gans, Herbert J. "The New Radicalism: Sect or Action Movement?" STUDIES ON THE LEFT. 5 (Summer, 1965), 126–140.

Gans, Herbert. "A Rational Approach to Radicalism," STUDIES ON THE LEFT, 6 (January/February, 1966), 37–47, 47–53.

Gitlin, Todd. "Whither the New Student Left?" FELLOWSHIP, 31 (December, 1965), 7–9.

Haber, Robert A. "From Protest to Radicalism: An Appraisal of the Student Movement," in M. Brown, ed. THE POLITICS AND ANTI-POLITICS OF THE YOUNG. Beverly Hills: Glencoe Press, 1969, 25–31.

Hayden, Tom. "The Politics of the Movement," in Irving Howe, ed. RADICAL PAPERS. New York: Doubleday, 1966, 362–377.

Hayden, Thomas. "Who Are the Student Boat Rockers?" MADEMOISELLE, 53 (August, 1961), 236–239.

Jacobs, James. "Growing Pains of the New Left," INTERNATIONAL SOCIALIST JOURNAL, 4 (February, 1967), 173–177.

Jacobson, Julius. "In Defense of the Young," NEW POLITICS, 8 (Spring, 1970), 4–13.

Joyce, Frank. "Letter to the New Left," LIBERATION, 10 (February, 1966), 47–48.

*Kofsky, Frank. "The Student Movement," MONTHLY REVIEW, 14 (October, 1962), 329–336.

Kramer, Bert. "Understanding the New Left," POLITICAL AFFAIRS, 45 (April, 1966), 56–62.

Lens, Sidney. "The New Left and the Old," PROGRESSIVE, 30 (June, 1966), 19–24.

Mandel, Ernest. "The New Vanguard," in Tariq Ali, ed. THE NEW REVOLUTIONARIES. New York: Morrow, 1969, 47–53.

*Mills, Herb. "In Defense of the Student Movement," NEW UNIVERSITY THOUGHT, 2 (Autumn, 1961), 8–12.

New University Conference. "The Student Rebellion," in Harold Jaffe and John Tytell, eds. THE AMERICAN EXPERIENCE: A RADICAL READER. New York: Harper and Row, 1970, 153–161.

Newfield, Jack. "In Defense of Student Radicals," in Gary Weaver and James Weaver, eds. THE UNIVERSITY AND REVOLUTION. Englewood Cliffs, New Jersey: Prentice-Hall, 1969, 43–55.

O'Brien, David J. "Eugene Genovese and the Student Left," LIBERATION, 14 (October, 1969), 29–33.

Parente, Michael and Mickey McCleery. "Campus Radicalism as a Relevant Political Science," JOURNAL OF HIGHER EDUCATION, 34 (June, 1968), 316–325.

Rogin, Michael. "Politics of Outrage:Notes on the Student Left," COMMONWEAL, 84 (April 15, 1966), 95–102.

Rossman, Michael. "The Sound of Marching, Changing Feet," ROLLING STONE, 30 (April 5, 1969), 1–8.

Roussopoulos, Dimitros. "What Is the New Radicalism?" OUR GENERATION, 6 (Summer, 1968), 15–27.

"Symposium: The Movement Ten Years from Now," LIBERATION, 14 (August–September, 1969), 5–48.

Waskow, Arthur I. "The New Student Movement," DISSENT, 7 (Autumn, 1965), 486–493.

Waskow, Arthur. "The New Student Movement," OUR GENERATION, 3 (May, 1966), 52–54.

Wolfe, Robert. "Beyond Protest," STUDIES ON THE LEFT, 7 (January–February, 1967), 3–21.

I.2. Comment and Analysis of the New Left

Bardis, Panos D. ENCYCLOPEDIA OF CAMPUS UNREST. New York: Exposition Press, 1971.

234

Brownfeld, Allan. THE NEW LEFT: MEMORANDUM. Washington: U.S. Government Printing Office, 1968.

Cantelon, John E. COLLEGE EDUCATION AND THE CAMPUS REVOLUTION. Philadelphia, Pennsylvania: Westminister, 1969.

Hoffman, Donald A., ed., REBELS WITH A CAUSE. Philadelphia, Pennsylvania: U.S. National Student Association, 1961.

INTERDOC. RADICALISM AND SECURITY. Hague: Interdoc, 1970.

Kennan, George F., et al. DEMOCRACY AND THE STUDENT LEFT. Boston: Little Brown, 1968.

Levine, Maryl and John Naisbitt. RIGHT ON. New York: Bantam, 1970.

Lipset, S. M. THE POSSIBLE EFFECTS OF STUDENT ACTIVISM ON INTERNATIONAL RELATIONS. Rand Corporation, Paper Number 3943. Santa Monica: Rand, 1968.

Lukas, Anthony J. DON'T SHOOT—WE ARE YOUR CHILDREN. New York: Random House, 1971.

*Nolfi, George J., jr. CASE STUDIES ON CURRENT CAMPUS ISSUES. Cambridge, Massachusetts: University Consultants, May, 1970.

Northwestern University Student Symposium. REFLECTIONS ON REBELLION. Evanston, Illinois: Northwestern University, 1966.

Pennsylvania. Department of Education. Bureau of Administrative Leadership Services. STUDENT UNREST. Harrisburg, Pennsylvania, Department of Education, 1969.

Rinzler, Alan, ed. MANIFESTO ADDRESSED TO THE PRESIDENT OF THE UNITED STATES FROM THE YOUTH OF AMERICA. New York: Macmillan, 1970.

Smith, Mark W. and Jerry H. Godard, eds. THE STUDENT AND THE PUBLIC IMAGE—THE DEAN SPEAKS OUT. Detroit: National Association of Student Personnel Administratives, 1967.

Thayer, George. THE FURTHER SHORES OF POLITICS. New York: Simon and Schuster, 1967.

U.S. Congress. House. Committee on Education and Labor. CAMPUS UNREST HEARING. (91st Congress. First Session). Washington: Government Printing Office, 1969.

U.S. Congress. House. Special Subcommittee to Inquire into the Capability of the National Guard to Cope with Civil Disturbances. HEARINGS. Washington, D.C.: Government Printing Office, 1967.

U.S. Congress. Senate. Committee on Government Operations Permanent Subcommittee on Investigations. STAFF STUDY OF CAMPUS RIOTS AND DISORDERS. Washington, D.C.: Government Printing Office, 1969.

U.S. Congress. Senate. Committee on the Judiciary. COMMUNIST YOUTH PROGRAM. Washington: Government Printing Office, 1966.

U.S. Congress. Senate. Committee on the Judiciary. EXTENT OF SUBVERSION IN CAMPUS DISORDERS. Part I. Washington, D.C.: Government Printing Office, 1969.

U.S. Congress. Senate. Committee on the Judiciary. Subcommittee to Investigate the Administration of the Internal Security Act and Other Internal Security Laws. EXTENT OF SUBVERSION IN THE "NEW LEFT": TESTI-

MONY OF ROBERT J. THOMAS HEARINGS. 91st Conference. 2nd session. Washington: Government Printing Office, 1970.

U.S. Congress. Senate. Committee on the Judiciary. Subcommittee to Investigate the Administration of the Internal Security Act and Other Internal Security Laws. EXTENT OF SUBVERSION IN CAMPUS DISORDERS: TESTIMONY OF ERNESTO E. BLANCO. HEARINGS. 91st Congress. First Session. Washington, D.C.: Government Printing Office, 1969.

U.S. Federal Bureau of Investigation. FUTURE OF NEW LEFT AND BLACK STUDENT MOVEMENTS. Washington, D.C.: Federal Bureau of Investigation, N.D.

U.S. Federal Bureau of Investigation. IMPACT OF NEW LEFT AND BLACK EXTREMIST STUDENT MOVEMENTS. Washington,D.C.: Federal Bureau of Investigation, N.D.

U.S. Federal Bureau of Investigation. NEW LEFT MOVEMENT. Washington, D.C.: Federal Bureau of Investigation, N.D.

U.S. Federal Bureau of Investigation. THE NEW LEFT: ROAD TO ANARCHY. Washington, D.C.: Federal Bureau of Investigation, N.D.

U.S. Federal Bureau of Investigation. THE STUDENT NEW LEFT—A THREAT TO DEMOCRATIC LAW AND ORDER. Washington, D.C.: Federal Bureau of Investigation, N.D.

U.S. Task Force on Law and Law Enforcement. RIGHTS IN CONCORD: THE RESPONSE TO COUNTER-INAUGURAL PROTEST ACTIVITIES IN WASHINGTON. A Staff Report of the National Commission on Causes and Prevention of Violence. Washington, D.C.: U.S. Government Printing Office, 1969.

Weber, Clarence A. ROOTS OF REBELLION. St. Louis, Missouri: Warren H. Green, 1971.

Weiss, A. Von. THE NEW LEFT. Hague: Interdoc, 1968.

Wittenberg, Rudolph M. THE TROUBLED GENERATION; TOWARD UNDERSTANDING AND HELPING THE YOUNG ADULT. New York: Association Press, 1967.

Wolfgang, Marvin E. YOUTH AND VIOLENCE. Washington, D.C.: U.S. Youth Development and Delinquency Prevention Administration, 1970.

Abcarian, Gilbert. "Romantics and Renegades: Political Defection and the Radical Left," JOURNAL OF SOCIAL FORCES, 27 (Number 1, 1971), 123-140.

Abram, Morris B. "Liberalism: A Response to the Campus." SOUTHWESTERN LAW JOURNAL, 23 (October, 1969), 662–668.

Abram, Morris. "The Restless Campus," COLLEGE AND UNIVERSITY JOURNAL, 8 (Fall, 1969), 34–39.

Adams, B. S. "Ceremony of Innocence," COLLEGE AND UNIVERSITY, 45 (Fall, 1969), 5-14.

Aiken, Henry David. "How Late Is It?" in W. J. Minter and Patricia Snyder, eds. VALUE CHANGE AND POWER CONFLICT IN HIGHER EDU-

236

CATION. Boulder, Colorado; Western Interstate Commission on Higher Education, 1970, 22–46.

Albjerg, H. "Role of the Activist on Today's Campus," COLLEGE AND UNIVERSITY, 42 (Spring, 1967), 301–307.

Allen, J. E., jr. "Campus Activism and Unrest," SCHOOL AND SOCIETY, 96 (October 26, 1968), 357–359.

Altbach, Philip G. "The Student Movement and the American University," PHI DELTA KAPPAN, 47 (April, 1966), 424–428.

Anonymous. "Our Son is a Campus Radical," READER'S DIGEST, 71 (April, 1969), 71–75.

"Are We in the Middle of the Second American Revolution? Symposium," NEW YORK TIMES MAGAZINE, (May 17, 1970), 26–27+.

Aron, R. "Student Rebellion: Vision of the Future or Echo from the Past?" POLITICAL SCIENCE QUARTERLY, 84 (June, 1969), 289–310.

Athos, A. G. "Is the Corporation Next to Fall?" HARVARD BUSINESS REVIEW, 48 (January, 1970), 49–61.

Austin, C. G. "Disruption and Immaturity," JOURNAL OF HIGHER EDUCATION, 41 (October, 1970), 562–565.

Austin, C. G. "Student Protests and the Establishment," JOURNAL OF HIGHER EDUCATION, 39 (April, 1968), 223–225.

Averill, L. J. "Ecology of Discontent," CHRISTIAN CENTURY, 86 (June, 18, 1969), 835–838.

Barnes, H. E. "The Ivory Tower Rebel and His Philosophy," JOURNAL OF THE NATIONAL ASSOCIATION OF WOMEN DEANS AND COUNSELORS, 28 (Winter, 1965), 66–73.

Barns, Hardial. "Necessity for Change," in Gerald McGuigan, ed. STUDENT PROTEST. Toronto: Methuen Publications, 1968, 133–162.

Barr, D. "Parents' Guide to the Age of Revolt," MCCALLS, 97 (October, 1969), 73+.

Barr, S. "Why Students Revolt," EDUCATION DEGEST, 34 (May, 1969), 4–5.

Bentley, Eric. "Defensive Conservatism" in Immanuel Wallerstein and Paul Starr, eds. THE UNIVERSITY CRISIS READER, 1. New York: Random House, 1971, 552–558.

Berg, Irwin A. "What's Really Behind Our Students' Unrest?" COLLEGE BOARD REVIEW, 60 (Summer, 1966), 11–14.

Berman, Ronald. "The New Left," in Ronald Berman, ed. AMERICA IN THE SIXTIES. New York: Harper Colophon Books, 1970, 110–171.

"Beyond the Barricades: Activist Universities," NEWSWEEK, 72 (July 22, 1968), 86–87.

Blocker, C. E. "Dissent and the College Student in Revolt," SCHOOL AND SOCIETY, 98 (January, 1970), 20–23.

Boulding, Kenneth. "Reflections on Protest," in Bruce Douglass, ed. REFLECTIONS ON PROTEST. Richmond, Virginia: John Knox Press, 1967, 61–70.

Bowen, H. R. "Student Unrest in the United States," INTERNATIONAL BUREAU OF EDUCATION BULLETIN, 42 (4th Quarter, 1968), 236–240.

Brademas, J. "Campus: Left? Right? Or Neither?" NEW YORK TIMES MAGAZINE, (April 22, 1962), 10+.

Bradley, G. E. "What Businessmen Need to Know about the Student Left," HARVARD BUSINESS REVIEW, 46 (September, 1968), 49–60.

Brann, James. "The Straight Kids Lose Faith," CHANGE, 2 (November–December, 1970), 66–71.

Braungart, R. B., and M. M. Braungart. "Administration, Faculty, and Student Reaction to Campus Unrest," JOURNAL OF COLLEGE STUDENT PERSONNEL, 13 (March, 1972), 112–119.

Brennan, W. J. "A Judge Looks at Student Dissent," HARVARD LAW SCHOOL BULLETIN, 19 (July, 1968), 9–13.

Brewster, K., jr. "If Not Reason, What?" AMERICAN SCHOLAR, 39 (Spring, 1970), 243–252.

Brewster, Kingman, jr. "New Responsibilities for an Old Generation," in Lawrence Dennis and Joseph Kauffman, eds. THE AMERICAN COLLEGE AND THE STUDENT. Washington: American Council on Education, 1966, 71–74.

Brewster, K., jr. "Politics and Academia," SCHOOL AND SOCIETY, 98 (April, 1970), 211–214.

Bridgeman, Phyllis and Alan N. Sabrosky. "The Student Speaks: Pros and Cons of Revolution," in Hans H. Indorf, ed. POLITICS 1970. Greenville, North Carolina: Political Science Department, East Carolina University, 1970, 129–140.

Brownfeld, A. C. "Student Rebels: Radical or Reactionary," CHRISTIAN CENTURY, 85 (October 9, 1968), 1268–1272.

Buchanan, J. M. "Student Revolts, Academic Liberalism, and Constitutional Attitudes," SOCIAL RESEARCH, 35 (Winter, 1968), 666–680.

Burck, C. "Student Activists: Free-Form Revolutionaries," FORTUNE, 79 (January, 1969), 108–111+.

Butler, W. R. "Meaning of Community; One Point of View," NATIONAL ASSOCIATION OF STUDENT PERSONNEL ADMINISTRATORS JOURNAL, 7 (January, 1970), 131–142.

Cahn, Judah. "Where Is Violence Justified?" RECONSTRUCTIONIST, 36 (June 19, 1970), 17–20.

"Campus Unrest," TODAY'S EDUCATION, 58 (November, 1969), 25–33.

Cass, James. "What Are They Telling Us," SATURDAY REVIEW, 51 (September, 1968), 57–58.

Cassata, M. B. "Student Unrest and the Library," WILSON LIBRARY BULLETIN, 45 (September, 1970), 78–85.

"Chaos on Campus," NEW REPUBLIC, 158 (January 6, 1968), 14–15.

Chesebro, J. W. "Rhetorical Strategies of the Radical-Revolutionary," TODAY'S SPEECH, 20 (Winter, 1972), 37–48.

Clark, Kenneth. "Efficiency as a Prod to Social Action," in Sidney Hook, ed. IN DEFENSE OF ACADEMIC FREEDOM. New York: Pegasus, 1971, 150–156.

Coffin, William Sloane, jr. "Dont' Tell them to Play It Safe," in Christopher Katope and Paul Zolbrod, eds. BEYOND BERKELEY. Cleveland: World, 1966, 217–220.

238

Coffman, Dale C. "Campus Unrest—Why?" NEW YORK STATE BAR JOURNAL, 42 (February, 1970), 106–111.

"College Ferment '71: Symposium," TODAY'S HEALTH, 49 (April, 1971), 25–40.

Commager, Henry Steele. "Students in Rebellion," in Alexander Klein, ed. NATURAL ENEMIES? YOUTH AND THE CLASH OF GENERATIONS. New York: Lippincott, 1969, 119–126.

Commager, H. S. "Why Student Rebellion?" CURRENT, 97 (July, 1968), 10–15.

Conant, Ralph W. "Rioting, Insurrection and Civil Disobedience," AMERICAN SCHOLAR, 37 (Summer, 1968), 420–433.

Conner, F. W. "Anarchist Echoes in Academia," IMPROVING COLLEGE AND UNIVERSITY TEACHING, 17 (Summer, 1969), 157–161.

Cottle, Thomas J. "The Politics of Pronouncement." HARVARD EDU-CATIONAL REVIEW, 39 (Number 3, 1969), 558–570.

Crane, Robert M. "Unrest on Campus—Revolution or Evolution," COLLEGE AND UNIVERSITY, 42 (Winter, 1967), 209–217.

Cranston, M. "Are Student Rebels Neo-Communists?" CURRENT, 104 (February, 1969), 19–25.

Culbert, Samuel A. and James M. Elder. "An Anatomy of Activism for Executives: the Social Unrest of Students Today Will Have a Strong Impact on Companies Tomorrow: As Employees, What Changes Will They Demand?" HARVARD BUSINESS REVIEW, 48 (November, December, 1970), 131–142.

Dalbey, E. G., jr. "Great White Son Turns Left," CHRISTIAN CENTURY, 88 (June 9, 1971), 716–720.

Davidson, Glen W. "Creative Tensions on Campus," COLLEGE AND UNIVERSITY JOURNAL, 6 (Winter, 1967), 2–9.

Davis, James. "Communists are Part of New Left," POLITICAL AFFAIRS, 45 (March, 1966), 49–53.

de Jouvenal, Bertrand. "Academic Youth and Social Revolution," in John Coffrey, ed. THE FUTURE ACADEMIC COMMUNITY: CONTINUITY AND CHANGE. Washington: American Council on Education, 1969, 150–168.

Deming, Barbara. "On Revolution and Equilibrium," LIBERATION, 12 (February, 1968), 10–21.

Dennis, Gene. "From Protest to . . .?" POLITICAL AFFAIRS, 47 (April, 1968), 51–57.

Dowd, Douglas, "Campus Disruptions and the Liberal-Left," MONTHLY REVIEW, 21 (September, 1969), 28–39.

Drucker, P. F. "Romantic Generation," HARPER, 232 (May, 1966), 12+.

Duberman, M. "On Misunderstanding Student Rebels," ATLANTIC, 222 (November, 1968), 63–70.

Eble, Kenneth E. "The Student as Polite Revolutionist," JOURNAL OF THE NATIONAL ASSOCIATION OF STUDENT PERSONNEL ADMINISTRATORS, 2 (October, 1964), 3–8.

Eisenberg, L. "Student Unrest: Sources and Consequences," SCIENCE, 167 (March 27, 1970), 1688–1692.

Etzioni, Amitai. "Challenge to Liberalism," NEW LEADER, 2 (May 20, 1968), 16–20.

Etzioni, Amitai. "University: Strike!" EDUCATIONAL RECORD, 51 (Summer, 1970), 219–222.

Fairlie, Henry. "How to Keep a Campus Together," INTERPLAY, 3 (July, 1970), 4–12.

Faultz, L. W. "Campus Conflict: A New Approach," JOURNAL OF THE COLLEGE AND UNIVERSITY PERSONNEL ASSOCIATION, 22 (December, 1970), 108–112.

Feinstein, Otto. "Is there a Student Movement?" NEW UNIVERSITY THOUGHT, 1 (Summer, 1961), 23–28.

Feldman, Paul. "New Winds on the Campus," DISSENT, 13 (March–April, 1966), 183–190.

Fellows at the Center for Advanced Study in the Behavioral Sciences. "Students Protests: A Phenomenon for Behavioral Sciences Research," SCIENCE, 161 (July 5, 1968), 20–23.

Feigenbaum, J. "Students and Society," in Johnathan Allen, ed. SCIENTISTS, STUDENTS AND SOCIETY, March 4. Cambridge, Massachusetts: Massachusetts Institute of Technology Press, 1970, 2–7.

Ferm, D. W. "Why College Students Demand Changes Now," REDBOOK, 131 (September, 1968), 81+.

Ferrer, Terry. "Those Restless Students–A Prophetic Warning," in Esther Lloyd-Jones and Herman Estrin, eds. THE AMERICAN STUDENT AND HIS COLLEGE. Boston: Houghton Mifflin, 1967, 27–30.

Fertig, L. "Hysteria on the Campus: Who is Responsible," VITAL SPEECHES, 37 (May 15, 1971), 454–459.

Fiedler, Leslie. "The New Mutants," in Alexander Klein, ed. NATURAL ENEMEIS? YOUTH AND THE CLASH OF GENERATIONS. New York: J. B. Lippincott, 1969, 206–217.

Finch, Robert. "Statement of the Secretary of Health, Education and Welfare Before a House Education Subcommittee," in W. Brickman and S. Lehrer, eds. CONFLICT AND CHANGE ON THE CAMPUS: THE RESPONSE TO STUDENT HYPERACTIVISM. New York: School and Society Books, 1970, 429–437.

Fischer, J. "Case for the Rebellious Students and their Counterevolution," HARPER'S 237 (August, 1968), 9–12.

Fischer, John. "Letter to a New Leftist, From a Tired Liberal," HARPER'S 232 (March, 1966), 16–28.

*Foster, Julian. "Student Protest: Aims and Strategies," in Julian Foster and Durward Long, eds. PROTEST! STUDENT ACTIVISM IN AMERICA. New York: Morrow, 1970, 401–418.

Freedman, M. B. "Post-Industrial Generation: Roots of Student Discontent," NATION, 200 (June 14, 1965), 639–643.

Freedman, Mervin. "Roots of Student Discontent," in Christopher Katope and Paul Zolbrod, eds. BEYOND BERKELEY. Cleveland: World, 1966, 236–248.

Frymier, J. R. "Why Students Rebel," EDUCATIONAL LEADERSHIP, 27 (January, 1970), 346–350.

Gallagher, B. G. "Speaking Out; Our Students Have No Utopia," SATURDAY EVENING POST, 240 (May 6, 1967), 8+.

Gallagher, B. G. "Student Unrest," COLLEGE AND UNIVERSITY BUSINESS, 38 (1965), 51–55.

Gallahue, J. J. "White Rage," AMERICA, 119 (October 5, 1968), 289–292.

Gandy, S. "Youth, Establishments, and Protest," THEOLOGY TODAY, 23 (Number 2, 1966), 216–223.

Genovese, E. "The Fortunes of the Left," NATIONAL REVIEW, 22 (December 1, 1970), 1266–1270.

Gilbert, J. "Left Young and Old," PARTISAN REVIEW, 36 (Number 3, 1969), 343–363.

Glass, J. C., jr. "Campus Unrest: Some Causes and Recommendations," NORTH CENTRAL ASSOCIATION QUARTERLY, 45 (Fall, 1970), 248–252.

Glazer, Nathan. "New Left and Its Limits," COMMENTARY, 46 (July, 1968), 31–39.

Glazer, Nathan. "On Being Deradicalized," COMMENTARY, 50 (October, 1970), 74–80.

*Glazer, Nathan. "Student Politics in a Democratic Society," AMERICAN SCHOLAR, 36 (Spring, 1967), 202–217.

Glazer, N. and F. G. Hutchins. "Campus Crucible," ATLANTIC, 224 (July, 1969), 43–56.

Gleason, Ralph. "The Times They Are A-Changin," RAMPARTS, 4 (April, 1965), 36–48.

Glenn, Edmund. "The University and the Revolution: New Left or New Right," in Gary Weaver and James Weaver, eds. THE UNIVERSITY AND REVOLUTION. Englewood Cliffs, New Jersey: Prentice-Hall, 1969, 99–120.

Good, Paul. "Odyssey of a Man—and a Movement," in William O'Neill, ed. AMERICAN SOCIETY SINCE 1945. Chicago: Quadrangle Books, 1969, 229–242.

Goodheart, Eugene. "The Rhetoric of Violence," NATION, (April 6, 1970), 399–402.

Goodman, W. "Liberal Establishment Faces the Black, the Young, the New Left," NEW YORK TIMES MAGAZINE, (December 29, 1968), 8–9+.

Gordon, E. W. "Relevance or Revolt," PERSPECTIVES IN EDUCATION, 3 (Fall, 1969), 10–16.

Gossett, William T. "The Politics of Dissent: A Lawyer Speaks for a New Confrontation," MICHIGAN QUARTERLY REVIEW, 8 (October, 1969), 263–267.

Grambs, J. D. "Riots and Disorders: Getting Your Money's Worth from American Education," CATHOLIC EDUCATION REVIEW, 67 (November, 1969), 123–132.

Graves, S. M. "Description of Student Unrest," NATIONAL ASSOCIATION OF SECONDARY SCHOOL PRINCIPALS BULLETIN, 53 (May, 1969), 191–197.

Greason, A. L., jr. "Protest and Reaction: Students and Society in Conflict," NORTH AMERICAN REVIEW, 6 (Summer, 1969), 48–53.

Greeley, Andrew M. "The College Blight on Idealism," EDUCATIONAL RECORD, 49 (Fall, 1968), 429–434.

Greene, Maxine. "The Spectrum of Disenchantment," in Richard L. Hart and J. Galen Saylor, eds. STUDENT UNREST: THREAT OR PROMISE. Washington, D.C.: Association for Supervision and Curriculum Development, 1970, 12–34.

Greenlief, June. "Static on the Left: Politics of Masquerade," VILLAGE VOICE, 12 (October, 12–18, 1967).

Groves, Eugene W. "Who's Having the Identity Crisis: Businessmen or Students?" AMERICAN SCHOLAR, 36 (Autumn, 1967), 631–635.

Guitar, M. A. "Unbugged Student: Communication between Activists and Non activists," MADEMOISELLE, 63 (August, 1966), 300–301+.

Gusfield, Joseph. "The Pluralist Campus and the Student Movement," ACTIVIST, 6 (March, 1966), 12–18.

Hall, Douglas K. "Student Freedom and the Development of Creative Education," in L. Vaccaro and J. T. Covert, eds. STUDENT FREEDOM IN AMERICAN HIGHER EDUCATION. New York: Teachers' College Press, 1969, 147–154.

Hallberg, E. C. "Campus Radical: Separation and Defeat," JOURNAL OF THE NATIONAL ASSOCIATION OF STUDENT PERSONNEL ADMINISTRATORS, 8 (October, 1970), 97–105.

Halle, Louis F. "Bringing About Change: a Matter of Manners?" NEW REPUBLIC, 159 (November 23, 1968), 19–22.

Hammerquist, Don. "Once Again on the New Left," POLITICAL AFFAIRS, 45 (May, 1966), 45–50.

Hanson, V. S. "College Student: Ants in Industry's Pants?" JOURNAL OF THE COLLEGE AND UNIVERSITY PERSONNEL ASSOCIATION, 21 (May, 1970), 1–10.

Harbison, F. H. "Campus Revolt from an Industrial Relations Perspective," MONTHLY LABOR REVIEW, 93 (March, 1970), 33–36.

Harbison, Frederick H. "Comparing Power Bids of Labor and Students: CIO of the '30's and Today's Campus Activists," UNIVERSITY, (Spring, 1970), 10–15.

Hassenger, R. "Conflict in the Catholic Colleges," ANNALS OF THE AMERICAN ACADEMY OF POLITICAL AND SOCIAL SCIENCE, 382 (March, 1969), 95–108.

Hassenger, Robert. "Protest and the Catholic Colleges," in Julian Foster and Durward Long, eds. PROTEST! STUDENT ACTIVISM IN AMERICA. New York: Morrow, 1970, 483–497.

Hately, William T. "Could This Financial Aid Plan Help End Student Unrest?" COLLEGE BOARD REVIEW, Number 72 (Summer, 1969), 18–25.

Hauser, Philip M. "Graduation Into Chaos," EDUCATIONAL RECORD, 48 (Fall, 1967), 304–314.

Havice, Charles. "Creative Criticism and Campus Protest," in C. Havice, ed. CAMPUS VALUES. New York: Scribner's, 1968, 116–126.

242

Hedgeman, Anna Arnold. "The Gift of Chaos," MOTIVE, 26 (December, 1965), 12–16.

Heist, Paul. "Activist Students Challenge the Social Scientists," in F. F. Korten, S. W. Cook and J. I. Lacey, eds. PSYCHOLOGY AND THE PROBLEMS OF SOCIETY. Washington: American Psychological Association, 1970, 395-405.

Henderson, A. D. "Brick Throwing at the Colleges," JOURNAL OF THE NATIONAL ASSOCIATION OF STUDENT PERSONNEL ADMINISTRATORS, 8 (July, 1970), 17–28.

Hentoff, Nat. "Youth–the Oppressed Majority," in Alexander Klein, ed. NATURAL ENEMIES? YOUTH AND THE CLASH OF GENERATIONS. New York: Lippincott, 1969, 11–31.

Herzog, A. "Dozen Duds in the Canons of Youth," EDUCATION DIGEST, 36 (November, 1970), 37–40.

Hesburgh, Theodore M. "Comments on Campus Unrest," SOCIAL SCIENCE, 44 (October, 1969), 195–199.

Hesburgh, Rev. Theodore, C. S. C. "Letter on Student Confrontation," in W. Brickman and S. Lehrer, eds. CONFLICT AND CHANGE ON THE CAMPUS: THE RESPONSE TO STUDENT HYPERACTIVISM. New York: School and Society Books, 1970, 397–404.

Hitchcock, J. "Revolution in the University," YALE REVIEW, 60 (December, 1970), 161–174.

Hitchcock, J. "Romantic Rebel on the Campus," YALE REVIEW, 57 (October, 1967), 31–37.

Hobbs, Nicholas. "The Art of Getting Students in Trouble," in Lawrence Dennis and Joseph Kauffman, eds. THE AMERICAN COLLEGE AND THE STUDENT. Washington: American Council on Education, 1966, p. 202–205.

Horn, John. "Student Dissent and the Values of the University: A Problem of Coexistence," MIDWEST QUARTERLY, 13 (April, 1972), 247–271.

Horowitz, I. L. "Radicals and the Revolt against Reason," NEW POLITICS, 6 (Fall, 1967), 30–41.

Horowitz, I. L. "Trade-Unionization of Students," CURRENT, 122 (October, 1970), 55–59.

Horowitz, I. L. "Young Radicals and Professional Critics," COMMON-WEALTH, 89 (January 31, 1969), 552–556.

Hosford, P. L. and M. Dyreson. "Dissent Without Dissension? Perhaps," EDUCATIONAL LEADERSHIP, 26 (April, 1969), 680–683.

Hoult, T. F. et al. "On Keeping our Cool in the Halls of Ivy," AAUP BULLETIN, 55 (June, 1969), 186–191.

Howe, Irving. "The Agony of the Campus," DISSENT, 16 (September/October 1969), 387–394.

Howe, I. "New Confrontations: Politics is a Dangerous Game," NEW YORK TIMES MAGAZINE, (October 20, 1968), 27–29+.

Howe, Irving. "The New Radicalism," PARTISAN REVIEW, 32 (Summer, 1965), 341–346.

Howe, Irving, "New Styles in 'Leftism,' " DISSENT, 12 (Summer, 1965), 295–323.

Howe, Irving. "Radical Questions and the American Intellectual," PARTISAN REVIEW, 33 (Spring, 1966), 174–192, 312–324.

Howe, I. and P. Rahv. "An Exchange on the Left," NEW YORK REVIEW OF BOOKS, 9 (November 23, 1967), 36–41.

Hudgins, G. "The Student Quake," COLLEGE AND UNIVERSITY JOURNAL, (Spring, 1969), 38–44.

Humphries, F., *et al.* "Are College Students a Defrauded Majority?" JOURNAL OF THE NATIONAL ASSOCIATION OF COLLEGE ADMISSIONS COUNSELORS, 14 (November, 1969), 10–14.

Humphrey, Richard A. "Three Reports on Campus Tensions: A Comparison," EDUCATIONAL RECORD, 52 (Winter, 1971), 47–51.

Indorf, Hans H. "Syndicalism: International Link and Common Denominator of Student Militants," in Hans H. Indorf, ed. POLITICS 1970. Greenville, North Carolina: Political Science Department, East Carolina University, 1970, 59–82.

Jackson, Ronald. "Responsible Individual Expression," in C. Havice, ed. CAMPUS VALUES. New York: Scribners, 1968, 109–115.

Jencks, C. "Limits of the New Left," NEW REPUBLIC, 157 (October 21, 1967), 19–21.

Jencks, Christopher. "Politics is for Other People," NEW REPUBLIC, 143 (October 3, 1960), 14–15.

Johansen, R. C. "Of Politics and Prophecy: Student Activism Today," CHRISTIAN CENTURY, 88 (February 17, 1971), 219–223.

Johnston, Richard J. "Student Revolt and Social Revolution," EDUCATIONAL RECORD, 51 (Winter, 1970), 22–27.

Jones, William H. "The New Radicals," JOHNS HOPKINS MAGAZINE, 17 (October, 1965), 9–13, 39–42.

Kahn, Tom. "The Problems of the New Left," COMMENTARY, 42 (July, 1966), 30–38.

Kahn, Tom. "The Student Movement: A New Social Force," WORLDVIEW, 9 (July/August, 1966), 9–13.

Kaminsky, Marc. "Radical Affirmatives," AMERICAN SCHOLAR, 36 (Autumn, 1967), 621–630.

Kauffman, Joseph F. "The Time of the Student: Shall We Overcome?" in Lawrence Dennis and Joseph Kauffman, eds. THE AMERICAN COLLEGE AND THE STUDENT. Washington: American Council on Education, 1966, 385–390.

Kearns, F. E. "Campus Activism," YALE REVIEW, 58 (October, 1968), 28–44.

Kelman, Steven. "The Contented Revolutionists," NEW LEADER, 52 (April 28, 1969), 12–14.

Kelman, Steven. "You Force Us to Rebel," in Alexander Klein, ed. NATURAL ENEMIES? YOUTH AND THE CLASH OF GENERATIONS, New York: J. B. Lippincott, 1969, 36–40.

Kelman, Steven. "Youth and Politics," NEW LEADER, 48 (February 1, 1965), 18–21.

Keniston, Kenneth. "Young Radicals and the Fear of Power," NATION, 206 (March 18, 1968), 370–373.

*Kerr, C. "Clark Kerr Calls it the Exaggerated Generation," NEW YORK TIMES MAGAZINE, (June 4, 1967), 28-29+.

Kerr, C. "Cure for Campus Strife: Interview," U.S. NEWS AND WORLD REPORT, 65 (December 30, 1968), 52-56.

*Kerr, Clark. "Student Dissent and Confrontation Politics," in Julian Foster and Durward Long, eds. PROTEST! STUDENT ACTIVISM IN AMERICA. New York: Morrow, 1970, 3-10.

Kerr, Clark. "Turmoil in Higher Education," LOOK, 31 (April 18, 1967), 17-21.

Ketels, Violet and Renee Weber. "The Student Revolt," MAIN CURRENTS IN MODERN THOUGHT, (1968), 123-129.

Kifner, J. "Spectator's Guide to the Troublemakers," ESQUIRE, 71 (February, 1969), 86-91.

Knop, E. "Student Dilemma: Role Conflict," IMPROVING COLLEGE AND UNIVERSITY TEACHING, 17 (Summer, 1969), 171-175.

Knowles, A. S. "President's View of Campus Unrest," SCHOOL AND SOCIETY, 99 (February, 1971) 81-84.

Kolden, Rolf. "Growing Up Revoluting," ACTIVIST, 8 (Fall, 1967), 24-25.

Krickus, Richard L. "Revolution Without the Masses," NEW LEADER, 52 (December 22, 1969), 8-10.

Kronenberger, J. "Counter-Establishment: Seven You Can Trust, None Over Thirty," LOOK, 34 (December 15, 1970), 68-73.

Kudela, R. M. "Facing Student Unrest," CLEARING HOUSE, 44 (May, 1970), 547-552.

Kurtz, Paul, Howard Zinn and Arisian Khoren, jr. "Liberals versus Radicals: Is There a Radical Difference?" HUMANIST, 30 (July/August, 1970), 7-14.

Leonard, G. B. "Beyond Campus Chaos: A Bold Plan for Peace," LOOK, 33 (June 10, 1969), 73+.

Leonard, George. "The Explosive Generation," LOOK, 25 (January 3, 1961), 16-25.

Lerner, Max. "The Revolutionary Frame of Our Time," in Lawrence Dennis and Joseph Kauffman, eds. THE AMERICAN COLLEGE AND THE STUDENT. Washington: American Council on Education, 1966, 8-22.

*Levine, Louis S. "Why Students Seize Power," NATION, 206 (May 13, 1968), 622-624.

Levitt, M. and B. Rubenstein. "The Children's Crusade," AMERICAN JOURNAL OF ORTHOPSYCHIATRY, 38 (July 1968), 591-598.

Lipset, S. M. "Political Thrust Motivating Campus Turmoil," SATURDAY REVIEW, 52 (March 1, 1969), 23-25+.

Lipset, S. M. "Rebellion on Campus," AMERICAN EDUCATION, 4 (October, 1968), 28-31.

Lipset, S. M. "Student Activism," CURRENT AFFAIRS BULLETIN, (Sydney), 42 (July 15, 1968), 50-64.

Lipset, S. M. "University Student Politics," in Robert Sigel, ed. ABOUT POLITICS. New York, Random House, 1970, 74-82.

Lobenthal, J. S., jr. "Catabolism of a Student Revolt," JOURNAL OF HIGHER EDUCATION, 40 (December, 1969), 717-730.

Logan, John, jr. "American Colleges and the Student Revolt," in Esther Lloyd-Jones and Herman Estrin, eds. THE AMERICAN STUDENT AND HIS COLLEGE. Boston: Houghton Mifflin, 1967.

Lowenthal, Richard. "Unreason and Revolution," in Irving Howe, ed BEYOND THE NEW LEFT. New York: McCall, 1970, 55–84.

Lowman, Dean. "The New Student Left," JOURNAL OF THE NATIONAL ASSOCIATION OF WOMEN DEANS AND COUNSELORS, 31 (Winter, 1968), 57–63.

Lustig, Jeff. "Not Foolproof, but Foolish," in Immanuel Wallerstein and Paul Starr, eds. THE UNIVERSITY CRISIS READER, II. New York: Random House, 1971, 41–50.

Lyford, Joseph P. "Who's Brainwashing Whom? The Theater of Violence on America's Campuses Is Being Tailored for Television as Carefully as Network and Sponsor Make a TV Special," CENTER MAGAZINE, 2 (March, 1969), 2–6.

*Lynch, James J. "Disorder, Power and the Students," VIRGINIA QUARTERLY REVIEW, 43 (Winter, 1967), 36–52.

*Lynd, S. "New Left," ANNALS OF THE AMERICAN ACADEMY OF POLITICAL AND SOCIAL SCIENCE, 382 (March, 1969), 64–72.

McArthur, Charles C. "The Movement," in G. B. Blaine, jr. and C. C. McArthur, eds. EMOTIONAL PROBLEMS OF THE STUDENT. New York: Appleton-Century-Crofts, 1971, 268–306.

McCain, James A. "Unrest on the Campus," in Joseph Arelrod and Mervin B. Freedman, ed. ISSUES OF THE SEVENTIES. San Francisco: Jossey-Bass, 1970, 131–140.

MacInnis, C. "Old Youth and Young," ENCOUNTER, 29 (September, 1967), 29–35.

MacLeish, R. "Youth in Dissent: Rebellion or Renewal?" READER'S DIGEST, 92 (May, 1968), 75–80.

Maes, J. L. "Cultural Causes for Student Activism," JOURNAL OF EDUCATION, 151 (February, 1969), 36–41.

Malone, D. H. "Testimony on Student Unrest Before California Legislative Committee," AMERICAN ASSOCIATION OF UNIVERSITY PROFESSORS BULLETIN, 55 (March, 1969), 91–93.

Marine, G. and R. Erlich. "School's Out," RAMPARTS, 7 (December 14, 1968), 19–25.

*Mauss, Armaud L. "The Lost Promise of Reconciliation: New Left versus Old Left," JOURNAL OF SOCIAL ISSUES, 27 (Number 1, 1971), 1–20.

Mayhew, Lewis. "Campus Conflict and Confluence," in L. B. Mayhew, ed. HIGHER EDUCATION IN THE REVOLUTIONARY DECADES. Berkeley, California: McCutchan, 1967, 457–466.

Mayhew, Lewis B. "Faith and Despair," in Kerry G. Smith, ed. STRESS AND CAMPUS RESPONSE. San Francisco: Jossey-Bass, 1968, 265–279.

Means, R. L. "Who Is Responsible for Student Violence," AMERICA, 120 (March 29, 1969), 352–355.

Mendel, Arthur. "Robots and Rebels," NEW REPUBLIC, 160 (January 11, 1969), 16–20, 33+.

246

*Miller, Michael V. "The Student State of Mind," DISSENT, 12 (Spring, 1965), 176–183.

Mitchell, Maurice B. "College Campus and Student Unrest," INSURANCE COUNSEL JOURNAL, 36 (October, 1969), 529–541.

Moore, R. S. "Protest and Beyond," in Bruce Douglass, ed. REFLECTIONS ON PROTEST. Richmond, Virginia: John Knox Press, 1967, 51–60.

Murphy, Franklin D. "The Time-Honored Student Restlessness," INTER-COLLEGIAN, 85 (Summer, 1967), 10–13.

Murray, N. "Silent Majority Myth," NATIONAL ASSOCIATION OF STUDENT PERSONNEL ADMINISTRATORS JOURNAL, 9 (July, 1971), 32–36.

Myers, John Holt. "Political Reactions," in Grace Holmes, ed. LAW AND DISCIPLINE ON CAMPUS. Ann Arbor, Michigan: Institute of Continuing Legal Education, 1971, 139–149.

"New Radicalism," PARTISAN REVIEW, 32, 33 (Spring, Summer, Fall, 1965, Winter 1966), 183–210, 341–408, 526–542, 34–77.

Newfield, Jack. "New Politics: More Mood than Movement," NATION, 209 (July 28, 1969), 70–73.

Newfield, J. "Real Revolt on Campus," COMMONWEAL, 75 (December 15, 1961), 309–311.

Nieburg, H. L. "Living with Violence: Excerpts from Political Violence," CURRENT, 112 (November, 1969), 36–42.

Nisbet, Robert. "Who Killed the Student Movement?" ENCOUNTER, 34 (February, 1970), 10–18.

Ohlsen, M. M. "Dissident Students," CONTEMPORARY EDUCATION, 42 (Fall, 1971), 157–163.

Olafson, Frederick. "Student Activism and the Social Role of the Univer-sities," in Sidney Hook, ed. IN DEFENSE OF ACADEMIC FREEDOM. New York: Pegasus, 1971, 130–150.

Osher, David. "Politics and Strategy in Resistance," NEW POLITICS, 7 (Fall, 1968), 58–64.

Padgett, Jack F. "The New Breed in Search of a New Morality," LIBERAL EDUCATION, 54 (October, 1968), 435–442.

Perkins, James A. "The Restless Student," MINERVA, 6 (Summer, 1968) 487–497.

"Perspectives on Students and the University," YALE REVIEW, 60 (December, 1970), 161–198.

Pietrofesa, J. J. and W. H. Van Hoose. "Student Dissent: An Analysis," CLEARING HOUSE, 44 (March, 1970), 395–400.

Podhoretz, Norman. "Yes and No," in Alexander Klein, ed. NATURAL ENEMIES? YOUTH AND THE CLASH OF GENERATIONS. New York: Lippincott, 1969, 227–233.

Pollitt, Daniel. "Student Demonstrations," NATIONAL ASSOCIATION OF STUDENT PERSONNEL ADMINISTRATORS JOURNAL, 47 (1965), 186–210.

Powell, Lewis, jr. "A Strategy for Campus Peace," in W. Brickman and S. Lehrer, eds. CONFLICT AND CHANGES ON THE CAMPUS: THE

RESPONSE TO STUDENT HYPERACTIVISM. New York: School and Society Books, 1970, 268–278.

Powell, Robert S., jr. "More than a Number," in Joseph Axelrod and Mervin B. Freedman, eds. ISSUES OF THE SEVENTIES. San Francisco: Jossey-Bass, 1970, 71–85.

Powledge, Fred. "The Student Left: Spurring Reform," NEW YORK TIMES, (March 25, 1965), 1–26.

Preis, J. "UW: The Unrevolutionary Present," NORTH AMERICAN REVIEW, 6 (Summer, 1969), 16–21.

"Problems of the Student Movement," MONTHLY REVIEW, 20 (December, 1968), 1–6.

Proctor, John. "The New Left," POLITICAL AFFAIRS, 44 (December, 1965), 32–47.

Proshansky, H. M. and R. M. Evans, eds. "Political Extremism in the 1960's," JOURNAL OF SOCIAL FORCES, 19 (Number 2, 1963), 1–131.

Punke, H. H. "Age of Protest," SOCIAL STUDIES, 59 (December, 1968), 318–325.

Pyke, L. H. "Student Dissent and Activism," VESTES, 15 (1972), 2–9.

Quann, C. J. "Student Unrest. A Double Image," COLLEGE AND UNI-VERSITIES, 44 (Spring, 1969), 256–262.

"Radicals in America: Who, What, Where and Why?" SENIOR SCHOLAS-TIC, 98 (April 19, 1971), 4–14.

Rahv, Philip. "A Guide to the Left," NEW YORK REVIEW OF BOOKS, 9 (October 12, 1967), 10–13.

Rawls, Betty. "Student Unrest Justified," COLLEGE AND UNIVERSITY JOURNAL, 8 (Fall, 1969), 40–45.

Reak, Jack E. "Student Unrest on American College and University Campuses," NORTH CENTRAL NEWS BULLETIN, 28 (April–May, 1967), 26–33.

Reiman, R. E. and Keith Clark. "Student Research Organizations: A Response to Campus Tensions," in Clifford T. Stewart, ed. INSTITUTIONAL RESEARCH AND INSTITUTIONAL POLICY FORMULATION. Claremont: California Association for Institutional Research, 1971, 170–174.

"The Resistance Movement," BOWDITCH REVIEW, 1 (Summer–Fall, 1967), 21–40.

"Restless Campus: Search for Understanding and Support: 1969 Conference Section," COLLEGE AND UNIVERSITY JOURNAL, 8 (Fall, 1969), 34–63.

Reynolds, Neil R. "Student Dissent and the Mass Media," COLLEGE AND UNIVERSITY JOURNAL, 9 (Spring, 1970), 9–12.

Rhinelander, Philip H. "Styles of Anti-Americanism," PER/SE, 3 (Fall, 1968), 8–15.

Rise, James. "The Campus Climate: A Reminder," in Samuel Baskin, ed. HIGHER EDUCATION AND SOME NEWER DEVELOPMENTS. New York: McGraw-Hill, 1965, 304–308.

Rich, John Martin. "Intellectual Sources of Student Militancy," in W. Brickman and S. Lehrer, eds. CONFLICT AND CHANGE ON THE CAMPUS:

THE RESPONSE TO THE STUDENT HYPERACTIVISM. New York: School and Society Books, 1970, 144–150.

Ridgeway, J. "Cops and the Kids," NEW REPUBLIC, 159 (September 7, 1968), 11–14.

*Riesman, David. "Styles of Response to Social Change," JOURNAL OF SOCIAL ISSUES, 17 (Number 1, 1961), 78–92.

Roche, John P. "The Rebellion of the Clerks," NEW LEADER, 52 (June 23, 1969), 14–18.

Ross, Dan. "American Youth on the Move," POLITICAL AFFAIRS, 39 (August, 1960), 24–83.

Ross, M. "Industrial Jurisprudence and the Campus," EDUCATIONAL RECORD, 51 (Winter, 1970), 28–33.

Rossman, Michael, Morris Abram, Seymour M. Lipset and Michael Vozick, et al. "Violence and Power on Campus, A Debate," CHANGE, 1 (March–April, 1969), 28–41.

Rosten, L. "To an Angry Young Man," LOOK, 32 (November 12, 1968), 28.

Rovitt, Earl. "On the Contemporary Apocalyptic Imagination," AMERI-CAN SCHOLAR, 37 (Summer, 1968), 453–468.

Rubinstein, Eli A. "Paradoxes of Student Protests," AMERICAN PSY-CHOLOGIST, 24 (February, 1969), 133–141.

Ruether, R. "Confrontation and Communication," CHRISTIAN CENTURY, 86 (September 10, 1969), 1163–1165.

Rustin, Bayard. "The New Radicalism: Round III," PARTISAN REVIEW, 32 (Fall, 1965), 526–542.

Ryan, J. J. "Student Unrest: The Educational Reasons," CATHOLIC WORLD, 208 (October, 1968), 7–10.

Ryman, E. C. "Student Revolt against Society or against Institutions?" INTERNATIONAL BUREAU OF EDUCATION BULLETIN, 42 (Fourth Quarter, 1968), 247–250.

Sachar, Abram. "A Climate of Commitment," in Eli Ginzberg, ed. VALUES AND IDEALS OF AMERICAN YOUTH. New York: Columbia University Press, 1961, 317–325.

Sanford, Nevitt. "Loss of Talent," in Joseph Axelrod and Mervin B. Freedman, ed. ISSUES OF THE SEVENTIES. San Francisco: Jossey-Bass, 1970, 56–71.

Schaar, J. H. and S. S. Wolin. "Where We Are Now," NEW YORK REVIEW OF BOOKS, 14 (May 7, 1970), 3–10.

Schickel, Richard. "Why Youth Seeks New Values," in Alexander Klein, ed. NATURAL ENEMIES? YOUTH AND THE CLASH OF GENERATIONS. New York: Lippincott, 1969, 1–10.

Schlesinger, Arthur M., jr. "McCarthyism Is Threatening Us Again," SATURDAY EVENING POST, 239 (August 13, 1966), 10–16.

Schlesinger, A., et al. "When, If Ever, Do You Call in the Cops," NEW YORK TIMES MAGAZINE, (May 4, 1969), 34–36.

Schrag, P. "Covering the Academic Fires," CHANGE, 2 (July–August, 1970), 10–13.

Schrag, Peter. "Stirrings on the Campus," in Samuel I. Bellman, ed. THE COLLEGE EXPERIENCE. San Francisco: Chandler, 1962, 135–140.

Schroth, A. "Students, Politics and Power," AMERICA, 119 (September 28, 1968), 258–259.

Schwab, Joseph J. "Diagnoses of Student Protest," UNIVERSITY OF CHICAGO MAGAZINE, 62 (March/April, 1970), 15–21.

Schwartz, Charles. "The Movement versus the Establishment," NATION, 210 (June 22, 1970), 747–751.

Schwartz, Ed. "On Demonstration," in Julian Foster, and Durward Long, eds. PROTEST! STUDENT ACTIVISM IN AMERICA. New York: Morrow, 1970, 394–400.

*Schwartz, Edward. "What the Students Want," PROGRESSIVE, 32 (June, 1968), 32–35.

Scott, R. L. "Messages Gouged on Ivied Walls," QUARTERLY JOURNAL OF SPEECH, 55 (April, 1969), 183–187.

Seabury, Paul. "Gideon's Army and Moynihan's Pros," in A. Kopkind, ed. THOUGHTS OF THE YOUNG RADICALS. New York: New Republic, 1966.

Searle, John. "A Foolproof Scenario for Student Revolt," NEW YORK TIMES MAGAZINE, (December 19, 1968), 4–6.

Seeley, John R. "Stance and Substance," ANNALS OF THE AMERICAN ACADEMY OF POLITICAL AND SOCIAL SCIENCE, 395 (May, 1971), 95–104.

Seligman, D. "Special Kind of Rebellion," FORTUNE, 79 (January, 1969), 66–69.

Sewell, William H. "Students and the University," AMERICAN SOCIOLO-GIST, 6 (May, 1971), 111–117.

Sharp, Samuel. "University and Revolution: A Question of Relevance," in James Weaver and Gary Weaver, eds. THE UNIVERSITY AND REVOLUTION. Englewood Cliffs, New Jersey: Prentice-Hall, 1969, 55–59.

Shoben, E. J., jr. "Demonstrations, Confrontations and Academic Business as Usual," WESTERN HUMANITIES REVIEW, 23 (Winter, 1969), 63–72.

*Shoben, E. J., jr. "Student Unrest: The Climate of Protest." COUNSELING PSYCHOLOGIST 1 (Fall, 1969), 14–32.

Shoben, E. J. "Students and Civil Disobedience," JOURNAL OF GENERAL EDUCATION, 20 (October, 1968), 218–226.

Shoben, E. J., jr. "Thoughts on the Decay of Morals," in G. K. Smith, et al, eds. STRESS AND CAMPUS RESPONSE. San Frnacisco: Jossey-Bass, 1968, 134–144.

Siegel, Jules. "Revolution," in D. Myrus, ed. THE YOUTH CULTURE, Chicago: Playboy Press, 1971, 140–146.

Silver, Allan. "Orwell, Thou Should'st Be Living at This Hour!" in Immanuel Wallerstein and Paul Starr, eds. THE UNIVERSITY CRISIS READER, II. New York: Random House, 1971, 85–92.

Silver, Allan. "The University Rebellion," NEW YORK REVIEW OF BOOKS, 12 (January 30, 1969), 15–23.

Singletary, Otis, A. "Student Unrest: Activists and Issues." AGB REPORTS, 11 (November, 1968), 3–10.

Smith, B. E., ed. "Natural Law Institute 1969: The Student Revolt: A Symposium," LOYOLA LAW REVIEW, 15 (1968–1969), 219–262.

Sobel, Michael. "An Encouraging Sign in the Recent Student Protests," JOURNAL OF HIGHER EDUCATION, 34 (May, 1968), 152–155.

"Social Changes and the College Student," EDUCATIONAL RECORD, 41 (October, 1960), 329–358.

Sparzo, Frank. "Facing the Issues of Student Unrest," in W. Brickman and S. Lehrer, eds. CONFLICT AND CHANGE ON THE CAMPUS: THE RESPONSE TO STUDENT HYPERACTIVISM. New York: School and Society Books, 1970, 215–227.

"Special Section on Involved Youth: Symposium," AMERICAN EDUCATION, 5 (August, 1969), 11–25.

Spencer, M. J. "Why is Youth So Revolting Nowadays? Various Manifestations Including the Underground Press," WILSON LIBRARY BULLETIN, 43 (March, 1969), 640–647.

Spender, S. "What the Rebellious Students Want." NEW YORK TIMES MAGAZINE, (March 30, 1969), 56+.

Spitz, David. "Pure Tolerance: A Critique of Criticisms," in Irving Howe, ed. BEYOND THE NEW LEFT. New York: McCall, 1970, 101–120.

Starr, R. "Consciousness III: Theories of C. A. Reich," COMMENTARY, 50 (December, 1970), 46–54.

Steinberg, J. "Dangerous Enthusiasm? Report on Student Political Involvement," MADEMOISELLE, 67, (August, 1968), 278–279.

Stucker, G. "Youth, Rebellion and the Environment," NATIONAL PARKS AND CONSERVATION MAGAZINE, 45 (April, 1971), 6–9.

"Student Activism; Channeling Activism into Accomplishment," NATIONS SCHOOLS, 84 (September, 1969), 39–50.

"Student Protests: How Far Is Too Far?" SENIOR SCHOLASTIC, 95 (October 20, 1969), 6–13.

"Student Rebels: How To Tame the Turmoil," NEWSWEEK, 73 (March 10, 1969), 66–73.

"Student Unrest: Why?" Symposium, TEXAS OUTLOOK, 52 (July, 1968), 14–17.

"Students USA: A Survey of Their World Affairs Activities," INTERCOM, 9 (July–August, 1967), 29–72.

"Symposium of New and Old Leftists: What's Happening to America?" PARTISAN REVIEW, 34 (Winter, 1967), 13–63.

Swados, Harvey. "What's Left of the Left?" in D. Boroff, ed. THE STATE OF THE NATION. Englewood Cliffs, New Jersey: Prentice Hall, 1965, 59–72.

Taylor, Harold. "The Ambiguities of Public Morality: A Problem for World Youths," in R. M. MacIver, ed. DILEMMA OF YOUTH IN AMERICA TODAY. New York: Harper and Brothers, 1961, 113–127.

Taylor, H. "New Young Are Now Heard," NEW YORK TIMES MAGAZINE, (January 29, 1961), 5+.

Taylor, H. "Student Revolution," PHI DELA KAPPAN, 51 (October, 1969), 62–67.

Taylor, Harold. "Student Unrest," in Joseph Axelrod and Mervin B.

Freedman, eds. ISSUES OF THE SEVENTIES. San Francisco: Jossey-Bass, 1970, 108–131.

Thompson, P. A. "American Student Revolt," CONTEMPORARY REVIEW, 198 (November, 1960), 613–616+.

Thomson, D. C. "Scranton Commission Report," NORTH AMERICAN REVIEW, 7 (Winter, 1970), 62–68.

Thomson, S. D. "Activism: A Game for Unloving Critics," EDUCATION DIGEST, 35 (September, 1969), 1–4.

Thomson, S. D. "Overview of Activism," JOURNAL OF SECONDARY EDUCATION, 44 (October, 1969), 252–259.

Thomson, S. D. "Perspective on Student Activism," THEORY INTO PRACTICE, 8 (October, 1969), 279–283.

Treuhaft, Jessica Mitford. "The Indignant Generation," NATION, 192 (May 27, 1961), 451–456.

Trevor, Fisk. "The Nature and Causes of Student Unrest," POLITICAL QUARTERLY, 40 (October/December, 1969), 419–425.

"Troubled Campus: Symposium," ATLANTIC, 216 (November, 1965), 107–112+.

Troutman, William F., jr. "The New Student Left: Liberal or Radical? The Case of the Southern Student Organizing Committee," in Hans H. Indorf, ed. POLITICS 1970. Greenville, North Carolina: Political Science Department, East Carolina University, 1970, 83–102.

Trump, J. L. and J. Hunt. "Nature and Extent of Student Activism," NATIONAL ASSOCIATION OF SECONDARY SCHOOL PRINCIPALS BULLETIN, 53 (May, 1969), 150–158.

"Turn from Campus Violence; the Reasons," U.S. NEWS AND WORLD REPORT, 71, (October 25, 1971), 40–43.

Tyler, Gus. "Insurrection of the In Between," NEW LEADER, 52 (April 28, 1969), 16–20.

Tyrmand, L. "Revolutionaries: European versus American," NEW YORK TIMES MAGAZINE, (February 15, 1970), 24–25+.

"Vanguard of the Campus Revolt," LOOK, 32 (October 1, 1968), 23+.

Vaughan, R. "Confrontation and Disruption," LIFE, 65 (October 18, 1968), 76–81+.

Voss, V. "College Barometer," MADEMOISELLE, 54 (April, 1962), 139–141+.

Wald, George. "Generation in Search of a Future," in I. Wallerstein and P. Starr, eds. THE UNIVERSITY CRISIS READER, I. New York: Random House, 1971, 4–12.

Walsh, J. L. "Student Protest Movement: History or Prelude?" COMMON-WEAL, 95, (February 4, 1972), 422–424+.

Walsh, Joseph L. "What the Students Want: The Meaning of the Protests," COMMONWEAL, 83 (November 19, 1965), 206–209.

Walzer, Michael. "Violence: The Police; The Militants and the Rest of Us," DISSENT, 18 (April, 1971), 119–127.

Ward, Barbara. "Why Students Revolt," NATION, 200 (January 25, 1965), 81–85.

252

Warnecke, Steven. "American Student Politics," YALE REVIEW, 60 (December, 1970), 185–199.

Waskow, Arthur I. "Young America's Newest Vocation: Awakening the Disadvantaged and the Disinterested to Their Political Opportunities and Responsibilities," SATURDAY REVIEW, 48 (June 5, 1965), 12–14.

*Ways, Max. "On the Campus: A Troubled Reflection of the United States," FORTUNE, 72 (September, 1965 and October, 1965), 130–135 and 140–147.

Weber, P. J. "Revolution on American Campuses: an Analysis," CATHOLIC WORLD, 210 (March, 1970), 248–252.

Weiss, John. "On the Youth Question," POLITICAL AFFAIRS, 42 (November, 1963), 64–65.

"What Student Activists Are Doing," NATIONS SCHOOLS, 83 (March, 1969), 61–66.

Williams, D. T., jr. "Awesome Effectiveness of Confrontation," EDUCATIONAL RECORD, 51 (Spring, 1970), 130–133.

Williamson, E. G. "Should Students Be Activists?" JOURNAL OF COLLEGE STUDENT PERSONNEL, 11 (September, 1970), 342–347.

Williamson, E. G. "Student Discontent Today: A Call for Educational Statesmanship," AGB REPORTS, 8 (December, 1965), 1–34.

Wilson, Thurlow R. "The Defiant and Disruptive Student: Three Models for Education," EDUCATION AND URBAN SOCIETY, 1 (January, 1968), 47–60.

Wingfield, C. J. "Campus Conflict and Institutional Maintenance: An Agenda for Public Administration," PUBLIC ADMINISTRATION REVIEW, 30 (March, 1970), 96–101.

Witten, E. "The New Left: Rhetoric of Ambivalence," NATION, 207 (December 16, 1968), 646–648.

Wolfe, Burton. "The Hoover Report," in Albert Anderson and Bernice Biggs, eds. A FOCUS ON REBELLION. San Francisco: Chandler, 1962, 115–118.

Woodring, P. "View from the Campus: Latitude of Protest," SATURDAY REVIEW, 51 (August 17, 1968), 52–53.

"World Campus: Points from Press and Platform," ROTARIAN, 117 (October, 1970), 34–38.

"You Can't Turn Off Concern," AMERICAN EDUCATION, 5 (August, 1969), 12–16.

Young, J. P. "In a Time of Campus Crises, College Publishers Ponder Future Role," PUBLISHERS WEEKLY, 195 (April 21, 1969), 28–31.

"Youth: A Social Force?" INTERNATIONAL SOCIAL SCIENCE JOURNAL, 24 (Number 2, 1972), 216–373.

"Youth in Ferment: What's It All About: Symposium," SENIOR SCHOLASTIC, 94 (March 7, 1969), 4–12.

"Youth 'Liberates' America: Symposium," AMERICA, 122 (April 25, 1970), 429–442.

Zaremba, E. "Student Voices: What Makes a Social Issue a Library Issue?" WILSON LIBRARY BULLETIN, 45 (September, 1970), 54–61.

Zinn, Howard. "Thou Shalt not Kill," in Immanuel Wallerstein and Paul

Starr, eds. THE UNIVERSITY CRISIS READER, I. New York: Random House, 1971, 248–255.

I.3. Conservative Commentary

Bloomberg, Edward. STUDENT VIOLENCE. Washington: Public Affairs Press, 1970.

Bradley, Gene H. WHAT BUSINESSMEN NEED TO KNOW ABOUT THE STUDENT LEFT. Boston; Harvard University, Graduate School of Business Administration, 1968.

Brustein, Robert. REVOLUTION AS THEATRE: NOTES ON THE NEW RADICAL STYLE. New York: Liverright, 1971.

Buckley, William F. GOD AND MAN AT YALE; THE SUPERSTITION OF ACADEMIC FREEDOM. Chicago: Regnery, 1951.

COMMUNISM AND THE NEW LEFT: WHAT THEY'RE UP TO NOW. Washington: U.S. News and World Report, 1969.

Coyne, John, jr. THE KUMQUAT STATEMENT. New York: Cowles, 1970.

Divale, William Tulio. I LIVED INSIDE THE CAMPUS REVOLUTION. New York: Cowles 1970.

Estrada, J. ed. THE UNIVERSITY UNDER SIEGE. Los Angeles, Nash, 1971.

Free Society Association. THE NEW STUDENT LEFT. Washington: Free Society Association, 1965.

*Gerberding, William and Duane Smith, eds. THE RADICAL LEFT: THE ABUSE OF STUDENT DISCONTENT. Boston: Houghton Mifflin, 1970.

Hammowy, R. LEFT AND RIGHT MEET. Berkeley, California: Alliance of Libertarian Activists, 1966.

Hook, Sidney, ed. IN DEFENSE OF ACADEMIC FREEDOM. New York: Pegasus, 1971.

Hoover, J. Edgar. COMMUNIST TARGET-YOUTH. Washington: House Committee on un-American Activities. Government Printing Office, 1961.

Kobetz, Richard W. and Carl W. Hamm, eds. CAMPUS UNREST: DIALOGUE OR DESTRUCTION? Proceedings of the International Association of Chiefs of Police Workshop for State Police Officials and Campus Security Directors. The University of Nebraska, May, 1970, International Association of Chiefs of Police, 1970, 160.

*Luce, Philip Abbott. THE NEW LEFT. New York: McKay, 1966.

Luce, Philip Abbott. ROAD TO REVOLUTION: COMMUNIST GUERILLA WARFARE IN THE U.S.A. San Diego, California; Viewpoint Books, 1967.

National Association of Manufacturers. THUNDER ON THE CAMPUS. New York: National Association of Manufacturers, 1967.

Noebel, D. A. COMMUNISM, HYPNOTISM AND THE BEATLES. Tulsa: Christian Crusade Publications, 1965.

Noebel, D. A. RHYTHM, RIOTS, AND REVOLUTION. Tulsa: Christian Crusade Publications, 1966.

*Root, Edward Merrill. COLLECTIVISM ON THE CAMPUS; THE BATTLE

254

FOR THE MIND IN AMERICAN COLLEGES. New York: Devin-Adair, 1955.

Shinto, William Mamoru. THE DRAMA OF STUDENT REVOLT. Valley Forge, Pennsylvania: Judson Press, 1970.

Toole, Kenneth Ross. THE TIME HAS COME TO SAY THE THINGS THAT NEED TO BE SAID ABOUT CAMPUS VIOLENCE, THE TYRANNY OF A MINORITY, THE CRUSADE OF THE SPOILED CHILDREN, THE PARENTAL ABDICATION OF RESPONSIBILITY AND THE LACK OF COURAGE, INTEGRITY AND WISDOM ON THE PART OF OUR EDUCATIONAL LEADERS. New York: Morrow, 1971.

U.S. Federal Bureau of Investigation. YOUTH IN REBELLION. Washington: Federal Bureau of Investigation, 1969.

Weaver, Ben H. THE STUDENT EXPLOITERS. Enid, Oklahoma: Phillips University Press, 1970.

Widener, Alice. STUDENT SUBVERSION. The Origin of America's Leftist Agitators, How They Emerged in the 1960's—slowly, When No One Was Aware—and How in 1968 They Burst Forth with Disruption, Violence and "Guerilla Politics." New York: U.S.A., 1968.

Widener, Alice. TEACHERS OF DESTRUCTION: THEIR PLANS FOR A SOCIALIST REVOLUTION: AN EYEWITNESS ACCOUNT. Washington: Citizens Evaluation Institute, 1971.

Wilhelmsen, Fredrick D. SEEDS OF ANARCHY: A STUDY OF CAMPUS REVOLUTION. Dallas: Argus Academic Press, 1969.

Young Americans for Freedom, University Research Committee. A FACULTY-STUDENT INQUIRY INTO THE CAUSES OF CAMPUS DIS-ORDERS. Washington, D.C.: Young Americans For Freedom, 1970.

Bettelheim, B. "College Student Rebellion: Explanations and Answers," PHI DELTA KAPPAN, 50 (May, 1969), 511–514.

Bettelheim, B. "Student Revolt: the Hard Core" Statement before the House Special Committee on Education," VITAL SPEECHES, 35 (April 15, 1969), 405–410.

Bradley, Thomas. "A Plea for Heresy," LIBERATION, 11 (August, 1966), 34–36, 40.

Brann, Eva. The Student's Problem," LIBERAL EDUCATION, 54 (October, 1968), 369–385.

Brown, S. "We Can't Appease the Younger Generation," NEW YORK TIMES MAGAZINE, (November 27, 1966), 56–67+.

Buckley, William F., jr. "The Responsibilities of the Student," in Alexander Klein, ed. NATURAL ENEMIES? YOUTH AND THE CLASH OF GENERA-TIONS. New York: J. B. Lippincott, 1969, 144–152.

Bunzel, John. "Student Power, Relevance and the Academy," INTER-COLLEGIATE REVIEW, 7 (Spring, 1971), 165–170.

"Campus Agitation versus Education," LIFE, 581 (January 22, 1965), 4.

"Can American Education Survive One More Year Like the One We Have Just Been Through?" NATIONAL REVIEW, 22 (July 14, 1970), 722–728.

Capell, E. "The Communist Student Plan," HERALD OF FREEDOM, (May 17, 1968).

"Communism and the New Left: What They're Up to Now," U.S. NEWS AND WORLD REPORT, 66 (January 20, 1969), 56–57.

Csikszentmihalyi, Mihaly. "The Eclipse of Education," MODERN AGE, 13 (Fall, 1969), 389–392.

Dallos, Robert E. "The Taxpayer and Campus Unrest," JOURNAL OF CALIFORNIA LAW ENFORCEMENT, 5 (October, 1970), 61–68.

Deane, Herbert A. "The New Nihilists," THE COLUMBIA UNIVERSITY FORUM, 10 (Summer, 1967), 36–39.

Deane, Herbert. "On the New Student Nihilism," in Sidney Hook, ed. IN DEFENSE OF ACADEMIC FREEDOM. New York: Pegasus, 1971, 26–35.

*Drachkovitch, M. "The 'New Left' in the United States: A Critical Appraisal," WESTERN POLITICS, 1 (Spring, 1966), 3–21.

Drachkovitch, M. "Radicalization and Fragmentation of the New Left," in LIBERTY UNDER LAW, ANARCHY TOTALITARIANISM: THIS IS THE CHOICE. Chicago: American Bar Association, 1970, 7–36.

Dyke, W. "Bombings, Campus Disorder: Interview," U.S. NEWS AND WORLD REPORT, 69 (October 5, 1970), 74–79.

East, John P. "Student Radicalism and Moral Authority: Some Personal Reflections," in Hans H. Indorf, ed. POLITICS 1970. Greenville, North Carolina: Political Science Department: East Carolina University, 1970, 47–58.

"End of the Youth Revolt?" U.S. NEWS AND WORLD REPORT, 71 (August 9, 1971), 26–31.

Evans, M. Stanton. "The New Totalitarians," INTERCOLLEGIATE REVIEW, 5 (Spring, 1969), 159–166.

Evans, M. Stanton. "Nihilism, a product of the Liberal system," in Immanuel Wallerstein and Paul Starr, eds. THE UNIVERSITY CRISIS READER, I. New York, Random House, 1971, 430–436.

*Feuer, Lewis. "Pornopolitics and the University," NEW LEADER, 48 (April 12, 1965), 14–19.

Garwood, John D. "Capitalism's Greatest Threat," PUBLIC UTILITIES FORTNIGHTLY, 83 (February 13, 1969), 25–31.

Gelliner, Ernest. "Myth, Ideology and Revolution," POLITICAL QUARTERLY, 40 (October/December, 1969), 472–484.

Geltman, M. "New Left and Old Right," NATIONAL REVIEW, 19 (June 13, 1967), 632–635.

Gray, R. T. "Campus Outlook: More Turmoil," NATION'S BUSINESS, 57 (August, 1969), 36–41.

*Greeley, Andrew M. "The End of the Movement," CHANGE, 4 (April, 1972), 42–47.

"The Guard versus Disorder," NATIONAL GUARDSMEN, 24 (June, 1970), 2–7, 9–13, 40.

Haley, P. Edward. "Students, Politics and Education: Notes on the Crisis." COLLEGE AND UNIVERSITY, 46 (Fall), 1970, 61–67.

Halle, L. J. "Student Drive to Destruction," NEW REPUBLIC, 159 (October 19, 1968), 10–13.

Hayakawa, S. I. "Gangsters Cash in on Student Revolt: Interview," U.S. NEWS AND WORLD REPORT, 66 (February 24, 1969), 38–41.

Hayakawa, S. I. "Protests, Pigs and Power Politics," LIBERAL EDUCA-
TION, 56 (March, 1970), 17–21.

Herberg, Will. "Anarchy on the Campus," MODERN AGE, 14 (Winter,
1969–1970), 2–10.

Hook, Sidney. "Barbarism, Virtue and the University," PUBLIC
INTEREST, (Spring, 1969), 23–29.

Hook, Sidney. "From the Platitudinous to the Absurd," in Sidney Hook,
ed. IN DEFENSE OF ACADEMIC FREEDOM. New York: Pegasus, 1971,
249–257.

Hook, S. "War against the Democratic Process," ATLANTIC, 223 (February, 1969), 45–49.

Hook, S. "Real Crisis on Campus: Interview," U.S. NEWS AND WORLD
REPORT, 66 (May 19, 1969), 40–44.

Hook, S. "Trojan Horse in American Higher Education," EDUCATIONAL
RECORD, 50 (Winter, 1969), 21–27.

Hook, Sidney. "Violence and Responsibility in the Academy," in W.
Brickman and S. Lehrer, eds. CONFLICT AND CHANGE ON THE CAMPUS:
THE RESPONSE OF STUDENT HYPERACTIVISM. New York: School and
Society Books, 1970, 281–292.

Hook, S. "Who's Responsible for Campus Violence?" SATURDAY REVIEW,
52 (April 19, 1969), 22–25+.

Hoover, J. Edgar. "An Analysis of the New Left: A Gospel of Nihilism,"
COLLEGIATE SCENE, 2 (October, 1967).

Hoover, J. Edgar. "Communist Target–Youth: Communist Infiltration and
Agitation Tactics," in Albert Anderson and Bernice Biggs, eds. A FOCUS ON
REBELLION. San Francisco: Chandler, 1962, 101–115.

Kennan, G. F. "Radicals Without a Program: Radical Left on Campus,"
NEW YORK TIMES MAGAZINE, (January 21, 1968), 22–23+ and (February
4, 1968), 19.

Kirk, Russel A. "The University and Revolution: An Insane Conjunction,"
THE INTERCOLLEGIATE REVIEW, 6 (Winter, 1969–1970), 13–23 and in
Gary Weaver and James Weaver, eds. THE UNIVERSITY AND REVOLUTION.
Englewood Cliffs, New Jersey: Prentice-Hall, 1969, 67–82.

Kirk, Russell. "What's Relevant!" in E. Bander, ed. TURMOIL ON THE
CAMPUS. New York: H. W. Wilson, 1970, 78–82.

Knopfelmacher, F. "The Parasite As Revolutionary: The Fleecing of
America," INTERCOLLEGIATE REVIEW, 7 (Summer, 1971), 227–234.

Kristol, Irving. "New Right, New Left," PUBLIC INTEREST, Number 4
(Summer, 1966), 3–7.

*Kristol, Irving. "What's Bugging the Students?" ATLANTIC, 216
(November, 1965), 108–111.

Kurty, Paul. "Inside the Buffalo Commune: Or, How to Destroy a University," in Sidney Hook, ed. IN DEFENSE OF ACADEMIC FREEDOM. New
York: Pegasus, 1971.

Methvin, Eugene. "Students Against Campus Violence," READER'S
DIGEST, 98 (January, 1971), 62–69.

Mitchell, John. "Statement of the Attorney General Before a House Edu-

cation Subcommittee," in William Brickman and Stanley Lehrer, eds. CON-
FLICT AND CHANGE ON THE CAMPUS: THE RESPONSE TO STUDENT
HYPERACTIVISM. New York: School and Society, 1970, 455–462.

Mitchell, Maurice B. "Dissent: Divine or Diabolical? An Educator Noted
for Bridging Gaps on Campus Explores Causes and Solutions," ROTARIAN,
117 (October, 1970), 20–25.

"New Mood: A Harder Line on College Disturbances," U.S. NEWS AND
WORLD REPORT, 66 (March, 1969), 30–37.

Niemeyer, G. "Homesickness of the New Left," NATIONAL REVIEW,
22 (July 28, 1970), 779–783.

Peterson, Douglas. "The American Cause and the University," NEW
GUARD, 8 (March, 1968), 6–9.

"Quiet Majority: Other Side of Campus Revolt," U.S. NEWS AND WORLD
REPORT, 66 (May 26, 1969), 34–37.

Reagan, Ronald, "Academic Freedom and Academic Order," CHANGE,
1 (July–August, 1969), 33–36.

"Red Diaper Babies," NEW GUARD, (September, 1965), 6–12.

Rogge, Benjamin A. "New Conservatives and Old Liberals," NEW
INDIVIDUALIST REVIEW, 2 (Autumn, 1962), 31–34.

Schlesinger, A. "Existential Politics and the Cult of Violence," PHI DELTA
KAPPAN, 50 (September, 1968), 9–15.

"Student Violence: into a More Dangerous Era," U.S. NEWS AND WORLD
REPORT, 68 (May 18, 1970), 28–31.

"Students on the Rampage All Around the World," U.S. NEWS AND
WORLD REPORT, 66 (February 3, 1969), 8, 10–11.

Van Den Haag, Ernest. "Student Seizures: The New Element," MODERN
AGE, 14 (Summer–Fall, 1970), 257–269.

Wilson, L. "Where Campus Violence is Heading: Interview," U.S. NEWS
AND WORLD REPORT, 64 (May 20, 1968), 41–44.

Zoll, Donald A. "The Right of Revolution Reconsidered," INTER-
COLLEGIATE REVIEW, 5 (Spring, 1969), 167–176.

Zoll, Donald Atwell. "Violence in the Civilized Society," INTERCOLLE-
GIATE REVIEW, 5 (Fall, 1968), 8–12.

I.4. Political Reaction and Opinion on Activism

Eulau, Heinz and Harold Quinley. STATE OFFICIALS AND HIGHER
EDUCATION: A SURVEY OF THE OPINIONS AND EXPECTATIONS OF
POLICY MAKERS IN NINE STATES. New York: McGraw-Hill, 1970.

Reynolds, Rushian Neil. "The Characterization of American Student Dissent in Selected General Circulation Magazines." Unpublished Ph.D. dissertation, Florida State University, 1969.

*Urban Research Corporation. LEGISLATIVE RESPONSE TO STUDENT
PROTEST. Chicago: Urban Research Corporation, 1970.

Bemesderfer, Karl. "The Legislators Strike Back," in Grace Holmes, ed. LAW AND DISCIPLINE ON CAMPUS. Ann Arbor, Michigan: Institute of Continuing Education, 1971, 149–159.

Biggs, Donald A. and C. Edwin Vanghan. "Some Parents' Attitudes toward Campus Dissent," JOURNAL OF COLLEGE STUDENT PERSONNEL, 12 (September, 1971), 347–352.

Boffey, P. M. "Campus Unrest: Riots Bring Danger of Punitive Backlash," SCIENCE, 164 (April 11, 1969), 161–165.

Epstein, Yakov M., Peter Suedfeld and Daniel M. Bresnahan. "Reaction to A Campus Confrontation," JOURNAL OF APPLIED SOCIAL PSYCHOLOGY, 1 (January, 1971), 57–65.

Green, E. "Congress and College Violence; with Discussion," COMPACT 3 (August, 1969), 19–27.

Hickey, Neil. "What Is Television's Most Critical Failure? Some Think It Could Well Be Its Coverage of the Unrest on American College Campuses," TV GUIDE, 19 (January 23, 1971), 7–10+; 19 (January 30, 1971), 6–11; 19 (February 6, 1971), 35–36+; 19 (February 13, 1971), 43+; 19 (February 20, 1971), 36–38

Osmunson, R. L. "Higher Education as Viewed by College and University Presidents," SCHOOL AND SOCIETY, 98 (October, 1970), 367–370.

*Pommer, Matt. "State and Multiversity," in P. G. Altbach, R. Laufer, and S. McVey, eds. ACADEMIC SUPERMARKETS. San Francisco: Jossey-Bass, 1971, 112–120.

PRESIDENT'S COMMISSION ON CAMPUS UNREST. "Government and Campus Unrest," in REPORT OF THE PRESIDENT'S COMMISSION ON CAMPUS UNREST. New York: Arno Press, 1970, 213–231.

Turner, Ralph H. "The Public Perception of Protest," AMERICAN SOCIOLOGICAL REVIEW, 34 (December, 1969), 815–831.

Spaeth, Joe L. "Public Reactions to College Student Protests," SOCIOLOGY OF EDUCATION, 42 (Spring, 1969), 199–206.

"Student Unrest Seen as Nation's Top Problem," GALLUP POLITICAL INDEX, Number 61 (July, 1970).

Walsh, J. "Campus Unrest: Congress Ponders Federal Sanctions on Universities," SCIENCE 165 (July 4, 1969), 46–49.

White, Kevin. "Confrontation: The Campus and the City: The View from City Hall," CHANGE, 1 (January–February, 1969), 6–10.

I.5. Official Reports on Dissent and Activism

American Bar Association. Commisson on Campus Governance and Student Dissent. REPORT. Chicago: American Bar Association, 1970.

California. Legislature. Assembly. Select Committee on Campus Disturbance. REPORT. Sacramento, California: Assembly of the State of California, 1969.

*Carnegie Commission on Higher Education: DISSENT AND DISRUPTION:

PROPOSALS FOR CONSIDERATION OF THE CAMPUS. New York: McGraw-Hill, 1971.

*Committee on the Student in Higher Education. REPORT ON THE STUDENT IN HIGHER EDUCATION. New Haven, Connecticut: Hazen Foundation, 1968.

CONFRONTATION OR PARTICIPATION? THE FEDERAL GOVERNMENT AND THE STUDENT COMMUNITY. A REPORT TO THE PRESIDENT OF THE UNITED STATES BY THE WHITE HOUSE FELLOWS ASSOCIATION. Washington, D.C.: White House Fellows Association, 1969.

CONSTRUCTIVE CHANGES TO EASE CAMPUS TENSIONS. Washington, D.C.: National Association of State Universities and Land Grant Colleges, 1970.

*Harris, Daniel. STAFF STUDY OF CAMPUS RIOTS AND DISORDERS, OCTOBER 1967–MARCH 1969. Washington, D.C.: U.S. Government Printing Office, 1969.

*Linowitz, Sol M. CAMPUS TENSIONS: ANALYSIS AND RECOMMENDATIONS; REPORT. Washington, D.C.: American Council on Education, Special Commission on Campus Tensions, 1970.

Michigan State Senate. Committee to Investigate Campus Disorders and Student Unrest. FINAL STAFF REPORT. Lansing, Michigan, 1970.

National Association of State Universities and Land-Grant Colleges, Office of Institutional Research. CONSTRUCTIVE CHANGES TO EASE CAMPUS TENSIONS: STATE AND LAND-GRANT UNIVERSITIES TAKE POSITIVE STEPS TO INVOLVE STUDENTS AND CURTAIL CAMPUS DISRUPTIONS. Washington, D.C.: National Association of State Universities and Land-Grant Colleges, Office of Institutional Research, 1970, 54.

National Conference on Youth and the Institutions, Washington, 1968. YOUTH AND THE ESTABLISHMENT: THE REPORT. Washington: National Committee for Children and Youth, 1969.

*Newman, Frank, et al. REPORT ON HIGHER EDUCATION–REPORT TO THE SECRETARY, U.S. DEPARTMENT OF HEALTH, EDUCATION AND WELFARE. Washington, D.C.: U.S. Department of Health, Education and Welfare, March, 1971.

New York (State). Temporary Commission to Study the Causes of Campus Unrest. THE ACADEMY IN TURMOIL: FIRST REPORT. Albany, New York, 1970.

Pennsylvania. Department of Education. Bureau of Administrative Leadership. STUDENT UNREST. Harrisburg, 1970, (revised edition).

Special Committee on Campus Tensions. CAMPUS TENSIONS: ANALYSIS AND RECOMMENDATIONS. Washington, D.C.: American Council on Education, 1970.

*"Student Protest," in Jerome Skolnick, THE POLITICS OF PROTEST, (Report to the National Commission on the Causes and Prevention of Violence). New York: Bantam, 1969, 81–124.

U.S. National Commission on the Causes and Prevention of Violence. TO ESTABLISH JUSTICE, TO INSURE DOMESTIC TRANQUILITY: FINAL REPORT. Washington, D.C.: U.S. Government Printing Office, 1969.

U.S. Office of Education. Subcommittee on Easing Tensions in Education. REPORT. Washington: U.S. Office of Education, 1969.

*U.S. President's Commission on Campus Unrest. THE REPORT OF THE PRESIDENT'S COMMISSION ON CAMPUS UNREST: INCLUDING SPECIAL REPORTS: THE KILLINGS AT JACKSON STATE, THE KENT STATE TRAGEDY. New York: ARNO Press, 1970, (reprint).

U.S. President. CONFRONTATION OR PARTICIPATION? THE FEDER-AL GOVERNMENT AND THE STUDENT COMMUNITY. Washington, D.C.: Government Printing Office, 1968.

Washington (State). Council on Higher Education. CAMPUS UNREST: PRIORITIES FOR WASHINGTON, Olympia, 1971.

Washington (State). Governor's Commission for Youth Involvement. TOWARD A NEW ACTIVISM: YOUTH'S ROLE IN A CHANGING SOCIETY: FINAL REPORT. Olympia: 1970.

Brock, W. E., et al. "Congress Looks at the Campus: The Brock Report on Student Unrest," AAUP BULLETIN, 55 (September, 1969), 327–336.

"Campus Unrest; Excerpts from the Scranton Commission Report; With Discussion," TODAY'S EDUCATION, 60 (January, 1971), 41–48+.

*Special Committee on Campus Tensions. "Campus Tensions: Analysis and Recommendations," AMERICAN PSYCHOLOGIST, 25 (August, 1970), 694–726.

I.6. Autobiographical Accounts

Cowan, Paul. THE MAKING OF AN UNAMERICAN. New York: Viking, 1967.

Gerzon, Mark. THE WHOLE WORLD IS WATCHING: A YOUNG MAN LOOKS AT YOUTH'S DISSENT. New York: Viking, 1969.

*Kunen, James S. THE STRAWBERRY STATEMENT: NOTES OF A COLLEGE REVOLUTIONARY. New York: Random House, 1969.

*Mungo, Raymond. FAMOUS LONG AGO: MY LIFE AND HARD TIMES WITH THE LIBERATION NEWS SERVICE. Boston: Beacon, 1970.

Myerson, Michael. THESE ARE THE GOOD OLD DAYS: COMING OF AGE AS A RADICAL IN AMERICA'S LATE, LATE YEARS. New York: Grossman, 1970.

Potter, Paul. A NAME FOR OURSELVES. Boston: Little Brown, 1971.

*Powers, Thomas. DIANA: THE MAKING OF A TERRORIST. Boston: Houghton Mifflin, 1970.

Rader, Dotson. I AIN'T MARCHIN ANYMORE. New York: McKay, 1969.

Reeves, Donald. NOTES OF A PROCESSED BROTHER. New York: Pantheon, 1972.

Rosenbaum, Robert, ed. GROWING UP IN AMERICA. Garden City, New York: Doubleday, 1969.

Rossman, Michael. THE WEDDING WITHIN THE WAR. Garden City, New York: Anchor Books, 1971.

Sigal, Clancy. GOING HOME. Boston: Houghton, Mifflin, 1962.

Von Hoffman, Nicholas. TWO, THREE, MANY MORE. New York: Quadrangle Books, 1969.

Chickering, Sherman. "How We Got that Way," AMERICAN SCHOLAR, 36 (Autumn, 1967), 602–607.

Haracz, Kate. "The Education of Kate Haracz; Journal of an Undergraduate," CHANGE, 2 (May–June, 1970), 12–26.

Leggett, John. "The Metamorphosis of the Campus Radical," NEW YORK TIMES MAGAZINE, (January 30, 1972), 14–20.

Rossman, Michael. "Barefoot in a Marshmallow World," RAMPARTS, 4 (January, 1966), 70–74.

Rossman, Michael. "Notes from the County Jail," NEW YORK REVIEW OF BOOKS, 5 (February 15, 1968), 19–24.

Rossman, Michael. "Look, Ma: No Hope–A New Left Memoir," COMMONWEAL, 88 (April 12, 1968), 101–103.

J. THE "COUNTER CULTURE"

J.1. Counter-Culture–The "Beats"

Lipton, Lawrence. THE HOLY BARBARIANS. New York: Julian Messner, 1959.

Ostergaard, Geoffrey Nielson. LATTER-DAY ANARCHISM: THE POLITICS OF THE AMERICAN BEAT GENERATION. Ahmedabad (India): Harold Laski Institute of Political Science, 1964.

Parkinson, Thomas, ed. A CASEBOOK ON THE BEAT. New York: Crowell, 1961.

Rigney, Francis J. and L. B. Smith. THE REAL BOHEMIA. New York: Basic Books, 1961.

Spate, James L. "Structure and Trends in Values Systems in the 'Hip' Underground Contraculture and the American Middle Class, 1957–1959." Unpublished Ph.D. dissertation, Department of Sociology, Boston University, 1971.

Baldwin, J. "A Question of Identity," PARTISAN REVIEW, 21 (July, 1954), 402–410.

*Berger, R. M. "On the Youthfulness of Youth Cultures," SOCIAL RESEARCH, 30 (Autumn, 1963), 319–342.

Burdick, Eugene. "The Politics of the Beat Generation," WESTERN POLITICAL QUARTERLY, 12 (June, 1959), 553–559.

Butler, F. A. "On the Beat Nature of Beat," AMERICAN SCHOLAR, 30 (1960–61), 79–92.

Holmes, C. "This Is the Beat Generation," NEW YORK TIMES MAGAZINE, (November 16, 1952), 10+.

Moody, H. R. "Reflections on the Beat Generation," RELIGION IN LIFE, 28 (Summer, 1959), 426–432.

Podhoretz, N. "Know-nothing Bohemians," PARTISAN REVIEW, 25 (Spring, 1958), 305–311+.

Ross, Tim. "The Rise and Fall of the Beats," NATION, 192 (May 27, 1961), 456–458.

Scott, J. "Beat Literature and the American Teen Culture," AMERICAN QUARTERLY, 14 (Summer, 1962), 150–160.

Werner, A. "Bohemia and Anti-Bohemia in Art, "SOUTH ATLANTIC QUARTERLY, 61 (January, 1952), 97–106.

White, Burton. "On-Campus Politics: Juvenile Delinquents, Beats, Students: An Attempt at a Distinction," in Albert Anderson and Bernice Biggs, eds. A FOCUS ON REBELLION. San Francisco: Chandler, 1962, 115–118.

J.2. Counter-Culture of the 1960s and 1970s

Cross Reference. The problem of drugs and drug abuse has been dealt with in a separate section. See Section III F 1.

Aldridge, John W. IN THE COUNTRY OF THE YOUNG. New York: Harper's Magazine Press, 1970.

Berke, Joseph, ed. COUNTER CULTURE. London: Peter Owen, 1969.

Birmingham, John, ed. OUR TIME IS NOW: NOTES FROM THE HIGH SCHOOL UNDERGROUND. New York: Praeger, 1970.

Bloustein, Edward J. THE UNIVERSITY AND THE COUNTERCULTURE. New Brunswick, New Jersey: Rutgers University Press, 1972.

Blum, Jeffery and Judith Smith. NOTHING LEFT TO LOSE: STUDIES OF STREET PEOPLE. Boston: Beacon, 1972.

*Braden, William. AGE OF AQUARIUS. Chicago: Quadrangle, 1970.

Brown, Joe David. THE HIPPIES. New York: Time-Life Books, 1967.

*Cavan, Sherri. HIPPIES OF THE HAIGHT. St. Louis, Missouri: New Critics Press, 1971.

Diamond, Stephen. WHAT THE TREES SAID: LIFE ON A NEW AGE FARM. New York: Dell, 1971.

Earisman, Delbert L. HIPPIES IN OUR MIDST: THE REBELLION BEYOND REBELLION. Philadelphia, Pennsylvania: Fortress Press, 1968.

Editors of Ramparts, eds. CONVERSATIONS WITH THE NEW REALITY: READINGS IN THE CULTURAL REVOLUTION. San Francisco: Canfield Press, 1972.

Eisen, Jonathan, ed. ALTAMONT: DEATH OF INNOCENCE IN THE WOODSTOCK NATION. New York: Random House, 1970.

Fairfield, Richard. COMMUNES USA: A PERSONAL TOUR. Baltimore, Maryland: Penguin, 1972.

Foss, Daniel. FREAK CULTURE: LIFE STYLE AND POLITICS. St. Louis, Missouri: New Critics Press, 1972.

*Goodman, Mitchell, ed. THE MOVEMENT TOWARD A NEW AMERICA. Philadelphia, Pennsylvania: Pilgrim Press, 1970.

Gruen, John. THE NEW BOHEMIA. New York: Grosset and Dunlap, 1966.

Gustaitis, Rasa. TURNING ON. New York: Macmillan, 1969.

Hoffman, Abbie. WOODSTOCK NATION: A TALK-ROCK ALBUM. New York: Vintage Books, 1969.

Hopkins, Jerry, ed. THE HIPPIE PAPERS: NOTES FROM THE UNDERGROUND PRESS. New York: New American Library, 1968.

Houriet, Robert. GETTING BACK TOGETHER. New York: Coward, McCann, Georhegan, 1971.

Howard, John. THE HIPPIE COLLEGE DROPOUT: A FINAL REPORT. Eugene, Oregon: Oregon University, 1969.

Kanter, Rosabeth. COMMITMENT AND COMMUNITY: COMMUNES AND UTOPIAS IN SOCIOLOGICAL PERSPECTIVE. Cambridge, Massachusetts: Harvard University Press, 1972.

Katz, Elia. ARMED LOVE. New York: Holt, Rinehart, and Winston, 1971.

Kelly, Kevin D. YOUTH, HUMANISM, AND TECHNOLOGY. New York: Basic Books, 1972.

Kornbluth, Jesse, ed. NOTES FROM THE NEW UNDERGROUND. New York: Viking, 1968.

Lewis, Roger. OUTLAWS OF AMERICA: THE UNDERGROUND PRESS AND ITS CONTEXT: NOTES ON A CULTURAL REVOLUTION, Baltimore, Maryland: Penguin Books, 1973.

Malcolm, Henry. GENERATION OF NARCISSUS. Boston: Little, Brown, 1971.

Many, Seth, ed. LEWD. Boston: Beacon Press, 1972.

Melville, Keith. COMMUNES IN THE COUNTER-CULTURE: ORIGINS, THEORIES. New York: Morrow, 1972.

Myrus, Donald, ed. THE YOUTH CULTURE. Chicago: Playboy Press, 1971.

Paul, Jon and Charlotte, eds. FIRE! REPORTS FROM THE UNDERGROUND PRESS. New York: Dutton, 1970.

Roberts, Ron E. THE NEW COMMUNES: COMING TOGETHER IN AMERICA. Englewood Cliffs, New Jersey: Prentice-Hall, 1971.

*Roszak, Theodore. THE MAKING OF A COUNTER CULTURE: REFLECTIONS ON THE TECHNOCRATIC SOCIETY AND ITS YOUTHFUL OPPOSITION. Garden City, New York: Doubleday, 1969.

Simmons, J. I. and Barry Winograd. IT'S HAPPENING: A PORTRAIT OF THE YOUTH SCENE TODAY. Santa Barbara, California: Marc-Laird, 1966.

*Speck, Ross V. THE NEW FAMILIES: YOUTH, COMMUNES AND THE POLITICS OF DRUGS. New York: Basic Books, 1972.

Spinrad, Norman. FRAGMENTS OF AMERICA. North Hollywood, California: Now Library Press, 1970.

Wilson, Bryan. THE YOUTH CULTURE AND THE UNIVERSITIES. London: Faber, 1970.

264

Winter, Gibson. BEING FREE: REFLECTIONS ON AMERICA'S CULTURAL REVOLUTION. New York: Macmillan, 1970.

Wolf, Leonard. VOICES FROM THE LOVE GENERATION. Boston: Little, Brown, 1968.

Wolfe, Burton H. THE HIPPIES. New York: New American Library, 1968.

*Yablonsky, Lewis. THE HIPPIE TRIP. New York: Pegasus, 1968.

Abel, Bob. "Up from the Underground: Notes on the New Comix," in Bernard Rosenberg and David White, eds. MASS CULTURE REVISITED. New York: Van Nostrand Reinhold, 1971, 423–444.

Andrews, L. M. "Communes and the Work Crisis: Rebellion Against the Work Ethic," NATION, 211 (November 9, 1970), 460–463.

Ardery, P. P., jr. "Upon a Time in Woodstock," NATIONAL REVIEW, 21 (September 9, 1969), 908+.

Bealer, Robert C., Fern K. Willits and Peter R. Maida. "The Rebellious Youth Subculture—A Myth," CHILDREN, 11 (1964), 43–48.

Benello, C. George. "Wasteland Culture," in Gerald McGuigan, ed. STUDENT PROTEST. Toronto: Methuen, 1968, 192–222.

Berger, Bennett M. "Hippie Morality: More Old than New," TRANS-ACTION, 5 (December, 1967), 19–26.

Berger, B. L. and Berger, B. "Blueing of America," NEW REPUBLIC, 164 (April 3, 1971), 20–23.

Bloy, Myron B., jr. "Culture and Counter-Culture: Alienated Youth's Risky Challenge to the Enlightenment," COMMONWEAL, 89 (January 17, 1969), 493–496.

Brickman, H. "The Psychedelic 'Hip Scene': Return of the Death Instinct," AMERICAN JOURNAL OF PSYCHIATRY, 125 (December, 1968), 766–772.

Brown, Michael E. "The Condemnation and Persecution of Hippies," TRANS-ACTION, 6 (September, 1969), 33–46.

Buhle, Paul. "Komix Kountermedia," LEVIATHAN, 1 (July–August, 1969), 13–18.

Burks, John. "The Underground Press: A Special Report," ROLLING STONE, No. 43 (October 4, 1969), 11–32.

Chenoweth, L. "Rhetoric of Hope and Despair: A Study of the Jimi Hendrix Experience and the Jefferson Airplane," AMERICAN QUARTERLY, 23 (Spring, 1971), 25–45.

Coles, Robert. "The Words and Music of Social Change," in Michael Wertheimer, ed. CONFRONTATION: PSYCHOLOGY AND THE PROBLEMS OF TODAY. Glenview, Illinois: Scott Foresman, 1970, 365–373.

Corry, J. "Politics of Style: Radical Culture," HARPER, 241 (November, 1970), 60–64.

Cox, Harvey. "An Open Letter to Allen Ginsberg," in Alexander Klein, ed. NATURAL ENEMIES? YOUTH AND THE CLASH OF GENERATIONS. New York: Lippincott, 1969, 427–431.

Culver, Elsie Thomas. "The 'Free' Church of Berkeley's Hippies," CHRISTIAN CENTURY, 85 (April 10, 1968), 462–470.

Davis, Fred. "Why All of Us May Be Hippies Someday," TRANS-ACTION, 5 (December, 1967), 10–18.

DeCecco, J. P. "Tired Feelings, New Life-Styles, and the Daily Liberation of the Schools," PHI DELTA KAPPAN, 53 (November, 1971), 168–171.

Denhardt, Robert and H. David Allen. "Youth Responses to Cultural Incongruities," YOUTH AND SOCIETY, 3 (December, 1971), 237–255.

Denisoff, R. S. "Protest Movements: Class Consciousness and the Propaganda Song," SOCIOLOGICAL QUARTERLY, 9 (Spring, 1968), 228–247.

Denisoff, R. S. "Urban Folk 'Movement' Research: Value Free?" WESTERN FOLKLORE, 28 (July, 1969), 228–231.

Denisoff, R. S. and M. H. Levine. "Generations and Counter-Culture: A Study in the Ideology of Music," YOUTH AND SOCIETY, 21 (September, 1970), 33–58.

Distler, Luther. "The Adolescent 'Hippie' and the Emergence of a Matristic Culture," PSYCHIATRY, 33 (August, 1970), 362–371.

"Documents: Problems and Perspectives: New Morality," in M. Teodori, ed. THE NEW LEFT: A DOCUMENTARY HISTORY. Indianapolis, Indiana: Bobbs-Merrill, 1969, 348–361.

Dworkin, Gerald. "The Hippies: Permanent Revolution?" DISSENT, 16 (March–April, 1969), 180–183.

Ferrandino, Joseph. "From Rock Culture and the Development of Social Consciousness," in William Slate, ed. POWER TO THE PEOPLE! NEW LEFT WRITINGS. New York: Tower, 1970, 173–196.

Frazier, C. S. "Hippies: Not So Old, Not So Different," MIDWEST QUARTERLY, 10 (Autumn, 1968), 61–71.

Fredenburgh, F. A. "Apologia for the Hippie-Generation," MENTAL HYGIENE, 52 (July, 1968), 341–348.

Geis, Gilbert. "Hypes, Hippies and Hypocrites," YOUTH AND SOCIETY, 1 (June, 1970), 365–379.

Gitlin, Todd. "Requiem for the Youth Culture," LIBERATION, 14 (February, 1970), 34–40.

Gennrich, G. "Beat Wanderers," ATLAS, 11 (March, 1966), 146–151.

Gleason, Ralph. "Like a Rolling Stone," in Alexander Klein, ed., YOUTH AND THE CLASH OF GENERATIONS. New York: Lippincott, 1969, 486–497.

Goldberg, Herb. "Rock Music and Sex," SEXUAL BEHAVIOR, 1 (August, 1971), 25–31.

Gottwald, N. K. "Hippies, Political Radicals and the Church," CHRISTIAN CENTURY, 84 (August 16, 1967), 1043–1045.

Gregory, T. B. "Continuing Search for Identity: The New Culture," EDUCATIONAL LEADERSHIP, 29 (November, 1971), 125–128.

Greeley, Andrew. "Implications for the Sociology of Religion of Occult Behavior in the Youth Culture," YOUTH AND SOCIETY, 2 (December, 1970), 131–140.

Greeley, Andrew. "There's a New-Time Religion on Campus: Interest in the Occult and Witchcraft," NEW YORK TIMES MAGAZINE, (June 1, 1969), 14–15+.

Grinder, Robert E. "Distinctiveness and Thrust in the American Youth Culture," JOURNAL OF SOCIAL ISSUES, 25 (No. 2, 1969), 7-19.

Gutmann, David. "The Premature Gerontocracy: Themes of Aging and Death in the Youth Culture," SOCIAL RESEARCH, 39 (Autumn, 1972), 419-448.

Hall, Stuart. "The Hippies: an American 'Movement,' " in J. Nagel, ed. STUDENT POWER. London: Merlin Press, 1969, 170-202.

Harris, Mark. "The Flowering of the Hippies," ATLANTIC, 220 (September, 1967), 63-72.

Heath, G. L. "Counter Culture as Counter Technoversity; Stanford Mid-Peninsula Free University," EDUCATION FORUM, 36 (January, 1972), 247-253.

*Hinkle, Warren. "A Social History of the Hippies," RAMPARTS, 5 (March, 1967), 5-28.

"Hippies—1968," RELIGION IN LIFE, 37 (Winter, 1968), 498-539.

*"Hippies: Their Past and Future," TRANS-ACTION, 5 (December, 1967), 10-32.

Hitchcock, James. "Comes the Cultural Revolution," NEW YORK TIMES MAGAZINE, (July 27, 1969), 5, 40.

Horowitz, Irving L. "Rock on the Rocks, or Bubblegum, Anybody?" in Bernard Rosenberg and David White, eds. MASS CULTURE REVISITED. New York: Van Nostrand Reinhold, 1971, 450-465.

Howard, John R. "The Flowering of the Hippie Movement," ANNALS OF THE AMERICAN ACADEMY OF POLITICAL AND SOCIAL SCIENCE, 382 (March, 1969), 43-55.

Jarmon, James E. "The New Music and Counter Culture Values," YOUTH AND SOCIETY, 4 (September, 1972), 61-84.

Johnson, J. J. "The Hippy as a Developmental Task," ADOLESCENCE, 4 (Spring, 1969), 35-42.

Keniston, Kenneth. "Social Change and Youth in America," DAEDALUS, 91 (Winter, 1962), 145-171.

Kirby, Douglas. "A Counter-Culture Explanation of Student Activism," SOCIAL PROBLEMS, 19 (1971), 203-216.

Klein, Robert A. "Hippies as the Focus of Violence; or, Disaffected Society and Its Stand Against Youth," in Morton Levitt and Ben Rubenstein, eds. YOUTH AND SOCIAL CHANGE. Detroit: Wayne State University Press, 1972, 97-110.

Kloman, William. "The Groove of the Future," in Alexander Klein, ed, YOUTH AND THE CLASH OF GENERATIONS. New York: Lippincott, 1969, 502-507.

Kolodney, D. "Peace in Middle Earth: Escapist Trend," RAMPARTS, 9 (October, 1970), 35-38.

Langman, Lauren. "Dionysus—Child of Tomorrow: Notes on Post-industrial Youth," YOUTH AND SOCIETY, 3 (Fall, 1971), 80-100.

Laqueur, W. "Uses of History: Hippies and the New Left of Yesteryear," CURRENT, 93 (March, 1968), 57-62.

Lerner, Michael. "Where To?" CHANGE, 3 (September, 1971), 26-34.

Levenson, Edgar A., Arthur Feiner and Nathan Stockhamer. "Youth Culture: the New Sensibility," in Morton Levitt and Ben Rubenstein, eds. YOUTH AND SOCIAL CHANGE. Detroit: Wayne State University Press, 1972, 89-96.

Levin, Jack and James Spates. "Hippie Values: An Analysis of the Underground Press," YOUTH AND SOCIETY, 2 (September, 1970), 59-73.

Lewis, George. "Capitalism, Contra-Culture and the Head Shop; Explorations in Structural Change," YOUTH AND SOCIETY, 4 (September, 1972) 85-102.

Litwak, Leo. "Joy is the Prize: A Trip to Esalen Institute," in Harold Jaffe and John Tytell, eds. THE AMERICAN EXPERIENCE: A RADICAL READER. New York: Harper and Row, 1970, 212-222.

Lofland, J. "The Youth Ghetto: A Perspective the 'Cities of Youth' Around Our Large Universities," JOURNAL OF HIGHER EDUCATION, 39 (March, 1968), 121-143.

Molnar, Thomas. "The Counter Culture: An Historical Perspective," INTERCOLLEGIATE REVIEW, 8 (Winter, 1972-1973), 91-98.

Mungo, R. "If Mr. Thoreau Calls, Tell Him I've Left the Country," ATLANTIC, 225 (May, 1970), 72-86.

Moynihan, Daniel. "Nirvana Now," in Alexander Klein, ed. NATURAL ENEMIES? YOUTH AND THE CLASH OF GENERATIONS. New York: Lippincott, 1969, 41-53.

*Myerhoff, Barbara. "The Revolution as a Trip: Symbol and Paradox," in P. G. Altbach and R. S. Laufer, eds. THE NEW PILGRIMS. New York: McKay, 1972, 251-266.

*Nagel, Julian. "A World Cultural Revolution?" in Julian Nagel, ed. STUDENT POWER. London: Merlin Press, 1969, 203-224.

Oglesby, Carl. "The Hippies: Suburbanites with Beads," ACTIVIST, 8 (Fall, 1967), 9+.

Ohles, John F. "The University and the Unstudent," in W. Brickman and S. Lehrer, eds. CONFLICT AND CHANGE ON THE CAMPUS. New York: School and Society Books, 1970, 101-104.

Pepper, Thomas. "Growing Rich on the Hippie," NATION, 206 (April 29, 1968), 569-572.

Pitts, Jesse. "The Hippies as Contrameritocracy," DISSENT, 16 (July-August, 1969), 326-338.

Richardson, J. "Romantic Bohemia," HISTORY TODAY, 19 (July, 1969), 460-467.

Riley, Ned. "Activists, Radicals and Yippies," CAREERS TODAY, 1 (January, 1969), 22-28.

Rodnitzky, J. L. "The Evolution of the American Protest Song," JOURNAL OF POPULAR CULTURE, 3 (Summer, 1969), 35-45.

Rosenstone, Robert. "The Times They Are A-Changin': The Music of Protest," ANNALS OF THE AMERICAN ACADEMY OF POLITICAL AND SOCIAL SCIENCE, 382 (March, 1969), 131-144.

Roszak, Theodore. "Youth and the Great Refusal," NATION, 206 (March 25, 1968), 400-407.

Rudikoff, Sonya. "O Pioneers! Reflections on the Whole Earth People," COMMENTARY, 54 (July, 1972), 62–74.

Rule, P. C. "Decline of Flower Power," AMERICA, 124 (February 13, 1971), 141–145.

Schwartzkopf, G. W. "Culture and Counterculture in U.S. Politics," AMERICA, 123 (November 14, 1970), 396–398.

Scott, John F. "The Sounds of the Tuned-In Generation," in Morton Levitt and Ben Rubenstein, eds. YOUTH AND SOCIAL CHANGE. Detroit: Wayne State University Press, 1972, 342–356.

Seaton, S. Lee and Karen Ann Watson. "Counter Culture and Rock: A Cantometric Analysis," YOUTH AND SOCIETY, 4 (September, 1972), 3–20.

Shmueli, Efraim. "Modern Hippies and Ancient Cynics: a Comparison of Philosophical and Political Developments and Its Lessons," CAHIERS D'HISTOIRE MONDIALE, 12 (1970), 490–514.

Simon, Geoffrey and Gafton Trout. "Hippies in College—From Teeny Boppers to Drug Freaks," TRANS-ACTION, 5 (December, 1967), 27–32.

Simon, William and John Gagnon. "Children of the Drug Age," SATURDAY REVIEW, 51 (September 21, 1968), 496–499, 511–512.

Sklar, R. "Tolkien and Hesse: Top of the Pops," NATION, 204 (May 8, 1967), 598–601.

Solnit, Albert. "War and Tear in the Communes," NATION, 212 (April 26, 1971), 524–527.

Spates, James and Jack Levin. "Beats, Hippies, the Hip Generation and the American Middle Class: An Analysis of Values," INTERNATIONAL SOCIAL SCIENCE JOURNAL, 24 (No. 2, 1972), 326–353.

Starr, Roger. "The Counter-Culture and Its Apologists," COMMENTARY, 50 (December, 1970), 46–54.

Steele, Robert. "Art, Youth Culture, and the Movies," in Bernard Rosenberg and David White, eds. MASS CULTURE REVISITED. New York: Van Nostrand Reinhold, 1971, 222–232.

Thompson, Hunter. "The 'Hashbury' Is the Capital of the Hippies," in William O'Neill, ed. AMERICAN SOCIETY SINCE 1945. Chicago: Quadrangle Books, 1969, 123–140.

Todd, R. "Alternatives: Underground Media Conference at Goddard College," ATLANTIC, 226 (November, 1970), 112+.

Tonsor, Stephen. "Science, Technology, and the Cultural Revolution," INTERCOLLEGIATE REVIEW, 8 (Winter, 1972–1973), 83–90.

Trow, Martin. "Cultural Sophistication and Higher Education," in SELECTION AND EDUCATIONAL DIFFERENTIATION: REPORT OF A CONFERENCE. Berkeley, California: Center for the Study of Higher Education, University of California, Berkeley, 1959, 107–124.

Watts, William A. and David Whittaker. "Profile of a Nonconformist Youth Culture: A Study of the Berkeley Non-Students," SOCIOLOGY OF EDUCATION, 41 (No. 2, 1968), 178–200.

"When, If Ever, Do You Call in the Cops?: Symposium," NEW YORK TIMES MAGAZINE, (May 4, 1969), 34–35+.

Whittaker, David and William Watts. "Personality Characteristics of a Nonconformist Youth Subculture: A Study of the Berkeley Non-Student," JOURNAL OF SOCIAL ISSUES, 25 (April, 1969), 65–89.

Widmer, Kingsley. "Thrust of the Underculture," NATION, 207 (December 30, 1968), 716–719.

"Wish I Could Give All I Wanted to Give: Thoughts on Living in a Political Commune," LIBERATION, 15 (August–September–October, 1970), 24–31.

Yinger, M. J. "Contraculture and Subculture," AMERICAN SOCIOLOGICAL REVIEW, 25 (October, 1960), 625–635.

K. EFFECTS OF ACTIVISM ON AND IN THE UNIVERSITY

K.1. Civil Liberties and Academic Freedom: General

American Bar Association, ed. LIBERTY UNDER LAW-ANARCHY TOTALITARIANISM—THIS IS THE CHOICE. Chicago: American Bar Association, 1970.

American Civil Liberties Union. ACADEMIC FREEDOM AND ACADEMIC RESPONSIBILITIES. New York: American Civil Liberties Union, 1956.

Baade, Hans W. and Robinson O. Everett, eds. ACADEMIC FREEDOM. Dobbs Ferry, New York: Oceana Publications, 1964.

Fellman, David. THE LIMITS OF FREEDOM. New Brunswick, New Jersey: Rutgers University Press, 1959.

Gardner, David P. THE CALIFORNIA OATH CONTROVERSY. Berkeley, California: University of California Press, 1967.

Hofstadter, Richard. ACADEMIC FREEDOM IN THE AGE OF THE COLLEGE. New York: Columbia University Press, 1964.

Hofstadter, Richard and Walter P. Metzger. THE DEVELOPMENT OF ACADEMIC FREEDOM IN THE UNITED STATES. New York: Columbia University Press, 1969.

Hook, Sidney. ACADEMIC FREEDOM AND ACADEMIC ANARCHY. New York: Cowles Book, 1970.

Hunt, John F. and Terrence R. Connelly. THE RESPONSIBILITY OF DISSENT: THE CHURCH AND ACADEMIC FREEDOM. New York: Sheed and Ward, 1970.

Iversen, Robert W. THE COMMUNISTS AND THE SCHOOLS. New York: Harcourt Brace, 1959.

Johnson, Julia E., ed. ACADEMIC FREEDOM. New York: Wilson, 1925.

Joughin, George Louis, ed. ACADEMIC FREEDOM AND TENURE: A HANDBOOK OF THE AMERICAN ASSOCIATION OF UNIVERSITY PROFESSORS. Madison, Wisconsin: University of Wisconsin Press, 1969.

Kirk, Russell A. ACADEMIC FREEDOM: AN ESSAY IN DEFINITION. New York: Regnery, 1955.

MacIver, Robert M. ACADEMIC FREEDOM IN OUR TIME. New York: Columbia University Press, 1955.

Manier, Edward and John Houck. ACADEMIC FREEDOM AND THE CATHOLIC UNIVERSITY. South Bend, Indiana: Fides, 1967.

Meiklejohn, A. FREEDOM AND THE COLLEGE. New York: Century, 1923.

*Metzger, Walter P. ACADEMIC FREEDOM IN THE AGE OF THE UNIVERSITY. New York: Columbia University Press, 1961.

Metzger, Walter P. *et al*, ed. DIMENSIONS OF ACADEMIC FREEDOM. Urbana, Illinois: University of Illinois Press, 1969.

Ray, Robert F. PARTISAN POLITICS ON THE CAMPUS: POLICIES REGARDING THE APPEARANCE OF POLITICAL FIGURES ON THE CAMPUSES OF PUBLICLY SUPPORTED INSTITUTIONS OF HIGHER LEARNING IN THE UNITED STATES. Iowa City, Iowa: Institute of Public Affairs, State University of Iowa, 1950.

Rose, A. M. LIBEL AND ACADEMIC FREEDOM: A LAWSUIT AGAINST POLITICAL EXTREMISM. Minneapolis, Minnesota: University of Minnesota Press, 1968.

Stewart, George R. THE YEAR OF THE OATH: THE FIGHT FOR ACADEMIC FREEDOM AT THE UNIVERSITY OF CALIFORNIA. Garden City, New York: Doubleday, 1950.

Summers, Robert E., ed. FREEDOM AND LOYALTY IN OUR COLLEGES. New York: H. W. Wilson, 1954.

U.S. Congress. Senate. Committee on the Judiciary. Subcommittee to Investigate the Administration of the Internal Security Act and Other Internal Security Laws. PROPOSED ACADEMIC FREEDOM PROTECTIVE ACT OF 1969. HEARINGS. 91st Congress. 1st Session. Washington, D.C.: Government Printing Office, 1969.

"Academic Freedom," (special issue) LAW AND CONTEMPORARY PROBLEMS, 28 (Summer, 1963), 429–635.

"Anti-intellectualism in California," ANTIOCH REVIEW, 10 (December, 1950), 537–542.

Aptheker, Herbert. "Academic Freedom in the United States," POLITICAL AFFAIRS, 44 (July, 1965), 53–60.

Aptheker, Herbert. "The Academic Rebellion in the United States," POLITICAL AFFAIRS, 44 (August, 1965), 34–41.

Beichman, Arnold. "Academic Freedom and the Failure of Nerve," in Sidney Hood, ed. IN DEFENSE OF ACADEMIC FREEDOM. New York: Pegasus, 1971, 184–206.

Ben-David, Joseph and Randall Collins. "A Comparative Study of Academic Freedom and Student Politics," COMPARATIVE EDUCATION REVIEW, 10 (June, 1966), 220–249.

Bryant, U. S. "Academic Freedom," SOUTH ATLANTIC QUARTERLY, 53 (October, 1954), 441–453.

Butler, Edward T. "Intellectual Freedom and the Academic Community," CALIFORNIA LIBRARIAN, 30 (July, 1969), 149–157.

Chalfant, Edward. "Academic Freedom for the Student in the Classroom," in Sidney Hook, ed. IN DEFENSE OF ACADEMIC FREEDOM. New York: Pegasus, 1971, 82–93.

Chickering, Arthur W. "Civil Liberties and the Experience of College," JOURNAL OF HIGHER EDUCATION, 41 (November, 1970), 599–606.

"Climate of Opinion and the State of Academic Freedom," AMERICAN SOCIOLOGICAL REVIEW, 21 (June, 1956), 353–357.

Commager, Henry S. "The University and Freedom: 'Lehrfreiheit' and 'Lernfreiheit,' " JOURNAL OF HIGHER EDUCATION, 34 (October, 1963), 361–370.

"Comment. Mississippi's Campus Speaker Ban: Constitutional Consideration and the Academic Freedom of Students," MISSISSIPPI LAW REVIEW. 488 (1967).

"Developments in the Law-Academic Freedom," HARVARD LAW REVIEW, 81 (March, 1968), 1045–1159.

Dumke, G. S. "Is Freedom Academic? California State Colleges," VITAL SPEECHES, 36 (February 15, 1970), 272–276.

Dwyer, Charles. "Freedom, Dissent, Responsibility in the Academic Community," in W. Brickman and S. Lehrer, eds. CONFLICT AND CHANGE ON THE CAMPUS: THE RESPONSE TO STUDENT HYPERACTIVISM. New York: School and Society Books, 1970, 293–302.

Emerson, T. I. and D. Haber. "Academic Freedom of the Faculty Member as Citizen," LAW AND CONTEMPORARY PROBLEMS, 28 (Spring, 1963), 525–572.

Esch, Marvin and John Chandler. "Government and Institutional Autonomy, and Academic Freedom," LIBERAL EDUCATION, 56 (March, 1970), 51–61.

Fellman, David. "Academic Freedom in American Law," WISCONSIN LAW REVIEW, (January, 1961).

Fidler, William P. "Academic Freedom in the South Today," AAUP BULLETIN, 51 (Winter, 1965), 413–421.

Franklin, H. Bruce. "The Real Issues of My Case," CHANGE, 4 (June, 1972), 31–39.

Fuchs, R. F. and R. M. Hunter. "Communists in the Colleges: Two Views," ANTIOCH REVIEW, 9 (June, 1949), 199–209.

Gideonse, H. D. "Changing Issues in Academic Freedom in the U.S. Today," AMERICAN PHILOSOPHICAL SOCIETY, 94 (April, 1950), 91–104.

Gideonse, H. D. "Academic Freedom: A Decade of Challenge and Clarification," in Neal Johnston, ed. ACADEMIC FREEDOM. Philadelphia, Pennsylvania: U.S. National Student Association, 1962.

Glazer, N. "Campus Rights and Responsibilities: A Role for Lawyers," AMERICAN SCHOLAR, 39 (Summer, 1970, 445–462.

Glazer, N. "Why a Faculty Cannot Afford a Franklin," CHANGE, 4 (June, 1972), 40–45.

Gleason, P. "Academic Freedom: Catholic Higher Education," AMERICA, 115 (July 16, 1966), 60–63.

Gleason, P. "Freedom and the Catholic University," NATIONAL CATHO-

LIC EDUCATION ASSOCIATION BULLETIN, 65 (November, 1968), 21–29.

Hacker, Andrew. "Academic Freedom—How Much IS There?" NEW YORK TIMES MAGAZINE, (June 17, 1964), 122–123.

Hacker, Louis M. "The Role of the College and University in Preserving the Freedoms of Faculty and Students," NATIONAL ASSOCIATION OF STUDENT PERSONNEL ADMINISTRATORS JOURNAL, 44 (April, 1962), 80–92.

Hausknecht, Murray. "Speakers on the Campus: A Reexamination," AAUP BULLETIN, 53 (September, 1967), 503–506.

Hill, J. I. "Discharge of Employee/Alumnus/SDS Member Arbitration Award, Yale University," JOURNAL OF THE COLLEGE AND UNIVERSITY PERSONNEL ASSOCIATION, 22 (March, 1971), 10–17.

Hook, Sidney. "Academic Integrity and Academic Freedom," COMMENTARY, 8 (October, 1949), 239–249.

Hook, Sidney. "Freedom to Learn, But not to Riot," NEW YORK TIMES MAGAZINE, (January 3, 1965), 8–9+.

Hook, Sidney. "Neither Blind Obedience Nor Uncivil Disobedience," NEW YORK TIMES MAGAZINE, (June 5, 1966), 52+.

Hook, Sidney. "The Survival of the Free University," HUMANIST, 30 (September/October, 1970), 26–29.

Jones, H. M. "American Concept of Academic Freedom," AMERICAN SCHOLAR, 29 (Winter, 1959–1960), 94–103.

Joughin, Louis. "Academic Freedom: 1865–1965," NATION, 201, (September 20, 1965), 176–182.

Kaufman, A. S. "Communist and the Governor," NEW REPUBLIC, 162 (January 3, 1970), 21–24.

Kelman, H. C. "Apprehension and Academic Freedom," PUBLIC OPINION QUARTERLY, 23 (Summer, 1959), 181–189.

Kilgore, Jack. "Academic Freedom in the Southwest," COLLEGE AND UNIVERSITY JOURNAL, 3 (Fall, 1964), 20–25.

Kirk, R. "Massive Subsidies and Academic Freedom," LAW AND CONTEMPORARY PROBLEMS, 28 (Spring, 1963), 607–612.

Kreyche, G. F. "Academic Freedom and the Christian College," CHRISTIAN CENTURY, 86 (September 24, 1969), 1217–1220.

Kreyche, Gerald. "Academic Freedom in Catholic Colleges," COLLEGE AND UNIVERSITY JOURNAL, 3 (Summer, 1964), 8–12.

Kurn, H. B. "Academic Freedom and the Educational Task," CHRISTIANITY TODAY, 13 (April 25, 1969), 5–8 and (May 9, 1969), 16–18.

Lepawsky, Albert. "Academic Freedom and Political Liberty," SCIENCE, 150 (December 17, 1965), 1559–1563.

Lewis, L. S. "Faculty Support of Academic Freedom and Self Government," SOCIAL PROBLEMS, 13 (Spring, 1966), 450–461.

Louisell, David W. "Responding to the December 8th Resolution: Of Politics, Free Speech, and Due Process," CALIFORNIA LAW REVIEW, 54 (March, 1960), 107–118.

Machlup, Fritz. "On Some Misconceptions Concerning Academic Freedom," AAUP BULLETIN, 41 (Winter, 1955), 753–784.

McKay, Robert B. "Academic Freedom: The New Threat," AGB REPORTS, 11 (May–June, 1969), 13–23.

McLeod, R. "Dissent and Reaction in Missouri: Free Speech Conflict," with Letter by J. Bodger. WILSON LIBRARY BULLETIN, 44 (November, 1969), 269–276.

Mayhew, Lewis B. "Dissent: A Campus View," CHANGE, 4 (June, 1972), 48–52.

Metzger, Walter P. "Academic Freedom and Big Business," in Hugh Hawkins, ed. THE EMERGING UNIVERSITY AND INDUSTRIAL AMERICA. Lexington, Massachusetts: D. C. Heath, 1970, 69–79.

Metzger, Walter P. "Case Studies in Academic Freedom," in O. A. Knorr and W. J. Minter, eds. ORDER AND FREEDOM ON CAMPUS. Boulder, Colorado: Western Interstate Commission for Higher Education, 1965, 23–33.

Metzger, Walter P. "The Crisis of Academic Authority," DAEDALUS, (Summer, 1970), 568–608.

Miller, John Perry. "Tenure: Bulwark of Academic Freedom and Brake on Change," EDUCATIONAL RECORD, 51 (Summer, 1970), 241–245.

Moneypenny, Phillip. "University Purpose, Discipline and Due Process," NORTH DAKOTA LAW REVIEW, 43 (Summer, 1967), 739–752.

Mothershead, J. L., jr. "Freedom of the Mind and American Higher Education," EDUCATIONAL RECORD, 34 (January, 1953), 5–16.

Myers, A. F. "National Security and Freedom in Higher Education," COLLEGE AND UNIVERSITY, 26 (October, 1950), 27–34.

Neumann, Harry. "Philosophers and Intellectuals: the Question of Academic Freedom," SOCIAL RESEARCH, 36 (Autumn, 1969), 562–584.

Pierce, Martin. "The Challenge to Academic Freedom: A Case History," LIBERATION, 11 (October, 1966), 26–30.

Pollitt, D. Y. "Campus Censorship: Statute Bearing Speakers from State Educational Institutions," NEW YORK CITY LAW REVIEW, 42 (December, 1963), 179.

Spencer, T. E. "Beyond Democracy, Beyond the Law: A New Statement on Academic Freedom," EDUCATIONAL THEORY, 21 (Fall, 1971), 434–443.

Stoke, H. W. "Invitation of Speakers to the College Campus," SCHOOL AND SOCIETY, 90 (March 10, 1962), 107–108.

Taylor, Harold. "Dismissal of Fifth Amendment Professors," ANNALS OF THE AMERICAN ACADEMY OF POLITICAL AND SOCIAL SCIENCE, 300 (July, 1955), 79–86.

Taylor, Harold. "Freedom and Authority on the Campus," in Nevitt Sanford, ed. THE AMERICAN COLLEGE. New York: John Wiley and Sons, 1964, 774–804.

Tisdel, Richard. "Academic Freedom—Its Constitutional Context," UNIVERSITY OF COLORADO LAW REVIEW, 40 (Summer, 1968), 600–616.

Van Alstyne, William. "The Constitutional Rights of Teachers and Professors," DUKE LAW REVIEW, (1970),

Van Alstyne, William. "Political Speakers at State Universities: Some Constitutional Considerations," UNIVERSITY OF PENNSYLVANIA LAW REVIEW, 11 (January, 1963), 328–342.

Van Waes, Robert. "Student Freedoms and Educational Reform," in G. K. Smith *et al*, eds. STRESS AND CAMPUS RESPONSE. San Francisco: Jossey-Bass, 1968, 73–77.

Vick, George R. "Confrontation in the University: Academic Freedom Versus Social Commitment," INTER-COLLEGIATE REVIEW, 6 (Spring, 1970), 91–97.

Wallerstein, I. "Academic Freedom and Collective Expressions of Opinion," JOURNAL OF HIGHER EDUCATION, 42 (December, 1971), 713–720.

Weissman, Stephen and Doug Tuthill. "Freedom and the University," MOTIVE, 26 (October, 1965), 4–14.

Wilson, Logan. "Campus Freedom and Order," DENVER LAW JOURNAL, 45 (No. 4, 1968), 502–510.

Wilson, Logan. "Freedom and Responsibility in Higher Education," in Lawrence Dennis and Joseph Kauffman, eds. THE AMERICAN COLLEGE AND THE STUDENT. Washington, D.C.: American Council on Education, 1966, 333–339.

Wright, Quincy. "Do Changing Conditions Require a New Definition of the Freedom to Learn and the Freedom to Teach?" CURRENT ISSUES IN HIGHER EDUCATION, (1953), 226–232.

K.2. Student Rights

ACADEMIC FREEDOM AND CIVIL LIBERTIES OF STUDENTS IN COLLEGES AND UNIVERSITIES. New York: American Civil Liberties Union, 1972.

American Civil Liberties Union. ACADEMIC FREEDOM AND CIVIL LIBERTIES OF STUDENTS. New York: American Civil Liberties Union, 1959.

American Civil Liberties Union. ACADEMIC FREEDOM AND CIVIL LIBERTIES OF STUDENTS IN COLLEGES AND UNIVERSITIES. New York: American Civil Liberties Union, 1970.

American Civil Liberties Union. WHAT FREEDOM FOR AMERICAN STUDENTS: A SURVEY OF PROCEDURES AFFECTING STUDENT ACTIVITIES AND EXPRESSION. New York: American Civil Liberties Union, 1941.

Blair, J. W., ed. STUDENT RIGHTS AND RESPONSIBILITIES. Washington, D.C.: Association of Student Governments, 1968.

California. Coordinating Council for Higher Education. THE UNDERGRADUATE STUDENT AND HIS HIGHER EDUCATION: POLICIES OF CALIFORNIA COLLEGES AND UNIVERSITIES IN THE NEXT DECADE. Sacramento, California: 1969.

Collins, Charles C. STUDENTS RIGHTS AND FREEDOMS: TOWARD

IMPLEMENTATION MODELS. Berkeley, California: University of California, 1970.

    FREEDOM OF EXPRESSION ON CAMPUS. Philadelphia, Pennsylvania: U.S. National Student Association, 1963.

    Gaddy, Dale Everette. "Judicial Interpretations and Certain Other Aspects of Student Academic Freedom in American Higher Education. Unpublished Ed.D. thesis, Duke University, 1968.

    Indiana University. Board of Trustees. FREEDOM, RESPONSIBILITY AND STUDENT ORGANIZATIONS: A SUMMARY REPORT ON THE SURVEY OF FACULTY-STUDENT OPINIONS ON THE ISSUE OF THE REGISTRATION OF STUDENT ORGANIZATIONS. Bloomington, Indiana: Indiana University, 1967

    Johnston, Neal, ed. ACADEMIC FREEDOM. Philadelphia, Pennsylvania: U.S. National Student Association, 1962.

    Johnston, Neal, ed. IN LOCO PARENTIS. Philadelphia, Pennsylvania: U.S. National Student Association, 1962.

    Kinney, Stanley Newell. "The Selection of Outside Speakers by Student Organizations at the University of Michigan, 1854–1935. Unpublished Ph.D. dissertation, University of Michigan, 1957.

    Liebert, Roland. PROBLEMS IN STUDENT RIGHTS AND FREEDOMS. Washington, D.C.: U.S. National Student Association, 1966.

    Liebert, Roland, ed. STUDENT CONDUCT AND SOCIAL FREEDOM. Washington, D.C.: U.S. National Student Association, 1966.

    *Knorr, O. W. and W. J. Minter, eds. ORDER AND FREEDOM ON THE CAMPUS: THE RIGHTS AND RESPONSIBILITIES OF FACULTY AND STUDENTS. Boulder, Colorado: Western Interstate Commission for Higher Education, 1965.

    Michigan. State University, East Lansing. Faculty Committee on Student Affairs. ACADEMIC FREEDOM FOR STUDENTS AT MICHIGAN STATE UNIVERSITY. East Lansing, Michigan, 1967.

    Noffsinger, Mark George. "The Evolution of Student Rights at the University of Michigan." Unpublished Ph.D. dissertation, University of Michigan, 1964.

    Nussbaum, Michael. STUDENT LEGAL RIGHTS: WHAT THEY ARE AND HOW TO PROTECT THEM. New York: Harper and Row, 1970.

    Ratcliff, Richard. CONSTITUTIONAL RIGHTS OF COLLEGE STUDENTS: A STUDY IN CASE LAW. Metuchen, New Jersey: Scarecrow Press, 1972.

    Schwartz, Edward. ACADEMIC FREEDOM OF STUDENTS: A SUMMARY AND ANALYSIS. Washington, D.C.: U.S. National Student Association, 1967.

    Vaccaro, Louis and James T. Covert, eds. STUDENT FREEDOM IN AMERICAN HIGHER EDUCATION. New York: Teachers College Press, 1969.

    *Williamson, E. G. and John Cowan. THE AMERICAN STUDENT'S FREEDOM OF EXPRESSION: A RESEARCH APPRAISAL. Minneapolis, Minnesota: University of Minnesota Press, 1967.

"Administrator's Handbook: Understanding the Joint Statement on Rights and Freedoms of Students," COLLEGE AND UNIVERSITY BUSINESS, 45 (July, 1968), 31–38.

American Civil Liberties Union. "Academic Freedom and Civil Liberties of Students in Colleges and Universities," AAUP BULLETIN, 48 (June, 1962), 110–115.

"Are the Rights of Students Expanding?" OKLAHOMA BAR ASSOCIATION JOURNAL, 38 (July 29, 1967), 1585–1596.

Armacost, Peter. "The American Association of University Professors and the Association of American Colleges Statements on Student Freedoms—A Comparison and Discussion of Viewpoints," in PROCEEDINGS, NATIONAL ASSOCIATION OF STUDENT PERSONNEL ADMINISTRATORS, Seattle, June, 1966, 94–105.

Association of American Colleges. "Joint Statement on Rights and Freedoms of Students," LIBERAL EDUCATION, 54 (March, 1968), 152–158.

Bakken, Clarence J. "Student Rights as Seen by a Lawyer Educator," JOURNAL OF COLLEGE STUDENT PERSONNEL, 6 (March, 1965), 136–144.

Barrington, Thomas M. "The Rights of College Students," NATIONAL ASSOCIATION OF STUDENT PERSONNEL ADMINISTRATORS JOURNAL, 4 (July, 1966), 19–24.

Bissell, Claude, "Academic Freedom: The Student Version," QUEEN'S QUARTERLY, 76 (Summer, 1969), 171–184.

Blackman, Edward. "The Campus Environment and Student Freedom," in Louis Vaccaro and James Covert, eds. STUDENT FREEDOM IN AMERICAN HIGHER EDUCATION. New York: Teachers College Press, 1969.

Britt, Laurence V. "Some Concepts of Student Academic Freedom," in Lawrence Dennis and Joseph Kauffman, eds. THE AMERICAN COLLEGE AND THE STUDENT. Washington, D.C.: American Council on Education, 1966, 284–287.

Buess, Thomas. "A Step Toward Guaranteed Student Rights, the University as Agency," in J. W. Blair, ed. STUDENT RIGHTS AND RESPONSIBILITIES, Cincinnati, Ohio: Associated Student Governments of the U.S.A., 1968.

Callahan, Daniel. "Student Freedom," in E. Manier and J. W. Houch, eds. ACADEMIC FREEDOM AND THE CATHOLIC UNIVERSITY. Notre Dame, Indiana: Fides Publishers, 1967, 123–144.

Casey, Thomas J. "Some Reflections on Student Rights," CATHOLIC EDUCATIONAL REVIEW, 66 (May, 1968), 297–306.

College Students Personnel Institute. "Rights and Responsibilities of College Students: An Annotated Bibliography," STUDENT PERSONNEL METHODS BULLETIN, (December, 1962)

Committee on Academic Freedom. "Academic Freedom and Civil Liberties of Students in Colleges and Universities," AAUP JOURNAL, 48 (June, 1962), 110–115.

Conley, William. "Pressures from Students for Emancipation from Institutional Controls—and Vice Versa," in G. K. Smith, ed. CURRENT ISSUES IN HIGHER EDUCATION 1965: PRESSURES AND PRIORITIES IN HIGHER EDUCATION. Washington, D.C.: National Education Association, 1965, 88–92.

Crookston, B. B. and J. M. Carlson. "Third Party Mediation in Campus Disputes," JOURNAL OF COLLEGE STUDENT PERSONNEL, 12 (November, 1971), 410–416.

Frankel, Charles. "Rights and Responsibilities in the Student-College Relationship," in Lawrence Dennis and Joseph Kauffman, eds. THE AMERICAN COLLEGE AND THE STUDENT. Washington, D.C.: American Council on Education, 1966, 232–251.

Giermanski, James R. "Student Civil Liberties," COMMONWEAL, 87 (January 26, 1968), 494–496.

Glasser, I. "Protecting Student Rights," CURRENT, 115 (February, 1970), 46–54.

Gordon, K. W. "Due Process: A Swing Toward Student Rights," JOURNAL OF COLLEGE STUDENT PERSONNEL, 12 (March, 1971), 95–101.

Gumacost, Peter. "Student Rights and Responsibilities," AGB REPORTS, 11 (April, 1969), 6–11.

Hall, Mary Jo. "Academic Freedom for Students: Some Thoughts on the Current Debate," in L. Vaccaro and J. Covert, eds. STUDENT FREEDOM IN AMERICAN HIGHER EDUCATION. New York: Teachers College Press, 1969, 62–72.

Hanson, D. J. "Student Rights and the Institutional Response," NATIONAL ASSOCIATION OF WOMEN DEANS AND COUNSELORS JOURNAL, 35 (Fall, 1971), 40–48.

Hassenger, Robert. "Freedom and the Quality of Student Life," in E. Manier and J. W. Houch, eds. ACADEMIC FREEDOM AND THE CATHOLIC UNIVERSITY. Notre Dame, Indiana: Fides Publishers, 1967, 145–164.

Hawes, Gene R. "Civil Liberties for College Students," SATURDAY REVIEW, 49 (June 18, 1966), 61–63+.

Heimberger, F. "Grass Roots of Campus Freedom," SATURDAY REVIEW, 48 (July 17, 1965), 60–62+.

Hentoff, N. "Students Want Their Constitutional Rights," EDUCATION DIGEST, 37 (October, 1971), 39–42.

Hentoff, N. "Why Students Want Their Constitutional Rights," SATURDAY REVIEW, 54 (May 22, 1971), 60–63+.

Hollister, C. A. "Scope of Student Freedom," JOURNAL OF THE COLLEGE AND UNIVERSITY PERSONNEL ASSOCIATION, 22 (March, 1971), 18–24.

Hopkins, Ernest Mattin. "A Student's Right to Hear: a Presidential Defense," in Esther Lloyd-Jones and Herman Estrin, eds. THE AMERICAN STUDENT AND HIS COLLEGE. Boston: Houghton Mifflin, 1967, 325–330.

Jacobson, Sol. "Student Academic Freedom and Communist Speakers on Campus," SCHOOL AND SOCIETY, 92 (November 14, 1964), 336–337.

Jacobson, Sol. "Student and Faculty Due Process: A Study in Contrasts at the City University of New York," AAUP BULLETIN, 52 (June, 1966), 196–204.

Jenison, L. M. "Attitudes of Students and Faculty Toward Selected Disciplinary Situations," NATIONAL ASSOCIATION OF STUDENT PERSONNEL ADMINISTRATORS JOURNAL, 9 (April, 1972), 291–294.

Johnson, Michael T. "The Constitutional Rights of College Students," TEXAS LAW REVIEW, 42 (February, 1964), 344–363.

"Joint Statement on Rights and Freedoms of Students," AAUP BULLETIN, 54 (June, 1968), 258–261.

Koile, Earl. A. "The Student Nobody Knows," in Ronald E. Barnes, *et al,* eds. THE AIM OF HIGHER EDUCATION: SOCIAL ADJUSTMENT OR HUMAN LIBERATION? St. Louis, Missouri: United Campus Christian Fellowship, 1966,

Kreuzer, James R. "A Student 'Right' Examined," AAUP BULLETIN, 53 (June, 1967), 196–200.

Lipscomb, Greg. "A Student Looks at Academic Freedom," in Lawrence Dennis and Joseph Kauffman, eds. THE AMERICAN COLLEGE AND THE STUDENT. Washington, D.C.: American Council on Education, 1966, 288–292.

McIntosh, Carl W. "Why Students Should Be Allowed to Listen," LIBERAL EDUCATION, 51 (December, 1965), 512–516.

McKay, Robert. "The Student as Private Citizen," DENVER LAW JOURNAL, 45 (No. 4, 1968), 558–580.

Miller, T. K. and G. P. Pilkey. "College Student Personnel and Academic Freedom for Students," PERSONNEL AND GUIDANCE JOURNAL, 46 (June, 1968), 954–960.

Monroe, Charles R. "Student Rights and Activism," in C. Monroe. PROFILE OF THE COMMUNITY COLLEGE. San Francisco: Jossey-Bass, 1972, 217–244.

Moneypenny, Philip. "Academic Freedom—Students and the Institution," NATIONAL ASSOCIATION OF STUDENT PERSONNEL ADMINISTRATORS JOURNAL, 4 (April, 1965), 3–9.

Moneypenny, Philip. "Statement on Faculty Responsibility for the Academic Freedom of Students," AAUP BULLETIN, 50 (September, 1964), 254–257.

Moneypenny, Philip. "The Student as a Student," DENVER LAW JOURNAL, 45 (No. 4 (1968), 649–675.

Moneypenny, Philip. "A Teacher Looks at Student Academic Freedom," in Lawrence Dennis and Joseph Kauffman, eds. THE AMERICAN COLLEGE AND THE STUDENT. Washington, D.C.: American Council on Education, 1966, 293–297.

Moneypenny, Philip. "Toward a Standard for Student Academic Freedom," LAW AND CONTEMPORARY PROBLEMS, 28 (Summer, 1963), 625–635.

Ratterman, P. H. "Student Rights and Freedoms on the Catholic University Campus: Background Considerations and Norms," NATIONAL CATHOLIC EDUCATION ASSOCIATION BULLETIN, 63 (August, 1966), 223–231.

Richardson, Richard, jr. "Recommendations on Student Rights and Freedoms: Some Procedural Considerations for the Two-Year College," JUNIOR COLLEGE JOURNAL, 39 (February, 1969), 34–44.

Seigel, Kalman. "College Freedoms Being Stifled by Students' Fear of Red Label," NEW YORK TIMES, (May 10, 1953), 1, 28.

Shoben, Edward J. "Academic Freedom for Students," NATIONAL ASSO-CIATION OF STUDENT PERSONNEL ADMINISTRATORS JOURNAL, 5 (July, 1967), 25-30.

Strickland, Donald A. "In Loco Parentis—Legal Mots and Student Morals," JOURNAL OF COLLEGE STUDENT PERSONNEL, 6 (November, 1965), 335-340.

Stroup, Herbert. "Freedom in Student Activities," in Esther Lloyd-Jones and Herman Estrin, eds. THE AMERICAN STUDENT AND HIS COLLEGE. Boston: Houghton Mifflin, 1967, 223-236.

"Student Bill of Rights," COLLEGE AND UNIVERSITY BUSINESS, 43 (September, 1967), 78-81.

"Student Rights and Campus Rules: A Symposium," CALIFORNIA LAW REVIEW, 54 (March, 1966), 1-178.

Szamek, P. "Colonels Will Get You if You Don't Watch Out; Case of Academic Freedom at Newark State College, New Jersey," NATIONAL RE-VIEW, 24 (April 14, 1972), 395-397+.

"Toward a Standard for Student Academic Freedom," in PROBLEMS IN STUDENT RIGHTS AND FREEDOMS. Philadelphia, Pennsylvania: U.S. National Student Association, 1964.

Tripp, Philip A. "Current and Developing Issues in Student Life," in REPORT OF COMMISSION III, Council of Student Personnel Associations in Higher Education, 1968.

Van Alstyne, William. "Student Rights and University Authority," THE COLLEGE COUNSEL, 2 (1967), 44-67.

Weiss, Donald H. "Freedom of Association for Students," JOURNAL OF HIGHER EDUCATION, 38 (April, 1967), 184-189.

Williamson, E. G. "Do Students Have Academic Freedom?" COLLEGE AND UNIVERSITY, 39 (Summer, 1964), 466-487.

Williamson, E. G. "Institutional Policy in Relation to Student Rights in Controversial Situations," in CURRENT ISSUES IN HIGHER EDUCATION. Washington, D.C.: Association for Higher Education, 1961, 93-96.

Williamson, E. G. "Rights and Responsibilities of Students," in O. A. Knorr and W. J. Minter, eds. ORDER AND FREEDOM ON CAMPUS. Boulder, Colorado: Western Interstate Commission for Higher Education, 1965, 33-40.

Williamson, E. G. "Students' Academic Freedom," EDUCATIONAL RECORD, 44 (July, 1963), 214-222.

Williamson, E. G. "Students' Rights and Responsibilities: Competing Concepts of Freedom," JOURNAL OF THE NATIONAL ASSOCIATION OF WOMEN DEANS AND COUNSELORS, 28 (Winter, 1965), 81-87.

Williamson, E. G. and John L. Cowan. "Academic Freedom for Students: Issues and Guidelines," in Lawrence Dennis and Joseph Kauffman, eds. THE AMERICAN COLLEGE AND THE STUDENT. Washington, D.C.: American Council on Education, 1966, 252-283.

Williamson, E. G. and John L. Cowan. "The Role of the President in

280

the Desirable Enactment of Academic Freedom for Students," EDUCATIONAL
RECORD, 46 (Fall, 1965), 351–372.

Yegge, Robert. "Emerging Legal Rights for Students," in G. K. Smith, *et al*,
eds. STRESS AND CAMPUS RESPONSE. San Francisco: Jossey-Bass, 1968,
77–90.

K.3. Legal Aspects of Student Activism and Discipline

American Civil Liberties Union. POLICY STATEMENT ON CIVIL
DISOBEDIENCE. New York: American Civil Liberties Union, 1968.

Bakken, Clarence J. THE LEGAL BASIS FOR COLLEGE STUDENT PER-
SONNEL WORK. Washington, D.C.: American College Personnel Association,
1968.

Blackwell, Thomas. COLLEGE LAW: A GUIDE FOR THE COLLEGE AND
UNIVERSITY ADMINISTRATORS. Washington, D.C.: American Council on
Education, 1961.

Bork, Robert H., Howard G. Krane and George D. Webster, *et al*. POLITI-
CAL ACTIVITIES OF COLLEGES AND UNIVERSITIES: SOME POLICY AND
LEGAL IMPLICATIONS. Washington: American Enterprise Institute for
Public Policy Research, 1970.

Brady, Thomas and Leverne Snoxell. STUDENT DISCIPLINE IN HIGHER
EDUCATION, Washington, D.C.: American College Personnel Association, 1968.

Brubacher, John S. THE COURTS ON HIGHER EDUCATION. San
Francisco: Jossey-Bass, 1971.

Chambers, M. M. CHANCE AND CHOICE IN HIGHER EDUCATION.
Danville, Illinois: Interstate Printers and Publishers, 1962.

Chambers, M. M. THE COLLEGES AND THE COURTS, 1936–1941. New
York: Merry Mount Press, 1942.

Chambers, M. M. THE COLLEGES AND THE COURTS, 1941–1945. New
York: Merry Mount Press, 1945.

Chambers, M. M. THE COLLEGES AND THE COURTS, 1946–1950. New
York: Columbia University Press, 1952.

Chambers, M. M. THE COLLEGE AND THE COURTS SINCE 1950.
Danville, Illinois: Interstate, 1964.

Chambers, M. M. THE COLLEGES AND THE COURTS, 1962–1966.
Danville, Illinois: Interstate, 1967.

Chambers, M. M. THE COLLEGES AND THE COURTS: THE DEVELOP-
ING LAW STUDENT AND THE COLLEGE. Danville, Illinois: Interstate, 1972.

Chambers, M. M. THE DEVELOPING LAW OF THE STUDENT AND THE
COLLEGE. Danville, Illinois: Interstate Publishers, 1972.

Chambers, Merritt. FREEDOM AND REPRESSION IN HIGHER EDUCA-
TION. Bloomington, Indiana: Bloomcraft Press, 1965.

CODES OF STUDENT CONDUCT: A BREAKDOWN OF STATEMENTS
OF SIXTEEN COLLEGES AND UNIVERSITIES. New York: National Industrial Conference Board, 1968.

Cox, Robert Leslie. "The Disposition of Student Misconduct in Institutions of Higher Education." Unpublished Ed.D. dissertation, University of
Houston, 1967.

Dutton, Thomas B., *et. al.* INSTITUTIONAL APPROACHES TO THE ADJUDICATION OF STUDENT MISCONDUCT. Detroit: National Association of Student Personnel Administrators, 1969.

Fischer, Thomas. DUE PROCESS IN THE STUDENT-INSTITUTIONAL RELATIONSHIP. Washington: American Association of State Colleges and Universities, 1970.

Flicker, Barbara. THE CAMPUS CRISIS: LEGAL PROBLEMS OF UNIVERSITY DISCIPLINE, ADMINISTRATION AND EXPANSION. New York: Practising Law Institute, 1969.

Georgia. University of Georgia. Institute of Higher Education. THE LEGAL ASPECTS OF STUDENT DISCIPLINE IN HIGHER EDUCATION. Athens, Georgia: University of Georgia, Institute of Higher Education, 1970.

Holmes, Grace W., ed. STUDENT PROTEST AND THE LAW. Ann Arbor, Michigan: Institute of Continuing Legal Education, 1969.

Iowa. University of Iowa. Institute of Public Affairs. PARTISAN POLITICS ON THE CAMPUS: POLICIES REGARDING THE APPEARANCE OF POLITICAL FIGURES ON THE CAMPUSES OF PUBLICALLY SUPPORTED INSTITUTIONS OF HIGHER LEARNING IN THE UNITED STATES. Iowa City, 1950.

Liebert, Roland. CAMPUS JUSTICE. Philadelphia, Pennsylvania: U.S. National Student Association, 1965.

Louisiana. State University and Agricultural and Mechanical College. Faculty Council. SELF STUDY. Baton Rouge, Louisiana, 1963.

Malm, Ivan Carl. "Written Policies and Rules Governing Junior College Student Conduct and Discipline." Unpublished Ph.D. dissertation. University of Southern California, 1963.

Metzger, Jerome Charles. "Litigation, 1960–1970, Involving Students and Higher Education Institutions." Unpublished Ed.D. dissertation, Indiana University, 1971.

*O'Hara, William and John Hill, jr. THE STUDENT, THE COLLEGE, THE LAW. New York: Teachers College Press, 1972.

Otten, Charles Michael. "From Paternalism to Private Government: The Patterns of University Authority Over Students." Unpublished Ph.D. dissertation, University of California, Berkeley, 1968.

Ratliff, Richard C. CONSTITUTIONAL RIGHTS OF COLLEGE STUDENTS. Metuchen, New Jersey: Scarecrow Press, 1972.

Seligman, Richard Penn. "Student and Administrator Perceptions of Campus Discipline." Unpublished Ed.D. dissertation, University of California, Los Angeles, 1969.

Walker, Paul. "Court Decisions Dealing with Legal Relationships Between American Colleges and Universities and their Students." Unpublished Ph.D. dissertation, University of Southern California, 1961.

West, Elonya, jr. JUDICIAL OPINION GOVERNING ADMISSION AND EXPULSION OF COLLEGE STUDENTS. Unpublished Ph.D. dissertation, Duke University, 1965.

CONFERENCE ON HIGHER EDUCATION: THE LAW AND STUDENT PROTEST. Athens: University of Georgia, Institute of Higher Education, 1970.

"ACLU on Student Demonstrations," SCHOOL AND SOCIETY, 96 (October, 1968), 376–377

Armstrong, Timothy J. "College Searches and Seizures: Privacy and Due Process Problems on Campus," CRIMINAL LAW BULLETIN, 5 (December, 1969), 537–571.

Banks, Charles G. "Campus Justice: A Workable System," STUDENT GOVERNMENT BULLETIN, 11 (Spring, 1966), 1–15.

Bealle, J. Rufus, "NACUA Report to the American Council on Education on the Use of Injunctions against Campus Disorders," COLLEGE COUNSEL, 4 (Number 2, 1969), 1–10.

Beaney, William M. "Some Legal Problems of Higher Education, JOURNAL OF THE NATIONAL ASSOCIATION OF WOMEN DEANS AND COUNSELORS, 32 (Summer, 1969), 162–169.

Beaney, William. "Students, Higher Education and the Law," with Commentaries, DENVER LAW JOURNAL, 45 (Number 4, 1968), 511–544.

Beder, H. W. and S. T. Ridcard. "Residence Hall Regulations and Staff Roles: A Substitute Model for in loco parentis," NATIONAL ASSOCIATION OF STUDENT PERSONNEL ADMINISTRATORS JOURNAL, 9 (July, 1971), 57–61.

Blackwell, T. E. "Court Affirms University's Right to Discipline Students," COLLEGE AND UNIVERSITY BUSINESS, 43 (September, 1967), 16-20.

Blackwell, Thomas E. "Right to Expel Student is Limited," COLLEGE AND UNIVERSITY BUSINESS, 42 (January, 1967), 59–62.

Boyle, James. "The Office of the Students' Attorney: A New Development," in Grace Holmes, ed. LAW AND DISCIPLINE ON CAMPUS. Ann Arbor, Michigan: Institute of Continuing Legal Education, 1971, 33–41.

Broiles, R. David. "Due Process and Dismissal of Students at State-Supported Colleges and Universities," GEORGIA STATE BAR JOURNAL, 3 (August, 1966), 101–111.

Byse, Clark. "Procedure in Student Dismissal Proceedings: Law and Policy," JOURNAL OF COLLEGE STUDENT PERSONNEL, 4 (March, 1963), 130–143.

"Campus Confrontation: Resolution by Injunction; Campus Confrontation; Resolution by Legislation," COLUMBIA JOURNAL OF LAW AND SOCIAL PROBLEMS, 6 (January, 1970), 1–48.

Chambers, M. M. "The courts and colleges since Mid-century," EDUCATIONAL RECORD. Volume 45 (Spring, 1964), 182–189.

Chambers, M. M. "A Decade of Progress in Higher Education Law," EDUCATIONAL FORUM, 26 (November, 1964), 79–84.

Chambers, M. M. "Discipline of College Students," YEARBOOK OF SCHOOL LAW, (1971), 297–322.

Chambers, M. M. "Speakers Bans and the Courts," EDUCATIONAL FORUM, 35 (May, 1971), 471–478.

Chambers, M. M. "The University President in Court," ASSOCIATION OF AMERICAN COLLEGES BULLETIN, 32 (May, 1964), 280–286.

Chambers, M. M. "What the Judges say About Higher Education Today," JOURNAL OF HIGHER EDUCATION, 35 (June, 1964), 299–307.

"College Disciplinary Proceedings," VANDERBILT LAW REVIEW, 18 (March, 1965), 819–837.

"College Searches and Seizures: Privacy and Due Process Problems on Campus," GEORGIA LAW REVIEW, 3 (Winter, 1969), 426–458.

"Comment. The College Student and Due Process in Disciplinary Proceedings," SOUTH DAKOTA LAW REVIEW, 13 (Winter, 1968), 87–112.

"Comment: The University and the Public: The Right of Access by Nonstudents to University Property," CALIFORNIA LAW REVIEW, 54 (March, 1966), 132–174.

"Constitution Law—Student Academic Freedom—'State Action' and Private Universities," TULANE LAW REVIEW, 44 (December, 1969), 184–192.

Cox, Joseph J. "Higher Education and the Student Unrest Provisions," OHIO STATE LAW JOURNAL, 31 (Winter, 1970), 111–124.

Crary, J. C., jr. "Control of Campus Disorders: A New York Solution." ALBANY LAW REVIEW, 34 (Fall, 1969), 85–94.

"Degree of Discretionary Authority Possessed by University Officials in Student Disciplinary Matters—the Availability of Mandamus," SOUTHWEST LAW JOURNAL, 21 (Fall, 1967), 664–678.

"Discipline of College Students," YEARBOOK OF SCHOOL LAW, (1970), 341–361.

"Due Process and Dismissal of Students at State-Supported Colleges and Universities," ST. LOUIS UNIVERSITY LAW JOURNAL, 10 (Summer, 1966), 542–554.

Etheridge, E. W. "Student Rights and the Campus Riots," COLLEGE AND UNIVERSITY, 45 (Fall, 1969), 15–23.

Fisk, Winston M. "A System of Law for the Campus: Some Reflections," GEORGE WASHINGTON LAW REVIEW, 38 (July, 1970), 1006–1025.

Fley, Jo Ann. "Changing Approaches to Disciplines in Student Personnel Work," JOURNAL OF THE NATIONAL ASSOCIATION OF WOMEN DEANS AND COUNSELORS, 27 (Spring, 1964), 105–113.

"Fourteenth Amendment and University Disciplinary Procedures," MISSOURI LAW REVIEW, 34 (Spring, 1969), 236–259.

Furay, Sally M. " Legal Relationship Between the Student and the Private College or University," SAN DIEGO LAW REVIEW, 7 (May, 1970), 244–267.

Goldman, Alvin. "The University and the Liberty of Its Students—a Fiduciary Theory," KENTUCKY LAW JOURNAL, 54 (Spring, 1966), 643–682.

Greene, J. R. "Due Process in Public Colleges and Universities—Need for Trial-type Hearings," HOWARD LAW JOURNAL, 13 (Spring, 1967), 414–420.

Greene, JeRoyd W., jr. "University Discipline and Student Rights: A Suggested Hearing Model," HOWARD LAW JOURNAL, 15 (Summer, 1969), 481–517.

Goodman, Richard. "A Trial Lawyer's View of Lawsuits Against Schools," in Grace Holmes, ed. LAW AND DISCIPLINE ON CAMPUS. Ann Arbor, Michigan: Institute of Continuing Education, 1971. 173–185.

Habbell, Robert N. "Varying Perceptions of Alleged Misbehavior and Resultant Disciplinary Action," JOURNAL OF COLLEGE STUDENT PERSONNEL, 7 (September, 1966), 260–265.

Hagie, Daryl G. "The Law and Student Dismissal Procedures, EDUCATIONAL RECORD, 47 (Fall, 1966), 518–524.

Hall, Ridgway, "Expulsion and the Student," MODERATOR, 5 (April, 1966), 8–12.

Harwood, C. E. "Suspension: a Valid Disciplinary Tool?" CLEARING HOUSE, 44 (September, 1969), 29–32.

Herman, Joseph. "Injunctive Control of Disruptive Student Demonstrations," VIRGINIA LAW REVIEW, 56 (March, 1970), 215–238.

Heyman, Ira. "Some Thoughts on University Disciplinary Proceedings," CALIFORNIA LAW REVIEW, 54 (March, 1966), 73–87.

Hoffman, R. W. "Encounter with Rockwell," NATIONAL ASSOCIATION OF STUDENT PERSONNEL ADMINISTRATORS JOURNAL, 4 (April, 1965), 13–18.

Holloway, John. "Injunctive Orders," in Grace Holmes, ed. LAW AND DISCIPLINE ON CAMPUS. Ann Arbor, Michigan: The Institute of Continuing Legal Education, 1971, 115–130.

Hubbell, R. N. "Varying Perceptions of Alleged Misbehavior and Resultant Disciplinary Action," JOURNAL OF COLLEGE STUDENT PERSONNEL, 7 (1966), 260–265.

Jacobson, Sol. "The Expulsion of Students and Due Process of Law," JOURNAL OF HIGHER EDUCATION, 34 (May, 1963), 250–255.

Johnson, A. W. "Double Jeopardy: A Misnomer; The Relation of the Student to the College and the Courts," JOURNAL OF HIGHER EDUCATION, 37 (January, 1966), 16–23.

Johnson, S. "The Constitutional Rights of College Students," TEXAS LAW REVIEW, 42 (February, 1964), 344–363.

Joyce, W. E. "Need for Greater Due Process in Student Disciplinary Procedures," NATIONAL ASSOCIATION OF STUDENT PERSONNEL ADMINISTRATORS JOURNAL, 7 (April, 1970), 235–240.

"Judicial Document on Student Discipline," EDUCATIONAL RECORD, 50 (Winter, 1969), 12–20.

Katzenbach, Nicholas de B. "Demonstrations, Freedom, and the Law," in Lawrence Dennis and Joseph Kauffman, eds. THE AMERICAN COLLEGE AND THE STUDENT. Washington: American Council on Education,1966, 298–304.

Kluge, Donald A. and Jacqueline Smith. "Recent Statements of Principles, Rights, and Procedures in Student Behavior," JOURNAL OF THE NATIONAL ASSOCIATION OF WOMEN DEANS AND COUNSELORS, 31 (Winter, 1968), 64–68.

Kovacevich, George J. "Student Unrest in a Legal Perspective: Focus on San Francisco State College," UNIVERSITY OF SAN FRANCISCO LAW REVIEW, 4 (April, 1970), 255–281.

Kramer, Eugene L. "Note. Expulsion of College and Professional Students— Rights and Remedies," NOTRE DAME LAWYER, 38 (March, 1963), 174–187.

Kutner, Luis. "Habeas Scholastica: An Ombudsman for Academic Due

Process–A Proposal," UNIVERSITY OF MIAMI LAW REVIEW, 23 (Fall, 1968), 107–159.

LaMorte, M. W. "Courts and the Governance of Student Conduct," SCHOOL AND SOCIETY, 100 (February, 1972), 89–93.

"Legislative Note. State's Right to Abrogate First Amendment Guarantees in Regulation of State University Speaker Programs," TULANE LAW REVIEW, 42 (February, 1968), 394–400.

LeMay, Morris. "College Disciplinary Problems: A Review," JOURNAL OF COLLEGE STUDENT PERSONNEL, 9 (May, 1968), 180–189.

Lenning, Oscar T. "Understanding the Student Lawbreaker," JOURNAL OF COLLEGE STUDENT PERSONNEL, 11 (January, 1970), 62–68.

Levine, Martin. "Private Government on the Campus: Judicial Review of University Expulsions," YALE LAW JOURNAL, 72 (June, 1963), 1362–1410.

Linde, Hans A. "Campus Law: Berkeley Viewed From Eugene," CALIFORNIA LAW REVIEW, 54 (March, 1966), 40–72.

Lunsford, Terry. "Who are Members of the University Community?" DENVER LAW JOURNAL, 45 (Number 4, 1968), 545–558.

McIlhenny, Edmund. "Due Process and the 'Private' Institution," in Lawrence Dennis and Joseph Kauffman, eds. THE AMERICAN COLLEGE AND THE STUDENT. Washington: American Council on Education, 1966, 326–332.

McKenney, Richard I. "Disciplinary Philosophy and Procedures in a Small College," ASSOCIATION OF AMERICAN COLLEGES BULLETIN, 42 (December, 1956), 548–552.

Mash, D. J. "Student Discipline in Higher Education: Collision Course with the Courts?" NATIONAL ASSOCIATION OF STUDENT PERSONNEL ADMINISTRATORS JOURNAL, 8 (January, 1971), 148–155.

Moneypenny, Philip. "University Purpose, Discipline and Due Process," NORTH DAKOTA LAW REVIEW, 43 (Summer, 1967), 739–752.

Mueller, K. H. "Problems in the Discipline Program: Standards of Right and Wrong," PERSONNEL AND GUIDANCE JOURNAL, 34 (March, 1956), 413–416.

Mueller, Kate Hevner. "Theory for Campus Discipline," PERSONNEL AND GUIDANCE JOURNAL, 36 (January, 1958), 302–309.

"Note. Private Government on the Campus–Judicial Review of University Expulsions," YALE LAW JOURNAL, 72 (June, 1963), 1362–1380.

O'Leary, Richard E. and John J. Templin. "Note: The College Student and Due Process in Disciplinary Proceedings," ILLINOIS LAW FORUM, (Fall, 1962), 438–443.

O'Neil, Robert. "The Litigator's Response," in Grace Holmes, ed. LAW AND DISCIPLINE ON CAMPUS. Ann Arbor, Michigan: Institute of Continuing Education, 1971, 159–173.

O'Neil, Robert M. "Private Universities and Public Law," BUFFALO LAW REVIEW, 19 (Winter, 1970), 155–168.

O'Toole, George, "Recent California Campus Disorder Legislation: A

286

Comment," HARVARD JOURNAL OF LEGISLATION, 8 (January, 1971), 310–332.

Parker, Douglas. "Some Legal Implications for Personnel Officers," JOURNAL OF THE NATIONAL ASSOCIATION OF WOMEN DEANS AND COUNSELORS, 24 (June, 1961), 198–202.

Perkins, J. A. "University and Due Process," AMERICAN LIBRARY ASSOCIATION BULLETIN, 62 (September, 1968), 977–983.

Pettigrew, H. W. "Bail and the Arrested University Student," COLLEGE AND UNIVERSITY, 46 (Spring, 1971), 211–219.

Phay, Robert E. "Higher Education and Due Process of Law," POPULAR GOVERNMENT, 37 (April, 1971), 9–19.

"Private Government on the Campus—Judicial Review of University Expulsions," YALE LAW JOURNAL, 72 (June, 1963), 1362–1410.

Prusok, Ralph E. "Student, Student Personnel Worker, and Parent Attitudes toward Student Discipline," PERSONNEL AND GUIDANCE JOURNAL, 40 (November, 1961), 247–253.

"Reasonable Rules, Reasonably Enforced Guidelines for University Disciplinary Proceedings," MINNESOTA LAW REVIEW, 53 (December, 1968), 301–341.

Rhatigan, J. J. "One Approach to Academic Due Process," NATIONAL ASSOCIATION OF STUDENT PERSONNEL ADMINISTRATORS JOURNAL, 8 (April, 1971), 284–288.

Rosenthal, Robert R. "Injunctive Relief Against Campus Disorders," UNIVERSITY OF PENNSYLVANIA LAW, 118 (April, 1970), 746–765.

Ross, Arthur M. "Industrial Jurisprudence on the Campus," EDUCATIONAL RECORD, 51 (Winter, 1970), 28–32.

Roth, J. A. "Study of Academic Success and Failure," EDUCATIONAL RESEARCH BULLETIN, 35 (October, 1956), 176–182.

Saxbe, W. B. "Student Unrest and the Law," CLEVELAND STATE LAW REVIEW, 18 (September, 1969), 429–439.

Schwartz. "The Student, The University and the First Amendment," OHIO STATE LAW JOURNAL, (1970).

"Scope of University Discipline," BROOKLYN LAW REVIEW, 35 (Spring, 1969), 486–497.

Scott, D. R. "Due Process in Higher Education," AAUP BULLETIN, 32 (June, 1946), 367–373.

Searey, Warren A. "Dismissal of Students: 'Due Process!'" HARVARD LAW REVIEW, 70 (June, 1957), 1406–1410.

Seward, Doris M. "Educational Discipline," JOURNAL OF THE NATIONAL ASSOCIATION OF WOMEN DEANS AND COUNSELORS, 24 (June, 1961), 192–197.

Shaul, Dennis. "Due Process: a Student's Viewpoint," in Lawrence Dennis and Joseph Kauffman, eds. THE AMERICAN COLLEGE AND THE STUDENT. Washington: American Council on Education, 1966, 323–325.

Sherry, Arthur H. "Governance of the University: Rules, Rights and Responsibilities," CALIFORNIA LAW REVIEW, 54 (March, 1966), 23–39.

Smith, F. B., ed. "Symposium: The Campus Crisis," WILLIAM AND MARY LAW REVIEW, 11 (Spring, 1970), 575–635.

Smith, G. P. and H. P. Kirk. "Student Discipline in Transition," NATIONAL ASSOCIATION OF STUDENT PERSONNEL ADMINISTRATORS JOURNAL, 8 (April, 1971), 276–282.

Smith, P. M. "Control of Behavior on the Small College Campus," SOCIOLOGY AND SOCIAL RESEARCH, 31 (November, 1946), 132–137.

Stein, R. H. "Discipline: On Campus, Downtown, or Both, A Need for a Standard," NATIONAL ASSOCIATION OF STUDENT PERSONNEL ADMINISTRATORS JOURNAL, 10 (July, 1972), 41–47.

"Student Due Process in the Private University: the State Action Doctrine," SYRACUSE LAW REVIEW, 20 (Summer, 1969), 911–923.

Tautfest, P. B. and F. C. Young. "Student-Parent Attitudes toward College Regulations," NATIONAL ASSOCIATION OF WOMEN DEANS AND COUNSELORS JOURNAL, 33 (Spring, 1970), 105–111.

Taylor, F. W. "A Comparison of University and Industrial Discipline and Methods," SCIENCE, 24 (1906), 577–583.

Tisdale, J. R. and F. G. Brown. "Characteristics of College Misconduct Cases," JOURNAL OF COLLEGE STUDENT PERSONNEL, 6 (November, 1965), 359–366.

Triezenberg, G. "How to Live with Due Process," EDUCATION DIGEST, 36 (May, 1971), 18–21.

Twohig, R. R., jr. "Uncertainty in College Disciplinary Regulations," OHIO STATE LAW JOURNAL, 29 (Fall, 1968), 1023–1037.

Van Alstyne, William. "The Judicial Trend Toward Student Academic Freedom," University of Florida Law Review, 20 (1968), 290–306.

Van Alstyne, William W. "The Prerogatives of Students, the Powers of Universities, and the Due Process of Law," JOURNAL OF THE NATIONAL ASSOCIATION OF WOMEN DEANS AND COUNSELORS, 30 (Fall, 1966), 11–16.

Van Alstyne, William. "Procedural Due Process and State University Students," UNIVERSITY OF CALIFORNIA, LOS ANGELES LAW REVIEW, 10 (1963), 368–389.

*Van Alstyne, William. "Student Academic Freedom and the Rule Making Powers of Public Universities: Some Constitutional Considerations," LAW IN TRANSITION QUARTERLY, 2 (Winter, 1965), 1–34.

Van Alstyne, William W. "Student Activism, The Law and the Courts," in Julian Foster and Durward Long, eds. PROTEST! STUDENT ACTIVISM IN AMERICA. New York: William Morrow, 1970, 531–553.

*Van Alstyne, William. "The Student as University Resident," DENVER LAW JOURNAL, 45 (Fall, 1968), 582–642.

Van Alstyne, William W. "Suggested Seminar in Student Rights," JOURNAL OF LEGAL EDUCATION, 21 (Number 5, 1969), 547–559.

Wagner, Carroll. "The Administrator's Dilemma, in Grace Holmes, ed. LAW AND DISCIPLINE ON CAMPUS. Ann Arbor, Michigan: The Institute of Continuing Education, 1971, 185–195.

Weigel, Rev. Gustave A. S. J. and John S. Brubacher. "Institutional Limits Upon Student Freedoms," NATIONAL ASSOCIATION OF STUDENT PERSONNEL ADMINISTRATORS JOURNAL, (April, 1962), 294–308.

"What's New on Campus? Parietal Hours," AMERICA, 118 (April 13, 1968), 480–483.

Wilkinson, Ernest L. and R. Richards Rolapp. "The Private College and Student Discipline," AMERICAN BAR ASSOCIATION JOURNAL, 56 (February, 1970), 121–126.

Williams, G. D. and J. A. Rhodes. "Satisfaction with the Environment and Attitudes toward the Disciplinary Process," JOURNAL OF COLLEGE STUDENT PERSONNEL, 10 (November, 1969), 391–396.

Wright, Charles A. "The Constitution on the Campus," VANDERBILT LAW REVIEW, 22 (October, 1969), 1027–1088.

Yarbrough, Tinsley E. "University-Student Relations and the Courts," in Hans H. Indorf, ed. POLITICS 1970. Greenville, North Carolina, Political Science Department, East Carolina University, 1970, 27–46.

Young, D. P. "Due Process Standards and Guidelines for Student Discipline in Higher Education," JOURNAL OF COLLEGE STUDENT PERSONNEL, 12 (March, 1971), 102–106.

K.4. The Crisis of the American University:
Pre 1960

Earnest, E. THE ACADEMIC PROCESSION. Indianapolis: Bobbs-Merrill, 1953.

Goodman, Paul. THE COMMUNITY OF SCHOLARS. New York: Random House, 1962.

Gordon, Richard and Katherine Gordon. THE BLIGHT ON THE IVY. Englewood Cliffs, New Jersey: Prentice Hall, 1963.

Hunt, Everett Lee. THE REVOLT OF THE COLLEGE INTELLECTUAL. Chicago: Aldine, 1963.

Hutchins, Robert M. THE HIGHER LEARNING IN AMERICA. New Haven: Yale University Press, 1962.

*Kerr, Clark. THE USES OF THE UNIVERSITY. New York: Harper Torchbooks, 1963.

Moss, Malcolm and Francis Rourke. THE CAMPUS AND THE STATE. Baltimore: Johns Hopkins Press, 1959.

Orlans, Harold. THE EFFECTS OF FEDERAL PROGRAMS ON HIGHER EDUCATION. Washington: Brookings, 1962.

Pusey, Nathan M. THE AGE OF THE SCHOLAR: OBSERVATIONS ON EDUCATION IN A TROUBLED DECADE. Cambridge: Belknap Press of Harvard University Press, 1963.

Riesman, D. CONSTRAINT AND VARIETY IN AMERICAN EDUCATION. Lincoln, Nebraska: University of Nebraska Press, 1956.

*Sanford, Nevitt, ed. THE AMERICAN COLLEGE. New York: John Wiley & Sons, 1962.

Sinclair, Upton. THE GOOSE-STEP: A STUDY OF AMERICAN EDU-
CATION. New York: AMS Press, 1970, (originally published in 1923).

Veblen, Thorstein. THE HIGHER LEARNING IN AMERICA. New York:
Huebsch, 1913.

Alexander, H. "Troubles of College Deans," COLLIERS, 124 (October 1,
1949), 13–15+.

Brown, J. Douglas. "The Squeeze on the Liberal University," ATLANTIC,
213 (May, 1964), 84–87.

Carmen, H. J. "Campus Issues and Problems," ANNALS OF THE
AMERICAN ACADEMY OF POLITICAL AND SOCIAL SCIENCE, 301
(September, 1955), 46–57.

"Crisis in the Colleges: Report of Nation-wide Survey," U.S. NEWS AND
WORLD REPORT, 42 (June 14, 1957), 48–50+.

Goodman, Paul. "The Freedom to Be Academic," in M. R. Stein, et al,
eds. IDENTITY AND ANXIETY. New York: Free Press of Glencoe, 1960,
351–367.

Kimball, S. T. "Social Science Research and Higher Education," HUMAN
ORGANIZATION, 21 (Winter, 1962), 271–279.

McLachlan, G. "Knowledge, Power, Survival; University Problems," TWEN-
TIETH CENTURY, 169 (March, 1961), 246–254.

Nemetz, Anthony. "The University and Society," JOURNAL OF HIGH-
ER EDUCATION, 32 (November, 1961), 425–435.

Raskin, A. H. "Corporation and the Campus," NEW YORK TIMES MAGA-
ZINE, (April 17, 1955), 2+.

Riesman, D. "Changing Colleges and Changing Students," NATIONAL
CATHOLIC EDUCATION ASSOCIATION BULLETIN, 58 (August, 1961),
104–115.

"A Special Report on the Universities," NEW REPUBLIC, 125 (October
29, 1951), 11–25.

Williams, Lloyd P. "Quiescence, Tradition, and Disorder—Cross-Section
of a Small College," AMERICAN ASSOCIATION OF UNIVERSITY PROFES-
SORS BULLETIN, 43 (December, 1957), 624–625.

K.5. The Crisis of the American University:
1960-

*Adelman, Howard and Dennis Lee, eds. THE UNIVERSITY GAME.
Toronto: Anansi, 1968.

*Aiken, Henry David. THE PREDICAMENT OF THE UNIVERSITY.
Bloomington, Indiana: Indiana University Press, 1971.

Aptheker, Bettina. THE ACADEMIC REBELLION IN THE UNITED
STATES: A MARXIST APPRAISAL. Secaucus, New Jersey: Citadel Press,
1972.

*Ashby, Eric. ANY PERSON, ANY STUDY: AN ESSAY ON HIGHER
EDUCATION IN THE UNITED STATES. New York: McGraw-Hill, 1971.

290

Birenbaum, William M. OVERLIVE: POWER, POVERTY AND THE UNIVERSITY. New York: Dial-Delacourte Press, 1969.

Buchanan, James M. and Nicos E. Deuletoglou. ACADEMIA IN ANARCHY: AN ECONOMIC DIAGNOSIS. New York: Basic Books, 1970.

Caffrey, John, ed. THE FUTURE ACADEMIC COMMUNITY: CONTINUITY AND CHANGE. Washington: American Council on Education, 1969.

Carnegie Commission on Higher Education. THE MOST EFFECTIVE USE OF RESOURCES: AN IMPERATIVE FOR HIGHER EDUCATION. New York: McGraw-Hill, 1972.

Davidson, Carl. THE MULTIVERSITY: CRUCIBLE OF THE NEW WORKING CLASS. Chicago: S.D.S., 1967.

*Driver, Christopher. THE EXPLODING UNIVERSITY. London: Hodder and Stoughton, 1971.

Feinstein, Otto. THE ECONOMICS OF HIGHER EDUCATION IN THE UNITED STATES: ECONOMICS, PERSONALISM, QUALITY. Lexington, Massachusetts: Heath Lexington Books, 1971.

Gorovitz, Samuel, ed. FREEDOM AND ORDER IN THE UNIVERSITY. Cleveland, Ohio: Western Reserve University Press, 1967.

Harcleroad, Fred F., ed. ISSUES OF THE SEVENTIES: THE FUTURE OF HIGHER EDUCATION. San Francisco: Jossey-Bass, 1970, 192.

Harris, Seymour. CHALLENGE AND CHANGE IN AMERICAN EDUCATION. Berkeley: McCutchen, 1965.

Hodgkinson, Harold L. and Myron B. Bloy, jr., eds. IDENTITY CRISIS IN HIGHER EDUCATION. San Francisco: Jossey-Bass, 1971.

Horowitz, D. THE UNIVERSITIES AND THE RULING CLASS: HOW WEALTH PUTS KNOWLEDGE IN ITS POCKET. San Francisco: Bay Area Radical Education Project, 1969.

Hutchins, Robert M., et al. THE UNIVERSITY IN AMERICA: AN OCCASIONAL PAPER ON THE ROLE OF EDUCATION IN THE FREE SOCIETY. Santa Barbara: Center for the Study of Democratic Institutions, 1967.

*Jencks, Christopher, and David Riesman. THE ACADEMIC REVOLUTION. Garden City, New York: Doubleday, 1968.

Keats, John. THE SHEEPSKIN PSYCHOSIS. Philadelphia, Pennsylvania: Lippincott, 1965.

Morison, Robert S., ed. THE CONTEMPORARY UNIVERSITY: USA. Boston: Beacon, 1967.

*Nichols, David C., ed. PERSPECTIVES ON CAMPUS TENSIONS. Washington, D.C.: American Council on Education, 1970.

*Nisbet, R. A. THE DEGRADATION OF THE ACADEMIC DOGMA. New York: Basic Books, 1970.

Perkins, James. THE UNIVERSITY IN TRANSITION. Princeton, New Jersey: Princeton University Press, 1966.

Ridgeway, James. THE CLOSED CORPORATION: AMERICAN UNIVERSITIES IN CRISIS. New York: Random House, 1968.

Riesman, D., J. Gusfield and Z. Gamson, et al. ACADEMIC VALUES AND MASS EDUCATION. Garden City, New York: Doubleday, 1970.

*Roszak, Theodore, ed. THE DISSENTING ACADEMY. New York: Vintage, 1968.

*Searle, John. THE CAMPUS WAR: A SYMPATHETIC LOOK AT THE UNIVERSITY IN AGONY. New York: World, 1971.

Smith, G. Kerry, ed. AGONY AND PROMISE: CURRENT ISSUES IN HIGHER EDUCATION. San Francisco: Jossey-Bass, 1969.

Smith, G. Kerry, ed. STRESS AND CAMPUS RESPONSE: CURRENT ISSUES IN HIGHER EDUCATION. San Francisco: Jossey-Bass, 1968.

Spiegel, John P. and Donald W. Light, jr. THE DIVIDED ACADEMY: THREE ESSAYS ON CONFLICT IN THE UNIVERSITIES. Waltham, Massachusetts: Brandeis University, Lemberg Center, 1970.

*Taylor, Harold. STUDENTS WITHOUT TEACHERS: THE CRISIS IN THE MULTIVERSITY. New York: McGraw-Hill, 1969.

U.S. President's Task Force on Higher Education. PRIORITIES IN HIGHER EDUCATION: THE REPORT. Washington: U.S. Government Printing Office, 1970.

*Von Hoffman, Nicholas. THE MULTIVERSITY. New York: Holt, Rinehart and Winston, 1966.

*Wallerstein, Immanuel. UNIVERSITY IN TURMOIL: THE POLITICS OF CHANGE. New York: Atheneum, 1969.

*Wallerstein, Immanuel and Paul Starr, eds. THE UNIVERSITY CRISIS READER. New York: Random House, 1971, (2 volumes).

*Wolff, Robert Paul. THE IDEAL OF THE UNIVERSITY. Boston: Beacon, 1969.

Woodring, Paul. THE HIGHER LEARNING IN AMERICA: A REASSESSMENT. New York: McGraw-Hill, 1968.

Abram, Morris B. "Reflections on the University in the New Revolution," DAEDALUS, 99 (Winter, 1970), 122–140.

Ackerman, J. S. "Two Styles: A Challenge to Higher Education," DAEDALUS, 98, (Summer, 1969), 855–869.

Aptheker, Bettina. "Aspects of the Crisis in Higher Education," POLITICAL AFFAIRS, 46 (October, 1967), 9–18.

Astin, Alexander W. "A Researcher's Proposal for Changes in Higher Education," EDUCATIONAL RECORD, 51 (Summer, 1970), 225–231.

Bailey, Stephen K. "Public Money and the Integrity of the Higher Academy," EDUCATIONAL RECORD, 50 (Spring, 1969), 149–154.

Barzun, Jacques. "Tomorrow's University—Reactionary Either Way," in Sidney Hook, ed. IN DEFENSE OF ACADEMIC FREEDOM. New York: Pegasus, 1971, 120–129.

Becker, Carl. "Freedom of Learning and Teaching," in Christopher Katope and Paul Zolbrod, eds. BEYOND BERKELEY. Cleveland: World, 1966, 184–202.

Bloustein, E. J. "New Student and His Role in American Colleges," LIBERAL EDUCATION, 54 (October, 1968), 345–364.

Bonham, George W. "The Ivory Tower Crumbles," SATURDAY REVIEW, 49 (May 21, 1966), 66–69+.

Brien, Richard H. "The 'Managerialization' of Higher Education," EDU-CATIONAL RECORD, 51 (Summer, 1970), 273–280.

Brownfeld, Allan C. "The New Left and the University: The Perilous State of Liberal Education," MICHIGAN QUARTERLY REVIEW, 8 (October, 1969), 253–258.

Clark, Burton R. "The New University," AMERICAN BEHAVIORAL SCIENTIST, 11 (May–June, 1968), 1–5.

Coffin, William Sloane, jr. "Moral Values and Our Universities," in Esther Lloyd-Jones and Herman Estrin, eds. THE AMERICAN STUDENT AND HIS COLLEGE. Boston: Houghton Mifflin, 1967, 151–155.

Coffin, William Sloane, jr. "Universities and Social Order: 1964," in G. K. Smith, ed. 1945–1970 TWENTY-FIVE YEARS. San Francisco: Jossey-Bass, 1970, 193–199.

Devall, W. B. "Academic Entrepreneurs: New Men of Power," LIBERAL EDUCATION, 54 (December, 1968), 566–572.

"Does the University Have A Future?" HUMANIST, 30 (September–October, 1970), 5–39, (Special Issue).

Ellmann, Richard. "Dissent and the Academy," NEW YORK REVIEW OF BOOKS, 10 (February 15, 1968), 6–8.

"Embattled University," DAEDALUS, 99 (Winter, 1970), 1–221.

Friedenberg, Edgar Z. "The University Community in an Open Society," DAEDALUS, 99 (Winter, 1970), 56–74.

Galbraith, John K. "Facing Political Reality: How the University Can Protect Itself," COLLEGE MANAGEMENT, 2 (September, 1967), 32–36.

Gardner, John W. "Agenda for the Colleges and Universities," JOURNAL OF HIGHER EDUCATION, 36 (1965), 359–365.

Glazer, Nathan. "The Campus and Its Critics," COMMENTARY, 47 (April, 1969), 40–48.

Glenny, Lyman A. "Institutional Autonomy for Whom?" in G. Kerry Smith, ed. THE TROUBLED CAMPUS. San Francisco: Jossey-Bass, 1970, 153–163.

Goldberg, K. and R. C. Linstromberg. "The University as an Anachronism," THE JOURNAL OF HIGHER EDUCATION, 40 (March, 1969), 193–204.

Gould, Samuel B. "Higher Education: In the Eye of the Hurricane," JOURNAL OF HIGHER EDUCATION, 40 (March, 1969), 169–180.

Greeley, A. M. "Malice in Wonderland," CHANGE, 2 (September–October, 1970), 32–38.

Green, Edith. "Through a Glass Darkly: Campus Issues in 1980," in G. K. Smith, et al, eds. STRESS AND CAMPUS RESPONSE. San Francisco: Jossey-Bass, 1968, 280–290.

Handlin, O. "Vulnerability of the American University," ENCOUNTER, 35 (July, 1970), 22–30.

Hinckle, Warren, Robert Scheer and Sol Stern, et al. "The University on the Make: or How MSU Helped Arm Madame Nhu," RAMPARTS, 4 (April, 1966), 12–22.

Hook, Sidney. "Conflict and Change in the Academic Community," in

Sidney Hook, ed. IN DEFENSE OF ACADEMIC FREEDOM. New York: Pegasus, 1971, 106–119.

Hook, Sidney. "The Long View," in Sidney Hook, ed. IN DEFENSE OF ACADEMIC FREEDOM. New York: Pegasus, 1971, 11–20.

Hook, S. "Prospects of Academe," ENCOUNTER, 31 (August, 1968), 60–66.

Howe, Harold, II. "Our Colleges Aren't Ready for Today's Students," SATURDAY REVIEW, 48 (May 15, 1965), 77–79+.

Hutchins, Robert M. "The University and the Multiversity," NEW REPUBLIC, 156 (April 1, 1967), 15–17.

Janson, Donald. "State Department on Campus," NATION, 200 (May 24, 1965), 547–550.

Johnston, J. Richard. "Classified Military Research on the Campus," JOURNAL OF HIGHER EDUCATION, 38 (June, 1967), 297–304.

Kateb, G. "Campus and Its Critics," COMMENTARY, 47 (April, 1969), 40–48.

Keniston, Kenneth. "Responsibility for Criticism and Change," in Charles Dobbins and Calvin Lee, eds. WHOSE GOALS FOR AMERICAN HIGHER EDUCATION? Washington, D.C.: American Council on Education, 1968, 145–163.

Keniston, K. and M. Lerner. "Unholy Alliance against the Campus," NEW YORK TIMES MAGAZINE, (November 8, 1970), 28–29+.

Kerr, Clark. "Conservatism, Dynamism, and the Changing University," in Alvin Eurich, ed. CAMPUS, 1980. New York: Delacourte Press, 1968, 299–323.

Kerr, Clark. "The Frantic Pace to Remain Contemporary," in R. S. Morison, ed. THE CONTEMPORARY UNIVERSITY: U.S.A. Boston: 1966, 19–38.

Kertesz, S. "Universities and the Universal," REVIEW OF POLITICS, 33 (April, 1971), 279–286.

Kirk, R. "The Scholar Is Not a Lion or a Fox," NEW YORK TIMES MAGAZINE, (May 1, 1966), 28–29+.

Kolko, G. "Universities and the Pentagon," NATION, 205 (October 9, 1967), 328–332 and (December 18, 1967), 645–648.

Kristol, I. "What Business is a University In?" NEW YORK TIMES MAGAZINE, (March 22, 1970), 30–31+.

*Kruytbosch, C. E. and S. L. Messinger, eds. "State of the University: Authority and Change," AMERICAN BEHAVIORAL SCIENTIST, 11 (May, 1968), 1–48.

Lichtman, Richard. "The Ideological Function of the University," INTERNATIONALIST SOCIALIST JOURNAL, 4 (December, 1967), 887–904.

Lichtman, Richard. "The University: Mask for Privilege?" THE CENTER MAGAZINE, 1 (January, 1968), 2–10.

Locher, Michael. "Campus Reconnaissance (1968)," in John and Susan Erlich, eds. STUDENT POWER, PARTICIPATION, AND REVOLUTION. New York: Association Press, 1970, 209–225.

Long, Durward. "Faculty Responsibility and the Executive Conquest of Academe," SCHOOL AND SOCIETY, 94 (February 19, 1966), 89–92.

294

Luria, S. E. and Zella Luria. "The Role of the University: Ivory Tower, Service Station, or Frontier Post?" DAEDALUS, 99 (Winter, 1970), 75–83.

Maccoby, H. "Controversy, Neutrality and Higher Education," AMERICAN SOCIOLOGICAL REVIEW, 25 (December, 1960), 884–893.

Macpherson, C. B. "The Violent Society and the Liberal University," AAUP BULLETIN, 55 (December, 1969), 435–439.

Main, J. "Square Universities Are Rolling Too," FORTUNE, 79 (January, 1969), 104–107+.

Martin, David. "The Dissolution of the Monasteries," in D. Martin, ed. ANARCHY AND CULTURE: THE PROBLEM OF THE CONTEMPORARY UNIVERSITY. London, Routledge and Kegan Paul, 1969, 1–12.

Martin, Warren B. "The University as Community," EDUCATIONAL RECORD, 48 (Fall, 1967), 320–326.

Mayhew, Lewis B. "The Future of American Higher Education," LIBERAL EDUCATION, 53 (December, 1967), 453–462.

Miles, Michael. "Whose University? A View from the Other Side of the Fence," NEW REPUBLIC, 160 (April 12, 1969), 17–20.

Moore, B., jr. "Reason and Radicalism in the University," NEW YORK REVIEW OF BOOKS, 14:8 (April 23, 1970), 30–37.

Morley, F. "Education's Faceless Factories Shortchange Out Students," NATION'S BUSINESS, 53 (February, 1965), 27–31.

Moynihan, Daniel P. "On Universal Higher Education," MINERVA, 9 (April, 1971), 256–271.

Mullaney, Antony," The University As a Community of Resistance," HARVARD EDUCATIONAL REVIEW, 40 (November, 1970), 628–641.

Munster, Joe H., jr. "The University in the Market Place," JOURNAL OF HIGHER EDUCATION, 35 (November, 1964), 417–425.

Newcomb, T. "University, Heal Thyself," POLITICAL SCIENCE QUARTERLY, 84 (June, 1969), 351–366.

Pake, G. E. "Whither United States Universities?" SCIENCE, 172 (May 28, 1971), 908–916.

Parsons, Talcott. "The Academic System: A Sociologist's View," PUBLIC INTEREST, 13 (Fall, 1968), 173–197.

Parsons, Talcott and Gerald M. Platt. "Considerations on the American Academic System," MINERVA, 6 (Summer, 1968), 497–523.

Perkins, James A. "Higher Education in the 1970's," EDUCATIONAL RECORD, 51 (Summer, 1970), 246–252.

Pinner, Frank. "The Crisis of the State Universities: Analysis and Remedies," in Nevitt Sanford, ed. THE AMERICAN COLLEGE: A PSYCHOLOGICAL AND SOCIAL INTERPRETATION OF THE HIGHER LEARNING. New York: Wiley, 1962, 940–971.

Sale, Kirk J. "Men of Low Profile," CHANGE, 2 (July/August, 1970), 35–40.

*Spiegel, John P. "Campus Conflict and Professorial Egos," TRANSACTION, 6 (October, 1969), 41–50.

Stewart, Campbell. "The Place of Higher Education in a Changing Society," in Nevitt Sanford, ed. THE AMERICAN COLLEGE. New York: John Wiley, 1964, 894–939.

Strickland, Stephen and Theodore Vallance. "Classified Research: To Be or Not To Be Involved," EDUCATIONAL RECORD, 48 (Summer, 1967), 224–336.

Stumpf, Samuel. "Freedom and Order on the Campus," LIBERAL EDUCATION, 56 (March, 1970), 22–28.

Sunderland, Stephen C. "Changing Universities: A Cross Cultural Approach," JOURNAL OF APPLIED BEHAVIORAL SCIENCE, 3 (October/November/December, 1967), 461–468.

Trow, Martin. "Admissions and the Crisis in American Higher Education," in W. T. Furniss, ed. HIGHER EDUCATION FOR EVERYBODY? Washington, D.C.: American Council on Education, 1971, 26–52.

Trow, Martin. "Reflections on the Transition from Mass to Universal Higher Education," DAEDALUS, 99 (Winter, 1970), 1–42.

Ward, John William. "The Trouble with Higher Education," PUBLIC INTEREST, Number 4 (Summer, 1966), 76–88.

Weiss, John. "The University as a Corporation," NEW UNIVERSITY THOUGHT, 4 (Summer, 1965), 31–45.

Wilson, Robert C. and Jerry Gaff. "Faculty Supporters of Change," RESEARCH REPORTER, 5 (Number 4, 1970), 1–4.

Windmiller, M. "Agents of the New Empire," NATION, 212 (May 10, 1971), 592–596.

Windmiller, M. "Scholars and Soldiers, A Crisis of Values," NATION, 205 (December 18, 1967), 651–654.

Wolff, Robert Paul. "The College as Rat Race," in Irving Howe, ed. THE RADICAL PAPERS. Garden City, New York: Doubleday, 1966, 296–306.

Wolff, Robert Paul. "The Myth of Value Neutrality," in Immanuel Wallerstein and Paul Starr, eds. THE UNIVERSITY CRISIS READER, I. New York: Random House, 1971, 63–69.

K.6. The Faculty and Student Activism

Cross Reference: See Section III C1 for further material relating to faculty, faculty attitudes, and teaching.

*Bayer, A. E. INSTITUTIONAL CORRELATES OF FACULTY SUPPORT OF CAMPUS UNREST. Washington, D.C.: American Council on Education, 1970.

Blackburn, Robert. THE PROFESSOR'S ROLE IN A CHANGING SOCIETY. Washington, D.C.: ERIC Clearing House in Higher Education, 1971.

Boruch, R. F. VARIETIES OF FACULTY INVOLVEMENT IN CAMPUS UNREST. Washington, D.C.: American Council on Education, 1969.

Daniels, Arlene, *et al.* ACADEMICS ON THE LINE. San Francisco: Jossey-Bass, 1970.

Haber, Barbara and Al Haber, GETTING BY WITH A LITTLE HELP FROM OUR FRIENDS. Boston: New England Free Press, 1968.

Lazarsfeld, Paul F. and Wagner Thielens, jr. THE ACADEMIC MIND. Glencoe, Illinois: Free Press of Glencoe, 1958.

Litwak, Leo and Herbert Wilner. COLLEGE DAYS IN EARTHQUAKE COUNTRY: A PERSONAL RECORD. New York: Random House, 1971.

Metzger, Loya Ferguson. "Faculty Activism in a Campus Crisis." Unpublished M.A. thesis, Columbia University.

Noll, C. E. and Rossi, P. H. GENERAL SOCIAL AND ECONOMIC ATTITUDES OF COLLEGE AND UNIVERSITY FACULTY MEMBERS. Chicago: National Opinion Research Center, n.d.

Abramson, H. J. and R. Wences. "Campus Dissent and Academic Punishment: The Response of College Professors to Local Political Activism," SOCIOLOGY OF EDUCATION, 41 (Winter, 1972), 61-75.

Armor, David J. et al. "Professors' Attitudes Toward the Vietnam War," PUBLIC OPINION QUARTERLY, 31 (No. 2, 1967), 159-175.

Axen, Richard. "Faculty Response to Student Dissent," in G. K. Smith, ed. STRESS AND CAMPUS RESPONSE. San Francisco: Jossey-Bass, 1968, 106-112.

Baldridge, J. Victor. "Faculty Activism and Influence Patterns in the University," in J. V. Baldridge, ed. ACADEMIC GOVERNANCE. Berkeley, California: McCutcheon, 1971, 293-313.

Baxter, W. F. "Faculty and Government Roles in Student Unrest," EDUCATIONAL RECORD, 50 (Fall, 1969), 411-419.

*Bayer, Alan E. "The Faculty Role in Campus Unrest," CHANGE, 3 (Winter, 1971-1972), 10-13+.

*Bayer, Alan E. "Institutional Correlates of Faculty Support of Campus Unrest," SOCIOLOGY OF EDUCATION, 45 (Winter, 1972), 76-94.

Birnbaum, N. "Dilemmas of Resistance: New Universities Conference," NATION, 206 (April 22, 1968), 535-538.

Brustein, Robert. "A Debate: the Case for Professionalism," in Immanuel Wallerstein and Paul Starr, eds. THE UNIVERSITY CRISIS READER, I. New York: Random House, 1971, 546-551.

Buchanan, J. M. "Student Revolts, Academic Liberalism, and Constitutional Attitudes," SOCIAL RESEARCH, 35 (Winter, 1968), 666-680.

Cantarow, Ellen. "The Radicalizing of a Teacher of Literature," CHANGE, 4 (May, 1972), 50-61.

Cole, Stephan and H. Adamsons. "Determinants of Faculty Support for Student Demonstrations," SOCIOLOGY OF EDUCATION, 42 (Fall, 1969), 315-329.

Cole, Stephan and H. Adamsons. "Professional Status and Faculty Support of Student Demonstrations," PUBLIC OPINION QUARTERLY, 34 (Fall, 1970), 389-394.

Dick, H. R. "Student-Faculty Role Consensus and Conflict," SOUTHWESTERN SOCIAL SCIENCE QUARTERLY, 41 (March, 1961), 415-423.

Edgar, R. W. "Moral Professor in the Immoral University," AAUP BULLETIN, 50 (December, 1964), 323-326.

"Faculty Participation in Strikes," AAUP BULLETIN, 54 (June, 1968), 155–159.

Glazer, Nathan. "Why a Faculty Cannot Afford a Franklin," CHANGE, 4 (May, 1972), 40–44.

Green, Jim. "Intellectuals and Activism: The Dilemma of the Radical Historians," ACTIVIST, 11 (No. 28, 1970), 3–6.

Hacker, Andrew. "The Rebelling Young Scholars," COMMENTARY, 30 (November, 1960), 404–412.

Hechinger, Fred. "Student Targets: Professors Are Next," CHANGE, 1 (January–February, 1969), 36–39.

Hitchcock, J. "Short Course in the Three Types of Radical Professors," NEW YORK TIMES MAGAZINE, (February 21, 1971), 30–31+.

Kadish, Sanford. "The Strike and the Professoriat," in W. P. Metzger *et al.*, DIMENSIONS OF ACADEMIC FREEDOM. Urbana, Illinois: University of Illinois Press, 1969, 34–69.

Kampf, Louis. "The Radical Faculty: What Are Its Goals," in Immanuel Wallerstein and Paul Starr, eds. THE UNIVERSITY CRISIS READER, II. New York: Random House, 1971, 522–526.

Kaplan, Abraham. "The Travesty of the Philosophers," CHANGE, 2 (January–February, 1970), 12–19.

Knauss, Robert. "The Faculty," in Grace Holmes, ed. LAW AND DISCI-PLINE ON CAMPUS. Ann Arbor, Michigan: Institute of Continuing Legal Education, 1971, 27–33.

Knoll, Erwin. "Revolt of the Professors," SATURDAY REVIEW, 48 (June, 1965), 60–61+.

Kristol, Irving. "The Troublesome Intellectuals," PUBLIC INTEREST, No. 2 (Winter, 1966), 3–6.

Kristol, Irving. Malcontent Professors," FORTUNE, 76 (December, 1967), 229–230.

Ladd, E. C., jr. "Professors and Political Petitions," SCIENCE, 163 (March 28, 1969), 1425–1430.

Ladd, E. C., jr. and Seymour Martin Lipset. "American Social Scientists and the Growth of Campus Political Activism in the 1960's," SOCIAL SCIENCE INFORMATION, 10 (No. 2, 1971), 105–120.

Ladd, E. C., jr. and Seymour Martin Lipset. The Politics of American Political Scientists," PS, 4 (Spring, 1971), 135–144.

*Laufer, Robert S. "Sources of Generational Conflict Among Faculty," YOUTH AND SOCIETY, 3 (June, 1972), 477–490.

Lehrer, Stanley. "Higher Education and the Disenchanted Students," SCHOOL AND SOCIETY, 97 (November, 1969), 427–431.

*Lipset, Seymour Martin. "Academia and Politics in America," in T. J. Nossiter, ed. IMAGINATION AND PRECISION IN THE SOCIAL SCIENCES. London: Faber, 1972, 211–289.

*Lipset, Seymour Martin. "The Politics of Academia," in D. C. Nichols, ed. PERSPECTIVES ON CAMPUS TENSIONS. Washington, D.C.: American Council on Education, 1970, 85–118.

Lipset, Seymour Martin and E. C. Ladd, jr. ". . . And What Professors Think," PSYCHOLOGY TODAY, 4 (November, 1970), 49–52.

*Lipset, Seymour Martin and E. C. Ladd, jr. "The Divided Professoriate," CHANGE, 3 (May–June, 1971), 54–60.

Lipset, Seymour Martin and E. C. Ladd, jr. "Jewish Academics in the United States: Their Achievements, Culture and Politics," in AMERICAN JEWISH YEAR BOOK, 1971. New York: Jewish Publication Society, 1971, 89–128.

Lynd, Staughton. "Intellectuals, the University and the Movement," in William Slate, ed. POWER TO THE PEOPLE! NEW LEFT WRITINGS. New York: Tower Publications, 1970, 191–206.

Morgan, William R. "Faculty Mediation in Campus Conflict," in Julian Foster and Durward Long, eds. PROTEST! STUDENT ACTIVISM IN AMERICA. New York: William Morrow, 1970, 365–382.

Morgenthau, Hans J. "Student-Faculty Participation in National Politics," in G. K. Smith, ed. AGONY AND PROMISE: CURRENT ISSUES IN HIGHER EDUCATION, 1969. San Francisco: Jossey-Bass, 1969, 5–9.

Novak, M. "End of Ideology?" COMMONWEAL, 87 (March 8, 1968), 679–682.

Nulle, S. H. "Academic Liberal," SOUTH ATLANTIC QUARTERLY, 69 (Summer, 1969), 307–316.

Paige, Glenn D. "The Professor and Politics," AAUP BULLETIN, 52 (March, 1966), 52–56.

Petras, James. "Ideology and the United States Political Scientists," SCIENCE AND SOCIETY, 29 (Spring, 1965), 192–216.

Price, Don. "Purists and Politicians," in Sidney Hook, ed. IN DEFENSE OF ACADEMIC FREEDOM. New York: Pegasus, 1971.

Rabinowitz, D. "Radicalized Professor: A Portrait," COMMENTARY, 50 (July, 1970), 62–64.

Rice, R. R. "Professors in Politics—Half a Century of Participation," WESTERN POLITICAL QUARTERLY, 12 (June, 1959), 582–584.

Riesman, David. "The Academic Career: Notes on Recruitment and Colleagueship," DAEDALUS, 85 (Winter, 1959), 147–169.

Riesman, David. "Student Culture and Faculty Values," in M. L. Habein, ed. SPOTLIGHT ON THE COLLEGE STUDENT. Washington, D.C.: American Council on Education, 1959, 8–31.

Robbins, Richard. "Up Against the Statler-Hilton Wall," DISSENT, 17 (March–April, 1970), 162–170.

Rossberg, Robert H. "The Professor and the Activist," NATIONAL ASSOCIATION OF STUDENT PERSONNEL ADMINISTRATORS JOURNAL, 6 (October, 1968), 59–68.

Sklar, Bernard. "Anatomy of Faculty Conflict," in P. G. Altbach, R. Laufer and S. McVey, eds. ACADEMIC SUPERMARKETS, San Francisco: Jossey-Bass, 1971, 190–209.

Schuman, H. and E. O. Laumann. "Do Most Professors Support the War?" TRANS-ACTION, 5 (November, 1967), 32–35.

Spaulding, Charles B. and Henry A. Turner. "Political Orientation and Field of Specialization Among College Professors," SOCIOLOGY OF EDUCATION, 41 (Summer, 1968), 247–262.

*Spiegel, J. P. "Campus Conflict and Professorial Egos," TRANS-ACTION, 6 (October, 1969), 41–50.

"Statement on Professors and Political Activity," AAUP BULLETIN, 53 (September, 1967), 307–308.

Tonsor, S. J. "Mess in Higher Education: Faculty Responsibility," VITAL SPEECHES, 36 (February 1, 1970), 250–253.

Trachtenberg, Alan. "Culture and Rebellion: Dilemmas of Radical Teachers," DISSENT, 16 (November–December, 1969), 497–504.

Trachtenberg, Alan. "Student Rebellion: Dilemma for Faculty," JOURNAL OF GENERAL EDUCATION, 21 (October, 1969), 163–175.

Ways, M. "Faculty is the Heart of the Trouble," FORTUNE, 79 (January, 1969), 94–97+.

Wences, Rosalio and Harold J. Abramson. "Faculty Opinion on the Issues of Job Placement and Dissent in the University," SOCIAL PROBLEMS, 18 (Summer, 1970), 27–38.

White, H. "Do American Colleges and Universities Encourage Their Faculties and Students to Participate Actively in Politics?" COLLEGE AND UNIVERSITY, 30 (April, 1955), 327–333.

Word, J. W. "Cleric or Critic? The Intellectual in the University," AMERICAN SCHOLAR, 35 (Winter, 1965-1966), 101-113.

K.7. University Reform

Altman, Robert A. and Carolyn Byerly, eds. THE PUBLIC CHALLENGE AND THE CAMPUS RESPONSE. Boulder, Colorado: Western Interstate Commission on Higher Education, 1971.

Atkinson, Carroll. TRUE CONFESSIONS OF A PH.D. AND RECOM-MENDATIONS FOR REFORM. Boston: Beacon, 1939 (revised 1945).

Baskin, Samuel, ed. HIGHER EDUCATION: SOME NEWER DEVELOP-MENTS. New York: McGraw-Hill, 1965.

Bell, Daniel. THE REFORMING OF GENERAL EDUCATION: THE COLUMBIA COLLEGE EXPERIENCE IN ITS NATIONAL SETTING. Garden City, New York: Anchor Books, 1968.

Brick, Michael and Earl McGrath. INNOVATION IN LIBERAL ARTS COLLEGES. New York: Teachers College Press, 1969.

Carnegie Commission on Higher Education. LESS TIME, MORE OPTIONS: EDUCATION BEYOND THE HIGH SCHOOL. New York: McGraw-Hill, 1971.

Carnegie Commission on Higher Education. NEW STUDENTS AND NEW PLACES: POLICIES FOR THE FUTURE GROWTH AND DEVELOPMENT OF AMERICAN HIGHER EDUCATION. New York: McGraw-Hill, 1971.

*Carnegie Commission on Higher Education. REFORM ON CAMPUS: CHANGING STUDENTS, CHANGING ACADEMIC PROGRAMS. New York: McGraw-Hill, 1972.

Danish, Paul. CAMPAIGN REPORT: A CONFERENCE ON EDUCA-

300

TIONAL REFORM. Washington, D.C.: U.S. National Student Association, 1966.

*Foote, Caleb, *et al.* THE CULTURE OF THE UNIVERSITY: GOVERN-ANCE AND EDUCATION. San Francisco: Joseey-Bass, 1968.

*Hefferlin, J. B. Lon. DYNAMICS OF ACADEMIC REFORM. San Francisco: Jossey-Bass, 1969.

Helms, Erwin. DIE HOCHSCHULREFORM IN DEN U.S.A. UND IHRE BEDEUTUNG FÜR DIE B.R.D. Hannover: Schroedel, 1971.

Henderson, Algo D. THE INNOVATIVE SPIRIT: CHANGE IN HIGHER EDUCATION. San Francisco: Jossey-Bass, 1970.

Hodgkinson, Harold L. INSTITUTIONS IN TRANSITION: A STUDY OF CHANGE IN HIGHER EDUCATION. Berkeley, California: Carnegie Commission on Higher Education, 1970.

*Jerome, Judson. CULTURE OUT OF ANARCHY. New York: Herder and Herder, 1971.

Johnson, B. Lamar. ISLANDS OF INNOVATION EXPANDING. Beverly Hills, California: Glencoe Press, 1969.

*Kean, Rick, ed. RUMORS OF CHANGE. Washington, D.C.: U.S. National Student Association, 1970.

*Ladd, Dwight R. CHANGE IN EDUCATIONAL POLICY: SELF-STUDIES IN SELECTED COLLEGES AND UNIVERSITIES. New York: McGraw-Hill, 1970.

Lowell, A. L. AT WAR WITH ACADEMIC TRADITIONS IN AMERICA. Cambridge, Massachusetts: Harvard University Press, 1934.

Lynd, Staughton. RESTRUCTURING THE UNIVERSITY. Chicago: New University Conference, n.d.

Martin, Warren Bryan. ALTERNATIVE TO IRRELEVANCE: A STRATEGY FOR REFORM IN HIGHER EDUCATION. Nashville, Tennessee: Abingdon, 1968.

Martin, Warren Bryan. CONFORMITY: STANDARDS AND CHANGE IN HIGHER EDUCATION. San Francisco: Jossey-Bass, 1969.

Patterson, Franklin and Charles Longsworth. THE MAKING OF A COLLEGE; PLANS FOR A NEW DEPARTURE IN HIGHER EDUCATION. Cambridge, Massachusetts: M.I.T. Press, 1966.

Perkins, James A. REFORM OF HIGHER EDUCATION: MISSION IMPOSSIBLE? New York: International Council for Educational Development, 1971 (Occasional Paper No. 2.)

Rossman, Michael. ON LEARNING AND SOCIAL CHANGE. New York: Vintage Books, 1972.

Shulman, Carol. GOVERNANCE. Washington, D.C.: ERIC Clearing House on Higher Education, 1970.

THE STUDY OF EDUCATION AT STANFORD. Stanford, California: Stanford University, 1969.

Taylor, Harold. HOW TO CHANGE COLLEGES: NOTES ON RADICAL REFORM. New York: Holt, Rinehart and Winston, 1971.

Tussman, Joseph. EXPERIMENT AT BERKELEY. New York: Oxford, 1969.

UNIVERSITY REFORM: U.S.A., 1970: A SYMPOSIUM. Washington, D.C.: Georgetown University Press, 1970.

Weiner, Harry. STUDENT TASK FORCES: AN EXPERIMENT IN INTER-DISCIPLINARY EDUCATION. New York: Alfred P. Sloan Foundation, 1972.

Bell, D. "Reforming of General Education," AMERICAN SCHOLAR, 37 (Summer, 1968), 401–406.

Botstein, Leon. "What is Innovation, Really?" CHANGE, 4 (April, 1972), 14–16+.

Bowen, Howard R. "Governance and Educational Reform," in G. K. Smith, ed. AGONY AND PROMISE. San Francisco: Jossey-Bass, 1970, 173–186.

Bromell, Henry. "The Great Experiment at Hampshire," CHANGE, 3 (November, 1971), 47–51.

Carrington, Paul. D. "The Many Mansions of a University," AMERICAN JOURNAL OF COMPARATIVE LAW, 17 (No. 3, 1969), 331–336.

Caws, Peter J. "Design for a University," DAEDALUS, 99 (Winter, 1970), 84–107.

Clecak, Peter. "The Limits of University Reform," OUR GENERATION, 5 (May, 1967), 74–86.

Clecak, Peter. "Reforming the Universities," NATION, 204 (March 27, 1967), 407–411.

Coyne, John and Thomas Hebert. "Goddard College: A Fresh Look at an Old Innovator," CHANGE, 3 (Winter, 1971–1972), 46–51.

Davidson, Carl. "University Reform Revisited," EDUCATIONAL RECORD, 48 (Winter, 1967), 5–10.

Davis, Paul. "An Educator's View: Six Crucial Changes Colleges Need," NATION'S BUSINESS, 58 (May, 1970), 60–64.

Flack, Michael. "Innovation and the University in Crisis: Three Proposals," EDUCATIONAL RECORD, 49 (Summer, 1968), 347–349.

Flexner, H. "Institutional Response to Change," JOURNAL OF GENERAL EDUCATION, 20 (January, 1969), 233–243.

Gallagher, Buell G. "Mandate for Change," in G. K. Smith, ed. THE TROUBLED CAMPUS. San Francisco: Jossey-Bass, 1970, 5–16.

Habermas, Jürgen. "The Priorities of Radical Reform," CHANGE, 2 (July–August, 1970), 29–34.

Hall, Mary Harrington. "Clark Kerr: The Nation's Most Famous Educator Speaks Out on Students, the Crisis in Higher Education, and the Future," PSYCHOLOGY TODAY, 1 (October, 1967), 25–32.

Hallberg, Edmond. "An Academic Congress: A Direction in University Governance," PHI DELTA KAPPAN, 50 (May, 1969), 538–540.

Halsey, A. H. "The Changing Functions of Universities," HARVARD EDUCATIONAL REVIEW, 30 (Spring, 1960), 119–127.

Hefferlin, J. B. L. "Ritualism, Privilege, and Reform," JOURNAL OF HIGHER EDUCATION, 41 (October, 1970), 516–523.

Helwig, David. "A Place to Grow," QUEEN'S QUARTERLY, 76 (Spring, 1969), 74–80.

302

Keeton, M. "A Productive Voice for Students," in S. Vetter, ed. NEW PROSPECTS FOR THE SMALL LIBERAL ARTS COLLEGES. New York: Teachers College Press, 1968.

Keyes, Ralph, *et al.* "The College That Students Helped Plan," CHANGE, 1 (March–April, 1969), 12–23.

King, J. "Reform of a College," MASSACHUSETTS REVIEW, 11 (Summer, 1970), 522–536.

Knowles, A. S. "Changes in the Traditional Concepts of Higher Education," SCHOOL AND SOCIETY, 99 (November, 1971), 405–409.

Kristol, Irving. "Different Ways to Restructure the University," NEW YORK TIMES MAGAZINE, (December 8, 1968), 50–51+ and (January 5, 1969), 90–93.

Landy, Marc and Mieko Landy. "Higher Learning in Appalachia: A Model for Change," JOURNAL OF HIGHER EDUCATION, 42 (March, 1971), 169–174.

Main, Jeremy. "The 'Square' Universities Are Rolling, Too," FORTUNE, 79 (January, 1969), 104+.

Maguire, John. "Strategies for Academic Reform," in H. L. Hodgkinson and M. B. Bloy, jr., eds. IDENTITY CRISIS IN HIGHER EDUCATION. San Francisco: Jossey-Bass, 1971, 91–112.

Martin, Warren B. "A Conservative Approach to Radical Reform," in W. J. Minter, ed. THE INDIVIDUAL AND THE SYSTEM. Boulder, Colorado: Western Interstate Commission for Higher Education, 1967, 37–56.

Muller, Steven. "Restructuring the University," COLLEGE AND UNIVERSITY JOURNAL, 8 (Fall, 1969), 49–55.

Mundinger, Donald C. "A Brief for a University Ombundsman," LIBERAL EDUCATION, 15 (October, 1969), 373–380.

Nyquist, E. B. and A. W. Cordier. "Role of the College and University in a Political World," COLLEGE AND UNIVERSITY, 46 (Summer, 1971), 275–293.

"Participation and Power: Should the University Be Restructured?" in I. Wallerstein and P. Starr, eds. THE UNIVERSITY CRISIS READER, 1. New York: Random House, 1971.

Pearl, Arthur. "Academic Reform: The More We Change, the Worse We Get," CHANGE, 2 (March–April, 1970), 39–43.

Peterson, R. E. "Reform in Higher Education: Demands of the Left and Right," LIBERAL EDUCATION, 55 (March, 1969), 60–77.

Potter, Paul. "Student Discontent and Campus Reform," in L. B. Mayhew, ed. HIGHER EDUCATION IN THE REVOLUTIONARY DECADES. Berkeley, California: McCutchon, 1967, 247–264.

Ravitz, Diane. "The Dreams of Livingston College," CHANGE, 1 (May-June, 1960), 36–40.

Redfield, J. M. "Reforming College Education," CURRENT, 96 (June, 1968), 6–14.

Riesman, David. "Innovation and Reaction in Higher Education," JOURNAL OF GENERAL EDUCATION, 16 (October, 1964), 177–196.

Riesman, David. "Notes on Educational Reform," JOURNAL OF GENERAL EDUCATION, 23 (July, 1971), 321–324.

Riesman, David. "The Search for Alternate Models in Education," AMERICAN SCHOLAR, 38 (Summer, 1969), 377–388.

Rossman, Michael. "How Do We Learn Today?" SATURDAY REVIEW, 55 (August 19, 1972), 27–33.

Rossman, Michael. "The Movement and Educational Reform," AMERICAN SCHOLAR, 36 (Autumn, 1967), 594–600.

Savio, Mario. "The University Becomes a Factory," LIFE, 58 (February, 1965), 18–23.

Schwartz, Edward. "The Cool Schools," CHANGE, 4 (February, 1972), 28–33.

Shaffer, Helen B. "Reorganization of the Universities," EDITORIAL RESEARCH REPORTS, (August 21, 1968), 605–624.

Silber, John. "Campus Reform: from Within or Without?" in R. Altman and C. Byerly, eds. THE PUBLIC CHALLENGE AND THE CAMPUS RESPONSE. Boulder, Colorado: Western Interstate Commission on Higher Education, 1971, 39–49.

Silberman, C. E. "Remaking of American Education," CURRENT ISSUES IN HIGHER EDUCATION, (1971), 227–233.

Tolley, William B. "Twenty-One Colleges Examine Themselves," EDUCATIONAL RECORD, 22 (July, 1941), 303–312.

"University Reform," in PRESIDENT'S COMMISSION ON CAMPUS UNREST, REPORT. New York: Arno Press, 1970, 185–211.

Villet, B. "Old Idea Flowers Anew at Santa Cruz," LIFE, 68 (May 8, 1970), 52–60+.

Williamson, E. G. "Social Change on the Campus," NATIONAL ASSOCIATION FOR STUDENT PERSONNEL ADMINISTRATORS JOURNAL, (April, 1960), 163–180.

Wilson, Logan. "Protest Politics and Campus Reform," ADMINISTRATIVE LAW REVIEW, 21 (November, 1968), 45–64.

K.8. Administrative Response to Activism

Seligman, Richard. "Measuring the Institutional Stance on Matters of Student Conduct," CSE Report No. 55, (Los Angeles, California: Center for the Study of Evaluation, UCLA Graduate School of Education, University of California, Los Angeles, 1969.

Carter, L. J. "Student Unrest: Administrators Seek Ways to Restore Peace," SCIENCE, 160 (June 14, 1968), 1205–1208.

"College Presidents Warn: Don't Let Protests Catch You Unprepared," SCHOOL MANAGEMENT, 13 (June, 1969), 59–62+.

Engel, R. A. and G. K. Widmer. "Crisis on the Campus: A Challenge to Administrators," EDUCATIONAL FORUM, 35 (March, 1971), 344–352.

Fearon, C. P. "Campus Protest and the Administrator," NATIONAL ASSOCIATION OF SECONDARY SCHOOL PRINCIPALS BULLETIN, 53 (September, 1969), 28–35.

304

Foster, Julian. "The Trustees and Protest," in Julian Foster and Durwood Long, eds. PROTEST! STUDENT ACTIVISM IN AMERICA. New York: William Morrow, 1970, 383–393.

Gusfield, J. R. "Student Protest and University Response," ANNALS OF THE AMERICAN ACADEMY OF POLITICAL AND SOCIAL SCIENCE, 395 (May, 1971), 26–38.

Henderson, Algo. "The Administrator/Student Conflict," ADMINISTRATIVE LAW REVIEW, 21 (November, 1968), 65–77.

Herr, Edwin L. "The Impact of Recent Student Protests and Student Movements: Implications for Counselors and Counselor Educators," COUNSELOR EDUCATION AND SUPERVISION, 6 (Summer, 1967), 236–247.

"How Should A University Administrator Respond to Radical Activism Among Students?" CALIFORNIA MANAGEMENT REVIEW, 12 (Winter, 1969), 89–94.

"How to Deal with Student Dissent," NEWSWEEK, 73 (March 10, 1969), 66–71.

Jenkins, Leo W., Robert W. Williams and John M. Howell. "Student Unrest: an Administrative Point of View," in Hans H. Indorf, ed. POLITICS 1970. Greenville, North Carolina: Political Science Department, East Carolina University, 1970, 113–120.

Levi, Albert W. "Violence and the University," JOURNAL OF COLLEGE STUDENT PERSONNEL, 10 (March, 1969), 87–95.

Lyman, R. W. "Professionalization: Are the Critics Justified?" EDUCATIONAL RECORD, 50 (Winter, 1969), 89–94.

Park, Rosemary. "Value Change and Power Conflict: the Administrative Interest," in W. J. Minter and Patricia Snyder, eds. VALUE CHANGE AND POWER CONFLICT IN HIGHER EDUCATION. Boulder, Colorado: Western Interstate Commission for Higher Education, 1970, 115–128.

Passalacqua-Garcia, Juan M. "Decision! The College Administrator and Student Unrest," EDUCATIONAL RECORD, 50 (Fall, 1969), 420–425.

Peters, C. E. "Activism: The Message it Holds for Placement and Recruitment," JOURNAL OF COLLEGE PLACEMENT, 29 (February, 1969), 49–52.

President's Commission on Campus Unrest. "The University's Response to Campus Disorder," in REPORT OF THE PRESIDENT'S COMMISSION ON CAMPUS UNREST. New York: Arno Press, 1970, 117–147.

Pusey, Nathan M. "Student Protest and Commitment," SCHOOL AND SOCIETY, 93 (December 11, 1965), 471–474.

Rapport, V. A. "Some Ways Toward Campus Peace," in William Brickman and Stanley Lehrer, eds. CONFLICT AND CHANGE ON THE CAMPUS. New York: School and Society Publications, 1970, 264–267.

Salk, M. "Styles of Handling Student Demonstrations," BULLETIN OF ATOMIC SCIENTISTS, 25 (June, 1969), 36–38.

Schroth, R. A. "Student Unrest: Administrators Seek Ways to Restore Peace," SCIENCE, 160 (June 14, 1968), 1205–1208.

Williamson, E. G. "The Dean of Students as Educator," EDUCATIONAL RECORD, 38 (July, 1957), 230–240.

Williamson, Edmund G. "The Need for Consultation Between Students and Administration," COLLEGE AND UNIVERSITY, 26 (April, 1951), 323–329.

Zumwinkle, Robert. "An Administrator's View," in Grace Holmes, ed. LAW AND DISCIPLINE ON CAMPUS. Ann Arbor, Michigan: Institute of Continuing Legal Education, 1971, 13–21.

K.9. Politics of Higher Education

Cross Reference: This section should be read in conjunction with the sections on faculty and student activism (K6), university reform (K7), and administrative response to activism (K8).

Altbach, P. G., R. Laufer, and S. McVey, eds. ACADEMIC SUPER-MARKETS. San Francisco: Jossey-Bass, 1971.

Baldridge, J. Victor. POWER AND CONFLICT IN THE UNIVERSITY: RESEARCH IN THE SOCIOLOGY OF COMPLEX ORGANIZATIONS. New York: Wiley, 1971.

Barzun, Jacques. THE AMERICAN UNIVERSITY: HOW IT RUNS, WHERE IT IS GOING. New York: Harper and Row, 1968.

Fashing, Joseph and Steven E. Deutsch. ACADEMICS IN RETREAT. Albuquerque, New Mexico: University of New Mexico Press, 1971.

Gross, Edward and Paul V. Grambach. UNIVERSITY GOALS AND ACADEMIC POWER. Washington, D.C.: American Council on Education, 1968.

Martin, Warren Bryan. CONFORMITY: STANDARDS AND CHANGE IN HIGHER EDUCATION. San Francisco: Jossey-Bass, 1969.

Millett, John D. THE ACADEMIC COMMUNITY. New York: McGraw-Hill, 1962.

Bunzel, John H. "Costs of the Politicized College," EDUCATIONAL RECORD, 50 (Spring, 1969), 131–137.

Chamberlain, P. C. "Obstacles to Change in the University," NATIONAL ASSOCIATION OF STUDENT PERSONNEL ADMINISTRATORS JOURNAL, 8 (July, 1971), 29–34.

Flower, J. A. "University: Community for Learning or Arena of Power Struggles?" NORTH CENTRAL ASSOCIATION QUARTERLY, 24 (Spring, 1970), 319–324.

Foster, Julian and Durward Long. "The Dynamics of Institutional Response," in Julian Foster and Durward Long, eds. PROTEST! STUDENT ACTIVISM IN AMERICA. New York: Morrow, 1970, 419–446.

Gross, Neal. "Organization Lag in Universities," HARVARD EDUCATIONAL REVIEW. 33 (Winter, 1963), 58–73.

Henderson, A. D. "Control in Higher Education: Trends and Issues," JOURNAL OF HIGHER EDUCATION, 40 (January, 1969), 1–11.

Kammerer, G. M. "State University as a Political System," JOURNAL OF POLITICS, 31 (May, 1969), 289–310.

Miles, R. E. "Pathology of Institutional Breakdown," JOURNAL OF HIGHER EDUCATION, 40 (May, 1969), 351–368.

Mirsky, M. J. "Show Me the Way to Go Home," PARTISAN REVIEW, 36 (No. 3, 1969), 517–520+.

Muller, S. "Reforming Higher Education: Administration-Faculty Impasse," CURRENT, 98 (August, 1968), 13–20.

Shaw, P. "Politics of Reform in Higher Education," COLLEGE ENGLISH, 33 (December, 1971), 294–303.

K.10. Police on Campus

Baker, Michael A. et al. POLICE ON CAMPUS: THE MASS POLICE ACTION AT COLUMBIA UNIVERSITY, SPRING, 1968. New York: New York Civil Liberties Union, 1969.

Hormachea, C. R. and Marion Hormachea, eds. CONFRONTATION: VIOLENCE AND THE POLICE. Boston: Holbrook Press, 1971.

Iannarelli, Alfred Victor. THE CAMPUS POLICE. Haywood, California: Precision Photo Form, 1968.

International Association of Chiefs of Police, Research and Development Division. POLICE CAPABILITIES, PROBLEMS AND NEEDS IN DEALING WITH CIVIL DISORDERS. (A Report submitted to the President's Advisory Committee on Civil Disorders), Washington, D.C., 1967.

Kobetz, Richard and Carl W. Hamm, eds. IACP WORKSHOP FOR STATE POLICE OFFICIALS AND CAMPUS SECURITY DIRECTORS, UNIVERSITY OF NEBRASKA, 1970. CAMPUS UNREST: DIALOGUE OR DESTRUCTION. Washington, D.C.: International Association of Chiefs of Police, 1970.

Smith, R. Dean and Richard Kobetz. GUIDELINES FOR CIVIL DISORDER AND MOBILIZATION PLANNING. Washington, D.C.: International Association of Chiefs of Police, 1968.

U.S. Army Military Police School, Ft. Gordon, Georgia. RIOT CONTROL, SPECIAL TEXT. Ft. Gordon, Georgia, 1964.

U.S. Federal Bureau of Investigation. PREVENTION AND CONTROL OF MOBS AND RIOTS. Washington, D.C.: Federal Bureau of Investigation, 1967.

Wagenhals, Nils D. EVALUATING A PUBLIC SERVICE FUNCTION: THE LARGE STATE UNIVERSITY CAMPUS POLICE UNIT. Los Angeles: Bureau of Governmental Research, University of California, 1962.

Berman, David R. "Law and Order on Campus: an Analysis of the Role and Problems of Security Police," JOURNAL OF URBAN LAW, 49 (February, 1972), 513–531.

Brest, Paul. "Intelligence Gathering on the Campus," in Grace Holmes, ed. LAW AND DISCIPLINE ON CAMPUS. Ann Arbor, Michigan: Institute of Continuing Legal Education, 1971, 97–107.

Coles, R., ed. "Policeman Complains: Interview: Excerpt from Middle Americans," NEW YORK TIMES MAGAZINE, (June 13, 1971), 11+.

Creamer, T. F. "I Was a Campus Cop," SATURDAY EVENING POST, 234 (January 28, 1961), 24–25+.

Davis, Donna G. "Security Problems in College and University Libraries: Student Violence," COLLEGE AND RESEARCH LIBRARIES, 32 (January, 1971), 15–22.

Gilbert, Ben. "Thursday Night and Friday Morning: The Police Problem," in C. R. Hormachea and Marion Hormachea, eds. CONFRONTATION: VIOLENCE AND THE POLICE. Boston: Holbrook Press, 1971, 94–112.

Greenbaum, C. W. and M. Zemach. "Role-Playing and Change of Attitude Toward the Police After a Campus Riot: Effects of Situational Demand and Justification," HUMAN RELATIONS, 25 (February, 1972), 87–99.

International Association of Chiefs of Police. "Anarchy on the Campus," POLICE CHIEF. (April, 1965).

International Association of Chiefs of Police. "Campus Disorders," in THE POLICE YEARBOOK 1970: CONTAINING THE PAPERS AND PRO-CEEDINGS OF THE 76TH ANNUAL CONFERENCE OF THE INTER-NATIONAL ASSOCIATION OF CHIEFS OF POLICE, INC. MIAMI, FLORIDA, SEPTEMBER 27–OCTOBER 2, 1969. Washington, D.C., 1970, 46–58.

Lankes, George. "Campus Violence and the Law," POLICE CHIEF, 37 (March, 1970), 38–42.

Misner, Gordon. "The Response of Police Agencies," ANNALS OF THE AMERICAN ACADEMY OF POLITICAL AND SOCIAL SCIENCE, 382 (March, 1969), 109–119.

Oblander, E. R. "Palo Alto Police Are No Longer Pigs," NASSP BULLETIN, 55 (April, 1971), 55–59.

President's Commission on Campus Unrest. "The Law Enforcement's Response," in REPORT OF THE PRESIDENT'S COMMISSION ON CAMPUS UNREST. New York: Arno Press, 1970, 149–183.

Stevens, Walter. "The Police," in Grace Holmes, ed. LAW AND DISCI-PLINE ON CAMPUS. Ann Arbor, Michigan: Institute of Continuing Legal Education, 1971, 107–115.

Truitt, John W., Richard O. Bernitt, and Charles L. Walther. "The Pre-vention, Deterrent and Control of Irresponsible Student Mass Behavior," in SAFETY MONOGRAPHS FOR COLLEGES AND UNIVERSITIES, (Sixth National Conference on Campus Safety, 1959).

"When, If Ever, Do You Call in the Cops?" (A Symposium) NEW YORK TIMES MAGAZINE, (May 4, 1969), 34–35+.

2

Minority Students in American
Higher Education

A. BLACK STUDENTS IN HIGHER EDUCATION

A.1. Black Students: Demographic Trends

Cross Reference: See also Materials under ethnic and religious groups on campus (IF5, IIC).

Bayer, Alan E. THE BLACK COLLEGE FRESHMAN: CHARACTERISTICS AND RECENT TRENDS. Washington, D.C.: American Council on Education, 1972.

Bayer, A. E. and R. F. Boruch. "The Black Student in American Colleges," ACE RESEARCH REPORTS. Volume 4. Number 2, American Council on Education, 1969.

Caliver, Ambrose. A BACKGROUND STUDY OF NEGRO COLLEGE STUDENTS. Westport, Connecticut: Greenwood, 1971.

Caliver, Ambrose. A PERSONNEL STUDY OF NEGRO COLLEGE STUDENTS: A STUDY OF THE RELATIONS BETWEEN CERTAIN BACKGROUND FACTORS OF NEGRO COLLEGE STUDENTS AND THEIR SUBSEQUENT CAREERS IN COLLEGE. Westport, Connecticut: Greenwood, 1971, (originally published in 1931).

Crossland, Fred E. MINORITY ACCESS TO COLLEGE: A FORD FOUNDATION REPORT. New York: Schocken, 1971.

Egerton, John. STATE UNIVERSITY AND BLACK AMERICANS: AN INQUIRY INTO DESEGREGATION AND EQUITY FOR NEGROES IN 100 PUBLIC UNIVERSITIES. Atlanta: Southern Education Foundation, 1969.

Morgan, Gordan Daniel. THE GHETTO COLLEGE STUDENT: A DESCRIPTIVE ESSAY ON COLLEGE YOUTH FROM THE INNER CITY. Iowa City: American College Testing Program, 1970.

Needham, Walter Evans. "Intellectual, Personality and Biographical Characteristics of Southern Negro and White College Students." Unpublished Ph.D. dissertation, University of Utah, 1966.

PUBLIC NEGRO COLLEGES: A FACT BOOK. Washington, D.C.: Office for Advancement of Public Negro Colleges, 1969.

U.S. Office of Education. STATISTICS OF NEGRO COLLEGES AND UNIVERSITIES: STUDENTS, STAFF, AND FINANCES, 1900–1950, Washington, D.C.: U.S. Office of Education, 1951.

Wisonsin State Commission of Civil Rights. THE BLACK STUDENT IN WISCONSIN STATE UNIVERSITIES, Washington: United States Commission on Civil Rights, 1971.

Astin, Alexander W. "Racial Considerations in Admissions," in D. C. Nichols and Olive Mills, eds. THE CAMPUS AND THE RACIAL CRISIS. Washington, D.C.: American Council on Education, 1970, 113–141.

Blumenfeld, W. S. "College Preferences of Able Negro Students: A Comparison of Those Naming Predominantly Negro Institutions and Those Naming Predominantly White Institutions," COLLEGE AND UNIVERSITY, 43 (Spring, 1968), 330–341.

Davis, Samuel C. et al. "A Comparison of Characteristics of Negro and White College Freshman Classmates," JOURNAL OF NEGRO EDUCATION, 39 (Fall, 1970), 359–366.

Doddy, Hurley H. "The Progress of the Negro in Higher Education: 1950–1960," JOURNAL OF NEGRO EDUCATION, 32 (Fall, 1963), 485–492.

Eells, W. C. "Higher Education of Negroes in the United States," JOURNAL OF NEGRO EDUCATION, 24 (Number 4, 1955), 426–434.

Froe, O. D. "Comparative Study of a Population of Disadvantaged College Freshmen," JOURNAL OF NEGRO EDUCATION, 37 (Fall, 1968), 370–382.

Lee, J. O. and A. S. Kramer, "Racial Inclusion in Church Related Colleges in the South," JOURNAL OF NEGRO EDUCATION, 22 (Number 1, 1953), 16–25.

Ohlendorf, G. W. and W. P. Kuvlesky. "Racial Differences in the Educational Orientations of Rural Youths," SOCIAL SCIENCE QUARTERLY, 49 (September, 1968), 274–283.

Pecou, J. S. et al. "Occupational Projections of Louisiana Black High School Seniors," EDUCATION AND URBAN SOCIETY, 2 (August, 1971), 459–468.

Sowell, T. "Black Professor Say: Colleges Are Skipping Over Competent Blacks to Admit Authentic Ghetto Types," NEW YORK TIMES MAGAZINE, (December, 13, 1970), 36–37+.

Walster, E. et al. "The Effect of Race and Sex on College Admission," SOCIOLOGY OF EDUCATION, 44 (Spring, 1970), 237–244.

A.2. Higher Education for Black Students

Ahmann, Mathew, ed. THE NEW NEGRO: A SYMPOSIUM. Notre Dame, Indiana: Fides Press, 1962.

Benedict College Convocation on the Second Century of Negro Higher Education. DIRECTIONS IN NEGRO HIGHER EDUCATION, 1970. Columbia, South Carolina: Benedict College, 1970.

Clift, Virgil A., A. W. Anderson and H. G. Hullfish, eds. NEGRO EDUCATION IN AMERICA, ITS ADEQUACY, PROBLEMS AND NEEDS. New York: Harper and Row, 1963.

Commission on Higher Educational Opportunities in the South. THE NEGRO AND HIGHER EDUCATION IN THE SOUTH: A STATEMENT. Atlanta: Southern Regional Education Board, 1967.

*Jones, Ann. UNCLE TOM'S CAMPUS. New York: Praeger, 1973.

Miller, Arthur S. RACIAL DISCRIMINATION AND PRIVATE EDUCATION. Chapel Hill, University of North Carolina Press, 1957.

Noble, Jeanne L. THE NEGRO WOMAN'S COLLEGE EDUCATION. New York: Teachers College, Columbia University, 1956.

Southwide Conference on Discrimination in Higher Education (1st, Atlanta University, 1950). DISCRIMINATION IN HIGHER EDUCATION. New Orleans: Southern Conference Educational Fund, 1951.

Wiggins, Sam P. THE DESEGREGATION ERA IN HIGHER EDUCATION. Berkeley: McCutchan, 1966.

Willie, Charles V. and Arline McCord. BLACK STUDENTS AT WHITE COLLEGES. New York: Praeger, 1972.

Woodson, Carter G. THE MIS-EDUCATION OF THE NEGRO. Washington: Associated Publishers, 1969.

"The Affirmative Duty to Integrate in Higher Education," YALE LAW JOURNAL, 79 (March, 1970), 666–697.

Bittle, W. E. "Desegregated All-White Institution: The University of Oklahoma," JOURNAL OF EDUCATIONAL SOCIOLOGY, 32 (February, 1959), 275–282.

Bond, Julian. "The Black Mind on the American Campus," BLACK POLITICIAN, 2 (July, 1970), 2–5.

Brazeal, B. R. "Some Problems in the Desegregation of Higher Education in the Hard Core States," JOURNAL OF NEGRO EDUCATION, 27 (Summer, 1958), 352–372.

Cooke, P. "Desegregated Higher Education in the District of Columbia," JOURNAL OF NEGRO EDUCATION, 27 (Summer, 1958), 342–351.

Cuninggim, M. "Integration in Professional Education: Story of Perkins, Southern Methodist University," ANNALS OF THE AMERICAN ACADEMY OF POLITICAL AND SOCIAL SCIENCE, 304 (March, 1956), 109–115.

Dorsen, Norman, "Racial Discrimination in 'Private' Schools," WILLIAM AND MARY LAW REVIEW, 9 (Fall, 1967), 39–58.

Dugan, Willis E. "Opportunity for All," in Joseph Axelrod and Mervin B. Freedman, eds. ISSUES OF THE SEVENTIES. San Francisco: Jossey-Bass, 1970, 45–56.

Engs, R. F. and J. B. Williams. "Integration by Evasion," NATION, 209 (November 17, 1969), 537–540.

Foreman, P. B. "Race Confronts Universities: A Preface for Policy," JOURNAL OF GENERAL EDUCATION, 20 (July, 1968), 81–97.

Green, R. L. "Black Quest for Higher Education: An Admissions Dilemma," PERSONNEL AND GUIDANCE JOURNAL, 47 (May, 1969), 905–911.

Hare, Nathan. "Final Reflections on a 'Negro' College: A Case Study," NEGRO DIGEST, 17 (March, 1968), 40–46+, 70–76.

Harleston, Bernard. "Higher Education for the Negro," ATLANTIC 216 (November, 1965), 139–144.

Harris, Nelson. "Desegregation in Institutions of Higher Learning," in Virgil Clift, et al., eds. NEGRO EDUCATION IN AMERICA. New York: Harper, 1962, 235–250.

Holland, Jerome. "The Negro and Higher Education," NATIONAL EDUCATION ASSOCIATION JOURNAL, 54 (March, 1965), 22–24.

"Integration at Ole Miss," EBONY, 21 (May, 1966), 29–32+.

"Integration in the University of Mississippi," CURRENT HISTORY, 43 (November, 1962), 307–311+.

Jans, R. T. "Racial Integration at Berea College, 1950–1952," JOURNAL OF NEGRO EDUCATION, 22 (Number 1, 1953), 26–37.

Janssen, Peter. "New Style Segregation," PROGRESSIVE, 30 (May, 1967), 28–31.

Jenkins, J. "Segregation and the Professor," YALE REVIEW, 46 (December, 1956), 311–320.

Johnson, C. S. "Next Steps in Education in the South," PHYLON, 15 (Number 1, 1954), 7–20.

Johnson, G. B. "Progress in the Desegregation of Higher Education," JOURNAL OF EDUCATIONAL SOCIOLOGY, 32 (February, 1959), 254–259.

Johnson, G. W. "Meditation on 1963," VIRGINIA QUARTERLY REVIEW, 39 (Spring, 1963), 161–171.

Lash, J. S. "Upteenth Crisis in Negro Higher Education," JOURNAL OF HIGHER EDUCATION, 22 (November, 1951), 432–436+.

Lyou, E. W. "University in the South," VIRGINIA QUARTERLY REVIEW, 44 (Summer, 1968), 458–469.

Martin, Robert. "General Education, Its Problems and Promise in the Education of Negroes," in Virgil Clift et al., eds. NEGRO EDUCATION IN AMERICA. New York: Harper, 1962, 183–198.

Meeth, L. Richard. "Breaking Racial Barriers, Part I: Interracial Student Exchange Programs," JOURNAL OF HIGHER EDUCATION, 37 (March, 1966), 137–143.

Meeth, L. Richard. "Breaking Racial Barriers, Part II: Interinstitutional Cooperative Programs Between Colleges for Negroes and Colleges for Whites," JOURNAL OF HIGHER EDUCATION, 37 (April, 1966), 211–217.

Miller, C. L. "Issues and Problems in the Higher Education of Negro Americans," JOURNAL OF NEGRO EDUCATION, 35 (Fall, 1966), 485–493.

Moore, Gilbert. "Blacks and Colleges," CHANGE, 4 (April, 1972), 33–41.

Mulherin, K. "California's Academic Fault," COMMONWEAL, 90 (May 23, 1969), 281–286.

Parrish, C. H., jr. "Desegregated Higher Education in Kentucky," JOURNAL OF NEGRO EDUCATION, 27 (Summer, 1958), 260–268.

Plant, R. L. "Racial Integration in Higher Education in the North," JOURNAL OF NEGRO EDUCATION, 23 (Number 3, 1954), 310–316.

Plant, Richard L. "A Second Front in the Fight on Segregated Education," THE CRISIS, 57 (January, 1950), 21–23+.

Reddick, L. O. "Critical Review: The Politics of Desegregation," JOURNAL OF NEGRO EDUCATION, 31 (Summer, 1962), 414–420.

Remmers, H. H. "Some Determinants of Discrimination in Higher Education," SCHOOL AND SOCIETY, 77 (April 11, 1953), 230–233.

Sarratt, Reed. "Report on Developments in Segregation-Desegregation," CURRENT ISSUES IN HIGHER EDUCATION 1961: GOALS FOR HIGHER EDUCATION IN A DECADE OF DECISION. Washington, D.C.: Association for Higher Education, 1961, 235–236.

Saveth, E. N. "Discrimination in the Colleges Dies Hard; Progress Report on an American Sore Spot," COMMENTARY, 9 (February, 1950), 115–121.

Schackelford, Laurel. "High Risk for Higher Education," CIVIL RIGHTS DIGEST, 2 (Summer, 1969), 45–50.

Sorkin, Alan L. "A Comparison of Quality Characteristics in Negro and White Public Colleges and Universities in the South," JOURNAL OF NEGRO EDUCATION, 38 (Spring, 1969), 112–119.

Sorkin, A. L. "Comparison of Quality Characteristics of Negro and White Private and Church-Related Colleges and Universities in the South," COLLEGE AND UNIVERSITY, 46 (Spring, 1971), 199–210.

Stembridge, Barbara Penn. "A Student's Appraisal of the Adequacy of Higher Education for Black Americans," JOURNAL OF NEGRO EDUCATION, 37 (Summer, 1968), 316–322.

Stuart, Reginald. "The Dilemma of a Dual System," NEW SOUTH, 26 (Winter, 1971), 171–196.

"Studies in the Higher Education of Negro Americans," JOURNAL OF NEGRO EDUCATION, 35 (Fall, 1966), 293–513.

Thompson, C. H. "Desegregation Pushed Off Dead Center," JOURNAL OF NEGRO EDUCATION, 29 (Spring, 1960), 107–111.

Thompson, C. H. "Prospect of Negro Higher Education," JOURNAL OF EDUCATIONAL SOCIOLOGY, 32 (February, 1959), 309–316.

Tyler, Ralph W. "Epilogue: Academic Excellence and Equal Opportunity," in Joseph Axelrod and Mervin B. Freedman, eds. ISSUES OF THE SEVENTIES. San Francisco: Jossey-Bass, 1970, 166–185.

Vairo, Philip D. "The Dilemma in Negro Higher Education," JOURNAL OF HIGHER EDUCATION, 48 (November, 1967), 448–450.

Wilkins, W. D. "College Education for Negroes," JOURNAL OF NEGRO EDUCATION, 23 (Number 4, 1954), 487–491.

A.3. Black Students: General Materials

*Bayer, Alan and Robert Boruch. THE BLACK STUDENT IN AMERICAN COLLEGES. Washington, D.C.: American Council on Education, 1969.

Bradley, Nolen Eugene, jr. "The Negro Undergraduate Student: Factors Relative to Performance in Predominantly White State Colleges and Universities in Tennessee." Unpublished Ed.D. dissertation, University of Tennessee, 1966.

CAREER COUNSELING AND PLACEMENT NEEDS OF BLACK STUDENTS AT INTEGRATED COLLEGES. Bethlehem, Pennsylvania: College Placement Services, 1970.

Check, John Felix. AN ANALYSIS OF DIFFERENCES IN CREATIVE ABILITY BETWEEN WHITE AND NEGRO STUDENTS, PUBLIC AND PAROCHIAL, THREE DIFFERENT GRADE LEVELS, AND MALES AND FEMALES. Washington, D.C.: U.S. Office of Education, Bureau of Research, 1969.

*Corson, William R. PROMISE OR PERIL: THE BLACK COLLEGE STUDENT IN AMERICA. New York: Norton, 1970.

314

Knoell, Dorothy. BLACK STUDENT POTENTIAL. Washington, D.C.: American Association of Junior Colleges, 1970.

Owens, Robert L. "Financial Assistance for Negro College Students in America: A Social Historical Interpretation of the Philosophy of Negro Higher Education." Unpublished Ph.D. dissertation, State University of Iowa, 1954.

Scott, Will Braxton, "Race Consciousness and the Negro Student at Indiana University." Unpublished Ed.D. dissertation, Indiana University, 1965.

Willie, Charles V. and Arline S. McCord. BLACK STUDENTS AT WHITE COLLEGES. New York: Praeger, 1972.

Wilson, Kenneth M. "Black Students Entering CRC Colleges: Their Characteristics and Their First-Year Academic Performance." RESEARCH MEMORANDUM No. 69-1. College Research Center, Vassar College, April 1969.

Alcindor, L. (J. Olsen, ed.) "UCLA Was a Mistake: Racial Prejudice on Campus," SPORTS ILLUSTRATED. 31 (November 3, 1969), 34–40+.

Bond, Julian. "The Black Mind on the American Campus," BLACK POLITICIAN, 2 (July, 1970), 2–5.

Bond, Julian, "The Failure of the White Minority," in Immanuel Wallerstein and Paul Starr, eds. THE UNIVERSITY CRISIS READER, I. New York: Random House, 1971, 311–317.

Berry, C. A. and A. L. Jones. "Factors Involved in Withdrawal of Students from Grambling College at or Before End of Their Freshman Year," JOURNAL OF NEGRO EDUCATION. 25 (Fall, 1956), 445–447.

Bradley, Nolen E. "The Negro Undergraduate Student: Factors Relative to Performance in Predominantly White State Colleges and Universities in Tennessee," JOURNAL OF NEGRO EDUCATION, 36 (Winter, 1967), 15–23.

Cardoso, J. J. "Ghetto Blacks and College Policy," LIBERAL EDUCATION, 55 (October, 1969), 363–372.

*Centra, John A. "Black Students at Predominantly White Colleges: A Research Description," SOCIOLOGY OF EDUCATION, 43 (Summer, 1970), 325–339.

Clark, Kenneth. "Black Youth Search for Identity," in Alexander Klein, ed. NATURAL ENEMIES? YOUTH AND THE CLASH OF GENERATIONS. New York: J. B. Lippincott, 1969, 268–273.

Conyers, J. E. and T. H. Kennedy. "Reported Knowledge Negro and White College Students Have of Negroes Who Have Passed as Whites," JOURNAL OF NEGRO EDUCATION, 33 (Fall, 1964), 454–459.

Elshorst, Hansjorg. "Two Years After Integration: Race Relations at a Deep South University," PHYLON, 28 (Spring, 1967), 41–51.

Emil, Sister Mary. "Race Relations and Higher Education," RELIGIOUS EDUCATION, 59 (January, 1964), 107–111.

Evans, J. C. and A. J. Parker. "ROTC Programs and Negro Youth," JOURNAL OF NEGRO EDUCATION, 25 (No. 2, 1956), 130–138.

Four Students. "On Being Black at Yale," in Immanuel Wallerstein and Paul Starr, eds. THE UNIVERSITY CRISIS READER, I. New York: Random House, 1971, 378–392.

Hamilton, C. E. "Problems of Negro College Students," JOURNAL OF NEGRO EDUCATION, 23 (No. 1, 1954), 88–91.

Hare, Nathan. "Conflicting Racial Orientations of Negro College Students and Professors," JOURNAL OF NEGRO EDUCATION, 34 (Fall, 1965), 431–434.

Heath, G. L. "Inquiry into a University's Noble Savage Program: Illinois State University's High Potential Program," INTEGRATED EDUCATION, 8 (July, 1970), 4–9.

Hedegard, J. M. and D. R. Brown. "Encounters of Some Negro and White Freshmen with a Public Multiversity," JOURNAL OF SOCIAL ISSUES, 25 (Summer, 1969), 131–144.

Henry, Oliver. "A Negro Student on Campus Turmoil," DISSENT, 16 (July-August, 1969), 297–300.

Henry, Oliver. "A Negro Student's Observations on Blacks," in Christopher Reaske and Robert Willson, eds. STUDENT VOICES/ONE. New York: Random House, 1971, 211–216.

Kendrick, S. A. "Minority Students on Campus," in R. A. Attman and P. O. Snyder, eds. THE MINORITY STUDENT ON THE CAMPUS: EXPECTA-TIONS AND POSSIBILITIES. Boulder, Colorado: Western Interstate Commission for Higher Education, 1971, 43–50.

Knight, J. H. "Counseling Black Students on Integrated Campuses," JOURNAL OF COLLEGE PLACEMENT, 32 (April, 1972), 30–37.

Lloyd, R. G. "Teaching Economics to Black Students," AMERICAN ECONOMIC REVIEW, PAPERS AND PROCEEDINGS, 61 (May, 1971), 249–255.

"Long March: Negro Students at University of Alabama," TIME, 81 (June 21, 1963), 13–17.

McSwine, Bartley. "Black Visions, White Realities," CHANGE, 3 (May-June, 1971), 28–37.

Marcus, Stanley. "Who Is Responsible? A Businessman Looks at Civil Rights," BUSINESS HORIZONS, 11 (June, 1968), 23–28.

Monro, J. U. "Escape from a Dark Cave," NATION, 209 (October 27, 1969), 434–439.

Moore, Gilbert. "Blacks and Colleges," CHANGE, 4 (April, 1972), 33–41.

Naughton, Ezra. "What You See Is What You Get: Black Student-White Campus," in D. Vermilye, ed. THE EXPANDED CAMPUS, San Francisco: Jossey-Bass, 1972, 49–66.

Olsen, J. "Cruel Deception," SPORTS ILLUSTRATED. 29 (July 1, 1968), 15–27.

Pasca, A. E. "Business Career for the Negro Male; BOOST Program," JOURNAL OF NEGRO EDUCATION, 38 (Winter, 1969), 64–68.

Pierce, R. M. and G. Norrell. "White Tutors for Black Students," JOURNAL OF COLLEGE STUDENT PERSONNEL, 11 (May, 1970), 169–172.

Pride, Richard and Ronald Donaldson. "Black Students at a White University," JOURNAL OF THE ASSOCIATION OF SOCIAL AND BEHAVIORAL SCIENCES, 15 (Fall), 22–38.

Rabinowitz, D. "Power in the Academy: A Reminiscence and a Parable," COMMENTARY, 47 (June, 1969), 42–49.

Rosenthal, M. et al. "Blacks at Brandeis," COMMONWEAL, 89 (March 14, 1969), 727–730.

Rothbart, G. S. "Legitimation of Inequality: Objective Scholarship vs. Black Militance," SOCIOLOGY OF EDUCATION, 43 (Spring, 1970), 159–174.

Rousseve, R. J. "Counselor Education and the Culturally Isolated: An Alliance for Mutual Benefit," JOURNAL OF NEGRO EDUCATION, 34 (Fall, 1965), 395–403.

Sampel, D. D. and W. R. Seymour. "Academic Success of Black Students: A Dilemma," JOURNAL OF COLLEGE STUDENT PERSONNEL, 12 (July, 1971), 243–247.

Samuels, G. "Alabama U.: a Story of Two Among 4,000," NEW YORK TIMES MAGAZINE, (July 28, 1963), 12+.

Shaffer, Helen B. "Blacks on Campus," EDITORIAL RESEARCH REPORTS, (September 6, 1972), 667–684.

Simon, R. J. et al. "Selective Evaluation of Their University by Negro and White Undergraduates," PHYLON, 30 (Spring, 1969), 11–16.

Simon, Rita J. and James Carey. "The Phantom Racist," in H. Becker, ed. CAMPUS POWER STRUGGLE. Chicago: Aldine, 1970, 101–120.

Staples, Robert. "The Black Scholar in Academe," CHANGE, 4 (November, 1972), 42–48.

Steif, William. "Blacks in College: 'the most Exciting Thing Around,' " PROGRESSIVE, 35 (September, 1971), 32–34.

Student Voice (Atlanta). "Black Body, White Mind," in Immanuel Wallerstein and Paul Starr, eds. THE UNIVERSITY CRISIS READER, I. New York: Random House, 1971, 749–756.

Turner, J. "Student's View: Black Students and Their Changing Prospective," EBONY, 24 (August, 1969), 135–140.

Wisdom, P. E. and K. A. Shaw. "Black Challenge to Higher Education," EDUCATIONAL RECORD, 50 (Fall, 1969), 351–359.

A.4. Historical Materials on Black Students

Bond, Horace Mann. THE EDUCATION OF THE NEGRO IN THE AMERICAN SOCIAL ORDER. New York: Octagon Books, 1966.

Bullock, Henry Allen. A HISTORY OF NEGRO EDUCATION IN THE SOUTH. Cambridge, Massachusetts: Harvard University Press, 1967.

DuBois, W. E. B. THE COLLEGE BRED NEGRO. Atlanta: Atlanta University Press, 1900 and 1910.

Noble, Jeanne L. THE NEGRO WOMAN'S COLLEGE EDUCATION. New York: Teachers College, Columbia University, 1956.

Aptheker, H. "Negro College Student in the 1920s–Years of Preparation and Protest: an Introduction," SCIENCE AND SOCIETY, 33 (Spring, 1969), 150–167.

Holmes, D. O. W. "Seventy Years of the Negro College, 1860 to 1930," PHYLON, 10 (No. 4, 1949), 307–313.

Johnson, Marcia L. "Student Protest at Fisk University in the 1920s," NEGRO HISTORY BULLETIN, 33 (October, 1970), 137–140.

Johnson, O. C. "Negro-Caucasian Club: A History: The American Students' First Inter-Racial Organization," NEGRO HISTORY BULLETIN, 33 (February, 1970), 35–41.

Jones, Claudia. "New Problems of the Negro Youth Movement," CLARITY, 1 (Summer, 1940), 54–64.

McPherson, D. "White Liberals and Black Power in Negro Education, 1865-1915," AMERICAN HISTORICAL REVIEW, 75 (June, 1970), 1357-1386.

A.5. Psychological Study of Black Students

Brewer, J. H. "An Ecological Study of the Psychological Environment of a Negro College and the Personality Needs of Its Students." Unpublished Ph.D. dissertation, University of Texas, 1963.

Clark, Kenneth B. and Lawrence Plotkin. THE NEGRO STUDENT AT COLLEGES. New York: National Scholarship and Service Fund for Negro Students, 1963.

Gurin, Patricia and Daniel Katz. MOTIVATION AND ASPIRATION IN THE NEGRO COLLEGE. Ann Arbor, Michigan: Survey Research Center, Institute for Social Research, University of Michigan, 1966.

Touchstone, Frank Virgil. "A Comparative Study of Negro and White College Students" Aggressiveness by Means of Sentence Completion." Unpublished Ph.D. dissertation, Purdue University, 1957.

Anderson, C. S. and J. S. Himes. "Dating Values and Norms on a Negro College Campus," MARRIAGE AND FAMILY LIVING, 21 (August, 1959), 227-229.

Atchinson, C. O. "Relationships Between Some Intellectual and Non-Intellectual Factors of High Anxiety and Low Anxiety Negro College Students," JOURNAL OF NEGRO EDUCATION, 37 (Spring, 1968), 174-178.

Banks, W. M. "Changing Attitudes of Black Students," PERSONNEL AND GUIDANCE JOURNAL, 48 (May, 1970), 739-745.

Bennett, W. S., jr. and N. D. Gist. "Aspirations of Negro and White Students," SOCIAL FORCES, 42 (October, 1963), 40-48.

Boykin, L. L. "Adjustment of 2,078 Negro Students," JOURNAL OF NEGRO EDUCATION, 26 (No. 1, 1957), 75-79.

Brewster, E. E. and M. D. Trigg. "Moral Values Among Negro College Students: A Study of Cultural and Racial Determinants," PHYLON, 23 (Fall, 1962), 286-293.

Charnofsky, Stanley. "Counseling for Power," PERSONNEL AND GUIDANCE JOURNAL, 49 (January, 1971), 351-357.

Clinard, M. B. and D. L. Noel. "Role Behavior of Students from Negro Colleges in a Non-Segregated University Situation," JOURNAL OF NEGRO EDUCATION, 27 (Spring, 1958), 182-188.

Derbyshire, R. L. and E. Brody. "Social Distance and Identity Conflict in Negro College Students," SOCIOLOGY AND SOCIAL RESEARCH, 48 (April, 1964), 301-314.

318

Dexter, E. S. and Stein, B. "The Measurement of Leadership in White and Negro Women Students," JOURNAL OF ABNORMAL AND SOCIAL PSYCHOLOGY, 51 (September, 1955), 219–221.

Eagleson, O. and E. S. Bell. "Values of Negro Women College Students," JOURNAL OF SOCIAL PSYCHOLOGY, 22 (November, 1945), 149–155.

Edlefsen, J. B. "Social Distance Attitudes of Negro College Students," PHYLON, 17 (March, 1956), 79–83.

*Erikson, Erik. "A Memorandum on Identity and Negro Youth," JOURNAL OF SOCIAL ISSUES, 20 (October, 1964), 29–43.

Fighter, J. H. "Career Preparation and Expectations of Negro College Seniors," JOURNAL OF NEGRO EDUCATION, 35 (Fall, 1966), 322–335.

Gaier, E. L. and W. A. Watts, "Current Attitudes and Socialization Patterns of White and Negro Students Entering College," JOURNAL OF NEGRO EDUCATION, 38 (Fall, 1969), 342–350.

Gist, N. and W. S. Bennett, jr. "Aspirations of Negro and White Students," SOCIAL FORCES, 42 (October, 1963), 40–48.

Grafton, Thomas H. "An Attitude Scale on Accepting Negro Students," SOCIAL FORCES, 43 (October, 1964), 38–41.

Gray, J. S. and A. H. Thompson. "The Ethnic Prejudices of White and Negro College Students," JOURNAL OF ABNORMAL AND SOCIAL PSYCHOLOGY, 48 (1953), 311–313.

*Gurin, P. "Motivation and Aspirations of Southern Negro College Youth," AMERICAN JOURNAL OF SOCIOLOGY, 75 (January, 1970), 607–631.

Hargrett, A. J. "Feelings of Depression Among Students of Savannah State College, 1957–1958," JOURNAL OF NEGRO EDUCATION, 27 (Fall, 1958), 539–543.

Harris, E. E. "Family and Student Identities: An Exploratory Study in Self and We-Group Attitudes," JOURNAL OF NEGRO EDUCATION, 34 (Winter, 1965), 17–22.

Harrison, E. C. "Study of Occupational Attitudes," JOURNAL OF NEGRO EDUCATION, 22 (No. 4, 1953), 471–475.

Hines, Ralph H. "Social Distance Components in Integration Attitudes of Negro College Students," JOURNAL OF NEGRO EDUCATION, 37 (Winter, 1968), 23–30.

Howard, Lawrence C. "Black Consciousness and Identity Crisis," in H. L. Lodgkinson and M. B. Bloy, jr., eds. IDENTITY CRISIS IN HIGHER EDUCATION. San Francisco: Jossey-Bass, 1971, 177–206.

Johnson, J. K. "Moral Attitudes of White and Negro Students," SOCIOLOGY AND SOCIAL RESEARCH, 20 (May-June, 1936), 463–472.

Maddox, George. "Drinking and Abstinence: Emerging Patterns Among Selected Negro Freshman," in George Maddox, ed. THE DOMESTICATED DRUG: DRINKING AMONG COLLEGIANS. New Haven, Connecticut: College and University Press, 1970, 146–176.

Maddox, George and Jay R. Williams. "Drinking Behavior of Negro Collegians," QUARTERLY JOURNAL OF STUDIES ON ALCOHOL, 29 (March, 1968), 117–129.

McClain, Edwin W. "Personality Characteristics of Negro College Students in the South—a Recent Appraisal," JOURNAL OF NEGRO EDUCATION, 36 (Summer, 1967), 320–325.

Mathis, W. J. and E. W. McClain. "Peak Experiences of White and Negro College Students," JOURNAL OF CLINICAL PSYCHOLOGY, 24 (July, 1968), 318–319.

Ostlund, L. A. "Occupational Choice Patterns of Negro College Women," JOURNAL OF NEGRO EDUCATION, 26 (No. 1, 1957), 86–91.

Pettigrew, Thomas F. "A Social Psychological View of the Predominantly Negro College," JOURNAL OF NEGRO EDUCATION, 36 (Summer, 1967), 274–285.

Poussaint, A. and C. Atkinson. "Black Youth and Motivation," BLACK SCHOLAR, 1 (March, 1970), 43–51.

Prothro, E. T. and J. A. Jensen. "Comparison of Some Ethnic and Religious Attitudes of Negro and White College Students in the Deep South," SOCIAL FORCES, 30 (May, 1952), 426–428.

Ratliffe, S. A. and L. K. Steil. "Attitudinal Differences Between Black and White College Students," SPEECH TEACHER, 19 (September, 1970), 190–198.

Sumner, F. C. and J. A. Lee. "Some Resemblances Between Friends of Like Sex and Between Friends of Unlike Sex Among a Group of Negro College Students," JOURNAL OF PSYCHOLOGY, 12 (October, 1941), 199–201.

Taylor, D. A. "Relationship Between Authoritarianism and Ethnocentrism in Negro College Students," JOURNAL OF NEGRO EDUCATION, 31 (Fall, 1962), 455–459.

Thomas, Charles W. "Black-White Campus Issues and the Function of Counseling Centers," in F. F. Korten, S. W. Cook, and J. I. Lacey, eds. PSYCHOLOGY AND THE PROBLEMS OF SOCIETY, Washington, D.C.: American Psychological Association, 1970, 420–426.

Thompson, M. L. "Attitudes of Twenty Negro Graduate Students Toward Education in the South," JOURNAL OF NEGRO EDUCATION, 25 (No. 4, 1956), 448–451.

Vittenson, Lillian K. "Areas of Concern to Negro College Students As Indicated by Their Responses to the Mooney Problem Check List," JOURNAL OF NEGRO EDUCATION, 36 (Winter, 1967), 51–57.

Wright, W. "Vocational and Learning Attitudes of Black Students," JOURNAL OF COLLEGE STUDENT PERSONNEL, 12 (July, 1971), 253–258.

A.6. Black Colleges and Their Students

Fichter, Joseph H. GRADUATES OF PREDOMINANTLY NEGRO COLLEGES: CLASS OF 1964; PREPARED FOR THE NATIONAL INSTITUTES OF HEALTH, WITH JOINT SPONSORSHIP BY THE U.S. DEPARTMENT OF LABOR AND NATIONAL SCIENCE FOUNDATION. Washington, D.C.: Public Heath Service, Publication No. 1571, 1967.

Gallagher, Buell G. AMERICAN CASTE AND THE NEGRO COLLEGE. New York: Columbia University Press, 1938.

320

Jaffe, A. J. *et al*. NEGRO HIGHER EDUCATION IN THE 1960's. New York: Praeger, 1968.

*Jones, Ann. UNCLE TOM'S CAMPUS. New York: Praeger, 1973.

Le Melle, Tilden J. and Wilbert J. Le Melle. THE BLACK COLLEGE: A STRATEGY FOR ACHIEVING RELEVANCY. New York: Praeger, 1969.

McGrath, Earl J. THE PREDOMINANTLY NEGRO COLLEGES AND UNIVERSITIES IN TRANSITION. New York: Teachers College, Columbia University, 1965.

Atwood, R. B. "Public Negro College in a Racially Integrated System of Higher Education," JOURNAL OF NEGRO EDUCATION, 21 (No. 3, 1952), 352-363.

Centra, J. A., R. L. Linn and M. E. Parry. "Academic Growth in Predominately Negro and Predominately White Colleges," AMERICAN EDUCATIONAL RESEARCH JOURNAL, 7 (January, 1970), 83-98.

Chappelle, Y. R. "The Black Woman on the Negro College Campus," BLACK SCHOLAR, 1 (January-February, 1970), 36-40.

Clement, R. E. "Present and Future Role of Private Colleges for Negroes," PHYLON, 10 (No. 4, 1949), 323-327.

Cozart, L. S. "Critical Problems in the Education of Negroes in the Southern Region," JOURNAL OF NEGRO EDUCATION, 25 (No. 2, 1956), 169-174.

Dent, Thomas C. "Blues for the Negro College," FREEDOMWAYS, 8 (Fall, 1968), 385-394.

Friedman, Neil. "Experiment on a Black Campus: Miles College," in Philip Runhel, *et al.*, eds. THE CHANGING COLLEGE CLASSROOM. San Francisco: Jossey-Bass, 1969, 52-68.

Friedman, N., ed. "Learning in Black Colleges: Symposium," WILSON LIBRARY BULLETIN, 44 (September, 1969), 49-74.

"The Future of Private Negro College," EBONY, 16 (July, 1961), 88-90+.

Greene, Thomas W. "After the Explosion, Two Years of Fallout," SOUTHERN EDUCATION REPORT, 4 (May, 1969), 32-37.

Gurin, P. "Social Class Constraints on the Occupational Aspirations of Students Attending Some Predominantly Negro Colleges," JOURNAL OF NEGRO EDUCATION, 35 (Fall, 1966), 336-350.

Gurin, P. and E. Epps. "Some Characteristics of Students from Poverty Backgrounds Attending Predominantly Negro Colleges in the Deep South," SOCIAL FORCES, 45 (September, 1966), 27-40.

Harrison, E. C. "The Negro College in a Changing Economy," JOURNAL OF HIGHER EDUCATION, 36 (May, 1965), 259-266.

*Hartnett, Rodney T. "Differences in Selected Attitudes and College Orientations Between Black Students Attending Traditionally Negro and Traditionally White Institutions," SOCIOLOGY OF EDUCATION, 43 (February, 1970), 419-436.

Himes, J. S., jr. "Factor of Social Mobility in Teaching Marriage Courses in Negro Colleges," SOCIAL FORCES, 30 (May, 1952), 439-443.

Himes, J. S., jr. and A. E. Manley. "Success of Students in a Negro Liberal

Arts College," JOURNAL OF NEGRO EDUCATION, 19 (No. 4, 1950), 466–473.

Hobson, F. C., jr. "Portrait of a Black College," COMMONWEAL, 88 (May 24, 1968), 295–298.

Hodkinson, J. Raymond. "What is Wrong with Negro Colleges? NEW SOUTH STUDENT, (April, 1966).

"Integration: Negro Colleges' Newest Challenge," EBONY, 21 (March, 1966), 36–38+.

*Jencks, Christopher and David Riesman, "Negroes and Their Colleges," in C. Jencks and D. Riesman, THE ACADEMIC REVOLUTION, Garden City, New York: Doubleday, 1968, 406–479.

Jenkins, M. D. "Future of the Desegregated Negro College: A Critical Summary," JOURNAL OF NEGRO EDUCATION, 27 (Summer, 1958), 419–429.

Johnson, G. B. "Desegregation and the Future of the Negro College: A Critical Summary," JOURNAL OF NEGRO EDUCATION, 27 (Summer, 1958), 430–435.

Johnson, O. C. "Importance of Black Colleges," EDUCATIONAL RECORD, 52 (Spring, 1971), 165–170.

Miles, Michael. "Colonialism on the Black Campus," NEW REPUBLIC, 157 (August 5, 1967), 15–16.

Morris, E. W. "Admissions in Predominantly Negro Colleges: A View from the Inside," COLLEGE AND UNIVERSITY, 44 (Winter, 1969), 130–144.

Myers, A. F. "Colleges for Negroes," SURVEY, 86 (May, 1950), 233–239.

Nabrit, S. M. "Desegregation and the Future of Graduate and Professional Education in Negro Institutions," JOURNAL OF NEGRO EDUCATION, 27 (Summer, 1958), 414–418.

"The Negro Public College," JOURNAL OF NEGRO EDUCATION, 21 (Summer, 1962), 215–428.

Patterson, F. D. "Colleges for Negro Youth and the Future," JOURNAL OF NEGRO EDUCATION, 27 (Spring, 1958), 107–114.

Payne, J. A., jr. "Role of the Negro College in the Light of Integrative Trends," JOURNAL OF NEGRO EDUCATION, 22 (No. 1, 1953), 80–83.

Payne, William. "Forgotten, But Not Gone: The Negro Landgrant Colleges," CIVIL RIGHTS DIGEST, 3 (Spring, 1970), 12–17.

Pittman, J. A. "Study of the Prediction of Academic Achievement in Publicly-Supported Colleges for Negroes," JOURNAL OF NEGRO EDUCATION, 23 (No. 2, 1954), 123–132.

Poinsett, A. "Reverse Integration in Mississippi: Tougaloo College," EBONY, 18 (January, 1963), 23–26+.

Robbins, Richard. "The Future of Negro Colleges," NEW SOUTH STUDENT, (April, 1966).

Roth, R. M. "Self-Selection Process by Northern Negroes Existing in a Southern Negro College," JOURNAL OF NEGRO EDUCATION, 28 (Winter, 1959), 35–41.

Rust, V. "Negro Schools: A Model for Nazi Colonial Education," JOURNAL OF NEGRO EDUCATION, 40 (Spring, 1971), 103–107.

322

*Sekora, J. "Murder Relentless and Impassive: The American Academic Community and the Negro College," SOUNDINGS, 51 (Fall, 1968), 237–271.

Sekora, J. "On Negro Colleges: A Reply to Jencks and Riesman," ANTIOCH REVIEW, 28 (Spring, 1968), 5–26.

Sisk, Glenn. "The Negro Colleges in Atlanta," JOURNAL OF NEGRO EDUCATION, 33 (Spring, 1964), 131–135; (Fall, 1964), 404–408.

Smith, Stanley H. "Administrators Should Heed Student Views," SOUTHERN EDUCATION REPORT, 4 (June, 1969), 41–45.

Sorkin, Alan. "A Comparison of Quality Characteristics in Negro and White Public Colleges and Universities in the South," JOURNAL OF NEGRO EDUCATION, 38 (Spring, 1969), 112–119.

Sorkin, Alan. "Comparison of Quality Characteristics of Negro and White Private and Church Related Colleges and Universities in the South," COLLEGE AND UNIVERSITY, 46 (Spring, 1971), 199–210.

Stephens, Ernest. "The Black University in America Today," FREEDOMWAYS, 7 (Spring, 1967), 131–137.

Stevenson, J. "Ignorant Armies," ATLANTIC, 224 (October, 1969), 57–63.

Stone, Raymond H. "The White Businessman and the Black Campus," BELL TELEPHONE MAGAZINE, 47 (November-December, 1968), 22–27.

Woodward, C. Van. "The Unreported Crisis in the Southern Colleges," HARPER'S, 225 (October, 1962), 82–89.

Zinn, Howard. "A New Direction for Negro Colleges," HARPER'S, 232 (May, 1966), 75.

B. BLACK STUDENT ACTIVISM

B.1. Civil Rights Movement: Pre-1965

Broderick, Francis L. and August Meier, eds. BLACK PROTEST THOUGHT IN THE TWENTIETH CENTURY. New York: Bobbs-Merrill, 1971.

Clarke, Jacquelyne. THESE RIGHTS THEY SEEK: A COMPARISON OF GOALS AND TECHNIQUES OF LOCAL CIVIL RIGHTS ORGANIZATIONS, Washington, D.C.: Public Affairs Press, 1962.

*Coles, Robert. CHILDREN OF CRISIS, A STUDY OF COURAGE AND FEAR. Boston: Little, Brown, 1967.

Dowd, Douglas and Mary Nichols, eds. STEP BY STEP. New York: Norton, 1965.

Ehle, J. THE FREE MEN. New York: Harper and Row, 1965.

Forman, James. SAMMY YOUNGE, jr., THE FIRST BLACK COLLEGE STUDENT TO DIE IN THE BLACK LIBERATION MOVEMENT. New York: Grove Press, 1968.

Friedman, Leon, ed. THE CIVIL RIGHTS READER, BASIC DOCUMENTS OF THE CIVIL RIGHTS MOVEMENT. New York: Walker, 1967.

*Grant, Joanne, ed. BLACK PROTEST: HISTORY, DOCUMENTS AND ANALYSIS: 1619 TO THE PRESENT. Greenwich, Connecticut: Fawcett Publications, 1968.

Hansberry, Lorraine. THE MOVEMENT: DOCUMENTARY OF A STRUGGLE FOR EQUALITY. New York: Simon and Schuster, 1964.

*Hentoff, Nat. THE NEW EQUALITY. New York: Viking, 1964.

Jones, Lewis W. THE INFLUENCE OF STUDENT DEMONSTRATIONS ON SOUTHERN NEGRO COLLEGES: PART I—INTRODUCTION AND SUMMARY. (A Report from the Department of Race Relations of Fisk University to the Field Foundation.) Nashville, Tennessee: Fisk University, 1960.

Lakey, George. "The Sociological Mechanisms of Nonviolent Action." Unpublished M.A. thesis, University of Pennsylvania, 1962.

Laue, James. "Direct Action and Desegregation: A Study in Social Spontaneity and Institutionalization." Unpublished Ph.D. dissertation, Harvard University, 1965.

Levy, Charles J. VOLUNTARY SERVITUDE: WHITES IN THE NEGRO MOVEMENT. New York: Appleton-Century-Crofts, 1968.

Lomax, Louis E. THE NEGRO REVOLT. New York: Harper and Brothers, 1962.

Matthews, Donald R. and James W. Prothro. NEGROES AND THE NEW SOUTHERN POLITICS. New York: Harcourt, Brace and World, 1966.

Oppenheimer, Martin. "The Genesis of the Southern Negro Student Movement: A Study in Contemporary Negro Protest." Unpublished Ph.D. dissertation, University of Pennsylvania, 1963.

Orbell, John Macleod. "Social Protest and Social Structure: Southern Negro College Student Participation in the Protest Movement." Unpublished Ph.D. dissertation, University of North Carolina, 1965.

Peck, Jim. CRACKING THE COLOR LINE, New York: Congress of Racial Equality, 1960.

Pinkney, Alphonso. THE COMMITTED: WHITE ACTIVISTS IN THE CIVIL RIGHTS MOVEMENT. New Haven, Connecticut: College and University Press, 1968.

Proudfoot, Merrill. DIARY OF A SIT-IN. Chapel Hill, North Carolina: University of North Carolina Press, 1962.

Ramsey, Paul. CHRISTIAN ETHICS AND THE SIT-INS. New York: Associated Press, 1961.

SIT-INS, THE STUDENTS REPORT. New York: Congress of Racial Equality, 1960.

*Southern Regional Council. THE STUDENT PROTEST MOVEMENT: A RECAPITULATION. Atlanta, Georgia: Southern Regional Council, 1961.

Stoper, Emily S. "The Student Nonviolent Coordinating Committee: the Growth of Radicalism in a Civil Rights Organization." Unpublished Ph.D. dissertation, Harvard University, 1968.

A SURVEY OF THE SOUTHERN STUDENT SIT-IN MOVEMENT AND NATIONWIDE STUDENT ACTIVITY. Philadelphia, Pennsylvania: U.S. National Student Association, 1960.

Wakefield, Dan. REVOLT IN THE SOUTH. New York: Grove Press, 1960.

*Watters, Pat. ENCOUNTER WITH THE FUTURE. Atlanta, Georgia: Southern Regional Council, 1965.

Watters, Pat and Reese Cleghorn, CLIMBING JACOB'S LADDER: THE

ARRIVAL OF NEGROES IN SOUTHERN POLITICS. New York: Harcourt, Brace and World, 1967.

Wehr, Paul. "The Sitdown Strikes: A Study of the Passive Resistance Movement in North Carolina," Unpublished M.A. thesis, University of North Carolina, 1960.

Westin, Alan F., ed. FREEDOM NOW! THE CIVIL RIGHTS STRUGGLE IN AMERICA. New York: Basic Books, 1964.

Wilkins, Roy. THE MEANING OF SIT-INS. New York: NAACP, 1960.

*Zinn, Howard. S.N.C.C.: THE NEW ABOLITIONISTS. Boston: Beacon Press, 1964.

Adams, Averna. "Sharecropper Is Me, the Small Farmer Is Me, the Domestic Is Me: Tougaloo College," WILSON LIBRARY BULLETIN, 44 (September, 1969), 58–63.

Atwater, James. " 'If We Can Crack Mississippi . . . ,' " SATURDAY EVENING POST, 237 (July 25, 1964), 15–19.

Baker, B. "Documentation of Communist Influences in Racial Turmoil," CONSERVATIVE JOURNAL, (May-June, 1968).

Bennett, Lerone. "The Plight of Negro College Presidents," EBONY, 15 (October, 1960), 138–142.

Bennett, Lerone. "SNCC: Rebels With a Cause," EBONY, 20 (July, 1965), 146–153.

Bennett, Lerone. "What Sit-Downs Means to America," EBONY, 15 (June, 1960), 35–40.

Bond, Julian. "Impetus and Impact: Students and the Civil Rights Movement," MOTIVE, 26 (October, 1965), 40–46.

Bond, Julian. "The Southern Student Movement," FREEDOMWAYS, 2 (Summer, 1962), 308–310.

Braden, Anne. "Mobilization at the Grass Roots: 1961–1962," MONTHLY REVIEW, 17 (July-August, 1965), 35–60.

*Braden, Anne. "The Southern Freedom Movement in Perspective," MONTHLY REVIEW, 17 (July-August, 1965), entire issue.

Bromley, Dorothy and Susan McCabe. "Impact of the Sit-In Movement on Academic Freedom," NEGRO EDUCATION REVIEW, 12 (April, 1961), 63–71.

Carmichael, Stokely. "Who Is Qualified?" in A. Kopkind, ed. THOUGHTS OF THE YOUNG RADICALS, New York: New Republic, 1966, 26–35.

Carr, Lester and S. Oliver Roberts. "Correlates of Civil-Rights Participation," JOURNAL OF SOCIAL PSYCHOLOGY, 67 (December, 1965), 259–267.

Clark, Jacqueline J. "Standard Operational Procedures in Tragic Situations," PHYLON, 27 (Winter, 1961), 318–329.

Clark, Septima P. "Literacy and Liberation," FREEDOMWAYS, 4 (Winter, 1964), 113–124.

*Coles, Robert. "Serpents and Doves: Non-Violent Youth in the South," in Erik Erikson, ed. THE CHALLENGE OF YOUTH. Garden City, New York: Doubleday, 1965, 223–259.

Constable, John. "Negro Student Protests Challenge North Carolina Leaders," NEW SOUTH, 15 (March, 1960), 3–10.

Cothraw, Tilman C. "The Negro Protest Against Segregation in the South," ANNALS OF THE ACADEMY OF POLITICAL AND SOCIAL SCIENCE, 357 (January, 1965), 65–72.

Countryman, Peter. "With Our Minds Stayed on Freedom," FELLOWSHIP, 29 (November 1, 1963), 17–18+.

Delavan, V. et al. "Why They Sat In," SOCIAL PROGRESS. 51 (February, 1961), 3–46.

"The Demonstrations in the South," NEW UNIVERSITY THOUGHT, 1 (Spring, 1960), 21–27.

DeMuth, Jerry. "Black Belt, Alabama," COMMONWEAL, 80 (August 7, 1964), 536–539.

DeMuth, Jerry. "Tired of Being Sick and Tired . . . ," NATION, 198 (June 1, 1964), 548–551.

DeVree, Charlotte. "The Young Negro Rebels," HARPER'S, 222 (October, 1961), 133–138.

Dienstfrey, T. "Conference on the Sit-Ins," COMMENTARY, 29 (June, 1960), 524–528.

"Direct Action in the South," NEW SOUTH, 18 (October-November, 1963), 1–32.

Doddy, Hurley. "The 'Sit-In' Demonstration and the Dilemma of the Negro College President," JOURNAL OF NEGRO EDUCATION, 30 (Winter, 1961), 1–3.

Fini, Benjamin. "College Color Line Cracking in the South," INTER-COLLEGIAN, 60 (January, 1951).

Fischer, John. "A Small Band of Practical Heroes," HARPER'S, 227 (October, 1963), 16+.

*Fishman, J. R. and F. Solomon. "The Psychosocial Meaning of Non-violence in Student Civil Rights Activity," PSYCHIATRY, 27 (May, 1964), 91–99.

*Fishman, Jacob and Fredric Solomon. "Youth and Social Action: An Introduction," JOURNAL OF SOCIAL ISSUES, 20 (October, 1964), 1–29.

*Fishman, Jacob and Fredric Solomon. "Youth and Social Action I: Perspectives on the Student Sit-In Movement," AMERICAN JOURNAL OF ORTHOPSYCHIATRY, 33 (October, 1963), 872–882.

Fleming, Harold C. "The Changing South and the Sit-Ins," JOURNAL OF INTERGROUP RELATIONS, 2 (Winter, 1960–1961), 56–60.

Freeman, Donald, "The Northern Student and Civil Rights," VENTURE, 2 (September, 1960), 12–14+.

Fuller, Helen. "Southern Students Take Over," NEW REPUBLIC, 142 (May, 1960), 14–16.

Gates, Maurice. "Negro Students Challenge Social Forces," THE CRISIS, 42 (August, 1935), 232–233+.

Geschwinder, James A. "Social Structure and the Negro Revolt: An Examination of Some Hypotheses," SOCIAL FORCES, 43 (December, 1964), 248–256.

Goldberg, C. L. "Southern Youth Points the Way," NEW REPUBLIC, 112 (May 7, 1945), 641–642.

326

Graham, Frank. "Students 'Standing Up' For the American Dream," NEW SOUTH, 15 (July-August, 1960), 7–8.

Graham, Shirley. "A Cup of Coffee, Please!" POLITICAL AFFAIRS, 39 (June, 1960), 23–36.

Hare, A. P. "Nonviolent Action From a Social-Psychological Perspective," SOCIOLOGICAL INQUIRY, 38 (Winter, 1968), 5–12.

Hayden, Tom. "Just a Matter of Timing?" LIBERATION, 7 (October, 1962), 24–26.

*Hayden, Tom. "SNCC: The Qualities of Protest," STUDIES ON THE LEFT, 5 (Winter, 1965), 113–124.

Hentoff, Nat. "Beyond Civil Rights," LIBERATION, 9 (May, 1964), 13–20.

Jencks, Christopher. "Mississippi. From Conversion to Coercion," NEW REPUBLIC, 151 (August 22, 1964), 17–21.

Johnson, G.W. "To Live and Die in Dixie," ATLANTIC, 206 (July, 1960) 29–34.

*Jones, Charles. "SNCC: Non-Violence and Revolution," NEW UNIVERSITY THOUGHT, 3 (September-October, 1963), 8–19.

*Kahn, Tom. "Problem of the Negro Movement: A Special Report," DISSENT, 11 (Winter, 1964), 108–138.

Kalikow, D. W. and L. Carr. "Determinants of Civil Rights Activities," JOURNAL OF SOCIAL PSYCHOLOGY, 74 (February, 1968), 111–116.

Keating, Edward, Warren Hinckle, and David Welsh. "The South at War," RAMPARTS, 4 (June, 1965), 17–52.

Killian, Lewis M. and Charles U. Smith. "Negro Protest Leaders in a Southern Community," SOCIAL FORCES, 38 (March, 1960), 253–257.

King, Mary. "In the South: Two Kinds of Students," FELLOWSHIP, 29 (November 1, 1963), 13+.

Kopkind, A. "New Radicals in Dixie," NEW REPUBLIC, 152 (April 10, 1965), 13–16.

Kopkind, A. "Seat Belts for Mississippi's Five," NEW REPUBLIC, (July 24, 1965), 17–18.

Lincoln, Eric. "The Strategy of a Sit-In," THE REPORTER, 24 (January 5, 1961), 20–23.

"Lincoln University—Missouri: The Student Thrust Against Segregation in the 40s," adapted from Lewis Jones, THE INFLUENCE OF STUDENT DEM-ONSTRATIONS ON SOUTHERN NEGRO COLLEGES, PART II–THE NEGRO STUDENT MOVEMENT, in Report from the Department of Race Relations of Fisk University to the Field Foundation. Nashville, Tennessee: Fisk University, 1962, 37–51.

Lomax, L. E. "Negro Revolt Against the Negro Leaders," HARPER, 220 (June, 1960), 41–48.

Lumer, Hyman. "The Sit-Ins: Negro Students Show the Way," POLITICAL AFFAIRS, 39 (April, 1960), 1–14.

Lynd, Staughton. "SNCC: The Beginning of Ideology," ACTIVIST, (Fall, 1964).

*Lynd, Staughton and Roberta Yancy. "Southern Negro Students: The College and the Movement," DISSENT, 11 (Winter, 1964), 39–45.

Mabee, Carleton. "Evolution of Non-Violence," NATION, 193 (August 12, 1961), 78–81.

Mabee, Carleton. "Sit-ins and Marches," NATION, 195 (October, 6, 1962), 197–199.

McKinney, Theophilus E., jr. "The Race Question and Student Demonstrations in the Deep South, 1962," QUARTERLY REVIEW OF HIGHER EDUCATION AMONG NEGROES, 30 (April, 1962), 61–65.

McMillan, G. E. "Sit-Downs: The South's New Time Bomb," LOOK, 24 (July 5, 1960), 21–25.

Massaquoi, H. J. "South Carolina's Moment of Truth," EBONY, 18 (May, 1963), 96–98+.

Meier, A. "Negro Protest Movements and Organizations," JOURNAL OF NEGRO EDUCATION, 32 (Fall, 1963), 437–450.

Meier, August. "The Successful Sit-In in a Border City," JOURNAL OF INTERGROUP RELATIONS, 2 (Summer, 1961), 230–237.

"Mississippi Tragedy: What It All Means," U.S. NEWS AND WORLD REPORT, 53 (October 15, 1962), 39–52.

Moses, Bob. "Mississippi: 1960–1962," LIBERATION, 14 (January, 1970), 6–17.

Nash, Diana. "Inside the Sit-Ins and Freedom Rides: Testimony of a Southern Student," in M. H. Ahmann, ed. THE NEW NEGRO. South Bend, Indiana: Fides Publishers, 1961, 43–60.

"The Negroes Act." DISSENT, 7 (Summer, 1960), 219–243.

Olds, Victoria M. "Freedom Rides: A Social Movement as an Aspect of Social Change," SOCIAL WORK, 8 (July, 1963), 16–23.

Olds, Victoria M. "Sit-Ins: Social Action to End Segregation," SOCIAL WORK, 6 (April, 1961), 66–105.

Oppenheimer, Martin. "Current Negro Protest Activities and the Concept of Social Movement," PHYLON, 24 (Summer, 1963), 154–159.

Oppenheimer, Martin. "Institutions of Higher Learning and the 1960 Sit-Ins: Some Clues for Social Action," JOURNAL OF NEGRO EDUCATION, 32 (Summer, 1963), 286–288.

*Oppenheimer, Martin. "Southern Student Movement: Year 1," JOURNAL OF NEGRO EDUCATION, 33 (Fall, 1964), 396–403.

Oppenheimer, Martin. "Southern Student Sit-Ins: Intra-Group and Community Conflict," PHYLON, 27 (Spring, 1966), 20–26.

*Orbell, John. "Protest Participation Among Southern Negro College Students," AMERICAN POLITICAL SCIENCE REVIEW, 61 (June, 1967), 446–456.

Orum, Anthony M. and Amy W. Orum. "The Class and Status Bases of Negro Student Protest," SOCIAL SCIENCE QUARTERLY, 49 (December, 1968), 521–533.

Payne, Bruce. "SNCC: An Overview Two Years Later," ACTIVIST, 6 (November, 1965), 4–9.

Petrof, John U. "The Effect of Student Boycotts Upon the Purchasing Habits of Negro Families in Atlanta, Georgia," PHYLON, 24 (Fall, 1963), 266–270.

Pinard, Maurice, Jerome Kirk, and Donald Von Eschen. "Processes of Recruitment in the Sit-In Movement," PUBLIC OPINION QUARTERLY, 33 (Fall, 1969), 355–369.

Pollit, Daniel H. "Dime Store Demonstrations: Events and Legal Problems of the First Sixty Days," DUKE LAW JOURNAL, (Summer, 1960), 315–365.

*Rabinowitz, Victor and Norman Fruchter. "An Exchange on S.N.C.C.," STUDIES ON THE LEFT, 5 (Spring, 1965), 82–95.

Randolph, Harland. "The Northern Student Movement," EDUCATIONAL RECORD, 45 (Fall, 1964), 389–394.

Record, Wilson. "Intellectuals in Social and Racial Movements," PHYLON, 15 (Fall, 1954), 231–242.

Reddick, L. D. "The State vs. the Student," DISSENT, 7 (Summer, 1960), 219–228.

Rinker, Charles. "Organizing in the Ghetto," in Bruce Douglass, ed. REFLECTIONS ON PROTEST. Richmond, Virginia: John Knox Press, 1967, 95–102.

Roberts, Steven V. "Something Had to Be Done . . . ," NATION, 194 (March 3, 1962), 187–190.

Rothbard, Murray N. "The Negro Revolution," NEW INDIVIDUALIST REVIEW, 3 (Summer, 1963), 29–37.

*Searles, Ruth and A. J. Williams, jr. "Negro College Students' Participation in Sit-Ins," SOCIAL FORCES, 40 (March, 1962), 215–220.

Sinclair, Hamish. "Hazard, Kentucky: Document of a Struggle," RADICAL AMERICA, 2 (January-February, 1968), 1–24.

"The Sit-In Demonstrations and the Dilemma of the Negro College President," JOURNAL OF NEGRO EDUCATION, 30 (Winter, 1961), 1–3.

Smith, Charles U. "The Sit-Ins and the New Negro Student," JOURNAL OF INTERGROUP RELATIONS, 2 (Summer, 1961), 223–229.

*Solomon, Fredric and Jacob Fishman. "The Psychosocial Meaning of Nonviolence in Student Civil Rights Activities," PSYCHIATRY, 27 (May, 1964), 91–99.

*Solomon, Fredric, Walter L. Walker, Garret O'Connor and Jacob Fishman. "Civil Rights Activity and Reduction in Crime Among Negroes," ARCHIVES OF GENERAL PSYCHIATRY, 2 (March, 1965), 227–236.

Stokely, James and Wilma Dykeman. "Sit down Chilun, Sit Down!" PROGRESSIVE, 24 (June, 1960), 8–12.

Strickland, William. "The Movement and Mississippi," FREEDOMWAYS, 5 (Spring, 1965), 310–313.

Stroud, Virgil C. "The Sit-Ins and the Fabric of the South," QUARTERLY REVIEW OF HIGHER EDUCATION AMONG NEGROES," 20 (October, 1961), 297–306.

Survace, Samuel J. and Melvin Seeman. "Some Correlates of Civil Rights Activism," SOCIAL FORCES, 46 (December, 1967), 197–207.

Thompson, Phillip A. "American Negro College Student Revolt," CONTEMPORARY REVIEW, 42 (November, 1960), 613–616.

Vander Zanden, James W. "The Non-Violent Resistance Movement Against Segregation," AMERICAN JOURNAL OF SOCIOLOGY, 68 (March, 1963), 544–550.

Vander Zanden, James W. "Sit Ins in Dixie," MIDWEST QUARTERLY, 2 (October, 1960), 11–19.

*Walzer, Michael. "A Cup of Coffee and a Seat," DISSENT, 7 (Spring, 1960), 111–120.

Walzer, Michael. "The Politics of the New Negro," DISSENT, 7 (Summer, 1960), 235–243.

Warren, Robert Penn. "Two for SNCC," COMMENTARY, 39 (April, 1965), 38–48.

Watson, J. E. "Place of Controversy on the Campus," JOURNAL OF HIGHER EDUCATION, 36 (January, 1965), 18–24.

Watts, Marzette. "Sit-Ins and Pickets: The Students Move in Montgomery," NEW UNIVERSITY THOUGHT, 1 (Spring, 1960), 16–20.

Westfeldt, Wallace. "Settling a Sit-In," MOTIVE, 21 (October, 1960), 32–29.

Zietlow, Carl P. "Race, Students, and Non-Violence," RELIGIOUS EDUCATION, 59 (January-February, 1964), 116–120.

Zinn, Howard. "Finishing School for Pickets," NATION, 191 (August 6, 1960), 71–73.

*Zinn, Howard. "SNICK: The Battle Scarred Youngsters," NATION, 197 (October 5, 1963), 193–196.

B.2. Civil Rights Movement: 1965–

Barbour, Floyd, ed. THE BLACK POWER REVOLT. Boston: Porter Sargent, 1968.

Cain, Arthur H. YOUNG PEOPLE AND REVOLUTION. New York: John Day, 1970.

Carmichael, Stokely and Charles Hamilton. BLACK POWER, THE POLITICS OF LIBERATION IN AMERICA. New York: Vintage Books, 1967.

Hayden, Thomas. REVOLUTION IN MISSISSIPPI. New York: Students for a Democratic Society, 1962.

Kleemann, Susanne. URSACHEN UND FORMEN DER AMERIKANISCHEN STUDENTEN OPPOSITION. Frankfurt am Main: Suhrkamp, 1971.

Meier, A., ed. THE TRANSFORMATION OF ACTIVISM. New York: Aldine, 1970.

*Meier, A. and E. Rudwick. CORE: A STUDY IN THE CIVIL RIGHTS MOVEMENT. New York: Oxford University Press, 1973.

Oppenheimer, Martin. THE URBAN GUERRILLA. Chicago: Quadrangle Books, 1969.

Pickney, A. THE COMMITTED: WHITE ACTIVISTS IN THE CIVIL RIGHTS MOVEMENT. New Haven, Connecticut: College and University Press, 1969.

Proctor, Samuel D. THE YOUNG NEGRO IN AMERICA; 1960–1980. New York: Association, 1966.

Watters, Pat. DOWN TO NOW; REFLECTIONS ON THE SOUTHERN CIVIL RIGHTS MOVEMENT. New York: Pantheon, 1971.

Allen, Robert. "The Politics of Black Power," in William Slate, ed. POWER TO THE PEOPLE. NEW LEFT WRITINGS. New York: Tower, 1970, 237–252.

Braden, Anne. "The SNCC Trends: Challenge to White America," SOUTHERN PATRIOT, (May 5, 1966).

Arthur, T. C. "Black Power as a Visable Force in Society," JOURNAL OF THE NATIONAL ASSOCIATION OF WOMEN DEANS AND COUNSELORS, 32 (Winter 1969), 55–58.

Caplan, Nathan. "Identity in Transition: A Theory of Black Militancy," in Roderick Aya and N. Miller, eds. THE NEW AMERICAN REVOLUTION. New York: Free Press, 1971.

Carmichael, Stokely. "Black Power and the Third World," in Taig Ali, ed. NEW REVOLUTIONARIES. London, Peter Owen, 1969, 91–105.

Carr, Lester and S. Oliver Roberts. "Correlators of Civil Rights Participation," JOURNAL OF SOCIAL PSYCHOLOGY, 67 (December, 1965), 259–267.

Carter, J. N. "Boll Weevil Six Feet Long; Mississippi Librarian's Action in Battle Against Campus Speaker Ban," LIBRARY JOURNAL, 94 (October 15, 1969), 3615–3618.

*Clark, Kenneth B. "The Civil Rights Movement: Momentum and Organization," DAEDALUS, 95 (Winter, 1966), 239–267.

Cleaver, Eldridge. "Letter From Jail," in Tariq Ali, ed. NEW REVOLUTIONARIES. London: Peter Owen, 1969, 79–90.

"Documents: The Radicalization of the Movement: Black Power," in M. Teodori, ed. THE NEW LEFT: A DOCUMENTARY HISTORY. Indianapolis, Indiana: Bobbs-Merrill, 1969, 271–296.

Doggert, David. "Resigning from the Southern Student Organizing Committee," in Christopher Reashe and Robert Wilson, jr., eds. STUDENT VOICES/ONE. New York: Random House, 1971, 51–57.

Forman, James. "United States 1967: High Tide of Black Resistance," TRICONTINENTAL, (May-June, 1968), 22–51.

Goodman, Walter. "When Black Power Runs the New Left," in William O'Neill, ed. AMERICAN SOCIETY SINCE 1945. Chicago: Quadrangle, 1969, 243–256.

Hamilton, C. V. "Black Rebels Are Not Pranksters: They Are Raising Vital Issues," NEW YORK TIMES MAGAZINE, (May 4, 1969), 138+.

Hannah, John A. "Civil Rights and the Public Universities," JOURNAL OF HIGHER EDUCATION, 37 (February, 1966), 61–67.

Harrington, Michael. "The Mystical Militants," NEW REPUBLIC, 154 (February 19, 1966), 20–22.

Henderson, Lennal, jr. "Engineers of Black Liberation," BLACK POLITICIAN, 1 (April, 1970), 12–15.

*Jacobs, H. "SNCC and Black Power," INTERNATIONAL SOCIALIST JOURNAL, 4 (August, 1967), 647–672.

Kopkind, Andrew. "The Birth of Black Power," RAMPARTS, 5 (October, 1966), 4–8.

Krueger, Marlis. "Zum Begriff der 'black culture'," BLÄTTER FÜR DEUTSCHE UND INTERNATIONALE POLITIK, 6 (1970), 627–638.

La Rue, Linda. "The Black Movement and Women's Liberation," BLACK SCHOLAR, 1 (May 1970), 36–42.

Lawson, James M., jr. "From a Lunch-Counter Stool," MOTIVE, 25 (February, 1966), 41–43.

*Levitt, Morris. "Negro Student Rebellion Against Parental Political Beliefs," SOCIAL FORCES, 45 (March, 1967), 438–440.

Lowe, Gilbert A., jr. "Howard University Students and the Community Project," JOURNAL OF NEGRO EDUCATION, 36 (Fall, 1967), 368–376.

Lynd, Staughton. "Radical Speaks in Defense of SNCC," NEW YORK TIMES MAGAZINE, (September 10, 1967), 50.

Marx, Gary T. and Michael Useem. "Majority Involvement in Minority Movements: Civil Rights, Abolition, Untouchability," JOURNAL OF SOCIAL FORCES, 27 (No. 1, 1971), 81–104.

Newfield, Jack. "The Question of SNCC," NATION, 201 (July 19, 1965), 37–40.

Newfield, Jack. "SSOC: Bridging the Gap Between Bureaucracy and Anarchy," MOTIVE, 26 (March 1966), 13–15.

Oppenheimer, Martin. "Institutions of Higher Education and the 1960 Sit-Ins: Some Clues for Social Action," JOURNAL OF NEGRO EDUCATION, 32 (Summer, 1963), 286–288.

Orum, Anthony M. "The Class and Status Bases of Negro Student Protest," SOCIAL SCIENCE QUARTERLY, 49 (December, 1968), 521–533.

Peavy, Charles D. "The Black Art of Propaganda: The Cultural Aim of the Black Power Movement," ROCKY MOUNTAIN SOCIAL SCIENCE JOURNAL, 7 (April, 1970), 9–16.

Redding, S. "Black Youth Movement," AMERICAN SCHOLAR, 38 (Autumn, 1969), 584–587.

*Roberts, Gene. "From 'Freedom High' to 'Black Power': The Story of SNICK," NEW YORK TIMES MAGAZINE, (September 25, 1966), 27–30+.

Roberts, Stephen V. "Black and White," NEW LEADER, 11 (May 20, 1968), 14–16.

Seale, Bobby. "Revolutionary Action on Campus and Community," BLACK SCHOLAR, 1 (December, 1969), 4–8.

Shoben, E. J. and P. Werdell. "SDS and SNCC: Profiles of Two Student Organizations," SCHOOL AND SOCIETY, 96 (October 26, 1968), 365–372.

Starr, P. "Black Panthers and White Radicals: Notes from New Haven," COMMONWEAL, 92 (June 12, 1970), 294–297.

Surlace, Samuel J. and Melvin Seeman. "Some Correlates of Civil Rights Activism," SOCIAL FORCES, 46 (December, 1967), 197–207.

Thompson, W. "What's Left of the Black Left?" RAMPARTS, 10 (June, 1972), 46–53; 11 (August, 1972), 57–58.

Turner, James. "Social Origins of Black Consciousness," in Roderick Aya and Norman Miller, eds. THE NEW AMERCIAN REVOLUTION. New York: Free Press, 1971.

Von Eschen, Donald, Jerome Kirk and Maurice Pinard. "The Disintegration of the Negro Non-Violent Movement," JOURNAL OF PEACE RESEARCH, 3 (1969), 216–234.

Von Eschen, Donald, Jerome Kirk and Maurice Pinard. "The Organizational Sub-Structure of Disorderly Politics," SOCIAL FORCES, 49 (June, 1971), 529–544.

Walker, Alice. "The Civil Rights Movement: What Good Was It?" AMER-
ICAN SCHOLAR, 36 (Autumn, 1967), 550–554.

Walters, Patricia. "SNCC in Trouble: Report from Atlanta," DISSENT, 8
(November-December, 1966), 639–641.

Washington, K. S. "What Counselors Must Know About Black Power,"
PERSONNEL AND GUIDANCE JOURNAL, 47 (November, 1968), 204–208.

Wehr, P. E. "Nonviolence and Differentiation in the Equal Rights Movement," SOCIOLOGICAL INQUIRY, 38 (1968), 65–76.

Woodley, Richard. "It Will Be a Hot Summer in Mississippi," REPORTER,
30 (May 21, 1964), 21–24.

B.3. Mississippi Summer Project

*Aiken, Michael, N. J. Demerath III, and Gerald Marwell. CONSCIENCE
AND CONFRONTATION. East Lansing, Michigan: Christian Faith and Higher
Education Institute, 1965.

*Aiken, Michael, N. J. Demerath III, and Gerald Marwell. DYNAMICS OF
IDEALISM. San Francisco: Jossey-Bass, 1971.

*Belfrage, Sally. FREEDOM SUMMER. New York: Viking, 1965.

Holt, Len. THE SUMMER THAT DIDN'T END. New York: Morrow, 1965.

Huie, William B. THREE LIVES FOR MISSISSIPPI. New York: Trident
Press, 1965.

Lomax, Louis E., John Howard Griffin, and Dick Gregory. MISSISSIPPI
EYEWITNESS: THE THREE CIVIL RIGHTS WORKERS—HOW THEY WERE
MURDERED. San Francisco: RAMPARTS (Special Suplement), 1964.

McCord, William. MISSISSIPPI: THE LONG HOT SUMMER. New York:
Norton, 1965.

Sugarman, Tracy. STRANGER AT THE GATES: A SUMMER IN
MISSISSIPPI. New York: Hill and Wang, 1966.

Sutherland, E., ed. LETTERS FROM MISSISSIPPI. New York: McGraw-
Hill, 1965.

Aiken, Michael, N. J. Demerath III, and Gerald Marwell. "Conscience and
Confrontation," NEW SOUTH, 21 (Spring, 1966), 19–28.

Herbers, John. "Communiqué from the Mississippi Front," in William
O'Neill, ed. AMERICAN SOCIETY SINCE 1945. Chicago: Quadrangle Books,
1969, 208–216.

Howe, Florence. "Mississippi's Freedom Schools: The Politics of Education," HARVARD EDUCATIONAL REVIEW, 35 (Spring, 1965), 141–160.

Johnson, David W. "Racial Attitudes of Negro Freedom School Participants
and White Civil Rights Participants," SOCIAL FORCES, 45 (December, 1966),
266–273.

Keller, A., F. Mabutt, and D. Ruhe. "Summer 1965: The White 'Freedom
Fighters' in the South," KANSAS JOURNAL OF SOCIOLOGY, 1 (Summer,
1965), 119–122.

Mabee, Carleton. "Freedom Schools, North and South," REPORTER, 31
(September 10, 1964), 30–32.

Rossman, Michael. "Civil Rights and F.S.M.: Some Background Notes," OCCIDENT, (Fall, 1964-1965), 1-14.

"Summer in Smoke—The Mississippi Summer Project," MODERATOR, 4 (Winter, 1965), 18-22.

Sutherland, Elizabeth. "Mississippi: Summer of . . . Discontent," NATION, 201 (October 11, 1965), 212-215.

Vanderburgh, Charles. "A Draftee's Diary from the Mississippi Front," HARPER'S, 228 (February, 1964), 37-45.

B.4. Black Student Movements on Campus

*Anthony, Earl. THE TIME OF THE FURNACES: A CASE STUDY OF BLACK STUDENT REVOLT. New York: Dial Press, 1971.

BLACK MILITANCY AND THE UNIVERSITY: Report of a Conference for Campus Clergy, November 20-December 1, 1968 at Shaw University, Raleigh, North Carolina. Washington, D.C.: National Newman Apostolate, 1969.

*Edwards, Harry. BLACK STUDENTS. New York: Free Press, 1970.

Edwards, Harry. THE REVOLT OF THE BLACK ATHLETE. New York: Free Press, 1969.

*McEvoy, James and Abraham Miller, eds. BLACK POWER AND STUDENT REBELLION. Belmont, California: Wadsworth, 1969.

*Nelson, Jack and Jack Bass. THE ORANGEBURG MASSACRE. New York: World, 1970.

Nichols, David C. and Olive Mills, eds. THE CAMPUS AND THE RACIAL CRISIS. Washington, D.C.: American Council of Education, 1970.

*Orum, Anthony M. BLACK STUDENTS IN PROTEST: A STUDY OF THE ORIGINS OF THE BLACK STUDENT MOVEMENT. Washington, D.C.: American Sociological Association, 1972.

Ashbrook, James B. "A New Day Has Taken Place," JOURNAL OF HUMAN RELATIONS, 17 (2nd Quarter, 1969), 260-278.

Banks, Henry A. "Black Consciousness: A Student Survey," BLACK SCHOLAR, 2 (September, 1970), 44-51.

Bass, Jack and Paul Clancy. "Militant Mood in Negro Colleges," RE-PORTER, 38 (May 16, 1968), 21-23.

Bennett, L. "Confrontation on the Campus," EBONY, 23 (May, 1968), 27-30+.

"Black Mood on Campus: Symposium," NEWSWEEK, 73 (February 10, 1969), 53-59.

"A Black Scholar Special: Student Strikes: 1968-1969," BLACK SCHOLAR, 1 (January-February, 1970), 65-75.

Brooks, P. "Panthers at Yale," PARTISAN REVIEW, 37 (No. 3, 1970), 420-439.

Browne, Robert S. "The Challenge of Black Student Organizations," FREEDOMWAYS, 8 (Fall, 1968), 325-333.

Brudnoy, D. "Black Power and the Campus," NATIONAL REVIEW, 20 (October 8, 1968), 1001-1004.

Brudnoy, D. "New Left and Negro Extremism," NATIONAL REVIEW, 21 (July 1, 1969), 640–643.

Cass, James. "Can the University Survive the Black Challenge?" SATURDAY REVIEW, 52 (June 21, 1969), 68–72+.

Chrisman, Robert. "Observations on Race and Class at San Francisco State," in J. McEvoy and A. Miller, eds. BLACK POWER AND STUDENT REVOLT. Belmont, California: Wadsworth, 1969, 222–232.

Cleaver, Eldridge. "A Word to Students," in Gary Weaver and James Weaver, eds. THE UNIVERSITY AND REVOLUTION. Englewood Cliffs, New Jersey: Prentice-Hall, 1969, 153–164.

Cunningham, George. "The Negro Fights for Freedom, II: Alcorn College, Mississippi," ANVIL AND STUDENT PARTISAN, 7 (Fall, 1957), 5–7.

Dawson, Charles S. "Black Student Organizations on Predominantly White Campuses: Analysis by a 1970 Graduate," UNIVERSITY, (Winter, 1970–1971), 12–18.

Daum, Walt, et al. "Harlem on Their Minds: The CCNY Crisis," in M. Friedman, ed., THE NEW LEFT OF THE SIXTIES. Albany, California: Independent Socialist Press, 1972, 172–179.

Day, Kenneth. "Black Student Activities and Administrative Responses at Public Universities in North Carolina. A Preliminary Survey," in Hans H. Indorf, ed. POLITICS 1970. Greenville, North Carolina: Political Science Department, East Carolina University, 1970, 103–112.

de Graaf, Lawrence B. "Howard: The Evolution of a Black Student Revolt," in Julian Foster and Durward Long, eds. PROTEST! STUDENT ACTIVISM IN AMERICA. New York: Morrow, 1970, 319–344.

Dickinson, James C. "The Case for Black Student Power," NATIONAL ASSOCIATION OF STUDENT PERSONNEL ADMINISTRATORS JOURNAL, 6 (April, 1969), 189–200.

Donaldson, Robert and Richard Pride. "Black Students at a White University: Their Attitudes and Behavior in an Era of Confrontation," JOURNAL OF SOCIAL AND BEHAVIORAL SCIENCES, 15 (Fall, 1969), 22–38.

DuBois, W. E. B. "The Hampton Strike," NATION, 125 (November 2, 1927), 471–472.

Dunbar, E. "Black Revolt Hits the White Campus," LOOK, 31 (October 31, 1967), 27–31.

Eliot, Thomas H. "Administrative Response to Campus Turmoil," in THE CAMPUS AND THE RACIAL CRISIS. Washington, D.C.: American Council on Education, 1969, 51–64.

Fleming, J. W. "Congress for the Unity of Black Students: A Report and an Evaluation," NATIONAL ASSOCIATION OF WOMEN DEANS AND COUNSELORS JOURNAL, 32 (Winter, 1969), 75–79.

Friedberg, Bernard. "Houston and the TSU Riot," in W. McCord, jr., J. Howard, B. Friedberg and E. Harwood. LIFE STYLES IN THE BLACK GHETTO. New York: Norton, 1969, 36–51.

Ginzberg, Eli. "Black Power and Student Unrest: Reflections on Columbia University and Harlem," GEORGE WASHINGTON LAW REVIEW, 37 (May, 1969), 835–847.

Graham E. K. "Case Study in Student Protest," AMERICAN SCHOLAR, 38 (Autumn, 1969), 668–682.

Greene, D. L. and D. G. Winter. "Motives, Involvement, and Leadership Among Black College Students," JOURNAL OF PERSONALITY, 36 (1971), 319, 332.

Gross, K. G. "Angry and Alone Together," NATION, 208 (February 17, 1969), 207–210.

Halpern, Ben. "Brandeis University and Ocean Hill-Brownsville," MID-STREAM, 15 (February, 1969), 15–21.

Hare, Nathan. "Behind the Black College Student Revolt," EBONY, 22 (August, 1967), 58–61.

Harper, Frederick D. "Black Student Revolt on the White Campus," JOURNAL OF COLLEGE STUDENT PERSONNEL, 10 (September, 1969), 291–295.

Harrington, J. H. "L.A.'s Student Blow-Out," PHI DELTA KAPPAN, 50 (October, 1968), 74–79.

Harris, S. "San Fernando's Black Revolt," COMMONWEAL, 89 (January 31, 1969), 549–552.

Harrison, E. C. "Student Unrest on the Black College Campus," JOURNAL OF NEGRO EDUCATION, 41 (Spring, 1972), 113–120.

Hope, John II. "The Negro College, Student Protest and the Future," JOURNAL OF NEGRO EDUCATION, 30 (Fall, 1961), 368–376.

Horowitz, Irving Louis and William Friedland. "Black Experience and Campus Shock," in I. L. Horowitz and W. Friedland. THE KNOWLEDGE FACTORY. Chicago: Aldine, 1970, 185–201.

Jackson, John S. "The Political Behavior and Socio-economic Background of Black Students: The Antecedents of Protest," MIDWEST JOURNAL OF POLITICAL SCIENCE, 15 (November, 1971), 661–686.

Johnson, Marcie Lynn. "Student Protest at Fisk University," NEGRO HISTORY BULLETIN, 33 (October, 1970), 137–140.

Jones, Mack. "Some Observations on Student Rebellion on Black Campuses," JOURNAL OF SOCIAL AND BEHAVIORAL SCIENCES, 15 (Fall, 1969), 61–65.

King, H. H. "Eva Jefferson: Young Voice of Change: Associated Student Government of Northwestern University, Evanston, Illinois," EBONY, 26 (January, 1971), 71–74+.

Lewis, Arthur W. "Black Power and the American University," UNIVERSITY, (Spring, 1969), 8–12.

*Long, Durward. "Black Protest," in Julian Foster and Durward Long, eds. PROTEST! STUDENT ACTIVISM IN AMERICA. New York: Morrow, 1970, 459–482.

Lowe, G. A., jr. and S. F. McDowell. "Participant-Nonparticipant Differences in the Howard University Student Protest," JOURNAL OF NEGRO EDUCATION, 40 (Winter, 1971), 81–90.

McDowell, S. F., G. A. Lowe, jr. and D. A. Dockett. "Howard University's Student Protest Movement," PUBLIC OPINION QUARTERLY, 34 (Fall, 1970), 383–388.

Matthews, Donald and James Prothro. "Negro Students and the Protest Movement," in James McEvoy and Abraham Miller, eds. BLACK POWER AND STUDENT REBELLION. Belmont, California: Wadsworth, 1969, 379–418.

Mines, Stephanie and Phil Frazier. "Bringin It All Down Home (1969)," in John and Susan Erlich, eds. STUDENT POWER, PARTICIPATION AND REVOLUTION. New York: Association Press, 1970, 85–94.

Nelson, B. "Brandeis: How a Liberal University Reacts to a Black Take-over," SCIENCE, 163 (March 28, 1969), 1431–1434.

. Noble, J. "Black Student Movement: A Search for Identity," NATIONAL ASSOCIATION OF WOMEN DEANS AND COUNSELORS JOURNAL, 32 (Winter, 1969), 49–54.

Obatala, J. K. "Black Students: Where Did Their Revolution Go?" NATION, 215 (October 2, 1972), 272–274.

Ogletree, E. "Negroes Want Separation," TIMES EDUCATIONAL SUP-PLEMENT, 2771 (June 28, 1968), 2122.

Payne, J. A., jr. "Problem of Student Unrest," NEGRO EDUCATION REVIEW, 20 (October, 1969), 114–120.

*President's Commission on Campus Unrest. "The Black Student Movement," in REPORT OF THE PRESIDENT'S COMMISSION ON CAMPUS UNREST. New York: Arno Press, 1970, 91–116.

Reed, Charles. "Crisis on the Negro Campus," NATION, 144 (February 10, 1962), 111–113.

Sacks, Herbert. " 'Bleep Kingman Brewster': A View from Calhoun College, Yale University, of the New Haven Black Panther Rally, May 1–3, 1970," in Morton Levitt and Ben Rubenstein, eds. YOUTH AND SOCIAL CHANGE. Detroit: Wayne State University Press, 1972, 243–266.

Seale, Bobby. "Revolutionary Action on Campus and Community," BLACK SCHOLAR, 1 (December, 1969), 4–7.

Simon, Rita James and James Carey. "The Phantom Racist," in H. Becker, ed. CAMPUS POWER STRUGGLE. Chicago: Aldine, 1970, 101–120.

Stanford, Max. "Black Nationalism and the Afro-American Student," BLACK SCHOLAR, 2 (June, 1971), 27–31.

Steinberg, David. "Black Power on Black Campuses," COMMONWEAL, 88 (April 19, 1968), 127–129.

*"Student Strikes: 1968, 1969," BLACK SCHOLAR, 1 (January-February, 1970), 65–76.

Terrell, Robert. "Lane College: The Fires of Discontent," NEW SOUTH, 24 (Spring, 1969), 2–16.

Terrell, Robert. "Up From Uncle Tomism: Demonstrations at Lane College, Jackson, Tennessee," COMMONWEAL, 92 (April 3, 1970), 87–88+.

Thelwell, Michael. ',From San Francisco State and Cornell: Two Black Radicals Report on Their Campus Struggles," RAMPARTS, 8 (July, 1969), 47–59.

"There Needs to Be Some Kind of Revolution in Education: The Black People Are Articulating That: A Student Forum," MADEMOISELLE, 69 (August, 1969), 266–267+.

United Black Population, University of Michigan. "Black Student Demands," in John and Susan Erlich, eds. STUDENT POWER, PARTICIPATION AND REVOLUTION. New York: Association Press, 1970, 177–181.

Weales, G. "Day LeRois Jones Spoke at Penn. Campus What Were the Blacks Doing in the Balcony?" NEW YORK TIMES MAGAZINE, (May 4, 1969), 38–40+.

Williams, F. H. "The University's Black Crisis," COLLEGE AND UNIVERSITY JOURNAL, 44 (Spring, 1969), 9–19.

B.5. Black Studies

Barksdale, Richard K. THE BLACK COLLEGE IN A TIME OF REVOLUTION. Atlanta Center for African and African-American Studies, Atlanta University 1969, Occasional Paper No. 2.

BLACK STUDIES: MYTHS AND REALITIES. New York: A. Philip Randolph Educational Fund, 1969.

*Blassingame, John W., ed. NEW PERSPECTIVES ON BLACK STUDIES. Urbana, Illinois: University of Illinois Press, 1971.

Furniss, W. Todd. BLACK STUDIES PROGRAMS AND CIVIL RIGHTS VIOLATIONS. Washington, D.C.: American Council on Education, 1969.

Lowe, K. TOWARDS A BLACK UNIVERSITY. Nashville, Tennessee: Southern Student Organizing Committee, 1968.

*Robinson, Arstead, *et al.* BLACK STUDIES IN THE UNIVERSITY: A SYMPOSIUM. New York: Bantam, 1969.

Baskin, D. "Black Separatism," JOURNAL OF HIGHER EDUCATION, 40 (December, 1969), 731–734.

Beckham, Edgar F. "What We Mean by 'the Black University,' " in Immanuel Wallerstein and Paul Starr, eds. THE UNIVERSITY CRISIS READER, I. New York: Random House, 1971, 356–360.

*Blassingame, J. W. "Black Studies: An Intellectual Crisis," AMERICAN SCHOLAR, 38 (Autumn, 1969), 548–561.

Brown, Ewart. "The Black University," in Gary Weaver and James Weaver, eds. THE UNIVERSITY AND REVOLUTION. Englewood Cliffs, New Jersey: Prentice-Hall, 1969.

*Bunzel, John H. "Black Studies at San Francisco State," PUBLIC INTEREST, No. 13 (Fall, 1968), 22–38.

Childs, C. "Black Studies at Cornell: The Troubled Path to Understanding," LIFE, (April 17, 1970), 56–60+.

Clark, K. B. "Charade of Power: Black Students at White Colleges," ANTIOCH REVIEW, 29 (Summer, 1969), 145–148.

Dunbar, E. "Black Studies Thing," NEW YORK TIMES MAGAZINE, (April 6, 1969), 25–27+.

Feinberg, W. and D. Tyock. "Black People, Not Student Personnel: The 'Disadvantaged' in Teacher Education," THE RECORD, 71 (December, 1969), 225–235.

338

*Genovese, Eugene. "Black Studies: Trouble Ahead," ATLANTIC, 223, (June, 1969), 37–41.

Hamilton, Charles V. "Relevance of Black Studies," in G. K. Smith, ed. AGONY AND PROMISE: CURRENT ISSUES IN HIGHER EDUCATION 1969. San Francisco: Jossey-Bass, 1969, 69–73.

Harding, Vincent. "Black Students and the Impossible Revolution," JOURNAL OF BLACK STUDIES, 1 (September, 1970), 75–100.

Harding, Vincent. "Educator's View: Black Students and the Impossible Revolution," EBONY, 24 (August, 1969), 141–146 and (September, 1969), 97–98+.

Harding, Vincent. "The Future of Black Studies," in G. K. Smith, ed. THE TROUBLED CAMPUS: CURRENT ISSUES IN HIGHER EDUCATION. San Francisco: Jossey-Bass, 1970, 212–219.

Hare, Nathan. "The Battle for Black Studies," BLACK SCHOLAR, 3 (May, 1972), 32–47.

Hare, Nathan. "What Black Studies Means to a Black Scholar—Interview," COLLEGE AND UNIVERSITY BUSINESS, 48 (May, 1970), 56–60.

Hatch, J. "Black Studies: The Real Issue," NATION, 208 (June 16, 1969), 755–758.

Henderson, S. "Toward a Black University," EBONY, 25 (September, 1970), 108–110+.

James, C. L. R. "Black Studies," RADICAL AMERICA, 5 (September-October, 1971), 79–96.

Lerner, Abba. "Black Studies: The Universities in Moral Crisis," in Sidney Hook, ed. IN DEFENSE OF ACADEMIC FREEDOM. New York: Pegasus, 1971, 75–81.

Lewis, W. A. "Black Power and the American University," AFRICA REPORT, 14 (May-June, 1969), 23–28.

Lewis, W. A. "Road to the Top Is Through Higher Education, Not Black Studies," NEW YORK TIMES MAGAZINE, (May 11, 1969), 34–35+.

Light, D. W. and D. Feldman. "Black and White at Brandeis," NORTH AMERICAN REVIEW, 6 (Summer, 1969), 25–29.

*Lythcott, Stephan. "The Case for Black Studies," ANTIOCH REVIEW, 29 (Summer, 1969), 149–154.

Meek, D. A. "Black Power and the Instructional Council: Development of an Afro-American Studies Curriculum at Merritt College," JUNIOR COLLEGE JOURNAL, 39 (October, 1968), 12–15+.

Rist, Ray C. "Black Staff, Black Studies and White Universities: A Study in Contradiction," JOURNAL OF HIGHER EDUCATION, 41 (November, 1970), 618–629.

Rosovsky, H. "Black Studies at Harvard: Personal Reflections Concerning Recent Events," AMERICAN SCHOLAR, 38 (Autumn, 1969), 562–572.

Staples, Robert. "Black Studies: A Review of the Literature," BLACK SCHOLAR, 2 (October, 1970), 53–56.

Turner, James. "Black Studies: Challenge to Higher Education," in G. K. Smith, ed. THE TROUBLED CAMPUS: CURRENT ISSUES IN HIGHER EDUCATION. San Francisco: Jossey-Bass, 1970, 201–211.

Walters, Hubert. "Black Music and the Black University," BLACK SCHOLAR, 3 (Summer, 1972), 14–21.

C. ETHNIC AND RELIGIOUS GROUPS IN HIGHER EDUCATION

C.1. Ethnic Students: General Materials

Artichoker, J., jr. and N. M. Palmer. SIOUX INDIAN GOES TO COLLEGE. Vermillion, South Dakota: University of South Dakota, Institute of Indian Studies, 1959.

Bennett, Howard. UNDERGRADUATE ENROLLMENT BY ETHNIC GROUP IN FEDERALLY FUNDED INSTITUTIONS OF HIGHER EDUCATION: FALL, 1968. Washington: Office for Civil Rights, United States Department of Health, Education and Welfare, 1969.

Berkowitz, David S. INEQUALITY OF OPPORTUNITY IN HIGHER EDUCATION. Albany: William Press, 1948.

Berry, Brewton. THE EDUCATION OF THE AMERICAN INDIANS. A SURVEY OF THE LITERATURE. Washington, D.C.: Office of Education, Bureau of Research, 1968.

Brown, Francis J. DISCRIMINATION IN COLLEGE ADMISSIONS: A REPORT OF A CONFERENCE HELD UNDER THE AUSPICES OF THE AMERICAN COUNCIL ON EDUCATION IN COOPERATION WITH THE ANTI-DEFAMATION LEAGUE OF B'NAI B'RITH, CHICAGO, NOVEMBER 4–5, 1950. Washington, D.C., 1950.

Brown, Francis J., Floyd W. Reeves, and Richard B. Anliot, eds. DISCRIMINATION IN HIGHER EDUCATION: REPORT OF MIDWEST EDUCATORS CONFERENCE IN CHICAGO, ILLINOIS, NOVEMBER 3–4, 1950. Washington, D.C., 1951.

Bryde, Reverend John Francis, S.J. "The Sioux Indian Student: A Study of Scholastic Failure and Personality Conflict." Unpublished Ph.D. dissertation, University of Denver, 1965.

Calvert, Robert, jr. EMPLOYING THE MINORITY GROUP COLLEGE GRADUATE: RECRUITING, EVALUATING QUALIFICATIONS, RETAINING EMPLOYEES. Garrett Park Press, 1968.

College and University Self-Study Institute. THE MINORITY STUDENT ON THE CAMPUS: EXPECTATIONS AND POSSIBILITIES. 12TH ANNUAL CONFERENCE. Boulder: Western Interstate Commission for Higher Education, 1970.

Connecticut Commission on Civil Rights. NEW STUDY OF COLLEGE ADMISSION PRACTICES WITH RESPECT TO RACE, RELIGION AND NATIONAL ORIGIN: BASED ON THE EXPERIENCES OF HIGH SCHOOL GRADUATES OF THE CLASSES OF 1949 AND 1950. Hartford, Connecticut, 1953.

Connecticut Inter-Racial Commission. COLLEGE ADMISSIONS PRACTICES WITH RESPECT TO RACE, RELIGION AND NATIONAL ORIGIN OF

CONNECTICUT HIGH SCHOOL GRADUATES, Hartford, Connecticut, 1949.

Davis, Helen E. ON GETTING INTO COLLEGE: A STUDY MADE FOR THE COMMITTEE ON DISCRIMINATION IN COLLEGE ADMISSIONS. Washington, D.C.: American Council on Education, 1949.

Franklin, Mayer J., Terry Martin and Corrine Sanchez, eds. CONFERENCE ON INCREASING OPPORTUNITIES FOR MEXICAN AMERICAN STUDENTS IN HIGHER EDUCATION, LOS ANGELES HARBOR COLLEGE, 1969. PROCEEDINGS. Los Angeles: California State College, 1969.

Ivy, Andrew C. and Irwin Ross. RELIGION AND RACE: BARRIERS TO COLLEGE? New York: Public Affairs Committee, 1949.

*Kimball, William Loyd. "Parent and Family Influences on Academic Achievement Among Mexican American Students." Unpublished Ph.D. dissertation, University of California at Los Angeles, 1968.

O'Brien, Robert W. THE COLLEGE NISEI. Palo Alto: Pacific Books, 1949.

Quimby, Robert Joseph. "American Indian Students in Arizona Colleges: A Discriminant Analysis of Select Variables That Contribute to Success and Failure." Unpublished Ph.D. dissertation, Arizona State University, 1963.

U.S. Department of Health, Education and Welfare, Office for Civil Rights. RACIAL AND ETHNIC ENROLLMENT DATA FROM INSTITUTIONS OF HIGHER EDUCATION, FALL, 1970. Washington, D.C.: Government Printing Office, 1972.

Barrett, Donald. "Demographic Characteristics," in Julian Samora, ed. LA RAZA: FORGOTTEN AMERICANS. Notre Dame, Indiana: University of Notre Dame Press, 1966.

Bongartz, R. "Chicano Rebellion: Demand for Courses in Mexican-American Studies," NATION 208 (March 3, 1969), 271–274.

Brown, D. R. and D. Bystryn. "College Environment, Personality and Social Ideology of Three Ethnic Groups," JOURNAL OF SOCIAL PSYCHOLOGY, 44 (November, 1956), 279–288.

Clurman, M. "How Discriminatory Are College Admissions?" COMMENTARY, 15 (June, 1953), 618–623.

Cottle, Thomas. "Run to Freedom: Chicanos and Higher Education," CHANGE, 4 (February, 1972), 34–41.

Gaither, Gerald, John Edgerly and Ralph Boston, "Ethnic Group Attitudes: A Behavioral Model for the Study of Attitude Intensity," in Cameron Fincher, ed. THE CHALLENGE AND RESPONSE OF INSTITUTIONAL RESEARCH PROCEEDINGS OF THE NINTH ANNUAL FORUM ON INSTITUTIONAL RESEARCH. Association for Institutional Research, 1970, 27–40.

Gordon, Edmund. "The Culturally Different, Deprived or Economically Marginal Student: A Challenge to Education," in L. B. Mayhew, ed., HIGHER EDUCATION IN THE REVOLUTIONARY DECADES. Berkeley, California: McCutchan, 1967, 363–381.

Greeley, A. M. "Note on Political and Social Differences among Ethnic College Graduates," SOCIOLOGY OF EDUCATION, 42 (Winter, 1969), 98–103.

Heath, G. Louis. "Berkeley's Ethnic Studies College," INTEGRATED EDUCATION, 7 (July-August, 1969), 17–23.

Lusky, L. "Minority Rights and the Public Interest," YALE LAW JOUR-NAL 52 (December, 1942), 1–41.

Miller, Albert H. "Problems of the Minority Student on the Campus," LIBERAL EDUCATION, 55 (March, 1969), 18–23.

Nelson, Harold A. "Expressed and Unexpressed Prejudice Against Ethnic Groups in a College Community," JOURNAL OF NEGRO EDUCATION, 31 (Spring, 1962), 125–131.

Nunez, Rene. "Recruitment and Admission of Minority Students: The Glaring Reality," in R. A. Altman and P. O. Snyder, eds. THE MINORITY STUDENT ON THE CAMPUS: EXPECTATIONS AND POSSIBILITIES. Boulder, Colorado: Western Interstate Commission for Higher Education, 1971, 127–140.

Perrin, Robert. "Computing Minorities," CHANGE, 4 (October, 1972), 36–38.

Roberts, Virgil. "Minority Interests in Value Change and Power Conflicts," in W. J. Minter and Patricia Snyder, eds. VALUE CHANGE AND POWER CON-FLICT IN HIGHER EDUCATION. Boulder, Colorado: Western Interstate Commission for Higher Education, 1970, 99–114.

Russell, J. D. "New Factors Affecting Equality of Opportunity," in American Council on Education, Committee on Equality of Opportunity in Higher Education. APPROACHING EQUALITY OF OPPORTUNITY IN HIGHER EDUCATION. Washington, D.C.: American Council on Education, 1955, 27–48.

Seeman, M. "The Intellectual and the Language of Minorities," AMERICAN JOURNAL OF SOCIOLOGY, 64 (July, 1958), 25–35.

C.2. Jews in Higher Education

Angres, Selma. "Values and Socialization Practices of Jewish and Non-Jewish Parents of College Students," Unpublished M.A. thesis, Committee on Human Development, University of Chicago, 1969.

B'nai B'rith Hillel Foundations. CHANGING PATTERNS OF JEWISH LIFE ON THE CAMPUS. Washington, D.C.: B'nai B'rith Hillel Foundations, 1961.

Drew, David E. A PROFILE OF THE JEWISH FRESHMAN. AMERICAN COUNCIL ON EDUCATION REPORTS 5. Washington, D.C.: American Council on Education, 1970.

Friedman, Theodore. LETTERS TO JEWISH COLLEGE STUDENTS. New York: J. David, 1965.

Grand, Samuel. "A History of Zionist Youth Organizations in the United States from Their Inception to 1940." Unpublished Ph.D. dissertation, Columbia University, 1958.

Nathan, M. THE ATTITUDES OF THE JEWISH STUDENTS IN THE COL-LEGES AND UNIVERSITIES TOWARD HIS RELIGION. New York: Bloch, 1932.

Schwartz, Howard. JEWISH COLLEGE YOUTH SPEAK THEIR MINDS. New York: American Jewish Committee, Institute of Human Relations, 1969.

342

Avineri, S. "Israel and the New Left," TRANS-ACTION, 7 (July, 1970), 79–83.

Bikel, Theodore. "Jewish Campus Youth," in Alexander Klein, ed. NATURAL ENEMIES? YOUTH AND THE CLASH OF GENERATIONS. New York: Lippincott, 1969.

Braun, Jonathan, "The Student Revolt and the Jewish Student," MIDSTREAM, 16 (March, 1970), 41–44.

Carvan, R. S. "Jewish Student Attitudes toward Interreligious and Intra-Jewish Marriage," AMERICAN JOURNAL OF SOCIOLOGY, 76 (May, 1971), 1064–1071.

Chomsky, W. "The Youth Rebellion and Jewish Education," RECONSTRUCTIONIST, 36 (March 6, 1970), 16–21.

Drew, David E. "Jewish Students Today: Radical or Conservative," TRANS-ACTION, 8 (October, 1971), 45–48.

Fein, Leonard J. "The Dilemmas of Jewish Identity on the College Campus," JUDAISM, 171 (Winter, 1968), 10–21.

Feldstein, Donald, "Campus Jews and Jewish Institutions," MIDSTREAM, 16 (April, 1970), 58–64.

Feuer, Lewis S. "Jewish Students as Bearers of Generational Conflict," MIDSTREAM, 16 (April, 1970), 58–64.

Freedman, M. "The Jewish College Student, 1951 Model: Is the Old Idealism and Zeal for Learning Gone?" COMMENTARY, 12 (October, 1951), 305–313.

Glazer, Nathan. "The Jewish Role in Student Activism," FORTUNE, 79 (January, 1969), 112–113, 126–129.

Glazer, Nathan. "The New Left and the Jews," JEWISH JOURNAL OF SOCIOLOGY, 11 (December, 1969), 121–132.

Greenberg, I. "Jewish Survival and the College Campus," JUDAISM, 17 (Summer, 1968), 259–281.

Greenberg, I. "Jewish Values and the Changing American Ethic," TRADITION, 10 (Summer, 1968), 42–74.

Greenberg, M. B. "College and the Orthodox Student," JEWISH LIFE, 36 (February-March, 1969), 22–37.

Greenberg, Meyer, "Social Characteristics of the Jewish Students at the University of Maryland," JEWISH SOCIAL STUDIES, 23 (January, 1961), 21–36.

Grunblatt, J. "Jewish Perspectives on Campus Unrest," TRADITION, 11 (Spring, 1970), 58–63.

Horowitz, I. L. "Student as Jew," ANTIOCH REVIEW, 29 (Winter, 1969–1970), 537–546.

Lipset, S. M. "Socialism of Fools: The New Left Calls It Anti-Zionism," NEW YORK TIMES MAGAZINE (January 3, 1971), 6–7+.

Peretz, M. "The American Left and Israel," COMMENTARY, 44 (November, 1967), 27–34.

Podhoretz, Norman. "The Tribe of the Wicked Son," COMMENTARY, 51 (February, 1971), 6–10.

Rubenstein, Richard L., "Jewish Students in American Universities," RECONSTRUCTIONIST, 28 (June 29, 1962), 6–13.

Saks, Robert J. "Israel and the New Left," JOURNAL OF JEWISH COMMUNAL SERVICE, 45 (Winter, 1969), 139–146.

Segal, B. E. "Contact, Compliance, and Distance Among Jewish and Non-Jewish Undergraduates," SOCIAL PROBLEMS, 13 (Summer, 1965), 66–74.

Segal, B. E. "Fraternities, Social Distance, and Anti-Semitism among Jewish and Non-Jewish Undergraduates," SOCIOLOGY OF EDUCATION, 38 (Spring, 1965), 251–265.

Sleeper, J. A. "Activists and a New Judaism," CONSERVATIVE JUDAISM, 23 (Summer, 1969), 25–32.

West, V. "The Influence of Parental Background on Jewish University Students," JEWISH JOURNAL OF SOCIOLOGY, 10 (December, 1968), 267–280.

C.3. Catholics in Higher Education

Byrne, John T. A STUDY OF STUDENT PROBLEMS IN CATHOLIC MEN'S COLLEGES. Washington: Catholic University of America Press, 1957.

Huey, Ann Frances. A COMPARATIVE STUDY OF THE PROBLEMS AND GUIDANCE RESOURCES OF CATHOLIC COLLEGE WOMEN. Washington: Catholic University of America Press, 1957.

Shinn, Anna Hazel. SOCIAL LIVING IN CATHOLIC FOUR YEAR COLLEGE FOR WOMEN. Washington: Catholic University of America Press, 1959.

Trent, J. W. and Jenette Golds. CATHOLICS IN COLLEGE. Chicago: University of Chicago Press, 1967.

Berry, M. A. "Catholic Colleges for Women and Education for Leadership," CATHOLIC EDUCATION REVIEW, 56 (February, 1958), 73–81.

Campanelle, T. "Critique on Catholic Higher Education," CATHOLIC EDUCATION REVIEW, 61 (May, 1963), 313–321.

Clifford, R. J. and W. R. Callahan. "Catholics in Higher Education: Catholic Student on the Secular Campus," AMERICA, 111 (September 19, 1964), 288–291.

Gorman, M. A. F. "In Defense of the Four-Year Catholic Women's College," CATHOLIC EDUCATION REVIEW, 63 (September, 1965), 369–375.

Hassenger, Robert. "Portrait of a Catholic Women's College," in R. Hassenger, ed. THE SHAPE OF CATHOLIC HIGHER EDUCATION. Chicago: University of Chicago Press, 1967.

Hassenger, Robert and Gerald Rauch. "The Student," in R. Hassenger, ed. THE SHAPE OF CATHOLIC HIGHER EDUCATION. Chicago: University of Chicago Press, 1967, 213–222.

Honora, Sister M. "Integration of Catholic Education for Men and Women," in R. J. Deferrari, ed. INTEGRATION IN CATHOLIC COLLEGES AND UNIVERSITIES. Washington, D.C.: The Catholic University of America Press, 1950, 315–327.

Jencks, Christopher and David Riesman. "The Catholics and Their Colleges," PUBLIC INTEREST, (Spring, 1967), 79–101, (Summer, 1967), 49–74.

Kosa, J., *et al.* "Marriage, Career and Religiousness among Catholic College Girls," MARRIAGE AND FAMILY LIVING, 24 (November, 1960), 376–380.

Novak, M. "Catholics in College: Secular Campuses," COMMONWEAL, 78 (March 29, 1963), 16–20.

D. WOMEN IN AMERICAN HIGHER EDUCATION

D.1. Demographic Data, Personal Background and Status of Women Students

American Council on Education. HOW FARE AMERICAN WOMEN? Washington: American Council on Education, 1955.

REPORTS OF ASSOCIATED WOMEN STUDENTS COMMISSION ON THE STATUS OF WOMEN. 1969–1970, Topeka: Kansas University, 1970.

REPORT ON THE STATUS OF WOMEN AT THE UNIVERSITY OF WASHINGTON: PART II. "Undergraduate and Graduate Students," Seattle: University of Washington, 1971.

Rowe, F. B. CHARACTERISTICS OF WOMEN'S COLLEGE STUDENTS. SREB RESEARCH MONOGRAPH NUMBER 8. Atlanta, Georgia: Southern Regional Education Board, 1964.

Werts, C. E. SEX DIFFERENCES IN COLLEGE ATTENDANCE. NMSC RESEARCH REPORTS, VOLUME 2, NUMBER 6. Evanston, Illinois: National Merit Scholarship, 1966.

WOMEN IN THE UNIVERSITY OF CHICAGO. REPORT OF THE COMMITTEE ON UNIVERSITY WOMEN. Chicago: University of Chicago, 1970.

Converse, Philip E. and Jean M. Converse. "The Status of Women as Students and Professionals in Political Science," POLITICAL SCIENCE, 4 (Summer, 1971), 328–348.

Cross, K. P. "College Women: A Research Description," NATIONAL ASSOCIATION OF WOMEN DEANS AND COUNSELORS JOURNAL, 32 (Fall, 1968), 12–21.

Darling, R. W. "College Women: Do They Fit the Research Description?" NATIONAL ASSOCIATION OF WOMEN DEANS AND COUNSELORS JOURNAL, 32 (Fall, 1968), 22–25.

Davis, A. D. "Women as a Minority Group in Higher Academics," AMERICAN SOCIOLOGIST, 4 (May, 1969), 95–99.

Hawkes, Ann L. Rose. "Factors affecting College Attendance," in Opal David, ed. THE EDUCATION OF WOMEN: SIGNS FOR THE FUTURE. Washington, D.C.: American Council on Education, 1959.

Mowsesian, R. "Educational and Career Aspirations of High School Females," NATIONAL ASSOCIATION OF WOMEN DEANS AND COUNSELORS JOURNAL, 35 (Winter, 1972), 65–70.

Mueller, K. H. and J. H. Mueller. "Socio-Economic Background of Women

Students at Indiana University," EDUCATIONAL AND PSYCHOLOGICAL MEASUREMENT, 9 (Autumn, 1949), 321–329.

Rossi, Alice. "Status of Women in Graduate Departments of Sociology 1968–1969," AMERICAN SOCIOLOGIST, 5 (February, 1970), 1–12.

Simon, Rita James, et al. "The Woman Ph.D.: A Recent Profile," SOCIAL PROBLEMS, 15 (Fall, 1967), 221–236.

Turner, R. H. "Some Aspects of Women's Ambition," AMERICAN JOURNAL OF SOCIOLOGY, 170 (November, 1964), 271–285.

Ward, Paul. "Women's Share in College Enrollments," in G. K. Smith, ed. CURRENT ISSUES IN HIGHER EDUCATION 1965: PRESSURES AND PRIORITIES IN HIGHER EDUCATION. Washington, D.C.: National Education Association, 1965, 138–141.

Werts, C. E. "A Comparison of Male vs. Female College Attendance Probabilities," SOCIOLOGY OF EDUCATION, 41 (Winter, 1968), 103–110.

D.2. Philosophy and Structure of Higher Education for Women

Beatley, Bancroft. ANOTHER LOOK AT WOMEN'S EDUCATION. Boston: Simmons College, 1955.

David, Opal, ed. THE EDUCATION OF WOMEN. Washington: American Council on Education, 1959.

Komarovsky, M. WOMEN IN THE MODERN WORLD. Boston: Little, Brown, 1953.

Lewis, Edwin C. DEVELOPING WOMEN'S POTENTIAL. Ames: Iowa State University Press, 1968.

Lifton, Robert Jay, ed. THE WOMAN IN AMERICA. Boston: Houghton, Mifflin, 1965.

Millet, K. SEXUAL POLITICS. New York: Doubleday, 1970.

Mueller, K. H. EDUCATING WOMEN FOR A CHANGING WORLD. Minneapolis: University of Minnesota Press, 1954.

Newcomer, Mabel. A CENTURY OF HIGHER EDUCATION FOR WOMEN. New York: Harper, 1959.

Noble, Jeanne L. THE NEGRO WOMAN'S COLLEGE EDUCATION. New York: Teachers College, Columbia University, 1956.

WOMEN ON CAMPUS: A SYMPOSIUM. Ann Arbor, Michigan: Center for Continuing Education of Women, University of Michigan, 1970.

Ashton, J. W. "Experiment in Education for Women: Assistant Dean of Faculties, Indiana University," SCHOOL AND SOCIETY, 76 (August 23, 1952), 122–131.

Beatley, B. "Another Look at Women's Education," JOURNAL OF HIGHER EDUCATION, 22 (January, 1951), 9–18.

Benezet, L. T. "Modern Mythology in Women's Education," AMERICAN ASSOCIATION OF UNIVERSITY PROFESSORS BULLETIN, 36 (September, 1950), 487–496.

Bettelheim, B. "Growing Up Female," HARPER, 225 (October, 1962), 120–128.

Billings, J. E. "Are Parents Irrelevant?" NATIONAL ASSOCIATION OF WOMEN DEANS AND COUNSELORS JOURNAL, 33 (Spring, 1970), 112–117.

Blackwell, G. W. "College and the Continuing Education of Women," EDUCATIONAL RECORD, 44 (January, 1963), 33–39.

Carlson, L. H. "Role of the Women's Colleges in the Next Ten Years," ASSOCIATION OF AMERICAN COLLEGES BULLETIN, 44 (March, 1958), 78–88.

Clapp, M. A. "Realistic Education for Women," AMERICAN ASSOCIATION OF UNIVERSITY WOMEN JOURNAL, 43 (June, 1950), 199–202.

Cless, Elizabeth L. "A Modest Proposal for the Educating of Women," AMERICAN SCHOLAR, 38 (Fall, 1969), 618–627.

Cohen, A. C. "Women and Higher Education: Recommendations for Change," PHI DELTA KAPPAN, 53 (November, 1971), 164–167.

Dolan, E. F. "Educated Women, A Mid-Century Evaluation," EDUCATIONAL FORUM, 20 (January, 1956), 219–228.

Dolan, E. F. "Higher Education for Women: Time for Reappraisal," HIGHER EDUCATION, 20 (September, 1963), 5–13.

Dolan, E. F. "Women's Continuing Education: Some National Resources," NATIONAL ASSOCIATION OF WOMEN DEANS AND COUNSELORS JOURNAL, 29 (Fall, 1965), 34–38.

Drinker, S. L. H. and J. Schreier. "Patriarchal Values in Women's Education," JOURNAL OF HIGHER EDUCATION, 25 (March, 1954), 115–121+.

"Education and the Role of Women: Symposium," NATIONAL EDUCATION ASSOCIATION JOURNAL, 49 (December, 1960), 48–53.

"Education for Women Surveyed by AAUW," JOURNAL OF HOME ECONOMICS, 42 (February, 1950), 119.

"Education of Women for Expanding Responsibilities; Discussion," in American Council on Education, TOWARD UNITY IN EDUCATIONAL POLICY. Washington: American Council on Education, n.d., 179–202.

"Education of Women: Symposium," SATURDAY REVIEW, 46 (May 18, 1963), 64–70+.

Eells, W. C. "Women in the Universities of the World," HIGHER EDUCATION, 9 (November 15, 1952), 61–65.

Fred, E. B. "Women and Higher Education: With Special Reference to the University of Wisconsin," JOURNAL OF EXPERIMENTAL EDUCATION, 31 (December, 1962), 158–172.

Harris, A. S. "Second Sex in Academe," AAUP BULLETIN, 56 (September, 1970), 283–295.

Hilton, M. E. "Higher Education of Women," in NATIONAL CONFERENCE ON HIGHER EDUCATION, CURRENT ISSUES IN HIGHER EDUCATION, 1955, 117–122.

Hottel, A. K. "Do Present and Future Responsibilities of Higher Education Pose Special Problems in the Education of Women," in CURRENT ISSUES IN HIGHER EDUCATION, 1953, 217–222.

Hottel, A. K. "Perspectives for the Education of Women," EDUCATIONAL RECORD, 36 (April, 1955), 112–119.

Hottel, A. K. "Social Change and Women's Education," ASSOCIATION OF AMERICAN COLLEGES BULLETIN, 39 (May, 1953), 312–316.

Husbands, S. A. "Women's Place In Higher Education," SCHOOL REVIEW, 80 (February, 1972), 261–274.

Keyseiling, Mary. "Continuing Education for Women: A Growing Challenge," in G. K. Smith, ed. IN SEARCH OF LEADERS. Washington, D.C.: American Association for Higher Education, 1967, 218–223.

Komarovsky, Mirra. "Cultural Contradictions and Sex Roles," AMERICAN JOURNAL OF SOCIOLOGY, 52 (November, 1946), 184–189.

Komarovsky, Mirra. "Functional Analysis of Sex Roles," AMERICAN SOCIOLOGICAL REVIEW, 15 (August, 1950), 508–516.

Komarovsky, M. "What Should Colleges Teach Women?" HARPER, 199 (November, 1949), 33–37.

Krauschaar, O. F. "Science and the Education of Women," ASSOCIATION OF AMERICAN COLLEGES BULLETIN, 43 (March, 1957), 89–94.

Lloyd-Jones, E. N. "Women Today and Their Education," TEACHER COLLEGE RECORD, 57 (October, 1955), 1–7, (April, 1956), 431–437.

Louttit, C. M. "Women: Their Roles and Education," JOURNAL OF HIGHER EDUCATION, 22 (April, 1951), 202–208+.

Mannes, Marya. "Female Intelligence: Who Wants It?" NEW YORK TIMES MAGAZINE, (January 3, 1960), 11+.

Morgan, A. F. "New Look at the Old-fashioned Liberal Education of Women," AMERICAN ASSOCIATION OF UNIVERSITY PROFESSORS BULLETIN, 39 (June, 1953), 259–263.

Mueller, K. H. "Women's Education, for what?" AMERICAN ASSOCIATION OF UNIVERSITY WOMEN JOURNAL, 48 (March, 1955), 136–140.

Neugarten, B. L. "Women in a University; With Reply by J. Freedman," SCHOOL REVIEW, 79 (November, 1970), 109–118.

Neuman, R. R. "When Will the Educational Needs of Women Be Met? Some Questions for the Counselor," JOURNAL OF COUNSELING PSYCHOLOGY, 10 (Winter, 1963), 378–383.

Ozick, Cynthia. "Women and Creativity: The Demise of the Dancing Dog," in Vivian Gornick and Barbara K. Moran, ed. WOMEN IN SEXIST SOCIETY: STUDIES IN POWER AND POWERLESSNESS. New York: Basic Books, 1971, 307–322.

Park, R. "Women's Higher Education," SCHOOL AND SOCIETY, 94 (January 22, 1966), 35–39.

Pullen, Doris L. "The Educational Establishment: Wasted Women," in Mary Lou Thompson, ed. VOICES OF THE NEW FEMINISM. Boston: Beacon Press, 1970, 115–135.

Rauschenbush, E. "Second Chance: New Education for Women," HARPER, 225 (October, 1962), 147–152.

Riesman, David. "Some Continuities and Discontinuities in the Education of Women," in ABUNDANCE FOR WHAT? Garden City, New York: Doubleday, 1964, 320–344.

Riesman, D. "Some Dilemmas of Women's Education," EDUCATIONAL RECORD, 46 (Fall, 1965), 424–434.

348

Rudikoff, Sonya. "Feminism Reconsidered," HUDSON REVIEW, 9, (Summer, 1956), 178-198.

Sanders, Elizabeth. "What do Young Women Want?" YOUTH AND SOCIETY, 3 (Fall, 1971), 36-60.

Sanders, M. K. "Proposition for Women," HARPER, 221 (September, 1960), 41-48.

Sandler, B. "Women in Higher Education," VITAL SPEECHES, 38 (June 15, 1972), 532-537.

Sanford, N. "Changing Sex Roles, Socialization and Education," in W. Henry, ed. HUMAN DEVELOPMENT BULLETIN. Chicago: University of Chicago, Human Development Student Organization, 1958, 58-75.

Solomon, E. C. "Educational Needs of College Women for Marriage and Family Planning," NATIONAL ASSOCIATION OF WOMEN DEANS AND COUNSELORS JOURNAL, 26 (January, 1963), 43-50.

Tead, O. "Junior College for Your Daughter?" JUNIOR COLLEGE JOURNAL, 24 (October, 1953), 65-71.

Thorne, Alison. "Women and Higher Education," in F. R. Paulsen, ed. HIGHER EDUCATION: DIMENSIONS AND DIRECTIONS. Tuscon, Arizona: University of Arizona Press, 1970, 137-156.

"Tough Training Ground for Women's Minds," LIFE, 41 (December 24, 1956), 102-104+.

Truex, D. "Education of Women, the Student Personnel Profession, and the New Feminism," NATIONAL ASSOCIATION OF WOMEN DEANS AND COUNSELORS JOURNAL, 35 (Fall, 1971), 13-20.

Wallin, Paul. "Cultural Contradiction and Sex Role: A Repeat Study," in Theodore Newcomb, ed. THE ADOLESCENT. New York: Dryden Press, 1953, 436-446.

White, L. T., jr. "Changing Context of Women's Education," MARRIAGE AND FAMILY LIVING, 17 (November, 1955), 291-295.

White, L., jr. "Do Women's Colleges Turn Out Spinsters?" HARPER, 205 (October, 1952), 44-48.

White, L., jr. "Educating Women in a Man's World," ATLANTIC, 185 (February, 1950), 52-55.

Wilson, V. H. "Education of Women," JUNIOR COLLEGE JOURNAL, 24 (October, 1953), 96-101.

D.3. Women in College: General Material

Cirtautas, Kazys Claude. THE AMERICAN COLLEGE GIRL. New York: Citadel Press, 1962.

Conference on Talented Women and the American College. NEED RESEARCH ON ABLE WOMEN IN HONORS PROGRAMS, COLLEGE, AND SOCIETY, PROCEEDINGS. New York: Columbia University, 1964.

Gentry, Louise. SOME INTELLECTUAL ATTRIBUTES AND EDUCATIONAL INTERESTS OF UNIVERSITY WOMEN IN VARIOUS MAJORS. Columbus, Ohio: Ohio State University, 1960.

Grote, C. HOUSING AND LIVING CONDITIONS OF WOMEN STUDENTS IN THE WESTERN ILLINOIS STATE TEACHERS COLLEGE AT MACOMB—SCHOOL YEARS 1926-1927, 1927-1928, AND 1928-1929. Teachers College Contributions to Education, Number 507. New York: Bureau of Publications, Teachers College, Columbia University, 1932.

Hopwood, Kathryn L. THE STUDENT ASSISTANT IN THE WOMEN'S RESIDENCE HALLS OF OHIO STATE UNIVERSITY. Columbus: Ohio State University Press, 1954.

Istiphan, Isis. "Role Expectations of American Undergraduate Women in a Western Coeducational Institution." Unpublished Ph.D. dissertation, University of Southern California, 1962.

King, Charlyce Ross. "Attitudes of College Women Toward Student Organizations at the University of Oklahoma." Unpublished Ed.D. dissertation, University of Oklahoma, 1957.

Laird, Helene. NANCY GOES TO COLLEGE. Cleveland: World, 1950.

Lane, W. C. "The Lower-Class Girl in College: A Study of Stanford Freshman Women." Unpublished Ph.D. dissertation, Stanford University, 1960.

Likert, Jane Gibson, ed. CONVERSATIONS WITH RETURNING WOMEN STUDENTS. Ann Arbor: Center for Continuing Education of Women, University of Michigan, 1967.

Pennsylvania State University, Office of Student Affairs and Office of the Dean of Women. A SUMMARY STATEMENT OF RESEARCH CONDUCTED BY THE ASSOCIATION OF WOMEN STUDENTS IN COOPERATION WITH THE OFFICE OF STUDENT AFFAIRS RESEARCH AND THE OFFICE OF THE DEAN OF WOMEN. University Park, Pennsylvania: Pennsylvania State University, Office of Student Affairs, 1966.

Pope, Ruth V. FACTORS AFFECTING THE ELIMINATION OF WOMEN STUDENTS. New York: Columbia University Teachers College, 1931.

Snow, Barbara M. "An Analysis of the Relationship of Certain Factors to the Social Acceptance of College Freshman Women." Unpublished Ph.D. dissertation, Pennsylvania State University, 1958.

Ten American College Girls. THE AMERICAN COLLEGE GIRL: HER COLLEGE AND HER IDEALS. Boston: L. C. Page, 1930.

Albjerg, M. H. "Why Do Bright Girls Not Take Stiff Courses?" EDUCATIONAL FORUM, 25 (January, 1961), 141-144.

Asbell, B. "Housewives on Campus: I Feel Alive Again," MCCALLS, 91 (November, 1963), 136-137+.

Boals, K. "Opinion: On the Subtle Chauvinism of Princeton Males," MADEMOISELLE, 76 (April, 1971), 56+.

Bohen, H. H. "Today's Women Students Get 'Conflicting Signals,' " UNIVERSITY, (Winter, 1972), 12-17.

Brown, H. S. "Pennsylvania Colleges; Man's World or Woman's?" COLLEGE AND UNIVERSITY, 32 (Number 3, 1957), 342-346.

Bunting, M. I., et al. "Academic Freedom and Incentive for Women," EDUCATIONAL RECORD, 51 (Fall, 1970), 386-391.

Cameron, M. E. "Women's Colleges and Scholarships," ASSOCIATIONS

OF AMERICAN COLLEGES BULLETIN, 42 (May, 1956), 233–239.

"Changing Co-ed," LOOK, 22 (September 30, 1958), 61–65.

Chapelle, Y. R. "The Black Woman on the Negro College Campus," BLACK SCHOLAR, 1 (January, February, 1970), 36–40.

Dement, A. L. "College Woman as a Science Major," JOURNAL OF HIGHER EDUCATION, 33 (December, 1962), 487–490.

Dement, A. L. "What Brings and Holds Women Science Majors?" COLLEGE AND UNIVERSITY, 39 (Fall, 1963), 44–50.

Devree, C. "College Girl, Progressive Education Type," NEW YORK TIMES MAGAZINE, (December 2, 1956), 16–17+.

Durnall, E. J., jr. and R. R. Reichart. "Student Personnel Practices in Junior Colleges for Women," JUNIOR COLLEGE JOURNAL, 25 (September, 1954), 41–45.

Ehrlich, H. "Bright Young World of a Freshman: Sarajane Kramer at University of Kentucky," LOOK, 25 (November 21, 1961), 32–40.

Elton, C. I. and H. A. Rose. "Within-university Transfer: Its Relation to Personality Characteristics," JOURNAL OF APPLIED PSYCHOLOGY, 50 (December, 1966), 539–543.

Goodloe, Abbe C. "Undergraduate Life at Wellesley," in James Stone and Donald DeNevi, eds. PORTRAITS OF THE AMERICAN UNIVERSITY, 1890–1910. San Francisco: Jossey Bass, 1971, 311–334.

Gross, Pamela. "Pamela Goes to College," LOOK, 19 (November 29, 1955), 59–62.

Haracz, Kate. "The Education of Kate Haracz: Journal of an Undergraduate," CHANGE, 2 (May-June, 1970), 12–26.

Hardee, M. D. "Counseling Women Students," JUNIOR COLLEGE JOURNAL, 34 (December, 1963), 16–20.

Hembrough, B. L. "Two-Fold Educational Challenge: The Student Wife and the Mature Woman Student," NATIONAL ASSOCIATION OF WOMEN DEANS AND COUNSELORS JOURNAL, 29 (Summer, 1966), 163–167.

Isaacson, L. E. and L. C. Amos. "Participation in Part-Time Work by Women College Students," PERSONNEL AND GUIDANCE JOURNAL, 35 (March, 1957), 445–448.

Lafuze, M. "Study of the Learning of Fundamental Skills by College Freshman Women of Low Motor Ability," RESEARCH QUARTERLY, 22 (May, 1951), 149–157.

Lee, A. M. "Study of Married Women College Students," NATIONAL ASSOCIATION OF WOMEN DEANS AND COUNSELORS JOURNAL, 24 (April, 1961), 132–137.

Leopold, A. K. "Today's Women College Graduates," PERSONNEL AND GUIDANCE JOURNAL, 38 (December, 1959), 280–284.

Lewis, E. C. "Choice and Conflict for the College Woman," NATIONAL ASSOCIATION OF WOMEN DEANS AND COUNSELORS JOURNAL, 32 (Summer, 1969), 176–182.

Lovelace, W. B. "Talented Women," SUPERIOR STUDENT, 6 (May, 1964), 35–39.

Lynch, N. "Lady Chatterley Goes to College," MADEMOISELLE, 57 (August, 1963), 224–225+.

McKeachie, W. J. and Y. G. Lin. "Sex Differences in Student Response to College Teachers: Teacher Warmth and Teacher Sex," AMERICAN EDUCATIONAL RESEARCH JOURNAL, 8 (March, 1971), 221–226.

Marks, J. "College Women 1970: A Whole New Can of Worms," MADEMIOSELLE, 70 (February, 1970), 258+.

"Mary Goes to College," LIFE, 31 (October 15, 1951), 135–141.

Mercer, Margaret. "A Study of Student Mortality in a Home Economics College," JOURNAL OF EDUCATIONAL RESEARCH, 34 (March, 1941), 531–537.

Metzger, S. M., et al. "Comparison of Life Styles of Honors and non-Honors Women," PERSONNEL AND GUIDANCE JOURNAL, 47 (March, 1969), 671–674.

Mosbacker, W. "Women Graduates of Cooperative Work-Study Programs on the College Level," PERSONNEL AND GUIDANCE JOURNAL, 35 (April, 1957), 508–511.

Mothner, I. "Coed's Double Life: Ann Boyer, Junior at Washington University," LOOK, 27 (February 12, 1963), 45–48.

Neal, R. "Women Off-Campus," PERSONNEL AND GUIDANCE JOURNAL, 40 (September, 1962), 31–35.

Nelson, Helen Y. "Factors Related to the Extent of Mortality Among Home Economics Students in Certain Colleges of Minnesota, Wisconsin and Iowa, During 1943–1950," JOURNAL OF EXPERIMENTAL EDUCATION, 22 (September, 1953), 59–62.

Newman, D. and R. Benton. "Never Again, Coed: Special Position of the Coed," MADEMOISELLE, 59 (August, 1964), 24+.

Olesen, V. L. and E. W. Whittaker. "Instant Life: College Women Report on Immersion in the Adult World," NATIONAL ASSOCIATION OF WOMEN DEANS AND COUNSELORS JOURNAL, 29 (Spring, 1966), 131–135.

Oltman, R. M., "Women in Higher Education," CURRENT ISSUES IN HIGHER EDUCATION, 1971, 129–137.

"One Woman, Two Lives," TIME, 78 (November 3, 1961), 68–73.

Pannell, A. G. "College Women in the Current Crisis through Individual Service," ASSOCIATION OF AMERICAN COLLEGE BULLETINS, 38 (March, 1952), 54–60.

Procter, M. E. "Why a (Princeton) Woman Can't Be More Like a Man," PRINCETON ALUMNI BULLETIN, (May 13, 1969), 10–12.

*Riesman, David. "Observations on Contemporary College Students—Especially Women," INTERCHANGE, 1 (April, 1970), 52–62.

Sanford, N. "Impact of a Women's College on Its Students," EDUCATIONAL CONFERENCE REPORT, 22 (1957), 121–129.

Shepard, J. "California Classic: The Berkeley Girl," LOOK, 30 (June 28, 1966), 78–80+.

Shuey, A. M. "Academic Success of Public and Private School Students in Randolph-Macon Woman's College: The Freshman Year," JOURNAL OF EDUCATIONAL RESEARCH, 49 (March, 1956), 481–492.

Stafford, A. and R. Sommer. "A Comparison on On-Campus and Off-Campus Living for 144 Freshman Girls," in Association of Colleges and University Housing Offices Research and Information Committee. STUDENT HOUSING RESEARCH. (n. p.: The Association, 1967).

"Triumph of the Fair Co-ed," NEWSWEEK, 50 (September 23, 1957), 65–68.

Turkey, R. S. "Intellectually-Oriented and Socially-Oriented Superior College Girls," NATIONAL ASSOCIATION OF WOMEN DEANS AND COUNSELORS JOURNAL, 27 (February, 1964), 50–58.

Whitcomb, J. "Penny Goes to College," COSMOPOLITAN, 139 (September, 1955), 42–45.

D.3.a. Psychological Aspects and Attitudes of College Women

Brody, David S. "Developmental Factors Affecting Sociality Traits and Work Habits Among College Women." Unpublished Ph.D. dissertation, University of Minnesota, 1952.

Bromley, Ann. "A Study of Women Matriculants of the Chicago Under-Graduate Division of the University of Illinois." Unpublished Ph.D. dissertation, Northwestern University, 1954.

Dunbar, Donald Stuart. "Sex-Role Identification and Achievement Motivation in College Women." Unpublished Ph.D. dissertation, Ohio State University, 1959.

Faunce, Patricia Spencer. "Personality Characteristics and Vocational Interests Related to the College Persistence of Academically Gifted Women." Unpublished Ph.D. dissertation, University of Minnesota, 1966.

Forest, Cecile Agnes Sister. "The Religious Academic Woman: A Study of Adjustment to Multiple Roles." Unpublished Ph.D. dissertation, Fordham University, 1966.

Lazure, Martha C. "An Intercultural Study of Personality Development in College Women of the United States and French Canada." Unpublished Master's thesis, Bryn Mawr College, 1959.

Levitt, Morris Jacob. "Political Attitudes of American Women: A Study of the Effects of Work and Education on Their Political Role." Unpublished Ph.D. dissertation, University of Maryland, 1965.

Marksberry, M. L. and C. M. Louttit. UNIVERSITY WOMEN'S OPINIONS ON THEIR EDUCATION. Urbana, Illinois: University of Illinois, 1951.

Melniker, Robert C. "Self Acceptance and the Mechanism of Identification. A Q-Sort Investigation of the Relationship Between Levels of Self-Acceptance, Character, Parental Descriptions and Identification Patterns in College Women." Unpublished Ph.D. dissertation, New York University, 1957.

O'Neill, John Philip. "Prediction of College Women's Understanding of the Behavior of Preschool Children." Unpublished Ph.D. dissertation, Florida State University, 1963.

Reevy, William Robert. "Marital Prediction Scores of College Women

Relative to Behavior and Attitudes." Unpublished Ph.D. dissertation, Pennsylvania State University, 1954.

Simmons, Wilber D. SUPERIOR WOMEN COLLEGE STUDENTS: A STUDY OF THEIR SELF CONCEPTS AND ACADEMIC MOTIVATION, FINAL REPORT. Urbana, Illinois: University of Illinois, 1968.

Westoff, Charles F. and Raymond H. Potvin. COLLEGE WOMEN AND FERTILITY VALUES. Princeton: Princeton University Press, 1967.

Wood, R. L. "The Relationship of the College Characteristics Index to Achievement and Certain Other Variables for Freshman Women in the College of Education at the University of Georgia." Unpublished Ph.D. dissertation, University of Georgia, 1963.

Wightwich, M. I. VOCATIONAL INTEREST PATTERNS: A DEVELOPMENTAL STUDY OF A GROUP OF COLLEGE WOMEN. New York: Bureau of Publications, Teachers College, Columbia University, 1945.

Anders, Sarah. "Regionalism, Religion and the Political Attitudes of College Women," JOURNAL OF EDUCATIONAL SOCIOLOGY, 34 (March, 1961), 324–327.

Angrist, Shirley S. "Role Conception as a Predictor of Adult Female Roles," SOCIOLOGY AND SOCIAL RESEARCH, 50 (July, 1966), 448–459.

Ashby, W. "Something More of the Depths: Student Values at Woman's College, University of North Carolina," RELIGIOUS EDUCATION, 55 (March, 1960), 99–102.

Baruch, Rhoda. "The Achievement Motive in Women: Implications for Career Development," JOURNAL OF PERSONALITY AND SOCIAL PSYCHOLOGY, 5 (March, 1967), 260–267.

Bell, M. et al. "Attitudes of Women at the University of Michigan Toward Physical Education," RESEARCH QUARTERLY, 24 (December, 1953), 379–391.

Bereiter, Carl. "Liberalism Versus Attitude Sophistication in College Women," JOURNAL OF SOCIAL PSYCHOLOGY, 63 (June, 1964), 121–127.

Bernard, Jessie. "The Second Sex and the Cichlid Effect," JOURNAL OF THE NATIONAL ASSOCIATION OF WOMEN DEANS AND COUNSELORS, 31 (Fall, 1967), 8–17.

Binger, Carl A. "Emotional Disturbances Among College Women," in G. B. Blaine, jr. and C. C. McArthur, eds. EMOTIONAL PROBLEMS OF THE STUDENT. New York: Appleton-Century-Crofts, 1971, 306–320.

Binger, C. "Pressures on College Girls Today," ATLANTIC, 207 (February, 1961), 40–44.

Black, J. D. "MMPI Results for Fifteen Groups of Female College Students," in W. G. Dahlstrom and G. S. Welsh, eds. BASIC READINGS ON THE MMPI IN PSYCHOLOGY AND MEDICINE. Minneapolis: University of Minnesota Press, 1956, 562–573.

Brody, D. S. "Genetic Study of Sociality Patterns of College Women," EDUCATIONAL-PSYCHOLOGICAL MEASUREMENT, 10 (1950), 513–520.

Broer, M. R. et al. "Attitude of University of Washington Women Students

354

Toward Physical Education Activity," RESEARCH QUARTERLY, 26 (December, 1955), 379–384.

Brown, D. R. "Value Change in College Women," NATIONAL ASSOCIA-TION OF WOMEN DEANS AND COUNSELORS JOURNAL, 25 (June, 1962), 148–155.

Broxton, J. "Self-Concepts of Freshman Women," NATIONAL ASSOCIA-TION OF WOMEN DEANS AND COUNSELORS JOURNAL, 26 (June, 1963), 25–29.

Burgemeister, Bessie B. "The Permanence of Interests of College Women Students," ARCHIVES OF PSYCHOLOGY, 36 (No. 225, 1940), 60–64.

Christensen, H. T. and M. M. Swihart. "Postgraduation Role Preferences of Senior Women in College," MARRIAGE AND FAMILY LIVING, 18 (Fall, 1956), 52–57.

Clark, J. H. "Grade Achievement of Female College Students in Relation to Non-Intellective Factors: MMPI Items," JOURNAL OF SOCIAL PSYCHOLOGY, 37 (May, 1953), 275–281.

Cope, R. G. "Sex-Related Factors and Attrition Among College Women," NATIONAL ASSOCIATION OF WOMEN DEANS AND COUNSELORS JOUR-NAL, 33 (Spring, 1970), 118–124.

Corey, S. M. "Changes in the Opinions of Female Students After One Year at a University," JOURNAL OF SOCIAL PSYCHOLOGY, 11 (May, 1940), 341–351.

Crissman, P. "Temporal Change in and Sexual Difference in Moral Judg-ments," JOURNAL OF SOCIAL PSYCHOLOGY, 16 (1942), 29–38.

Davity, William A. *et al.* "Some Implications of a Pregnancy on Campus: A Research Study," JOURNAL OF THE AMERICAN COLLEGE HEALTH ASSOCIATION, 16 (February, 1968), 253–259.

Dellas, M. and E. L. Geier, "Modes of Conformity of Freshmen Women at Differently Oriented Colleges," JOURNAL OF EDUCATIONAL RESEARCH, 62 (April, 1969), 370–374.

Dolan, E. F. "Educational Goals for College Women," ASSOCIATION OF AMERICAN COLLEGES BULLETIN, 39 (October, 1953), 441–451.

Douvan, Elizabeth. "Adolescent Girls: Their Attitude Toward Education," in Opal David, ed. THE EDUCATION OF WOMEN. Washington, D.C.: American Council on Education, 1959, 23–29.

Dua, P. S. "Personality Characteristics Differentiating Women Leaders and Non-Leaders in a University," NATIONAL ASSOCIATION OF WOMEN DEANS AND COUNSELORS JOURNAL, 27 (Spring, 1964), 128–132.

Dunteman, G. H. "Discriminant Analysis of the SVIB for Female Students in Five College Curricula," JOURNAL OF APPLIED PSYCHOLOGY, 50 (December, 1966), 509–515.

Erou, L. D. "Responses of Women to the Thematic Apperception Test," JOURNAL OF CONSULTING PSYCHOLOGY, 17 (August, 1953), 269–282.

Faunce, P. S. "Personality Characteristics and Vocational Interests Related to the College Persistence of Academically Gifted Women," JOURNAL OF COUNSELING PSYCHOLOGY, 15 (January, 1968), 31–40.

Field, H. A. "Comparison of Major Groups of College Women on the Kuder

Preference Record, Personal," EDUCATIONAL AND PSYCHOLOGICAL MEASUREMENT, 12 (Number 4, 1952), 664–668.

Freedman, M. B. "Changes in Six Decades of Some Attitudes and Values Held by Educated Women," JOURNAL OF SOCIAL ISSUES, 17 (Number 1, 1961), 19–28.

Freedman, M. B. "A Half Century of Vassar Opinion," VASSAR COLLEGE ALUMNAE MAGAZINE, 44 (1959), 3–6.

Freedman, M. B. "The Role of the Educated Woman: An Empirical Study of the Attitudes of a Group of College Women," JOURNAL OF COLLEGE STUDENT PERSONNEL, 3 (March 1965), 145–155.

Freedman, M. "Some Observations on Personality Development in College Women," STUDENT MEDICINE, 8 (February, 1960), 228–245.

Glass, K. D. and E. W. Schoch. "Religious Belief and Practice Related to Anxiety and Dogmatism in College Women," NATIONAL ASSOCIATION OF WOMEN DEANS AND COUNSELORS JOURNAL, 34 (Spring, 1971), 130–133.

Grater, H. A. "Behavior Standards Held by University Females and Their Mothers," PERSONNEL AND GUIDANCE JOURNAL, 38 (January, 1960), 369–372.

Gurin, M. G. et al. "Effect of the Social Context in the Vocational Counseling of College Women," JOURNAL OF COUNSELING PSYCHOLOGY, 10 (Spring, 1963), 28–33.

Gysberg, N. C. et al. "Characteristics of Homemaker-and Career-Oriented Women," JOURNAL OF COUNSELING PSYCHOLOGY, 15 (November, 1968), 541–546.

Halfter, I. T. "Aging and Learning: An Achievement Study," SCHOOL REVIEW, 70 (Autumn, 1962), 287–302.

Halfter, I. T. "Comparative Academic Achievement of Women," ADULT EDUCATION, 12 (Winter, 1962), 106–115.

Halfter, I. T. "Comparative Academic Achievement of Young and Old," NATIONAL ASSOCIATION OF WOMEN DEANS AND COUNSELORS JOURNAL, 25 (January, 1962), 60–67.

Heist, P. "Commentary on the Motivation and Education of College Women," NATIONAL ASSOCIATION OF WOMEN DEANS AND COUNSELORS JOURNAL, 25 (January, 1962), 51–59.

Helson, Ravenna. "Personality Characteristics and Developmental History of Creative College Women," GENETIC PSYCHOLOGY MONOGRAPHS, 76 (November, 1967), 205–256.

Helson, Ravenna. "Personality of Women with Imaginative and Artistic Interests: The Role of Masculinity, Originality, and Other Characteristics in Their Creativity," JOURNAL OF PERSONALITY, 34 (March, 1966), 1–25.

Hewer, V. H. and G. Neubeck. "Attitudes of College Students Toward Employment among Married Women," PERSONNEL AND GUIDANCE JOURNAL, 42 (February, 1964), 587–592.

Horner, Matina. "Fail: Bright Women," in Elsie Adams and Mary Louise Briscoe, eds., UP AGAINST THE WALL, MOTHER . . . , Beverly Hills, California: Glencoe Press, 1971, 379–385.

Hunter, E. C. "Changes in General Attitudes of Women Students During

Four Years in College," JOURNAL OF SOCIAL PSYCHOLOGY, 16 (November, 1942), 243–257.

Jahoda, Marie and Joan Havel. "Psychological Problems of Women in Different Social Roles," EDUCATIONAL RESEARCH, 36 (1955), 325–335.

Johnson, Ray W. "Parental Identification and Vocational Interests of College Women," MEASUREMENT AND EVALUATION IN GUIDANCE, 3 (Fall, 1970), 147–151.

Kammeyer, K. "Birth Order and the Feminine Sex Role Among College Women," AMERICAN SOCIOLOGICAL REVIEW, 31 (Number 4, 1966), 508–516.

Kappes, E. E. "Inventory to Determine Attitudes of College Women Toward Physical Education and Student Services of the Physical Education Department," RESEARCH QUARTERLY, 25 (December, 1954), 429–438.

Klein, E. B. and L. J. Gould. "Alienation and Identification in College Women," JOURNAL OF PERSONALITY, 37 (September, 1969), 468–480.

Komaravsky, M. "Cultural Contradictions and Sex Roles," in E. Schuler et al., eds. OUTSIDE READINGS IN SOCIOLOGY. New York: Crowell, 1952, 133–142.

Lind, M. "College Values on the Balance Scales; AAUW's Questionnaire Survey," COLLEGE AND UNIVERSITY, 26 (October, 1950), 42–53.

Lloyd, B. J. "Questionnaire Portrait of the Freshman Coed: Early Adjustment," NATIONAL ASSOCIATION OF WOMEN DEANS AND COUNSELORS JOURNAL, 28 (Summer, 1965), 160–166.

Lough, O. M. "Women Students in Liberal Arts, Nursing and Teacher Training Curricula and the Minnesota Multiphasic Personality Inventory," JOURNAL OF APPLIED PSYCHOLOGY, 35 (1951), 125–126.

Lough, O.M. and M. E. Green. "Comparison of the Minnesota Multiphasic Personality Inventory and the Washburne S-A Inventory as Measures of Personality of College Women," JOURNAL OF SOCIAL PSYCHOLOGY, 32 (August, 1950), 23–30.

Louttit, C. M. and M. L. Marksberry, "Attitudes of Women on Higher Education," EDUCATIONAL ADMINISTRATION AND SUPERVISION, 37 (November, 1951), 385–395.

Lum, M. K. M. "Comparison of Under and Overachieving Female College Students," JOURNAL OF EDUCATIONAL PSYCHOLOGY, 51 (June, 1960), 109–114.

Marcia, J. E. and M. L. Friedman. "Ego Identity Status in College Women," JOURNAL OF PERSONALITY, 38 (June, 1970), 249–263.

McCue, B. F. "Flexibility Measurements of College Women," RESEARCH QUARTERLY, 24 (October, 1953), 316–324.

McKee, Betty, H. H. Remmers and Dorothy C. Stratton, "Women's Extracurricular Activities as Related to Certain Other Characteristics," PURDUE UNIVERSITY STUDIES IN HIGHER EDUCATION, 39 (December, 1940), 5–15.

Mista, N. J. "Attitudes of College Women Toward Their High School Physical Education Programs," AMERICAN ASSOCIATION FOR HEALTH,

PHYSICAL EDUCATION AND RECREATION RESEARCH QUARTERLY, 39 (March, 1968), 166–174.

Mull, H. K. "Ethical Discrimination of Various Groups of College Women," JOURNAL OF SOCIAL PSYCHOLOGY, 35 (February, 1952), 69–72.

Norfleet, M. A. W. "Personality Characteristics of Achieving and Under-achieving High Ability Senior Women," PERSONNEL AND GUIDANCE JOURNAL, 46 (June, 1968), 976–980.

Palubinskas, A. L. "Personality Changes in College Women During Four Years of College Experience," PROCEEDINGS OF THE IOWA ACADEMY OF SCIENCE, 59 (1952), 389–391.

Powell, M. "Relationship Existent Between Adjustment Traits of College Freshmen Women: As Measured by the Bell Adjustment Inventory," JOURNAL OF SOCIAL PSYCHOLOGY, 31 (February, 1950), 145–149.

Richardson, H. M. "Community of Values as a Factor in Friendships of College and Adult Women," JOURNAL OF SOCIAL PSYCHOLOGY, 11 (May, 1940), 303–312.

Rose, A. A. "Effects of the War on the Social and Emotional Adjustment of College Girls," JOURNAL OF SOCIAL PSYCHOLOGY, 24 (November, 1946), 177–185.

Rose, Arnold. "The Adequacy of Women's Expectations for Adult Roles," SOCIAL FORCES, 30 (October, 1951), 69–77.

Sanford, N. "Motivation of High Achievers," in Opal David, ed. THE EDUCATION OF WOMEN. Washington, D.C.: American Council on Education, 1959, 34–38.

Schmidt, H. O. "Comparison of Women Students in Occupational Therapy and in Nursing," JOURNAL OF PSYCHOLOGY, 31 (April, 1951), 161–174.

Schmidt, M. R. "Personality Changes in College Women," JOURNAL OF COLLEGE STUDENT PERSONNEL, 11 (November, 1970), 414–418.

Schofield, L. F. and R. B. Cable, "Self-Concepts of Mature and Young Women Students," JOURNAL OF COLLEGE AND STUDENT PERSONNEL, 12 (July, 1971), 297–302.

Schufletowski, Frank W. "Are College Women Satisfied With Their Equality and Freedom?" JOURNAL OF COLLEGE STUDENT PERSONNEL, 8 (March, 1967), 109–111.

Shuey, A. M. "Intelligence of College Women as Related to Family Size," JOURNAL OF EDUCATIONAL PSYCHOLOGY, 42 (April, 1951), 215–222.

Siegel, A. E. and E. A. Curtis. "Familial Correlates of Orientation Toward Future Employment Among College Women," JOURNAL OF EDUCATIONAL PSYCHOLOGY, 54 (February, 1963), 33–37.

Smith, J. C. "Casework on the Campus," SOCIAL CASEWORK, 33 (December, 1952), 423–429.

Standt, V. M. "Relationship of Certain Personality Traits to Errors and Correct Responses in Several Types of Tasks Among College Women Under Varying Test Conditions," JOURNAL OF PSYCHOLOGY, 27 (April, 1949), 465–478.

Steinmann, Anne. "Female-Role Perception as a Factor in Counseling,"

358

JOURNAL OF THE NATIONAL ASSOCIATION OF WOMEN DEANS AND
COUNSELORS, 34 (Fall, 1970), 27–33.

Steinmann, A., J. Levi and D. J. Fox. "Self-Concept of College Women
Compared with Their Concept of Ideal Woman and Men's Ideal Woman,"
JOURNAL OF COUNSELING PSYCHOLOGY, 11 (Winter, 1964), 370–374.

Summerskill, J. and C. D. Darling. "Sex Differences in Adjustment to
College," JOURNAL OF EDUCATIONAL PSYCHOLOGY, 46 (October, 1955),
355–361.

Tomeh, A. K. "Impact of Reference Groups on the Education and Occupational Aspirations of Women College Students," JOURNAL OF MARRIAGE
AND THE FAMILY, 30 (February, 1968), 102–110.

Veroff, J. "Achievement Motive in High School and College Age Women,"
JOURNAL OF ABNORMAL AND SOCIAL PSYCHOLOGY, 48 (January,
1953), 108–119.

Vetter, L. and E. C. Lewis. "Some Correlates of Homemaking vs. Career
Preference Among College Home Economics Students," PERSONNEL AND
GUIDANCE JOURNAL, 42 (February, 1964), 593–598.

Vincent, C. E. "Role Clarification for the Contemporary College-Educated
Woman," JOURNAL OF HOME ECONOMICS, 45 (October, 1953), 567–570.

Wallen, P. "Cultural Contradictions and Sex Roles: A Repeat Study,"
AMERICAN SOCIOLOGICAL REVIEW, 15 (April, 1950), 288–293.

Walters, C. E. "Study of the Effects of Prescribed Efficiency of Women,"
RESEARCH QUARTERLY, 24 (March, 1953), 102–111.

Walters, J. "Effects of an Introductory Course in Child Development on
the Attitudes of College Women Toward Child Guidance," JOURNAL OF
EXPERIMENTAL EDUCATION, 27 (June, 1959), 311–321.

Weitz, H. and R. M. Colver. "Relationship Between the Educational Goals
and the Academic Performance of Women, a Confirmation," EDUCATIONAL
AND PSYCHOLOGICAL MANUAL, 19 (Autumn, 1959), 373–380.

Westervelt, R. "Femininity in American Women: The Influence of Education," NATIONAL ASSOCIATION OF WOMEN DEANS AND COUNSELORS
JOURNAL, 35 (Fall, 1971), 2–12.

Westoff, C. F. and R. H. Potrin, "Higher Education, Religion and Women's
Family-Size Orientations," AMERICAN SOCIOLOGICAL REVIEW, 31 (August,
1966), 489–496.

Wright, Dorothy M. "Junior College Students View Women's Roles,"
JOURNAL OF THE NATIONAL ASSOCIATION OF WOMEN DEANS AND
COUNSELORS, 30 (Winter, 1967), 71–77.

Wright, John J. "Sex Role Crises in College Students," JOURNAL OF THE
AMERICAN HEALTH ASSOCIATION, 14 (December, 1965), 92–96.

*D.3.b. Sexual and Personal Liberty
of College Women*

Shrader, Wesley. COLLEGE RUINED OUR DAUGHTER: LETTERS TO
PARENTS CONCERNING THE BAFFLING WORLD OF THE COLLEGE STU-
DENT. New York: Harper and Row, 1969.

White, Julie Ellen. "Dimensions of Conformity and Evasion in Residence Halls for University Women: A Sociological Analysis of Normative Behavior in a Large-Scale Social Organization," Unpublished Ph.D. dissertation, University of Illinois, 1962.

Anderson, R. N. "Survey of Undergraduate Women's Social Regulations," PERSONNEL AND GUIDANCE JOURNAL, 44 (June, 1966), 1062–1066.

Bartlett, L. R. *et al.* "What Price Freedom? A Symposium," NATIONAL ASSOCIATION OF WOMEN DEANS AND COUNSELORS JOURNAL, 30 (Fall, 1966), 21–27.

Ellis, A. "Love and Family Relationships of American College Girls," with reply by E. W. Burgess. AMERICAN JOURNAL OF SOCIOLOGY, 55 (May, 1950), 550–558.

Fley, J. A. "Campus Regulations: Are Girls Different?" NATIONAL ASSOCIATION OF WOMEN DEANS AND COUNSELORS JOURNAL, 31 (Spring, 1968), 116–122.

Hartshorn, E. "Some Samples of Freedoms for Women Students in Higher Education," NATIONAL ASSOCIATION OF WOMEN DEANS AND COUN-SELORS JOURNAL, 24 (April, 1961), 138–144.

Lerner, M. "What Sex Means to College Girls Today," REDBOOK, 127 (June, 1966), 51+.

Mueller, K. H. "Sex Differences in Campus Regulations," PERSONNEL AND GUIDANCE JOURNAL, 32 (May, 1954), 528–532.

Schoemer, J. R. and W. A. McConnell, "Is There a Place for the Freshman Women's Residence Hall?" PERSONNEL AND GUIDANCE JOURNAL, 49 (September, 1970), 35–40.

Taves, I. "Young Girl's First Year of Freedom," WOMAN'S HOME COM-PANION, 80 (October, 1953), 28–31+.

Whitney, M. "Greater Freedom for Women Has Increased the Security Problem," COLLEGE AND UNIVERSITY BUSINESS, 48 (April, 1970), 97–98.

Wilkinson, D. Y. "Dating Status of American College Women as a Predictor of Interactional Patterns with Parents," INTERNATIONAL JOURNAL OF SOCIOLOGY, 20 (December, 1970), 300–306.

D.3.c. Women's Movement on Campus and Women in the Student Left

Committee on University Women. WOMEN IN THE UNIVERSITY OF CHICAGO: REPORT. Chicago: University of Chicago University Senate, 1970.

HOW HARVARD RULES WOMEN. Cambridge, Massachusetts: New University Conference, 1970.

*Lever, Janet and Pepper Schwartz. WOMEN AT YALE: LIBERATING A COLLEGE CAMPUS. Indianapolis: Bobbs-Merrill, 1971.

Oltman, Ruth M. CAMPUS 1970: WHERE DO WOMEN STAND?, Wash-ington, D.C.: American Association of University Women, 1970.

Tobias, S. FEMALE STUDIES NUMBER 1: A COLLECTION OF COL-LEGE SYLLABI AND READING LISTS. Pittsburgh: Know, 1970.

WOMEN IN ACTION: SPEECHES AND PANEL DISCUSSIONS OF THE CONFERENCE-WORKSHOP, MARCH 26, 1969. Ann Arbor: Center for Continuing Education of Women, University of Michigan, 1969.

Women's Research Group. WOMEN AT WISCONSIN. Madison: Women's Research Group, 1970.

Babcox, Peter. "Meet the Women of the Revolution, 1969," NEW YORK TIMES MAGAZINE, (February 9, 1969), 34.

Barnard, Jesse. "My Four Revolutions: An Autobiographical History of the ASA," AMERICAN JOURNAL OF SOCIOLOGY, 78 (January, 1973).

Bird, Caroline. "Women's Lib and the Women's Colleges," CHANGE, 4 (April, 1972), 60–65.

Brooks, R. M. "Woman's Place Is in the Wrong," VITAL SPEECHES, 28 (December 30, 1961), 151–154.

Brownmiller, S. "Sisterhood is Powerful," NEW YORK TIMES MAGAZINE, (March 15, 1970), 26–27+.

Brownmiller, Susan. "Up from Silence," ESQUIRE, 71 (March, 1969), 100–102, 150–153.

Cantarow, Ellen et al. "I am Furious (Female)," in Christopher Reaske and Robert Wilson, jr. eds. STUDENT VOICES/ONE. New York: Random House, 1971.

Cherniss, Cary. "Personality and Ideology: A Personological Study of Women's Liberation," PSYCHIATRY, 35 (May, 1972), 109–125.

Detlefsen, E. G., P. Schuman and G. W. Hathway, et al. "Overdue: the Women's Liberation Movement," WILSON LIBRARY BULLETIN, 44 (May, 1970), 962–965+.

*Freeman, J. "The Origins of the Women's Liberation Movement," AMERICAN JOURNAL OF SOCIOLOGY, 78 (January, 1973).

*Freeman, J. "Women's Liberation and Its Impact on the Campus," LIBERAL EDUCATION, 57 (December, 1971), 468–478.

Gardner, Jo Ann Evans. "The Feminist Movement," in G. K. Smith, ed. THE TROUBLED CAMPUS. San Francisco: Jossey-Bass, 1970, 46–53.

Goldfield, Evelyn, Sue Munaker and Heather Booth, et al. "Women in the Radical Movement," RADICALS IN THE PROFESSIONS NEWSLETTER, (March, 1968).

Gruchow, N. "Discrimination: Women Charge Universities, Colleges with Bias," SCIENCE, 168 (May 1, 1970), 559–561.

Hayden, Julie. "A Woman's View," in Atlantic Monthly ed. THE TROUBLED CAMPUS. Boston: Little, Brown, 1966, 32–40.

*Hinckle, W. and C. Hinckle. "History of the Rise of the Unusual Movements for Women Power in the United States. 1961–1968," RAMPARTS, (February, 1968), 22–31.

Hoffman, B. H. "Coeds in Rebellion," LADIES HOME JOURNAL, 82 (October, 1965), 82–84+.

Jackson, Molly "The New and the Newer: Women on Campus (1970)," in John and Susan Erlich, eds. STUDENT POWER, PARTICIPATION AND REVOLUTION. New York: Association Press, 1970, 74–80.

*Komisar, L. "New Feminism," SATURDAY REVIEW, 53 (February 21, 1970), 27–30+.

*McAfee, K. and Myrna Wood. "Bread and Roses," in William Slate, ed. POWER TO THE PEOPLE: NEW LEFT WRITINGS. New York: Tower, 1970, 217–236.

Millet, Kate. "Libbies, Smithies, Vassarites," CHANGE, 2 (September-October, 1970), 42–50.

The Old Mole, "Women and the University" in Immanuel Wallerstein and Paul Starr, eds. THE UNIVERSITY CRISIS READER, I. New York: Random House, 1971, 393–399.

Packer, Barbara and Karen Waggoner. "Yale and the New Sisterhood," YALE ALUMNI MAGAZINE, 33 (April, 1970), 26–31.

Pifer, A. "Newest Campus Crusade: Equal Rights for Women," U.S. NEWS AND WORLD REPORT, 71 (December 13, 1971), 79–82.

Rat, "Women's Liberation–'The Longest Revolution'," in Ethel Romm, ed. THE OPEN CONSPIRACY. New York: K. S. Giniger, 1970, 209–223.

Shapley, D. "Sex Discrimination on Campus: Michigan Wrestles with Equal Pay," SCIENCE, 173 (July 16, 1971), 214–216.

Truex, D. "Focus on Feminine Ferment," JOURNAL OF COLLEGE STUDENT PERSONNEL, 11 (September, 1970), 323–331.

"What? No Degree for Women's Lib?" COLLEGE MANAGEMENT, 5 (December, 1970), 14–17.

Wilson, Ray. "When Womens Lib Looks at Your Faculty," in Clifford T. Stewart, ed. INSTITUTIONAL RESEARCH AND INSTITUTIONAL POLICY FORMULATION. Claremont, California. Association for Institutional Research, 1971, 156–160.

"Women Profs Fight Back: Discrimination Against Women," NEWSWEEK, 77 (May 17, 1971), 99–100+.

Woodring, P. "Sexism on the Campus: Women's Rights in Teaching and Administration Positions," SATURDAY REVIEW, 53 (May 16, 1970), 80+.

D.4. Women and Graduate Schools

Lopate, Carol. WOMEN IN MEDICINE. Baltimore: John Hopkins University Press, 1968.

Mitchell, S. B. WOMEN AND THE DOCTORATE. Stillwater: Oklahoma State University, 1968.

Radcliffe College. Committee on Graduate Education for Women. GRADUATE EDUCATION FOR WOMEN: THE RADCLIFFE PH.D. Cambridge: Harvard University Press, 1956.

SPECIAL REPORT ON WOMEN AND GRADUATE EDUCATION. Washington, D.C.: U.S. Department of Health, Education and Welfare, National Institutes of Health, 1968.

U.S. National Institutes of Health, Resources Analysis Branch. SPECIAL REPORT ON WOMEN AND GRADUATE STUDY. Washington, D.C.: U.S. Government Printing Office, 1968.

362

Bakke, E. Wright. "Graduate Education for Women at Yale," VENTURES, 9 (Fall, 1969), 11–25.

*Converse, Philip and Jean Converse. "The Status of Women as Student Professionals in Political Science," PS, 4 (Summer, 1971), 328–348.

Feldman, Saul. "Marital Status and Graduate Education; Impediment or Stimulant?" AMERICAN JOURNAL OF SOCIOLOGY, 78 (January, 1973).

Le Fevre, Carole. "The Mature Woman as Graduate Student," SCHOOL REVIEW, 80 (February, 1972), 281–299.

Mitchell, S. B. and Robert Alciatore. "Women Doctoral Recipients Evaluate their Training," EDUCATIONAL FORUM, 34 (May, 1970), 533–540.

*Rossi, Alice. "Status of Women in Graduate Departments of Sociology," AMERICAN SOCIOLOGIST, 5 (Number 1, 1970), 1–12.

D.5. Education and Career Patterns of College Women

Almquist, Elizabeth M. "Occupational Choice and Career Salience Among College Women." Unpublished Ph.D. dissertation, University of Kansas, 1969.

Angel, Juvenal Londoño. MATCHING COLLEGE WOMEN TO JOBS. New York: World Trade Academy Press, 1970.

Arns, Josephine. "A Factorial Analysis of the Vocational Interests of Two Hundred Adult Female Students," Unpublished Ed.D. dissertation, Temple University, 1958.

*Astin, Helen S. THE WOMAN DOCTORATE IN AMERICA. New York: Russell Sage Foundation, 1969.

*Bernard, Jessie S. ACADEMIC WOMEN. University Park: Pennsylvania State University Press, 1964.

Conference on Opportunities for Women through Education, University of Michigan, 1965. OPPORTUNITIES FOR WOMEN THROUGH EDUCATION. Ann Arbor: University of Michigan, Center for Continuing Education of Women, 1965.

CONFERENCE ON WOMEN'S DESTINY—CHOICE OR CHANGE? Seattle, 1963. REPORT. Washington, D.C.: U.S. Department of Labor, Women's Bureau, 1965.

Davison, M. B. "Educational Outcomes and Implications of Academically or Vocationally Focused Small Groups of Undergraduate Students in a Women's Residence Hall." Unpublished Ph.D. dissertation, Pennsylvania State University, 1964.

*Epstein, Cynthia Fuchs. WOMAN'S PLACE: OPTIONS AND LIMITS IN PROFESSIONAL CAREERS. Berkeley: University of California Press, 1970.

Ginzberg, Eli and Alice M. Yohalem. EDUCATED AMERICAN WOMEN: SELF-PORTRAITS. New York: Columbia University Press, 1966.

JOB HORIZONS FOR COLLEGE WOMEN. United States Women's Bureau, Bulletin 288, 1967.

Jordan, Annie W. RELATIONSHIP BETWEEN SELECTED COLLEGIATE EXPERIENCES AND BEGINNING JOBS FOR WOMEN. Columbus, Ohio: Ohio State University, 1957.

Marksberry, Mary Lee. ATTITUDES OF COLLEGE WOMEN AND ALUMNAE TOWARD LIFE ROLES AND CERTAIN COLLEGE CHARACTERISTICS. Urbana: Committee on Education for Women, University of Illinois, 1951.

Mattfield, J. A. and C. Van Aken, eds. WOMEN AND THE SCIENTIFIC PROFESSIONS: THE M.I.T. SYMPOSIUM ON WOMEN IN SCIENCE AND ENGINEERING, Cambridge, Massachusetts: MIT Press, 1965.

Muller, Leo C. and Ovida G. Muller, eds. NEW HORIZONS FOR COLLEGE WOMEN. Washington: Public Affairs Press, 1960.

New York. Governor's Committee on the Education and Employment of Women. NEW YORK WOMEN AND THEIR CHANGING WORK: NEW WAYS TO ENCOURAGE THE EDUCATION OF WOMEN TO MAKE FULL USE OF THEIR TALENTS AND TRAINING, AND THE EDUCATION OF THE COMMUNITY TO MAKE FULL USE OF ITS TRAINED AND TALENTED WOMEN. Albany: State of New York, 1964.

Robinson, Lora H. THE STATUS OF ACADEMIC WOMEN. Washington, D.C.: ERIC Clearing House on Higher Education, 1971.

Shosteck, Robert. FIVE THOUSAND WOMEN COLLEGE GRADUATES REPORT: FINDINGS OF A NATIONAL SURVEY OF THE SOCIAL AND ECONOMIC STATUS OF WOMEN GRADUATES AND LIBERAL ARTS COLLEGES OF 1946–1949. Washington: B'nai B'rith Vocational Service Bureau, 1953.

Simpson, Lawrence Alan. "A Study of Employing Agents' Attitudes Toward Academic Women in Higher Education." Unpublished Ph.D. dissertation, Pennsylvania State University, 1968.

Slocum, W. L. and L. T. Empey. OCCUPATIONAL PLANNING BY YOUNG WOMEN. A STUDY OF OCCUPATIONAL EXPERIENCES, ASPIRATIONS, ATTITUDES AND PLANS OF COLLEGE AND HIGH SCHOOL GIRLS. Bulletin 568, Pullman, Washington: Institute of Agricultural Sciences, State College of Washington, 1956.

Tangri, Sandra Florence Schwartz. "Role Innovation in Occupational Choice Among College Women." Ann Arbor: University Microfilms, 1969.

U.S. Congress. House Committee on Education and Labor. Special subcommittee on Women. DISCRIMINATION AGAINST WOMEN. HEARINGS ... Washington, D.C.: U.S. Government Printing Office, 1970.

U.S. National Science Foundation. WOMEN IN SCIENTIFIC CAREERS. Washington, 1961.

U.S. Women's Bureau. EMPLOYMENT AFTER COLLEGE: REPORT ON WOMEN GRADUATES, CLASS OF 1955. Washington: Government Printing Office, 1956.

Watermulder, Georgia P. CAREERS FOR COLLEGE WOMEN: A BIBLIOGRAPHY OF VOCATIONAL MATERIALS. University of Michigan, Center for Continuing Education of Women, 1968.

Watley, D. F. CAREER OR MARRIAGE?: A LONGITUDINAL STUDY OF ABLE YOUNG WOMEN. Evanston, Illinois: National Merit Scholarship Corporation, 1969.

Wells, Jean Alice. COLLEGE WOMEN GO TO WORK: REPORT ON

WOMEN GRADUATES, CLASS OF 1956. Washington: U.S. Department of Labor, Women's Bureau, 1958.

Wilson, Pauline Park. COLLEGE WOMEN WHO EXPRESS FUTILITY: A STUDY BASED ON FIFTY SELECTED LIFE HISTORIES OF WOMEN COLLEGE GRADUATES. New York: Bureau of Publications, Teachers College, Columbia University, 1950.

Almquist E. M. and S. S. Angrist. "Role Model Influences on College Women's Career Aspirations," MERRILL PALMER QUARTERLY OF BEHAVIOR AND DEVELOPMENT, 17 (July, 1971), 263–279.

Astin, Helen S. "Career Development of Young Women during the Post High School Years," JOURNAL OF COUNSELING PSYCHOLOGY, 18 (July, 1971).

Astin, Helen S. and Alan E. Bayer. "Sex Discrimination in Academe," EDUCATIONAL RECORD, 53 (Spring, 1972), 101–118.

Berry, J. "Life Plans of College Women," NATIONAL ASSOCIATION OF DEANS OF WOMEN JOURNAL, 18 (January, 1955), 76–80.

Bunting, M. I. "Huge Waste: Educated Womanpower," NEW YORK TIMES MAGAZINE, (May 7, 1961), 23+.

Byrne, K. "Repentent Dropouts: Academic Comeback of the Mature Woman," AMERICA, 122 (May 16, 1970), 522–524.

Case, D. "Married Women and Young Women Students at a Day College of Education and in their First Year as Teachers," BRITISH JOURNAL OF EDUCATIONAL PSYCHOLOGY, 38 (February, 1968), 102–105.

Dement, A. L. "Higher Education of the Housewife," JOURNAL OF HIGHER EDUCATION, 31 (January, 1960), 28–32.

Dunbar, E. "Mother Returns to the Campus: Minnesota Plan for the Continuing Education of Women," LOOK, (October 23, 1962), 46–50.

Epperson, D. C. "Achieving Professional Commitment from College Women," JOURNAL OF TEACHER EDUCATION, 16 (March, 1965), 36–45.

Falk, L. L. "Occupational Satisfaction of Female College Graduates," JOURNAL OF MARRIAGE AND THE FAMILY, 28 (May, 1966), 177–185.

Faunce, Patricia Spencer. "Academic Careers of Gifted Women," PERSONNEL AND GUIDANCE JOURNAL, 46 (November, 1967), 252–257.

Fletcher, F.M., jr. "Supply of Women for Citical Occupations," EDUCATIONAL RESEARCH BULLETIN, 33 (October, 1954), 176–182.

*Graham, P. A. "Women in Academe," SCIENCE, 169 (September 25, 1970), 1283–1290.

Greene, F. D. "Follow-up Study of Non-Graduating Women from the College of Education of Ohio State University," EDUCATIONAL ADMINISTRATION AND SUPERVISION, 29 (October, 1943), 427–433.

Grumbach, "Women's Place," COMMONWEAL, 74 (April 28, 1961), 119–121.

Hawkins, Ruth R. "The Odds Against Women," CHANGE, 1 (November-December, 1969), 34–37.

Hoffel, A. H. K., "Changing Status of Women," NATIONAL ASSOCIA-

TION OF WOMEN DEANS AND COUNSELORS JOURNAL, 17 (January, 1954), 62–67.

Kiell, N. and B. Friedman, "Culture Lag and Housewifemanship: The Role of the Married Female College Graduate," JOURNAL OF EDUCATIONAL SOCIOLOGY, 31 (October, 1957), 87–95.

Knudsen, Dean D. "The Declining Status of Women: Popular Myths and the Failures of Functionalist Thought," SOCIAL FORCES, 48 (December, 1969), 183–202.

Leopold, A. K. "1955's Women College Graduates in 1956," PERSONNEL AND GUIDANCE JOURNAL, 35 (February, 1957), 342–346.

McKinney, John C. "Women in the Academic Labor Force," GRADUATE SCHOOL REPORT, 3 (1972).

Marksberry, M. L. "Attitudes of College Women toward Selected Roles in Life," SCHOOL AND SOCIETY, 75 (June 21, 1952), 394–396.

Murphy, F. "Women and the Scientific Revolution," AMERICAN ASSOCIATION OF UNIVERSITY WOMEN JOURNAL, 53 (October, 1959), 19–22.

Norris, L. W. "Role of Women in American Economic Life," ASSOCIATION OF AMERICAN COLLEGES BULLETIN, 42 (March, 1956), 51–60.

Ostlund, L. A. "Occupational Choice Patterns of Negro College Women," JOURNAL OF NEGRO EDUCATION, 26 (Number 1, 1957), 86–91.

Parrish, J. E. "College Women and Jobs: Another Look at the 1970s," JOURNAL OF COLLEGE PLACEMENT, 31 (April, 1971), 34–38+.

Prather, Jane. "Why Can't Women Be More Like Men: A Summary of the Sociopsychological Factors Hindering Women's Advancement in the Professions," AMERICAN BEHAVIORAL SCIENTIST, 14 (November-December, 1971), 172–182.

Rand, L. "Masculinity or Feminity? Differentiating Career-Oriented and Homemaking-Oriented College Freshman Women," JOURNAL OF COUNSELING PSYCHOLOGY, 15 (September, 1968), 444–450.

Roe, A. "Women in Science," PERSONNEL AND GUIDANCE JOURNAL, 44 (April, 1966), 784–787.

Rossi, A. "Discrimination and Demography Restrict Opportunities for Academic Women," COLLEGE AND UNIVERSITY BUSINESS, 48 (February, 1970), 74–78.

Rossman, J. E. and D. P. Campbell. "Why College-Trained Mothers Work," PERSONNEL AND GUIDANCE JOURNAL, 43 (June, 1965), 986–992.

Russin, J. M., ed. "What Educated Women Want: Report: Views of Vassar Seniors," NEWSWEEK, 67 (June 13, 1966), 68–72+.

Sanford, N. "Is College Education Wasted on Women?" LADIES HOME JOURNAL, 74 (May, 1957), 78–79+.

Scnaffer, Harry and Juliet. "Job Discrimination Against Faculty Wives," JOURNAL OF HIGHER EDUCATION, 37 (January, 1966), 10–15.

Searls, L. G. "Leisure Role Emphasis of College Graduate Homemakers," JOURNAL OF MARRIAGE AND THE FAMILY, 28 (February, 1966), 77–82.

Simon, Rita James, et al. "Of Nepotism, Marriage and the Pursuit of an Academic Career," SOCIOLOGY OF EDUCATION, 39 (Fall, 1966), 344–358.

Simpson, R. L. and I. H. Simpson. "Occupational Choice Among Career-

Oriented College Women," MARRIAGE AND FAMILY LIVING, 23 (November, 1961), 377–383.

Swerdloff, S. "Job Opportunities for Women College Graduates," MONTHLY LABOR REVIEW, 87 (April, 1964), 396–400.

Tobias, S. and E. Kusnetz, "For College Students: A Study of Women, Their Roles and Stereotypes," JOURNAL OF HOME ECONOMICS, 64 (April, 1972), 17–21.

Wells, J. A. "Employment of June 1955 Women College Graduates," MONTHLY LABOR REVIEW, 79 (September, 1956), 1057–1061.

Wells, J. A. "Employment of June 1956 Women College Graduates," MONTHLY LABOR REVIEW, 81 (July, 1958), 752–756.

Wells, J. A. "Employment of June 1957 Women College Graduates," MONTHLY LABOR REVIEW, 82 (June, 1959), 663–666.

Wells, J. A. "Women College Graduates Seven Years Later," MONTHLY LABOR REVIEW, 90 (July, 1967), 28–32.

White, M. S. "Psychological and Social Barriers to Women in Science," SCIENCE, 170 (October 23, 1970), 413–416.

Willig, J. "Class of '34 (female) Fifteen Years Later," NEW YORK TIMES MAGAZINE, (June 12, 1949), 10+.

Zissis, C. "Study of the Life Planning of 550 Freshman Women at Purdue University," NATIONAL ASSOCIATION OF WOMEN DEANS AND COUNSELORS JOURNAL, 27 (Summer, 1964), 153–159.

3

Students and Student Life in America

A. WHO ARE THE STUDENTS?

A.1. Socio-Economic and Statistical Studies of the General Student Body

Abe, C. and J. L. Holland. A DESCRIPTION OF COLLEGE FRESHMAN. (ACT Research Reports, Number 3.) Iowa City, Iowa: American College Testing Program, 1965.

Abe, C., *et al.* A DESCRIPTION OF AMERICAN COLLEGE FRESHMAN. (ACT Research Reports, Number 1.) Iowa City, Iowa: American College Testing Program, 1965.

ADMISSION TO AMERICAN COLLEGES. New York: Educational Records Bureau, 1964.

American Council on Education. FACTORS AFFECTING THE ADMISSION OF HIGH SCHOOL SENIORS TO COLLEGE. Washington: American Council on Education, 1949.

Astin, A. W. TRENDS IN THE CHARACTERISTICS OF ENTERING COLLEGE STUDENTS, 1961–65. (American Council on Education Research Reports, Volume 1, Number 4.) Washington, D.C.: Office of Research, American Council on Education, 1966.

Astin, A. W., R. J. Panos, and J. A. Creager, *et al.* NATIONAL NORMS FOR ENTERING COLLEGE FRESHMAN– FALL, 1966. (American Council on Education Research Reports, Volume 2, Number 1.) Washington, D.C.: Office of Research, American Council on Education, 1967.

Astin, Alexander, R. J. Panos and J. Creager, *et al.* NATIONAL NORMS FOR ENTERING COLLEGE FRESHMAN, 1968. Washington: American Council on Education, 1969.

Astin, A. W., R. J. Panos and J. A. Creager, *et al.* SUPPLEMENTARY NATIONAL NORMS FOR FRESHMAN ENTERING COLLEGE IN 1966. (American Council on Education Research Reports, Volume 2, Number 3.) Washington, D.C.: Office of Research, American Council on Education, 1967.

Athey, Irene and James Trent. STUDENT CHARACTERISTICS ASSOCIATED WITH VARYING COLLEGE ATTENDANCE PATTERNS. Berkeley, California: Center for Research and Development in Higher Education, 1966.

Bailey, Benjamin H. CHARACTERISTICS OF HIGH SCHOOL SENIORS AS RELATED TO SUBSEQUENT COLLEGE ATTENDANCE. Morgantown: West Virginia University, 1966.

Baird, L. L. FAMILY INCOME AND THE CHARACTERISTICS OF COL-

LEGE-BOUND STUDENTS. (ACT Research Reports, Number 17.) Iowa City: ACT Program, 1967.

Baird, L. L. and J. L. Holland. THE FLOW OF HIGH SCHOOL STUDENTS TO SCHOOLS, COLLEGES, AND JOBS. (ACT Research Reports, Number 26.) Iowa City:ACT Program, 1968.

Baird, Leonard L. FAMILY INCOME AND THE CHARACTERISTICS OF COLLEGE-BOUND STUDENTS. Iowa City: American College Testing Program, 1967.

Baird, Leonard L. and James M. Richards, jr. THE EFFECTS OF SELECT-ING COLLEGE STUDENTS BY VARIOUS KINDS OF HIGH SCHOOL ACHIEVEMENT. Iowa City: American College Testing Program, 1968.

Beezer, Robert H. and Howard F. Hjelm. FACTORS RELATED TO COL-LEGE ATTENDANCE. Washington: United States Department of Health, Education and Welfare, Office of Education, 1961.

Berdie, R. F. AFTER HIGH SCHOOL - WHAT? Minneapolis, Minnesota: University of Minnesota Press, 1954.

Berdie, Ralph F., et al. WHO GOES TO COLLEGE? COMPARISON OF MINNESOTA COLLEGE FRESHMEN, 1950–60. Minneapolis: University of Minnesota Press, 1962.

Berdie, R. F. and A. B. Hood. DECISIONS FOR TOMORROW: PLANS OF HIGH SCHOOL SENIORS FOR AFTER GRADUATION.Minneapolis, Minnesota: University of Minnesota Press, 1965.

Blee, Myron R. "Factors Associated with the College Attendance Plans of Florida High School Seniors." Unpublished Ed.D. dissertation, University of Illinois, 1958.

Bureau of Institutional Research. THIRTEENTH ANNUAL SURVEY OF MINNESOTA COLLEGE AND UNIVERSITY ENROLLMENTS: A TABULAR SUMMARY. Minneapolis: University of Minnesota, 1966.

Caro, Francis George. "A Social Class Comparison of Attitudes of Male High School Students Towards College and Dominant Occupational Goals." Unpublished Ph.D. dissertation, University of Minnesota, 1962.

Cohen, Elizabeth G. "Parental Factors in Educational Mobility." Unpublished Ph.D. dissertation, Harvard University, 1958.

Coleman, J. S. and P. Rossi. DETERMINANTS AND CONSEQUENCES OF COLLEGE CHOICE. Chicago: National Opinion Research Center, 1964.

Corcoran, Mary and R. F. Keller. COLLEGE ATTENDANCE OF MINNE-SOTA HIGH SCHOOL SENIORS. Minneapolis: Bureau of Institutional Research, University of Minnesota, 1957.

Creager, John, et al. NATIONAL NORMS FOR ENTERING COLLEGE FRESHMAN: FALL, 1969. Washington, D.C.: American Council on Education, 1969.

Dole, A. A. FOLLOW-UP STUDIES OF THE DETERMINANTS OF EDU-CATIONAL-VOCATIONAL CHOICES. (United States Department of Health, Education and Welfare, Cooperative Research Project Number 2109.) Honolulu, Hawaii: University of Hawaii, 1965.

Doew, David E. A PROFILE OF THE JEWISH FRESHMAN. Washington, D. C.: American Council on Education, Office of Research, 1970.

Educational Testing Service. BACKGROUND FACTORS RELATING TO COLLEGE PLANS AND COLLEGE ENROLLMENT AMONG PUBLIC HIGH SCHOOL STUDENTS. Princeton, New Jersey: Educational Testing Service, 1957.

Fenske, R. H. "A Study of Post-high School Plans in Communities with Differing Educational Opportunities." Unpublished Ph.D. dissertation, University of Wisconsin, 1965.

Fine, Benjamin. ADMISSION TO AMERICAN COLLEGES: A STUDY OF CURRENT POLICY AND PRACTICE. New York: Harper, 1946.

Goetsch, H. B. PARENTAL INCOME AND COLLEGE OPPORTUNITIES. New York: Bureau of Publications, Teachers College, Columbia University, 1940.

Grossman, Charles S., et al. MIGRATION OF COLLEGE AND UNIVERSITY STUDENTS, STATE OF WASHINGTON. Seattle: Washington University, State Census Board, 1967.

Groat, Harry Theodore. "College Student Migration: 1887 to 1958." Unpublished Ph. D. dissertation, Brown University, 1962.

*Havemann, Ernest and Patricia S. West. THEY WENT TO COLLEGE. New York: Harcourt and Brace, 1952.

Hollinshead, Byron S. WHO SHOULD GO TO COLLEGE? New York: Columbia University Press, 1953.

Iffert, R. E. and B. S. Clarke. COLLEGE APPLICANTS, ENTRANTS, DROPOUTS. (UNITED STATES DEPARTMENT OF HEALTH, EDUCATION AND WELFARE, OFFICE OF EDUCATION), BULLETIN, NUMBER 29. Washington, D.C.: United States Government Printing Office, 1965.

Jaffe, A.J. and W. Adams. SOCIAL AND ECONOMIC CHARACTERISTICS OF THE COLLEGE POPULATION AND OTHERS WITH SOME COLLEGE TRAINING. (United States Department of Health, Education and Welfare, Cooperative Research Project Number 1269.) New York: Bureau of Applied Social Research, Columbia University, 1965.

Kiefer, John U. A STUDY OF WHITE NON-FLORIDA RESIDENT STUDENTS ENROLLED IN SELECTED FLORIDA COLLEGES AND UNIVERSITIES FOR THE FIRST TIME IN THE FALL, 1958. Tallahassee: Office of Institutional Research and Service, Florida State University, 1961.

Learned, W. and C. Langmuir. MISPLACEMENT IN COLLEGE. New York: Carnegie Foundation, 1938.

Little, James Kenneth. EXPLORATIONS INTO THE COLLEGE PLANS AND EXPERIENCES OF HIGH SCHOOL GRADUATES. Madison, Wisconsin: School of Education, University of Wisconsin, 1959.

Moore, Elmer J., E. L. Baum and R. B. Glasgow. ECONOMIC FACTORS INFLUENCING EDUCATIONAL ATTAINMENTS AND ASPIRATIONS OF FARM YOUTH. Washington: United States Department of Agriculture, Economic Research Service, Resource Development Economic Division, 1964.

Medsker, Leland L., James W. Trent, et al. THE INFLUENCE OF DIFFERENT TYPES OF PUBLIC HIGHER INSTITUTIONS ON COLLEGE ATTENDANCE FROM VARYING SOCIOECONOMIC AND ABILITY LEVELS. Berkeley, California: Center for the Study of Higher Education, University of California, 1965.

Nam, C. B. and J. D. Cowhig. FACTORS RELATED TO COLLEGE AT-
TENDANCE OF FARM AND NON-FARM HIGH SCHOOL GRADUATES:
1960. (United States Department of Commerce, Bureau of the Census, Series
Census - ERS, Number 32.) Washington, D.C.: Department of Commerce and
United States Department of Agriculture, 1962.

New York (State) University. Division of Research in Higher Education (by
Philip Cowen). FACTORS RELATED TO THE COLLEGE PLANS OF HIGH
SCHOOL SENIORS. Albany, 1960.

Nichols, R. C. COLLEGE PREFERENCES OF ELEVENTH GRADE STU-
DENTS. (National Merit Scholarship Corporation Research Reports, Volume 2,
Number 9.) Evanston, Illinois: National Merit Scholarship Corporation, 1966.

Oklahoma. State Regents for Higher Education. IN AND OUT OF COL-
LEGE. Oklahoma City, 1964.

Pace, C. R. SELECTIVE EDUCATION FOR A DIVERSITY OF STU-
DENTS RESEARCH MEMORANDUM RM-65-1. Princeton, New Jersey: Educational Testing Service, 1965.

Panos, R. J. and A. W. Astin. THEY WENT TO COLLEGE: A DESCRIP-
TIVE SUMMARY OF THE CLASS OF 1965. (American Council on Education
Research Reports, Volume 2, Number 5.) Washington, D.C.: Office of Research,
American Council on Education, 1967.

Prehn, John Wilford. "Social Mobility Through Higher Education and its
Relationship to Internal Migration." Unpublished Ph. D. dissertation, State
University of Iowa, 1964.

Ramsey, Robert R., jr. and Kenneth Schultz. STUDENT ADMISSIONS
AND PERFORMANCE: VIRGINIA STATE CONTROLLED INSTITUTIONS
OF HIGHER EDUCATION, 1967–1968. Richmond: State Council of Higher
Education for Virginia, 1969.

Reynolds, O. Edgar. THE SOCIAL AND ECONOMIC STATUS OF COL-
LEGE STUDENTS. New York: Teachers College, Columbia University, 1927.

Sandis. Eva Elizabeth. "The Influence of Parents on Students' Educational
Plans." Unpublished Ph.D. dissertation, Columbia University, 1967.

Schoenfeldt, Lyle F. ABILITY, FAMILY SOCIOECONOMIC LEVEL AND
ADVANCED EDUCATION. Washington: ERIC Document Reproduction Service, 1968.

Simmons, N. G., jr. "College-going Plans and Actual College Attendance of
Academically Superior High School Seniors in the State of Georgia for the
1961–62 School Year." Unpublished Ed.D. dissertation, University of Georgia,
1963.

Smith, George Baxter. WHO WOULD BE ELIMINATED? A STUDY OF
SELECTIVE ADMISSIONS TO COLLEGE. Lawrence: University of Kansas,
Department of Education, 1956.

Stice, G., W. G. Mollenkopf, and W. S. Torgerson, et al. BACKGROUND
FACTORS AND COLLEGE GOING PLANS AMONG HIGH APTITUDE PUB-
LIC HIGH SCHOOL SENIORS. Princeton: Educational Testing Service, 1956.

Stice, G., W. G. Mollenkopf and W. S. Torgerson, et al. BACKGROUND
FACTORS RELATING TO COLLEGE PLANS AND COLLEGE ENROLL-
MENT AMONG PUBLIC HIGH SCHOOL STUDENTS. Princeton: Educational
Testing Service, 1957.

Strang, Ruth. BEHAVIOR AND BACKGROUND OF STUDENTS IN COL-LEGE AND SECONDARY SCHOOL. New York: Harper, 1937.

Stroup, Francis and Deane Andrew. BARRIERS TO COLLEGE ATTEN-DANCE: THE REPORT OF A STUDY OF FACTORS RELATED TO EDUCA-TIONAL DISCONTINUANCE OF HIGH SCHOOL GRADUATES. Magnolia, Arkansas: 1958.

Thistlethwaite, D. L. RECRUITMENT AND RETENTION OF TALENTED COLLEGE STUDENTS: FINAL REPORT OF FACTORS INFLUENCING THE RECRUITMENT AND TRAINING OF INTELLECTUALLY TALENTED STU-DENTS IN HIGHER EDUCATIONAL PROGRAMS. (United States Department of Health, Education and Welfare, Cooperative Research Project Number 6571) Nashville, Tennessee: Vanderbilt University, 1963.

*Trent, James W. PERSONAL FACTORS IN COLLEGE CHOICE. Berke-ley: Center for the Study of Higher Education, University of California, 1965.

*Trent, J. W. and L. L. Medsker. BEYOND HIGH SCHOOL: A STUDY OF 10,000 HIGH SCHOOL GRADUATES. Berkeley, California: Center for Research and Development in Higher Education, University of California, 1967.

Trent, James W. and Leland L. Medsker. PATTERNS OF COLLEGE AT-TENDANCE. Berkeley: Center for Research and Development in Higher Educa-tion, University of California, 1968.

U.S. Department of Commerce. FARM POPULATION: EDUCATIONAL STATUS AND SCHOOL PLANS OF FARM AND NONFARM YOUTH, OCTO-BER, 1959. U.S. Department of Commerce, Bureau of the Census Series Census - AMS (P-27). Washington, D.C.: U.S. Department of Commerce and U.S. Depart-ment of Agriculture, 1960.

U.S. Department of Health, Education and Welfare. OPENING FALL EN-ROLLMENT IN HIGHER EDUCATION, 1966. Washington: Government Printing Office, 1966.

U.S. Office of Education. Division of Educational Statistics. RESIDENCE AND MIGRATION OF COLLEGE STUDENTS, FALL, 1963. Washington, 1964.

Wasburn, Courtland L. THE FLOW OF STUDENTS INTO, AMONG, AND THROUGH THE PUBLIC INSTITUTION OF HIGHER EDUCATION IN CALI-FORNIA. Sacramento: California Coordinating Council for Higher Education, 1967.

White, R. C. THESE WILL GO TO COLLEGE: A STUDY OF FUTURE DEMAND FOR ADMISSION TO COLLEGE BY SECONDARY SCHOOL GRADUATES IN THE CLEVELAND-AKRON-LORAINE AREA. Cleveland, Ohio: Western Reserve University Press, 1952.

Adams, B. N. and M. T. Meidam, "Economics, Family Structure, and Col-lege Attendance," AMERICAN JOURNAL OF SOCIOLOGY, 74 (November, 1968), 230–239.

Alexander, C. N., jr. "Ordinal Position and Social Mobility," SOCIO-METRY, 31 (September, 1968), 285–293.

Alexander, C. N., jr. and E. Q. Campbell. "Peer Influences on Adolescent Educational Aspirations," AMERICAN SOCIOLOGICAL REVIEW, 29 (August, 1964), 568–575

Anderson, C. Arnold. "A Skeptical Note on Education and Mobility," in A. H. Halsey, Jean Floud and C. Arnold Anderson, eds. EDUCATION, ECONOMY AND SOCIETY. New York: Free Press, 1965, 164–179.

Astin, A. W. "Some Characteristics of Student Bodies Entering Higher Educational Institutions," JOURNAL OF EDUCATIONAL PSYCHOLOGY, 55 (October, 1964), 267–275.

*Astin, Alexander W. "Who Goes Where to College?" in Kaoru Yamamoto, ed. THE COLLEGE STUDENT AND HIS CULTURE: AN ANALYSIS. Boston: Houghton Mifflin, 1968, 144–160.

Baird, L. L. and J. L. Holland. "The Flow of High School Students to Schools, Colleges and Jobs: A Re-examination of Some Old Questions by the Use of Multiple Indices of Talent," JOURNAL OF HUMAN RESOURCES, 4 (Number 1, 1968), 22–37.

Bayer, A. E. "Birth Order and College Attendance," JOURNAL OF MARRIAGE AND THE FAMILY, 28 (November, 1966), 480–484.

Bayer, A. E. "Marriage Plans and Educational Aspiration," AMERICAN JOURNAL OF SOCIOLOGY, 75 (September, 1969), 239–244.

Bayer, A. E. and R. F. Boruch. "Black and White Freshmen Entering Four-Year Colleges," EDUCATIONAL RECORD, 50 (Fall, 1969), 371–386.

Bordua, D. J. "Educational Aspirations and Parental Stress on College," SOCIAL FORCES, 38 (March, 1960), 262–269.

Boyle, R. P. "The Effect of the High School on Students' Aspirations," AMERICAN JOURNAL OF SOCIOLOGY, 71 (May, 1966), 628–639.

Boyle, R. P. "On Neighborhood Context and College Plans," AMERICAN SOCIOLOGICAL REVIEW, 31 (October, 1966), 706–7.

Burchinal, L. G. "Differences in Educational and Occupational Aspirations of Farm, Small Town and City Boys," RURAL SOCIOLOGY, 26 (June, 1961), 107–121.

Campbell, E. Q. and C. N. Alexander. "Structural Effects and Interpersonal Relationships," AMERICAN JOURNAL OF SOCIOLOGY, 71 (November, 1965), 284–289.

Carlin, E. A. "Of Those Who Begin," in P. L. Dressel, ed. EVALUATION IN THE BASIC COLLEGE AT MICHIGAN STATE UNIVERSITY. New York: Harper, 1958, 31–46.

Centi, P. and R. Sullivan. "Motives for College: Utilitarian or Liberal?" JOURNAL OF COLLEGE STUDENT PERSONNEL, 8 (September, 1967), 305–307.

Chapman, D. and J. Volkman. "A Social Determinant of Level of Aspiration," JOURNAL OF ABNORMAL AND SOCIAL PSYCHOLOGY, 34 (April, 1939), 225–238.

"Comparative Study of Social Origin of Students in the Universities," YEAR BOOK OF EDUCATION, (1950), 594–644.

Cutright, P. "Students' Decision to Attend College," JOURNAL OF EDUCATIONAL SOCIOLOGY, 33 (February, 1960), 292–299.

Davis, J. S. "Social Class Factors and School Attendance," HARVARD EDUCATIONAL REVIEW, 23 (Summer, 1953), 175–185.

Davis, E. "Some Aspects of Teen Age Image of Higher Education," SOCIAL SCIENCE QUARTERLY, 49 (September, 1968), 262–273.

Dole, A. A. and J. M. Digman. "Factors in College Attendance," JOURNAL OF APPLIED PSYCHOLOGY, 51 (June, 1967), 247–253.

Douan, Elizabeth and Carol Kaye, "Motivation Factors in College Entrance," in Nevitt Sanford, ed. THE AMERICAN COLLEGE. New York: John Wiley and Sons, 1962, 199–224.

Duncan, O. D., A. D. Haller and A. Portes. "Peer Influences on Aspirations: A Reinterpretation," AMERICAN JOURNAL OF SOCIOLOGY, 74 (September, 1968), 119–137.

Elks, R. A. and W. C. Lane. "Social Mobility and Career Orientation," SOCIOLOGY AND SOCIAL RESEARCH, 50 (April, 1966), 280–296.

Ellis, Robert A. "Some New Perspectives on Upward Mobility," URBAN AND SOCIAL CHANGE REVIEW, 4 (Fall, 1970), 15–17.

Ellis, Robert A. and W. Clayton Lane. "Structural Supports for Upward Mobility: Re-examines the Social Mechanisms that Lead Lower-Class Youth to Make Use of College as a Mobility Channel," AMERICAN SOCIOLOGICAL REVIEW, 28 (October, 1963), 743–756.

Farwell, E. D., P. A. Heist, and J. R. McConnell. "Colleges and Universities-Student Population," in C. W. Harris, ed. ENCYCLOPEDIA OF EDUCATIONAL RESEARCH. New York: MacMillan, 1960, 289–300.

Feldmesser, R. A. "Social Status and Access to Higher Education: A Comparison of the United States and the Soviet Union," HARVARD EDUCATIONAL REVIEW, 27 (Spring, 1957), 92–106.

Grant, C. W. "A Follow Up Study of Spring, 1966, High School Graduates in the State of Utah," PERSONNEL AND GUIDANCE JOURNAL, 47 (October, 1968), 157–162.

Groat, Theodore. "An Enigma for Future Enrollment Planning: College Student Migration," NORTH CENTRAL ASSOCIATION QUARTERLY, 37 (Winter, 1963), 229–232.

Groat, Theodore H. "Internal Migration Patterns of a Population Subgroup: College Students, 1887–1958," AMERICAN JOURNAL OF SOCIOLOGY, 119 (January 1964), 383–394.

Gummere, R. M. "America's Wandering Scholars," HARPER, 222 (May, 1961) 73–76.

Gummere, Richard, jr. "America's Wandering Scholars," in Samuel Bellman, ed. THE COLLEGE EXPERIENCE. San Francisco: Chandler, 1962, 42–53.

Haller, A. O. and C. E. Butterworth. "Peer Influences on Levels of Occupational and Educational Aspiration," SOCIAL FORCES, 38 (May, 1960), 289–295.

Hartnett, R. T. and J. A. Centra. "Attitudes and Secondary School Backgrounds of Catholics Entering College," SOCIOLOGY OF EDUCATION, 42 (Spring, 1969), 188–198.

Havighurst, Robert J. and Robert P. Rogers. "The Role of Motivation in Attendance at Post-High School Educational Institutions," in Byron S. Hollinshead, ed. WHO SHOULD GO TO COLLEGE? New York: Columbia University Press, 1953, 135–165.

374

Heist, P. "The Entering College Student—Background and Characteristics," REVIEW OF EDUCATIONAL RESEARCH, 30 (1960), 285–297.

Herriott, R. E. "Some Social Determinants of Educational Aspiration," HARVARD EDUCATIONAL REVIEW, 33 (Spring, 1963), 157–177.

Jaffe, A.J. and Walter Adams. "College Education for U.S. Youth: The Attitudes of Parents and Children," AMERICAN JOURNAL OF ECONOMICS AND SOCIOLOGY, 23 (July, 1964), 269–283.

Jencks, Christopher. "Social Stratification and Higher Education," HARVARD EDUCATIONAL REVIEW, 38 (Spring, 1968), 277–316.

Jantzen, S. "Should Everyone go to College?" SENIOR SCHOLASTIC, 99 (November 15, 1971), 4–9.

Johnstone, John W. and Larry Rosenberg. "Sociological Observations on the Privileged Adolescent," in James E. Adams, ed. UNDERSTANDING ADOLESCENCE: CURRENT DEVELOPMENTS IN ADOLESCENT PSYCHOLOGY. Boston: Allyn and Bacon, 1968, 318–336.

Kandel, D. B. and G. S. Lesser. "Parental and Peer Influences on Educational Plans of Adolescents," AMERICAN SOCOLOGICAL REVIEW, 34 (April, 1969), 213–223.

Kandel, D. and G. S. Lesser. "School, Family, and Peer Influence on Educational Plans of Adolescents in the United States and Denmark," SOCIOLOGY OF EDUCATION, 43 (Summer, 1970), 270–289.

Keller, R. J., et al. "The Minnesota Public High School Graduates of 1945 - one year Later," in Minnesota Commission on Higher Education, HIGHER EDUCATION IN MINNESOTA. Minneapolis, Minnesota: University of Minnesota Press, 1950, 81–115.

Krauss, I. "Sources of Educational Aspirations Among Working Class Youth," AMERICAN SOCIOLOGICAL REVIEW, 29 (December, 1964), 867–879.

McDill, Edward L. and James S. Coleman. "Family and Peer Influences in College Plans of High School Students," SOCIOLOGY OF EDUCATION, 38 (Winter, 1965), 112–126.

Michael, J. A. "High School Climates and Plans for Entering College," PUBLIC OPINION QUARTERLY, 25 (Winter, 1961), 585–595.

Michael, J. A. "On Neighborhood Context and College Plans (II)," AMERICAN SOCIOLOGICAL REVIEW, 31 (October, 1966), 702–706.

Mulligan, R. A. "Social Characteristics of College Students," AMERICAN SOCIOLOGICAL REVIEW, 18 (June, 1953), 305–310.

Mulligan, R. A. "Socio-economic Background and College Enrollment," AMERICAN SOCIOLOGICAL REVIEW, 16 (April, 1951), 188–196.

Panos, R. J. and A. W. Astin. "They Went to College: a Descriptive Summary of the Class of 1965," in Galen N. Drewry, ed. THE INSTRUCTIONAL PROCESS AND INSTITUTIONAL RESEARCH. Proceedings of Seventh Annual Forum of the Association for Institutional Research. N. P.: Association for Institutional Research, 1967, 85–94.

Pavalko, R. M. and M. H. Walizer. "Parental Educational Differences and the College Plans of Youth," SOCIOLOGY AND SOCIAL RESEARCH, 54 (October 1969), 80–89.

Picow, Steven J., and Arthur Cosby. "Social Origins, Occupational Goals and Southern Youth," YOUTH AND SOCIETY, 2 (March, 1971), 307–322.

Rehberg, R. A., W. E. Schafer and J. Sinclair. "Toward a Temporal Sequence of Adolescent Achievement Variables," AMERICAN SOCIOLOGICAL REVIEW, 35 (February, 1970), 34–48.

Rhodes, A. L. and C. B. Nam. "The Religious Context of Educational Expectation," AMERICAN SOCIOLOGICAL REVIEW, 35 (April, 1970), 253–267.

Rogoff, N. "Local Social Structure and Educational Selection," in A. H. Halsey, J. Floud and C. A. Anderson, eds. EDUCATION, ECONOMY AND SOCIETY: A READER IN THE SOCIOLOGY OF EDUCATION. New York: Free Press, 1963, 241–251.

Sewell, W. H. "Community of Residence and College Plans," AMERICAN SOCIOLOGICAL REVIEW, 29 (February, 1964), 24–38.

Sewell, William H. and M. J. Armer. "Neighborhood Context and College Plans," AMERICAN SOCIOLOGICAL REVIEW, 3 (April, 1966), 159–168.

Sewell, William, Archie O. Haller and Murray A. Straus. "Social Status and Educational and Occupational Aspiration," AMERICAN SOCIOLOGICAL REVIEW, 22 (February, 1957), 67–73.

Sewell, W. H. and V. P. Shah. "Social Class, Parental Encouragement, and Educational Aspirations," AMERICAN JOURNAL OF SOCIOLOGY, 73 (March, 1968), 559–572.

Sewell, William H. and Vimal P. Shah. "Socioeconomic Status, Intelligence, and the Attainment of Higher Education," SOCIOLOGY OF EDUCATION, 40 (Winter, 1967), 1–23.

Shuttleworth, F. K. "Discrimination in College Opportunities and Admissions," SCHOOL AND SOCIETY, 74 (December 22, 1951), 398–402.

Sibley, E. "Some Demographic Clues to Stratification," AMERICAN SOCIOLOGICAL REVIEW, 7 (June, 1942), 322–330.

Simpson, Richard L. "Parental Influence, Anticipatory Socialization, and Social Mobility," AMERICAN SOCIOLOGICAL REVIEW, 27 (August, 1962), 517–522.

Smith, G. B. "Who Would be Eliminated?: A Study of Selective Admission to College," KANSAS STUDIES IN EDUCATION. 7, (Number 1, 1956).

Spady, W. G., jr. "Educational Mobility and Access: Growth and Paradoxes," AMERICAN JOURNAL OF SOCIOLOGY, 23 (November, 1967), 273–286.

Steahr, Thomas and Calvin Schmid. "College Student Migration in the United States," JOURNAL OF HIGHER EDUCATION, 43 (June, 1972), 441–463.

Stewart, D. W. and R. P. Chambers. "Status Background of the Veteran College Student," SOCIOLOGY AND SOCIAL RESEARCH, 35 (September, 1950), 12–21.

Stevens, E. H. "Motivation for College in High-school Boys," SCHOOL REVIEW, 66 (Autumn, 1958), 341–350.

Thaden, John Fred. "The Changing College Student Population," in Eric Gardener, ed. THE COLLEGE STUDENT. New York: Center for Applied Research in Education, 1965, 18–40.

Turner, R. H. "On Neighborhood Context and College Plans (I)," AMERI-CAN SOCIOLOGICAL REVIEW, 31 (October, 1966), 698–702.

Wagner, H. R., *et al.* "Religious Background and Higher Education," AMER-ICAN SOCIOLOGICAL REVIEW, 24 (December, 1959), 852–856.

Webster, H., *et al.* "Individual Differences among College Freshmen," in N. B. Henry, ed. NATIONAL SOCIETY FOR THE STUDY OF EDUCATION YEARBOOK, (pt. 1, 1961), 145–163.

West, Joseph V. "Characteristics and Changes in the 1961 Class, Baylor University," in C. H. Bagley, ed. DESIGN AND METHODOLOGY IN INSTITU-TIONAL RESEARCH. (Proceedings of Fifth Annual National Institutional Research Forum.) Pullman, Washington: Washington State University, Office of Institutional Research, 1965, 169–182.

Whalen, W. J. "Why Catholics Attend Non-Catholic Colleges," CATHOLIC WORLD, 182 (October, 1955), 31–36.

Wilson, A. B. "Residential Segregation of Social Classes and Aspiration of High School Boys," AMERICAN SOCIOLOGICAL REVIEW, 24 (December, 1959), 836–843.

Wolfle, Dael. "Educational Opportunity, Measured Intelligence, and Social Background," in A. H. Halsey, Jean Floud and Arnold C. Anderson, eds. EDU-CATION, ECONOMY AND SOCIETY, New York: Free Press, 1965, 216–240.

A.2. The Student Body at Varying Types of Institutions

Astin, Alexander W. WHO GOES WHERE TO COLLEGE. Chicago: Science Research Associates, 1965.

American College Testing Program. THE TWO YEAR COLLEGE AND ITS STUDENTS. Iowa City: American College Testing Program, 1969.

ACT Research and Development Division. COLLEGE STUDENT PRO-FILES. Iowa City: American College Testing Program, 1966.

Badgett, John L., jr. THE RELATIONSHIP BETWEEN SELF-CONCEPTS AND CERTAIN ACADEMIC, VOCATIONAL, BIOGRAPHICAL, AND PER-SONALITY VARIABLES OF ENTERING MALE FRESHMEN AT A MAJOR LAND GRANT UNIVERSITY. College Station: Texas A and M University, 1968.

Baird, L. L. THE UNDECIDED STUDENT—HOW DIFFERENT IS HE?" (ACT Research Reports, Number 22.) Iowa City: ACT Program, 1967.

Birney, R. C., H. R. Coplin, and R. F. Grose. THE CLASS OF 1959 AT AMHERST COLLEGE: A PRELIMINARY REPORT. Amherst, Massachusetts: Committee on Guidance and Counseling, Amherst College, 1960.

Bolick, Gerald M. SOCIO-ECONOMIC PROFILE OF CREDIT STUDENTS IN THE NORTH CAROLINA COMMUNITY COLLEGE SYSTEM. Washington: U.S. Department of Health, Education and Welfare, Office of Education, Bu-reau of Research, 1969.

Coker, D. L. "Diversity of Scholastic Aptitude, Non-Intellectual Attributes and Environmental Characteristics Among Students and Campuses." Unpub-lished Ph.D. dissertation, Indiana University, 1966.

Cross, Patricia. THE JUNIOR COLLEGE STUDENT: A RESEARCH DESCRIPTION. Princeton: Educational Testing Service, 1968.

Dunteman, G. H., H. E. Anderson, jr., and J. R. Barry, *et al.* CHARACTERISTICS OF STUDENTS IN THE HEALTH RELATED PROFESSIONS. (Rehabilitation Monograph Series, Number 2,) Gainesville, Florida: University of Florida, 1966.

Franklin, Elton. CHARACTERISTICS OF THE STUDENT POPULATION, UNIVERSITY OF ALABAMA RESIDENT CENTER, HUNTSVILLE, ALABAMA. Nashville: George Peabody College for Teachers, 1960.

Hall, E. and B. Borger, COLLEGE GOALS AND REASONS FOR SELECTING THE UNIVERSITY OF FLORIDA: LOWER DIVISION STUDENTS ENTERING SEPTEMBER 1965. Mental Health Project Bulletin Number 23. Gainsville, Florida: Student Mental Health Project, University of Florida, 1965.

Henry, M., *et al.* MONTEITH COLLEGE: PRELIMINARY REPORT ON THE ENTERING STUDENTS OF THE FALL TERM, 1966. Berkeley, California: Center for Research and Development in Higher Education, University of California, Berkeley, 1967.

Hood, Albert B. WHAT TYPE OF COLLEGE FOR WHAT TYPE OF STUDENT? Minnesota Studies in Student Personnel Work, Volume 4, 1968.

Kinney, Cherry Carter. "Social Origins of University Students: A Socio-Economic Analysis of the 1960 Indiana University Student Body." Unpublished Ph.D. dissertation, Indiana University, 1965.

Knueppel, M. L. "Distinguishing Characteristics of Students Entering the Public Versus Private Institutions of Higher Education in Wisconsin." Unpublished Ph.D. dissertation, University of Wisconsin, 1959.

Koos, Leonard V. THE COMMUNITY COLLEGE STUDENT. Gainesville, Florida: University of Florida Press, 1970.

LeCroy, Richard Jan. A STUDY OF STUDENTS WHO ENTERED TWO YEAR COLLEGES IN VIRGINIA AS FRESHMEN IN THE FALL 1963. Richmond: Higher Education Commission, 1966.

Medsker, Leland L. and Dale Tillery. BREAKING THE ACCESS BARRIERS: A PROFILE OF TWO YEAR COLLEGES. New York: McGraw Hill, 1971.

Morrill, W. H. "The Relationship of Student Personality, Area of Concentration and College Environment." Unpublished Ph.D. Dissertation, University of Missouri, 1966.

Nester, Emery Walter, jr. "The Relationship Between Certain Student Personality Characteristics and Choice of College and Related Curricula." Unpublished Ed.D. dissertation, Arizona State University, 1969.

Panos, R. J. SOME CHARACTERISTICS OF JUNIOR COLLEGE STUDENTS. (American Council on Education Research Reports, Volume 1, Number 2.) Washington, D.C.: Office of Research. American Council on Education, 1967.

Reeves, F. W. and J. D. Russell. ADMISSION AND RETENTION OF UNIVERSITY STUDENTS. Chicago: University of Chicago Press, 1933.

Richards, James M., jr. and John L. Holland. A FACTOR ANALYSIS OF STUDENT "EXPLANATION" OF THEIR CHOICE OF A COLLEGE. Iowa City: American College Testing Program, 1965.

Seron, Merron S. ANALYSIS OF FACTORS WHICH DETERMINE

CHOICE OF COLLEGE AMONG URBAN, SUBURBAN, AND RURAL HIGH SCHOOL STUDENTS. FINAL REPORT. Evanston, Illinois: Northwestern University, 1967.

Snyder, Fred A. and Clyde E. Blocker. A PROFILE OF STUDENTS. Harrisburg: Harrisburg Area Community College, 1969.

Sullivan, John Joseph. A LOOK AT THE UNIVERSITY OF GEORGIA CLASS OF 1966. Athens: Institute of Higher Education, University of Georgia, 1967.

Sussman, L. and G. N. Levine. THE ENTERING FRESHMAN AT MASSACHUSETTS INSTITUTE OF TECHNOLOGY: CLASS OF '61. Cambridge, Massachusetts: Massachusetts Institute of Technology, 1958.

Thistlethwaite, D. L. RECRUITMENT AND RETENTION OF TALENTED COLLEGE STUDENTS: FINAL REPORT OF FACTORS INFLUENCING THE RECRUITMENT AND TRAINING OF INTELLECTUALLY TALENTED STUDENTS IN HIGHER EDUCATION PROGRAM. U. S. Department of Health, Education and Welfare, Cooperative Research Project, Number 657. Nashville: Vanderbilt University, 1963.

Tillery, H. D. "Differential Characteristics of Entering Freshmen at the University of California and Their Peers at California Junior Colleges." Unpublished Ph.D. dissertation, University of California, Berkeley, 1964.

Washington (State). Department of Education. COMMUNITY COLLEGE STUDENT CHARACTERISTICS. Olympia, 1965.

Astin, A. W. "College Preferences of Very Able College Students." COLLEGE AND UNIVERSITY, 40 (Spring, 1965), 282–297.

Astin, Alexander W. "Distribution of Students Among Higher Educational Institutions," JOURNAL OF EDUCATIONAL PSYCHOLOGY, 55 (October, 1964), 276–287.

Astin, A. W. "The Distribution of 'Wealth' in Higher Education," COLLEGE AND UNIVERSITY, 37 (Winter, 1962), 113–125.

Boroff, David. "Smith: a College for ARG's with High IQ's," in Samuel I. Bellman, ed. THE COLLEGE EXPERIENCE. San Francisco: Chandler, 1962, 147–158.

Brown, R. D. "Student Characteristics and Institutional Impact of the Large Publicly Controlled versus the Small Private Institution," COLLEGE AND UNIVERSITY, 42 (Spring, 1967), 325–336.

Campbell, David P. "The Right College," in Fred F. Harcleroad, ed. ISSUES OF THE SEVENTIES. San Francisco: Jossey-Bass, 1970, 85–98.

Covan, J. T. "What Kind of College Gets the Bright Students?" JOURNAL OF HIGHER EDUCATION, 8 (May, 1937), 265–272.

Clark, B. R. "College Image and Student Selection," in SELECTION AND EDUCATIONAL DIFFERENTIATION. Berkeley, California: Field Service Center and Center for the Study of Higher Education, University of California, 1959.

Cooley, W. W. "Differences among College Students," in J. C. Flanagan and W. W. Cooley, eds. PROJECT TALENT: ONE YEAR FOLLOW-UP STUDIES. Pittsburgh: School of Education, University of Pittsburgh, 1966, 131–156.

Estadt, B. K. "Profile of a Small College Seminary," NATIONAL CATHO-LIC EDUCATIONAL ASSOCIATION BULLETIN, 64 (May, 1968), 43–51.

Farwell, E. D., *et al.* "Student Personality Characteristics Associated with Groups of Colleges and Fields of Study," COLLEGE AND UNIVERSITY, 37 (Number 3, Spring, 1962), 229–241.

Hawes, Gene. "The Colleges of America's Upper Class," in Esther Lloyd Jones and Herman Estrin, eds. THE AMERICAN STUDENT AND HIS COL-LEGE. Boston: Houghton Mifflin, 1967, 73–80.

Heist, P. and H. Webster. "Differential Characteristics of Student Bodies-Implications for Selection and Study of Undergraduates," in SELECTION AND EDUCATIONAL DIFFERENTATION. Berkeley, California: Center for Research and Development in Higher Education, 1960, 91–106.

Holland, J. L. "Determinants of College Choice," COLLEGE AND UNI-VERSITY, 35 (Fall, 1959), 11–28.

Holland, J. L. "Student Explanations of College Choice and Their Rela-tion to College Popularity, College Productivity and Sex Differences," COL-LEGE AND UNIVERSITY, 33 (Spring, 1958), 313–320.

Holland, J. L. "Parental Expectations and Attitudes about Colleges," COLLEGE AND UNIVERSITY, 34 (Winter, 1959), 164–170.

Hoyt, D. P. "Description and Prediction of Diversity among Junior Col-leges," PERSONNEL AND GUIDANCE JOURNAL, 46 (June, 1968), 997–1004.

McConnell, T.R. "Problems of Distributing Students Among Institutions with Varying Characteristics," NORTH CENTRAL ASSOCIATION QUAR-TERLY, 35 (January, 1961), 226–238.

*McConnell, T. R. and Paul Heist. "The Diverse College Student Population," in Nevitt Sanford, ed. THE AMERICAN COLLEGE. New York: Wiley, 1964, 225–252.

Milholland, J. E., F. B. Worner and H. Walker, *et al.* "College Enrollments of the Highest Ten Per Cent of Michigan High School Graduates, 1960," COL-LEGE AND UNIVERSITY, 39 (Fall, 1963), 64–71.

Power, E. J. "Changing Student in the Catholic College: Excerpt from Cath-olic Higher Education in America: A History," SCHOOL AND SOCIETY, 99 (December, 1971), 493–496.

Richards, J. M. and L. S. Braskamp. "Who Goes Where to Junior College?" in THE TWO-YEAR COLLEGE AND ITS STUDENTS: AN EMPIRICAL REPORT. Iowa City: American College Testing Program, 1969.

Schoenfeldt, L. S. "Education after High School," SOCIOLOGY OF EDU-CATION, 41 (Spring, 1968), 350–359.

Sims, V. M. "Social Class Affiliation of Students in a Southern State Uni-versity," JOURNAL OF SOCIAL PSYCHOLOGY, 32 (November, 1956), 163–175.

Snelling, W. R. and R. Boruch. "Factors Influencing Student Choice of College and Course of Study," JOURNAL OF CHEMICAL EDUCATION, 47 (May, 1970), 326–330.

Stordahl, K. E. "Student Perceptions of Influences on College Choice," JOURNAL OF EDUCATIONAL RESEARCH, 63 (January, 1970), 209–212.

Trent, J. W. "A New Look at Recruitment Policies," COLLEGE BOARD REVIEW, 58 (Winter, 1965–66), 7–11.

A.3. Student Background and the Choice of Academic Fields

Abe, Clifford and John L. Holland. A DESCRIPTION OF COLLEGE FRESHMEN—STUDENTS WITH DIFFERENT CHOICES OF MAJOR FIELDS. Iowa City; American College Testing Program, 1965.

Astin, Helen S. and Ann Bisconti. TRENDS IN ACADEMIC AND CAREER PLANS OF COLLEGE FRESHMEN. Bethlehem, Pennsylvania: College Placement Council, 1972.

Bedison, George V. "A Comparative Study of the Social and Economic Status of Students Enrolled in Schools of Education in the Universities in Pennsylvania and Neighboring States. Unpublished Ed. D. dissertation, University of Pittsburgh, 1955.

Brass, R. O. "An Investigation of Selected Personal Background Factors and Reasons Related to Students who Change Schools within Purdue University." Unpublished Ph.D. dissertation, Purdue University, 1956.

Brown, Frederick Gramm. "Measured Personality Characteristics of Liberal Arts College Freshmen." Unpublished Ph.D. dissertation, University of Minnesota, 1958.

Campbell, James Patrick. "A Multivariate Analysis of the Relationship of Selected Academic Interest and Aptitude Variables in Choice of Major Field." Unpublished Ph.D. dissertation, Temple University, 1966.

Clayton, Howard. AN INVESTIGATION OF PERSONALITY CHARACTERISTICS AMONG LIBRARY STUDENTS AT ONE MIDWESTERN UNIVERSITY. Brockport, New York: State University of New York, Brockport, 1968.

Copp, Carol Mary. "The Student of Nursing as a Marginal Person." Unpublished Ph.D. dissertation, University of Colorado, 1968.

Educational Testing Service. STATISTICAL STUDIES OF SELECTIVE SERVICE TESTING, 1951–1953. Statistical Report SR-55-30. Princeton, New Jersey: Educational Testing Service, 1957.

Filbeck, R. W. "The Differentiation of Freshman Curricular Groups by Means of Empirically Derived Academic Interest Scales." Unpublished Ph.D. dissertation, University of Missouri, 1959.

Henry, Joan Louise. "Student Characteristics and Perceptions of Indiana University." Unpublished Ed.D. dissertation. Indiana University, 1966.

Johnson, Cecil H. and Kinsler B. Mack. WHY STUDENTS SELECT AGRICULTURE AS A MAJOR COURSE OF STUDY. Clemson University, South Carolina Department of Agricultural Education, 1963.

King, R. G. "The Prediction of Choice of Undergraduate Field of Concentration in Harvard College." Unpublished Ph.D. dissertation, Howard University, 1958.

Kitchell, Myrtle Elizabeth. "A Study of the Relationship of Certain Socio-economic Factors to the Choice of Educational Institution and Program of First-year Students in Nursing in the North Central Region." Unpublished Ph.D. dissertation, University of Minnesota, 1955.

Koprowski, Eugene J. "Ego Strength and Realism in Curriculum Choice." Unpublished Ph.D. dissertation, University of Denver, 1962.

LeBold, William Kerns. "A Longitudinal Study of Purdue Engineering Students." Unpublished Ph.D. dissertation, Purdue University, 1957.

Lionberger, Herbert F., C. L. Gregory and H. C. Chang. EDUCATIONAL CHOICES AND EXPECTATIONS OF MALE STUDENTS ENTERING A MIDWESTERN UNIVERSITY. Columbia: University of Missouri, 1967.

McCarthy, Thomas J. PERSONALITY TRAITS OF SEMINARIANS. Washington, D.C.: Catholic University of America Press, 1942.

Parton, Ronald Burton. "Selection of Education as a Major at the University of Puget Sound." Unpublished Ph.D. dissertation, University of Missouri, Columbia, 1966.

Pavalko, Ronald Michael. "The Predental Student: A Study of Occupational Choice and Professional Recruitment." Unpublished Ph.D. dissertation, University of California, Los Angeles, 1963.

Regan, M. C. and O. E. Thompson. THE ENTERING STUDENT: COLLEGE OF AGRICULTURE. Research Monograph. Number 1. Davis, California: Department of Agricultural Education, University of California, Davis, 1965.

Rubenstein, Frank Jay. "A Study of Freshman Nursing Students' Role Conceptions." Unpublished Ph. D. dissertation, University of Pittsburgh, 1964.

Saddler, L. E. "A Comparison of Students Remaining in an Engineering Curriculum and Students Transferring from Engineering to Other Curricula." Unpublished Ph. D. dissertation, University of Missouri, 1949.

Sherry, N. M. "Inconsistency Between Measured Interest and Choice of College Major." Unpublished Ph. D. dissertation, University of California, Berkeley, 1963.

Stellwagen, Walter Richard. "An Examination of the Use of Linear and Nonlinear Discriminant Functions in the Classification of College Students Into Academic Groups." Unpublished Ph. D. dissertation, Syracuse University, 1958.

Steinberg, Carl. "The Relation of Interests, Values and Personality to the Major Field of Study in College." Unpublished Ph. D. dissertation, New York University, 1953.

Stevens, William Charles. "The Quantification of Personal Data For Use in A Multivariate Statistical Analysis of Differences Between Selected Groups of College Students." Unpublished Ph. D. dissertation, University of Minnesota, 1953.

Sundheim, Betty Jean Madden. "The Relationships Between "N" Achievement, "N" Affiliation, Sex-role Concepts, Academic Grades, and Curricular Choice." Unpublished Ph. D. dissertation, Columbia University, 1962.

Akenson, D. H. and R. S. Beecher. "Speculations on Change of College Major," COLLEGE AND UNIVERSITY, 42 (Winter, 1967), 175–180.

Barrett, D. M. "Aptitude and Interest Patterns of Art Majors in a Liberal Arts College," JOURNAL OF APPLIED PSYCHOLOGY, 29 (December, 1945), 483–492.

382

Bereiter, Carl and Mervin B. Freedman. "Field Study and the People in Them," in Nevitt Sanford, ed. THE AMERICAN COLLEGE. New York: Wiley, 1964, 563–596.

Bordin, E. S. and E. H. Wilson. "Change of Interest as a Function of Shift in Curricular Orientation," EDUCATIONAL AND PSYCHOLOGICAL MEASUREMENT, 13 (Summer, 1953), 297–307.

Borg, W. R. "Personality Characteristics of a Group of College Art Students," JOURNAL OF EDUCATIONAL PSYCHOLOGY, 43 (March, 1952), 149–156.

Brown, R. D. "Curricular Changers and Persisters: How Do They Differ?" JOURNAL OF COLLEGE STUDENT PERSONNEL, 11 (September, 1970), 366–372.

Clark, J. H. "The Interpretation of the M M P I Profiles of College Students: A Comparison by College Major Subject," JOURNAL OF CLINICAL PSYCHOLOGY, 9 (October, 1953), 382–384.

Congdon, Robert G. "Personality Factors and the Capacity to Meet Curriculum Demands," PERSONNEL AND GUIDANCE JOURNAL, 42 (April, 1964), 766–775.

Cook, M. D. "College Students Change Majors," SCHOOL AND SOCIETY, 93 (May 1, 1965), 271–273.

Eickhorn, R. L. and G. J. Kallas. "Social Class Background as a Predictor of Academic Success in Engineering," Journal of Engineering Education, 52 (April, 1962), 507–512.

Elton, C. F. and H. A. Rose. "Personality Characteristics of Students who Transfer Out of Engineering," PERSONNEL AND GUIDANCE JOURNAL, 45 (May, 1967), 911–915.

Friedenberg, Edgar Z. "Why Students Leave Science," COMMENTARY, 32 (August, 1961), 144–155.

Fullmer, D. W. "Success and Perseverance of University Students," JOURNAL OF HIGHER EDUCATION, 27 (November, 1956), 445–447.

Gamble, G. W. "Pre-College Experiences and Curriculum Changes by College Students," PERSONNEL AND GUIDANCE JOURNAL, 40 (February, 1962), 561–564.

Goodman, C. H. "A Comparison of the Interests and Personality Traits of Engineers and Liberal Arts Students," JOURNAL OF APPLIED PSYCHOLOGY, 26 (December, 1942), 721–737.

Hancock, J. W. and G. C. Carter. "Student Personality Traits and Curriculae of Enrollment," JOURNAL OF EDUCATIONAL RESEARCH, 43 (November, 1954), 225–227.

Harder, D. F. "Differentiation of Curricular Groups Based upon Responses to Unique Items of the M M P I," JOURNAL OF COUNSELING PSYCHOLOGY, 6 (Spring, 1959), 28–34.

Holland, J. L. and R. C. Nichols. "Exploration of a Theory of Vocational Choice III. A Longitudinal Study of Change in Major Field of Study." PERSONNEL AND GUIDANCE JOURNAL, 43 (November, 1964), 235–242.

Korn, H. A. "Differences between Majors in Engineering and Physical Sciences on CPI and SVIB Scores," JOURNAL OF COUNSELING PSYCHOLOGY, 9 (Fall, 1962), 306–312.

Kraushopf, C. J., Dorothy Elder and Delia Mapeli *et al.* "Some Characteristics of Students who Transfer from Engineering to Arts and Sciences," VOCATIONAL GUIDANCE QUARTERLY, 12 (Spring, 1964), 187–191.

Lehmann, I. F. "Curricular Differences in Selected Cognitive and Affective Characteristics," JOURNAL OF EDUCATIONAL MEASUREMENT, 2 (June, 1965), 103–110.

Manbeck, M. W. "Why Veterans Change Registration in Courses," JOURNAL OF EDUCATIONAL RESEARCH, 46 (April, 1953), 621–625.

Matteson, R. W. "Concomitants of Changing Curriculum Preference," COLLEGE AND UNIVERSITY, 28 (January, 1953), 223–235.

Medalia, N. Z. "Choice of College Major by Contest Mobility," SOCIOLOGY OF EDUCATION, 41 (Spring, 1968), 282–290.

Norman, R. D. and M. Redlo. "MMPI Personality Patterns for Various College Major Groups," JOURNAL OF APPLIED PSYCHOLOGY, 36 (December, 1952), 404–409.

Pierson, R. R. "Changes of Majors by University Students," PERSONNEL AND GUIDANCE JOURNAL, 40 (January, 1962), 458–461.

Sternberg, Carl. "Personality Traits Patterns of College Students Majoring in Different Fields," PSYCHOLOGICAL MONOGRAPHS: GENERAL AND APPLIED, 69 (Number 18, 1955), 1–21.

Stewart, L. H. "Characteristics of Junior College Students in Occupationally Oriented Curricula," JOURNAL OF COUNSELING PSYCHOLOGY, 13 (Spring, 1966), 46–52.

Teevan, L. C. "Personality Correlates of Undergraduate Field of Specialization," JOURNAL OF CONSULTING PSYCHOLOGY, 18 (Number 3, 1954), 212–214.

Tisdale, J. R. "The Selection of College Majors," JOURNAL OF EDUCATIONAL RESEARCH, 61 (October, 1967), 90–91.

Trow, Martin. "Some Implications of the Social Origins of Engineers," in SCIENTIFIC MANPOWER, 1958. Washington: Government Printing Office, 1959, 67–74.

Walters, A. and A. C. Eurich. "A Quantitative Study of the Major Interests of College Students," JOURNAL OF EDUCATIONAL PSYCHOLOGY, 27 (November, 1936), 561–571.

Warren, J. R. "Self Concept, Occupational Role Expectation, and Change in College Major," JOURNAL OF COUNSELING PSYCHOLOGY, 8 (Summer, 1961), 164–169.

Weitz, H. *et al.* "Relationships Between the Choice of a Major Field of Study and Academic Preparation and Performance," EDUCATIONAL AND PSYCHOLOGICAL MEASUREMENT, 15 (Number 1, 1955), 28–38.

Wolfle, D. and T. Oxtoby. "Distributions of Ability of Students Specializing in Different Fields," SCIENCE, 116 (September 26, 1952), 311–314.

A.4. Why Students Get Into College

A.4.a. The College Admission System

Miller, Robert Emil. "Policies and Practices Relating to Admission of Non-Resident Students to State Universities." Unpublished Ph. D. dissertation, University of Connecticut, 1966.

Nichols, R. C. THE ORIGIN AND DEVELOPMENT OF TALENT. National Merit Scholarship Corporation Research Reports, Volume 2, Number 70. Evanston, Illinois: National Merit Scholarship Corporation, 1966.

Brookover, Wilbur. "Selection and Admission Policies and Practice," in Eric Gardner, ed. THE COLLEGE STUDENT, New York: Center for Applied Research in Education, 1965, 41–57.

Cohen, Irving. "The Obsolescence and Replacement of College Admissions Criteria," in Patricia Wright, ed. INSTITUTIONAL RESEARCH AND COMMUNICATION IN HIGHER EDUCATION. Proceedings of the Tenth Annual Forum on Institutional Research. N. P.: Association for Institutional Research, 1970, 250–254.

Fishman, Joshua A. "Non-Intellective Factors as Prediction, as Criteria, and as Contingencies in Selection and Guidance," in SELECTION AND EDUCATIONAL DIFFERENTIATION. Report of a Conference, 1959. Berkeley: Field Service Center and Center for the Study of Higher Education, University of California, Berkeley, 1959, 55–78.

Fishman, Joshua A. "Some Social-Psychological Theory for Selecting and Guiding College Students," in Nevitt Sanford, ed. THE AMERICAN COLLEGE. New York: John Wiley and Sons, 1964, 666–689.

Fishman, J. A. "Unsolved Criterion Problems in the Selection of College Students," HARVARD EDUCATION REVIEW, 28 (Fall, 1958), 340–349.

Hampton, Robert E. "Testing and Equality of Career Opportunity," in F. F. Korten, S. W. Cook and J. I. Lacey, eds. PSYCHOLOGY AND THE PROBLEMS OF SOCIETY. Washington: American Psychological Association, 1970, 289–294.

Heist, P. and H. Webster. "A Research Orientation to Selection Admission, and Differential Education," in H. T. Sprague, ed. RESEARCH ON COLLEGE STUDENTS: INSTITUTE LECTURES CONSIDERING RECENT RESEARCH ON COLLEGE STUDENTS MOTIVATION, VALUES AND ATTITUDES AND CAMPUS CULTURES. Boulder, Colorado: Western Interstate Commission for Higher Education and Berkeley: Center for Higher Education, 1960.

Hills, John. "Issues in College Admissions," COLLEGE AND UNIVERSITY, Journal 1 (Fall, 1962), 15–21.

Kinkead, K. T. "Reporter at Large: Selecting the Yale Freshman Class," NEW YORKER, 36 (September 10, 1960), 132–136+.

Knoell, D. M. "Are Our Colleges Really Accessible to the Poor?" JUNIOR COLLEGE JOURNAL, 39 (October, 1968), 9–11.

McConnell, T. R. "Differential Selectivity of American Higher Education," in K. E. Anderson, ed. THE COMING CRISIS IN THE SELECTION OF STU-

DENTS FOR COLLEGE ENTRANCE. Washington, D.C.: American Educational Research Association, 1960, 3–9.

Rosen, B. "Use of Potentially Discriminatory Questions on College Applications in the Southern United States," JOURNAL OF NEGRO EDUCATION, 38 (Spring, 1969), 120–124.

Wring, Cliff W., jr. "Student Selection, the Educational Environment, and the Cultivation of Talent," DAEDALUS, 94 (Summer, 1965), 632–641.

Wolff, R. P. "Race to College," ATLANTIC, 216 (November, 1965), 145–148.

A.4.b. Reform Of College Admissions: The Open Door

*Astin, Helen, et al. HIGHER EDUCATION AND THE DISADVANTAGED STUDENT. Washington, D.C.: Human Services Press, 1972.

*Clark, B. R. THE OPEN DOOR COLLEGE: A CASE STUDY. New York: McGraw Hill, 1960.

Cole, C. C., jr. ENCOURAGING SCIENTIFIC TALENT: A STUDY OF AMERICA'S ABLE STUDENTS WHO ARE LOST TO COLLEGE AND WAYS OF ATTRACTING THEM TO COLLEGE AND SCIENCE CAREERS. New York: College Entrance Examination Board, 1956.

*Cross, K. Patricia. BEYOND THE OPEN DOOR: NEW STUDENTS IN HIGHER EDUCATION. San Francisco: Jossey Bass, 1972.

Gordon, Edmund W. and D. A. Wilkerson. COMPENSATORY EDUCATION FOR THE DISADVANTAGED. New York: College Entrance Examination Board, 1966.

Invitational Conference on Encouraging Personal Incentive for Higher Education among Talented but Disadvantaged Youth. Washington, 1959. Nicholas C. Brown, ed. HIGHER EDUCATION: INCENTIVES AND OBSTACLES: A REPORT. Washington: American Council on Education, 1960.

Katz, Jerry Martin. "The Educational Shibboleth: Equality of Opportunity in a Democratic Institution, the Public Junior College." Unpublished Ph. D. dissertation, University of California, Los Angeles, 1967.

Kroepsh, Robert H. and Ian M. Thompson. URBAN AND MINORITY CENTERED PROGRAMS IN WESTERN COLLEGES AND UNIVERSITIES, 1969–1970. Boulder, Colorado: Western Interstate Commission for Higher Education, 1969.

Martyn, Kenneth A. INCREASING OPPORTUNITIES FOR DISADVANTAGED STUDENTS: FINAL REPORT. A REPORT TO THE JOINT COMMITTEE ON HIGHER EDUCATION, CALIFORNIA LEGISLATURE. Los Angeles, 1969.

New York (State) University. OPEN ADMISSIONS TO POST-SECONDARY EDUCATION: A STATEMENT BY THE REGENTS OF THE UNIVERSITY OF THE STATE OF NEW YORK. Albany, 1969.

Adams, W. Sam "Meeting the Challenges of open Admissions and Maintenance of Academic Standards" in Clifford T. Stewart, ed. INSTITUTIONAL

RESEARCH AND INSTITUTIONAL POLICY FORMULATION. Claremont: California Association for Institutional Research, 1971, 160–167.

Butler, Broadus. "Pressures on Higher Education for the Education of Disadvantaged Groups," in G. K. Smith, ed. CURRENT ISSUES IN HIGHER EDUCATION, 1965: PRESSURES AND PRIORITIES IN HIGHER EDUCATION. Washington, D.C.: National Education Association, 1965.

Clecak, P. "Snare of Preparation," AMERICAN SCHOLAR, 38 (Autumn, 1969), 657–667.

Dennis, Lawrence. "Equalizing Educational Opportunity for the Disadvantaged," in G. K. Smith, ed. CURRENT ISSUES IN HIGHER EDUCATION, 1964: UNDERGRADUATE EDUCATION. Washington, D.C.: National Education Association, 1964, 186–193.

Dugan, Willis E. "Opportunity for All," in Fred F. Harcleroad, ed. ISSUES OF THE SEVENTIES. San Francisco: Jossey Bass, 1970, 45–56.

Froe, D. D. "Educational Planning for Disadvantaged College Youth," JOURNAL OF NEGRO EDUCATION, 33 (Summer, 1964), 290–303.

Healy, T. S. and A. W. Astin. "Challenge of Open Admissions," SATURDAY REVIEW, 52 (December 20, 1969), 54–58+.

*Holt, John. "In Defense of Open Admissions," in Immanuel Wallerstein and Paul Starr, eds. THE UNIVERSITY CRISIS READER, I. New York: Random House, 1971, 308–335.

Moore, William, jr. "Opportunity for the Disadvantaged," in G. K. Smith, et al., eds. STRESS AND CAMPUS RESPONSE. San Francisco: Jossey-Bass, 1968, 232–240.

O'Neil, Robert M. "Preferential Admissions Equalizing the Access of Minority Groups to Higher Education," YALE LAW REVIEW, 80 (March, 1971), 699–767.

Resnik, S. and B. Kaplan. "Report Card on Open Admissions: Remedial Work Recommended: City University of New York," NEW YORK TIMES MAGAZINE, (May 9, 1971), 26–28+.

Tyler, Ralph W. "Epilogue: Academic Excellence and Equal Opportunity" in Fred F. Harcleroad, ed. ISSUES OF THE SEVENTIES. San Francisco: Jossey-Bass, 1970, 166–185.

B. ASPECTS OF STUDENT LIFE: GENERAL AND HISTORICAL

B.1. Before 1900

Bagg, L. H. FOUR YEARS AT YALE, BY A GRADUATE OF '69. New Haven: Charles C. Chatfield, 1871.

Beatty, Richard C. JOURNAL OF SOUTHERN STUDENT, 1846–48 WITH LETTERS OF A LATER PERIOD. Nashville, Tennessee: Vanderbilt University Press, 1944.

Brubacher, John Seiler. HIGHER EDUCATION IN TRANSITION, A HISTORY OF AMERICAN COLLEGES AND UNIVERSITIES 1636–1968. New York: Harper and Row, 1968.

Coulter, Ellis Merton. COLLEGE LIFE IN THE OLD SOUTH. Athens, Georgia: University of Georgia Press, 1951.

Cutting, George R. STUDENT LIFE AT AMHERST: ITS ORGANIZA-TION, THEIR MEMBERSHIP, AND HISTORY. Amherst: Hatch and Williams, 1871.

Fletcher, Robert Samuel. A HISTORY OF OBERLIN COLLEGE FROM THE FOUNDATION THROUGH THE CIVIL WAR. Oberlin: Oberlin College, 1943.

Hall, G. Stanley. STUDENT CUSTOMS. Worcester, Massachusetts: American Antiquarian Society Proceedings, 1900.

Hammond, William. REMEMBRANCE OF AMHERST, AN UNDERGRAD-UATE'S DIARY, 1846–1848. New York, Columbia University Press, 1946.

Hangartner, Carl, S. J. "Movements to Change American College Teaching 1700–1830." Unpublished Ph.D. dissertation, Yale University, 1967.

Olin, Stephan. COLLEGE LIFE: ITS THEORY AND PRACTICE. New York, Harper, 1867.

Patton, Cornelius H. and Walter T. Field. EIGHT O'CLOCK CHAPEL: A STUDY OF NEW ENGLAND COLLEGE LIFE IN THE EIGHTIES. Boston: Houghton Mifflin, 1927.

Pike, Frederic A. A STUDENT AT WISCONSIN FIFTY YEARS AGO: REMINISCES AND RECORDS OF THE EIGHTIES. Madison: Democrat Printing, 1935.

Porter, N. THE AMERICAN COLLEGES AND THE AMERICAN PUBLIC. New Haven: Chatfield, 1870.

*Sheldon, Henry D. THE HISTORY AND PEDAGOGY OF AMERICAN STUDENT SOCIETIES. New York: D. Appleton, 1901.

*Sheldon, Henry D. STUDENT LIFE AND CUSTOMS. New York: Arno Press, 1969.

Stine, George Frederick. "Male Undergraduate Student Life and Services at the Pennsylvania State University: 1850–1965." Unpublished Ph.D. dissertation, Pennsylvania State University, 1966.

Stokes, Anson, MEMORIALS OF EMINENT YALE MEN. A BIOGRAPH-ICAL STUDY OF STUDENT LIFE AND UNIVERSITY INFLUENCES IN THE EIGHTEENTH AND NINETEENTH CENTURIES. (2 volumes), New Haven, 1914.

Thwing, C. F. THE AMERICAN COLLEGE IN AMERICAN LIFE. New York: Putnam's Sons, 1897.

*Thwing, C. F. AMERICAN COLLEGES: THEIR STUDENTS AND WORK. New York: Putnam's Sons, 1883.

Broome, Edwin C. "A Historical and Critical Discussion of College Admission Requirements," COLUMBIA UNIVERSITY CONTRIBUTIONS TO PHILOSOPHY, PSYCHOLOGY AND EDUCATION, 11 (April, 1903), reprinted Princeton, New Jersey: College Entrance Examination Board, 1968.

"College Discipline," CRITIC, 1 (July 30, 1881).

Dexter, Franklin B. "On Some Social Distinctions at Harvard and Yale Before the Revolution," PROCEEDINGS OF THE AMERICAN ANTIQUAR-IAN SOCIETY, (October, 1893), 34–59.

388

Dexter, Franklin B. "Student Life at Yale in the Early Days of Connecticut Hall," PAPERS OF THE NEW HAVEN COLONIAL HISTORICAL SOCIETY, 7 (1908), 288–297.

Emerson, Ralph Waldo. "Emerson's Opinion of Southern Students, 1837," in R. Hofstadter and W. Smith, eds. AMERICAN HIGHER EDUCATION: A DOCUMENTARY HISTORY, VOLUME I. The University of Chicago Press, 1961, 419–433.

Grant, Robert. "Harvard College in the Seventies," in James Stone and Donald DeNevi, eds. PORTRAITS OF THE AMERICAN UNIVERSITY, 1890–1910. San Francisco: Jossey-Bass, 1971, 216–228.

Martin, Edward. "Undergraduate Life at Harvard," in James Stone and Donald DeNevi, eds. PORTRAITS OF THE AMERICAN UNIVERSITY, 1890–1910. San Francisco: Jossey-Bass, 1971, 193–215.

Sack, Saul. "Student Life in the Nineteenth Century," PENNSYLVANIA MAGAZINE OF HISTORY AND BIOGRAPHY, 85 (July, 1961), 255–288.

Shaler, N. S. "The Problem of Discipline in Higher Education," ATLANTIC, 54 (June, 1889).

Urofsky, Melvin. "Reforms and Response: The Yale Report of 1828," HISTORY OF EDUCATION QUARTERLY, 5 (March, 1965), 53–67.

Woodward, F. C. "Student Life in Southern Colleges," EDITORS REVIEW, 10 (1895), 461–475.

B.2. 1900 to 1930

Angell, Robert C. THE CAMPUS, A STUDY OF CONTEMPORARY UNDERGRADUATE LIFE IN THE AMERICAN UNIVERSITY. New York: D. Appleton, 1928.

Benn, John A. COLUMBUS-UNDERGRADUATE. Philadelphia: Lippincott, 1928

Benson, Elizabeth. THE YOUNGER GENERATION. New York, 1927.

Book, William. HOW TO SUCCEED IN COLLEGE. Baltimore: Warwick and York, 1927.

Bourne, Randolph. EDUCATION AND LIVING. New York: Century, 1917.

Bourne, Randolph. YOUTH AND LIFE. Boston: Houghton Mifflin, 1913.

Bowden-Smith, A. C. AN ENGLISH STUDENT'S WANDER YEAR IN AMERICA. London: Edwin Arnold, 1910.

Briggs, Le Baron Russell. COLLEGE LIFE. Boston: Houghton Mifflin, 1904.

Canby, Henry S. COLLEGE SONS AND COLLEGE FATHERS. New York: Harper, 1915.

Clark, Thomas A. DISCIPLINE AND THE DERELICT; BEING A SERIES OF ESSAYS ON SOME OF THOSE WHO TREAD THE GREEN CARPET. New York, 1921.

Crane, R. T. THE DEMORALIZATION OF COLLEGE LIFE: REPORT ON AN INVESTIGATION AT HARVARD. Chicago: Shepard, 1911.

Edwards, Richard H., J. M. Artman and Galen Fisher, *et al.* UNDERGRAD-UATES; A STUDY OF MORALE IN TWENTY-THREE AMERICAN COLLEGES AND UNIVERSITIES. Garden City, New York: Doubleday, Doran, 1928.

Foster, W. T. SHOULD STUDENTS STUDY? New York: Harper, 1917.

Gavit, John Palmer. COLLEGE. New York: Harcourt, Brace, 1925.

Hicks, Granville. JOHN REED: THE MAKING OF A REVOLUTIONARY. New York: MacMillan, 1937.

Irwin, Wallace A. THE SHAME OF THE COLLEGES. New York: Outing, 1907.

Johnson, Owen M. STOVER AT YALE. New York: Grosset and Dunlop, 1912.

Keppel, Frederick Paul. THE UNDERGRADUATE AND HIS COLLEGE. Boston: Houghton Mifflin, 1917.

*Lee, Calvin B. T. THE CAMPUS SCENE: 1900–1970. New York: McKay, 1970.

McConn, Charles Maxwell. COLLEGE OR KINDERGARTEN? New York: New Republic, 1929.

Poole, Ernest. THE BRIDGE: MY OWN STORY. New York: MacMillan, 1940.

Pyre, James F. A. WISCONSIN. New York: Oxford University Press, 1920.

*Sinclair, Upton. THE GOOSE STEP. Pasadena, California: "The Author," 1923.

Thwing, C. F. THE AMERICAN COLLEGES AND UNIVERSITIES IN THE GREAT WAR. New York: MacMillan, 1920.

Thwing, Charles F. LETTERS FROM A FATHER TO HIS SON ENTERING COLLEGE. New York: Platt and Peck, 1912.

Tucker, William F. MY GENERATION: AN AUTOBIOGRAPHICAL INTERPRETATION. Boston: Houghton Mifflin, 1919.

Veblen, Thorstein. THE HIGHER LEARNING IN AMERICA. Stanford, California: Academic Reprints, 1954.

Comer, Cornelia. "A Letter to the Rising Generation," ATLANTIC MONTHLY, 107 (February, 1911), 147–149.

Cooper, Clayton S. "The American Undergraduate," in James Stone and Donald DeNevi, eds. PORTRAITS OF THE AMERICAN UNIVERSITY, 1890–1910. San Francisco: Jossey-Bass, 1971, 171–192.

Corbin, John. "The Struggle for College Democracy," in James Stone and Donald DeNevi, eds. PORTRAITS OF THE AMERICAN UNIVERSITY, 1890–1910. San Francisco: Jossey-Bass, 1971, 244–251.

Cutler, Addison T. and Talcott Parsons. "A Word From Amherst Students," NEW STUDENT, 3 (October 20, 1923), 6–7.

Davies, J. "Princeton: Excerpts from Tiger in the Ivy, the Princeton Man and His University, 1900–1967," HORIZON, 9 (Winter, 1967), 57–66+.

Duffus, D. L. "Students Change With the Colleges: The Rah-Rah Boy has Gone and in His Place is One Not Ashamed to Seek Scholastic Honors," NEW YORK TIMES MAGAZINE, (January 22, 1928).

Hutchinson, Ruth and Mary Connard. "What's in a College Week?" SCHOOL AND SOCIETY, 24 (December 18, 1926).

"Is the Younger Generation in Peril?" LITERARY DIGEST, 59 (May 14, 1921), 9–12.

Johnson, Owen M. "Dink Stover at Yale, About 1909," in Samuel I. Bellman, ed. THE COLLEGE EXPERIENCE. San Francisco: Chandler, 1962, 3–12.

Pringle, Henry. "Young Men on the Make," HARPER'S, 158 (January, 1929), 149–157.

Showerman, Grant. "Intellect and the Undergraduate," SCHOOL AND SOCIETY, 13 (February 26, 1921), 241–242.

"What the Undergraduate Wants," NEW REPUBLIC, 39 (July 30, 1924), 258–260.

B.3. 1930 to 1950

Allaway, William Harris. RELIEF EFFORTS IN THE EDUCATIONAL COMMUNITY. Madison, Wisconsin: U.S. National Student Association, 1949.

Bell, H. M. YOUTH TELL THEIR STORY. Washington, D.C.: American Council on Education, 1938.

Bevis, A. M. DIETS AND RIOTS. Boston: Marshall Jones, 1936.

Congdon, Don, ed. THE THIRTIES: A TIME TO REMEMBER. New York: Simon and Schuster, 1962.

Crawford, Mary M. STUDENT FOLKWAYS AND SPENDING AT INDIANA UNIVERSITY: 1940–1941. New York: Columbia University Press, 1943.

Davis, Kingsley. YOUTH IN THE DEPRESSION. Chicago: University of Chicago Press, 1935.

Davis, Maxine. THE LOST GENERATION: A PORTRAIT OF AMERICAN YOUTH TODAY. New York: Macmillan, 1936.

First, Wesley, ed. UNIVERSITY ON THE HEIGHTS. Garden City, New York: Doubleday, 1969.

Fisher, Dorothy Canfield. OUR YOUNG FOLKS. New York: Harcourt, Brace, 1943.

Gauss, Christian. LIFE IN COLLEGE. New York: Scribner's, 1931.

Gould, Leslie A. AMERICAN YOUTH TODAY. New York: Random House, 1940.

Hand, Harold C., et al., eds. CAMPUS ACTIVITIES. New York: McGraw-Hill, 1938.

Hawes, James Anderson. TWENTY YEARS AMONG THE TWENTY YEAR OLDS. New York: E. P. Dutton, 1945.

Johnson, Burgess. CAMPUS VERSUS CLASSROOM, A CANDID APPRAISAL OF THE AMERICAN COLLEGE. New York: I. Washburn, 1946.

Kelley, Janet Agnes. COLLEGE LIFE AND THE MORES. New York: Bureau of Publications, Teachers College, Columbia University, 1949.

McNeeley, J. COLLEGE STUDENT MORALITY. Washington, D.C.: U.S. Government Printing Office, 1938.

National Conference of College and University Presidents. HIGHER EDU-
CATION AND THE WAR. Washington, D.C.: American Council on Education,
1942.

Rainey, Homer, P., *et al.* HOW FARE AMERICAN YOUTH? New York: D.
Appleton-Century, 1937.

Rawick, George. "The New Deal and Youth." Unpublished Ph.D. dissertation, University of Wisconsin, 1957.

Spectorsky, A. C., ed. THE COLLEGE YEARS. New York: Hawthorne
Press, 1958.

Strang, Ruth. BEHAVIOR AND BACKGROUND OF STUDENTS IN COL-
LEGE AND SECONDARY SCHOOL. New York: Harper Brothers, 1937.

Todd, John Edward. SOCIAL NORMS AND THE BEHAVIOR OF COL-
LEGE STUDENTS. New York: Teachers College, Columbia University, 1941.

Butts, Porter. "The Undergraduate: A Case Study," NEW YORK TIMES
MAGAZINE, (January 12, 1936), 8+.

Clark, Eunice. "Lo, the Poor Student," NEW REPUBLIC, 77 (February 17,
1934), 277–278.

Conant, J. B. "Mobilizing American Youth," ATLANTIC, 170 (July, 1942),
48–53.

Cowley, W. H. and Willard Waller. "A Study of Student Life," JOURNAL
OF HIGHER EDUCATION, 6 (March, 1935), 132–142.

Edman, Irwin. "A Portrait of an Undergraduate of 1934," NEW YORK
TIMES MAGAZINE, (May 6, 1934), 3+.

Gauss, Christian. "The New Morality in the Colleges," SCRIBNER'S MAG-
AZINE, 90 (November, 1931), 525–532.

Heck, C. R. "The 'American Way' in College," HARVARD EDUCATION-
AL REVIEW, 8 (March, 1938), 228–236.

Hutchings, H. B. "When I Was an Undergraduate," MICHIGAN ALUMNUS
QUARTERLY REVIEW, 45 (1939), 129.

"Life Goes to a Summer Prom at the University of Wisconsin," LIFE, 27
(August 22, 1949), 88–90+.

Monroe, P. "Modern Student and His Political and International Influence,"
in P. Monroe. ESSAYS IN COMPARATIVE EDUCATION. Vol. 2. New York:
Teachers College, Columbia University, 1932, 232–241.

Neblett, Thomas. "Youth Movements in the United States," ANNALS OF
THE AMERICAN ACADEMY OF POLITICAL AND SOCIAL SCIENCE, 194
(November, 1937), 141–151.

Pressey, L. C. "A Class of Probation Students," JOURNAL OF HIGHER
EDUCATION, 2 (December, 1931), 506–510.

Sherman, Arthur Wesley, jr. "Emancipation Status of College Students,"
JOURNAL OF GENETIC PSYCHOLOGY, 68 (June, 1946), 171–180.

Strang, Ruth. "Student Activities and Organizations," in P. F. Valentine,
ed. THE AMERICAN COLLEGE. New York: Philosophical Library, 1949.

Turner, Fred H. "Students and the Depression," SATURDAY EVENING
POST, 12 (February 2, 1935), 12–13+.

"Youth in College," FORTUNE, 13 (June, 1936), 99–102, 155–162.

Zolotow, M. "Bohemia on the Campus: Sex, Poetry, and the Higher Emancipation at Wisconsin," AMERICAN MERCURY, 48 (December, 1939), 471–476.

B.4. 1950–1960

Abbott, Frank C., ed. STUDENT LIFE IN THE UNITED STATES. Report of the Conference on Student Life, Haverford College, 1953.

American Council on Education. STUDENT LIFE IN THE UNITED STATES. Washington, D.C.: American Council on Education, 1953.

Bennett, M. E. and M. Levin. GETTING THE MOST OUT OF COLLEGE. New York: McGraw-Hill, 1957.

Chi Psi. THE MAN AND HIS COLLEGE. Chicago: Chi Psi Educational Trust, 1952.

Deutsch, Monroe E. THE COLLEGE FROM WITHIN. Berkeley, California: University of California Press, 1952.

Devane, William. THE AMERICAN UNIVERSITY IN THE TWENTIETH CENTURY. Baton Rouge, Louisiana: Louisiana State University Press, 1957.

Engeman, J. COLLEGE: THE LIFE OF A STUDENT. New York: Lathrop, Lee and Shepard, 1959.

Gamelin, Francis Clifford. "Intercollege Comparisons of Student Satisfaction With College Life." Unpublished Ph.D. dissertation, University of Minnesota, 1953.

Habein, Margaret L., ed. SPOTLIGHT ON THE COLLEGE STUDENT. Washington, D.C: American Council on Education, 1959.

*MacIver, R. M., ed. DILEMMAS OF YOUTH IN AMERICA TODAY. New York: Harper, 1961.

Mayer, Frederick. CREATIVE UNIVERSITIES. New York: College and University Press, 1961.

Sigal, Clancy. GOING AWAY: A REPORT, A MEMOIR. Boston: Houghton Mifflin, 1962.

Stanford University. Study of Undergraduate Education. THE UNDERGRADUATE IN THE UNIVERSITY. Stanford University, 1957.

U.S. National Student Association. THE IDEA OF A STUDENT. Philadelphia, Pennsylvania: U.S. National Student Association, 1959.

Werner, Fred, ed. THE WORLD OF THE AMERICAN STUDENT. Philadelphia, Pennsylvania: U.S. National Student Association, 1958.

Wilson, Howard E. AMERICAN COLLEGE LIFE, Washington, D.C.: American Council on Education, 1956.

Barclay, D. "The Silent Generation Speaks Up," NEW YORK TIMES MAGAZINE, (May 15, 1960), 96+.

"Beer and Bikes From Yale to Vassar," LIFE, 32 (April 28, 1952), 136–138+.

Butz, O. "Defense of the Class of '58," NEW YORK TIMES MAGAZINE, (May 25, 1958), 20+.

"Campus Love Left Out in Cold: University of Michigan," LIFE, 42 (March 11, 1957), 49–50+.

"Campuses Enjoy a Riotous Spring," LIFE, 32 (May 26, 1952), 28–31.

"Class of '58 Speaks Up: Symposium by College Students," NATION, 186 (May 17, 1958), 432–439.

"College Life in the U.S.A.," HOUSE AND GARDEN, 104 (August, 1953), 60–71+.

Collins, Mary. "The College Experience Through the Eyes of the Students," in Lois Murphy and Esther Raushenbush, eds. ACHIEVEMENT IN THE COLLEGE YEARS. New York: Harper, 1960, 58–90.

"Conversations on the College Lawn, University of New Mexico," LIFE, 30 (May 14, 1951), 105–106+.

Cronin, M. J. "Students Are Supposed to Be Dumb," AMERICAN ASSOCIATION OF UNIVERSITY PROFESSORS BULLETIN, 41 (June, 1955), 359–365.

*Davis, James and A. Paul Hare. "Button-down Collar Culture: A Study of Undergraduate Life at a Men's College," HUMAN ORGANIZATION, 14 (Winter, 1956), 13–20.

Deutzer, W. T. "Introduction to Panel Discussion: Student Looks at Higher Education," in NATIONAL CONFERENCE ON HIGHER EDUCATION, CURRENT ISSUES IN HIGHER EDUCATION, (1952), 45–49.

Dorson, R. M. "Folklore of College Students: Excerpt from American Folklore," SCIENCE DIGEST, 49 (April, 1961), 21–26.

Durflinger, G. W. "Fundamentals Forgotten by College Students," JOURNAL OF EDUCATIONAL RESEARCH, 49 (April, 1956), 571–579.

Eddy, Edward. "Paradox in a Parenthesis," NATION, 188 (May 16, 1959), 440–444.

Ellison, J. "Are We Making a Playground Out of College," SATURDAY EVENING POST, 231 (March 7, 1959), 19–21+.

Emmanuel, Pierre. "American As Students," ATLANTIC, 194 (August, 1954), 59–62.

. Engle, Paul. "In Defense of the State University," SATURDAY EVENING POST, 232 (February 13, 1960), 22–23+.

"Farewell to Bright College Years," LIFE, 42 (June 24, 1957), 130–136.

Fiedler, Leslie A. "The Un-Angry Young Men: America's Post-War Generation," ENCOUNTER, 10 (January, 1958), 3–12.

" '55 Class: First of a Generation," BUSINESS WEEK, (June 11, 1955), 124–126+.

*Freedman, Mervin. "The Dangers of Non-Conformism," AMERICAN SCHOLAR, 28 (Winter, 1958), 25–33.

Funkenstein, Daniel. "What Does Higher Education Need to Know About the Student in Today's Changing Society?" CURRENT ISSUES IN HIGHER EDUCATION 1960: GUIDELINE FOR THE 60's. Washington, D.C.: Association for Higher Education, 1960, 160–165.

Gibson, Walker. "How Different We Were," in Esther Lloyd-Jones and Herman Estrin, eds. THE AMERICAN STUDENT AND HIS COLLEGE. Houghton Mifflin, 1967, 362–367.

Glicksberg, C. I. "In Vindication of College Youth," EDUCATIONAL RECORD, 37 (October, 1956), 336-343.

Goodman, W. "Bicker at Princeton: The Eating Clubs Again," COMMENTARY, 25 (May, 1958), 406–415.

Graham, E. K. "Academic Policy and the Gentle Art of Survival,"NATIONAL ASSOCIATION OF WOMEN DEANS AND COUNSELORS JOURNAL, 17 (June, 1954), 149–155.

Hamilton, A. "Madness on the Campus," SATURDAY EVENING POST, 228 (April, 28, 1956), 26–27+.

Hechinger, G. and F. Hechinger. "Case for Campus Life," NEW YORK TIMES MAGAZINE, (March 29, 1959), 11+.

Highet, G. "Her Sons, Alert and Grateful: Columbia Students," LIFE, 36 (February 15, 1954), 126–128+.

Himstead, R. E. "Colleges, Ethics and the Public," ANNALS OF THE AMERICAN ACADEMY OF POLITICAL AND SOCIAL SCIENCE, 280 (March, 1952), 133–141.

Hirshberg, A. "Prodigy at Harvard: F. Safler," SATURDAY EVENING POST, 230 (September 14, 1957), 38–39+.

Hymes, Dell H. "Robin Hood Goes to College," NATION, 178 (June 5, 1954), 472.

James, W. "University and Its Students," FORTNIGHTLY, 175 (New style 169) (May, 1951), 292–297.

Jencks, Christopher. "Politics Is For Other People," in Samuel I. Bellman, ed. THE COLLEGE EXPERIENCE. San Francisco: Chandler Publishing, 1962, 129–133.

Kimball, P. "Terribly Normal Class of '52," NEW YORK TIMES MAGAZINE, (June 8, 1952), 14–15+.

Kimbrough, E. "Bryn Mawr," HOLIDAY, 11 (May, 1952), 60–65+.

Kohn, H. "This Generation of College Youth," EDUCATIONAL FORUM, 16 (November, 1951), 65–71.

"Life Goes Polynesian in Pasadena: City College Party," LIFE, 31 (December 10, 1951), 170–172+.

"Look on the Campus," COSMOPOLITAN, 143 (September, 1957), 60–65.

Malleson, N. B. "University Student, 1953," UNIVERSITIES QUARTERLY, 13 (May, 1959), 287–298; 14 (November, 1959), 42–56; 15 (February, 1960), 156–164; 15 (December, 1960), 54–63.

Miller, Perry. "Liberty and Conformity," GRADUATE JOURNAL, 2 (Spring, 1959), 34–41.

Mitgang, Herbert. "What College Youth is Thinking," SURVEY, 77 (February, 1951), 58–59.

Moore, Forest. "The Student in Colleges and Universities of the United States," in Ray Billington, ed. EDUCATION AND STUDENT LIFE IN THE UNITED STATES; REPORT OF THE CONFERENCE HELD AT NORTHWESTERN UNIVERSITY. EVANSTON, ILLINOIS, JUNE 18–21, 1957. Evanston, Illinois: Northwestern University, 1967.

Nielson, B. W. "Vassar '58 Looks at the World of '58," NEW YORK TIMES MAGAZINE, (June 8, 1958), 34+.

Owen, L. "Anatomy of School Spirit," AMERICAN MERCURY, 70 (February, 1950), 143–149.

Poore, Charles. "Class of '54–New Generation, New Hope," NEW YORK TIMES MAGAZINE, (October 22, 1950), 17+.

*Rawick, George. "The American Student: A Profile," DISSENT, 1 (Autumn, 1954), 393–398.

*Riesman, David. "The College Student in an Age of Organization," CHICAGO REVIEW, 12 (Autumn, 1958), 50–68.

*Riesman, David. "The Found Generation," AMERICAN SCHOLAR, 25 (Autumn, 1956), 421–435.

*Riesman, David. "Where is the College Generation Headed?" ATLANTIC, 207 (April, 1961), 39–45.

Sanford, Nevitt. "Knowledge of Students Through the Social Studies," in Margaret Habein, ed. SPORTLIGHT ON THE COLLEGE STUDENT. Washington, D.C.: American Council on Education, 1959, 86–93.

Sanford, Nevitt. "The Professor Looks at the Student," in R. M. Cooper, ed. THE TWO ENDS OF THE LOG: LEARNING AND TEACHING IN TODAY'S COLLEGE. Minneapolis: Univerity of Minnesota Press, 1958.

Schickel, Richard. "The Island of the Present: A Report on the American College Student," PROGRESSIVE, 19 (April, 1955), 29–32.

Seigel, K. "Style Note: The Campus Strait Jacket," NATION, 174 (June 28, 1952), 661–662+.

Seligman, Daniel. "The Confidential Twenty-five Year-Olds," FORTUNE, 51 (February, 1955), 100–102.

Smith, G. G. "Freshman Mixer: or, the Wallflower Must Go," NEW YORK TIMES MAGAZINE, (October 9, 1955), 26–27+.

Smith, G. Gaddis. "Lo, the Old College Spirit," NEW YORK TIMES MAGAZINE, (January 17, 1954), 18+.

Smith, N. "Sad News from the Campus: Nobody Loves the Football Hero Now," LIFE, 43 (November 11, 1957), 149–150+.

Speier, H. "Risk, Security, and Modern Hero Worship," in H. Speier. SOCIAL ORDER AND THE RISKS OF WAR. New York: George Stewart, 1952, 112–130.

Stone, H. E. "Project in Campus-Community Co-operation; the Development of a Campus-City Co-ordinating Council for Student Affairs," JOURNAL OF HIGHER EDUCATION, 30 (May, 1959), 255–259.

Strozier, Robert. "Analysis of the Student Community," in Erich Walter, ed. RELIGION AND THE STATE UNIVERSITY. Ann Arbor, Michigan: University of Michigan Press, 1958, 195–213.

Syrkin, M. "Youth and Lady Macduff," AMERICAN ASSOCIATION OF UNIVERSITY PROFESSORS BULLETIN, 40 (June, 1954), 317–323.

Taylor, H. A. "World of the American Student," JOURNAL OF HIGHER EDUCATION, 27 (May, 1956), 244–250.

*"Tension Beneath Apathy: Symposium," NATION, 188 (May 16, 1959), 440–455.

Trask, W. R. and L. Marcuse. "Oldest Younger Generation," PARTISAN REVIEW, 19 (March, 1952), 211–216.

"Under the Biltmore Clock," LIFE, 32 (April 21, 1952), 158–160+.

"U.S. Campus Kids of 1953: Unkiddable and Unbeatable," NEWSWEEK, 42 (November 2, 1953), 52–55.

Varney, H. L. "Our College Graduate Snobocracy," AMERICAN MERCURY, 84 (January, 1957), 98–101.

Walsh, C. "Flat Minds, Kind Hearts, and Fine Arts," CHRISTIAN SCHOLAR, 36 (June, 1953), 100–109.

Weales, G. "Ritual in Georgia," SOUTHERN FOLKLORE QUARTERLY, 21 (June, 1957), 104–109.

Weaver, P. "Pursuit of Learning and the Undaily Male," MADEMOISELLE, 46 (January, 1958), 80–84+.

Wilson, H. E. "College Way of Life," TEACHERS COLLEGE RECORD, 58 (March, 1957), 310–315.

"The Younger Generation," TIME, 58 (November 5, 1951), 46–52.

B.5. 1960–

American Council on Education. THE STUDENT IN HIGHER EDUCATION. Washington, D.C.: American Council on Education, 1965.

Bell, Norman T., *et al.* INTRODUCTION TO COLLEGE LIFE. Second Edition. Boston: Houghton Mifflin, 1969.

*Bellman, Samuel, ed. THE COLLEGE EXPERIENCE. San Francisco: Chandler, 1962.

*Boroff, David. CAMPUS: U.S.A. New York: Harper, 1961.

Bowman, Norman. COLLEGE IS A QUESTION MARK. Nashville, Tennessee, Convention Press, 1968.

Brookover, Wilbur, ed. THE COLLEGE STUDENT. New York: Center for Applied Research in Education, 1965.

*Committee on the Student in Higher Education. THE STUDENT IN HIGHER EDUCATION. New Haven, Connecticut: Hazen Foundation, 1968.

*Dennis, Lawrence E. and Joseph F. Kauffman. THE COLLEGE AND THE STUDENT. Washington, D.C.: American Council on Education, 1966.

DeVane, W. C. HIGHER EDUCATION IN TWENTIETH-CENTURY AMERICA. Cambridge, Massachusetts: Harvard University Press, 1965.

Donovan, John D. THE ACADEMIC MAN IN THE CATHOLIC COLLEGE. New York: Sheed and Ward, 1964.

Ellsworth, Henry. THE COLLEGE MALE; AN EXAMINATION OF THE PROBLEMS AND PITFALLS OF CAMPUS LIFE. Derby, Connecticut: Monarch Books, 1964.

Estrin, Herman A. and Ester Lloyd-Jones. HOW MANY ROADS? . . . THE '70s. Beverly Hills, California: Glencoe Press, 1970.

Ferm, V. INSIDE IVY WALLS. New York: Citadel Press, 1964.

Freedman, Mervin. THE COLLEGE EXPERIENCE. San Francisco: Jossey-Bass, 1967.

Geier, Woodrow A. TODAY'S STUDENT AND HIS UNIVERSITY. Nashville, Tennessee: Board of Education, Methodist Church, Bureau of Higher Education, 1966.

Halladay, D.W., *et al.* THE ROLE OF THE STUDENT. Washington, D.C.: American Association of State Colleges and Universities, 1968.

Herman, I. M. STUDENTS AND UNIVERSITIES: REPORT OF A CONFERENCE AT DITCHLEY PARK, FEBRUARY 7–10, 1969, American Ditchley Foundation, 1969.

Higgins, George C., jr. "A Factor Analytic Study of Some Dimensions of College Experience," Unpublished Ph.D. dissertation, University of Rochester, 1964.

Kammeyer, Kenneth and Charles Bolton. THE UNIVERSITY STUDENT. New Haven, Connecticut: College and University Press, 1967.

Kavanaugh, Robert. THE GRIM GENERATION. New York: Trident Press, 1970.

*Lloyd-Jones, Esther and Herman Estrin, eds. THE AMERICAN STUDENT AND HIS COLLEGE. Boston: Houghton Mifflin, 1967.

Nygreen, Glen T. THE CONTEMPORARY COLLEGE STUDENT. Woodstock, Maryland: Woodstock College, 1969.

Preu, J. A. THE ROLE AND SCOPE OF THE FLORIDA STATE UNIVERSITY. STUDENTS AND STUDENT LIFE. Florida State University Self Study Series, Vol. 25. Tallahassee, Florida: Florida State University, n.d.

Raushenbush, Esther. THE STUDENT AND HIS STUDIES. Middletown, Connecticut: Wesleyan University Press, 1964.

Situationist International. ON THE POVERTY OF STUDENT LIFE. New York: Situationist International, 1967.

*THE STUDENT IN HIGHER EDUCATION. New Haven, Connecticut: Hazen Foundation, 1968.

Sutherland, Robert, ed. PERSONALITY FACTORS ON THE COLLEGE CAMPUS. Austin, Texas: Hogg Foundation for Mental Health, 1962.

Warren, J. R. PATTERNS OF COLLEGE EXPERIENCES. U.S. Department of Health, Education and Welfare Cooperative Research Project S-327. Claremont, California: College Graduate School and University Center, 1966.

*Yamamoto, Kaoru, ed. THE COLLEGE STUDENT AND HIS CULTURE: AN ANALYSIS. Boston: Houghton Mifflin, 1968.

Boroff, D. "College Intellectual, 1965 Model," NEW YORK TIMES MAGAZINE, (December 6, 1964), 36–37+.

Braiman, Alex. "Riotous Behavior in the College: a Psychosocial View," JOURNAL OF THE AMERICAN COLLEGE HEALTH ASSOCIATION, 14 (February, 1966), 147–153.

*"Campus Report: Mood of the Students," NEW YORK TIMES MAGAZINE, (November 17, 1963), 24–25, 127+.

Cross, K. Patricia. "New Students of the 70's," THE RESEARCH REPORTER, 6 (No. 4, 1971), 1–8.

Dennis, Lawrence E. "On Discovering College Students," in Lawrence Dennis and Joseph F. Kauffman, eds. THE COLLEGE AND THE STUDENT. Washington, D.C.: American Council on Education, 1966, 1–5.

Ellison, E. J. "Trouble on Sun-Tan U.," SATURDAY EVENING POST, 234 (September 16, 1961), 109–113+.

Estes, J. "Gifted Boy Finds His Way: B. Wichmann's Escape from Mediocrity," LIFE, 57 (December 4, 1964), 79–80+.

"Five Freshman at Harvard: Symposium," SEVENTEEN, 25 (May, 1966), 154–155+.

"Four Mademoiselle Editors Go to Ten Campuses to Find Out What They're Like in 1971," MADEMOISELLE, 73 (August, 1971), 248–253+.

Frede, Richard. "The College Experience," in Samuel I. Bellman, ed. THE COLLEGE EXPERIENCE. San Francisco: Chandler, 1962, 160–165.

Freedman, Mervin B. "College Students Under Pressure," JOURNAL OF GENERAL EDUCATION, 17 (July, 1965), 85–90.

"Freshman Class: 1960," LIFE, 49 (October 3, 1960), 94–101.

Gallagher, Buell G. "The Vanguard of the Dysphoric Generation," in Lawrence Dennis and Joseph Kauffman, eds. THE AMERICAN COLLEGE AND THE STUDENT. Washington, D.C.: American Council on Education, 1966, 368–371.

Gilbert, Richard. "A Good Time at UCLA: An English View," HARPER'S, 230 (April, 1965), 75–83.

Giusti, J. P. "Students and the 1970's: Calm After the Storm," SCHOOL AND SOCIETY, 97 (October, 1969), 360–363.

Glickman, I. J. "College Students: Children or Adults?" MOMENTUM, 1 (April, 1970), 23–31.

Glynn, Lenny. "Hacking Around," in Christopher Reaske and Robert Wilson, jr. STUDENT VOICES/ONE. New York: Random House, 1971, 151–156.

Goodman, Mary Ellen. "Campus Youth in an Age of Anomie," JOURNAL OF THE NATIONAL ASSOCIATION OF WOMEN DEANS AND COUNSELORS, 29 (Summer, 1966), 188–192.

Goodman, Paul. "The Calling of American Youth," COMMENTARY, 29 (March, 1960), 217–229.

Goodman, Paul. "The New Reformation," NEW YORK TIMES MAGAZINE, (September 14, 1969), 32–33, 142–155.

Gottlieb, David. "The Rise and Fall of the American Teenager," YOUTH AND SOCIETY, 1 (June, 1970), 420–436.

Grace, H. A. "Perspectives on Student Life," PEABODY JOURNAL OF EDUCATION, 40 (September, 1962), 89–93.

"Graduate: Snapshots of Three Generations: Interviews," NEWSWEEK, 71 (June 24, 1968), 66–71.

"Graduation Day for '70: with Excerpts from Commencement Addresses," LIFE, 68 (June 19, 1970), 20–29.

Grafton, S. "Tense Generation," LOOK, 27 (August 27, 1963), 17–23.

Greeley, A. M. "Campus Community: Experiment in Living," AMERICA, 115 (November 12, 1966), 588–591.

Greeley, A. M. "New Breed," AMERICA, 110 (May 23, 1964), 706–709.

Greeley, Andrew. "The Teaching of Moral Wisdom," in G. K. Smith, *et al.* eds. STRESS AND CAMPUS RESPONSE. San Francisco: Jossey-Bass, 1968, 209–217.

Green, A. W. "Young America Takes Over the Colleges," COMMENTARY, 7 (June, 1949), 524–534.

Grinnell, J. E. "Goodbye, Joe College," PHI DELTA KAPPAN, 49 (May, 1968), 517–521.

Guitar, M. A. "Knitted Brows on the Subway: A Profile of New York's Barnard College," MADEMOISELLE, 58 (April, 1964), 169–171+.

Gross, R. "Challenge to this Generation of Students," EDUCATION DIGEST, 33 (May, 1968), 26–29.

Gummere, R. M., jr. "(1) Money (2) Book (3) Going Steady," NEW YORK TIMES MAGAZINE, (June, 1962), 30+.

Hacker, A. "College Grad Has Been Short-Changed," NEW YORK TIMES MAGAZINE, (June 6, 1965), 25+.

Hacker, Andrew. "Cornell: Campus Closeup," NATION, 194 (May 19, 1962), 437–439.

Hall, C. S. "Disquiet After Hours: Basic Conflicts of Undergraduates Revealed in Their Dreams," MADEMOISELLE, 64 (January, 1967), 77+.

Hall, William E. "Taking Advantage of Change," in Richard L. Hart and J. Galen Saylor, eds. STUDENT UNREST: THREAT OR PROMISE. Washington, D.C.: Association for Supervision & Curriculum Development, 1970, 93–100.

Halleck, Seymour. "The Roots of Student Despair," THINK, 33 (March-April, 1967), 20–24.

Hamalian, L. "Class of 1966: Loss of Tragedy," NATION, 202 (June 6, 1966), 676–679.

*Harrington, Michael. "The American Campus: 1962," DISSENT, 9 (Spring, 1962), 164–168.

Harris, David. "Foundations of Community: American Students," BOWDITCH REVIEW, (Fall, 1967), 3–9.

Hechinger, Grace and Fred. "The Case for Campus Life," in Samuel Bellman, ed.THE COLLEGE EXPERIENCE. San Francisco: Chandler Publishing, 1962, 167–175.

Hefferlin, J. B. Lon. "Recent Research on College Students," in E. J. McGrath, ed. THE LIBERAL ARTS COLLEGE'S RESPONSIBILITY FOR THE INDIVIDUAL STUDENT. New York: Teachers College Press, 1966, 80–85.

Heist, P. A. "Implications from Recent Research on College Students," JOURNAL OF NATIONAL ASSOCIATION OF WOMEN DEANS AND COUNSELORS, 22 (1959), 116–124.

Heist, P. A. "Student," NATIONAL SOCIETY FOR THE STUDY OF EDUCATION YEARBOOK, (Part 2, 1961), 211–234.

Hodgkinson, H. L. "Students and an Intellectual Community," EDUCA-TIONAL RECORD, 49 (Fall, 1968), 398–406.

"How Much Student Life?" JOURNAL OF HIGHER EDUCATION, 32 (October, 1961), 402–408.

Jarrett, J. L. "College Students: the New Breed," SATURDAY REVIEW, 48 (March 20, 1965), 64–65+.

Jencks, Christopher. "A New Breed of B.A.'s," NEW REPUBLIC, 153 (October 23, 1965), 17–21.

Kamber, G. "Cool Look at the Campus," TWENTIETH CENTURY, 177 (No. 1038, 1968), 26–30.

Katz, F. M. and C. N. Katz. "Appraisal of Students: Evaluations by Academics Visiting the United States of America," JOURNAL OF EDUCATIONAL RESEARCH, 62 (January, 1969), 231–237.

Katz, Joseph. "Four Years of Growth, Conflict and Compliance," in Joseph Katz et al. NO TIME FOR YOUTH, San Francisco: Jossey-Bass, 1968, 3–72.

Katz, Joseph and Nevitt Sanford. "Stanford Undergrads: 17 to 22: The Turbulent Years," STANFORD TODAY, (January, 1966), 7–10.

*Kauffman, Joseph F. "The Student in Higher Education," in Lawrence Dennis and Joseph Kauffman, eds. THE AMERICAN COLLEGE AND THE STUDENT. Washington, D.C.: American Council on Education, 1966, 141–162.

*Keniston, Kenneth. "Social Change and Youth in America," DAEDALUS, 91 (Winter, 1962), 145–171.

King, L. L. "Blowing My Mind at Harvard," HARPER, 241 (October, 1970), 95–98+.

Kile, Earl. "The Student Nobody Knows," in Esther Lloyd-Jones and Herman Estrin, eds. THE AMERICAN STUDENT AND HIS COLLEGE. Boston: Houghton Mifflin, 1967, 19–26.

Koin, Harold. "Incomplete Liberation: Two Premedical Students," in Joseph Katz et al. NO TIME FOR YOUTH. San Francisco: Jossey-Bass, 1968, 230–254.

Kressy, Michael. "The Community College Student: a Lession in Humility," COLLEGE ENGLISH, 32 (April, 1971), 772–777.

Lloyd-Jones, Esther. "What Are College Students Made of?" in Esther Lloyd-Jones and Herman Estrin, eds. THE AMERICAN STUDENT AND HIS COLLEGE. Boston: Houghton Mifflin, 1967, 38–46.

Lukas, J. A. "Fairly Old Grad ('55) Looks at Harvard (in '69)," NEW YORK TIMES MAGAZINE, (June 8, 1969), 28–29+.

Malnig, L. R. and T. V. Tuleja. "Goodbye, Mr. Chips?" NATIONAL CATH-OLIC GUIDANCE CONFERENCE JOURNAL, 13 (Summer, 1969), 107–115.

Margolis, R. J. "Two Nations at Wesleyan University," NEW YORK TIMES MAGAZINE, (January 18, 1970), 9+.

Martin, Reed. "Student Non Politics, or, How To Make Irrelevancy a Virtue," AMERICAN STUDENT, (Winter, 1966), 7–10.

*Martinson, Robert. "State of the Campus, 1962," NATION, 194 (May 19, 1962), 432–437.

Mayer, L. A. "Young America: by the Numbers," FORTUNE, 79 (January, 1969), 72–76.

*Meyerson, Martin. "Ethos of the American College Student: Beyond the Protests," DAEDALUS, (Summer, 1966), 713–739.

Michael, Donald N. "The Next Generation," in Kaoru Yamamoto, ed. THE COLLEGE STUDENT AND HIS CULTURE: AN ANALYSIS. Boston: Houghton Mifflin, 1968, 466–470.

Moore, G. "Who Says College Kids Have Changed," LIFE, 62 (May 19, 1967), 90–90B+.

Morgan, T. B. "Class of '68," LOOK, 28 (September 22, 1964), 19–33.

Mundinger, Donald C. "Campus Life in a Litigious Age," in Lawrence Dennis and Joseph Kauffman, eds. THE AMERICAN COLLEGE AND THE STUDENT. Washington, D.C.: American Council on Education, 1966, 318–322.

"The No-Nonsense Kids," in Samuel I. Bellman, ed. THE COLLEGE EXPERIENCE. San Francisco: Chandler, 1962, 219–223.

Norton-Taylor, D. "Private World of the Class of '66," FORTUNE, 73 (February, 1966), 102+, 128–132+.

"Our Angry Under-graduates: Symposium," SATURDAY EVENING POST, 241 (September 21, 1968), 4, 23–27+.

Poppy, J. "Perils of Big Brotherhood," LOOK, 27 (March 12, 1963), 53–56+.

Possony, Stefan T. "The University and Its Students," MODERN AGE, 13 (Summer, 1969), 258–269, (Fall, 1969), 378–388.

Pruitt, William. "College Students, Their Community, and Their Activities," in Gordon Klopf, ed. COLLEGE STUDENT PERSONNEL WORK IN THE YEARS AHEAD. Washington, D.C.: American Personnel and Guidance Association, 1966, 10–21.

Ratterman, P. H. "The New Breed of Student," in CURRENT ISSUES IN HIGHER EDUCATION, 1966. Washington, D.C.: Association for Higher Education, 1966, 158–163.

Richards, Robert. "The College Student in Changing America," in Eric Gardener, ed. THE COLLEGE STUDENT. New York: Center for Applied Research in Education, 1965, 3–19.

Riesman, David. "Where is the College Generation Headed?" ATLANTIC, 207 (April, 1961), 39–45.

Sanford, Nevitt. "The College Student of Today and Tomorrow," NATIONAL ASSOCIATION OF STUDENT PERSONNEL ADMINISTRATORS JOURNAL, 5 (October, 1967), 221–228.

Sanford, Nevitt. "The College Student of 1980," in Alvin Eurich, ed. CAMPUS 1980. New York: Delacorte Press, 1968, 176–200.

Sanford, Nevitt and A. Kinsolving. "Morals on the Campus: a Professor and a Minister Disagree on the Present State of Student Morality," NATIONAL EDUCATION ASSOCIATION JOURNAL, 54 (April, 1965), 20–24.

Schlesinger, Arthur, jr. "Joe College Is Dead," SATURDAY EVENING POST, 241 (September 21, 1968), 24–26, 66+.

Schurchman, H. P. "The Double Life of the Commuter College Student," MENTAL HYGIENE, 50 (January, 1966), 104–110.

Sherriffs, A. C. "Convenient Myths: Today's Students," VITAL SPEECHES, 33 (August 15, 1967), 669–672.

Silber, E., et al. "Competent Adolescents Coping With College Decisions," ARCHIVES OF GENERAL PSYCHIATRY, 5 (1961), 517–527.

Stanton, Charles M. "The Committed Student—a New and Rare Breed," in CURRENT ISSUES IN HIGHER EDUCATION, 1966. Washington, D.C: Association for Higher Education, 1966, 164–168.

Stein, Robert. "The Average Student: A Useful Fiction," DISSENT, 18 (April, 1971), 174–178.

"Students Are Big Business," LOOK, 25 (September 13, 1960), 64–67.

Subcommittee to Study Student Life at Amherst College. "Report to the Committee on Educational Policy," AMHERST ALUMNI NEWS, Special Issue (Winter, 1965).

Todd, R. "Ins and Outs at M.I.T.," NEW YORK TIMES MAGAZINE, (May 18, 1969), 32–33+.

Todd, R. "Voices of Harvard '70," NEW YORK TIMES MAGAZINE, (June 7, 1970), 26–29+.

Trent, James W. and Judith L. Craise. "Commitment and Conformity in the American College," JOURNAL OF SOCIAL ISSUES, 23 (July, 1967), 34–51.

*Trow, Martin. "The Undergraduate Dilemma in Large State Universities," UNIVERSITIES QUARTERLY, 21 (December, 1966), 17–43.

Voss, V. "College Crowd," MADEMOISELLE, 58 (January, 1964), 77+.

"What the College Catalogues Didn't Tell Us," SEVENTEEN, 27 (September, 1968), 146–147+.

"What the College Catalogues Don't Tell You," SEVENTEEN, 24 (August, 1965), 238–239+.

Wilson, C. R. "Ugly American Undergraduates," SCHOOL AND SOCIETY, 92 (November 28, 1964), 351–354.

Wilson, L. "American College Student Today," COLLEGE AND UNIVERSITY, 38 (Summer, 1963), 381–390.

Wilson, L. "Is the College Student Becoming a 'Forgotten Man?' " SCHOOL AND SOCIETY, 93 (February 6, 1965), 78–81.

Young, Donald F. "Today's College Student," PUBLIC RELATIONS QUARTERLY, 14 (No. 3, 1970), 14–24.

Younge, G. D. "Students," REVIEW OF EDUCATIONAL RESEARCH, 35 (October, 1965), 253–263.

"Youth in America: Cultural and Educational Problems: Symposium," SCHOOL AND SOCIETY, 99 (April, 1971), 245–254.

*"Youth 1967: The Challenge of Change," AMERICAN SCHOLAR, 36 (Autumn, 1967), 527–646.

Zimmerman, William David. "The Changing Nature of the Personnel Dimension of Education," LIBERAL EDUCATION, 49 (December, 1963), 520–528.

C. THE STUDENT AND ACADEMIC LIFE

C.1. Relationship to Faculty

C.1.a. The Impact of Teachers on Students and General Studies

Cross Reference: See also section on attitude change in students (D7e).

Barry, Ruth, *et al.* CASE STUDIES IN COLLEGE STUDENT-STAFF RELATIONSHIPS. New York: Teachers College, Columbia University, 1956.

Hardee, Melveno Drahein. FACULTY ADVISING IN COLLEGES AND UNIVERSITIES. Washington: American College Personnel Association, 1970.

Hedegard, James Meredith. "Student-instructor Interaction and its Affects on Student Achievement and Attitudes." Unpublished Ph.D. dissertation, University of Michigan, 1968.

Hickerson, John Douglas. "Student and Faculty Expectations and Perceptions of the Faculty Role and Student Role in Kalamazoo College and Western Michigan University." Unpublished Ed.D. dissertation, Pennsylvania State University, 1970.

Jacob, Philip E. CHANGING VALUES IN COLLEGE: AN EXPLORATORY STUDY OF THE IMPACT OF COLLEGE TEACHING. New York: Harper, 1957.

McGehee, Nan. FACULTY AND STUDENTS OR FACULTY VS. STUDENTS. Washington, D.C.: National Association of State Universities and Land-Grant Colleges, 1969.

Mahler, Clarence Angus. "A Study of Student and Faculty Reactions to Student Personnel Work." Unpublished Ph.D. dissertation, University of Minnesota, 1955.

Martin, David Houston. "An Experimental Investigation of the Effects of a Dyadic Teaching Program on Prospective Teachers' Attitudes." Unpublished Ph.D. dissertation, George Peabody College for Teachers, 1966.

Martoccia, Charles T. "Instructor Influence on Subsequent Student Progress in a Physical Science Course." Unpublished Ph.D. dissertation, University of Florida, 1960.

Matlin, Norman. THE EDUCATIONAL ENCLAVE: COERCIVE BARGAINING IN COLLEGES AND UNIVERSITIES, New York: Funk and Wagnalls, 1969.

Menges, Robert John. "Student Instructor Cognitive Compatibility in the Large Lecture Class: An Exploratory Study." Unpublished Ed.D. dissertation, Columbia University, 1967.

Meyer, E. E., jr. "A Study of Undergraduate Student Faculty Relationship At a Large University." Unpublished Ph.D. dissertation, University of Wisconsin, 1965.

404

Milton, Ohmer. SURVEY OF FACULTY VIEWS ON STUDENT PARTICI-PATION IN DECISION MAKING. Washington: U.S. Office of Education, Bureau of Research, 1968.

Milton, Ohmer and Edward Joseph Shoben, jr., eds. LEARNING AND THE PROFESSORS. Athens: Ohio University Press, 1968.

Schwartz, Alvin. UNIVERSITY: THE STUDENTS, FACULTY, AND CAMPUS LIFE AT ONE UNIVERSITY. New York: Viking Press, 1969.

Sutherland, Robert L., *et al.* STUDENTS AND STAFF IN A SOCIAL CONTEXT. Washington: American Council on Education, 1953.

Theilens, W., jr. THE STRUCTURE OF FACULTY INFLUENCE: A CASE STUDY OF THE INSTRUCTOR'S ROLE IN THREE KINDS OF CHANGE AMONG COLUMBIA COLLEGE STUDENTS. New York: Bureau of Applied Social Research, Columbia University, 1966.

Webb. M. M. "Differential Perceptions of a College Teacher's Role." Unpublished Master's Thesis, Florida State University, 1962.

*Wilson, Robert and Jerry Gaff. STUDENT VOICE—FACULTY RESPONSE. Berkeley: Center for Research and Development in Higher Education, University of California, 1969.

Zander, Alvin F., Theodore Curtis, Howard Rosenfeld, *et al.* THE INFLUENCE OF TEACHERS AND PEERS ON ASPIRATIONS OF YOUTH. Ann Arbor: Research Center for Group Dynamics, Institute for Social Research, University of Michigan, 1961.

Adelson, Joseph. "The Teacher as a Model," in Sanford, Nevitt, ed. THE AMERICAN COLLEGE. New York: John Wiley and Sons, 1964, 396–417.

Alberti, R. E. "Influence of the Faculty on College Student Development," JOURNAL OF COLLEGE STUDENT PERSONNEL, 13 (January, 1972), 18–23.

Anderson, Valborg. "My Students Wear a Mask," ATLANTIC, 204 (June, 1961), 67–70.

Barber, Bernard. "Professors, Authority, and University Change," AMERICAN COUNCIL OF LEARNED SOCIETIES NEWSLETTER, 19 (December, 1968), 1–11.

Barrett, P. "Student-Faculty—Administration Relations in Higher Education," CATHOLIC EDUCATIONAL REVIEW, 58 (October, 1960), 473–478.

Brown, Donald R. "Non-Intellective Qualities and the Perceptions of the Ideal Student by College Faculty," JOURNAL OF EDUCATIONAL SOCIOLOGY, 33 (February, 1960), 269–278.

Brown, Ralph. "Rights and Responsibilities of Faculty," in O. A. Knorr and W. J. Minter, eds. ORDER AND FREEDOM ON CAMPUS. Boulder, Colorado: Western Interstate Commission for Higher Education, (October, 1965), 11–22.

Burkhardt, Frederick H. "The Changing Role of the Professor," in Lawrence Dennis and Joseph Kauffman, eds. THE AMERICAN COLLEGE AND THE STUDENT. Washington: American Council on Education, 1966, 206–210.

Cashman, P. H. "Working With the Modern Student," JOURNAL OF HIGHER EDUCATION, 41 (April, 1970), 264–274.

Cancilla, B., *et al.* "Behavior of College Students under an Unlimited Cut

System," JOURNAL OF EXPERIMENTAL EDUCATION, 36 (Spring, 1968), 11–16.

Combs, J. "Responses to the One-Year-Follow-Up Questionnaires," in J. C. Flanagan and W. W. Cooley, eds. PROJECT TALENT: ONE YEAR FOLLOW-UP STUDIES, U.S. DEPARTMENT HEALTH, EDUCATION AND WELFARE RESEARCH PROJECT NUMBER 2333. Pittsburgh, Pennsylvania: School of Education, University of Pittsburgh, 1966, 27–74.

Dilley, Josiah S. "Student-Faculty Noncommunication," JOURNAL OF COLLEGE STUDENT PERSONNEL, 8 (September, 1967), 282–285.

Duncan, H. G. and W. C. Duncan. "Student-Teacher Relationship," SOCIOLOGY AND SOCIAL RESEARCH, 18 (July–August, 1934), 530–540.

Ericksen, Stanford. "The Teacher, the Book and the Student's Private Knowledge," in W. J. Minter, ed. THE INDIVIDUAL AND THE SYSTEM. Boulder, Colorado: Western Interstate Commission for Higher Education, 1967, 83–100.

"Faculty Perceptions of Students," in CEEB, RESEARCH AND DEVELOPMENT REPORTS. Princeton, New Jersey: Educational Testing Service, 1966, 65–66.

Feinberg, L. "Faculty-Student Interaction: How Students Differ," JOURNAL OF COLLEGE STUDENT PERSONNEL, 13 (January, 1972), 24–27.

Finicher, C. "Of Students, Professors, and Computers," SCHOOL AND SOCIETY, 95 (March 4, 1967), 144–148.

Gamson, Zelda F. "Performance and Personalism in Student-Faculty Relations," SOCIOLOGY OF EDUCATION, 40 (Fall, 1967), 279–301.

Geiger, L. G. "Student Response to Faculty Power," SCHOOL AND SOCIETY, 99 (November, 1971), 424–426.

Gibson, William. "Students and Faculty," DISSENT, 7 (Summer, 1960), 232–235.

Gideonse, D. "Student Activists and Faculty Irrelevance," AMERICAN ASSOCIATION OF COLLEGES FOR TEACHER EDUCATION YEARBOOK, 21 (1968) 180–189.

Guagey, W. J. "Student Attitude Learning as a Function of Parental Acceptance and Sex of Teacher," JOURNAL OF TEACHER EDUCATION, 19 (Fall, 1968), 313–316.

Gusfield, Joseph. "The Academic Milieu: Students and Teachers in India and the United States," in Philip G. Altbach, ed. TURMOIL AND TRANSITION. New York: Basic Books, 1968, 93–127.

Gusfield, J. R. "Community or Communities: the Faculty Impact on Student Life," LIBERAL EDUCATION, 53 (March, 1967), 23–32.

Hechinger, Fred M. "Student Targets: Professors are Next," CHANGE, 1 (January–February, 1969), 36–39.

Hobbs, W. C. "Academicians Are Not Gods and Students are Not Persons," JOURNAL OF HIGHER EDUCATION, 39 (May, 1968), 281–283.

Howe, Irving. "Beleaguered Professors," ATLANTIC, 216 (November, 1965), 115–118.

Katz, Joseph. "Personality and Interpersonal Relations in the College Class-

406

room," in Sanford, Nevitt, ed. THE AMERICAN COLLEGE. New York: John Wiley and Sons, 1964, 365–395.

Kerlinger, F. N. "The Factor Structure and Content of Perceptions of Desirable Characteristics of Teachers," EDUCATIONAL AND PSYCHOLOGICAL MEASUREMENT, 27, (Fall, 1967), 643–656.

Kinnane, M. "Social Aspects of the Life of the College Teacher: Some Perceptions of Undergraduates and Woodrow Wilson Fellows," VOCATIONAL GUIDANCE QUARTERLY, 14 (Fall, 1965), 51–54.

Kitchen, W. W. "Teachers View Students: An Attitude Assessment through Personality Profiles," ADULT EDUCATION, 22 (Winter, 1972), 136–149.

Konvitz, Milton R. "Why One Professor Changed His Vote," in Immanuel Wallerstein and Paul Starr, eds. THE UNIVERSITY CRISIS READER, II. New York: Random House, 1971, 404–410.

Lehman, I. J. "The College Faculty as Perceived by Graduates and Non-Graduates," JOURNAL OF EDUCATIONAL MEASUREMENT, 3 (Summer, 1966), 169–173.

Leslie, Larry. "Faculty React to Student Participation," JOURNAL OF TEACHER EDUCATION, 21 (Spring, 1970), 53–59.

Lewis, Lionel S. "University Faculty and Students: A Profile," COLLEGE AND UNIVERSITY, 42 (Spring, 1967), 345–350.

*Lipset, S. M. "Faculty and Students: Allied and in Conflict," in S. M. Lipset, REBELLION IN THE UNIVERSITY, Boston: Little, Brown, 1972.

Lipset, Seymour Martin and Everett Carrill Ladd, jr. "And What Professors Think about Student Protest and Manners, Morals, Politics, and Chaos on the Campus," PSYCHOLOGY TODAY, 4 (November, 1970), 49–51, 106.

McKeachie, Wilbert J. "Significant Student and Faculty Characteristics Relevantt to Personalizing Higher Education," in W. J. Minter, ed. THE INDIVIDUAL AND THE SYSTEM. Boulder, Colorado: Western Interstate Commission for Higher Education, 1967, 21–36.

McKeachie, W. J. and Y. Lin "Sex Differences in Student Response to College Teachers: Teacher Warmth and Teacher Sex," AMERICAN EDUCATIONAL RESEARCH JOURNAL, 8 (March, 1971), 221–226.

Mayhew, Lewis. "Faculty and Students as Adversaries," COMPACT, 3 (October, 1969), 22–26.

Mollenkott, V. R. "Teachers, Students, and Selfishness in the Seventies," CHRISTIANITY TODAY, 14 (April 10, 1970), 6–8+.

Neumann, H. "Permanent War of Students and Teachers," JOURNAL OF GENERAL EDUCATION, 21 (January, 1970), 271–279.

Riesman, David. "The Influence of Student Culture and Faculty Values in the American College," in G. Bereday and P. Lauwreys, eds. YEARBOOK OF EDUCATION, 1959, Yonkers on Hudson, New York: World, 1959, 386–404.

Roche, J. P. "On Being an Unfashionable Professor," NEW YORK TIMES MAGAZINE, (October 18, 1970), 30–31+.

Roche, John P. "Retreat of the Faculty," NEW LEADER, 52 (November 10, 1969), 12–16.

Rusalem, H. "Physically Handicapped Student and the College Faculty," COLLEGE AND UNIVERSITY, 37 (Winter, 1962), 161–167.

Sanford, Nevitt. "The Students We Teach Today," JOURNAL OF THE CANADIAN ASSOCIATION OF UNIVERSITY STUDENT PERSONNEL SERVICES, 1 (Winter, 1967), 8–16.

Schoenwald, R. L. "Can We Hold On?" LIBERAL EDUCATION, 55 (December, 1969), 513–518.

Shapiro, S. A. "The Student and the Teacher: Face to Face," MOTIVE, 28 (February, 1968), 26–33.

Smith, A. A. "What Is Good College Teaching?" JOURNAL OF HIGHER EDUCATION, 15 (April, 1944), 216–218.

Spaulding, K. C. "Why Don't you Let Students Think Independently, Professor?" EDUCATIONAL FORUM, 27 (January, 1963), 151–155.

Stroup, H. H. "Values and Disvalues of Faculty-Student Committees," PERSONNEL AND GUIDANCE JOURNAL, 35 (January, 1957), 289–292.

Tanner, D. "Influencing Student Opinion in the College Classroom," JOURNAL OF EDUCATIONAL RESEARCH, 62 (September, 1968), 30–33.

Thielens, Wagner, jr. "The Teacher-Student Relationship in the College Classroom," in Lee C. Deighton. ENCYCLOPEDIA OF EDUCATION, Volume 9. New York: MacMillan, 1971, 305–310.

Whitaker, J. R. "Students as Persons: A Letter to a Young Instructor," PEABODY JOURNAL OF EDUCATION, 47 (March, 1970), 265–569.

White, R. E. "Rights of Students in the Classroom," SCHOOL AND SOCIETY, 95 (April 15, 1967), 263–264.

Wilson, R. and J. Gaff. "Student Voice—Faculty Response," in C. E. Kruytbosch and S. Messinger, eds. THE STATE OF THE UNIVERSITY. Beverly Hills, California: Sage, 1968, 181–188.

Young, Kenneth E. "The Coming and Conflict Between Students and Faculty," NASPA JOURNAL, 5 (January, 1968), 277–282.

Yourglich, A. "Study on Correlations Between College Teachers' and Students' Concepts of Ideal-Student and Ideal-Teacher," JOURNAL OF EDUCATIONAL RESEARCH, 49 (September, 1955), 59–64.

C.1.b. The Teaching Aspect

Dubin, R. and T. C. Taveggia. THE TEACHING-LEARNING PARADOX: A COMPARATIVE ANALYSIS OF COLLEGE TEACHING METHODS. Eugene, Oregon: Center for the Advanced Study of Educational Administration, University of Oregon, 1968.

Hatch, W. R. and A. Bennet. EFFECTIVENESS IN TEACHING. (New Dimensions in Higher Education, Number 3. U.S. Department of Health, Education and Welfare), Washington, D.C.: United States Government Printing Office, 1960.

Lean, A. E. AND MERELY TEACH: IRREVERENT ESSAYS ON THE MYTHOLOGY OF EDUCATION. Carbondale, Illinois: Southern Illinois University Press, 1968.

McKeachie, W. J. TEACHING TIPS: A GUIDEBOOK FOR THE BEGINNING COLLEGE TEACHER, Ann Arbor, Michigan: George Wahr, 1968.

408

Patton, J. A. "A Study of the Effects of Student Acceptance of Responsibility and Motivation on Course Behavior." Unpublished Ph.D. dissertation, University of Michigan, 1955.

Williams, Paul Leon. "A Study of Variables Related to Students' Perception of Classroom Tests." Unpublished Ph.D. dissertation, Illinois Institute of Technology, 1966.

Dearing, Bruce. "Abuses in Undergraduate Teaching: 1965," in G. K. Smith, ed. 1945–1970 TWENTY FIVE YEARS. San Francisco: Jossey-Bass, 1970, 220–226.

Di Vesta, F. J. "Evaluation of Several Teaching Methods by Adult Students," JOURNAL OF EDUCATIONAL RESEARCH, 46 (May, 1953), 659–671.

Evans, Ellis D. "Student Activism and Teaching Effectiveness: Survival of the Fittest?" JOURNAL OF COLLEGE STUDENT PERSONNEL, 10 (March, 1969), 102–108.

Harold, Brent. "Beyond Student Centered Teaching," CHANGE, 4 (October, 1972) 48–53.

Killian, James R., jr. "Teaching Is Better Than Ever," in THE TROUBLED CAMPUS. Boston: Little, Brown, 1966, 100–114.

McKeachie, W. J. "Students, Groups, and Teaching Methods," AMERICAN PSYCHOLOGIST, 13 (Oct. 1958), 580–584.

Paschal, Elizabeth. "Organizing for Better Instruction," in Alvin Eurich, ed. CAMPUS 1980. New York: Delacorte Press, 1968, 220–235.

Perry, R. R. "Criteria of Effective Teaching Behavior in an Institution of Higher Education," in G. N. Drewry, ed., THE INSTRUCTIONAL PROCESS AND INSTITUTIONAL RESEARCH: PROCEEDINGS OF SEVENTH ANNUAL FORUM OF THE ASSOCIATION FOR INSTITUTIONAL RESEARCH, 1967, 49–59.

Rossman, Michael. "The Totalitarian Classroom—A Learning Game," in Immanuel Wallerstein and Paul Stan, eds. THE UNIVERSITY CRISIS READER, I. New York: Random House, 1971, 537–546.

Taylor, H. "Individual Student," in Harold Taylor, ed. ESSAYS IN TEACHING. New York: Harper, 1950, 212–235.

Voeks, V. "Ridicule and Other Detriments to Effective Teaching," AMERICAN ASSOCIATION OF UNIVERSITY PROFESSORS BULLETIN, 40 (Winter, 1954–55), 621–630.

*Wilson, Robert C. and J. G. Gaff. "Faculty Culture and Interdisciplinary Studies," JOURNAL OF HIGHER EDUCATION, 62 (March, 1971), 186–201.

Wilson, Robert C. and J. G. Gaff. "Faculty Values and Improving Teaching," in G. Kerry Smith, ed. NEW TEACHING NEW LEARNING. San Francisco: Jossey-Bass, 1971, 39–46.

*Wilson, Robert C. and J. G. Gaff. "The Teaching Environment," AMERICAN ASSOCIATION OF UNIVERSITY PROFESSORS BULLETIN, 57 (Winter, 1971), 475–493.

Williams, E. M. "Innovation in Undergraduate Teaching," SCIENCE, 155 (February 24, 1967), 974–979.

Wolfe, Alan. "Working with the Working Class," CHANGE, 4 (February, 1972), 48–54.

C.1.c. Student Evaluation of Faculty

French, Grace Marian. "College Students' Concept of Effective Teaching Determined By an Analysis of Teacher Ratings." Unpublished Ph.D. dissertation, University of Washington, 1957.

Hodgson, Thomas Frances. "The General and Primary Factors in Student Evaluation of Teaching Ability." Unpublished Ph.D. dissertation, University of Washington, 1958.

Illinois. University. Student Senate. THE ADVISER: AN EVALUATION OF TEACHERS AND COURSES AT THE UNIVERSITY OF ILLINOIS. Urbana-Champaign, 1968.

Jenks, R. Stephan. THE STUDENT ROLE IN FACULTY SELECTION, EVALUATION AND RETENTION. Washington, D.C.: National Association of State Universities and Land Grant Colleges, 1969.

Leftwich, William Hensley. "A Comparison of Graphic and Forced-Choice Ratings of Teaching Performance at the College and University Level." Unpublished Ph.D. dissertation, Purdue University, 1962.

*Miller, Richard I. EVALUATING FACULTY PERFORMANCE. San Francisco: Jossey-Bass, 1972.

Riley, John W., Bryce F. Ryan, and Marcia Lifshitz. THE STUDENT LOOKS AT HIS TEACHER. New Brunswick, New Jersey: Rutgers University Press, 1950.

Wolthuis, Ronald Marvin. "A Study of Factors Related to Sudent Ratings of College Instructors." Unpublished Ed.D. dissertation, Western Michigan University, 1970.

Bousfield, W. A. "Students' Ratings of Qualities Considered Desirable in College Professions," SCHOOL AND SOCIETY, 51 (February 24, 1940), 253–256.

Clark, K. E. and R. J. Keller. "Student Ratings of College Teaching," in Ruth Eckert and R. J. Keller, eds. A UNIVERSITY LOOKS AT ITS PROGRAM: THE REPORT OF THE UNIVERSITY OF MINNESOTA BUREAU OF INSTITUTIONAL RESEARCH, 1942–1952. Minneapolis, Minnesota: The University of Minnesota Press, 1954, 197–212.

Clinton, R. J. "Qualities College Students Desire in College Instructors," SCHOOL AND SOCIETY, 32 (November 22, 1930), 702.

Coffman, W. E. "Determining Students' Concepts of Effective Teaching From Their Ratings of Instructors," JOURNAL OF EDUCATIONAL PSYCHOLOGY, 45 (May, 1953), 659–671.

Feuer, Lewis S. "Should College Students Grade Their Teachers?" NEW YORK TIMES MAGAZINE, (September 18, 1966), 56–60.

Fosmire, F. R. "Generality of Some Academic Reputations," SCIENCE, 124 (October 12, 1956), 680–681.

410

Gadrella, B. M. "College Students Views and Ratings of an Ideal Professor," COLLEGE AND UNIVERSITY, 44 (Fall, 1968), 89–96.

Haggard, W. W. "Some freshman Describe the Desirable College Teacher," SCHOOL AND SOCIETY, 58 (September 25, 1943), 238–240.

Hoffman, R. W. "Students Portray the Excellent Teacher," IMPROVING COLLEGE AND UNIVERSITY TEACHING, 11 (Winter, 1963), 21–24.

Kinnane, M. "Interpretation of College Teaching: Views of Undergraduates and Woodrow Wilson Fellows," EDUCATIONAL RECORD, 45 (Spring, 1964), 167–172.

Krueger, L. M. "Traits in College Teachers Preferred by Students: A Study in Leadership," PHI DELTA KAPPAN, 19 (September, 1936), 14–19.

Lewis, L. S. "Students' Images of Professors," EDUCATIONAL FORUM, 32 (January, 1968), 185–190.

McClelland, J. N. "Effect of Student Evaluations of College Instruction upon Subsequent Evaluations," CALIFORNIA JOURNAL OF EDUCATIONAL RESEARCH, 21 (March, 1970), 88–95.

McKeachie, W. J. "Student Ratings of Faculty: A Research Review," IMPROVING COLLEGE AND UNIVERSITY TEACHING, 5 (Winter, 1957), 31–38.

Musella, D. and R. Rusch. "Student Opinion on College Teaching," IMPROVING COLLEGE AND UNIVERSITY TEACHING, 16 (Spring, 1968), 137–140.

Pogue, F. G., jr. "Students' Ratings of the Ideal Teacher," IMPROVING COLLEGE AND UNIVERSITY TEACHING, 15 (Spring, 1967), 133–136.

Rayder, N. F. "College Student Ratings of Instructors," JOURNAL OF EXPERIMENTAL EDUCATION, 37 (Winter, 1968), 76–81.

Smith, A. A. "College Teachers Evaluated by Students," SOCIOLOGY AND SOCIAL RESEARCH, 28 (July–August, 1944), 471–478.

Werdell, Philip. "Student Participation in Effective Programs of Faculty Evaluation," in G. K. Smith, ed. IN SEARCH OF LEADERS. Washington, D.C.: American Association for Higher Education, 1967, 182–186.

Yamamoto, K. and H. F. Dizney. "Eight Professors: A Study on College Students Preferences Among Their Teachers," JOURNAL OF EDUCATIONAL PSYCHOLOGY, 57 (June, 1966), 146–150.

Yonge, G. D. and J. M. Sasseurath. "Student Personality Correlates of Teacher Ratings," JOURNAL OF EDUCATIONAL PSYCHOLOGY, 59 (February, 1968), 44–52.

C.1.d. Teachers or Researchers: the Question of Faculty Role

Cross Reference: See sections on Faculty Role in student activism (Ik6) and the politics of higher education (Ik9).

Eckert, R. E. and Sticklein, J. E. JOB MOTIVATIONS AND SATISFACTIONS OF COLLEGE TEACHERS: A STUDY OF FACULTY MEMBERS IN

MINNESOTA COLLEGES. U.S. Department of Health, Education, and Welfare Cooperative Research. Monograph Number 7 (OE-53009). Washington, D.C.: U.S. Government Printing Office, 1961.

Gardner, John. THE FLIGHT FROM TEACHING. New York: Carnegie Foundation for the Advancement of Teaching, 1964.

Beichman, A. "Will Teacher be the New Drop-Out?" NEW YORK TIMES MAGAZINE, (December 7, 1969), 48–49+.

Blank, B. "Student Opinion about Faculty Research," SCHOOL AND SOCIETY, 90 (March 24, 1962), 146–147.

Bresler, J. B. "Teaching Effectiveness and Government Awards," SCIENCE, 160 (April 12, 1968), 164–167.

Brustein, Robert. "The Case for Professionalism," in Irving Howe, ed. in BEYOND THE NEW LEFT. New York: McCall, 1970, 214–221.

Fischer, John. "Is There a Teacher on the Faculty? HARPER'S, 230 (February, 1965), 18–28.

Gwyn, Frederick L. "And Sadly Teach," in Lawrence Dennis and Joseph Kauffman, eds. THE AMERICAN COLLEGE AND THE STUDENT. Washington: American Council on Education, 1966, 196–201.

Hammond, P. E., et al. "Teaching versus Research: Sources of Misperceptions," JOURNAL OF HIGHER EDUCATION, 40 (December, 1969), 682–690.

Hayes, J. R. "Research, Teaching, and Faculty Fate," SCIENCE, 172 (April 16, 1971), 227–230.

Hutchinson, William R. "Yes, John, There Are Teachers on the Faculty," AMERICAN SCHOLAR, 35 (Summer, 1966), 430–441.

Johnson, Ernest. "The Professor's Dilemma," POLITICAL AFFAIRS, 44 (January, 1965), 63–64.

Knapp, R. H. "Changing Functions of the College Professor," in N. Sanford, ed. THE AMERICAN COLLEGE:A PSYCHOLOGICAL AND SOCIAL INTERPRETATION OF THE HIGHER LEARNING. New York: Wiley. 1962, 290–310.

Kolb, William. "The College Teacher as Professional Man Plus," in G. K. Smith, et al., eds. STRESS AND CAMPUS RESPONSE. San Francisco: Jossey-Bass, 1968, 173–177.

Martin, T. W. and K. J. Berry. "Teaching-Research Dilemma: Its Sources in the University Setting," JOURNAL OF HIGHER EDUCATION, 40 (December, 1969), 691–703.

Maslow, A. H. and W. Zimmerman. "College Teaching Ability, Scholarly Activity, and Personality," JOURNAL OF EDUCATIONAL PSYCHOLOGY, 47 (March, 1956), 185–189.

Parrish, K. and G. R. Weldy. "Good Scholarship: Do Students Really Care?" CLEARING HOUSE, 43 (January, 1969), 275–279.

Parsons, H. L. "Meletus or Socrates?" LIBERAL EDUCATION, 49 (October, 1963), 411–420.

Rudolph, Frederick. "Neglect of Students as a Historical Tradition," in Lawrence Dennis and Joseph Kauffman, eds. THE AMERICAN COLLEGE AND THE STUDENT. Washington: American Council on Education, 1966, 47–58.

412

C.2. Student Achievement: General Considerations

Cross Reference: To view this concept from the reverse side, see section on dropping out of the university (IIIF2).

Ashcraft, Marion Gilbert. AN ANALYSIS OF THE EFFECTS OF THE HIGH SCHOOL CURRICULUM UPON COLLEGE ACHIEVEMENT. Las Cruces: New Mexico Occupational Research and Development Coordinating Unit, 1967.

Borup, Jerry, Floyd Elliot and John Guinn. FRESHMAN STUDENT IDENTITY: ANALYSIS OF ATTITUDE, MOTIVATION AND ACHIEVEMENT. Kingsville: Texas A. and T. University, 1968.

Bronzaft, Arline Lilian. "Test-anxiety, Social Mobility and Academic Achievement." Unpublished Ph.D. dissertation, Columbia University, 1966.

Daniel, Lark Owen III. "Self-reported Academic Achievement as Related to Personal Data, Study Mechanics, and Knowledge of Learning Principles." Unpublished Ph.D. dissertation, Purdue University, 1935.

Darley, John G. PROMISE AND PERFORMANCE: A STUDY OF ABILITY AND ACHIEVEMENT IN HIGHER EDUCATION. Berkeley: Center for the Study of Higher Education, University of California, 1962.

Edgerton, H. A. and H. A. Toops. ACADEMIC PROGRESS: A FOUR YEAR FOLLOW-UP STUDY OF THE FRESHMAN ENTERING OHIO STATE UNIVERSITY IN 1923. OHIO STATE UNIVERSITY STUDENTS CONTRIBUTIONS IN SCHOOL ADMINISTRATION. Columbus, Ohio: Ohio State University Press, 1929.

Elliot, H. Chandler. THE EFFECTIVE STUDENT. New York: Harper and Row, 1966.

Frederiksen, N. O. and W. B. Schrader. ACADEMIC ACHIEVEMENT OF VETERAN AND NON-VETERAN STUDENTS. Washington, D.C.: American Psychological Association, 1952.

Gaffney, Louis B. "Likes and Dislikes of College Students in Relation to Adjustment and Achievement." Unpublished Ph.D. dissertation, University of Minnesota, 1956.

Garms, Joe Dewayne. "Predicting Scholastic Achievement With Nonintellectual Variables." Unpublished Ph.D. dissertation, Texas Technical University, 1967.

Gladstein, G. A. "The Relationship Between Study Behavior and Personality for Academically Successful Students." Unpublished Ph.D. dissertation, University of Chicago, 1957.

Holland, John L. and James M. Richards, jr. ACADEMIC AND NON-ACADEMIC ACCOMPLISHMENT IN A REPRESENTATIVE SAMPLE TAKEN FROM A POPULATION OF 612,000. Iowa City: American College Testing Program, 1966.

Hurst, Charles G., jr. "Speech and Functional Intelligence: An Experimental Study of Educational Implications of A Basic Speech Course." Unpublished Ph.D. dissertation, Wayne State University, 1961.

Kimball, Barbara. "Relationship Between Non-Intellective Factors and

Scholastic Achievement." Unpublished Ph.D. dissertation, Harvard University, 1950.

Klingelhofer, Edwin Lewis. "The Relationship of Academic Advisement to the Scholastic Performance of College Probationary Students." Unpublished Ph.D. dissertation, University of Iowa, 1953.

Kramer, Margaret Louise Lindsey. "An Evaluation of the Effectiveness of A Freshman Remedial English Program on Subsequent Academic Performance." Unpublished Ph.D. dissertation, University of Houston, 1962.

Laude, Leon A. "The Relationship of Selected Interests of Male College Freshmen to Three Academic Levels of Achievement." Unpublished Ph.D. dissertation, University of Michigan, 1958.

McLauglin, Roger James, D.S.S. "The Process of Decision in College Selection and its Relation to Student Achievement and Withdrawal." Unpublished Ph.D. dissertation, Syracuse University, 1966.

Mathieu, Phillippa L. and Janet P. Moursand. RELATIONSHIP OF GROUP COUNCILING TO SUBSEQUENT ACADEMIC PERFORMANCE AT THE COLLEGE LEVEL. Madison: Wisconsin University, Psychotherapy Research Group, 1962.

Meade, Martin James. "A Biographical Inventory as a Predictor of An Essentially Non-Intellectual Criterion of College success." Unpublished Ph.D. dissertation, Fordham University, 1963.

Missall, Ellswerth. TO HELP THEM ACHIEVE. Brooklyn: School of General Studies, Office of the Dean, Brooklyn College of the City University of New York, 1967.

*Murphy, Lois and Esther Raushenbush, eds. ACHIEVEMENT IN THE COLLEGE YEARS. New York: Harper and Row, 1960.

Newell, John M. PERFORMANCE BY HIGH AND LOW RISK COLLEGE FRESHMEN ON MEASURES OF CREATIVITY. Medford, Massachusetts: Tufts University, 1966.

Oxhorn, Joseph Lewis. "The Relation of Figure Drawings To Masculine-Feminine Orientation and Academic Achievement." Unpublished Ed.D. dissertation, Rutgers, 1965.

Pemberton, W. A. ABILITY: VALUES AND COLLEGE ACHIEVEMENT. (University of Delaware Studies in Higher Education, Number 1). Newark, Delaware, 1963.

Pride, Carl Wayne. "A Study of the Effect of An Experimental Guidance Program On Academic Achievement of a Selected Group of Students." Unpublished Ed.D. dissertation, University of Houston, 1968.

*Propper, Martin Michael. "Academic Achievement and Alienation in Intellectually Able Adolescents." Unpublished Ph.D. dissertation, St. John's University, 1968.

Rogers, George Walter. "Lecture Listening Skills: Their Nature And Relation To Achievement." Unpublished Ph.D. dissertation, Ohio State University, 1959.

Schlossberg, Nancy K. MEN-IN-TRANSITION, A STUDY OF ADULT MALE UNDERGRADUATES AT WAYNE STATE UNIVERSITY. Detroit, Michigan: Wayne State University, Montieth College, 1967.

414

Simms, James Carroll. "Values and Status Variables as Determinants of Academic Achievement." Unpublished Ph.D. dissertation, Emory University, 1962.

Smith, C. L. "Significant Differences Between High-Ability Achieving College Freshman as Revealed by Interview Data." Unpublished Ph.D. dissertation, University of Kentucky, 1962.

Suslow, Sidney, *et al*. STUDENT PERFORMANCE AND ATTRITION AT THE UNIVERSITY OF CALIFORNIA, BERKELEY: A FOLLOW-UP OF THE ENTERING FRESHMAN CLASSES OF FALL 1955 AND FALL 1960. Berkeley: University of California, Office of Institutional Research, 1968.

Walter, Verne Arthur. "The Effect of Need For Academic Achievement on the Performance of College Students in Learning Certain Study Skills." Unpublished Ph.D. dissertation, Ohio State University, 1956.

Wellington, J. A. "Factors Related to Academic Success of Resident Freshmen Men at a Midwestern Liberal Arts College During Academic Year 1952–1953." Unpublished Ph.D. dissertation, Northwestern University, 1954.

Werner, O. H. THE SCHOLASTIC PERSISTENCE OF 2,140 UNCLASSIFIED STUDENTS IN THE UNIVERSITY OF NEBRASKA. University of Nebraska Printing Division, 1955.

Alexander, H. and Ruth Woodruff. "Determinants of College Success," JOURNAL OF HIGHER EDUCATION, 11 (December, 1940), 479–484.

Andrew, D. C. "A Descriptive Analysis of 248 Non-High School Graduates Admitted to the University of Utah," JOURNAL OF EDUCATIONAL RESEARCH, 47 (April, 1954), 589–598.

Bauer, E. J. "Achievement and Role Definition of the College Student," U.S. DEPARTMENT OF HEALTH, EDUCATION, AND WELFARE COOPERATIVE RESEARCH PROJECT NUMBER 2605. Lawrence, Kansas: University of Kansas, 1965.

Berg, I. A. and R. P. Larsen. "A Comparative Study of Students Entering College One or More Semesters before Graduation from High School," JOURNAL OF EDUCATIONAL RESEARCH, 39 (September, 1939), 33–41.

Blanton, W. L. and R. F. Peck. "College Student Motivation and Academic Performance," EDUCATIONAL AND PSYCHOLOGICAL MEASUREMENT, 24 (Winter, 1964), 897–912.

Bluhm, H. P. and S. Couch. "Characteristics and Academic Performance of Readmitted Students," COLLEGE AND UNIVERSITY, 47 (Spring, 1972), 168–175.

Brown, W. F., N. Abeles, and I. Iscoe. "Motivational Differences between High and Low Scholarship Students," JOURNAL OF EDUCATIONAL PSYCOLOGY, 45 (April, 1954). 215–223.

Carter, G. C. "Student Traits and Progression through College," JOURNAL OF EDUCATIONAL PSYCHOLOGY, 40 (May, 1949), 306–308.

*Clark, B. R. "Cooling-Out Function in Higher Education," AMERICAN JOURNAL OF SOCIOLOGY, 65 (May, 1960), 569–576.

Coleman, J. S. "Academic Achievement and the Structure of Competition," HARVARD EDUCATIONAL REVIEW, 29 (Summer, 1959), 337–347.

Dwyer, P. "The Correlation between Age at Entrance and Success in College," JOURNAL OF EDUCATIONAL PSYCHOLOGY, 30 (April, 1939), 251–264.

Eckland, B. K. "Academic Ability, Higher Education, and Occupational Mobility," AMERICAN SOCIOLOGICAL REVIEW, 30 (October, 1965), 735–746.

Eddy, Edward D., jr. "The Possible and the Potential," in Kaoru Yamamoto, ed. THE COLLEGE STUDENT AND HIS CULTURE. Boston: Houghton Mifflin, 1968, 395–400.

Ellis, Robert A., Robert J. Parelius and Ann P. Parelius. "The Collegiate Scholar: Education for Elite Status," SOCIOLOGY OF EDUCATION, 44 (Winter, 1971), 27–58.

Erb, E. D. "Conformity and Achievement in College," PERSONNEL AND GUIDANCE JOURNAL, 39 (January, 1961), 361–366.

Farnsworth, D. S. "Academic Success or Failure in College Students," COLLEGE BOARD REVIEW, 24 (Fall, 1954), 3–7.

Farnsworth, D. S. "Some Non-Academic Causes of Success and Failure in College Students," COLLEGE ADMISSIONS, 2 (1955), 72–78.

Garrett, H. F. "A Review and Interpretation of Investigations of Factors Related to Scholastic Success in College of Arts and Sciences and Teachers Colleges," JOURNAL OF EXPERIMENTAL EDUCATION, 18 (December, 1949), 91–138.

Goldberg, Maxwell and Norman Ruiland. "The Abler Student," in Samuel Baskin, ed. HIGHER EDUCATION: SOME NEWER DEVELOPMENTS. New York: McGraw-Hill, 1965, 104–127.

Haggard, E. "Personality Dynamics and Intellectual Achievement," in Lois Murphy and Esther Raushenbush, eds. ACHIEVEMENT IN THE COLLEGE YEARS: A RECORD OF INTELLECTUAL AND PERSONAL GROWTH. New York: Harper, 1960, 116–133.

Heist, Paul, et al. "Personality and Scholarship," SCIENCE, 133 (February 10, 1961), 362–367.

Holmes, D. "Investigation of Student Attitudes Which May Be Related to Leaving College," JOURNAL OF EDUCATIONAL RESEARCH, 52 (September, 1958), 17–21.

Jensen, B. T. "Instruction and Personality as Factors in Student Performance," JOURNAL OF EDUCATIONAL RESEARCH, 47 (March, 1954), 529–535.

Jex, F. B., and R. M. Merrill. "A Study in Persistence: Withdrawal and Graduation Rates at the University of Utah," PERSONNEL AND GUIDANCE JOURNAL, 40 (May, 1962), 762–768.

Johnson, C. C. and C. E. Gearing. "Influences on Academic Performance," INSTITUTE FOR RESEARCH IN THE BEHAVIORAL, ECONOMIC, AND MANAGEMENT SCIENCES, INSTITUTE PAPER NUMBER 125. Lafayette, Indiana: Herman C. Krannert Graduate School of Industrial Administration, Purdue University, 1966.

Livesay, T. M. "Does Test Intelligence Increase at the College Level?" JOURNAL OF EDUCATIONAL PSYCHOLOGY, 30 (January, 1939), 63–68.

416

MacLachlan, P. S. and C. W. Burnett. "Who Are the Superior Freshmen in College?" PERSONNEL AND GUIDANCE JOURNAL, 32 (February, 1954), 345–349.

Marks, E., J. Adhley, and M. Zeigler. "Recommended Curricular Change and Scholastic Performance," JOURNAL OF COUNSELING PSYCHOLOGY, 12 (Spring, 1965), 17–22.

Miller, E. L. "The Success of Freshmen in College," NORTH CENTRAL ASSOCIATION QUARTERLY, 2 (September, 1927), 140–145.

Mountford, J. F. "Success and Failure at the University," UNIVERSITY QUARTERLY, 11 (May, 1957), 226–234.

Munger, P. "Factors Related to Persistence in College Who Ranked in Lower Third of Their High School Class," JOURNAL OF COUNSELING PSYCHOLOGY, 1 (Fall, 1954), 132–136.

Neidt, C. O. and D. E. Hedlund. "Relationship between Changes in Attitudes toward a Course and Final Achievement," JOURNAL OF EDUCATIONAL RESEARCH, 61 (October, 1967), 56–58.

Nixon, Robert E. "The Goals of Growth in College Students," JOURNAL OF THE NATIONAL ASSOCIATION OF WOMEN DEANS AND COUNSELORS, 29 (Winter, 1966), 71–75.

Olson, L. A. "Academic Attitudes, Expectations and Achievement," IMPROVING COLLEGE AND UNIVERSITY TEACHING, 13 (Winter, 1965), 39–41.

Pace, C. R. and C. E. Hawley. "Evaluation of Student Progress in Relation to Program and Course Objectives," in American Council on Education, IMPROVING COLLEGE INSTRUCTION, Washington, D.C.: American Council on Education, n.d., 93–113.

Pepinsky, H. B. "Productivity in the University," PERSONNEL AND GUIDANCE JOURNAL, 35 (November, 1956), 134–139.

Pepinsky, H. B. "Research on Productive Behavior," PERSONNEL AND GUIDANCE JOURNAL, 33 (November, 1954), 140–144.

Pressey, S. L. "Age of College Graduation and Success in Adult Life," PSYCHOLOGICAL REVIEW, 30 (June 1946), 226–233.

Rogers, Agnes L. "The Growth of Intelligence at the College Level," SCHOOL AND SOCIETY, 31 (May 24, 1930), 693–699.

Roth, J. A. "The Study of Academic Success and Failure," EDUCATIONAL RESEARCH BULLETIN, 35 (October, 1956), 176–182.

Rowe, F. B. "Non-intellective Factors Affecting Student Performance," in K. M. Wilson, ed. RESEARCH RELATED TO COLLEGE ADMISSIONS. Atlanta, Georgia: Southern Regional Educational Board, 1963, 135–144.

Schoenfeldt, L. F. "Post-high-school Education," in J. C. Flanagan and W. W. Cooley, eds. PROJECT TALENT: ONE-YEAR FOLLOW-UP STUDIES. (U.S. Department of Health, Education, and Welfare Cooperative Research Project Number 2333) Pittsburgh, Pennsylvania: School of Education, University of Pittsburgh, 1966, 91–129.

Schrammel, H. E. and E. R. Wood. "Success and Failure of College Students," KANSAS STATE TEACHERS COLLEGE STUDIES IN EDUCATION, 1931.

"The Selection, Retention and Promotion of Undergraduates," BULLETIN OF AMERICAN ASSOCIATION OF UNIVERSITY PROFESSORS, 12 October, 1926), 373–481.

Stright, I. L. "Some Factors Affecting College Success," JOURNAL OF EDUCATIONAL PSYCHOLOGY, 38 (April, 1947), 232–240.

Tom, Frederick K. T. "College Success of Former Students of Vocational Agriculture," AGRICULTURAL EDUCATION MAGAZINE, 32 (February, 1960), 172–176.

Weintraub, Ruth and Ruth Salley. "Graduation Prospects of an Entering Freshman," JOURNAL OF EDUCATIONAL RESEARCH, 39 (October, 1945), 116–126.

Weitz, Henry and Jean H. Wilkinson. "The Relationship Between Certain Non-Intellective Factors and Academic Success in College," JOURNAL OF COUNSELING PSYCHOLOGY, 4 (Spring, 1957), 54–60.

Williams, V. "Difficulties in Identifying Relatively Permanent Characteristics Related to Persistence in College," JOURNAL OF COUNSELING PSYCHOLOGY, 13 (1966), 108.

Williamson, E. G. "The Relationship of Number of Hours of Study to Scholarship," JOURNAL OF EDUCATIONAL PSYCHOLOGY, 26 (December, 1935), 638.

Woodman, E. M. "Description of a Guidance Instrument Designed to Measure Attitudes Related to Academic Success in College," EDUCATIONAL AND PSYCHOLOGICAL MEASUREMENT, 12 (Summer, 1952), 275–284.

Zaccaria, L. and J. Greaser. "Factors Related to Persistence in an Urban Commuter University," JOURNAL OF COLLEGE STUDENT PERSONNEL, 12 (July, 1971), 286–291.

C.2.a. Prediction and Quantified Correlates of Achievement

Abraham, A. A. THEY CAME TO COLLEGE. Tallahassee, Florida: Agricultural and Mechanical University, 1964.

Acey, Alfred A. TIME AS A RELEVANT VARIABLE WHEN PERSONALITY SCORES ARE USED TO PREDICT ACHIEVEMENT. Washington, D.C.: American Personnel and Guidance Association, 1968.

Alpert, R. S. "Anxiety in Academic Achievement Situations: Its Measurement and Relation to Aptitude," Unpublished Ph.D. dissertation, Stanford University, 1957.

Anastasi, Anne, *et al.* THE VALIDATION OF A BIOGRAPHICAL INVENTORY AS A PREDICTOR OF COLLEGE SUCCESS. New York: College Entrance Examination Board, 1960.

*Astin, Alexander W. PREDICTING ACADEMIC PERFORMANCE IN COLLEGE. New York: Free Press, 1971.

Baker, P. C. II. "Experiments in Variable Selection for Prediction of Academic Achievement." Unpublished Ph.D. dissertation, Purdue University, 1955.

Buel, William B. "A Study of Scholastic Achievement as Measured By Three

418

Forms of an Interest Inventory." Unpublished Ph.D. dissertation, Ohio State University, 1958.

Chase, Clinton I. PREDICTING THE SUCCESS OF UNIVERSITY FRESH-MEN. Bloomington, Indiana: Indiana University Bureau of Educational Studies and Testing, 1963.

Coombs, R. H. "A Socio-psychological Analysis of the Relationship Between High School and College Scholastic Achievement." Unpublished Ph.D. dissertation, Washington State University, 1964.

Donahue, Wilma T., C. Coombs, and R. M. W. Travers, eds. MEASURE-MENT OF STUDENT ADJUSTMENT TO ACHIEVEMENT. Ann Arbor, Michigan: University of Michigan Press, 1949.

Einspahr, M. H. "The Construction and Validation of Scales for Predicting Academic Success in College." Unpublished Ph.D. dissertation, University of Houston, 1959.

Fisher, Everett James. "A Longitudinal Study of the Prediction of Scholastic Success at the University of Tennessee." Unpublished Ph.D. dissertation, University of Tennessee, 1962.

Hartnett, Rodney T. "An Analysis of Factors Associated with Changes in Scholastic Performance Patterns." Unpublished Ph.D. dissertation, Michigan State University, 1963.

Hoyt, Donald P. FORECASTING ACADEMIC SUCCESS IN SPECIFIC COLLEGES. Iowa City, Iowa: American College Testing Program, 1968.

Johnson, Richard W. "The Effectiveness of Academic Interest Scales in Predicting College Achievement," Unpublished Ph.D. dissertation, University of Massachusetts, 1968.

Marks, Edmond. "Nonadditive Effects in the Prediction of Academic Achievement." Unpublished Ph.D. dissertation, Pennsylvania State University, 1964.

Messick, Samuel. PERSONALITY MEASUREMENT AND COLLEGE PER-FORMANCE. Princeton, New Jersey: Educational Testing Service, 1963.

*Richards, James M. ASSESSING STUDENT PERFORMANCE IN COL-LEGE Washington, D.C.: ERIC Clearing House on Higher Education, 1970.

Richards, J. M., et al. THE ASSESSMENT OF STUDENT ACCOMPLISH-MENT IN COLLEGE. Iowa City, Iowa: American College Testing Program, 1966.

Durflinger, G. W. "The Prediction of College Success: a Summary of Present Findings," JOURNAL OF AMERICAN ASSOCIATION OF COLLEGE REGISTRARS, 19 (1943), 68–78.

Feder, D. "Factors Which Affect Achievement and Its Prediction at the College Level," JOURNAL OF AMERICAN ASSOCIATION OF COLLEGE REGISTRARS, 15 (1940), 107–117.

Holland, John L. "The Prediction of College Grades from Personality and Aptitude Variables," JOURNAL OF EDUCATIONAL PSYCHOLOGY, 51 (October, 1960), 245–254.

Howard, V. and W. Warrington. "Inventory of Beliefs: Changes in Beliefs and Attitudes and Academic Success Prediction," PERSONNEL AND GUIDANCE JOURNAL, 37 (December, 1958), 299–302.

Jackson, R. A. "Prediction of the Academic Success of College Freshmen," JOURNAL OF EDUCATIONAL PSYCHOLOGY, 46 (May, 1955), 296–301.

Johnston, J. B. "Predicting Success or Failure in College at the Time of Entrance: II," SCHOOL AND SOCIETY, 20 (July 5, 1924), 27–34.

Long, J. M. "Sex Differences in Academic Prediction Based on Scholastic Personality and Interest Factors," JOURNAL OF EXPERIMENTAL EDUCATION, 32 (Spring, 1964), 239–248.

Lorge, Irving D. "Trends in the Measurement of Achievement," in Wilma Donahue, et al., eds. THE MEASUREMENT OF STUDENT ADJUSTMENT AND ACHIEVEMENT. Ann Arbor: University of Michigan Press, 1949.

"Prediction of the First Year College Performance of High Aptitude Students," PSYCHOLOGICAL MONOGRAPHS, 77 (No. 7, 1963), 1–29.

Richards, J. M., jr., and S. W. Lutz. "Predicting Student Accomplishment in College from the ACT Assessment," JOURNAL OF EDUCATIONAL MEASUREMENT, 5 (Spring, 1968), 17–29.

Richards, J. M., jr., J. L. Holland and S. W. Lutz. "The Assessment of Student Accomplishment in College," JOURNAL OF COLLEGE STUDENT PERSONNEL, 8 (November, 1967), 360–365.

Richards, J. M., jr., J. L. Holland and S. W. Lutz. "The Prediction of Student Accomplishment in College," JOURNAL OF EDUCATIONAL PSYCHOLOGY, 58 (December, 1967), 343–355.

Stanley, J. C. "Predicting College Success of the Educationally Disadvantaged," SCIENCE, 171 (February 19, 1971), 640–647.

Travers, Robert. "Significant Research on the Prediction of Academic Success," in Wilma Donahue, et al. eds. THE MEASUREMENT OF STUDENT ADJUSTMENT AND ACHIEVEMENT. Ann Arbor: University of Michigan Press, 1949. 147–190.

Wegner, Eldon and William Sewell. "Selection and Context as Factors Affecting the Probability of Graduation from College," AMERICAN JOURNAL OF SOCIOLOGY, 75 (January, 1970), 665–679.

C.2.b. Achievement in Specific Fields and Junior Colleges

Aiken, Lewis Roscoe jr. "Mathemaphobia and Mathemaphilia: An Analysis of Personal and Social Factors Affecting Performance in Mathematics." Unpublished Ph.D. dissertation, University of North Carolina at Chapel Hill, 1960.

Augustine, Rodger D. PERSISTENCE AND ATTRITION OF ENGINEERING STUDENTS, A STUDY OF FRESHMAN AND SOPHOMORE ENGINEERING STUDENTS AT THREE MIDWESTERN UNIVERSITIES. Washington: ERIC Clearing House, 1966.

Begarb, Michael Jay. "The Effect of Differences in Curricula and Experiences on Social Work, Student Attitudes and Knowledge About Mental Retarda-

420

tion." Unpublished Ph.D. dissertation, Catholic University of America, 1968.

Bonner, Leon William. "Factors Associated with the Academic Achievement of Freshman Students at a Southern Agricultural College." Unpublished Ph.D. dissertation, Pennsylvania State University, 1956.

Boyce, James Edward. "Comparison of Methods of Combining Scores to Predict Academic Success in a Cooperative Engineering Program." Unpublished Ph.D. dissertation, Purdue University, 1955.

Burgess, Elva. "Personality Factors in Over-and Under-achievers in Engineering." Unpublished Ph.D. dissertation, Pennsylvania State University, 1955.

Caro, Paul Wiley, jr. "The Effect of Class Attendance and 'Time Structured' Content on Achievement in General Psychology." Unpublished Ph.D. dissertation, University of Tennessee, 1961.

Champion, John Mills. "A Method for Predicting Success of Commerce Students." Unpublished Ph.D. dissertation, Purdue University, 1958.

Crooks, William Ramsden. "The Value of Personality Adjustment Questionnaire Items in the Prediction of Outcomes in College Engineering Training." Unpublished Ph.D. dissertation, University of Minnesota, 1952.

Foy, Glenn Arthur. "A Study of the Relationship Between Certain Factor-analyzed Ability Measures and Success in College Engineering." Unpublished Ph.D. dissertation, University of Southern California, 1959.

Gaza, Caesar Thomas. "The Prediction of Success in Nursing Training: The Use of the Interpersonal System or Multilevel Personality Diagnosis as an Adjunct to the Selection Program of a Hospital School of Nursing." Unpublished Ph.D. dissertation, New York University, 1963.

Goodman, Charles H. "Ability Patterns of Engineers and Success in Engineering School." Unpublished Ph.D. dissertation, Pennsylvania State University, 1941.

Grady, Michael jr. "The Interrelationships Between (1) Each of Three Motivational Needs of Officer Students (2) The Pattern of Scores on a Decision Making Test And (3) Academic Success in One of Three Air University Resident Courses." Unpublished Ph.D. dissertation, University of Alabama, 1964.

Herman, David Ovenden. "A Factorial Study of Research Potential in Chemistry." Unpublished Ph.D. dissertation, Ohio State University, 1959.

Landiss, Carl W. "Relative Influence of Various Physical Education Activities on Motor Ability and Physical Fitness on Male College Freshman." Ann Arbor, Michigan: University Microfilms, 1951.

McClelland, John B. A SUMMARY OF STUDIES IN ACHIEVEMENT OF VOCATIONAL AGRICULTURE GRADUATES IN COLLEGE. Ames: Iowa State University of Science of Technology. Iowa State Department of Public Instruction, 1965.

Mayfield, Eugene Cunliffe. "Interests as a Predictor of Graduation in Engineering." Unpublished Ph.D. dissertation, Purdue University, 1960.

Mercer, Carolyn Malina. "Reading and its Relationship with Parental Identification and Personality in a College Population." Unpublished Ph.D. dissertation, University of Houston, 1968.

Moore, Charles W. "Some Relationships Between Standardized Test Scores and Academic Performance in the College of Business Administration of the University of Houston." Unpublished Ph.D. dissertation, University of Houston, 1958.

Moore, W., jr. AGAINST THE ODDS: THE HIGH-RISK STUDENT IN THE COMMUNITY COLLEGE. San Francisco: Jossey-Bass, 1970.

Saunders, Walter Lane. VERBAL-NUMERICAL ACHIEVEMENT IN A RE-QUIRED COLLEGE PHYSICAL SCIENCE COURSE AND SOME PERSONAL-ITY CORRELATES. Corvallis: Oregon State University, 1968.

Smith, Harold T. AN ANALYSIS OF INTELLECTUAL FACTORS BEAR-ING SUCCESS IN THE COLLEGE OF BUSINESS, BRIGHAM YOUNG UNI-VERSITY. Provo, Utah: Brigham Young University, Graduate Department of Education, 1967.

South, John Craig. "An Item Factor Analysis of Some Value Dimensions and Their Relation to a Measure of Success in Student Nurse Training." Unpub-lished Ph.D. dissertation, Ohio State University 1959.

Trayford, Cyril. "A Study of the Effects of Curriculum-Related Out-of-School Experiences on Performance in Junior College." Unpublished Ph.D. dis-sertation, University of Chicago, 1957.

Waggoner, Jack T. "The Evaluation of Some New Three-Dimensional Spa-tial Vizualization Test Items as Predictors of Success in Art, Architecture, and Engineering Drawing." Unpublished Ph.D. dissertation, University of Houston, 1959.

Fallows, M. "Junior College: Social Experiment: Relationship Between Social Status and Academic Success," COMMONWEAL, 85 (October 7, 1966), 9–13.

Frumkin, R. M. "Dogmatism, Social Class, Values, and Academic Achieve-ment in Sociology," JOURNAL OF EDUCATIONAL SOCIOLOGY, 34 (May 1961), 398–403.

Hammond, Marjorie. "Attitudinal Changes of Successful Students in a Col-lege of Engineering," JOURNAL OF COUNSELING PSYCHOLOGY, 6 (Spring, 1959), 69–71.

Pattishall, E. G., jr. and F. W. Banghart, jr. "A Comparative Analysis of School of Education Graduates with Withdrawals," EDUCATION RESEARCH BULLETIN, (University of Virginia), (April, 1957).

Shuey, A. M. "Choice of Major Subject as Related to American Council Examination Score and College Grades," JOURNAL OF EDUCATIONAL PSY-CHOLOGY, 41, (May, 1950), 292–300.

Snyder, B. R. "How Creative Students Fare in Science," in P. Heist, ed. EDUCATION FOR CREATIVITY: A MODERN MYTH. Berkeley, California: Center for Research and Development in Higher Education, University of California, 49–66.

Thistlethwaite, D. L. "Fields of Study and Development of Motivation to Seek Advanced Training," JOURNAL OF EDUCATIONAL PSYCHOLOGY, 53 (April, 1962), 53–64.

422

C.2.c. Psychological Aspects of Achievement—
Motivation and Creativity

Benett, Margaret E. COLLEGE AND LIFE: PROBLEMS OF SELF DIS-
COVERY AND SELF DIRECTION. New York: McGraw-Hill, 1952.

George, Clay Edwin. "Emotional Adaptability and Intellectual Efficiency."
Unpublished Ph.D. dissertation, University of Houston, 1962.

Gumeson, George Gerald. "A Comparative Analysis of the Needs, Values,
Cognitive Abilities and Other Personality Characteristics of High and Low Creative Junior College Students." Unpublished Ph.D. dissertation, University of Denver, 1963.

*Heist, Paul. THE CREATIVE COLLEGE STUDENT. San Francisco: Jossey-
Bass, 1968.

Holmes, Paul Roger. "The Influence of Anxiety Upon Academic Performance Under Varying Conditions of Task Orientation and Evaluation." Unpublished Ph.D. dissertation, George Peabody College for Teachers, 1966.

Hsieh, Chen-tzu (Wei). "The Relationship of Two Experimental Measures
of Student Motivation to Academic Success in College." Ann Arbor: University
Microfilms, 1955.

Jensen, Diana Elizabeth. "The Effects of Delayed Auditory Feedback Stress
and Failure Stress on Selected Measures of Speech, Language, and Problem Solving Performance in College Students." Unpublished Ph.D. dissertation, Indiana
University, 1966.

Lindgren, Henry Clay. THE PSYCHOLOGY OF COLLEGE SUCCESS: A
DYNAMIC APPROACH. New York: Wiley, 1969.

Middleton, George, jr. "Personality Syndromes and Academic Achievement." Unpublished Ph.D. dissertation Pennsylvania State University, 1958.

Platt, Alexander Bradford. "The Relationships of Values to Academic
Goals, Attrition, Achievement, and Satisfaction." Unpublished Ph.D. dissertation, Columbia University, 1966.

Purkey, William Watson. SELF CONCEPT AND SCHOOL ACHIEVEMENT.
Englewood Cliffs, New Jersey: Prentice-Hall, 1970.

Weigand, G. "Motivational Factors Associated with Success and Failure of
Probational Students." Unpublished Ph.D. dissertation, University of Maryland,
1951.

Brazziel, W. F. "Needs, Values, and Academic Achievement," IMPROVING
COLLEGE AND UNIVERSITY TEACHING, (Summer, 1964), 159–163.

Brown, Donald. "Personality, College Environments and Academic Productivity," in N. Sanford, ed. THE AMERICAN COLLEGE. New York: Wiley, 1964.
536–562.

Bruner, Jerome. "The Conditions of Creativity," in M. Wertheimer, ed.
CONFRONTATION: PSYCHOLOGY AND THE PROBLEMS OF TODAY.
Glenview, Illinois: Scott Foresman, 1970. 352–356.

Cottle, Thomas J. "The Mosaic of Creativity," in M. Wertheimer, ed. CON-
FRONTATION: PSYCHOLOGY AND THE PROBLEMS OF TODAY. Glenview,
Illinois: Scott Foresman, 1970. 385–395.

Griffiths, G. R. "The Relationship Between Scholastic Achievement and

Personality Adjustment of Men College Students," JOURNAL OF APPLIED PSYCHOLOGY, 29 (October, 1945), 360–367.

Guilford, J. P. "Creativity: Retrospect and Prospect," JOURNAL OF CREATIVE BEHAVIOR, 4 (Summer, 1970), 149–168.

Jones, J. G. and R. W. Strowig. "Adolescent Identity and Self-Perception as Predictors of Scholastic Achievement," JOURNAL OF EDUCATIONAL RESEARCH, 62 (1968), 78–82.

Kosa, John, Leo D. Rachiele, Cyril O. Schommer, *et al.* "The Self Image and Performance of Socially Mobile College Students," JOURNAL OF SOCIAL PSYCHOLOGY, 56 (April, 1962), 301–316.

Kracht, C. R. and J. P. Casey. "Attitudes, Anxieties, and Student Teaching Performance," PEABODY JOURNAL OF EDUCATION, 45 (January 1968), 214–217.

MacKinnon, D. W. "Identifying and Developing Creativity," in T. R. McConnell, ed. SELECTION AND EDUCATIONAL DIFFERENTIATION. Berkeley: Field Service Center and Center for the Study of Higher Education, University of California, 1959.

Rezler, A. G. "Personal Values and Achievement in College," PERSONNEL AND GUIDANCE JOURNAL, 39 (October, 1960), 137–143.

Schafer, Roy. "Talent as Danger: Psychoanalytic Observations on Academic Difficulty," in L. A. Pervin, *et al.*, eds. THE COLLEGE DROPOUT AND THE UTILIZATION OF TALENT. Princeton, New Jersey: The Princeton University Press, 1966. 207–220.

Woods, A. H. and G. Chase. "Forms of Personality Obstructive to Progress in College," JOURNAL OF SOCIAL PSYCHOLOGY, 8 (November, 1937), 411–431.

C.2.d. Sociological Aspects of Achievement

Cross Reference: Studies of the Effects of Fraternities and Sororities, Residential Patterns, Peer Group Influence and Student Sub-Culture on Achievement Have Been Placed in Specific Sections on Those Aspects of Student Life.

Brennan, William Charles. "Primary Relationships and Academic Achievement: a Comparison of American and English Youth." Unpublished Ph.D. dissertation, St. Louis University, 1967.

Crowther, Betty Isabel. "A Sociological Analysis of Academic Achievement." Unpublished Ph.D. dissertation, University of Wisconsin, 1965.

McKnight, A. James. "The Relation of Certain Home Factors to College Achievement." Unpublished Ph.D dissertation, University of Minnesota, 1958.

Nishiyama, Rev. Toshihiko Peter, S.J. "Primary Relationships and Academic Achievement: A Comparative Study of American and Japanese Youth." Unpublished Ph.D. dissertation, St. Louis University, 1965.

Patrich, G. H. "A Comparative Study of Scholastic Aptitude, Scholastic Achievement and Personal Adjustment of Male Athletes and Male Non-Athletes

424

at Kansas State College." Unpublished Master's thesiŝ, Kansas State College, 1950.

Slater, John M. RELATIONSHIPS BETWEEN COLLEGE PERSISTENCE (ATTRITION), FATHER'S OCCUPATION, AND CHOICE OF CURRICULUM. University of Illinois, 1956.

Sprigle, Herbert A. "A Factor Analytic Study of Family Relationships in a Group of Academic Achievers and Underachievers." Unpublished Ph.D. dissertation, Pennsylvania State University, 1959.

Stechlein, J. E. and L. D. Dameron. INTERCOLLEGIATE ATHLETICS AND ACADEMIC PROGRESS: A COMPARISON OF ACADEMIC CHARAC-TERISTICS OF ATHLETES AND NON-ATHLETES AT THE UNIVERSITY OF MINNESOTA. Report Series Number 3. Minneapolis, Minnesota: Bureau of Institutional Research, University of Minnesota, 1965.

Wade, Durlyn E. "Student Success in a State Teachers College and the Dis-tribution of Social Class Status." Unpublished Ph.D. dissertation, New York University, 1956.

Wegner, Eldon Lowell. "The Relationship of College Characteristics to Graduation." Unpublished Ph.D. dissertation, University of Wisconsin, 1967.

Astin, A. W. "Undergraduate Achievement and Institutional 'Excellence'," SCIENCE, 161 (August 16, 1968), 661–668.

Brockington, F. and Z. Stein. "Admission, Achievement, and Social Class," UNIVERSITY QUARTERLY, 18 (December, 1963), 52–73.

Centra, J. A. and D. Rock. "College Environments and Student Academic Achievement," AMERICAN EDUCATIONAL RESEARCH JOURNAL, 8 November, 1971), 623–634.

Chickering, A. W. "Institutional Objectives and Student Development in College," JOURNAL OF APPLIED BEHAVIORAL SCIENCE, 3 (July/August/September, 1967), 287–304.

Dietrich, John E. "The Effect of Participation in Extracurricular Dramatics Upon Scholastic Achievement," PURDUE UNIVERSITY STUDIES IN HIGHER EDUCATION, 39 (December, 1940), 16–30.

Drasgow, J. "Differences Between College Students," JOURNAL OF HIGHER EDUCATION, 29 (April, 1958), 216–218.

Dunkelberger, G. F. "Do Extracurricular Activities Make for Poor Scholar-ship?" JOURNAL OF EDUCATIONAL SOCIOLOGY, 9 (December, 1935), 215–218.

Eckland, B. K. "Social Class and College Graduation: Some Misconceptions Corrected," AMERICAN JOURNAL OF SOCIOLOGY, 70 (July, 1964), 36–50.

Gibb, Leonard L. "Home Background and Self-Actualization Attainment," JOURNAL OF COLLEGE STUDENT PERSONNEL, 9 (January, 1968), 49–53.

Gottlieb, D. "Social Class, Achievement, and the College-going Experience," SCHOOL REVIEW, 70 (Autumn, 1962), 273–286.

Grosof, Elliott. "Social Class Backgrounds of College Seniors," AMERICAN CATHOLIC SOCIOLOGICAL REVIEW, 23 (Fall, 1962), 224–234.

Hartnett, R. T. "Involvement in Extra Curricular Activities as a Factor in Academic Performance," JOURNAL OF COLLEGE STUDENT PERSONNEL, 6 (September, 1965), 272–274.

Hill, R. "An Experimental Study of Social Adjustment: An Experimental Study of the Effects of Staff Stimulation to Participation in Extracurricular Activities on the Scholastic Achievement and Social Adjustment of College Students," AMERICAN SOCIOLOGICAL REVIEW, 9 (October, 1944), 481–494.

Holland, J. L. and J. M. Richards, jr. "Academic and Non-Academic Accomplishment: Correlated or UnCorrelated?" JOURNAL OF EDUCATIONAL PSYCHOLOGY, 56:4 (August 1956), 165–174.

Kinloch, G. C. and R. Perrucci. "Social Origins, Academic Achievement, and Mobility Channels: Sponsored and Contest Mobility Among College Graduates," SOCIAL FORCES, 48 (September 1969), 36–45.

Laura, L. and J. D. Perry. "Academic Achievements of Veterans and Non-Veterans at the City College of New York," JOURNAL OF EDUCATIONAL PSYCHOLOGY, 42 (January, 1951), 31–42.

Mehus, O. M. "Academic Achievement of College Students in Different Kinds of Extra-Curricular Activities," JOURNAL OF EDUCATIONAL SOCIOLogy, 8 (September, 1934), 50–56.

Mehus, O. M. "Extra-Curricular Activities and Academic Achievement," JOURNAL OF EDUCATIONAL SOCIOLOGY, 6 (1932).

Mueller, J. H. and K. H. Mueller. "Social-Economic Background and Campus Success," EDUCATIONAL AND PSYCHOLOGICAL MEASUREMENT, 3 (Summer, 1943), 143–150.

Mueller, K. H. and J. H. Mueller. "Class Structure and Academic and Social Success," EDUCATIONAL AND PSYCHOLOGICAL MEASUREMENT, 13 (Number 3, 1953), 486–496.

Sanders, W. B., et al. "Intelligence and Academic Performance of College Students of Urban, Rural, and Mixed Backgrounds," JOURNAL OF EDUCATIONAL RESEARCH, 49 (November, 1955), 185–193.

Sandford, C. T., et al. "Class Influences in Higher Education," BRITISH JOURNAL OF EDUCATIONAL PSYCHOLOGY, 35 (June, 1965), 183–194.

*Spady, W. G. "Lament for the Letterman: Effects of Peer Status and Extracurricular Activities on Goals and Achievement," AMERICAN JOURNAL OF SOCIOLOGY, 75 (January, 1970, part 2), 680–702.

Thistlethwaite, Donald L. "College Press and Student Achievement," JOURNAL OF EDUCATIONAL PSYCHOLOGY, 50 (October, 1959), 183–191.

Washburne, N. F. "Socioeconomic Status, Urbanism and Academic Performance in College," JOURNAL OF EDUCATIONAL RESEARCH, 53 (December, 1959), 130–137.

Wright, J. J. "The Impact of Perceived Stress on Academic Achievement When Family Income Level and Self-Concept are Taken Into Account," JOURNAL OF COLLEGE STUDENT PERSONNEL, 7 (March, 1966), 113–117.

426

C.2.e. Under-Achievement in College

Dula, Thomas C. "A Study of Academic Probation and Suspension Policies and Practices and the Outcome of These Policies and Practices in Representative Public Junior Colleges." Unpublished Ph.D. dissertation, Florida State University, 1961.

Kisch, Jeremy M. "A Comparative Study of Patterns of Underachievement Among Male College Students." Unpublished Ph.D. dissertation, University of Michigan, 1967.

Pearlman, Samuel. "An Investigation of the Problem of Academic Under-Achievement Among Intellectually Superior College Students." Unpublished Ph.D. dissertation, New York University, 1952.

Stewart, Lawrence H. INCREASING THE ACADEMIC ACHIEVEMENT OF CULTURALLY DISADVANTAGED YOUTH. Berkeley: University of California, 1966.

Abraham, W. "Solving the Dilemma of the Underachiever," TODAYS HEALTH, 43 (December 1965), 34–37+.

Brown, W. H. "Analysis and Comparison of the Academic Adjustment and Problems of Probation Students and Honor Students," COLLEGE AND UNIVERSITY, 28 (April 1953), 389–396.

Diener, C. L. "Similarities and Differences Between Over-achieving and Under-achieving Students," PERSONNEL & GUIDANCE JOURNAL, 38 (January 1960), 396–400.

Fischer, R. P. "The Role of Frustration in Academic Underachievement: An Experimental Investigation," JOURNAL OF AMERICAN ASSOCIATION OF COLLEGE REGISTRARS, 18 (1943), 227–238.

Margolis, J. D. "Non-Dropout Problem," JOURNAL OF HIGHER EDUCATION, 40 (May 1969), 394–397.

Owens, W. A. and W. C. Johnson. "Some Measured Personality Traits of Collegiate Underachievers," JOURNAL OF EDUCATIONAL PSYCHOLOGY, 40 (January 1949), 41–46.

Shaw, M. C. and D. J. Brown. "Scholastic Underachievement of Bright College Students," PERSONNEL & GUIDANCE JOURNAL, 36 (November 1957), 195–199.

Smith, C. P. and M. T. Winterbottom. "Personality Characteristics of College Students on Academic Probation," JOURNAL OF PERSONALITY, 38 (September 1970), 379–391.

Wedemayer, C. A. "Gifted Achievers and Non-Achievers," JOURNAL OF HIGHER EDUCATION, 24 (January 1953), 25–30.

Whitmer, C. A. "A Study of the Scholastic Progress of College Probationers," JOURNAL OF APPLIED PSCYHOLOGY, 17 (February, 1933), 39–49.

C.2.f. The Gifted Student

Krippner, Stanley. CHARACTERISTICS OF GIFTED AND TALENTED YOUTH. Brooklyn, New York: Maimonides Medical Center, 1967.

McConnell, Thomas R. THE REDISCOVERY OF THE GIFTED STUDENT. Berkeley, California: Center for the Study of Higher Education, 1959.

Roberts, Roy J. PREDICTION OF COLLEGE PERFORMANCE OF SUPERIOR STUDENTS. Evanston, Illinois: National Merit Scholarship Corporation, 1965.

Stedman, Edith. THE GIFTED STUDENT AND STUDENT PERSONNEL PROGRAMS IN COLLEGES AND UNIVERSITIES. Pasadena, California: Western Personnel Institute, 1959.

Wallach, Michael A. and Cliff W. Wing, jr. TALENTED STUDENT. New York: Holt, Rinehart and Winston, 1969.

Wolfle, Dael. AMERICA'S RESOURCES OF SPECIALIZED TALENT. New York: Harper, 1954.

Cadbury, William. "Challenging the Superior Student in the Small Private College," in Joseph Cohen, ed. THE SUPERIOR STUDENT IN AMERICAN HIGHER EDUCATION. New York: McGraw-Hill, 1966.

Friedenberg, E. Z. "Gifted Student and His Enemies," COMMENTARY, 33 (May 1962), 410–419.

Gladstein, G. A. "Study Behavior of Gifted Stereotype and Non-Stereotype College Students," PERSONNEL AND GUIDANCE JOURNAL, 38 (February 1960), 470–474.

Lindgreen, H. C., et al. "Academic Aptitude Test for Superior College Students," JOURNAL OF PSYCHOLOGY, 35 (April 1953), 229–233.

Little, J. K. "Persistence of Academically Talented Youth in University Studies," EDUCATIONAL RECORD, 40 (July 1959), 237–241.

Myers, R. C. "Academic Overachievers: Stereotyped Aspects," JOURNAL OF EXPERIMENTAL EDUCATION, 18 (March 1950), 229–238.

Neel, M. O. and C. O. Mathews. "Needs of Superior Students," JOURNAL OF HIGHER EDUCATION, 6 (January 1935), 29–34.

Robertson, James. "The Superior Student: Characteristics, Aspirations, and Needs," in Joseph Cohen, ed. THE SUPERIOR STUDENT IN AMERICAN HIGHER EDUCATION. New York: McGraw-Hill, 1966.

Stamatakos, L. C. and R. H. Shaffer. "Effects of Special Attention Upon Potentially Superior Freshman Students," PERSONNEL GUIDANCE JOURNAL, 38 (October 1959), 106–111.

Thistlethwaite, D. L. "College Press and Changes in Study Plans of Talented Students," JOURNAL OF EDUCATIONAL PSYCHOLOGY, 51 (Number 4, 1960), 222–234.

Wallach, Michael and Cliff W. Wing, jr. "The Talented Student," in M.

Wertheimer, ed. CONFRONTATION: PSYCHOLOGY AND THE PROBLEMS OF TODAY. Glenview, Illinois: Scott Foresman, 1970. 356–365.

Warren, J. R. and P. A. Heist. "Personality Traits of Gifted College Students," SCIENCE, 132 (August 5, 1960), 330–337.

C.3 Adjustment to College and Problems of the Course Through College

Angell, Robert Cooley. STUDY IN UNDERGRADUATE ADJUSTMENT. Chicago: University of Chicago Press, 1930.

Cassidy, Sally Whelan, *et al.* IMPACT OF A HIGH DEMAND COLLEGE IN A LARGE UNIVERSITY ON WORKING CLASS YOUTH. Detroit, Michigan: Wayne State University, Monteith College, 1968.

Coffelt, J. J. and D. S. Hobbs. IN AND OUT OF COLLEGE; A LONGITUDINAL STUDY OF THE 1962 FRESHMAN CLASS IN OKLAHOMA COLLEGES. REPORT I: THE FIRST YEAR. Oklahoma City: Oklahoma State Regents for Higher Education, 1964.

Costar, James W. "Academic Adjustment of Selected Male Students Reported for Disciplinary Action and Michigan State University." Unpublished Ph.D. dissertation, Michigan State University, 1959.

Demaree, Robert G., *et al.* PERCEPTIONS OF THE UNIVERSITY BY FRESHMAN AND SOPHOMORE ENROLLEES OF THE COLLEGE OF LIBERAL ARTS AND SCIENCES. Urbana, Illinois: University of Illinois, 1963.

Dick, Harry Richard. "Relationship of Conflicting Role Expectations of College Freshmen and Faculty Members to Some Aspects of Personal Disorganization of Freshmen Students." Unpublished Ph.D. dissertation, Washington State University, 1957.

Fredericksen, Norman. ADJUSTMENT TO COLLEGE: A STUDY OF 10,000 VETERANS AND NON-VETERAN STUDENTS IN 116 AMERICAN COLLEGES. Princeton, New Jersey: Educational Testing Service, 1951.

Glick, Lester Jay. "A Conceptualization and Operationalization of Social Functioning of College Sophomores." Unpublished D.S.W. dissertation, Washington University, 1961.

Hale, L. B. FROM SCHOOL TO COLLEGE: A STUDY OF THE TRANSITION EXPERIENCE. (Yale Studies in Religious Education, No. 11). New Haven, Connecticut: Yale University Press, 1939.

Hall, E. and B. Barger. TRANSITIONAL EXPERIENCES OF NEW STUDENTS AT THE UNIVERSITY OF FLORIDA: A REPORT OF INTERVIEWS CONDUCTED DURING THE FALL TRIMESTER, 1965. (Mental Health Project Bulletin No. 23), Gainesville, Florida: Student Mental Health Project, University of Florida, 1966.

Herr, E. L. and G. D. Moore. A PILOT STUDY OF COLLEGE EXPECTATIONS AND 'REALITY' PERCEPTIONS. New York: College Entrance Examination Board, 1967.

Hill, Walter Raymond. "A Multivariate Comparison of College Freshmen with Adequate or Deficient Reading Comprehension," Unpublished Ph.D. dissertation, State University of Iowa, 1959.

Hochbaum, Jerry. "Student Orientation to College—Their Sources, Correlates and Consequences." Unpublished Ph.D. dissertation, New York University, 1965.

Jones, John D. A STUDY OF THE RELATIONSHIP BETWEEN THE STUDENT'S SOCIO-ECONOMIC BACKGROUND AND HIS FRESHMAN YEAR IN COLLEGE. Washington, D.C.: American Personnel and Guidance Association, 1968.

Kerns, Byron L. "A Study of Under-Achieving and Over-Achieving First-Semester College Freshmen as Revealed by the Way in Which They View the College Situation and Themselves as College Students." Unpublished Ph.D. dissertation, 1957.

Krueger, Cynthia Sue. "Problems and Processes of Professional Socialization: The Student Nurses." Unpublished Ph.D. dissertation, Washington University, 1967.

Kurland, Norman D. TRANSITION FROM SCHOOL TO COLLEGE. NEW DIMENSIONS IN HIGHER EDUCATION. Durham, North Carolina: Duke University, 1967.

Lynch, Thomas H., *et al.* THE SELECTIVE EFFECTS OF DIFFERENT PRE-ENROLLMENT COUNSELING PROGRAMS ON ENTERING FRESHMEN. Washington, D.C.: American Personnel and Guidance Association, 1968.

McCabe, Joseph E. YOUR FIRST YEAR IN COLLEGE. Philadelphia, Pennsylvania: Westminster Press, 1967.

Scott, Judith V. THAT FRESHMAN FEELING. Philadelphia, Pennsylvania: Macrae Smith, 1960.

Spencer, George Minard. "An Investigation of Some Non-Intellectual Factors Presumably Affecting the Academic Adjustment of College Students at Florida State University." Unpublished Ph.D. dissertation, Florida State University, 1955.

Sussman, Leila Aline. FRESHMAN MORALE AT M.I.T.: THE CLASS OF 1961. Cambridge, Massachusetts: Massachusetts Institute of Technology, 1960.

Volpel, Marvin Chesley. "A Study to Determine Why Freshman Scholarship Students at Michigan State College Fail to Renew Their Scholarships." Unpublished Ph.D. dissertation, Michigan State College, 1952.

Adinolfi, A. A. "Characteristics of Highly Accepted, Highly Rejected and Relatively Unknown University Freshmen," JOURNAL OF COUNSELING PSYCHOLOGY, 17 (September, 1970), 456–464.

Baker, R. W. and L. J. Nidorf. "Pattern of Occurrence of Psychological Disturbances in College Students as a Function of Year Level," JOURNAL OF CLINICAL PSYCHOLOGY, 20 (October, 1964), 530–531.

Bergethon, K. R. "Preparation and Adjustment of College Freshmen," in Educational Conference, EDUCATION IN A FREE WORLD, 1954, 19–32.

Bryant, Lawrence C. "A Study of Psycho-Social Behavior of College Freshmen—1966–1967," QUARTERLY REVIEW OF HIGHER EDUCATION AMONG NEGROES, 35 (April, 1967), 84–87.

Camden, B. "For a Better Understanding of Entering Students," SCHOOL REVIEW, 61 (January, 1953), 39–42.

Coelho, G.V., *et al.* "Coping Strategies in a New Learning Environment: a Study of American College Freshman," ARCHIVES OF GENERAL PSYCHIATRY, 9 (November, 1963), 433–443.

Cooper, L. B. "A Study in Freshman Elimination in One College," NATION'S SCHOOLS, 2 (September, 1928), 25–29.

Cottle, Thomas J. "Billy Kowalski Goes to College," CHANGE, 3 (March–April, 1971), 36–42.

Deutsch, M. "Discussion and Critique of Some Variables in the Social Psychology of School-to-College Transition," JOURNAL OF EDUCATIONAL SOCIOLOGY, 33 (February, 1960), 300–304.

Fowler, B. P. "College Freshmen Tell Their Story; a Study by the Committee on School and College Relations of the Educational Records Bureau," in Educational Conference. SELECTION AND GUIDANCE OF GIFTED STUDENTS FOR NATIONAL SURVIVAL, 1955, 91–101.

Freedman, Mervin B. "The Passage Through College," JOURNAL OF SOCIAL ISSUES, 12 (No. 4, 1956), 13–28.

Freedman, Mervin B. "Some Observations of Students as They Relate to Orientation Procedures in Colleges and Universities," JOURNAL OF COLLEGE STUDENT PERSONNEL, 2 (October, 1960), 2–10.

Froe, O. D. and M. A. Lee. "New Emphasis in Freshman Orientation," PERSONNEL AND GUIDANCE JOURNAL, 34 (February, 1956), 360–365.

Gould, S. B. "September Undergraduate: Hope vs. Exasperation," SATURDAY REVIEW, 45 (September 15, 1962), 52–54+.

Greenfield, L. B. "Attrition Among First Semester Engineering Freshmen," PERSONNEL AND GUIDANCE JOURNAL, 42 (June, 1964), 1003–1010.

Gustad, J. W. "Factors Associated with Social Behavior and Adjustment: A Review of the Literature," EDUCATIONAL AND PSYCHOLOGICAL MEASUREMENT, 12 (Spring, 1952), 3–19.

Hardaway, C. W. "Study of Enrollment and Drop-out Factors of Freshmen on Non-Teaching Curricula at Indiana State," TEACHER'S COLLEGE JOURNAL, 27 (November, 1955), 30–34.

Harford, E. J. "Military Experience and Higher Education," PEABODY JOURNAL OF EDUCATION, 33 (November, 1955), 171–175.

Jackson, D. "Freshman Blues," LIFE, 58 (January 8, 1965), 63–72+.

Jones, J. D. "Study of the Relationship Between the Student's Socio-Economic Background and His Freshman Year in College," NATIONAL ASSOCIATION OF STUDENT PERSONNEL ADMINISTRATORS JOURNAL, 8 (April, 1971), 234–236.

Kipnis, D. "Social Immaturity, Intellectual Ability, and Adjustive Behavior in College," JOURNAL OF APPLIED PSYCHOLOGY, 52 (February, 1968), 71–80.

Klein, D. "What Makes Freshman Year So Dangerous," SEVENTEEN, 26 (September, 1967), 158–159+.

Kysai, J. E. "Social Class and Adaptation of College Students: A Review and Prospectus," MENTAL HYGIENE, 50 (July, 1966), 398–405.

Lins, L. J. and H. Pitt. "Staying Power and Rate of Progress of the University of Wisconsin Freshmen," COLLEGE AND UNIVERSITY, 29 (October, 1953), 86–99.

McDonagh, E. C. "Adjustment Problems and Characteristics of University Veterans," SOCIOLOGY AND SOCIAL RESEARCH, 31 (January–February, 1947), 220–225.

Matteson, R. W. "Self-Estimates of College Freshmen," PERSONNEL AND GUIDANCE JOURNAL, 34 (January, 1956), 280–284.

Mercer, Margaret. "Personal Factors in College Adjustment," JOURNAL OF EDUCATIONAL RESEARCH, 36 (April, 1943), 561–568.

Mitchell, F. T. "Why Freshmen Leave College," JOURNAL OF HIGHER EDUCATION, 13 (February, 1942), 95–100.

Mogar, Robert E. "Orientations of College Students: Preliminary Data and Review of the Literature," PSYCHOLOGICAL REPORTS, 15 (Monograph Supplement 5-V15) 1964, 739–770.

Newman, David and Robert Benton. "Pressure: Buckle Under, Winsocki," ESQUIRE, 62 (September, 1964), 97–100.

Richards, J. M., jr. "A Factor Analytic Study of the Self-Ratings of College Freshmen," EDUCATIONAL AND PSYCHOLOGICAL MEASUREMENT, 26 (1966), 861–870.

Ridlon, H. G. "Why Freshmen Fail," ATLANTIC, 208 (September, 1961), 56–60.

Romine, B. H., jr. and W. S. Gehman. "Tension in Freshman and Senior Engineering Students," EDUCATIONAL AND PSYCHOLOGICAL MEASUREMENT, 26 (Autumn, 1966), 565–576.

Rust, R. M. and J. S. Davie. "Differences in Behavior Among College Classes," PSYCHOLOGICAL REPORTS, 12 (April, 1963) 415–420.

Sanford, Nevitt. "Developmental Status of the Entering Freshman," in Nevitt Sanford, ed. THE AMERICAN COLLEGE. New York: Wiley, 1964, 253–282.

Sanford, Nevitt. "Uncertain Senior," NATIONAL ASSOCIATION OF WOMEN DEANS AND COUNSELORS JOURNAL, 21 (October, 1957), 9–15.

Silber, E., et al. "Adaptive Behavior in Competent Adolescents: Coping with the Anticipation of College," ARCHIVES OF GENERAL PSYCHIATRY, 5 (October, 1961), 354–365.

Silber, E., et al. "Competent Adolescents Coping with College Decisions," ARCHIVES OF GENERAL PSYCHIATRY, 5 (December, 1961), 517–527.

Stern, G. G. "Continuity and Contrast in the Transition from High School to College," in N. F. Brown, ed. ORIENTATION TO COLLEGE LEARNING— A RE-APPRAISAL. Washington, D.C.: American Council on Education, 1961, 33–58.

Tate, M. T. and V. Musick. "Adjustment Problems of College Students," SOCIAL FORCES, 33 (December, 1954), 182–185.

"That Crucial Freshman Year: Symposium," NATIONAL EDUCATION ASSOCIATION JOURNAL, 52 (September, 1963), 51–54.

Wallace, W. L. "Institutional and Life-Cycle Socialization of College Freshmen," AMERICAN JOURNAL OF SOCIOLOGY, 70 (November, 1964), 303–318.

Walsh, W. B. and J. H. Russel, III. "College Major Choice and Personal Adjustment," PERSONNEL AND GUIDANCE JOURNAL, 47 (March, 1969), 685–688.

Wertenbaker, W. "Reporter at Large: Harvard University," NEW YORKER, 38 (December 1, 1962), 68–70+.

Wilson, E. K. "The Entering Student: Attributes and Agents of Change," in J. M. Newcomb and E. K. Wilson, eds. COLLEGE PEER GROUPS: PROBLEMS AND PROSPECTS FOR RESEARCH. Chicago: Aldine, 1966, 71–106.

Yoshino, R. "College Drop-Outs at the End of the Freshman Year," JOURNAL OF EDUCATIONAL SOCIOLOGY, 32 (September, 1958), 42–48.

C.4. Educational Philosophy and Curriculum Patterns: Relevance and Change

*Axelrod, Joseph et al. SEARCH FOR RELEVANCE. San Francisco: Jossey-Bass, 1969.

Barnes, Ronald et al. eds. THE AIM OF HIGHER EDUCATION: SOCIAL ADJUSTMENT OR HUMAN LIBERATION? St. Louis, Missouri: UMHE Publications, 1966.

Baskin, Samuel, ed. HIGHER EDUCATION: SOME NEWER DEVELOPMENTS. New York: McGraw-Hill, 1965.

Bronowski, Jacob, et al. IMAGINATION AND THE UNIVERSITY. Toronto, Canada: University of Toronto Press, 1964.

Dressel, Paul L. THE UNDERGRADUATE CURRICULUM IN HIGHER EDUCATION. Washington, D.C.: Center for Applied Research in Education, 1963.

Faust, Clarence H. and Jessica Feingold. APPROACHES TO EDUCATION FOR CHARACTER: STRATEGIES FOR CHANGE IN HIGHER EDUCATION. New York: Columbia University Press, 1969.

Harcleroad, Fred F., jr. "Influence of Organized Student Opinion on American College Curricula: An Historical Survey." Unpublished Ph.D. dissertation, Stanford University, 1948.

Harvard University Committee. GENERAL EDUCATION IN A FREE SOCIETY. Cambridge, Massachusetts: Harvard University, 1945.

*Harvey, James. REFORMING UNDERGRADUATE CURRICULUM: PROBLEMS AND PROPOSALS. Washington, D.C.: ERIC Clearing House on Higher Education, 1971.

Heaton, Kenneth L. and G. Robert Koopman. A COLLEGE CURRICULUM BASED ON FUNCTIONAL NEEDS OF STUDENTS. Chicago: University of Chicago Press, 1936.

*Hutchins, Robert M. THE UNIVERSITY OF UTOPIA. Chicago: University of Chicago Press, 1953.

Learned, W. S. and B. D. Wood. THE STUDENT AND HIS KNOWLEDGE. (A Report to the Carnegie Foundation on the results of high school and college exams of 1928, 1930 and 1932) BULLETIN 29, New York: Carnegie Foundation for the Advancement of Teaching, 1938.

McGrath, Earl J., ed. THE LIBERAL ARTS COLLEGE'S RESPONSIBIL-
ITY FOR THE INDIVIDUAL STUDENT. New York: Teachers College, Columbia University, 1966.

Mayhew, Lewis B. CONTEMPORARY COLLEGE STUDENTS AND THE
CURRICULUM. Atlanta, Georgia: Southern Regional Education Board, 1969.

Meehan, Mary. STUDENT PROGRAMS TO SUPPLEMENT THE CURRIC-
ULUM. Washington, D.C.: U.S. National Student Association, 1966.

Morris, William H., ed. EFFECTIVE COLLEGE TEACHING: THE QUEST
FOR RELEVANCE. Washington, D.C.: American Association for Higher Education, 1970.

Newman, J. H. IDEA OF A LIBERAL EDUCATION. New York: Barnes
and Noble, 1952.

Reid, John Christopher. "An Investigation of Student Attitudes Toward
Instructional Television and Other University Experiences." Unpublished Ph.D.
dissertation, University of Missouri, 1965.

Riker, H. C. COLLEGE HOUSING AS LEARNING CENTERS. Student Personnel Series No. 3. Washington, D.C.: American Personnel and Guidance Association, 1965.

Runkel, Philip, Roger Harrison and Margaret Runkel, eds. THE CHANGING
COLLEGE CLASSROOM. San Francisco: Jossey-Bass, 1969.

Sachs, Benjamin M. THE STUDENT, THE INTERVIEW, THE CURRICU-
LUM, Boston: Houghton Mifflin, 1966.

Sanford, Nevitt and J. Katz. SEARCH FOR RELEVANCE. San Francisco:
Jossey-Bass, 1969.

Schoenfeld, Janet D. STUDENT INITIATED CHANGES IN THE ACA-
DEMIC CURRICULUM. Washington, D.C.: ERIC Clearing House on Higher Education, 1972.

*Schwab, Joseph. COLLEGE CURRICULUM AND STUDENT PROTEST.
Chicago: University of Chicago Press, 1969.

Sherman, Jerome Nathaniel. "An Evaluation of a Type of Special Counseling at the Undergraduate Level as Related to Academic Success." Unpublished
Ph.D. dissertation, University of Houston, 1968.

Slowinski, Donald Joseph. "An Investigation of Some of the Implications of
Educational Philosophy Relative to Change in Higher Education with Particular
Attention to the Role of Students as Change Agents." Unpublished Ed.D. thesis,
George Washington University, 1969.

Stickler, William Hugh, ed. EXPERIMENTAL COLLEGES: THEIR ROLE
IN AMERICAN HIGHER EDUCATION. Tallahassee, Florida: Florida State University Press, 1964.

*Suczek, Robert F. THE BEST LAID PLANS: STUDENT DEVELOPMENT
IN AN EXPERIMENTAL COLLEGE. San Francisco: Jossey-Bass, 1972.

Taylor, Harold. ON EDUCATION AND FREEDOM. Carbondale, Illinois:
Southern Illinois University Press, 1967.

*Tussman, Joseph. EXPERIMENT AT BERKELEY. New York: Oxford Uni-
versity Press, 1969.

Williams, Aston R. GENERAL EDUCATION IN HIGHER EDUCATION.
New York: Teachers' College Press, 1968.

Wilson, H.E. AMERICAN COLLEGE LIFE AS EDUCATION IN WORLD OUTLOOK. Washington, D.C.: American Council on Education, 1956.

Wilson, J.W. and E.H. Lyons. WORK-STUDY COLLEGE PROGRAMS. New York: Harper, 1961.

Abrams, Irwin. "The Student Abroad," in Samuel Baskin, ed. HIGHER EDUCATION: SOME NEWER DEVELOPMENTS. New York: McGraw-Hill, 1965, 78–103.

Axelrod, J. "An Experimental College Model," EDUCATIONAL RECORD, 48 (Fall, 1967), 327–337.

Bart, Peter. "Students of Left Set Up Colleges," NEW YORK TIMES, December 12, 1965, 1, 73.

Berke, Joseph. "The Free University of New York," in Joseph Berke, ed. COUNTER CULTURE. London: Peter Owen, 1969, 212–228.

Berte, N. R. and C. Upshaw. "Student Life Studies: an Action Research Option," NATIONAL ASSOCIATION OF STUDENT PERSONNEL ADMINIS-TRATORS JOURNAL, 9 (July, 1971), 77–80.

Black, Bob and Blair Hamilton. "The Spirit of the Free Universities," CHANGE, 1 (January–February, 1969), 54–55.

Black, I. "Berea College," PHYLON QUARTERLY, 8 (October, 1957), 267–276.

Brann, James W. "San Francisco Students Run Own 'College,'" CHRONI-CLE OF HIGHER EDUCATION. 1 (December 21, 1966).

Blatchford, J. H. "ACTION in the University," AMERICAN EDUCATION, 8 (March, 1972), 37–40.

Brinkley, S. G. "Mental Activity in College Classes," JOURNAL OF EDU-CATIONAL RESEARCH, 46 (March, 1953), 535–541.

Brinkley, S. G. "Mental Activity in College Classes: Student Estimate of Relative Value of Ten Learning Situations," JOURNAL OF EXPERIMENTAL EDUCATION, 20 (June, 1952), 373–378.

Brooks, Laverne A. and Louie R. Davis. "Student Opinion Regarding In-structional Procedures on the College Level," TEACHERS COLLEGE RECORD, 56 (March, 1955), 331–337.

Brown, C. M. "T.V. or the Herded Tour: Large Numbers of Entering Fresh-men," LIBRARY JOURNAL, 90 (May 15, 1965), 2214–2218.

Caffrey, John. "The Role of Computers: the Individualization of Educa-tion," in W. J. Minter, ed. THE INDIVIDUAL AND THE SYSTEM. Boulder, Colorado: Western Interstate Commission for Higher Education, 1967.

Carpenter, C. R. and L. P. Greenhill. "Providing the Conditions for Learn-ing the 'New' Media," in Samuel Baskin, ed. HIGHER EDUCATION: SOME NEWER DEVELOPMENTS. New York: McGraw-Hill, 1965, 128–152.

Clark, Robert. "Unsolved Problems in Honors," THE SUPERIOR STU-DENT, 7 (November–December, 1964), 5–11.

Clark, Terry. "Institutionalization of Innovation in Higher Education: Four Models," ADMINISTRATIVE SCIENCE QUARTERLY, 13 (June, 1968), 1–25.

Cottle, Thomas J. "Revolt and Repair: A Comparative Study of Two University Tutorial Movements," SOCIOLOGICAL QUARTERLY, 8 (Winter, 1967), 21–36.

Wilson, Howard E. and Florence H. Wilson. AMERICAN HIGHER EDUCATION AND WORLD AFFAIRS. Washington, D.C.: American Council on Education, 1963.

Armstrong, W. M. "Schools and Political Literacy," LIBERAL EDUCATION, 46 (December, 1960), 455–462.

Bay, Christian. "A Social Theory of Higher Education," in Nevitt Sanford, ed. THE AMERICAN COLLEGE. New York: Wiley, 1964, 972–1008.

Becker, H. S. "What Do They Really Learn at College?" TRANS-ACTION, 1 (May, 1964), 14–17.

Bell, D. "Social Change in Education and the Change in Educational Concepts: Excerpt from APPROACHES TO EDUCATION FOR CHARACTER, ed. by C. H. Faust and J. Feingold," SCHOOL AND SOCIETY, 97 (Summer, 1969), 322–326.

Bernstein, Jesse. "Doing the Assignment: A Search for Now and Tomorrow," in John and Susan Erlich, eds. STUDENT POWER, PARTICIPATION, AND REVOLUTION. New York: Association Press, 1970, 41–44.

Bess, J. L. and J. A. Bilournsky. "Curriculum Hypocrisies: Studies of Student Initiated Courses," UNIVERSITY QUARTERLY, 24 (Summer, 1970), 291–309.

Bloy, M. B., jr. "Counter Curriculum," COMMONWEAL, 91 (October 3, 1969), 8–12.

Brademas, John and Adolph Holtzman. "What is the Obligation of Higher Education to Prepare Students for Participation in Political Affairs?" CURRENT ISSUES IN HIGHER EDUCATION 1962. HIGHER EDUCATION IN AN AGE OF REVOLUTION. Washington, D.C.: Association for Higher Education, 1962, 141–150.

Braden, S. E. "Impact of Student Unrest on Teacher Education, as Viewed by a President," EDUCATION, 41 (October, 1969), 5–9.

Bowles, Frank H. "Changing Educational Values," in R. M. MacIver, ed. DILEMMAS OF YOUTH IN AMERICA TODAY. New York: Harper, 1961, 53–65.

Cantore, E. "Scientific Humanism and the University," THOUGHT, 43 (Autumn, 1968), 409–428.

Caviness, George. "To My Son on Finishing College," in Esther Lloyd-Jones and Herman Estrin, eds. THE AMERICAN STUDENT AND HIS COLLEGE. Boston: Houghton Mifflin, 1967, 375–379.

Cohen, C. "Democracy and the Curriculum," NATION, 208 (March 17, 1969), 334–338.

Dieterich, D. J. "Student Unrest and Student Participation in Curriculum Planning," ENGLISH JOURNAL, 61 (March, 1972), 443–449.

Dressel, Paul L. "Curriculum and Instruction," JOURNAL OF EDUCATIONAL PSYCHOLOGY, 38 (October, 1967), 393–396.

Dressel, Paul L. "General and Liberal Education," REVIEW OF EDUCATIONAL RESEARCH, 24 (October, 1954), 285–294.

Dressel, Paul L. "Meaning of a College Education," JOURNAL OF HIGHER EDUCATION, 39 (December, 1968), 481–489.

Eash, M. J. "Aberrant Curriculum Designs," EDUCATIONAL FORUM, 35 (January, 1971), 197–202.

"Elitism Is Said to Corrupt Liberal Arts," CHRONICLE OF HIGHER EDUCATION, 4 (May 11, 1970), 31–33.

Ellsworth, R. E. "College Students and Reading," AMERICAN SCHOLAR, 27 (Fall, 1958), 473–481.

Falk, Richard A. "The Revolution in Peace Education," SATURDAY REVIEW, 49 (May 21, 1966), 59–61+.

Frankel, Charles, "Pressures Away from Intellectuality," in R. M. MacIver, ed. DILEMMAS OF YOUTH IN AMERICA TODAY. New York: Harper, 1961, 65–67.

Garrity, Donald L. "Response to Student Demands for Relevance," in G. K. Smith, ed. STRESS AND CAMPUS RESPONSE. San Francisco: Jossey-Bass, 1968, 214–219.

Gutmann, J. "Toward a Philosophy of Educational Liberation," VIRGINIA QUARTERLY REVIEW, 46 (Summer, 1970), 433–438.

Hacker, L. M. "Free Society and Liberal Learning," JOURNAL OF GENERAL EDUCATION, 4 (July, 1950), 243–249.

Hand, Harold. "Practices in Determining Institutional Objectives," in Harold Benjamin, ed. DEMOCRACY IN THE ADMINISTRATION OF HIGHER EDUCATION. New York: Harper, 1950.

Hassenger, Robert. "A Rationale for Changing Student Values," EDUCATIONAL RECORD, 48 (Winter, 1967), 61–68.

Hayakawa, S. I. "A Reassessment of Our Educational Objectives," S.A.M. ADVANCED MANAGEMENT JOURNAL, 34 (October, 1969), 5–13.

Hilton, M. E. "Some Problems of Defining and Assuming Responsibilities in a Democratic Society," NATIONAL ASSOCIATION OF DEANS OF WOMEN JOURNAL, 19 (June, 1956), 143–150.

Hitch, Charles. "The Universities' Commitment to Contemporary Problems," CALIFORNIA MANAGEMENT REVIEW, 11 (Summer, 1969), 4–7.

Hull, W. F. "Formal Study of Higher Education for Under-Graduates at One Urban University: Of What Value Is It? NATIONAL ASSOCIATION OF STUDENT PERSONNEL ADMINISTRATORS JOURNAL, 10 (July, 1972), 48–54.

Jacob, P. "Humanistic Potentials in Higher Education," TEACHERS COLLEGE RECORD, 62 (November, 1960), 106–116.

Jacob, Philip. "Student Capabilities for Liberal Education," in Margaret Habein, ed. SPOTLIGHT ON THE COLLEGE STUDENT. Washington, D.C.: American Council on Education, 1959, 3–6.

Jones, Howard Mumford. "The Meaning of a University," in THE TROUBLED CAMPUS. Boston: Little, Brown, 1966, 172–182.

Kampf, L. "Humanities and Inhumanities," NATION, 207 (September 30, 1968), 309–313.

Korn, Harold. "Differences in Student Response to the Curriculum," in Joseph Katz, *et al.* NO TIME FOR YOUTH. San Francisco: Jossey-Bass, 1968, 187–206.

Kranzberg, Melvin. "The Liberal Curriculum in a Scientific and Technological Age," in Lawrence Dennis and Joseph Kauffman, eds. THE AMERICAN COLLEGE AND THE STUDENT. Washington, D.C.: American Council on Education, 1966, 177–184.

Lehman, I. J. "Curricular Differences in Selected Cognitive and Affective Characteristics," JOURNAL OF EDUCATIONAL MEASUREMENT, 2 (December, 1964), 103–110.

Lehner, A. P. "Laissez-faire Curriculum in the Democratic School," ENGLISH JOURNAL, 59 (September, 1970), 803–810.

Leland, Carole A. "The Atypical Student: His Alternatives and Ours," in ASSESSING THE CURRENT EDUCATIONAL CONGERIES: (Proceedings of the Sixteenth Annual Western Regional Conference on Testing Problems, May 5, 1967, San Francisco). Princeton, New Jersey: Educational Testing Service, 1967, 1–12.

McClatchy, Joseph D. "A Student Looks at the Curriculum," in Lawrence Dennis and Joseph Kauffman, eds. THE AMERICAN COLLEGE AND THE STUDENT. Washington, D.C.: American Council on Education, 1966, 185–188.

McKeachie, Wilbert J. "Effective Teaching: The Relevance of the Curriculum," in Lawrence Dennis and Joseph Kauffman, eds. THE AMERICAN COLLEGE AND THE STUDENT. Washington, D.C.: American Council on Education, 1966, 189–191.

McNeil, Donald R. "Undergraduate Education," in CONTEMPORARY ISSUES IN AMERICAN EDUCATION. Washington, D.C.: U.S. Office of Education, 1965, 138–143.

Maxwell, W. David. "Some Dimensions of Relevance," AAUP BULLETIN, 55 (September, 1969), 337–341.

Mayhew, Lewis. "The Future Undergraduate Curriculum," in Alvin Eurich, ed. CAMPUS 1980. New York: Delacorte Press, 1968, 200–219.

Millet, S. "Student Militancy and the College Curriculum," COLLEGE ENGLISH, 32 (December, 1970), 243–254.

Millet, John D. "The Ethics of Higher Education," EDUCATION RECORD, 48 (Winter, 1967), 11–21.

Morgan, Arthur. "Developing Community Responsibility," in W. D. Weatherford, jr., ed. THE GOALS OF HIGHER EDUCATION. Cambridge, Massachusetts: Harvard University Press, 1960, 99–120.

O'Brien, Kenneth B., jr. "The Under-graduate and American Higher Education: Notes for a Course," LIBERAL EDUCATION, 52 (May, 1966), 165–171.

O'Bryne, E. M. "Liberating the Liberal Arts Student," ASSOCIATION OF AMERICAN COLLEGES BULLETIN, 41 (March, 1955), 98–104.

Pace, C. Robert. "New Concepts in Institutional Goals for Students," in Earl J. McGrath, ed. THE LIBERAL ARTS COLLEGE'S RESPONSIBILITY FOR THE INDIVIDUAL STUDENT. New York: Teachers College Press, 1966, 38–47.

Pace, C. Robert. "University-wide Studies in Evaluation of General Education at Syracuse University," in P. L. Dressel, ed. EVALUATION IN GENERAL EDUCATION. Dubuque, Iowa: Brown, 1954, 1–27.

Sanford, Nevitt. "Aims of a College Education," in Charles Havice, ed. CAMPUS VALUES, New York: Charles Scribner's Sons, 1968, 1–16.

Sanford, Nevitt. "Implications of Personality Studies for Curriculum and Personnel Planning," in Robert Sutherland, et al. eds. PERSONALITY FACTORS ON THE COLLEGE CAMPUS. Auston, Texas: Hogg Foundation for Mental Health, 1962, 3–29.

Saurman, K. P. "Awakening Students to Society Through an Urban Dialogue," CATHOLIC EDUCATION REVIEW, 63 (October, 1965), 433–438.

Schick, Marvin and Albert Somit. "The Failure to Teach Political Activity," AMERICAN BEHAVIORAL SCIENTIST, 6 (January, 1963), 5–8.

Schwebel, Robert. "Wakening Our Sleepy Universities: Student Involvement in Curriculum Change," TEACHERS COLLEGE RECORD, 70 (October, 1968), 31–43.

Shoben, Edward J., jr. "On Student-Initiated Courses: Some Reflections," in G. K. Smith, ed. IN SEARCH OF LEADERS. Washington, D.C.: American Association for Higher Education, 1967, 178–182.

Taylor, Harold. "Individualism and the Liberal Tradition," in W. D. Weatherford, jr., ed. THE GOALS OF HIGHER EDUCATION. Cambridge, Massachusetts: Harvard University Press, 1960, 9–26.

Walters, A. "Motives, Values, and Realities in Catholic Higher Education, Excerpts from Address," CATHOLIC WORLD, 207 (April, 1968), 5–9.

Warren, J. R. "Changing Students and Constant Curricula," EDUCATIONAL RECORD, 51 (Spring, 1970), 182–187.

Zimmerman, Robert L. "The Student Response to College," JOURNAL OF HIGHER EDUCATION, 40 (January, 1969), 31–38.

C.5. The Changing Classroom and Institutional Innovation

Clair, Dean James. "Conscious but Unexpressed Thought Responses in Discussion Class," Unpublished Ph.D. dissertation, Northwestern University, 1955.

Cohen, Joseph W., ed. THE SUPERIOR STUDENT IN AMERICAN HIGHER EDUCATION. New York: McGraw-Hill, 1966.

Cross, K. Patricia. NEW STUDENTS AND NEW NEEDS IN HIGHER EDUCATION. Berkeley, California: Center for Research and Development in Higher Education, University of California, 1972.

Diemer, Ann Olmstead Henderson. "A Case Study of the Effects of Competition and Cooperation on Learning in an Introductory Sociology Class." Unpublished Ph.D. dissertation, Wayne State University, 1967.

Eichleay, R.W., et al. COOPERATIVE SELF-EDUCATION: A REPORT ON THE FIRST YEAR. Detroit, Michigan: Monteith College, Wayne State University, 1964.

Evans, Richard Isadore. RESISTANCE TO INNOVATION IN HIGHER EDUCATION: A SOCIAL PSYCHOLOGICAL EXPLORATION FOCUSED ON TELEVISION AND THE ESTABLISHMENT. San Francisco: Jossey-Bass, 1967.

FREE UNIVERSITIES AND EXPERIMENTAL COLLEGES. Washington, D.C.: U.S. National Student Association, 1971.

Gamson, Z. F. "Social Control and Modification: A Study of Responses to Students in a Small Nonresidential College." Unpublished Ph.D. dissertation, Harvard University, 1964.

Gruber, H. E. THE FARRAND HALL EXPERIMENT. University of Colorado Behavior Research Laboratory Report No. 17. Boulder, Colorado: Department of Psychology, University of Colorado, 1961.

Hamlin, W. and L. Porter, eds. DIMENSIONS OF CHANGE IN HIGHER EDUCATION. Yellow Springs, Ohio: Union for Research and Experimentation in Higher Education, 1966.

Hatch, W. R. THE EXPERIMENTAL COLLEGE. (New Dimensions in Higher Education, No. 2. U.S. Department of Health, Education and Welfare, Office of Education). Washington, D.C.: U.S. Government Printing Office, 1960.

Heist, Paul, ed. THE CREATIVE COLLEGE STUDENT: AN UNMET CHALLENGE. San Francisco: Jossey–Bass, 1968.

*Henderson, Algo Donayer. THE INNOVATIVE SPIRIT. San Francisco: Jossey-Bass, 1970.

Henderson, Algo Donayer and Dorothy Hall. ANTIOCH COLLEGE: ITS DESIGN FOR LIBERAL EDUCATION. New York: Harper, 1946.

Hirsh, W. INVENTING EDUCATION FOR THE FUTURE. San Francisco: Chandler, 1967.

Hofstadter, R. and C. Dewitt Haredr. THE DEVELOPMENT AND SCOPE OF HIGHER EDUCATION IN THE UNITED STATES. New York: Columbia University Press, 1952.

Jones, B. BENNINGTON COLLEGE: THE DEVELOPMENT OF AN EDUCATIONAL IDEA. New York: Harper, 1946.

Mann, Richard E., et al. THE COLLEGE CLASSROOM: CONFLICT, CHANGE, AND LEARNING. New York: Wiley, 1970.

Miles, B. INNOVATIONS IN EDUCATION. New York: Teachers College, Columbia University, 1964.

Porter, L. C., ed. DIMENSIONS OF CHANGE IN HIGHER EDUCATION. Yellow Springs, Ohio. Union for Research and Experimentation in Higher Education, 1967.

"Courses from Free University Catalogues," in Joseph Berke, ed. COUNTER CULTURE. London: Peter Owen, 1969, 46–51.

Coyne, John and Thomas Hebert. "Goddard College: A Fresh Look at an Old Innovator," CHANGE, 3 (Winter, 1971–1972), 46–51.

Dearing, Bruce. "The Student on his Own: Independent Study," in Samuel Baskin, ed. HIGHER EDUCATION: SOME NEWER DEVELOPMENTS. New York: McGraw-Hill, 1965, 49–77.

Dixon, James P. "Personalized Higher Education: Ideas and Issues," in W. J. Minter, ed. THE INDIVIDUAL AND THE SYSTEM. Boulder, Colorado: Western Interstate Commission for Higher Education, 1967, 3–20.

Dowse, E. M. and M. E. Harrison. "Educational Program of the Residence Hall," JOURNAL OF THE NATIONAL ASSOCIATION OF WOMEN DEANS AND COUNSELORS. 20 (January, 1957), 58–75.

Duberman, M. "Experiment in Education," DAEDALUS, 97 (Winter, 1968), 318–341.

Dykes, A. R. "Innovation in Higher Education," SCHOOL AND SOCIETY, 94 (April 2, 1966), 179–182.

Eberle, August. "Tricameral System Aligns at Policy Level," COLLEGE AND UNIVERSITY BUSINESS, 47 (July, 1969), 32–34.

Elzey, Roberta. "Founding an Anti-University," Joseph Berke, ed. COUNTER CULTURE, London: Peter Owen, 1969, 229–248.

"Experimental College," MODERATOR, 5 (November, 1966), 42–43.

Gaff, Jerry. "Innovation and Evaluation: A Case Study," EDUCATIONAL RECORD, 50 (Summer, 1969), 290–299.

Haak, L. A. "Acceleration by Examination," COLLEGE AND UNIVERSITY, 29 (October, 1953), 39–52.

Hobbs, D. "Student Choice as an Instrument of Higher Education Policy," in C. H. Bagley, ed. RESEARCH ON ACADEMIC INPUT: PROCEEDINGS OF THE SIXTH ANNUAL FORUM OF THE ASSOCIATION FOR INSTITUTIONAL RESEARCH. Cortland, New York: Office of Institutional Planning, State University of New York at Cortland, 1966, 53–58.

Hodgkinson, Harold. "Walden U." in H. L. Hodgkinson and M. B. Bloy, jr. IDENTITY CRISIS IN HIGHER EDUCATION. San Francisco: Jossey-Bass, 1971, 77–90.

Hornbühe, R. Lee. "Selecting and Developing Appropriate Institutional Activities," in Harold Benjamin, ed. DEMOCRACY IN THE ADMINISTRATION OF HIGHER EDUCATION. New York: Harper, 1950, 181–203.

*Jerome, Judson. "Portrait of Three Experiments," CHANGE, 2 (July–August, 1970), 40–54.

Junker, Howard. "The Free University: Academy for Mavericks," NATION, 201 (August 16, 1965), 78–81.

*Keyes, Ralph. "The Free Universities," NATION, 205 (October 2, 1967), 294–299.

*Keyes, Ralph, et al. "The College that Students Helped Plan," CHANGE, 1 (March-April, 1969), 12–23.

Lauter, P. and F. Howe. "What Happened to the Free University?" SATURDAY REVIEW, (June 20, 1970), 80–82, 93–94.

McLuhan, Marshall. "Classroom Without Walls," in Harold Jaffe and John Tytell, eds. THE AMERICAN EXPERIENCE: A RADICAL READER. New York: Harper, 1970, 293–299.

Mathews, Richard. "The Free University of New York: Society's Just Got to Go—We All Know That," SATURDAY REVIEW, 49 (September, 17, 1966), 514–516, 532–533.

"Must We Leave to Learn?" MODERATOR, 3 (Spring, 1964), 3–8.

"On Margaret Mead's Gender in the Honors Program; Discussion," SUPERIOR STUDENT, 4 (March, 1962), 16–23.

Perry, J.B., jr., *et al.* "New Wine in Old Bottles: a Post-Mortem Inquiry on a Free University," NEW DIRECTIONS IN TEACHING, 2 (1971), 29–36.

Perry, J., M. Gugh, E. Snyder, and E. Spreitzer. "Patterns of Student Participation in a Free University," YOUTH AND SOCIETY, 3 (December, 1971), 211–224.

Power, Keith. "Midpeninsula: the Jivy League," NATION, 208 (April 14, 1969), 463–464.

Rowland, H. R. "Campus Ombudsman: an Emerging Role," EDUCATION DIGEST, 35 (February, 1970), 28–31 and in G. K. Smith, ed. CURRENT ISSUES IN HIGHER EDUCATION, 1970. THE TROUBLED CAMPUS. San Francisco: Jossey-Bass, 1970. 122–130.

Ruedisili, C. H. "Student Revolt and the Honors Program," JOURNAL OF HIGHER EDUCATION, 41 (April, 1970), 283–290.

Schwartz, Edward. "The Cool Schools," CHANGE, 4 (February, 1972), 28–33.

Schwartz, Edward. "The New University," in H. L. Hodgkinson and M. B. Bloy, jr., eds. IDENTITY CRISIS IN HIGHER EDUCATION. San Francisco: Jossey-Bass, 1971, 127–151.

Scott, B. "Free University of Stanford?" UNIVERSITY QUARTERLY, 22 (September, 1968), 439–442.

Siegel, L., *et al.* "Effectiveness of Large Group Instruction at the University Level" HARVARD EDUCATIONAL REVIEW, 29 (Summer, 1959), 216–226.

Smithers, A. "What Do Students Expect of Lectures?" UNIVERSITY QUARTERLY, 24 (Summer, 1970), 330–336.

Stansil, Peter. "New Experimental College," in Joseph Berke, ed. COUNTER CULTURE. London: Peter Owen, 1969, 260–280.

Tanruther, E. M. "Program Designed to Encourage Democratic Procedures," EDUCATION, 72 (January, 1952), 305–314.

C.6. Grading

Becker, Howard, Blanche Geer, and Everett Hughes. MAKING THE GRADE: THE ACADEMIC SIDE OF COLLEGE LIFE. New York: Wiley, 1968.

Dressel, Paul L. and Lewis B. Mayhew. GENERAL EDUCATION: EXPLORATIONS IN EVALUATION. Washington, D.C.: American Council on Education, 1954.

Dunnette, Marvin Dale. "A Special Analogies Test for the Evaluation of Graduate Engineers," Unpublished Ph.D. dissertation, University of Minnesota, 1954.

Hewitt, Raymond G. THE STATUS OF PASS-FAIL OPTIONS AT TWENTY-TWO COLLEGES. Amherst, Massachusetts: Massachusetts University, Office of the Institutional Studies, 1967.

Hoyt, Donald P. THE RELATIONSHIP BETWEEN COLLEGE GRADES AND ADULT ACHIEVEMENT. A REVIEW OF THE LITERATURE. Iowa City, Iowa: American College Testing Program, Research and Development Division, 1965.

Pemberton, Carol F. AN EVALUATION OF THE CUMULATIVE GRADE AVERAGE AS A MEANS OF IDENTIFYING SUPERIOR STUDENTS. Newark, Delaware: University Impact Study, University of Delaware, 1966.

Spautz, Michael Edward. "The Relationships Between Academic Grades and Subsequent Salary and Creativity Measures for a Sample of Engineering Graduates." Unpublished Ph.D. dissertation, University of California, Los Angeles, 1965.

*Warren, Jonathan R. COLLEGE GRADING PRACTICES: AN OVERVIEW. Washington, D.C.: ERIC Clearinghouse on Higher Education, 1971.

Gardner, Geoffrey. "Some Notes on Academic Grading," LIBERATION, 12 (March, 1967), 15–18.

Goodman, Paul. "Abolishing the Grading System: 1964," in G. K. Smith, ed. 1945–1970. TWENTY-FIVE YEARS. San Francisco: Jossey-Bass, 1970, 189–192.

Harris, D. "Factors Affecting College Grades: A Review of the Literature, 1930–1937," PSYCHOLOGY BULLETIN, 37 (1940), 125–166.

Lehman, H. C. "Motivation: College Marks and the Fraternity Pledge," JOURNAL OF APPLIED PSYCHOLOGY, 19 (February, 1935), 9–28.

"More on Grading: Symposium," CLEARING HOUSE, 43 (February, 1969), 331–343.

Morishima, James K. "Student Perception of Grading Practices at the University of Washington," in Galen N. Drewry, ed. THE INSTRUCTIONAL PROCESS AND INSTITUTIONAL RESEARCH. N. p. Association for Institutional Research, 1967, 165–168.

Shuey, A. M. "Improvement in Scores on the American Council Psychological Examination Score and College Grades," JOURNAL OF EDUCATIONAL PSYCHOLOGY, 39 (November, 1948), 417–425.

Stallings, W. M., et al. "Fear of Failure and the Pass-Fail Grading Option," JOURNAL OF EXPERIMENTAL EDUCATION, 38 (Winter, 1969), 87–91.

Trout, David. "Academic Achievement and Subsequent Success in Life," in Wilma Donahue, et al., eds. THE MEASUREMENT OF STUDENT ADJUSTMENT AND ACHIEVEMENT. Ann Arbor, Michigan: University of Michigan Press, 1949, 201–218.

C.7. Student Cheating

Barton, Allen H. STUDENT DISHONESTY AND ITS CONTROL, New York: Columbia University Bureau of Applied Social Research, 1961.

Bowers, William Joseph. "Student Dishonesty and its Control in College." Unpublished Ph.D. dissertation, Columbia University, 1966.

Lewis, D. M. CHEATING AS RELATED TO THE SOCIAL SYSTEM IN A UNIVERSITY. Kalamazoo, Michigan: Western Michigan University, 1965.

McIntire, Walter Gordon. "A Comparative Study of Selected Personality Characteristics of Students Who Cheat and Do Not Cheat in an Academic Situation." Unpublished Ph.D. dissertation, University of North Dakota, 1968.

Poyourow; Donald Francis. "Risk Taking Patterns of Student Groups Differing in Degrees of Restraint Towards Cheating Opportunities." Unpublished Ph.D. dissertation, New York University, 1968.

Slocum, W. L. ACADEMIC MORALITY AT THE STATE COLLEGE OF WASHINGTON. Pullman, Washington: State College of Washington, 1956.

Anderson, William F., jr. "Attitudes of University Students Toward Cheating," JOURNAL OF EDUCATIONAL RESEARCH, 50 (April, 1957), 531–538.

Boujean, C. M. and R. McGee, "Scholastic Dishonesty Among Undergraduates in Differing Systems of Social Control," SOCIOLOGY OF EDUCATION, 38 (Winter, 1965), 127–137.

Bowers, William. "Confronting College Cheating," in Charles Havice, ed. CAMPUS VALUES. New York: Scribner's, 1968, 73–87.

Centra, J. A. "College Freshman Attitudes Toward Cheating," PERSONNEL AND GUIDANCE JOURNAL, 48 (January, 1970), 366–373.

Drake, Charles A. "Why Students Cheat," JOURNAL OF HIGHER EDUCATION, 12 (November, 1941), 418–420.

Ellison, J. "American Disgrace: College Cheating," SATURDAY EVENING POST, 232 (January 9, 1960), 13+.

Gordon, K. K. and R. E. Gordon. "College Cheating: a Problem for the College Mental Heath Services," JOURNAL OF THE AMERICAN COLLEGE HEALTH ASSOCIATION, 14 (April, 1966), 234–238.

Harp, J. and P. Taietz. "Academic Integrity and Social Structure: A Study of Cheating Among College Students," SOCIAL PROBLEMS, 13 (Spring, 1966), 365–373.

Herman, A. L. "College Cheating," JOURNAL OF HIGHER EDUCATION, 37 (May, 1966), 260–266.

Hetherington, E. M. and S. E. Feldman. "College Cheating as a Function of Subject and Situational Variables," JOURNAL OF EDUCATIONAL PSYCHOLOGY, 55 (August, 1964), 212–218.

Johnson, Richmond E. and Malcolm S. Klores. "Attitudes Toward Cheating as a Function of Classroom Dissatisfaction and Peer Norms," JOURNAL OF EDUCATIONAL RESEARCH, 62 (October, 1968), 60–64.

Knowlton, J. Q. and L. A. Hamerlynck. "Perception of Deviant Behavior: A Study of Cheating," JOURNAL OF EDUCATIONAL PSYCHOLOGY, 58 (December, 1967), 379–385.

Middlebrook, Samuel. "No Panacea for College Cheating," in Samuel I. Bellman, ed. THE COLLEGE EXPERIENCE. San Francisco: Chandler, 1962, 188–195.

Raimi, R. A. "Cheating in College," HARPER, 232 (May, 1966), 68–70+.

Rokens, R. W. and H. F. Dizney. "A Study of Unethical Academic Behavior in High School and College," JOURNAL OF EDUCATIONAL RESEARCH, 59 (January, 1966), 231–234.

Shurtleff, Ray. "Plagiarism: The Gray Area," in Charles Havice, ed. CAMPUS VALUES, New York: Scribner's, 1968, 88–94.

Steininger, Marion. "Attitudes Toward Cheating: General and Specific," PSYCHOLOGICAL REPORTS, 22 (June, 1968), 1101–1107.

Steininger, Marion, *et al.* "Cheating on College Examinations as a Function of Situationally Aroused Anxiety and Hostility," JOURNAL OF EDUCATIONAL PSYCHOLOGY, 55 (December, 1964), 317–324.

Stern, B. H. "What Should Be Done About Cheating in College?" EDUCATIONAL FORUM, 27 (November, 1962), 79–83.

Trabue, A. "Classroom Cheating: An Isolated Phenomenon?" EDUCATIONAL RECORD, 43 (October, 1962), 309–316.

Trachtenberg, Stephen J. "What Happened to the Buffalo," CHANGE, 4 (October, 1972), 45–47.

D. GENERAL SOCIAL AND PSYCHOLOGICAL ASPECTS OF STUDENT LIFE

D.1. Student Subcultures

Adams, D. V. "An Analysis of Student Subcultures at Michigan State University." Unpublished Ph.D. dissertation, Michigan State University, 1965.

Chickering, Arthur W. CAMPUS CLIMATE AND DEVELOPMENT STUDIES, THEIR IMPLICATIONS FOR FOUR YEAR CHURCH RELATED COLLEGES. Washington, D.C., Council for the Advancement of Small Colleges, 1967.

*Clark, Burton R. and Martin Trow. DETERMINANTS OF COLLEGE STUDENT SUBCULTURES. Berkeley, California: Center for Research and Development in Higher Education, 1963.

Ewalt, Robert Hermann, "Student Subcultures in University Residence Halls." Unpublished Ph.D. dissertation, University of Illinois, 1967.

Flacks, R. "Adaptations of Deviants in a College Community." Unpublished Ph.D. dissertation, University of Michigan, 1963.

Freedman, Mervin B. THE STUDENT AND CAMPUS CLIMATES OF LEARNING. NEW DIMENSIONS IN HIGHER EDUCATION. Durham, North Carolina: Duke University, 1967.

*Heiss, Ann M. TODAY'S AND TOMORROW'S STUDENTS. Berkeley: University of California, Center for Research and Development in Higher Education, 1967.

Hodgkins, B. J. "Student Subcultures: An Analysis of Their Origins and Effects on Student Attitude and Value Change in Higher Education." Unpublished Ph.D. dissertation, Michigan State University, 1964.

McCarley, R. "A Walk Around the Yard: A Study of the Freshman Year at Harvard." Undergraduate thesis, Department of Social Relations, Harvard University, 1959.

*Newcomb, T. and R. Flacks. DEVIANT SUBCULTURES ON A COLLEGE CAMPUS. Washington, D.C.: U.S. Office of Education, 1963.

Pace, Charles Robert. THE INFLUENCE OF ACADEMIC AND STUDENT SUBCULTURES IN COLLEGE AND UNIVERSITY ENVIRONMENTS. Washington, D.C.: U.S. Office of Education, 1964.

Pace, C. R. THE MEASUREMENT OF SUBCULTURES IN COMPLEX

UNIVERSITIES. COLLEGE ENTRANCE EXAMINATION BOARD REPORT NUMBER 4. Los Angeles, California: University of California, 1967.

*Peterson, Richard E. ON A TYPOLOGY OF COLLEGE STUDENTS. Princeton, New Jersey: Educational Testing Service, 1965.

Plasek, John Wayne. "Student Subculture and Professional Socialization: An Interaction Approach." Unpublished Ph.D. dissertation. University of California at Los Angeles, 1967.

Snyder, Eldon Eugene. "The School as a Social System: A Study of Selected Aspects of a Student Social Structure." Unpublished Ph.D. dissertation, University of Kansas, 1962.

Walker, Jimmy R. COLLEGE STUDENT SUBCULTURES: IMPLICATIONS FOR STUDENT PERSONNEL ADMINISTRATION. Washington: American Personnel and Guidance Association, 1968.

*Wallace, Walter L. STUDENT CULTURE. Chicago: Aldine, 1966.

Whittaker, David. STUDENT SUBCULTURES REVIEWED AND REVISITED. Berkeley: University of California, Center for Research and Development in Higher Education, 1968.

Apostal, R. A. "Personality Type and Preferred College Subculture," JOURNAL OF COLLEGE STUDENT PERSONNEL, 11 (May, 1970), 206–209.

Apostal, R. A. "Student Subculture and Personal Values," JOURNAL OF COLLEGE STUDENT PERSONNEL, 9 (January, 1968), 34–39.

*Becker, H. S. "Student Culture," in T. F. Lunsford, ed. THE STUDY OF CAMPUS CULTURES. Berkeley: Center for the Study of Higher Education, University of California, Berkeley, 1963, 1963, 11–25.

Berdie, Ralph. "The Study of Students at the University of Minnesota," INTELLECT, 101 (November, 1972), 123–126.

Bragg, E. W. "A Study of the College Campus or a Learning Environment," JOURNAL OF NEGRO EDUCATION, 37 (Winter, 1968), 82–85.

Brainard, S. R. and R. J. Dollar. "Personality Characteristics of Leaders Identifying with Different Students Subcultures," JOURNAL OF COLLEGE STUDENT PERSONNEL, 12 (May, 1971), 200–203.

Bushnell, John. "Student Culture at Vassar," JOURNAL OF SOCIAL ISSUES, 12, (Number 4, 1956), 489–514.

Clark, Burton R. "The Organizational Context," in Theodore Newcomb and Everett Wilson, eds. COLLEGE PEER GROUPS: PROBLEMS AND PROSPECTS FOR RESEARCH. Chicago: Aldine, 1966.

Coleman, J. S. "The Adolescent Subculture and Academic Achievement," AMERICAN JOURNAL OF SOCIOLOGY, 65 (January, 1960), 337–347.

Frantz, T. T. "Student Subcultures," JOURNAL OF COLLEGE STUDENT PERSONNEL, 10 (January, 1969), 16–20.

Goodman, Paul. "Youth Subculture and an Unteachable Generation," in Michael Wetheimer, ed. CONFRONTATION: PSYCHOLOGY AND THE PROBLEMS OF TODAY. Glenview, Illinois: Scott Foresman, 1970. 373–385.

Gottlieb, D. "College Climates and Student Subcultures," in W. B. Brookover, ed. THE COLLEGE STUDENT. New York: Center for Applied Research in Education, 1965, 78–99.

*Gottlieb, David and Benjamin Hodgkins. "College Student Subcultures," in Kaoru Yamamoto, ed. THE COLLEGE STUDENT AND HIS CULTURE: AN ANALYSIS. Boston: Houghton Mifflin, 1968, 238–255.

Gottlieb, David and Benjamin Hodgkins. "College Student Subcultures: Their Structure and Characteristics in Relation to Student Attitude Change," SCHOOL REVIEW, 71 (Autumn, 1963), 266–289.

Hand, H. C. "Studying the Students and their Communities," in Harold Benjamin, ed. DEMOCRACY IN THE ADMINISTRATION OF HIGHER EDUCATION. New York: Harper, 1950, 165–180.

Hartshorne, E. Y. "Undergraduate Society and the College Culture," AMERICAN SOCIOLOGICAL REVIEW, 8 (June, 1943), 321–332.

Hughes, Everett, Howard Becker and Blanche Geer, et al. "Student Culture and Academic Effort," in Sanford, Nevitt, eds. THE AMERICAN COLLEGE. New York: John Wiley, 1964, 515–535.

Keese, Sue. "Notes on Antioch Visit," in Morton Levitt and Ben Rubenstein, eds. YOUTH AND SOCIAL CHANGE. Detroit: Wayne State University Press, 1972, 303–320.

Kolb, William L. "Changing the Collegiate Culture," in Lawrence Dennis and Joseph Kauffman, eds. THE AMERICAN COLLEGE AND THE STUDENT. Washington, D.C.: American Council on Education, 1966, 67–70.

Lafore, Laurence. "One Campus, Two Cultures," SCIENCE, 145 (July 24, 1964), 371–373, 428.

Lewis, Lionel S. "The Value of College to Different Subcultures," SCHOOL REVIEW, 77 (March, 1969), 32–40.

McArthur, Charles C. "Sub-Culture and Personality During the College Years," JOURNAL OF EDUCATIONAL SOCIOLOGY, 33 (February, 1960), 360–368.

Maw, I. E. L. "Student Subcultures and Their Future Time Perspectives; Clark-Trow Typology," NASPA JOURNAL, 8 (January, 1971), 160–167.

Maw, I. E. L. "Student Subcultures and Activity Involvement," JOURNAL OF COLLEGE STUDENT PERSONNEL, 12 (January, 1971), 62–66.

Middleton, D. and J. Moland. "Humor in Negro and White Subcultures: A Study of Jokes Among University Students," AMERICAN SOCIOLOGICAL REVIEW, 24 (February, 1959), 61–69.

Pace, C. R. "The Influence of Student Culture and Faculty Values in the American College," in G. Z. Bereday and J. A. Lauwerys, eds. HIGHER EDUCATION: THE YEAR BOOK OF EDUCATION. New York: World Book, 1959.

Pace, C. Robert. "Interactions among Academic, Administrative, and Student Subcultures," in Terry Lunsford, ed. THE STUDY OF CAMPUS CULTURES. Boulder, Colorado: Western Interstate Commission for Higher Education, 1963, 55–80.

Pace, C. R. "Methods of Describing College Cultures," TEACHERS COLLEGE RECORD, 63, (January, 1962), 267–277.

Rasmussen, Karl. "College Students, a Natural Aristocracy?" SOUTH ATLANTIC QUARTERLY, 71 (Summer, 1972), 390–400.

Regan, Mary C. "Student Change: the New Student and Society," NASPA JOURNAL, 6 (January, 1969), 127–135.

Riesman, David. "College Subcultures and College Outcomes," in SELEC-TION AND EDUCATIONAL DIFFERENTIATION. Berkeley: Center for the Study of Higher Education, 1959.

Spike, Paul. "Phenomenology of Today's Students," in H. L. Hodgkinson and M. B. Bloy, jr., eds. IDENTITY CRISIS IN HIGHER EDUCATION. San Francisco: Jossey-Bass, 1971, 153–161.

"The Student Activist and his Subculture," COLLEGE AND UNIVERSITY BUSINESS, 45 (August, 1968), 41–49.

Taylor, W. "Student Culture and Residence," UNIVERSITIES QUARTER-LY, 19 (Spring, 1965), 331–344.

Thistlethwaite, Donald L. "Some Ecological Effects of Entering a Field of Study," JOURNAL OF EDUCATIONAL PSYCHOLOGY, 60 (August, 1969), 284–293.

Thistlethwaite, D. L. and N. Wheeler. "Effects of Teacher and Peer Subcul-tures Upon Student Aspirations," JOURNAL OF EDUCATIONAL PSYCHOL-OGY, 57 (February, 1966), 35–47.

Trow, Martin. "The Campus Viewed as Culture," in Hall T. Sprague, ed. RESEARCH ON COLLEGE STUDENTS. Boulder, Colorado: Western Interstate Commission for Higher Education, 1960, 105–124.

Trow, M. "Cultural Sophistication and Higher Education," in SELECTION AND EDUCATIONAL DIFFERENTIATION. Berkeley, California: University of California Field Service Center and Center for the Study of Higher Education, 1960, 107–124.

Trow, Martin. "Student Cultures and Administrative Action," in R.Suther-land, ed. PERSONALITY FACTORS ON THE COLLEGE CAMPUS. Austin, Texas: Hogg Foundation for Mental Health, 1962, 203–225.

Vaccaro, Louis. "The New Student Subculture and the Search for Meaning," in Louis Vaccaro and James Covert, eds. STUDENT FREEDOM IN AMERICAN HIGHER EDUCATION. New York: Teacher's College Press, 1969, 31–39.

Warren, J. R. "Student Perception of College Subcultures," AMERICAN EDUCATIONAL RESEARCH JOURNAL, 5 (March, 1968), 213–232.

Withey, Stephen. "Some Effects on Life Style," in S. Withey, ed. A DE-GREE AND WHAT ELSE? New York: McGraw Hill, 1972, 81–94.

Whiting, A. N. "The Student Culture and the Educational Enterprise," LIBERAL EDUCATION, 50 (December, 1964), 513–516.

Whittaker, David, "Student Subcultures Reviewed and Revisited," NASPA JOURNAL, 7 (July, 1969), 23–24.

D.2. The Idea of College Environment

Adolph, R., K. Harrison, and D. Peterson. PATTERNS OF COLLEGE CHARACTERISTICS OBTAINED FROM OREGON STATE UNIVERSITY STUDENTS, COUNSELING AND STUDENT PERSONNEL RESEARCH TEAM REPORT NO. 6. Corvallis, Oregon: Counseling Center, Oregon, State University, 1965–1966.

448

*Astin, Alexander. THE COLLEGE ENVIRONMENT. Washington, D.C.: American Council on Education, 1967.

Brown, R. D. "Manipulation of the Environmental Press in a College Residence Hall." Unpublished Ph.D. dissertation, University of Iowa, 1966.

Bruning, C. "Comparison of Institutional Press as Perceived by Selected Students in Church-Related Schools." Unpublished Ph.D. dissertation, University of Minnesota, 1965.

Califf, Stanley Norman. "Perception of College Environment by Achieving and Non-achieving Freshmen." Unpublished Ph.D. dissertation, Claremont Graduate School and University Center, 1967.

Campbell, Paul S. "Personality Needs of Community College and University Students and Their Perceptions of the Press of Their Institutions: an Experimental Investigation." Unpublished Ph.D. dissertation, Michigan State University, 1964.

Centra, J. A. THE COLLEGE ENVIRONMENT REVISITED: CURRENT DESCRIPTIONS AND A COMPARISON OF THREE METHODS OF ASSESSMENT. Princeton, New Jersey: Educational Testing Service, 1970.

Centra, J. A. "Student Perceptions of Total University and Major Field Environments." Unpublished Ph.D. dissertation, Michigan State University, 1965.

Centra, J. A. and R. L. Linn. ON THE INTERPRETATION OF STUDENT PERCEPTIONS OF THEIR COLLEGE ENVIRONMENTS. Princeton, New Jersey: Educational Testing Service, 1968.

Duling, John Anderson. "College Environment as Perceived by Selected Student Subgroups." Unpublished Ed.D. thesis, Colorado State College, 1966.

Dunham, E. A. COLLEGES OF THE FORGOTTEN AMERICANS: A PROFILE OF STATE COLLEGES AND REGIONAL UNIVERSITIES. New York: McGraw-Hill, 1969.

Ferm, Lois R. "Student Characteristics and Environments for Learning in Wesleyan Colleges." Unpublished Ph.D. dissertation, University of Minnesota, 1972.

Fisher, M. S. "Environment, Expectations, and the Significance of Disparity Between Actual and Expected Environment at the University of Utah." Unpublished Ph.D. dissertation, University of California, Los Angeles, 1966.

Foote, Caleb, et al. THE CULTURE OF THE UNIVERSITY. San Francisco: Jossey-Bass, 1968.

Hughes, Everett C. STUDENTS' CULTURE AND PERSPECTIVES: LECTURES ON MEDICAL AND GENERAL EDUCATION. Lawrence, Kansas: University of Kansas School of Law, 1961.

Kansas City Regional Council for Higher Education. Office of Institutional Research. CAMPUS ENVIRONMENT: AN ON GOING ASSESSMENT OF STUDENT ATTITUDES. Kansas City, Kansas, 1969.

McFee, A. "The Relation of Selected Factors to Students' Perception of a College Environment." Unpublished M.A. thesis, Syracuse University, 1959.

Pate, B. C. "Colleges as Environmental Systems: Toward the Codification Social Theory." Unpublished Ph.D. dissertation, Boston University, 1964.

Pervin, Lawrence A. SOURCES OF STRAIN IN THE COLLEGE ENVI-

RONMENT AS RELATED TO STUDENT DISSATISFACTION AND THE DROPOUT. Princeton: Princeton University, 1967.

Schuhle, William, jr. "Normative Homogeneity in a Social Group: a Measure of Agreement and Understanding in a small College." Unpublished Ph.D. dissertation, University of Minnesota, 1955.

Stern, G. G. STUDIES OF COLLEGE ENVIRONMENTS. Syracuse, New York: Psychological Research Center, 1966.

Stricker, George. STUDENTS' VIEWS OF THEIR COLLEGE ENVIRONMENT. Garden City, New York: Adelphi University, 1964.

Thistlethwaite, D. L. THE EFFECTS OF COLLEGE ENVIRONMENTS ON STUDENTS' DECISIONS TO ATTEND GRADUATE SCHOOL. U.S. Department of Health, Education and Welfare Project No. 2993. Nashville, Tennessee: Vanderbilt University, 1968.

Tiller, Thomas Columbus, jr. "A Study at Lynchburg College of the Relationship Between Congruence and Non-congruence of Student Needs with College Environmental press and Selected Attitudes and Behavior." Unpublished Ph.D. dissertation, Florida State University, 1968.

Trimble, Maxine Genevieve. "Measurement of Perceived Campus Press on Three Student Groups at the Kansas State Teachers College of Emporia." Unpublished Ed.D. thesis, University of Arkansas, 1969.

Weits, C. E. THE STUDY OF COLLEGE ENVIRONMENTS USING PATH ANALYSIS. (National Merit Scholarship Corporation Research Reports, Vol. 3, No. 4). Evanston, Illinois: National Merit Scholarship Corporation, 1967.

Astin, A. W. "Differential College Effects on the Motivation of Talented Students to Seek the Ph.D.," JOURNAL OF EDUCATIONAL PSYCHOLOGY, 54 (February, 1963), 63-71.

Astin, A. W. "Classroom Environment in Different Fields of Study," JOURNAL OF EDUCATIONAL PSYCHOLOGY, 56 (October, 1965), 275-282.

Astin, A. W. "Effects of Different College Environments on the Vocational Choices of High Aptitude Students," JOURNAL OF COUNSELING PSYCHOLOGY, 12 (Spring, 1965), 28-34.

Baird, L. L. "Big School, Small School: a Critical Examination of the Hypothesis," JOURNAL OF EDUCATIONAL PSYCHOLOGY, 60 (August, 1969), 253-260.

Barton, A. H. "The College as Social Organization," COLLEGE ADMISSIONS, 10 (1963), 31-45.

Berry, Margaret. "Campus Culture: A Product of its Own History," JOURNAL OF COLLEGE STUDENT PERSONNEL ADMINISTRATORS, 8 (January, 1967), 3-9.

Bickham, M. H. "Making Social Analyses of College Communities," JOURNAL OF EDUCATIONAL SOCIOLOGY, 2 (May, 1929), 514-519.

Boland, W. R. "Size, Organization and Environmental Mediation: a Study of Colleges and Universities," in W. Heydebrand, ed. COMPARATIVE ORGANIZATIONS: THE RESULTS OF EMPIRICAL RESEARCH. Englewood Cliffs, New Jersey: Prentice-Hall, 1971.

Boyer, E. L. and W. B. Michael. "Faculty and Student Assessments of the Environments of Several Small Religiously Oriented Colleges," CALIFORNIA JOURNAL OF EDUCATIONAL RESEARCH, 19 (March, 1968), 59–66.

*Brown, Donald R. "Student Stress and the Institutional Environment," JOURNAL OF SOCIAL ISSUES, 23 (July, 1967), 92–107.

Chickering, A. W. "Institutional Differences and Student Characteristics," JOURNAL OF THE AMERICAN COLLEGE HEALTH ASSOCIATION, 15 (1966), 168–181.

Clark, Burton R. "The College as Determinant," in Kaoru Yamamoto, ed. THE COLLEGE STUDENT AND HIS CULTURE: AN ANALYSIS. Boston: Houghton Mifflin, 1968. 255–269.

Clark, Burton and Martin Trow. "The Organizational Context," in A. Orum, ed. THE SEEDS OF POLITICS. Englewood Cliffs, New Jersey: Prentice-Hall, 1972, 149–164.

Cole, D. and B. Fields. "Student Perceptions of Varied Campus Climates," PERSONNEL AND GUIDANCE JOURNAL, 34 (February, 1961), 509–510.

Conway, Jill. "Styles of Academic Culture," DAEDALUS, 99 (Winter, 1970), 43–55.

Dundon, Mary Catherine. "The Christian Character of Certain Liberal Arts Colleges with a Focus on the Academic Arena," SOCIOLOGICAL ANALYSIS, 32 (Summer, 1971), 107–119.

Geager, J. A. and A. W. Astin. "Alternative Methods of Describing Characteristics of Colleges and Universities," EDUCATIONAL AND PSYCHOLOGICAL MEASUREMENT, 28 (Autumn, 1968), 719–734.

*Gusfield, Joseph R. "Intellectual Character and American Universities," JOURNAL OF GENERAL EDUCATION, 14 (January, 1963), 230–247.

*Gusfield, Joseph R. and David Riesman. "Academic Standards and 'The Two Cultures' in the Context of a New State College," SCHOOL REVIEW, 74 (Spring, 1966), 95–116.

Hand, Harold. "Studying the Students and Their Communities," in Harold Benjamin, ed. DEMOCRACY IN THE ADMINISTRATION OF HIGHER EDUCATION. New York: Harper, 1950, 165–181.

Haveman, Ernest and Patricia West. "Motorboards Come in All Sizes," in Samuel Bellman, ed. THE COLLEGE EXPERIENCE. San Francisco: Chandler, 1962, 209–218.

Hassenger, Robert and Robert S. J. Weiss. "The Catholic School Climate," SCHOOL REVIEW, 74 (Winter, 1966), 419–445.

Hoffman, R. "Swept with Confused Alarms: Psychological Climate on Campus," MADEMOISELLE, 59 (August, 1964), 260–261+.

Ivey, Allen and Ray Wilson. "Perceptions of College Environment: a Four-Year Longitudinal Study," JOURNAL OF COLLEGE STUDENT PERSONNEL, 12 (May, 1971), 177+.

King, Jonathan. "Campus Cultures and the Cultured Campus," in Institute on College Self-Study. THE STUDY OF CAMPUS CULTURES (4th Conference, 1962), Terry Lunsford, ed. Boulder, Colorado: Western Interstate Commission on Higher Education, 1963, 129–138.

Kirkland, William. "American Culture and Campus Culture," CHRISTIAN-ITY AND CRISIS, 20 (March 7, 1960), 20–24.

McConnell, T. R. "Recent Research on Institutional Climates: 2. The Vocational College Culture," in N. C. Brown, ed. ORIENTATION TO COLLEGE LEARNING—A REAPPRAISAL: REPORT OF A CONFERENCE ON INTRO-DUCTION OF ENTERING STUDENTS TO THE INTELLECTUAL LIFE OF THE COLLEGE. Washington, D.C.: American Council on Education, 1961, 59–73.

McConnell, R. T. and P. Heist. "Do Students Make the College?" COL-LEGE AND UNIVERSITY, 34 (Summer, 1959), 442–452.

McFee. A. "The Relation of Selected Factors to Students' Perception of a College Environment," JOURNAL OF EDUCATIONAL PSYCHOLOGY, 52 (February, 1961), 25–29.

McGee, Reece. "The Function of Institutional Inbreeding," AMERICAN JOURNAL OF SOCIOLOGY, 65 (March, 1966), 483–488.

Marks, E. "Individual Differences in Perceptions of the College Environ-ment," JOURNAL OF EDUCATIONAL PSYCHOLOGY, 61 (August, 1970), 270–279.

Mayhew, Lewis B. "Institutional Factors and the Learning Environment," in Lawrence Dennis and Joseph Kauffman, eds. THE AMERICAN COLLEGE AND THE STUDENT. Washington, D.C.: American Council on Education, 1966, 211–230.

Mulford, C. L. "Self-Actualization in a Small College Environment," JOUR-NAL OF COLLEGE STUDENT PERSONNEL, 8 (March, 1967), 100–104.

Newcomb, T. M. "The Influence of Attitude Climate Upon Some Determi-nants of Information," JOURNAL OF ABNORMAL AND SOCIAL PSYCHOL-OGY, 41 (July, 1946), 291–302.

Nichols, Robert C. "Effects of Various College Characteristics on Student Aptitude Test Scores," JOURNAL OF EDUCATIONAL PSYCHOLOGY, 55 (February, 1964), 45–54.

Nunnally, J. C. and Donald Thistlethwaite, "Factored Scales for Measur-ing Characteristics of College Environments," EDUCATIONAL AND PSYCHO-LOGICAL MEASUREMENTS, 23 (Summer, 1963), 239–248.

Pace, C. R. "College Environments," ENCYCLOPEDIA OF EDUCATIONAL RESEARCH, Fourth Edition, 1969, 169–173.

Pace, C. R. "Evaluating the Total Climate or Profile of a Campus," CUR-RENT ISSUES IN HIGHER EDUCATION, 1961: GOALS FOR HIGHER EDU-CATION IN A DECADE OF DECISION. Washington, D.C.: Association for Higher Education, 1961, 171–176.

Pace, C. R. "Five College Environments," In O. Milton and E. J. Shoben, eds. LEARNING AND THE PROFESSORS, Athens, Ohio: Ohio University Press, 1968, pp. 91–104.

Pace, C. R. "Implications of Differences in Campus Atmosphere for Evalua-tion and Planning of College Programs," in Robert Sutherland, et al., eds. PER-SONALITY FACTORS ON THE COLLEGE CAMPUS. Austin, Texas: Hogg Foundation for Mental Health, 1962, 43–63.

452

Pace, C. R. "Perspective on the Student and His College," in Lawrence Dennis and Joseph Kauffman, eds., THE AMERICAN COLLEGE AND THE STUDENT, (Washington, D.C.: American Council on Education, 1966), 76-100.

Pervin, L. W. "A Twenty-College Study of Student College Interaction Using TAPE (Transactional Analysis of Personality and Environment): Rationale, Reliability and Validity," JOURNAL OF EDUCATIONAL PSYCHOLOGY, 58 (October, 1967), 290-302.

Pervin, L. W., et al. "Personal Determinants and Their Interaction with the Environment," in L. A. Pervin, et al., THE COLLEGE DROPOUT AND THE UTILIZATION OF TALENT. Princeton, New Jersey: Princeton University Press, 1966, 111-130.

Pervin, L. A. "Satisfaction and Perceived Self-Environment Similarity: A Semantic Differential Study of Student-College Interaction," JOURNAL OF PERSONALITY, 35 (1967), 625-634.

Richards, J. M., R. Seligman, and P. K. Jones. "Faculty and Curriculum as Measures of College Environment," JOURNAL OF EDUCATIONAL PSYCHOLOGY, 61 (August, 1970), 324-332.

Schoen, W. T., jr. "Campus Climate: Student Perception and Faculty Idealism," JOURNAL OF EDUCATIONAL RESEARCH, 60 (September, 1966), 3-7.

School Review Staff. "Social Climates in School and College," SCHOOL REVIEW, 71 (Autumn, 1963), 249-388.

Stern, George G. "Characteristics of the Intellectual Climate in College Environments," HARVARD EDUCATIONAL REVIEW, 33 (Winter, 1963), 5-41.

Stern, George G. "Environments for Learning," in Nevitt Sanford, ed. THE AMERICAN COLLEGE. New York: Wiley, 1964, 690-730.

Stern, George G. "Research on Institutional Climates: 1. Continuity and Contrast in the Transition from High School To College," in N. C. Brown, ed. ORIENTATION TO COLLEGE LEARNING– A REAPPRAISAL. Washington, D.C.: American Council on Education, 1961, 33-58.

Stern, George G. "Student Ecology and College Environment," in RESEARCH IN HIGHER EDUCATION: GUIDE TO INSTITUTIONAL DECISIONS. New York: College Entrance Examination Board, 1964, 35-52.

Sutherland, Robert L. "Some Aspects of the Culture of a Campus," in E. G. Williamson, ed. TRENDS IN STUDENT PERSONNEL WORK. Minneapolis, Minnesota: University of Minnesota Press, 1949, 350-355.

Swados. H. "Joys and Terrors of Sending the Kids to College," NEW YORK TIMES MAGAZINE, (February 14, 1971), 12-13+.

Thistlethwaite, Donald L. "College Environments and the Development of Talent," SCIENCE, 130 (July 10, 1959), 71-76.

Thistlethwaite, Donald L. "Diversities in College Environments: Implications for Student Selection," in K. M. Wilson, ed. RESEARCH RELATED TO COLLEGE ADMISSIONS. Atlanta, Georgia: Southern Regional Education Board, 1963, 145-167.

Trow, Martin. "The Campus as a Context for Learning," NATIONAL ASSOCIATION OF STUDENT PERSONNEL ADMINISTRATORS JOURNAL, 46 (April, 1964), 135-145.

Tyler, Ralph. "The Study of Campus Cultures," in Institute on College Self-Study, THE STUDY OF CAMPUS CULTURES (4th Conference, 1962) Terry Lunsford, ed. Boulder, Colorado: Western Interstate Commission for Higher Education, 1963, 1–10.

Webb. S. C. and Dolores G. Crowder. "Analyzing the Psychological Climate of a Single College," TEACHERS COLLEGE RECORD, 66 (February, 1965), 425–433.

Weiss, Robert. "The Environment for Learning on the Catholic Campus," in R. Hassenger, ed. THE SHAPE OF CATHOLIC HIGHER EDUCATION. Chicago: University of Chicago Press, 1967, 57–82.

Werts, C. E. and D. J. Watley. "A Student's Dilemma: Big Fish—Little Pond or Little Fish—Big Pond," JOURNAL OF COUNSELING PSCYHOLOGY, 16 (January, 1969), 14–19.

Wright, Stephen J. "Institutional Expectations and Influences," in Lawrence Dennis and Joseph Kauffman, eds. THE AMERICAN COLLEGE AND THE STUDENT. Washington, D.C.: American Council on Education, 1966, 123–125.

Yonge, G. D. "Personality Correlates of the College and University Environment Scales," EDUCATIONAL AND PSYCHOLOGICAL MEASUREMENT, 28 (Spring, 1968), 115–123.

D.3. The Influence of Student Peer Groups

Alsobrook, J. M., jr. "A Study of Health-Engendering-People in a Campus Community." Unpublished Ph.D. dissertation, University of Florida, 1962.

Bates, Frederick L. and H. M. Miller. A STUDY OF THE RELATIONSHIP OF ASSOCIATIONAL PATTERNS TO ACADEMIC PERFORMANCE AT A STATE UNIVERSITY. Athens, Georgia: Georgia University, 1968.

Boyer, R. K. "The Student Peer Group: Its Effect on College Performance," Unpublished Ph.D. dissertation, Case Institute of Technology, 1965.

Broderick, C. B. "Predicting Friendship Behavior: a Study of the Determinates of Friendship Selection and Maintenance in a College Population." Unpublished Ph.D. dissertation, Cornell University, 1956.

Brodie, Donald Quentin. "Structural and Interpersonal Influences Upon Students' Educational Horizons." Unpublished Ph.D. dissertation, University of Pittsburgh, 1968.

Carter, T. M. "The Effect of Roommate Ability on the Academic Achievement of College Freshmen." Unpublished Ph.D. dissertation, University of Florida, 1966.

Efron, R. Homophily Among Undergraduates: A Study of Some of the Regularities in Their Choice of Friends." Unpublished Ph.D. dissertation, University of Michigan.

Fiedler, E. L. "The Relationship Between Scholastic Achievement and Social Participation in College." Unpublished Ph.D. dissertation, Kansas State College, 1943.

Fontana, A. F. "The Effects of Acceptance and Rejection by Desired Mem-

454

bership Groups on Self-Evaluation." Unpublished Ph.D. dissertation, University of Michigan, 1964.

Glick, D. W. "An Investigation of Changes in the Normative System of Behavioral Norms on the Selection of Associates." Unpublished Ph.D. dissertation, University of Kansas, 1963.

Hassan, Abd El-Bassit Mohammed Awad. "Social Interactions Between Foreign Students and Americans in a Mid-Western Community." Unpublished Ph.D. dissertation, Purdue University, 1961.

McKillop, D. P. "Compatibility and Stability in Relationships Between Roommates." Unpublished Ph.D. dissertation, Harvard University, 1965.

Masterton, George. "Friendship as a Situational Phenomenon: a Study of Friendship Among College Freshmen." University of Pittsburgh, 1956.

Mill, Cyril Ralph. "Personality Patterns of Socially Selected and Socially Rejected Male College Students," Unpublished Ph.D. dissertation, Michigan State University, 1953.

Mitchell, P. H. "An Evaluation of the Relationship of Values to Sociometric Choice." Unpublished Ph.D. dissertation, University of Michigan, 1951.

*Newcomb, Theodore and E. K. Wilson, eds. COLLEGE PEER GROUPS: PROBLEMS AND PROSPECTS FOR RESEARCH. Chicago: Aldine, 1966.

Slocum, John Wesley, jr. "Group Cohesiveness: a Salient Factor Affecting Students' Academic Achievement and Adjustment in a Collegiate Environment." Unpublished D.B.A. thesis, University of Washington, 1967.

Spady, W. G., jr. "Peer Integration and Academic Success: the Dropout Process Among Chicago Freshman." Unpublished Ph.D. dissertation, University of Chicago, 1967.

Turner, Edward Thomas, "The Effects of Viewing College Football, Basketball and Wrestling on the Elicited Aggressive Responses of Male Spectators." Unpublished Ph.D. dissertation, University of Maryland, 1968.

Wallace, W. L. PEER GROUPS AND STUDENT ACHIEVEMENT: THE COLLEGE CAMPUS AND ITS STUDENTS. Chicago: National Opinion Research Center, 1963.

Warwick, C. E. "Relationship of Scholastic Aspiration and Group Cohesiveness to the Academic Achievement of Male Freshman at Cornell University." Unpublished Ph.D. dissertation, University of Illinois, 1962.

Bauer, E. J. "Student Peer Groups and Academic Development," COLLEGE STUDENT SURVEY, 1 (Fall, 1967), 22–31.

Bonney, M. E. "A Sociometric Study of the Relationship of Some Factors to Mutual Friendships on the Elementary, Secondary, and College Levels," SOCIOMETRY, 9 (February, 1946), 21–47.

Bonney, M. E. "A Study of Friendship Choices in College in Relation to Church affiliation, In-Church Preferences, Family Size, and Length of Enrollment in College," JOURNAL OF SOCIAL PSYCHOLOGY, 29 (May, 1949), 153–166.

Bowers, W. J. "Normative Constraints on Deviant Behavior in the College," SOCIOMETRY, 31 (1968), 370–385.

Carew, D. K. "Comparison of Activities, Social Acceptance and Scholastic Achievements of Men Students," PERSONNEL AND GUIDANCE JOURNAL, 36 (October, 1957), 121–124.

Childe, Dennis. "Some Reference Groups of University Students," EDUCATIONAL RESEARCH, 12 (February, 1970), 145–149.

Cross, K. Patricia. "Students' Education of One Another," RESEARCH REPORTER, 3 (No. 2, 1968), 5–7.

Curry, T. J. and R. M. Emerson. "Balance Theory of Interpersonal Attraction?" SOCIOMETRY, 33 (1970), 216–238.

Day, B. R. "A Comparison of Personality Needs of Courtship Couples and Same-Sex-Friendships," SOCIOLOGY AND SOCIAL RESEARCH, 45 (July, 1961), 435–440.

Denzin, N. K. "Significant Others of a College Population," SOCIOLOGICAL QUARTERLY, 7 (Summer, 1966), 298–310.

Deutsch, S. E. "Impact of Cross-Cultural Relations on the Campus," SOCIOLOGY AND SOCIAL RESEARCH, 53 (January, 1969), 137–146.

Finger, J. A. "Academic Motivation and Youth-Culture Involvement: Their Relationships to School Performance and Career Success," SCHOOL REVIEW, 74 (Summer, 1966), 177–195.

Goldsen, R.K., et al. "Factors Associated with the Development of Cross-Cultural Social Interaction," JOURNAL OF SOCIAL ISSUES, 12 (No. 1, 1956), 26–32.

Grant, W. H. and F. A. Eigenbrod, jr. "Behavior Changes Influenced by Structured Peer Group Activities," JOURNAL OF COLLEGE STUDENT PERSONNEL, 11 (July, 1970), 291–295.

Grinder, R. E. "Relations of Social Dating Attractions to Academic Orientation and Peer Relations," JOURNAL OF EDUCATIONAL PSYCHOLOGY, 57 (February, 1966), 27–34.

Hall, D. T. "The Effect of Student-Student Congruence Upon Student Learning in College Classes," JOURNAL OF EDUCATIONAL PSYCHOLOGY, 61 (June, 1970), 205–213.

Hall, R. L. and B. Willerman, "The Educational Influence of Dormitory Roommates," SOCIOMETRY, 26 (September, 1963), 294–318.

Hilberry, Conrad and Morris T. Keeton. "Student Society in the Liberal Arts College: the Invisible Teacher," JOURNAL OF HIGHER EDUCATION, 39 (November, 1968), 431–441.

Horrocks, J. E. and B. A. Wear. "Analysis of Interpersonal Choice Relationships of College Students," JOURNAL OF SOCIAL PSYCHOLOGY, 38 (August, 1953), 87–98.

Kelley, H. H. "Two Functions of Reference Groups," in G. E. Swanson, T. Newcomb, E. L. Hartley, eds. READINGS IN SOCIAL PSYCHOLOGY. New York: Holt, 1952, 410–412.

Kemper, Theodore. "Reference Groups, Socialization and Achievement," AMERICAN SOCIOLOGICAL REVIEW, 33 (February, 1968), 31–43.

Lehmann, Irvin. "American College Students and the Socialization Process," in Eric Gardener, ed. THE COLLEGE STUDENT. New York: Center for Applied Research in Education, 1965.

Levine, R. A. "American College Experience as a Socialization Process," in T. M. Newcomb and E. K. Wilson, eds. COLLEGE PEER GROUPS: PROBLEMS AND PROSPECTS FOR RESEARCH. Chicago: Aldine, 1966.

Lindzey, G. and J. A. Urdan. "Personality and Social Choice," SOCIOMETRY, 17 (February, 1954), 47–63.

Lundberg, G. A., V. B. Hertzler, and L. Dickson. "Attraction Patterns in a University," SOCIOMETRY, 12 (1949), 158–169.

MacKay, W. R. "Interpersonal Relationships, a Factor in Academic Success," CALIFORNIA JOURNAL OF EDUCATIONAL RESEARCH, 16 (September, 1965), 189–196.

McKenna, H. V., et al. "Concepts of the Ideal Self and of the Friend," JOURNAL OF PERSONALITY, 24 (March, 1956), 262–271.

Merelman, Richard M. "Intimate Environments and Political Behavior," MIDWEST JOURNAL OF POLITICAL SCIENCE, 12 (August, 1968), 382–400.

Mowrer, O. H. "But the Peer Group Says . . . ," NATIONAL ASSOCIATION OF WOMEN DEANS AND COUNSELORS JOURNAL, 25 (April, 1962), 112–117.

Newcomb, Theodore. "Student Peer-Group Influence and Intellectual Outcomes of College Experience," in Robert Sutherland et al, eds. PERSONALITY FACTORS ON THE COLLEGE CAMPUS. Austin, Texas: Hogg Foundation for Mental Health, 1962, 69–93.

Newcomb, Theodore M. "Student Peer-Group Influence," in Nevitt Sanford, ed. THE AMERICAN COLLEGE. New York: Wiley, 1964, 469–488.

O'Shea, Arthur J. "Peer Relationships and Male Academic Achievement: A Review and Suggested Clarification," PERSONNEL AND GUIDANCE JOURNAL, 47 (January, 1969), 417–423.

Pervin, L. A. "A Twenty-College Study of Student College Interaction Using TAPE (Transactional Analysis of Personality and Environment): Rationale, Reliability and Validity," JOURNAL OF EDUCATIONAL PSYCHOLOGY, 58 (October, 1967), 290–302.

Sanford, N. "Factors Related to the Effectiveness of Student Interaction with the College Social System," in B. Barger and E. E. Hall, eds. HIGHER EDUCATION AND MENTAL HEALTH. Gainesville, Florida: Mental Health Project, University of Florida, 1963, 8–26.

Schoenfeld, Clarence A. "Student Press," in C. A. Schoenfeld, ed. THE UNIVERSITY AND ITS PUBLICS: APPROACHES TO A PUBLIC PROGRAM FOR COLLEGES AND UNIVERSITIES. New York: Harper, 1954, 67–70.

Siegel, Alberta E. and Sidney Siegel. "Reference Groups, Membership Groups, and Attitude Change," JOURNAL OF ABNORMAL AND SOCIAL PSYCHOLOGY, 55 (November, 1957), 360–363.

Sims, V. M. "Some Correlates of Social-Class Identification Among High School and College Students," SCHOOL REVIEW, 60 (March, 1952), 160–163.

Smucker, O. "The Campus Clique as an Agency of Socialization," JOURNAL OF EDUCATIONAL SOCIOLOGY, 21 (November, 1947), 163–168.

Spaulding, C. B. "Relative Attachment of Students to Groups and Organizations," SOCIOLOGY AND SOCIAL RESEARCH, 50 (July, 1966), 421–435.

Toby, Jackson. "The American College Student: A Candidate for Socialization," AAUP BULLETIN, 43 (June, 1957), 319–322.

Tomeh, A. K. "Reference-Group Supports Among Middle Eastern College Students," JOURNAL OF MARRIAGE AND THE FAMILY, 32 (February, 1970), 156–166.

Tunnell, James, jr. "The Proper Burden of Student Leadership," in Esther Lloyd-Jones and Herman Estrin, eds. THE AMERICAN STUDENT AND HIS COLLEGE. Boston: Houghton Mifflin, 1967, 237–341.

Wallace, W. L. "Peer Influences and Undergraduates' Aspirations for Graduate Study," SOCIOLOGY OF EDUCATION, 38 (Fall, 1965), 375–392.

Warwick, C. E. "Relationship of Scholastic Aspiration and Group Cohesiveness to the Academic Achievement of Male Freshmen at Cornell University," HUMAN RELATIONS, 17 (May, 1962), 155–168.

White, Robert W. "Sense of Interpersonal Competence," in Robert W. White, ed. THE STUDY OF LIVES. New York: Atherton Press, 1963, 72–93.

D.4. The Residential Pattern of Students

Cross Reference. The role of fraternities and sororities has been given separate consideration in a later section.

Andrews, Ernest E. THE RESIDENTIAL COLLEGE STUDENT—A STUDY IN IDENTITY CRISIS. Washington, D.C.: ERIC Clearinghouse, 1967.

College Student Personnel Institute. STUDENT HOUSING IN COLLEGES AND UNIVERSITIES, 1961–1966. Claremont, California: College Student Personnel Institute, 1966.

Dollar, R. J. "A Study of Certain Psychosocial Differences Among Dormitory, Fraternity, and Off-Campus Freshman men at Oklahoma State University." Unpublished Ph.D. dissertation, Oklahoma State University, 1963.

Florida State University, Tallahassee. Office of Education Research and Service. RELATIONSHIP BETWEEN TYPES OF HOUSING AND ACADEMIC ACHIEVEMENT: A STUDY OF FLORIDA STATE UNIVERSITY FRESHMEN, 1955–1956. Tallahassee, Florida, 1957.

Fritz, Roger J. "A Comparison of Attitude Differences and Changes of College Freshman Men Living in Various Types of Housing." Unpublished Ph.D. dissertation, University of Wisconsin, 1956.

Gamble, F. P. "Effects of Campus Living Groups on Academic Values and Performance." Unpublished M.A. thesis, University of California, Berkeley, 1961.

Griffeth, P. L. "Type of Residence as a Factor in Academic Achievement at the State University of Iowa." 1958.

Iowa. University. Housing Committee. STUDENT HOUSING AT THE UNIVERSITY OF IOWA: A REPORT. Iowa City, Iowa, 1967.

Kidd, John W. "An Analysis of Social Rejection in a College Men's Residence Hall." Unpublished Ph.D. dissertation, Michigan State College, 1951.

458

Powell, John R., *et al.* THE PERSONNEL ASSISTANT IN COLLEGE RESIDENCE HALLS. Boston: Houghton, Mifflin, 1969.

Strozier, R. M., *et al.* HOUSING OF STUDENTS. American Council on Education Studies Series 6, Student Personnel Work No. 14, Vol. 14. Washington, D.C.: American Council on Education, 1950.

Taylor, John Frances. "Success of College Freshmen in Community Class Centers and in Regular Residential Colleges." Unpublished Ph.D. dissertation, Pennsylvania State University, 1949.

Van Der Rym, Sim and Murray Silverstein. DORMS AT BERKELEY, AN ENVIRONMENTAL ANALYSIS. Berkeley, California: University of California, Center for Planning, Development and Research, 1967.

Walker, E. T. "The Relation of the Housing of Students to Success in a University," Unpublished Ph.D. dissertation, University of Chicago, 1934.

Alfert, E. "Housing Selection, Need Satisfaction, and Drop-Out from College," PSYCHOLOGICAL REPORTS, 19 (August, 1966), 183–186.

Baker, S. R. "The Relationship Between College Residence and Environmental Press," JOURNAL OF COLLEGE STUDENT PERSONNEL, 7 (July, 1966), 222–224.

Baird, L. L. "The Effects of College Residence Groups on Students' Self Concepts, Goals, and Achievements," PERSONNEL AND GUIDANCE JOURNAL, 47 (June, 1969), 1015–1021.

Brown, R. D. "Manipulation of the Environmental Press in a College Residence Hall," PERSONNEL AND GUIDANCE JOURNAL, 46 (February, 1968), 555–560.

Centra, J. A. "Student Perception of Residence Hall Environments: Living vs. Conventional Units." Research Memorandum RM67-13. Princeton, New Jersey: Educational Testing Service, 1967.

Chesin, S. E. "Effects of Differential Housing on Attitudes and Values," COLLEGE STUDENT SURVEY, 3 (1969), 62–66.

Chickering, A. W. "College Residences and Student Development," EDUCATIONAL RECORD, 48 (Spring, 1967), 179–186.

Chickering, A. W. and Ellen Kuper. "Educational Outcomes for Commuters and Residents," EDUCATIONAL RECORD, 52 (Summer, 1971), 255–261.

Cowley, W. H. "The History of Student Residential Housing," SCHOOL AND SOCIETY, 40 (December 1, 1934), 705–712.

Crew, J. L. and J. B. Giblette. "Academic Performance of Freshman Males as a Function of Residence Hall Housing," JOURNAL OF COLLEGE STUDENT PERSONNEL, 6 (March, 1965), 167–170.

Decoster, D. A. "Housing Assignments for High Ability Students," JOURNAL OF COLLEGE STUDENT PERSONNEL, 7 (January, 1966), 19–22.

Dollar, R. J. "Student Characteristics and Choice of Housing," JOURNAL OF COLLEGE STUDENT PERSONNEL, 7 (May, 1966), 147–150.

Ellis, R. A. and R. L. Bowlin. "Parent-Student Attitudes Toward Off-Campus Housing," NATIONAL ASSOCIATION OF WOMEN DEANS AND COUNSELORS JOURNAL, 11 (May, 1970), 182–187.

Elton, C. F. and W. S. Bate. "The Effect of Housing Policy on Grade-Point Average," JOURNAL OF COLLEGE STUDENT PERSONNEL, 7 (March, 1966), 73–77.

Herbert, D. J. "The Relationship Between the Percentage of Freshmen on a Residence Hall Corridor and the Grade Point Averages of the Occupants," COLLEGE AND UNIVERSITY, 41 (Spring, 1966), 348–352.

*Jencks, Christopher and David Riesman. "Patterns of Residential Education: A Case Study of Harvard," in Nevitt Sanford, ed. THE AMERICAN COLLEGE. New York: Wiley, 1962, 731–773.

Kohake, Cletus K. "Cooperative Campus Living," CATHOLIC EDUCATION REVIEW, 61 (January, 1963), 37–51.

Kysar, J. E. "Mental Health in an Urban Commuter University," ARCHIVES OF GENERAL PSYCHIATRY, 11 (November, 1964), 472–483.

Lantz, H. R. and J. S. McCrary. "An Analysis of Parent-Student Relationships of University Student Commuters and Non-Commuters," JOURNAL OF COUNSELING PSYCHOLOGY, 2 (Spring, 1955), 43–46.

Lindahl, C. "Impact of Living Arrangements on Student Environmental Perceptions," JOURNAL OF COLLEGE STUDENT PERSONNEL, 8 (January, 1967), 10–15.

Lozoff, Marjorie. "Residential Groups and Individual Development," in Joseph Katz, et al. NO TIME FOR YOUTH. San Francisco: Jossey-Bass. 1968.

McQuade, W. "New Style of Campus Living," FORTUNE, 79 (January, 1969), 98–103.

Matson, R. E. A Study of the Influence of Fraternity, Residence Hall, and Off-Campus Living on Students of High, Average and College Potential," JOURNAL OF THE NATIONAL ASSOCIATION OF WOMEN DEANS AND COUNSELORS. 26 (April, 1963), 24–29.

Olson, L. A. "Dormitory Environment and Student Attitudes," UNIVERSITY COLLEGE QUARTERLY, 11 (1966), 20–29.

Olson, L. A. "Living-Learning Units as Seen by the Faculty," JOURNAL OF HIGHER EDUCATION, 35 (February, 1964), 83–86.

Olson, L. A. "Student Opinions on 'the Cold Dorm,'" UNIVERSITY COLLEGE QUARTERLY, 8 (1963), 25–30.

Olson, L. A. "Students Live and Learn in Residence Halls," COLLEGE AND UNIVERSITY BUSINESS, 38 (1965), 73–75.

Olson, L. A. "Students' Reactions to Living, Learning Residence Halls," JOURNAL OF COLLEGE STUDENTS PERSONNEL, 6 (October, 1964), 29–31.

Peterson, B. H. "The Scholarship of Students Housed in Various Living Quarters," SCHOOL AND SOCIETY, 57 (February 20, 1943), 221–224.

Prosok, R. E. "The Off-Campus Students," JOURNAL OF COLLEGE STUDENT PERSONNEL, 2 (December, 1960), 2–9.

Prosok, R. E. and W. B. Walsh. "College Students Residence and Academic Achievement," JOURNAL OF COLLEGE STUDENT PERSONNEL, 5 (March, 1964), 180–184.

Riker, Harold. "The Changing Role of Student Housing," in Gordon Klopf, ed. COLLEGE STUDENT PERSONNEL WORK IN THE YEARS AHEAD. Washington, D.C.: American Personnel and Guidance Association, 1966.

Rollin, B. "Co-ed Living," LOOK, 33 (September 3, 1969), 22–24+.

Schuchman, H. P. "The Double Life of the Commuter College Student," MENTAL HYGIENE, 50 (January, 1966), 104–110.

Segal, S. J. "Implications of Residential Setting for Development During College," JOURNAL OF COLLEGE STUDENT PERSONNEL, 8 (September, 1967), 308–310.

Sommers, R. "Student Reactions to Four Types of Residence Halls," JOURNAL OF COLLEGE STUDENT PERSONNEL, 9 (July, 1968), 232–237.

Stark, M. "Commuter and Residence Hall Students Compared," PERSONNEL AND GUIDANCE JOURNAL, 44 (October, 1965), 277–281.

Stickler, W. H. "Yes, Freshman Do Better in Dorms," COLLEGE AND UNIVERSITY BUSINESS, 24 (1958), 39–40.

Thoday, D. R. "Halls of Residence," UNIVERSITIES QUARTERLY, 12 (November, 1957), 45–56.

Thorsen, K. "Co-ed Dorms, an Intimate Revolution in Campus Life: Oberlin College, Ohio," LIFE, 69 (November 20, 1970), 32–41.

Van Alstine, F., H. R. Douglass and P. Johnson. "The Relation Between the Housing of Students and Their Scholarship," SCHOOL AND SOCIETY, 56 (October 24, 1942), 388–392.

Van Der Ryn, S. and M. Silverstein. "Berkeley, How Do Students Really Live," ARCHITECTURAL FORUM, 127 (July, 1967), 90–97.

Warr, P. W. "Attitudes and Behaviour in a Hall of Residence," UNIVERSITY QUARTERLY, 19 (December, 1964), 56–68.

Williamson, E. G. "Students' Residence: Shelter or Education?" PERSONNEL AND GUIDANCE JOURNAL, 36 (February, 1958), 392–398.

Williamson, E. G. and W. M. Wise. "Symposium: Residence Halls in Higher Education," PERSONNEL AND GUIDANCE JOURNAL, 36 (February, 1958), 392–401.

Wise, W. M. "Residence Halls and Higher Learning," PERSONNEL AND GUIDANCE JOURNAL, 36 (February, 1958), 398–401.

D.5. Sex on the Campus

Ald, Roy. SEX OFF CAMPUS. New York: Grosset and Dunlap, 1969.

Bardis, Panos Demetrios. "Dating Attitudes and Patterns Among Foreign Students at Purdue University." Unpublished Ph.D. dissertation, Purdue University, 1955.

Bell, R. R. PREMARITAL SEX IN A CHANGING SOCIETY. Englewood Cliffs, New Jersey: Prentice-Hall, 1966.

Cavan, Ruth S. AMERICAN MARRIAGE: A WAY OF LIFE. New York: Thomas Y. Crowell, 1959.

*Committee on the College Student, Group for the Advancement of Psychiatry. SEX AND THE COLLEGE STUDENT. New York: Atheneum, 1966.

Greene, Gael. SEX AND THE COLLEGE GIRL. New York: Dell, 1964.

Hettlinger, Richard F. LIVING WITH SEX. New York: Seabury Press, 1966.

Keller, Dolores Elaine. "Personality Aspects Related to Misinformation About Sex: the Relationship Between Misinformation About Sex Manifested in a Group of College Students and Certain Social and Physical Aspects of Personality." Unpublished Ph.D. dissertation, New York University, 1956.

Kirkendall, Lester A. and Robert N. Whitehurst, eds. THE NEW SEXUAL REVOLUTION. New York: D. W. Brown, 1971.

Kirkendall, Lester A. PREMARITAL INTERCOURSE AND INTERPERSONAL RELATIONSHIPS: A RESEARCH STUDY OF INTERPERSONAL RELATIONSHIPS BASED ON CASE HISTORIES OF 668 PREMARITAL INTERCOURSE EXPERIENCES REPORTED BY 200 COLLEGE LEVEL MALES. New York: Julian Press, 1961.

Kronhausen, Phyllis and Eberhard Kronhausen. SEX HISTORIES OF AMERICAN COLLEGE MEN. New York: Ballantine, 1960

Packard, V. THE SEXUAL WILDERNESS: THE CONTEMPORARY UPHEAVAL IN MALE-FEMALE RELATIONSHIPS. New York: McKay, 1968.

Reiss, Ira R. PREMARITAL SEXUAL STANDARDS IN AMERICA. New York: Free Press, 1960.

Southard, Helen F. SEX BEFORE 20. New York: E. P. Dutton, 1967.

Barron, J. L. "Too Much Sex on Campus," LADIES HOME JOURNAL, 81 (January, 1964), 48+.

Bell, R. R. and J. B. Chaskes. "Premarital Sexual Experience Among Coeds, 1958 and 1968," JOURNAL OF MARRIAGE AND THE FAMILY, 32 (February, 1970), 81-84.

Blaine, Graham B., jr. "Sex and the Adolescent," NEW YORK STATE JOURNAL OF MEDICINE, 67 (July 15, 1967), 1967-1975.

Blood, R. O., jr. "Uniformities and Diversities in Campus Dating Preferences," MARRIAGE AND FAMILY LIVING, 18 (February, 1956), 37-45.

Blood, R. O., jr. and S. O. Nicholson. "Attitudes of American Men and Women Students Toward International Dating," MARRIAGE AND FAMILY LIVING, 24 (February, 1962), 35-41.

Blood, R. O., jr. and S. O. Nicholson. "International Dating Experiences of American Women," MARRIAGE AND FAMILY LIVING, 24 (May, 1962), 129-136.

Bowman, Henry A. "Sex and the College Student." PROCEEDINGS OF THE 47th ANNUAL CONFERENCE OF THE ASSOCIATION OF COLLEGE UNIONS-INTERNATIONAL, HOUSTON, TEXAS, MARCH, 1970, 2, 19-26.

Cole, C. W. "American Youth Goes Monogamous," HARPER, 214 (March, 1957), 29-33.

Coles, Robert. "Sex and Students," in A. Klein, ed. NATURAL ENEMIES? YOUTH AND THE CLASH OF GENERATIONS. New York: J. B. Lippincott, 1969, 406-410.

Conner, R. and E. F. Hall, "Dating Behavior of College Freshmen and Sophomores," JOURNAL OF HOME ECONOMICS, 44 (April, 1952), 278–281.

DeCoster, D. A. "New Morality," JOURNAL OF COLLEGE STUDENT PERSONNEL, 11 (July, 1970), 243–247.

Decter, Midge. "Sex, My Daughter, and Me," in A. Klein, ed. NATURAL ENEMIES? YOUTH AND THE CLASH OF GENERATIONS. New York: Lippincott, 1969, 310–321.

Delora, Jack. "Social System of Dating on a College Campus," JOURNAL OF MARRIAGE AND THE FAMILY, 25 (February, 1963), 81–84.

Dreyfus, Edward A. "The Search for Intimacy," ADOLESCENCE, 2 (Spring, 1967), 25–40.

Ehrmann, Winston. "Changing Sexual Mores," in Eli Ginzberg, ed. VALUES AND IDEALS OF AMERICAN YOUTH. New York: Columbia University, 1961, 53–70.

Ehrmann, Winston. "Dating Behavior of College Students," in Theodore Newcomb, ed. THE ADOLESCENT. New York: Dryden Press, 1953, 502–511.

Ehrmann, Winston. "Variety and Meaning of Premarital Heterosexual Experiences for the College Student," NATIONAL ASSOCIATION OF WOMEN DEANS AND COUNSELORS JOURNAL, 26 (January, 1963), 22–28.

Eldridge, D. A. "More on Campus Mores," SATURDAY REVIEW, 47 (June 20, 1964), 57–59+.

Elton, C. F. and H. A. Rose. "Traditional Sex Attitudes and Discrepant Ability Measures in College Women," JOURNAL OF COUNSELING PSYCHOLOGY, 14 (November, 1967), 538–543.

Fell, J. P. "Psychosocial Analysis of Sex-Policing on Campus," SCHOOL AND SOCIETY, 98 (October, 1970), 351–354.

Finger, F. W. "Sex Beliefs and Practices Among Male College Students," JOURNAL OF ABNORMAL AND SOCIAL PSYCHOLOGY, 42 (1947), 57–67.

Freedman, Mervin. "The Sexual Behavior of American College Women," MERRILL-PALMER QUARTERLY, 11 (January, 1965), 33–48.

Freeman, H. A. and R. S. Freeman. "Senior College Women: Their Sexual Standards and Activity, Part I: To Whom Does the College Woman Turn for Sex Counseling?" JOURNAL OF THE NATIONAL ASSOCIATION OF WOMEN DEANS AND COUNSELORS, 29 (January, 1966), 59–64.

Freeman, H. A. and R. S. Freeman. "Senior College Women: Their Sexual Standards and Activity, Part II: Dating: Petting-Coital Practices," JOURNAL OF THE NATIONAL ASSOCIATION OF WOMEN DEANS AND COUNSELORS, 29 (Spring, 1966), 136–143.

Glicksberg, C. I. "Morality of College Youth," JOURNAL OF HIGHER EDUCATION, 24 (June, 1953), 315–319.

Grant, A. "No Rings Attached: a Look at Premarital Marriage on Campus," MADEMOISELLE, 66 (April, 1968), 208–209+.

Grauss, Frank. "Why a Moral Revolution?" in Esther Lloyd-Jones and Herman Estrin, eds. THE AMERICAN STUDENT AND HIS COLLEGE. Boston: Houghton Mifflin, 1967, 204–208.

Grinder, R. E. and S. S. Schmitt, "Coeds and Contraceptive Information,"

JOURNAL OF MARRIAGE AND THE FAMILY, 28 (November, 1966), 471–479.

Grinker, Roy R., sr., Roy R. Grinker, jr. and J. Timberlake, " 'Mentally Healthy' Young Males (Homoclites): a Study," ARCHIVES OF GENERAL PSYCHIATRY, 6 (1962), 405–453.

Gross, Stanley J. "Student Sexual Expression," JOURNAL OF COLLEGE STUDENT PERSONNEL, 9 (January, 1968), 9–16.

Hacker, A. "Pill and Morality," NEW YORK TIMES MAGAZINE, (November 21, 1965), 32–33+.

Hamill, Robert. "What's Happening to Our Campus Morals?" in Esther Lloyd-Jones and Herman Estrin, eds. THE AMERICAN STUDENT AND HIS COLLEGE. Boston: Houghton Mifflin, 1967, 171–179.

*Hassenger, Robert. "A Campus Sexual Revolution?" in L. Vaccaro and J. Covert, eds. STUDENT FREEDOM IN AMERICAN HIGHER EDUCATION. New York: Teachers College Press, 1969, 125–146.

Hayman, H. S. "Sex and the American College Girls Today," JOURNAL OF SCHOOL HEALTH, 37 (February, 1967), 54–62.

Hechinger, G. and F. M. Hechinger. "College Morals Mirror Our Society," NEW YORK TIMES MAGAZINE, (April 14, 1963), 22+.

Herz, S. "Research Study on Behavioral Patterns in Sex and Drug Use on College Campus," ADOLESCENCE, 5 (Spring, 1970), 1–16.

Hettlinger, Richard. "Portrait of the Freshman as a Sexual Being," in Charles Havice, ed. CAMPUS VALUES. New York: Charles Scribner's Sons, 1968, 34–50.

Hewitt, L. E. "Student Perceptions of Traits Desired in Themselves as Dating and Marriage Partners," MARRIAGE AND FAMILY LIVING, 20 (November, 1958), 344–349.

Holverstott, Joanna. "Homosexuals in College," MODERATOR, 5 (March, 1966), 19–22.

Holverstott, Joanna. "Homosexuals on Campus," in Esther Lloyd-Jones and Herman Estrin, eds. THE AMERICAN STUDENT AND HIS COLLEGE. Boston: Houghton Mifflin, 1967, 213–220.

Jacob, P. E. "College Morals: Interview," COSMOPOLITAN, 143 (September, 1957), 52–55.

Johnson, L. B. "They Act as if We'd Invented Sin," McCALLS, 94 (June, 1967), 32+.

Johnson, N. "Sex and the College Girl," ATLANTIC, 204 (November, 1959), 56–60.

Kaats, G. R. "Dynamics of Sexual Behavior of College Students," JOURNAL OF MARRIAGE AND THE FAMILY, 32 (August, 1970), 390–399.

Kanin, Eugene J. "Reference Groups and Sex Conduct Norm Violations," SOCIOLOGICAL QUARTERLY, 8 (Autumn, 1967), 495–504.

Kanin, E. J. "Sexually Aggressive College Males," JOURNAL OF COLLEGE STUDENT PERSONNEL, 12 (March, 1971), 107–110.

Karlen, A. "Unmarried Marrieds on Campus," NEW YORK TIMES MAGAZINE, (January 26, 1969), 28–29+.

464

Keller, D. E. "Personality Aspects Related to Misinformation About Sex Among College Students: Questionnaire Analysis," SCIENCE EDUCATION, 43 (March, 1959), 163–168.

Kelley, J. A. "Varying Mores in School and College Cultures," JOURNAL OF EDUCATIONAL SOCIOLOGY, 31 (March, 1958), 244–252.

Kirkendall, L. A. "College Youth and Sexual Confusion," NATIONAL ASSOCIATION OF WOMEN DEANS AND COUNSELORS JOURNAL, 26 (January, 1963), 6–15.

Kirkendall, L. A. "The Tumult Over Morals and a Way Out," in Esther Lloyd-Jones and Herman Estrin, eds. THE AMERICAN STUDENT AND HIS COLLEGE, Boston: Houghton Mifflin, 1967, 180–185.

Kirkpatrick, C. and E. Kanin. "Male Sex Aggression on a University Campus," AMERICAN SOCIOLOGICAL REVIEW, 22 (February, 1957), 52-58.

Knox, D. H. jr. and M. S. Sprakowski. "Attitudes of College Students Toward Love," JOURNAL OF MARRIAGE AND THE FAMILY, 30 (November, 1968), 638–642.

Larson, R. F. and G. R. Leslie. "Prestige Influences in Serious Dating Relationships of University Students," SOCIAL FORCES, 47 (December, 1968), 195–202.

Lawrie, S. H. "Factors Involved in the Frequency of Dating," MARRIAGE AND FAMILY LIVING, 18 (February, 1956), 46–51.

Lear, M. W. "But Where Are the Chaperons?" NEW YORK TIMES MAGAZINE, (February 23, 1964), 22+.

Liebert, Robert. "The Gay Student Movement: a Psychopolitical View," CHANGE, 3 (October, 1971), 38–44.

McGinnis, R. "Campus Values in Mate Selections: A Repeat Study," SOCIAL FORCES, 36 (May, 1958), 368–373.

Malcolm, A. H. "Sex Goes to College," TODAY'S HEALTH, 49 (April, 1971), 26–29.

Manville, W. H. "The Wayward Co-ed and the Vulnerable Professor: New Love Team on Campus," COSMOPOLITAN, 164 (January, 1968), 44–47, 127–129.

Miller, H. and W. Wilson. "Relation of Sexual Behaviors, Values and Conflict to Avowed Happiness and Personal Adjustment," PSYCHOLOGICAL REPORTS, 23 (December, 1968), 1075–1086.

Mills, A. "Campus Romance: Steve Ambrose and Judy Dorlester of the University of Wisconsin," LADIES HOME JOURNAL, 74 (July, 1957), 109–112+.

"Morals Revolution on U.S. Campus," NEWSWEEK, 63 (April 7, 1964), 52–56+.

Noble, Charles C. "How Do Institutional Practices and the Institutional Environment Affect the Moral Standards of the Individual Student?" CURRENT ISSUES IN HIGHER EDUCATION, (1953), 212–217.

Offer, Daniel. "Sex and the Normal Adolescent," in Morton Levitt and Ben Rubenstein, eds. YOUTH AND SOCIAL CHANGE, Detroit, Michigan: Wayne State University Press, 1972, 333–341.

Packard, V. "Sex on Campus," McCALLS, 95 (August, 1968), 58–59+.

Peters, M. and W. Peters. "How College Students Feel About Love, Sex, and Marriage," GOOD HOUSEKEEPING, 170 (June, 1970), 84–85+.

Plante, Patricia R. "Morality and the Mod College Student," LIBERAL EDUCATION, 53 (December, 1967), 466–475.

Rama Rau, S. "Harvard's Girl Friend," HOLIDAY, 15 (April, 1954), 48–51+.

Reiss, I. L. "Social Class and Campus Dating," SOCIAL PROBLEMS, 13 (Fall, 1965), 193–204.

Richardson, J. "Ten-Dollar Understanding. Brothel Behavior of the College Boy," ESQUIRE, 62 (September, 1964), 101+.

Riesman, David. "Permissiveness and Sex Roles," MARRIAGE AND FAMILY LIVING, 21 (August, 1959), 211–217.

Rossi, A. S. "The Beginning of Ideology: Alternative Models of Sex Equality," HUMANIST, (September–October, 1969).

Rule, J. T. "Must Colleges Police Sex?" ATLANTIC, 213 (April, 1964), 55–58.

Puppel, Howard J., jr. "Religiosity and Premarital Sexual Permissiveness: A Methodological Note," SOCIOLOGICAL ANALYSIS, 30 (Fall, 1969), 176–188.

Salisbury, Winfield and Frances. "Youth and the Search for Intimacy," in L. A. Kirkendall and R. N. Whitehurst, eds. THE NEW SEXUAL REVOLUTION. New York: Donald-Brown, 1971, 169–182.

Shaffer, Helen. "Sex on the Campus," EDITORIAL RESEARCH REPORTS, 2 (December 30, 1963), 945–962.

Siddall, L. B. "Pregnant College Girl," NATIONAL ASSOCIATION OF WOMEN DEANS AND COUNSELORS JOURNAL, 34 (Winter, 1971), 84–88.

Simenson, W. and G. Geis. "Courtship Patterns of Norwegian and American University Students," MARRIAGE AND FAMILY LIVING, 18 (November, 1956), 334–338.

Simon, William and John Gagnon. "Psychosexual Development," in Michael Wertheimer, ed. CONFRONTATION: PSYCHOLOGY AND THE PROBLEMS OF TODAY. Glenview, Illinois: Scott Foresman, 1970, 43–51.

Smith, E. A. "Dating and Courtship at Pioneer College," SOCIOLOGY AND SOCIAL RESEARCH, 40 (November, 1955), 92–98.

Smith, E. and J. H. Greenbergmonane. "Courtship Values in a Youth Sample," AMERICAN SOCIOLOGICAL REVIEW, 18 (December, 1953). 635–640.

Smith, H. E. "Dating and Courtship Patterns, Some Explorations," JOURNAL OF EDUCATIONAL SOCIOLOGY, 35 (October, 1961), 49–58.

Smith, P. B. and K. Kommel. "Student-Parent Reactions to Off-Campus Cohabitation," JOURNAL OF COLLEGE STUDENT PERSONNEL, 11 (May, 1970), 188–193.

Spaulding, C. B. "Romantic Love Complex in American Culture," SOCIOLOGY AND SOCIAL RESEARCH, 55 (October, 1970), 82–100.

Stein, R. "Sex on the Campus," CORONET, 28 (May, 1950), 98–102.

Steinberg, J. "Next: A Sleep-in? Birth Control in Colleges," MADEMOISELLE, 62 (April, 1966), 10+.

Steinem, Gloria. "The Moral Disarmament of Betty Co-Ed," ESQUIRE, 58 (September, 1962), 97+.

Talmey, A., ed. "Sex, Virginity, Money: Interview with B. Bettelheim," VOGUE, 156 (August 1, 1970), 94–95+.

Thornburg, H. D. "Age and First Sources of Sex Information as Reported by 88 College Women," JOURNAL OF SCHOOL HEALTH, 40 (March, 1970), 156–158.

Van Horne, Harriet. "The Sexual Revolution—In Living Color," in A. Klein, ed. NATURAL ENEMIES? YOUTH AND THE CLASH OF GENERATIONS. New York: Lippincott, 1969, 410–414.

Vreeland, Rebecca S. "Is It True What They Say About Harvard Boys?" PSYCHOLOGY TODAY, 5 (January, 1972), 65–68.

Vreeland, Rebecca S. "Patterns of Heterosexual Relations Among Harvard Men," JOURNAL OF THE AMERICAN COLLEGE HEALTH ASSOCIATION, 16 (April, 1968), 335–338.

Vreeland, Rebecca S. "Sex at Harvard," SEXUAL BEHAVIOR, 2 (February, 1972), 4–10.

Waller, W. "The Rating and Dating Complex," AMERICAN SOCIOLOGICAL REVIEW, 2 (October, 1937), 727–734.

Walsh, J. L. "Sex on Campus: a New Ethic but Not Sex for Kicks," COMMONWEAL, 83 (February 24, 1967), 590–591+.

Walters, Paul. "Promiscuity in Adolescence," AMERICAN JOURNAL OF ORTHOPSYCHIATRY, 35 (July, 1965), 670–675.

"What Parents Think About College Morals," READER'S DIGEST, 86 (May, 1965), 141–144.

Winch, R. F. "Courtship in College Women," AMERICAN JOURNAL OF SOCIOLOGY, 55 (November, 1949), 269–278.

Wood, Frederic C., jr. "New Sexual Attitudes," in G. K. Smith, AGONY AND PROMISE: CURRENT ISSUES IN HIGHER EDUCATION 1969. San Francisco: Jossey-Bass, 1969, 105–112.

D.6. Married Students

Eshleman, J. Ross and Chester L. Hunt. SOCIAL CLASS FACTORS IN THE COLLEGE ADJUSTMENT OF MARRIED STUDENTS. Kalamazoo, Michigan: Western Michigan University, 1965.

Aller, F. D. "Some Factors in Marital Adjustment and Academic Achievement of Married Students," PERSONNEL AND GUIDANCE JOURNAL, 41 (March, 1963), 609–616.

Beaty, J. K. "We Sweat Out Our Campus Marriage," SATURDAY EVENING POST, 228 (April 14, 1956), 58–59+.

Blyth, M. "Perils of a Ph.T.," READER'S DIGEST, 87 (October, 1965), 143–146.

Bossard, J. H. S. and E. S. Boll. "Campus Marriages, for Better or For Worse?" NEW YORK TIMES MAGAZINE, (April 5, 1959), 59+.

Bressler, B. and W. Kephart. "Marriage and Family Patterns of an Academic Group," MARRIAGE AND FAMILY LIVING, 16 (May, 1954), 121–127.

Carbine, P. "More Married Students," LOOK, 23 (October 27, 1959), 125–128.

Chambliss, R. "Married Students at a State University," JOURNAL OF EDUCATIONAL SOCIOLOGY, 34 (May, 1961), 409–416.

Chilman, C. S. and D. L. Meyer. "Single and Married Undergraduates' Measured Personality Needs and Self-Rated Happiness," JOURNAL OF MARRIAGE AND THE FAMILY, 28 (February, 1966), 67–76.

Christensen, H. T. and R. E. Philbrick. "Family Size as a Factor in the Marital Adjustments of College Couples," AMERICAN SOCIOLOGICAL REVIEW, 17 (June, 1952), 306–312.

Dressel, F. B. "Logic, Research and the Married College Student," PERSONNEL AND GUIDANCE JOURNAL, 43 (May, 1965), 920–924.

Grafton, S. "Young Marriages: What Happens When Parents Pay the Bills?" McCALLS, 94 (April, 1967), 67+.

Havemann, E. "To Love, Honor, Obey and Study," LIFE, 38 (May 23, 1955), 152–156+.

Hill, E. "How Successful Are College Marriages?" REDBOOK, 123 (May, 1964), 58–59+.

Jenson, V. H. and M. H. Clark. "Married and Unmarried College Students: Achievement, Ability and Personality," PERSONNEL AND GUIDANCE JOURNAL, 37 (October, 1958), 125–126.

Marshall, W. H. and M. P. King. "Undergraduate Student Marriage: a Compilation of Research Findings," JOURNAL OF MARRIAGE AND THE FAMILY, 28 (No. 3, 1966), 350–359.

" 'Maturity is the Key' to Successful College Marriage: Interview with Dr. David Henry," U.S. NEWS AND WORLD REPORT, (June 6, 1960), 86–89.

Neubeck, Gerhard. "The Decision to Marry While in College," ACTA SOCIOLOGICA, 8 (1964), 56–67.

"A New Look at Early Marriages: Interview with Dr. Margaret Mead," U.S. NEWS AND WORLD REPORT, (June 6, 1960), 80–86.

Rogers, E. M. "Effect of Campus Marriages on Participation in College Life," COLLEGE AND UNIVERSITY, 33 (Winter, 1958), 193–199.

Pope, Elizabeth. "Why Do They Marry?" GOOD HOUSEKEEPING, (May, 1959), 159, 142–144+.

Sanber, S. R. "Money and Marriage in College," COLLEGE AND UNIVERSITY, 46 (Spring, 1971), 245–250.

Schab, Fred. "The Married College Student: A Comparison of Male Undergraduate and Graduate Students' Attitudes and Values," JOURNAL OF COLLEGE STUDENT PERSONNEL, 7 (May, 1966), 154–158.

Sibley, E. "Higher Education and Earlier Parenthood: A Changing Cycle of Family Life," ANTIOCH REVIEW, 17 (Spring, 1957), 45–59.

468

D.7. The Study of Student Attitudes

Cross Reference. For student attitudes dealing with moral or political questions see the first part of this bibliography.

D.7.a. Student Attitudes Toward Education and Educational Goals

Cross Reference. Attitudes toward initial college attendance are listed in sections under "Who are the students?"

Almos, Kermit O. "A Study of Interrelationships Between Measured Satisfaction with College and Certain Academic and Personality Variables." Unpublished Ph.D. dissertation, University of Minnesota, 1957.

Baird, L. L. THE EDUCATIONAL GOALS OF COLLEGE-BOUND STUDENTS, (ACT Research Reports, No. 19). Iowa City, Iowa: ACT Program, 1967.

Berdie, Ralph Freimuth, Bonifacio Pilapil and In Jae Im. GRADUATING SENIORS' SATISFACTION WITH THE UNIVERSITY. Minneapolis, Minnesota: Bureau of Institutional Research, University of Minnesota, 1968.

Bradley, W. N. "An Analysis of Selected Cognitive and Non-Cognitive Variables Relating to a Student's Persistence in a Major Area of Study at Michigan State University." Unpublished Ph.D. dissertation, Michigan State University, 1962.

Henderson, Robert William. "The Measurement of Academic Interest." Unpublished Ph.D. dissertation, University of Kentucky, 1949.

Koval, John Patrick. "The Drifters and the Directed: An Analysis of Educational Involvement." Unpublished Ph.D. dissertation, University of Oregon, 1967.

Longino, Charles Freeman, jr. "Students' Orientations Toward College Life: Some Sources and Consequences." Unpublished Ph.D. dissertation, University of North Carolina, 1968.

*Mock, K. THE POTENTIAL ACTIVIST AND HIS PERCEPTION OF THE UNIVERSITY. Berkeley, California: Center for the Study of Higher Education, 1968.

Weiss, R. F. "Student and Faculty Perceptions of Institutional Press at St. Louis University." Unpublished Ph.D. dissertation, University of Minnesota, 1964.

*Wise, M. Max. THEY COME FOR THE BEST OF REASONS: COLLEGE STUDENTS TODAY. Washington, D.C.: American Council on Education, 1958.

Zander, Donald Richard. "The Influence of an Orientation Program on Attitudes Toward Higher Education." Unpublished Ph.D. dissertation, University of Minnesota, 1959.

Zeigler, Martin L. "Validation of Scholastic Orientation scales for Freshmen Males in Engineering and Architecture and Liberal Arts." Unpublished Ph.D. dissertation, Pennsylvania State University, 1954.

Allman, R. W. "Evaluation of the Goals of Higher Education by 294 College Seniors of Alabama," JOURNAL OF NEGRO EDUCATION, 29 (Spring, 1960), 198–203.

Baird, L. L. "Degree Goals of College Applicants," COLLEGE AND UNIVERSITY, 43, (Spring, 1968), 308–327.

Bendig, A. W. and P. T. Hountras. "Anxiety, Authoritarianism, and Student Attitude Toward Departmental Control of College Instruction." JOURNAL OF EDUCATIONAL PSYCHOLOGY, 50 (February, 1959), 1–7.

Berdie, R. F. "College Expectations, Experiences, and Perceptions," JOURNAL OF COLLEGE STUDENT PERSONNEL, 7 (November, 1966), 336–344.

Cole, J. W., K. Wilson and D. Tiedeman. "Dispersion Analysis and the Search for Educational Goals in College: a Study in Duplicate," JOURNAL OF EDUCATIONAL PSYCHOLOGY, 55 (June, 1964), 121–131.

Constantinople, Anne. "Perceived Instrumentality of the College as a Measure of Attitudes Toward College," JOURNAL OF PERSONALITY AND SOCIAL PSYCHOLOGY, 5 (February, 1967), 196–201.

Davie, J. S. "Satisfaction and the College Experience," in B. M. Wedge, ed. PSYCHOSOCIAL PROBLEMS OF COLLEGE MEN. New Haven, Connecticut: Yale University Press, 1958, 15–44.

Dole, A. A. "Reported Determinants of Educational Choice," PERSONNEL AND GUIDANCE JOURNAL, 42 (February, 1964), 564–571.

Egner, R. E. and A. J. Obelsky. "Significance of Stereotyped Conditioning for Education," JOURNAL OF HIGHER EDUCATION, 28 (June, 1957), 329–336.

Evans, T. D. "Parent and Student Perceptions of a Commuter Campus," NATIONAL ASSOCIATION OF STUDENT PERSONNEL ADMINISTRATORS JOURNAL, 7 (Winter, 1971), 164–169.

Fey, Nancy. "The Educational Process Through a Student's Eyes," in Esther Lloyd-Jones and Herman Estrin, eds. THE AMERICAN STUDENT AND HIS COLLEGE. Boston: Houghton Mifflin, 1967, 367–374.

Fraser, T. P. "Study of the Opinion of Students on College General Education Science," SCIENCE EDUCATION, 39 (April, 1955), 213–219.

French, J. W. "Aptitude and Interest Score Patterns Related to Satisfaction with College Major Field," EDUCATIONAL AND PSYCHOLOGICAL MEASUREMENT, 21 (Summer, 1961), 287–294.

Gamson, Z. F. "Utilitarian and Normative Orientations Toward Education," SOCIOLOGY OF EDUCATION, 39 (Winter, 1966), 46–73.

Herr, E. L. "Student Needs, College Expectations, and Reality Perceptions," EDUCATIONAL RESEARCH, 65 (October, 1971), 51–56.

Jaffe, A. J. and Walter Adams. "College Education for U.S. Youth: the Attitudes of Parents and Children," AMERICAN JOURNAL OF ECONOMICS AND SOCIOLOGY, 23 (July, 1964), 269–283.

Jervis. F. M. and R. G. Congdom. "Student and Faculty Perceptions of Educational Values," AMERICAN PSYCHOLOGIST, 13 (August, 1958), 464–466.

Kidd, J. W., et al. "Student Attitudes Toward General Education," JOURNAL OF HIGHER EDUCATION, 25 (April, 1954), 209–213+.

470

Kirk, B. A. and R. W. Cummings. "Changing Patterns of Interest Within a University Culture," MEASUREMENT AND EVALUATION IN GUIDANCE, 3 (Winter, 1971), 238–242.

LeMay, Morris L., *et al.* "Student Attitudes Toward University Rules and Regulations," COLLEGE STUDENT SURVEY, 2 (Fall, 1968).

McPeck, B. L. "The University as Perceived by Its Subcultures: an Experimental Study," NATIONAL ASSOCIATION OF WOMEN DEANS AND COUNSELORS JOURNAL, 30 (Spring, 1967), 129–132.

Marks, E. "Student Perceptions of College Persistence, and Their Intellective, Personality and Performance Correlates," JOURNAL OF EDUCATIONAL PSYCHOLOGY, 58 (August, 1967), 210–221.

Martorana, S. V. and S. Gittler. "Student Attitudes Toward the Objectives of General Education," JUNIOR COLLEGE JOURNAL, 21 (December, 1950), 226–235.

Nosow, S. "Educational Value: Orientations of College Students," JOURNAL OF EDUCATIONAL RESEARCH, 52 (December, 1958), 123–128.

Pervin, L. A. "Reality and Nonreality in Student Expectations of College," JOURNAL OF PSYCHOLOGY, 64 (September, 1966), 41–48.

Preston, R. C. "Education Graduates View Education and Academic Courses," SCHOOL AND SOCIETY, 92 (Summer, 1964), 233–237.

Rosenberg, M. "Psychological Depression and Educational Attitudes," STUDENT MEDICINE, 5 (1956), 5–20.

Standing, G. R. and C. A. Parker. "The College Characteristics Index as a Measure of Entering Students Preconceptions of College Life," JOURNAL OF COLLEGE STUDENT PERSONNEL, 6 (October, 1964), 2–6.

Stewart, L. H. "Interests of Junior College Students in Occupationally Oriented Curricula: Interest Assessment Scale," VOCATIONAL GUIDANCE QUARTERLY, 19 (March, 1971), 165–170.

Wenkert, R. and H. C. Selvin. "School Spirit in the Context of a Liberal Education," SOCIAL PROBLEMS, 10 (Fall, 1962), 156–168.

Winkie, Joy. "Responsibility and Cooperative Education," in Charles Havice, ed. CAMPUS VALUES, New York: Scribner's, 1968, 143–156.

D.7.b. Student Attitudes Toward Job Orientation

*Astin, Alexander W. and Robert Panos. THE EDUCATIONAL AND VOCATIONAL DEVELOPMENT OF COLLEGE STUDENTS, Washington, D.C.: American Council of Education, 1969.

Austin, C. G. "Self Identity and Role-Identity in the Selection of Teaching as a Career," Unpublished Ph.D. dissertation, University of Michigan, 1965.

Cross, Theodore R. "An Exploratory Investigation of Personality and Background Factors Characterizing Entering College Men Who Possess a Low Intensity of Vocational Interests." Unpublished Ph.D. dissertation, University of Minnesota, 1955.

*Davis, James A. UNDERGRADUATE CAREER DECISIONS. Chicago: Aldine, 1965.

Dixon, Marlene Davidson. "Professionals, Experts and Managers: Student Career Orientations in Engineering." Unpublished Ph.D. dissertation, University of California, Los Angeles, 1967.

Doyle, Robert Edward. "A Study of Career Patterns of Alumni of a Metropolitan Liberal Arts College." Unpublished Ph.D. dissertation, New York University, 1963.

Dunphy, Philip W., ed. CAREER DEVELOPMENT FOR THE COLLEGE STUDENT. Cranston, Rhode Island: Carroll Press, 1969.

Feather, Don B. "The Relation of Personality Maladjustments of 503 University of Michigan Students to Their Occupational Interests." Unpublished Ph.D. dissertation, University of Michigan, 1949.

Gaither, James Wallace. "A Factorial Analysis of the Occupational Interests of Two Hundred Vocationally Inexperienced Adult Male Students." Unpublished Ed.D. thesis, Temple University, 1958.

Greeley, A. M. "The Influence of Religion on the Career Plans and Occupational Values of June, 1961, College Graduates." Unpublished Ph.D. dissertation, University of Chicago, 1962.

Hearn, Hershel LeRoy. "The Student Actress: A Case Study in the Process of Professionalization." Unpublished Ph.D. dissertation, University of Missouri, 1966.

Holland, J. L. and S. W. Lutz. PREDICTING A STUDENT'S VOCATIONAL CHOICE, (ACT Research Reports, No. 18). Iowa City, Iowa: American College Testing Program, 1967.

Holland, J. L. and D. Whitney. CHANGES IN THE VOCATIONAL PLANS OF COLLEGE STUDENTS: ORDERLY OR RANDOM? ACT Research Reports, No. 26. Iowa City, Iowa: American College Testing Program, 1968.

HOW COLLEGE STUDENTS SEE BUSINESS AS A CAREER AND HOW THEY VIEW THE ROLE OF BUSINESS AND GOVERNMENT. New York: Society for the Advancement of Management, March, 1968.

Jaeger, Eloise. "An Investigation of a Projective Test in Determining Attitudes of Prospective Teachers of Physical Education." Unpublished Ph.D. dissertation, University of Iowa, 1952.

Kanter, S. A. "The Social Psychology of Premature Occupational Choice: an Investigation of Student Careers in an Undergraduate Engineering School." Unpublished Ph.D. dissertation, University of Michigan, 1967.

Kinane, M. ATTITUDES OF UNDERGRADUATES TOWARD COLLEGE TEACHING AS A CAREER. Winchester, Massachusetts: New England Board of Higher Education, 1961.

Knebel, Lewis McBurney. "College Placement and College Relations: A Study of the Process of Occupational Development." Unpublished Ph.D. dissertation, University of Maryland, 1964.

Krulee, G., R. O'Keefe, and M. Goldberg. INFLUENCE OF IDENTITY PROCESSES ON STUDENT BEHAVIOR AND OCCUPATIONAL CHOICE. Evanston, Illinois: Northwestern University, 1966.

Lane, Paul Anthony. "The Relationship Among Some Measures of Preferred Interest, Vocational Objectives and Academic Performance." Unpublished Ph.D. dissertation, University of Connecticut, 1959.

472

Martin, Ann Mildred. "The Development and Cross-Validation of an Academic Interest Scale for the Strong Vocational Interest Blank." Unpublished Ph.D. dissertation, University of Pittsburgh, 1962.

Miller, Jerry Lee Lamasney. "Occupational Choice. The Construction and Testing of a Paradigm of Occupational Choice for the College Graduate." Unpublished Ph.D. dissertation, Florida State University, 1959.

Mitchell, Elmer D. THE RELATIONSHIP BETWEEN STUDENT INTERESTS AND VOCATIONAL CHOICES: A 25 YEAR STUDY OF STUDENTS ENTERING THE UNIVERSITY OF MICHIGAN. Ann Arbor, Michigan: University of Michigan, 1954.

Nachman, Barbara. "Childhood Experiences and Vocational Choice: a Study of Lawyers, Dentists, and Social Workers." Unpublished Ph.D. dissertation, University of Michigan, 1957.

Odiorne, George S. and Arthur S. Hann. EFFECTIVE COLLEGE RECRUITING. Ann Arbor, Michigan: University of Michigan, Bureau of Industrial Relations, 1961.

O'Dowd, D. D. and D. C. Beardslee. COLLEGE STUDENT IMAGES OF A SELECTED GROUP OF PROFESSIONS AND OCCUPATIONS. (Final Report, Cooperative Research Project No. 562. U.S. Office of Education). Middletown. Connecticut: Wesleyan University, 1960.

Powell, F. V. "A Comparison Between the Vocational Interest Patterns of Students in Five Colleges of a State University." Unpublished Ph.D. dissertation, University of Wisconsin, 1955.

Rosenberg, Morris. OCCUPATIONS AND VALUES. Glencoe, Illinois: Free Press, 1957.

Sharp, Laure (Metzger). EDUCATION AND EMPLOYMENT: THE EARLY YEARS OF COLLEGE GRADUATES. Baltimore, Maryland: Johns Hopkins Press, 1970.

Sparkling, E. J. DO COLLEGE STUDENTS CHOOSE VOCATIONS WISELY? TEACHERS COLLEGE CONTRIBUTIONS TO EDUCATION, No. 561. New York: Bureau of Publications, Teachers College, Columbia University, 1933.

Stephens, Everett W. CAREER COUNSELING AND PLACEMENT IN HIGHER EDUCATION: A STUDENT PERSONNEL FUNCTION. Bethlehem, Pennsylvania: College Placement Council, 1970.

Stephenson, Richard Ryle. "A Comparison of the Strong VIB Profiles of High Ability Male S.L.A. Freshmen Who Change Expressed Vocational Choice with those Who do not Change Such Expressions." Unpublished Ph.D. dissertation, University of Minnesota, 1959.

Taves, M. J., R. Corwin and J. Hass. ROLE CONCEPTION AND VOCATIONAL SUCCESS AND SATISFACTION: A STUDY OF STUDENT AND PROFESSIONAL NURSES. Bureau of Business Research Monograph No. 112. Columbus, Ohio: Bureau of Business Research, College of Commerce and Administration, Ohio State University, 1963.

Thistlethwaite, D. L. EFFECTS OF COLLEGE UPON STUDENT ASPIRATIONS. (U.S. Department of Health, Education and Welfare Cooperative Research Project No. D-098). Nashville, Tennessee: Vanderbilt University, 1965.

Tripp, L. Reed and H. Allan Hunt. ATTITUDES OF COLLEGE STUDENTS TOWARD CAREERS IN BUSINESS. Bethlehem, Pennsylvania: College Placement Council, 1967.

West, Patricia Salter. "The College Graduate in American Society. A Survey Analysis." Unpublished Ph.D. dissertation, Columbia University, 1951.

Anderson, W. A. "Occupational Attitudes of College Men," JOURNAL OF SOCIAL PSYCHOLOGY, 5 (1934), 435–465.

Astin, A. W. "Effects of Different College Environments on the Vocational Choices of High Aptitude Students," JOURNAL OF COUNSELING PSYCHOLOGY, 12 (Spring, 1965), 28–34.

Beardslee, D. C. and D. D. O'Dowd. "College-Student Image of the Scientist," SCIENCE, 133 (March 31, 1961), 997–1001.

Beardslee, D. C. and D. D. O'Dowd. "Student and the Occupational World," in Nevitt Sanford, ed. THE AMERICAN COLLEGE. New York: Wiley, 1964, 597–626.

Bennett, W. S., jr. and N. P. Gist. "Class and Family Influences on Student Aspirations," SOCIAL FORCES, 43 (December, 1964), 167–173.

Bidwell, C. E., et al. "Undergraduate Careers: Alternatives and Determinants," SCHOOL REVIEW, 71 (Autumn, 1963), 299–316.

Blum, L. P. "A Comparative Study of Students Preparing for Five Selected Professions Including Teaching," JOURNAL OF EXPERIMENTAL EDUCATION, 16 (September, 1947), 31–65

Blum, S. H. "Desire for Security: an Element in the Vocational Choice of College Men," JOURNAL OF EDUCATIONAL PSYCHOLOGY, 52 (December, 1961), 317–321.

Brown, W. H. "Vocational Aspirations of Freshmen," COLLEGE AND UNIVERSITY, 27 (January, 1952), 206–218.

Campbell, D. P. "The Vocational Interests of Dartmouth College Freshmen: 1947–1967," PERSONNEL AND GUIDANCE JOURNAL, 47 (February, 1969) 521–530.

"College Students View Business and Vice Versa," CONFERENCE BOARD RECORD, 5 (May, 1968), 38–50.

Currie, Ian D., et al. "Images of the Professor and Interest in the Academic Profession," in R. Pavalko, ed. SOCIOLOGY OF EDUCATION. Itaska, Illinois: Peacock, 1968, 532–554.

Davis, James. "The Campus as a Frog Pond: An Application of the Theory of Relative Deprivation to Career Decisions of College Men," AMERICAN JOURNAL OF SOCIOLOGY, 72 (July, 1966), 17–31.

Dilley, N. E. "Personal Values Held by College Students Who Enter a Teacher Education Program," JOURNAL OF TEACHER EDUCATION, 8 (September, 1957), 289–294.

"Disenchanted Campus: Attitudes Towards Business; L. Harris Poll," NEWSWEEK, 67 (May 2, 1966), 85–86+.

Doyle, R. E. "Career Patterns of Male College Graduates," PERSONNEL

474

AND GUIDANCE JOURNAL, 44 (December, 1965), 410–415.

Ellis, R. A. and W. C. Lane. "Social Mobility and Career Orientation," SOCIOLOGY AND SOCIAL RESEARCH, 50 (April, 1966), 280–296.

Filley, Alan C. "Today's College Graduates and Small Business," MANAGEMENT OF PERSONNEL QUARTERLY, 8 (Winter, 1969), 8–12.

Frederickson, George H. "Understanding Attitudes Toward Public Employment," PUBLIC ADMINISTRATION REVIEW, 27 (December, 1967), 411–420.

Gibson, Frank K. and George A. James. "Student Attitudes Toward Government Employees and Employment," PUBLIC ADMINISTRATION REVIEW, 27 (December, 1967), 429–435.

Goodwin, L. "Academic World and the Business World: a Comparison of Occupational Goals," SOCIOLOGY OF EDUCATION, 42 (Spring, 1969), 170–187.

Habbe, S. "Business and the College Student," CONFERENCE BOARD RECORD, 4 (September, 1967), 18–26.

Haller, A. and C. Butterworth. "Peer Influences on Levels of Occupational and Educational Aspiration," SOCIAL FORCES, 38 (May, 1960), 289–295.

Heath, Clark W., J. P. Monks, and W. H. Woods. "The Nature of Career Selection in a Group of Harvard Undergraduates," HARVARD EDUCATION REVIEW, 17 (May, 1947), 190–197.

Hewer, V. H. "Vocational Interests of College Freshmen and Their Social Origins," JOURNAL OF APPLIED PSYCHOLOGY, 49 (December, 1965), 407–411.

Hilgert, R. L. and L. A. Eason. "How Students Weigh Recruiters," JOURNAL OF COLLEGE PLACEMENT, 28 (February, 1968), 99–100+.

Hind, R. R. and T. E. Wirth. "Effect of University Experience on Occupational Choice Among Undergraduates," SOCIOLOGY OF EDUCATION, 42 (Winter, 1969), 50–70.

Holland, J. L. "Explorations of a Theory of Vocational Choice and Achievement: A Longitudinal Study Using a Sample of Typical College Students," JOURNAL OF APPLIED PSYCHOLOGY MONOGRAPH SUPPLEMENT, 52, (February, 1968), 1–37.

Holland, J. L. "Explorations of a Theory of Vocational Choice and Achievement: II. A Four-Year Prediction Study." PSYCHOLOGICAL REPORTS, 12 (April, 1963), 547–594.

Holland, J. L. "Some Explorations of a Theory of Vocational Choice: I. One-and Two-Year Longitudinal Studies," PSYCHOLOGICAL MONOGRAPHS: GENERAL AND APPLIED, 76 (No. 26, 1962), 1–49.

Inlow, G. M. "Job Satisfaction of Liberal Arts Graduates," JOURNAL OF APPLIED PSYCHOLOGY, 35 (June, 1951), 175–181.

Kamens, D. H. "College Charter and College Size: Effects on Occupational Choice and College Atrition," SOCIOLOGY OF EDUCATION, 44 (Summer, 1971), 270–296.

Kinane, Mary. "Attitudes of College Students Toward College Training as a Career," EDUCATIONAL RECORD, 43 (April 1962), 139–147.

Korn, Harold. "Careers: Choice, Chance or Inertia?" in Joseph Katz, et al. NO TIME FOR YOUTH. San Francisco: Jossey-Bass, 1968, 206–230.

Lawrie, J. W. "Attitudes Toward Business as a Function of Student Quality and Career Intentions," PERSONNEL AND GUIDANCE JOURNAL, 46 (May, 1968), 903–908.

Lesly, P. "Corporate Image and the Future Leaders of Business," PUBLIC OPINION QUARTERLY, 23 (Winter, 1959–1960), 547–553.

Mcdouagh, E. C. et al. "Relative Professional Status as Perceived by American and Swedish University Students," SOCIAL FORCES, 38 (October, 1959), 65–69.

McGuire, Joseph W. "Business and the Generation Gap," CALIFORNIA MANAGEMENT REVIEW, 13 (Winter, 1970), 78–88.

Maurer, H. "Twenty Minutes to a Career," FORTUNE, 53 (March, 1956), 116–119+.

Mitias, R. G. E. "Concepts of Science and Scientists Among College Students," JOURNAL OF RESEARCH IN SCIENCE TEACHING, 7 (No. 2, 1970), 135–140.

Olive, L. E. "Relationships of Values and Occupational Role Perceptions for Freshmen and Senior Students in a College of Engineering: Poe Inventory of Values," JOURNAL OF COUNSELING PSYCHOLOGY, 16 (March, 1969), 114–120.

Petrik, N. D. "Socio-Economic Status, Vocational Interests, and Persistence in Selected College Curricula," VOCATIONAL GUIDANCE QUARTERLY, 16 (September, 1967), 39–44.

Salley, R. E. "Recent Alumnae Report on Employment, Hunter College, New York," SCHOOL AND SOCIETY, 71 (June 17, 1950), 375–378.

Selvin, H. C. "The Impact of University Experiences on Occupational Plans," SCHOOL REVIEW, 71 (Autumn, 1963), 217–229.

Sewell, W. H. and A. M. Oriensteen. "Community of Residence and Occupational Choice," AMERICAN JOURNAL OF SOCIOLOGY, 70 (March, 1965), 551–563.

Simpson, R. L. and J. H. Simpson. "Values, Personal Influence and Occupational Choice," SOCIAL FORCES, 39 (December, 1960), 116–125.

Sisson, E. D. "The Predictive Value of Vocational Choices of College Students," SCHOOL AND SOCIETY, 47 (May 14, 1938), 646–648.

Spaeth, J. L. "Occupational Attainment Among Male College Graduates," AMERICAN JOURNAL OF SOCIOLOGY, 75 (January, 1970), 632–644.

Spaeth, J. L. "Occupational Prestige Expectations Among Male College Graduates," AMERICAN JOURNAL OF SOCIOLOGY, 73 (March, 1968), 548–558.

Spohn, Herbert. "Vocational Orientation and Growth," in Lois Murphy and Esther Raushenbush, eds. ACHIEVEMENT IN THE COLLEGE YEARS. New York: Harper, 1960, 156–194.

Stessin, L. "They're Not Trying to Succeed in Business: College Seniors," NEW YORK TIMES MAGAZINE, (March 28, 1965), 76+.

Stevens, N. D. and E. W. Stephens. "Who and What Influence Student Attitudes Toward Occupations?" JOURNAL OF COLLEGE PLACEMENT, 28 (February, 1968), 50–53+.

476

Strong, E. K., jr. "Amount of Change in Occupational Choice of College Freshmen," EDUCATIONAL AND PSYCHOLOGICAL MEASUREMENT, 12 (Winter, 1952), 677–691.

"Student Attitudes on Science: Summary of Interviews," BULLETIN OF THE ATOMIC SCIENTISTS, 27 (May, 1971), 31–35.

Taylor, H. G. "Campus Image of Business," DUNS REVIEW, 88 (November, 1966), 21–22+.

Vacchiano, R. B. and R. J. Adrian. "Multiple Discrimination Prediction of College Career Choice," EDUCATIONAL AND PSYCHOLOGICAL MEASURE-MENT, 26 (Winter, 1966), 985–995.

Vener, A. M. "College Education and Vocational Career," in W. B. Brook-over, ed. THE COLLEGE STUDENT. New York: Center for Applied Research in Education, 1965, 100–116.

Werts, C. E. "Career Changes in College," SOCIOLOGY OF EDUCATION, 40 (Winter, 1967), 90–95.

Werts, C. E. "Social Class and Initial Career Choice of College Freshmen," SOCIOLOGY OF EDUCATION, 39 (Winter, 1966), 74–85.

Winch, R. F. and P. A. Trash. "Aspects of College Experience and Their Relevance to the Activities of Later Life: A Story of 740 Northwestern Alumnae," NATIONAL ASSOCIATION OF WOMEN DEANS AND COUNSELORS JOUR-NAL, 26 (June, 1963), 30–37.

Wingo, W. "How Students See You Now," NATION'S BUSINESS, 58 (May, 1970), 54–58.

Yankelovich, Daniel. "Karl Marx vs. American Business: Round 2. A New Student Attack on Business, Centered Around an Updated Version of the Classic Marxian Analysis, Is Building and Can Present Corporations with the most Potent Challenge They Have Confronted Since the 1930's," BELL TELEPHONE MAGAZINE, 48 (September–October, 1969), 2–9.

D.7.c. Student Attitudes Toward Religion

Barkman, Paul F. "A Study of the Relationship of the Needs for Belonging and Conformity to Religious Beliefs and Values in a Christian College." Unpub-lished Ph.D. dissertation, New York University, 1960.

Covington, G. WHAT THEY BELIEVE: A SURVEY OF RELIGIOUS FAITH AMONG GROUPS OF COLLEGE STUDENTS. New York: Philosophical Library, 1956.

Educational Reviewer, Inc. A SURVEY OF THE POLITICAL AND RELI-GIOUS ATTITUDES OF AMERICAN COLLEGE STUDENTS. New York: Edu-cational Reviewer, 1964.

Ferman, Louis Abbott. "Religious Change on a College Campus." Unpub-lished Ph.D. dissertation, Cornell University, 1961.

Flanagan, George F. "An Investigation of Religious Attitudes Among Cath-olic Seniors in College Who Have Had Varying Amounts of Catholic Schooling." Unpublished Ph.D, dissertation, University of Minnesota, 1958.

Funk, Ruth Anne. "A Survey of Religious Attitudes and Manifest Anxiety in a College Population," Unpublished Ph.D. dissertation, Purdue University, 1955.

Gold, Benjamin. RELIGIOUS ATTITUDES OF COLLEGE STUDENTS AT HARVARD UNIVERSITY, RADCLIFFE COLLEGE AND LOS ANGELES CITY COLLEGE—HIGHLIGHTS OF COMPARATIVE STUDIES MADE IN 1946–1948 AND IN 1966–1967. Los Angeles: Los Angeles City College, 1967.

Hall, R. M. "Religious Beliefs and Social Values of Syracuse University Freshmen and Seniors, 1950." Unpublished Ph.D. dissertation, Syracuse University, 1951.

Hammond, Phillip E. THE CAMPUS CLERGYMAN. New York: Basic Books, 1966.

Hardon, John A. THE HUNGRY GENERATION: RELIGIOUS ATTITUDES AND NEEDS AT A STATE UNIVERSITY. Westminster, Maryland: Newman Press, 1967.

Harvard Student Council. RELIGION AT HARVARD. Cambridge, Massachusetts: Harvard Student Council, 1956.

Hassenger, R. "The Impact of a Value-Oriented College on the Religious Orientations of Students with Various Backgrounds, Traits and College Exposures." Unpublished Ph.D. dissertation, University of Chicago, 1965.

Hoge, Dean "College Students' Religion: A Study of Trends in Attitudes and Behavior," Unpublished Ph.D. dissertation, Harvard University, 1969.

Kuhre, Bruce Edward. "Multi-Dimensional Religiosity and Its Social Correlates Among a College Population," Unpublished Ph.D. dissertation, Pennsylvania State University, 1966.

McNamara, R. J. "The Interplay of Intellectual and Religious Values." Unpublished Ph.D. dissertation, Cornell University, 1963.

Mott, Johanna Katherine. "Religious Interests of College Students at the University of Oklahoma." Unpublished Ph.D. dissertation, University of Oklahoma, 1957.

Ramshaw, Warren Clement. "Religious Participation and the Fate of Religious Ideology on a Resident and a Nonresident College Campus: an Exploratory Study." Unpublished Ph.D. dissertation, University of Illinois, 1966.

Salisbury, William Seward. RELIGION AND THE COLLEGE STUDENT. Albany, New York: Research Foundation, State University of New York, 1957.

Silverman, Hirsch Lazaar. "Relationships of Personality Factors and Religious Background Among College Students." Unpublished Ph.D. dissertation, Yeshiva University, 1951.

Symington, T. A. RELIGIOUS LIBERALS AND CONSERVATIVES: A COMPARISON OF THOSE WHO ARE LIBERAL IN THEIR RELIGIOUS THINKING AND THOSE WHO ARE CONSERVATIVE. Teachers College Contributions to Education, No. 640. New York: Bureau of Publications, Teachers College, Columbia University, 1935.

Trent, J. W. CATHOLICS IN COLLEGE: RELIGIOUS COMMITMENT AND THE INTELLECTUAL LIFE. Chicago: University of Chicago Press, 1967.

Vincent, Lena P. (Duell). "The Religious Concepts and Attitudes of One

478

Hundred College Students." Unpublished Ph.D. dissertation, University of Michigan, 1957.

Weeks, S. Marion. THE STUDENT VIEWS RELIGION. Nashville, Tennessee: Parthenon Press, 1951.

Alexander, C. Norman, jr. and Ernest Campbell. "Normative Milieux and Social Behaviors: Church Affiliations and Collegiate Drinking Patterns," in George Maddox, ed. THE DOMESTICATED DRUG: DRINKING AMONG COLLEGIANS. New Haven, Connecticut: College and University Press, 1970, 268-290.

Allport, G. W., J. M. Gillespie and J. Young. "The Religion of the Post-War College Student," JOURNAL OF AMERICAN PSYCHOLOGY, 25 (1948), 3-33.

Bain, R. "Religious Attitudes of College Students," AMERICAN JOURNAL OF SOCIOLOGY, 32 (March, 1927), 762-770.

Bender, I. E. "Changes in Religious Interest: a Retest After 15 Years," JOURNAL OF ABNORMAL AND SOCIAL PSYCHOLOGY, 57 (July, 1958), 41-46.

Brown, D. G. and W. L. Lowe. "Religious Beliefs and Personality Characteristics of College Students," JOURNAL OF SOCIAL PSYCHOLOGY, 33 (February, 1951), 103-124.

Campbell, Douglas and Dennis Magill. "Religious Involvement and Intellectuality Among University Students," SOCIOLOGICAL ANALYSIS, 29 (Spring, 1968), 79-93.

Dudycha, G. J. "The Religious Beliefs of College Students," JOURNAL OF APPLIED PSYCHOLOGY, 17 (October, 1933), 585-603.

Dudycha, G. J. "The Religious Beliefs of College Freshmen in 1930 and 1949," RELIGIOUS EDUCATION, 49 (May–June, 1950), 165-169.

Emme, E. E. "Factors in the Religious Development of Thirty-Eight College Students," RELIGIOUS EDUCATION, 36 (April–June, 1941), 116-120.

Feldman, K. A. "Change and Stability of Religious Orientations During College. Part I. Freshman-Senior Comparisons," REVIEW OF RELIGIOUS RESEARCH, 11 (Fall, 1969), 40-60.

Ferguson, L. W. "Socio-Psychological Correlates of the Primary Attitude Scales: I. Religionism, II. Humanitarianism," JOURNAL OF SOCIAL PSYCHOLOGY, 19 (February, 1944), 81-98.

Ferman, L. A. "Religious Change on a College Campus," JOURNAL OF COLLEGE STUDENT PERSONNEL, 1 (March, 1960), 2-12.

Ferrer, Terry. "Religion in Our Colleges," in Samuel I. Bellman, ed. THE COLLEGE EXPERIENCE. San Francisco: Chandler, 1962, 109-115.

"From Freaks to Followers," CHURCH TODAY, 16 (October 22, 1971), 33-34.

Gilliland, A. R. "The Attitude of College Students Toward God and the Church," JOURNAL OF SOCIAL PSYCHOLOGY, 11 (August, 1940), 11-18.

Gilliland, A. R. "Changes in Religious Beliefs of College Students," JOURNAL OF SOCIAL PSYCHOLOGY, 37 (February, 1953), 113-116.

Gray, J. G. "Salvation on the Campus: Why Existentialism Is Capturing the Students," HARPER, 230 (May, 1965), 53–59.

Hadden, Jeffery and Robert Evans. "Religious Participation Among College Freshmen," in Shirley and John Clark, eds. YOUTH IN MODERN SOCIETY. New York: Holt Rinehart and Winston, 1972, 388–399.

Hadden, Jeffery K. and Robert Evans. "Some Correlates of Religious Participation Among College Freshmen," RELIGIOUS EDUCATION. (July–August, 1965), 277–285.

Hartnett, R. T. and R. E. Peterson. "Religious Preference as a Factor in Attitudinal and Background Differences Among College Freshmen," SOCIOLOGY OF EDUCATION, 41 (Spring, 1968), 227–237.

Hassenger, R. "Catholic College Impact on Religious Orientations," SOCIOLOGICAL ANALYSIS, 27 (Summer, 1966), 67–79.

Hassenger, R. "College and Catholics: an Introduction," in R. Hassenger, ed. THE SHAPE OF CATHOLIC HIGHER EDUCATION. Chicago: University of Chicago Press, 1967, 3–14.

*Hastings, Phillip and Dean R. Hoge. "Religious Change Among College Students Over Two Decades," SOCIAL FORCES, 49 (September, 1970), 16–28.

Havens, J. "Course of College Religious Conflict," RELIGIOUS EDUCATION, 65 (May, 1970), 257–264.

Havens, J. "A Study of Religious Conflict in College Students," JOURNAL OF SOCIAL PSYCHOLOGY, 64 (February, 1964), 77–87.

Havice, Charles. "Religion on Campus," in Charles Havice, ed. CAMPUS VALUES. New York: Scribner's, 1968, 127–140.

Heath, Douglas H. "Secularization and Maturity of Religious Beliefs," RELIGION AND HEALTH, 8 (October, 1969), 335–358.

Herberg, W. "Religious Stirring on the Campus: A Student Generation Accessible to God," COMMENTARY, 13 (March 1952), 242–248.

Hites, R. W. "Change in Religious Attitudes During Four Years of College," JOURNAL OF SOCIAL PSYCHOLOGY, 66 (June, 1965), 51–63.

Hoge, Dean R. "Religious Commitments of College Students Over Five Decades," in INTERNATIONAL YEARBOOK OF THE SOCIOLOGY OF RELIGION. 1971, 184–211.

Horton, P. B. "Student Interest in the Church," RELIGIOUS EDUCATION, 35 (October–December, 1940), 215–219.

Jacks, I. "Religious Affiliation and Educational, Political and Religious Values of College Freshmen and Sophomores," ADOLESCENCE, 7 (Spring, 1972), 95–120.

Jones, Vernon. "Attitudes of College Students and Their Changes: A 37-Year Study," GENETIC PSYCHOLOGY MONOGRAPHS, 81 (February, 1970), 3–80.

Jospe, A. "Religion in the University: A Terminal Case?" RELIGIOUS EDUCATION, 67 (March, 1972), 123–130.

McCabe, Sheridan. "Religious Commitment and Student Freedom on the Church-Related Campus," in L. Vaccaro and J. T. Covert, eds. STUDENT FREE-

DOM IN AMERICAN HIGHER EDUCATION. New York: Teachers College Press, 1969, 115–124.

Maier, J. and W. Spinrad. "Comparison of Religious Beliefs and Practices of Jewish, Catholic and Protestant Students," PHYLON QUARTERLY, 18 (January, 1958), 355–360.

Michaelsen, R. "Study of Religion: A Quiet Revolution in American Universities," JOURNAL OF HIGHER EDUCATION, 37 (April, 1966), 181–186.

Nelson, E. N. P. "Patterns of Religious Attitude Shifts From College to Fourteen Years Later," PSYCHOLOGICAL MONOGRAPHS: GENERAL AND APPLIED, 70 (No. 16, 1956), 1–15.

Nelson, E. N. P. "Student Attitudes Toward Religion," GENETIC PSYCHOLOGY MONOGRAPHS, 22 (August, 1940), 323–423.

"Religion on the Campus; Symposium," RELIGIOUS EDUCATION, 60 (July, 1965), 259–289.

Shannon, J. B. "Religious Revolution on the Campus," SATURDAY EVENING POST, 230 (March 29, 1958), 19–21+.

Stark, Rodney, "Class, Radicalism and Religious Involvement," AMERICAN SOCIOLOGICAL REVIEW, 29 (October, 1964), 698–708.

"A Survey of the Political and Religious Attitudes of American College Students," NATIONAL REVIEW, 15 (October 8, 1963), 279–302.

Thompson, Hugo W. "College Students and the Church," in Samuel I. Bellman, ed. THE COLLEGE EXPERIENCE. San Francisco: Chandler Publishing, 1962, 117–123.

Van Tuyl, M. C. T. "Where Do Students 'Lose' Religion?" RELIGIOUS EDUCATION, 33 (January–March, 1938), 19–29.

Wickenden, A. C. "The Effect of the College Experience Upon Students' Concepts of God," JOURNAL OF RELIGION, 12 (1932), 242–267.

Zelan, J. "Religious Apostasy, Higher Education and Occupational Choice," SOCIOLOGY OF EDUCATION, 41 (Fall, 1968), 370–379.

D.7.d. Students' Attitudes (Miscellaneous)

Ford, Imogene Morrow. "Differences in Campus Clothing Usage as Related to Selected Attitudes: An Exploratory Study." Unpublished Ph.D. dissertation, Pennsylvania State University, 1968.

Lloyd, John W. STUDENT PERCEPTIONS OF CAUSES OF LABOR-MANAGEMENT CONFLICT. Iowa City, Iowa: Center for Labor and Management, University of Iowa, 1968.

Matteson, David Roy. "Changes in Attitudes Toward Authority Figures in Selected College Freshmen." Unpublished Ph.D. dissertation, Boston University, 1968.

Perkins, John Chester. "Marital Prediction Scores of College Men Relative to Behavior and Attitudes: A Comparison of Two Groups of Males with Favorable and Unfavorable Marital Happiness Predictions." Unpublished Ph.D. dissertation, Pennsylvania State University, 1954.

Peterson, Roger Kermit. "An Analysis of Student Opinion Concerning the University Center as it Pertains to the Needs of Special Interest Groups at the University of Northern Colorado." Unpublished Ph.D. dissertation, University of Northern Colorado, 1970.

Riss, Eric. "Originality and Personality: An Exploratory Investigation to Study the Relationship of Originality to Certain Personality Variables in Art Students." Unpublished Ph.D. dissertation, New York University, 1958.

Rizzo, John Raymond "Value Dimensions, Value Commitments, and In-Basket Performance of Business Students." Unpublished Ph.D. dissertation, Ohio State University, 1964.

Weissman, M. P. "An Approach to the Assessment of Intellectual Disposition Among High-Ability Students." Unpublished Ph.D. dissertation, University of California, 1958.

Bott, M. M. "Measuring the Mystique: SVIB Masculinity-Femininity Scale," PERSONNEL AND GUIDANCE JOURNAL, 46 (June, 1968), 967–970.

*Braga, Joseph and R. P. Doyle. "Student Activism and Social Intelligence," YOUTH AND SOCIETY, 2 (Summer, 1971), 425–440.

Burma, J. H. "Attitudes of College Youth on War Marriage," SOCIAL FORCES, 24 (October, 1945), 96–100.

Burma, John H. "Student Attitudes Toward and Participation in Campus Organizations," SOCIOLOGY AND SOCIAL RESEARCH, 32 (November-December, 1947), 625–629.

Cantey, E. and H. K. Mull. "A Comparison of Freshmen and Seniors in a Liberal Arts College in Respect to Their Understanding of Social Issues," JOURNAL OF SOCIAL PSYCHOLOGY, 16 (November, 1942), 335–339.

Cooper, L. "Predisposition Toward Parenthood: A Comparison of Male and Female Students," SOCIOLOGY AND SOCIAL RESEARCH, 42 (September-October, 1957), 31–36.

Dole, A. A. "Accuracy of Retrospective Self-Reports by College Students," VOCATIONAL GUIDANCE QUARTERLY, 17 (Summer, 1968), 33–40.

Dudycha, G. J. "Superstitious Beliefs of College Freshmen in 1930 and 1949," SCHOOL AND SOCIETY, 72 (December 9, 1950), 376–379.

Gezi, K. I. and E. R. Kruschke, "Law-Abidingness Among Conservative and Liberal Students," EDUCATION, 91 (November, 1970), 97–102.

Holmes, D. C. "Student's Attitudes Toward the Worth and Dignity of Others," EDUCATIONAL RESEARCH BULLETIN, 31 (March, 1952), 63–66.

Kinnane, M. "Catholic Students' Attitudes Toward College Authority," CATHOLIC EDUCATION REVIEW, 61 (May, 1963), 294–301.

Kovach, E. M. A. "Latin Curricula: Student Attitudes," THE CLASSICAL JOURNAL, 63 (December, 1967), 109–114.

Laybourng, G. P. and H. P. Longstaff. "College Students Opinion of Radio Advertising," JOURNAL OF APPLIED PSYCHOLOGY, 32 (February, 1948), 81–87.

Richek, Herbert G. "Attitudes Toward Authority and Mental Health in Adolescent College Students," PSYCHIATRIC QUARTERLY, 45 (No. 3, 1971), 357–371.

Sermul, M. J. "Effects of Coeducation on Attitudes of Male College Students," JOURNAL OF EDUCATIONAL SOCIOLOGY, 34 (September, 1961), 11–17.

Smith, P. M. and N. C. Johnson. "Attitudes and Academic Status of Freshmen," JOURNAL OF NEGRO EDUCATION, 35 (Winter, 1966), 95–99.

Standt, V. M. "Attitudes of College Students Toward Marriage and Related Problems: Age, Educational, Familial, and Economic Factors in Marriage," JOURNAL OF PSYCHOLOGY, 34 (July, 1952), 95–106.

Vail, J. P. and V. M. Standt. "Attitudes of College Students Toward Marriage and Related Problems: Dating and Mate Selection," JOURNAL OF PSYCHOLOGY, 30 (July, 1950), 171–182.

Williams, R., et al. "Reactions of College Students to Manpower Policies and the Military Service Prospect," EDUCATIONAL RECORD, 34 (April, 1953), 101–107.

Wilson, L. L. "Study of Opinions Related to the Nature of Science and Its Purpose in Society," SCIENCE EDUCATION, 38 (March, 1954), 159–164.

Wilson, Mathews. "Students Against the Law: the Power of Negative Thinking," MODERATOR, 6 (November, 1967), 11–16.

D.7.e. Attitude Change in Students

Cross Reference. This is a general section; for attitude change in a specific area (like religion) see that area.

Astin, Alexander W. and Robert J. Panos. THE EDUCATIONAL AND VOCATIONAL DEVELOPMENT OF COLLEGE STUDENTS. Washington, D.C.: American Council on Education, 1969.

Astin, Alexander W., Robert J. Panos, and J. A. Creager. IMPLICATIONS OF A PROGRAM OF RESEARCH ON STUDENT DEVELOPMENT IN HIGHER EDUCATION, (ACE Research Reports). Washington, D.C.: Office of Research, American Council on Higher Education, 1967.

Barton, Allen H. STUDYING THE EFFECTS OF COLLEGE EDUCATION: A METHODOLOGICAL EXAMINATION OF CHANGING VALUES IN COLLEGE. New Haven, Connecticut: Hazen Foundation, 1959.

Clark, Burton, et al. STUDENTS AND COLLEGES: INTERACTION AND CHANGE. Berkeley, California: Center for Research and Development in Higher Education, University of California, 1972.

Commission to Study the Impact of the University on Its Under-Graduates. REPORT. Newark, Delaware: University of Delaware, 1964.

Eckert, R. E. OUTCOMES OF GENERAL EDUCATION. Minneapolis, Minnesota: University of Minnesota Press, 1955.

Eddy, Edward D. THE COLLEGE INFLUENCE ON STUDENT CHARACTER. Washington, D.C.: American Council on Education, 1959.

*Feldman, Kenneth A. and Theodore M. Newcomb. THE IMPACT OF COLLEGE ON STUDENTS. (2 Volumes). San Francisco: Jossey-Bass, 1969.

Fisher, Margaret B. and Jeanne L. Noble. COLLEGE EDUCATION AS PERSONAL DEVELOPMENT. Englewood Cliffs, New Jersey: Prentice-Hall, 1960.

Foster, F. S., et al. THE IMPACT OF A VALUE-ORIENTED UNIVERSITY ON STUDENT ATTITUDES AND THINKING. (U.S. Department of Health, Education and Welfare Cooperative Research Program Project, No. 729). Santa Clara, California: University of Santa Clara, 1961.

Freedman, Mervin B. IMPACT OF COLLEGE. Washington, D.C.: U.S. Department of Health, Education and Welfare, Office of Education, 1960.

Garrison, Charles Lee. "The Introductory Political Science Course As An Agent of Political Socialization. Unpublished Ph.D. Dissertation, University of Oregon, 1966.

Gruen, Richard. "A Study of Attitude Change and Change in Self-Concept Among Liberal Arts College Students." Unpublished Ph.D. dissertation, New York University, 1963.

Harrington, T. F., jr. "The Interrelation of Personality Variables and College Experiences of Engineering Students over a Four Year Span." Unpublished Ph.D. dissertation, Purdue University, 1965.

Heath, Roy. THE REASONABLE ADVENTURER: A STUDY OF THE DEVELOPMENT OF THIRTY-SIX UNDERGRADUATES AT PRINCETON. Pittsburgh, Pennsylvania: University of Pittsburgh, Press, 1964.

Hodgkinson, Harold L., William R. Rogers, Frederick Q. Shafer. THE IMPACT OF THE AMERICAN COLLEGE ON STUDENT VALUES. New York: Commission on Higher Education, National Council of Churches, 1964.

Kirk, Jerome Richard. "Cultural Diversity and Character Change at Carnegie Tech." Unpublished Ph.D. dissertation, Johns Hopkins University, 1965.

Kopans, Albert. "A Comparison of Some Social Science and Natural Science Upper Classmen on Prejudice and Critical Thinking Ability." Unpublished Ph.D. dissertation, Yeshiva University, 1963.

Lyles, James A. "A Study of Changes in Capacity and Development of Students During a Four Year College Program." Unpublished Ed.D. thesis, Temple University, 1959.

Madison, Peter. PERSONALITY DEVELOPMENT IN COLLEGE. Reading, Massachusetts: Addison-Wesley, 1969.

Nichols, R. C. PERSONALITY CHANGE AND THE COLLEGE. Evanston, Illinois: National Merit Scholarship Corporation, 1965.

Nichols, R. C. and A. W. Astin. PROGRESS OF THE MERIT SCHOLAR: AN EIGHT–YEAR FOLLOW-UP. Evanston, Illinois: National Merit Scholarship Corporation, 1965.

Perry, William G., jr. FORMS OF INTELLECTUAL AND ETHICAL DEVELOPMENT IN THE COLLEGE YEARS. Cambridge, Massachusetts: Bureau of Study Counsel, Harvard University, 1968.

Perry, William G., jr. PATTERNS OF DEVELOPMENT IN THOUGHT AND VALUES OF STUDENTS IN A LIBERAL ARTS COLLEGE. Cambridge, Massachusetts: Bureau of Study Council, Harvard University, 1968.

484

Plant, W. T. PERSONALITY CHANGES ASSOCIATED WITH A COLLEGE EDUCATION. U.S. Department of Health, Education and Welfare Cooperative Research Branch Project 348 (SAE 7666) San Jose, California: San Jose State College, 1962.

Sanford, Nevitt. SELF AND SOCIETY: SOCIAL CHANGE AND INDIVIDUAL DEVELOPMENT. New York: Atherton, 1966.

Sites, Paul LaBonte. "The Impact of the University Experience Upon Students' Willingness to Accept the Advice and Opinions of Experts." Unpublished Ph.D. dissertation, Purdue University, 1960.

Skager, R., J. Holland, and L. Brakamp. CHANGES IN SELF-RATING AND LIFE GOALS AMONG STUDENTS AT COLLEGES WITH DIFFERENT CHARACTERISTICS, (ACT Research Reports No. 14), Iowa City, Iowa: American College Testing Program, 1966.

Stember, Charles H. EDUCATION AND ATTITUDE CHANGE. New York: Institute of Human Relations Press, 1961.

Tead, Ordway. CHARACTER BUILDING AND HIGHER EDUCATION. New York: Macmillan, 1953.

Trent, J. W. "The Development of Intellectual Disposition Within Catholic Colleges." Unpublished Ph.D. dissertation, University of California, Berkeley, 1964.

Walizer, Michael and Robert Herriott. THE IMPACT OF COLLEGE ON STUDENTS' COMPETENCE TO FUNCTION IN A LEARNING SOCIETY. Iowa City, Iowa: American College Testing Program, 1971.

Warwick, D. P. "Socialization and Value Change in a College Community." Unpublished Ph.D. dissertation, University of Michigan, 1963.

Willer, D. E. "Value Change: A Panel Study of Purdue Engineers." Unpublished M.A. thesis, Purdue University, 1962.

Alfert, E. and R. F. Suczek. Personality Development and Cultural Change." JOURNAL OF HIGHER EDUCATION, 42 (January, 1971), 21–26.

Allport, Gordon W. "Crises in Normal Personality Development," TEACHERS COLLEGE RECORD, 66 (1964), 235–241.

Arsenian, S. "Change in Evaluative Attitudes During Four Years of College," JOURNAL OF APPLIED PSYCHOLOGY, 27 (August, 1943), 338–349.

*Astin, Alexander. "The Methodology of Research on College Impact, Part I," SOCIOLOGY OF EDUCATION, 43 (Summer, 1970), 223–254.

*Astin, Alexander. "The Methodology of Research on College Impact, Part II," SOCIOLOGY OF EDUCATION, 43 (Fall, 1970), 437–450.

Bain, Reed. "Changed Beliefs of College Students," JOURNAL OF ABNORMAL AND SOCIAL PSYCHOLOGY, 31 (April–June, 1936), 1–11.

Bardis, P. D. "Influence of a Functional Marriage Course on Attitudes Toward Familism," JOURNAL OF EDUCATIONAL SOCIOLOGY, 32 (January, 1959), 232–239.

Barkley, K. L. "Relative Influence of Commercial and Liberal Arts Curricula Upon Changes in Students' Attitudes," JOURNAL OF SOCIAL PSYCHOLOGY, 15 (February, 1942), 129–144.

Barton, Allen H. "Studying the Effects of College Education," in Kaoru Yamamoto, ed. THE COLLEGE STUDENT AND HIS CULTURE: AN ANALYSIS. Boston: Houghton Mifflin, 1968, 326–330.

Beach, L. R. "Personality Change in the Church-Related Liberal Arts College," PSYCHOLOGICAL REPORTS, 19 (December, 1966), 1257–1258.

Blank, B. D. "Do Collegians Conform?" SCHOOL AND SOCIETY, 88 (March 26, 1960), 157–160.

Bloom, B. S. and H. Webster. "The Outcomes of College," REVIEW OF EDUCATIONAL RESEARCH, 30 (October, 1960), 321–333.

Boldt, W. J. and J. B. Stroud. "Changes in the Attitudes of College Students," JOURNAL OF EDUCATIONAL PSYCHOLOGY, 25 (November, 1934), 611–619.

Boyer, E. L. and W. B. Michael. "Outcomes of College," REVIEW OF EDUCATIONAL RESEARCH, 35 (October, 1965), 277–291.

Brontman, Manuel and Werner I. Halpern. "Character Formation Problems in Today's Adolescent," in Morton Levitt and Ben Rubenstein, eds. YOUTH AND SOCIAL CHANGE. Detroit, Michigan: Wayne State University Press, 1972, 323–332.

Brown, D. R. "Student Characteristics and Institutional Impact of the Large Publically Controlled vs. the Small Private Institution," COLLEGE AND UNIVERSITY, 42 (Spring, 1967), 325–336.

Bugelski, R. and Olive Lester. "Changes in Attitudes of College Students During Their College Course and After Graduation," JOURNAL OF SOCIAL PSYCHOLOGY, 12 (November, 1940), 319–332.

Chickering, A. W. "Cultural Sophistication and College Experience," EDUCATIONAL RECORD, 52 (Spring, 1971), 125–128.

Chickering, A. W., et al. "Institutional Differences and Student Development," JOURNAL OF EDUCATIONAL PSYCHOLOGY, 60 (August, 1969), 315–326.

Corey, S. M. "Attitude Changes Between College Classes: A Summary and Criticism," JOURNAL OF EDUCATIONAL PSYCHOLOGY, 27 (May, 1936), 321–330.

Dressel, Paul L. "Factors Involved in Changing the Values of College Students," EDUCATIONAL RECORD, 46 (Spring, 1965), 104–113.

Dressel, Paul L. "Interests-Stable or Unstable? JOURNAL OF EDUCATIONAL RESEARCH, 48 (October, 1954), 95–102.

Dressel, Paul L. and I. J. Lehmann. "The Impact of Higher Education on Student Attitudes, Values and Critical Thinking Abilities," EDUCATIONAL RECORD, 46 (Summer, 1965), 248–258.

Eddy, E. D., jr. "College Influence on Student Character," NATIONAL ASSOCIATION OF WOMEN DEANS AND COUNSELORS JOURNAL, 22 (June, 1959), 183–186.

Elton, C. F. and H. A. Rose. "The Face of Change," JOURNAL OF COUNSELING PSYCHOLOGY, 15 (July, 1968), 372–375.

Eron, Leonard D. and Robert S. Redmount. "The Effect of Legal Education on Attitudes," JOURNAL OF LEGAL EDUCATION, 9 (No. 4, 1957), 431–443.

486

*Feldman, K. A. "Studying the Impacts of Colleges on Students," SOCIOL-OGY OF EDUCATION, 42 (Summer, 1969), 207–237.

*Feldman, Kenneth and Theodore Newcomb. "Some Methods for Assessing College Impacts," SOCIOLOGY OF EDUCATION, 44 (Spring, 1971), 133–150.

Flanders, J. P. and Donald L. Thistlethwaite. "Effects of Informative and Justificatory Variables Upon Imitation," JOURNAL OF EXPERIMENTAL SOCIAL PSYCHOLOGY, 6 (1970), 316–328.

Florence, Louise M. "Mental Growth and Development at the College Level," JOURNAL OF EDUCATIONAL PSYCHOLOGY, 38 (February, 1947), 65–82.

Flory, C. D. "The Intellectual Growth of College Students," JOURNAL OF EDUCATIONAL RESEARCH, 33 (February, 1940), 443–451.

Foster, Julien. "Some Effects of Jesuit Education: A Case Study," in R. Hassenger, ed. THE SHAPE OF CATHOLIC HIGHER EDUCATION. Chicago: University of Chicago Press, 1967.

Freedman, M. B. "Personality Growth in the College Years," COLLEGE BOARD REVIEW, 56 (Spring, 1965), 25–32.

Gilbert, G. M. "Stereotype Resistance and Change Among College Students," JOURNAL OF ABNORMAL AND SOCIAL PSYCHOLOGY, 46 (April, 1951), 245–254.

Glazer, N. "What Americans Get Out of College: Higher Income and What Else?" COMMENTARY, 13 (May, 1952), 486–490.

*Goertzel, T. "Changes in Values of College Students," PACIFIC SOCIO-LOGICAL REVIEW, 15 (April, 1972), 235–244.

*Gurin, Gerald. "The Impact of the College Experience," in S. Withey ed. A DEGREE AND WHAT ELSE: CORRELATES AND CONSEQUENCES OF A COLLEGE EDUCATION, New York: McGraw-Hill, 1972. 25–54.

Gustad, J. W. "Changes in Social Attitudes and Behavior: A Review of the Literature," EDUCATIONAL AND PSYCHOLOGICAL MEASUREMENT, 11 (Spring, 1951), 87–102.

Haagen, C. H. "Research at Wesleyan University," in C. E. Bidwell, ed. THE AMERICAN COLLEGE AND STUDENT PERSONALITY: A SURVEY OF RESEARCH PROGRESS AND PROBLEMS. Report of a conference on Research on College Influences on Personality, Social Science Research Council Committee on Personality Development in Youth. Andover, Massachusetts. New York: Social Science Research Council, 1959.

Hassenger, Robert. "The Impact of Catholic Colleges," in Robert Hassenger, ed. THE SHAPE OF CATHOLIC HIGHER EDUCATION. Chicago: University of Chicago Press, 1967, 103–161.

Heath, G. R., jr. "Personality and Student Development," in John Dodds, et al. NEW DIMENSIONS OF LEARING IN A FREE SOCIETY. Pittsburgh, Pennsylvania: University of Pittsburgh Press, 1958, 225–245.

Hearn, H. L., et al. "Identity and Institutional Imperatives: the Socialization of the Student Actress," SOCIOLOGICAL QUARTERLY, 9 (Winter, 1968), 47–63.

Hilton, T. L. and J. H. Korn. "Measured Change in Personal Values," EDU-CATIONAL AND PSYCHOLOGICAL MEASUREMENT, 24 (1964), 609–622.

Hoggart, Richard, "Higher Education and Personal Life: Changing Attitudes," in W. R. Niblett, ed. HIGHER EDUCATION: DEMAND AND RESPONSE. London: Tavistock Publications, 1969, 231–242.

Hopwood, K. L. "Stability in Freshman Attitudes," NATIONAL ASSOCIATION OF DEANS OF WOMEN JOURNAL, 17 (March, 1954), 125–129.

Hunter, E. C. "Change in Scores of College Students on the American Council Psychological Examinations at Yearly Intervals During the College Course," JOURNAL OF EDUCATIONAL RESEARCH, 36 (December, 1942), 284–291.

Huntley, C. W. "Changes in Study of Values Scores During the Four Years of College," GENETIC PSYCHOLOGY MONOGRAPHS, 71 (May, 1965), 349–383.

*Jacob, Philip E. "Changing Values in College," in Kaoru Yamamoto, ed. THE COLLEGE STUDENT AND HIS CULTURE: AN ANALYSIS, Boston: Houghton Mifflin, 1968, 309–316.

Jones, Vernon. "Attitudes of College Students and the Changes in Such Attitudes During Four Years in College," JOURNAL OF EDUCATIONAL PSYCHOLOGY, Part 1: 29 (No. 1, 1938), 14–25; Part 2: 29 (No. 2, 1938), 114–134.

Kanter, S. A. and D. R. Brown. "Personality Change as a Validation of the Bereiter Differential Change Scales," EDUCATIONAL AND PSYCHOLOGICAL MEASUREMENT, 28 (Spring, 1968), 125–134.

Kelsey, I. B. "Philosophic Considerations of a Shift in Values," IMPROVING COLLEGE UNIVERSITY TEACHING, 12 (Summer, 1964), 154–158.

Korn, Harold. "Personality Scale Changes From the Freshman to the Senior Year," In Joseph Katz, et al. NO TIME FOR YOUTH. San Francisco: Jossey-Bass, 1968, 162–185.

Lehman, I. J. "Changes in Critical Thinking, Attitudes, and Values from Freshman to Senior Years," JOURNAL OF EDUCATIONAL PSYCHOLOGY, 54 (December, 1963), 305–315.

Lehmann, Irvin J., Birend K. Sinha and Rodney T. Hartnett. "Changes in Attitudes and Values Associated with College Attendance," JOURNAL OF EDUCATIONAL PSYCHOLOGY, 57 (1966), 89–98.

Levin, Max. "Changes in Authoritarianism," in Joseph Katz et al. NO TIME FOR YOUTH. San Francisco: Jossey-Bass, 1968, 376–385.

Lloyd-Jones, Susan. "Student Interests in Value Change and Power Conflict," in W. J. Minter and Patricia Snyder, eds. VALUE CHANGE AND POWER CONFLICT IN HIGHER EDUCATION. Boulder, Colorado: Western Interstate Commission for Higher Education, 1970, 87–98.

Louise, Sister M. F. "Mental Growth and Development at the College Level," JOURNAL OF EDUCATIONAL PSYCHOLOGY, 38 (February, 1947), 65–83.

*McDermott, J. "Laying on of Culture: Faculty Attempts to Make Working Class Students Accept Culture of the University World on Their Own," NATION, 208 (March 10, 1969), 296–301.

McEvoy, T. L. "Cosmopolitanism," JOURNAL OF HIGHER EDUCATION, 39 (February, 1968), 84–91.

McFarland, S. G. and Donald L. Thistlethwaite. "An Analysis of a Logical

488

Consistency Model of Belief Change," JOURNAL OF PERSONALITY AND SOCIAL PSYCHOLOGY, 15 (No. 2, 1970), 133–143.

McKeachie, W. J. "Individual Conformity to Attitudes of Classroom Groups," JOURNAL OF ABNORMAL AND SOCIAL PSYCHOLOGY, 49 (1954), 282–289.

Matteson, R. W. "Experience-Interest Changes in Students," JOURNAL OF COUNSELING PSYCHOLOGY, 2 (Summer, 1955), 113–121.

Mayhew, L. B. "And in Attitudes," in P. Dressel, ed. EVALUATION IN THE BASIC COLLEGE. New York: Harper, 1958, 214–231.

Miller, E. D. Nonacademic Changes in College Students," EDUCATIONAL RECORD, 40 (April, 1959), 118–122.

Morris, Charles and Linwood Small. "Changes in Conceptions of the Good Life by American College Students from 1950 to 1970," JOURNAL OF PERSONALITY AND SOCIAL PSYCHOLOGY, 20 (November, 1971), 254–260.

Murphy, Lois. "The Students' Experience of Growth," in Lois Murphy and Esther Raushenbush, eds. ACHIEVEMENT IN THE COLLEGE YEARS. New York: Harper, 1960, 91–115.

*Newcomb, T. M. "Attitude Development as a Function of Reference Groups: the Bennington Study," in H. Proshansky and B. Seidenberg, eds. BASIC STUDIES IN SOCIAL PSYCHOLOGY. New York: Holt, Rinehart and Winston, 1965, 215–224.

Newcomb, Theodore. "College Experience and Attitude Development," in Theodore Newcomb, ed. THE ADOLESCENT. New York: Dryden Press, 1953, 397–406.

Nichols, R. C. "Personality Change and the College," AMERICAN EDUCATIONAL RESEARCH JOURNAL, 4 (May, 1967), 173–190.

Plant, W. T. and E. W. Minum. "Differential Personality Development in Young Adults of Markedly Different Aptitude Levels," JOURNAL OF EDUCATIONAL PSYCHOLOGY, 58 (June, 1967), 141–152.

Plant, W. T. and C. W. Telford. "Changes in Personality for Groups Completing Different Amounts of College Over Two Years," GENETIC PSYCHOLOGY MONOGRAPHS, 74 (August, 1966), 3–36.

Riesman, David. "Review: Changing Values in College: An Exploratory Study of the Impact of College Teaching," AMERICAN SOCIOLOGICAL REVIEW, 23 (December, 1958), 732–738.

Rettig, Salomon and Benjamin Pasamanick. "Changes in Moral Values Among College Students: A Factorial Study," AMERICAN SOCIOLOGICAL REVIEW, 24 (December, 1959), 856–863.

Rock, D. A., et al. "Interaction Between College Effects and Students' Aptitudes," AMERICAN EDUCATION RESEARCH JOURNAL, 9 (Winter, 1972), 149–161.

Rogers, R. W. and Donald L. Thistlethwaite. "An Analysis of Active and Passive Defenses in Inducing Resistance to Persuasion," JOURNAL OF PERSONALITY AND SOCIAL PSYCHOLOGY, 11 (No. 4, 1969), 301–308.

Rogers, R. W. and Donald L. Thistlethwaite. "Effects of Fear Arousal and Reassurance on Attitude Change," JOURNAL OF PERSONALITY AND SOCIAL PSYCHOLOGY, 15 (No. 3, 1970), 227–233.

Sanford, Nevitt. "The Development of Social Responsibility Through the College Experience," in E. J. McGrath, ed. THE LIBERAL ARTS COLLEGE'S RESPONSIBILITY FOR THE INDIVIDUAL STUDENT. New York: Teachers College Press, Columbia University, 1966, 22–36.

Sanford, Nevitt. "General Education and Personality Theory," TEACHERS COLLEGE RECORD, 66 (1965), 721–732.

Sanford, Nevitt. "Measuring the Success of a College," in K. M. Wilson, ed. RESEARCH RELATED TO COLLEGE ADMINISTRATION. Atlanta, Georgia: Southern Regional Education Board, 1963.

Sanford, Nevitt. "Personality Development During the College Years," JOURNAL OF SOCIAL ISSUES, 12 (January, 1956), 1–71.

Snyder, B. R. "Adaptation, Education and Emotional Growth," in L. A. Pervin, L. E. Reik and W. Dalrymple, eds. THE COLLEGE DROPOUT AND THE UTILIZATION OF TALENT. Princeton, New Jersey: Princeton University Press, 1966, 155–175.

Stalnaker, Elizabeth M. "A Four Year Study of the Freshman Class of 1935 at West Virginia University," JOURNAL OF EDUCATIONAL RESEARCH, 36 (October, 1942), 100–118.

Stalnaker, Elizabeth M. "A Four Year Study of the Freshman Class of 1935 at the West Virginia University," JOURNAL OF EDUCATIONAL RESEARCH, 39 (October, 1945), 81–108.

Stanley, J. C. "A Design for Comparing the Impact of Different Colleges," AMERICAN EDUCATIONAL RESEARCH JOURNAL, 4 (May, 1967), 223–228.

Steinzor, B. "The Development of Intellectual Qualities Through the College Years," in Lois Murphy and Esther Raushenbush, eds. ACHIEVEMENT IN THE COLLEGE YEARS: A RECORD OF INTELLECTUAL AND PERSONAL GROWTH. New York: Harper, 1960, 156–194.

Stewart, L. H. "Change in Personality Test Scores During College," JOURNAL OF COUNSELING PSYCHOLOGY, 11 (Fall, 1964), 211–230.

Stroup, Herbert. "Adventuring in Social Maturity," in Charles Havice, ed. CAMPUS VALUES. New York: Scribner's, 1968, 23–33.

Vreeland, R. S. and C. E. Bidwell. "Classifying University Departments: An Approach to the Analysis of Their Effects Upon Undergraduates' Values and Attitudes," SOCIOLOGY OF EDUCATION, 39 (Summer, 1966), 237–254.

Webb, S. C. "Changes in Student Personal Qualities Associated with Change in Intellectual Abilities," COLLEGE AND UNIVERSITY, 41 (Spring, 1966), 280–289.

Webster, Harold. "Changes in Attitudes During College," JOURNAL OF EDUCATIONAL PSYCHOLOGY, 49 (June, 1958), 109–117.

Webster, H. "The Impact of the Student on the College," in K. M. Wilson, ed. INSTITUTIONAL RESEARCH ON COLLEGE STUDENTS. Atlanta, Georgia: Southern College Personnel Association and Southern Regional Education Board, 1962, 1–34.

Webster, H. "Personality Development During the College Years: Some Quantitative Results," JOURNAL OF SOCIAL ISSUES, 12 (October, 1956), 29–43.

490

Webster, H. "Problems of Studying Educational Growth in College Students," in K. M. Wilson, ed. RESEARCH RELATED TO COLLEGE ADMISSIONS. Atlanta, Georgia: Southern Regional Educational Board, 1963, 17–30.

Webster, Harold, Mervin Freedman and Paul Heist. "Personality Changes in College Students," in Nevitt Sanford, ed. THE AMERICAN COLLEGE. New York: Wiley, 1964, 811–846.

Wells, D. A. "Creation of Values," NATIONAL ASSOCIATION OF WOMEN DEANS AND COUNSELORS JOURNAL, 28 (Winter, 1965), 51–56.

Wilson, Logan. "Changes in Student Opinions and Attitudes," SOCIOLOGY AND SOCIAL RESEARCH, 20 (July–August, 1936), 552–559.

Wright, J. C. and B. B. Scarborough. "Relationship of the Interests of College Freshmen to Their Interests as Sophomores and as Seniors," EDUCATIONAL AND PSYCHOLOGICAL MEASUREMENT, 18 (Spring, 1958), 153–158.

D.7.f. Persistence of Attitudes

Campbell, D. P. A STUDY OF COLLEGE FRESHMAN—25 YEARS LATER, (U.S. Department of Health, Education and Welfare Cooperative Research Project Number 2160). Minneapolis, Minnesota: University of Minnesota, 1965.

Jones, Vernon Augustus. ATTITUDES OF COLLEGE STUDENTS AND THEIR CHANGES: A 37 YEAR STUDY, in Genetic Psychological Monographs, Volume 81, 1970.

Lathrop, R. L. and R. S. Stein. THE PERSISTENCE OF COLLEGE TEACHING AS A CAREER CHOICE: A FOLLOW-UP STUDY OF FIFTY HONOR STUDENTS, TWO YEARS BEYOND THE BACCALAUREATE. Minneapolis, Minnesota: Bureau of Institutional Research, University of Minnesota, 1962.

Nelson, Erland. PERSISTENCE OF ATTITUDES OF COLLEGE STUDENTS FOURTEEN YEARS LATER. Washington: American Psychological Association, 1954.

*Newcomb, Theodore M., et al. PERSISTENCE AND CHANGE: BENNINGTON COLLEGE AND ITS STUDENTS AFTER TWENTY-FIVE YEARS. New York: Wiley, 1967.

Pace, C. R. THEY WENT TO COLLEGE: A STUDY OF 951 FORMER UNIVERSITY STUDENTS. Minneapolis, Minnesota: University of Minnesota Press, 1941.

Pollan, William D. "Stability of Interest of College Students." Unpublished Ed.D. dissertation, North Texas State University, 1956.

Smith, A. W. PARTICIPATION; ORGANIZATION: A STUDY OF COLUMBIA COLLEGE ALUMNI, (Teachers College Contribution to Education, Number 935). New York: Bureau of Publications, Teachers College, Columbia University, 1948.

Arsenian, Seth. "Change in Evaluative Attitudes During Twenty-Five Years," JOURNAL OF APPLIED PSYCHOLOGY, 54 (August, 1970), 302–304.

Buck, W. A. "A Measurement of Changes in Attitudes and Interests of University Students Over a 10 Year Period," JOURNAL OF ABNORMAL SOCIAL PSYCHOLOGY, 31 (April–June, 1936), 12–19.

Edelstein, Alex. "Since Bennington: Evidence of Change in Student Political Behavior," PUBLIC OPINION QUARTERLY, 26 (Winter, 1962), 564–577.

Greeley, Andrew M. and Joe L. Spaeth. "Political Change among College Alumni," SOCIOLOGY OF EDUCATION, 43 (Winter, 1970), 100–112.

Herzberg, F. and A. Bouton. "A Further Study of the Stability of the Kuder Preference Record," EDUCATIONAL AND PSYCHOLOGICAL MEASURE-MENT, 14 (Summer, 1954), 326–331.

Keller, R. J. and C. R. Carlson. "Students of Minnesota Liberal Arts Colleges: A Follow-Up Study of Former Minnesota Liberal Arts College Students," in Minnesota Commission on Higher Education, HIGHER EDUCATION IN MINNESOTA. Minneapolis: University of Minnesota Press, 1950, 210–235.

Keller, R. J. and R. M. Cooper. "A Follow-up Study of Former Students in the College of Science, Literature and the Arts," in Ruth E. Eckert and R. D. Keller, eds. A UNIVERSITY LOOKS AT ITS PROGRAM: THE REPORT OF THE UNIVERSITY OF MINNESOTA BUREAU OF INSTITUTIONAL RE-SEARCH, 1942-1952. Minneapolis, Minnesota: University of Minnesota Press, 1954, 47–63.

McBride, Katherine. "Alumnae-Bryn Mawr College," in CASE BOOK—EDUCATION BEYOND THE HIGH SCHOOL. Washington: U.S. Office of Education, 1958.

Nelson, Erland. Persistence of Attitudes of College Students Four Years Later," PSYCHOLOGICAL MONOGRAPHS, 68 (Number 2, 1954), 1–12.

Newcomb, T. M. "Persistence and Regression of Changed Attitudes: Long-Range Studies," JOURNAL OF SOCIAL ISSUES, 19 (October, 1963), 3–14.

Pressey, S. L. and A. W. Jones. "1923–1953 and 20–60, Age Changes in Moral Codes, Anxieties, and Interests as Shown by the 'X-O Tests'," JOURNAL OF PSYCHOLOGY, 39 (October, 1955), 485–502.

Stone, E. X., jr. "Permanence of Interest Scores Over 22 Years," JOURNAL OF APPLIED PSYCHOLOGY, (April, 1951), 89–91.

Von Hoffman, N. "Class of '43 Is Puzzled: 25th Reunion at Harvard," ATLANTIC, 322 (October, 1968), 69–76.

E. NON-ACTIVIST CAMPUS ACTIVITIES

E.1. The Role of the Fraternity and Sorority

*Baird, William Raimond. AMERICAN COLLEGE FRATERNITIES. New York, 1898.

Dahl, S. T. "A Study of the Relationship of Academic Achievement and Membership in a Male Social Unit at the Brigham Young University." Unpublished Ph.D. dissertation, Brigham Young University, 1961.

Havemeyer, Loomis. "GO TO YOUR ROOM:" A STORY OF UNDERGRADUATE SOCIETIES AND FRATERNITIES AT YALE. New Haven: 1960.

492

Ibrahim, Azmy Ishak. "Process of Group Identification in a Sorority: A Reformulation of Reference Group Theory." Unpublished Ph.D. dissertation, University of Colorado, 1964.

Kansas University, Men's Interfraternity Council. FRATERNITY LIFE AT THE UNIVERSITY OF KANSAS. Lawrence, Kansas, 1962.

Kellogg, H. L., ed. COLLEGE SECRET SOCIETIES. Chicago: Ezra Cook, 1874.

*Lee, Alfred M. FRATERNITIES WITHOUT BROTHERHOOD: A STUDY OF PREJUDICE ON THE AMERICAN CAMPUS. Boston: Beacon Press, 1955.

*Leemon, Thomas. THE RITES OF PASSAGE IN A STUDENT CULTURE: A STUDY OF THE DYNAMICS OF TRANSITION. New York: Teachers College Press, 1972.

Michigan Student Study. "Ten Fraternities at the University of Michigan: Preliminary Report from the Student Organizations Study." Ann Arbor: Institute for Social Research, University of Michigan, 1967.

Musgrave, Wayne. COLLEGE FRATERNITIES. New York: Interfraternity Conference, 1923.

Robson, John, ed. BAIRD'S MANUAL OF AMERICAN COLLEGE FRATERNITIES. Menasha, Wisconsin: George Banta, 1963.

*Scott, William A. VALUES AND ORGANIZATIONS: A STUDY OF FRATERNITIES AND SORORITIES. Chicago: Rand McNally, 1965.

Shutt, Darold L. ATTITUDE CHANGES AMONG FIRST YEAR COLLEGE MEN LIVING IN FRATERNITIES AND RESIDENCE HALLS. University of Illinois, 1955.

Sprinthall, Richard Clark. "Social Conformity in a College Fraternity." Unpublished Ph.D. dissertation, Boston University, 1958.

University of Vermont. FRATERNITY SELF-STUDY: PRELIMINARY REPORT. Burlington, Vermont: University of Vermont, 1965.

Van Riper, Paul P. THE CORNELL FRATERNITY SELF-STUDY PROGRAM: A REPORT ON SOME EDUCATIONAL AND SOCIAL ASPECTS OF FRATERNITY LIFE. Ithaca: Cornell Fraternities Research Committee of the Cornell Association of Resident Fraternity Advisors, 1961.

Widmar, G. E. "A Comparative Study of Fraternity and Sorority Membership Aspirations of Entering Freshmen at the Florida State University." Unpublished Ph.D. dissertation, Florida State University, 1966.

Wise, Wilmer Earle. "The Influence of the Greek-Letter Fraternity System at the Pennsylvania State University on Certain Student Attitudes, Achievements, and Knowledge." Unpublished Ed.D. dissertation, Pennsylvania State University, 1963.

Yardley, William Augustus. "An Analysis of Greek-Letter Social Fraternities as a Factor in Student Life at the Ohio State University." Unpublished Ph.D. dissertation, Ohio State University, 1953.

Beery, G. S. "Relationship of the College Administration with Fraternities and Sororities," EDUCATIONAL PSYCHOLOGY MAGAZINE, 7 (1947), 594–602.

Blackwell, Thomas E. "How Civil Rights Act Affects Fraternities," COLLEGE AND UNIVERSITY BUSINESS, 41 (December, 1966), 53–54.

Bohrnstedt, G. W. "Conservatism, Authoritarianism and Religiosity of Fraternity Pledges," JOURNAL OF COLLEGE STUDENT PERSONNEL, 10 (January, 1969), 36–43.

Bohrnstedt, G. W. "Social Mobility Aspirations and Fraternity Membership," SOCIOLOGICAL QUARTERLY, 10 (Winter, 1969), 42–52.

Brower, B. "Fraternities," ESQUIRE, 56 (October, 1961), 116–119+.

Butler, W. R. "Factors Associated with Scholastic Achievement in High and Low Achieving Fraternities," PERSONNEL AND GUIDANCE JOURNAL, 38 (October, 1959), 134–141.

Collins, W. P. and R. D. Whetstone. "A Comparison of Sorority and Independent Women Based on Retention, Academic Achievement, and Scholastic Aptitude," JOURNAL OF THE NATIONAL ASSOCIATION OF WOMEN DEANS AND COUNSELORS, 28 (Summer, 1965), 177–178.

Cronbach, L. J. "Stereotypes and College Sororities," JOURNAL OF HIGHER EDUCATION, 15 (April, 1944), 214–216.

Crookston, B. B. "Academic Performance of Fraternity Pledges," JOURNAL OF COLLEGE STUDENT PERSONNEL, 1 (June, 1960), 19–22.

Crookston, B. B. "Selectivity as a Factor in Fraternity Scholastic Achievement," PERSONNEL AND GUIDANCE JOURNAL, 40 (December, 1961), 355–357.

Divesta, F. J. and A. D. Woodruff. "Students' Concepts of Fraternities and Sororities," JOURNAL OF SOCIAL PSYCHOLOGY, 29 (February, 1949), 119–122.

Eurich, A. C. "The Relation of Achievement Between College Fraternity and Non-Fraternity Groups," SCHOOL AND SOCIETY, 26 (November 12, 1927), 624–630.

"Fraternity Rushing," LIFE, 41 (September 24, 1956), 141–149.

Gerson, W. M. "College Sorority as a Social System," SOCIOLOGY AND SOCIAL RESEARCH, 53 (April, 1969), 385–394.

Gordon, M. and S. R. Wilson. "Status Inconsistency and Satisfaction with Sorority Membership," SOCIAL FORCES, 48 (December, 1969), 176–183.

Harp, J. and P. Taiety. "On Fraternity Membership and College Cheating— A Reply to Bowers and Stannard," SOCIAL PROBLEMS, 15 (Fall, 1967), 122–124.

Higdon, H. "Troubled Heart of Sigma Chi: Attempt to Pledge a Negro at University of Michigan," NEW YORK TIMES MAGAZINE, (November 14, 1965), 48–49+.

Hopkins, J. M. "Segregated Fraternities in Our Colleges," CHRISTIAN SCHOLAR, 41 (June, 1958), 109–113.

Jackson, R. and R. C. Winkler, "A Comparison of Pledges and Independents," PERSONNEL AND GUIDANCE JOURNAL, 43 (December, 1964), 379–382.

Kaludis, G. and G. Zathen. "Anatomy of a Pledge Class," JOURNAL OF COLLEGE STUDENT PERSONNEL, 7 (September, 1966), 282–284.

494

Lepley, W. M. "A Comparison of Fraternity and Non-Fraternity Populations with Regard to Certain Personality Characteristics," JOURNAL OF APPLIED PSYCHOLOGY, 26 (February, 1942), 50–54.

Levine, G. N. and L. A. Sussman. "Social Class and Sociability in Fraternity Pledging," AMERICAN JOURNAL OF SOCIOLOGY, 65 (January, 1960), 391–399.

McCraken, Robert. "The Influence of the Fraternity," in Kenneth Knickerbocker, ed. IDEAS FOR WRITING. New York: Henry Holt, 1956, 244–249.

MacPhail, A. H. "A Comparative Study of the Quality of Academic Work Done by Fraternity and Non-Fraternity Students at Brown University," SCHOOL AND SOCIETY, 38 (December 30, 1933), 873–876.

Marcson, S. ed. "Segregation and Integration in College Fraternities," SOCIAL PROBLEMS, 2 (Number 3, 1955), 129–175.

Murphey, Raymond and Charles Havice. Part One: "Extracurricular Activities," "The Invisible Curriculum," Part Two: "Fraternities, to Join or Not to Join," in Charles Havice, ed. CAMPUS VALUES. New York: Charles Scribner's Sons, 1968, 95–109.

Plant, W. T. "Sex, Intelligence and Sorority or Fraternity Membership and Changes in Ethnocentrism Over a Two-Year Period," JOURNAL OF GENETIC PSYCHOLOGY, 93 (September, 1958), 53–57.

Porter, John A. "College Fraternities," in James Stone and Donald DeNevi, eds. PORTRAITS OF THE AMERICAN UNIVERSITY, 1890–1910. San Francisco: Jossey-Bass, 1971, 293–304.

Rorty, J. "Greek Letter Discrimination," COMMENTARY, 21 (February, 1956), 118–125.

Schmidt, M. R. "Relationship between Sorority Membership and Changes in Selected Personality Variables and Attitudes," JOURNAL OF COLLEGE STUDENT PERSONNAL, 12 (May, 1971), 208–213.

Schwartz, G. and D. Merten, "Social Identity and Expressive Symbols: The Meaning of an Initiation Ritual," AMERICAN ANTHROPOLOGIST, 70 (December, 1968), 1117–1131.

Scott, J. F. "The American College Sorority: Its Role in Class and Ethnic Endogamy," AMERICAN SOCIOLOGICAL REVIEW, 30 (August, 1965), 514–527.

Sherman, J.R. "Attitudes toward Men's Social Fraternities at the University of Colorado," JOURNAL OF COLLEGE STUDENT PERSONNEL, 8 (March, 1967), 75–79.

Stannard, Charles I. and William J. Bowers, "The College Fraternity as an Opportunity Structure for Meeting Academic Demands," SOCIAL PROBLEMS, 17 (Winter, 1970), 371–390.

Stone, C. L. "Sorority Status and Personality Adjustment," AMERICAN SOCIOLOGICAL REVIEW, 16 (August, 1951), 538–541.

"A Symposium on Segregation and Integration in College Fraternities," SOCIAL PROBLEMS, 2 (Number 3, 1955), 129–175.

Thal, Debbie. "A Girl's Diary of Sorority Rush . . . the Realities of Another World," in Christopher Reaske and Robert Wilson, jr., eds. STUDENT VOICES/ ONE. New York: Random House, 1971.

Thompson, Wade. "My Crusade Against Fraternities," NATION, 189 (September 26, 1959), 169–172.

Wallace, W. L. "Faculty and Fraternities: Organizational Influences on Student Achievement," ADMINISTRATIVE SCIENCE QUARTERLY, 11 (March, 1967), 643–670.

Warman, R. E. "Pledges View of Fraternity Effect on Scholarship," FRATERNITY MONTHLY, (October, 1962), 30–32.

"What Happens When Sigma Chi Pledges a Negro," LOOK, 29 (July 27, 1965), 36–40.

Williamson, E. G. and B. J. Borreson. "Learning to Resolve Social Conflicts," EDUCATIONAL RECORD, 31 (January, 1950), 26–38.

Willerman, B. "Changing the Attitudes of Fraternity Members toward University Control," PERSONNEL AND GUIDANCE JOURNAL, 37 (April, 1959), 542–550.

Willerman, B. and L. Swanson. "Group Prestige in Voluntary Organizations: A Study of College Sororities," HUMAN RELATIONS, 6 (Number 1, 1953), 57–77.

Willingham, W. W. "College Performance of Fraternity Members and Independent Students," PERSONNEL AND GUIDANCE JOURNAL, 41 (September, 1962), 29–31.

Wood, Martha Craig. "Sororities: I'm Glad I Joined," in Samuel I. Bellman, ed. THE COLLEGE EXPERIENCE. San Francisco: Chandler, 1962, 69–72.

"Zeta Beta Kaput?" in Samuel I. Bellman, ed. THE COLLEGE EXPERIENCE. San Francisco: Chandler, 1962, 74–77.

E.2. The Student Press

Boffa, Robert C. A STUDY OF THE LIABILITY OF A STATE EDUCATIONAL INSTITUTION FOR THE TORTS OF ITS STUDENT PRESS. Philadelphia: U.S. National Student Association, 1961.

Comcowich, Jerome M. "The Student Newspaper: A Comparative Examination of Ten Central Massachusetts College Student Newspapers," 1967–1968. Unpublished Ph.D. dissertation, University of Denver, 1968.

Delaware, University of. Office of the Dean of Students. SUPERVISION AND CONTROL OF STUDENT PUBLICATIONS. 1961.

Estrin, Herman A. and Arthur M. Sanderson, eds. FREEDOM AND CENSORSHIP OF THE COLLEGE PRESS. Dubuque, Iowa: W. C. Brown, 1966.

Green, Reginald H. and Edwin S. Kahn. MASS COMMUNICATION ON CAMPUS, THE COLLEGE EDITOR: ROLE AND RESPONSIBILITY. Philadelphia: U.S. National Student Association, 1958.

Ritter, Edward J. SURVEY OF COLLEGE PUBLICATIONS AND COLLEGE PUBLICATION BOARDS. Peoria, Illinois: Bradley University, 1962.

Schwerner, Stephen Abraham. "An Historical Study of the Changing Emphasis on Social, Political, and Educational Issues Since World War I in Undergraduate Newspapers at Four Eastern Colleges." Unpublished Ph.D. dissertation, New York University, 1970.

496

Special Commission on the Student Press. THE STUDENT NEWSPAPER: REPORT . . . TO THE PRESIDENT OF THE UNIVERSITY OF CALIFORNIA. Washington American Council on Education, 1970.

Abbott, C. Michael. "The Student Press: Some First Impressions," WAYNE LAW REVIEW, 16 (Winter, 1969), 1–36.

Abbott, C. Michael. "The Student Press: Some Second Thoughts," WAYNE LAW REVIEW, 16 (Summer, 1970), 989–1004.

Bing, Roland. "The Role of the College Press: Student Newspapers," JOURNAL OF HIGHER EDUCATION, 26 (October 1955), 382–385, 400.

Chase, Richard. "The New Campus Magazine," HARPERS, 223 (October, 1931), 168–172.

Ebert, Roger. "Toward a Free and Responsible Press," in Tom DeVoies, ed. READINGS ON STUDENT PRESS FREEDOM. Washington: U.S. Student Press Association, 1965. 8–12.

Greenfield, Jeff. "College Newspapers in Search of Their Own Voice," HARPERS, 232 (May 1966), 87–93.

Heidenheimer, Arnold J. "The College Press: 1.65% Free," NEW REPUBLIC, 125 (October 29, 1951), 15+.

"How Free is College Journalism?" NEW REPUBLIC, 134 (April 2, 1956), 11–14.

Hudjins, H. C. jr. "Academic Freedom and the Student Press," WAKE FOREST INTRAMURAL LAW REVIEW, 6 (December , 1969), 1–39.

Kirk, R. "Campus Conservative Journals," NATIONAL REVIEW, 16 (June 2, 1964), 449+.

Marsh, J. J. and B. C. Kinnick. "College Press: Freedom and Control," JOURNAL OF COLLEGE STUDENT PERSONNEL, 10 (November, 1969), 382–386.

Moderator. "Student Press Freedom: Liberty or License?" in E. Lloyd-Jones and Herman Estrin, eds. THE AMERICAN STUDENT AND HIS COLLEGE. Boston: Houghton Mifflin, 1967. 330–333.

O'Connell, M. "Censorship on Campus: A Student's Plea for Granting Responsible Freedom to Catholic College Editors," AMERICA, 3 (November 14, 1964), 611–613.

Politella, Dorio. "Student Power and the Student Press," COLLEGE PRESS REVIEW, 8 (Spring, 1968), 9–13.

Sorensen, G. "Do Student Newspapers Have a Place," PERSONNEL AND GUIDANCE JOURNAL, 33 (February, 1955), 339–343.

Stewart, M. "Gadfly to the Sacred Cow," WORLD STUDENT NEWS, 17 (Number 8, 1963), 1–4.

E.3. Other Campus Activities

American Association for Health, Physical Education and Recreation. CAMPUS RECREATION. Washington: AAHPER, 1968.

Bohrnstedt, G. W. "Processes of Seeking Membership in and Recruitment by Voluntary Social Organizations." Unpublished Ph.D. dissertation, University of Wisconsin, 1966.

Chapin, F. S. and O. M. Mehus. EXTRA CURRICULAR ACTIVITIES AT THE UNIVERSITY OF MINNESOTA. Minneapolis: University of Minnesota Press, 1929.

Frederick, R. W. STUDENT ACTIVITIES IN AMERICAN EDUCATION. New York: Center for Applied Research in Education, 1965.

Henningsen, Charles G., Ronald C. Moss, and Everett M. Rogers. PARTIC-IPATION IN CAMPUS LIFE. Ames: Iowa State College, 1956.

Hollis, Adelyn F. "Factors Related to Student Participation in Campus Activities in a Midwestern Teachers' College." Unpublished Ph.D. dissertation, University of Michigan, 1953.

Hyry, George Arthur. "Factors Associated with Participation by Men in Campus Activities in a Midwestern College." Unpublished Ph.D. dissertation, University of Michigan, 1957.

Lenfestey, Frederick Thomas. "The Degree of Participation in Student Activities in Relation to the Presence of Certain Personality Characteristics." Unpublished Ph.D. dissertation, University of Florida, 1956.

Miller, F. A., J. H. Moyer, and R. B. Patrick. PLANNING STUDENT AC-TIVITIES. Englewood Cliffs, New Jersey: Prentice-Hall, 1956.

Minkin, Vera F. "A Study of the Student Activity Program at Newark State College." Unpublished Ph.D. dissertation, New York University, 1960.

Paster, George N. "Evaluation and Analysis of Student Participation in Out-of-Class Activities at a City College." Unpublished Ph.D. dissertation, University of Chicago, 1952.

Permaul, Jane Szutu. "Behavioral Differences Among Selected Organized Student Groups." Unpublished Ph.D. dissertation, University of California at Los Angeles, 1970.

Robbins, Jerry H. and S. B. Williams. STUDENT ACTIVITIES IN THE IN-NOVATIVE SCHOOL. Minneapolis: Burgess, 1969.

Roselius, Roland Henry. "A Study of the Extra-Curricular Aspects of Cultural Assimilation on the College Campus." Unpublished Ph.D. dissertation, Ohio State University, 1957.

STUDENT INVOLVEMENT IN EXTRA-CAMPUS ACTIVITY. Philadelphia: U.S. National Student Association, 1963.

Struup, H. TOWARD A PHILOSOPHY OF ORGANIZED STUDENT ACTIVITIES. Minneapolis: University of Minnesota Press, 1964.

Umbarger, Carter C., et al. COLLEGE STUDENTS IN A MENTAL HOSPI-TAL: AN ACCOUNT OF ORGANIZED SOCIAL CONTACTS BETWEEN COLLEGE VOLUNTEERS AND MENTAL PATIENTS IN A HOSPITAL COM-MUNITY. New York: Grune and Stratton, 1962.

Willett, Lynn Howe. "Factors Related to Student Involvement in Student Government Elections." Unpublished Ph.D. dissertation, University of Iowa, 1970.

498

*Williamson, Edward G., W. L. Layton, and M. L. Snoke. A STUDY OF PARTICIPATION IN COLLEGE ACTIVITIES. Minneapolis: University of Minnesota Press, 1954.

Bach, Mary. "Factors Related to Student Participation in Campus Social Organizations," JOURNAL OF SOCIAL PSYCHOLOGY, 54 (August 1961), 337–348.

Bailard, V. "Developing Leadership Through Student Clubs," PERSONNEL AND GUIDANCE JOURNAL, 32 (November 1953), 135–138.

Dole, A. A. "College Students Report on Their Use of Time," PERSONNEL AND GUIDANCE JOURNAL, 37 (May 1959), 633–637.

Findikyan, N. and S. Sells. "Organizational Structure and Similarity of Campus Student Organizations," ORGANIZATIONAL BEHAVIOR AND HUMAN PERFORMANCE, 1 (December 1966), 169–190.

Goldsmith, A. G. and C. C. Crawford. "How College Students Spend Their Time," SCHOOL AND SOCIETY, 27 (March 31, 1928), 401.

Hare, A. P. "An Evaluation of Extracurriculum Activities," SCHOOL REVIEW, 63 (March 1955), 164–168.

Hutchings, R. "Student Union at Cornell University," RECREATION, 40 (September 1946), 296+.

Kalish, R. A. and O. J. Bartos. "Survey of Student Attitudes Toward Campus Activities at the University of Hawaii," PERSONNEL AND GUIDANCE JOURNAL, 39 (December 1960), 292–299.

Muse, W. V. "Management Skill in Student Organizations," PERSONNEL AND GUIDANCE JOURNAL, 48 (June 1970), 842–847.

Nelson, E. "Extra-Class Activities and Student Attitudes," AMERICAN SOCIOLOGICAL REVIEW, 4 (December 1939), 823–826.

Short, R. "Student Activities: A Two-Way Street," TEXAS OUTLOOK, 52 (November 1968), 36–37.

Spencer, S. M. "They Befrind the Mentally Ill: Volunteers from College Campuses," SATURDAY EVENING POST, 230 (October 5, 1957), 19–21+.

Strang, Ruth. "Student Activities and Organizations," in P. F. Valentine, ed. THE AMERICAN COLLEGE. New York: Philosophical Library, 1949.

Stroup, H. "Group Classification in Student Activities," PEABODY JOURNAL OF EDUCATION, 34 (January 1957), 195–204.

Stroup, H. H. "Role of Student Activities in the University," ASSOCIATION OF AMERICAN COLLEGES BULLETIN, 41 (October 1955), 436–447.

Swensen, J. and J. L. Rhulman. "Leisure Activities of a University Sophomore Class," EDUCATIONAL AND PSYCHOLOGICAL MEASUREMENT, 12 (Number 3, 1952), 452–466.

Wesik, J. L. and J. MacMillan. "A Survey of the Activities Interest of Students in a Technical Institute," COLLEGE STUDENT SURVEY, 4 (Spring, 1970), 10–16.

Williamson, E. G. "Learning Versus Fun in College," JOURNAL OF HIGHER EDUCATION, 28 (November 1957), 425–432+.

Wise, W. M. "What Changes in Campus-Life Activities for the Undergraduate Student Will be Necessary or Desirable in the Colleges and Universities?" in NATIONAL CONFERENCE ON HIGHER EDUCATION, CURRENT ISSUES IN HIGHER EDUCATION, 1957. 82–86.

F. THE PROBLEMS OF STUDENTS

Joint Committee on Health Problems in Education. AS OTHERS SEE US. Washington: National Education Association and the American Medical Association, 1959.

Lunden, Walter A. SHOPLIFTING AMONG COLLEGE STUDENTS. Ames: Iowa State University of Science and Technology, 1966.

New Jersey. Legislature. Senate. Committee on Education. REPORT REGARDING THE ALLEGED DISTRIBUTION OF LEWD AND OBSCENE LITERATURE TO STUDENTS AT PATTERSON STATE COLLEGE. Trenton: 1969.

Werner, Oscar H. EVERY COLLEGE STUDENT'S PROBLEMS. New York: Silver, Burdett, 1929.

Wiltsey, Robert Griffin. "Some Relationships Between Verbal Reports of Pleasant and Unpleasant Moods, Sleep Duration and Sleep Quality Variables in College Students." Unpublished Ph.D. dissertation, Rochester University, 1967.

Freedman, Mervin. "Pressures on Students," in G. K. Smith, ed. CURRENT ISSUES IN HIGHER EDUCATION 1965: PRESSURES AND PRIORITIES IN HIGHER EDUCATION. Washington, D.C.: National Education Association, 1965.

Jackson, K. R. and S. G. Clark. "Thefts Among College Students," PERSONNEL AND GUIDANCE JOURNAL, 36 (April 1958), 557–562.

Katz, Joseph. "Sociatal Expectations and Influences," in L. E. Dennis and J. K. Kauffman, eds. THE COLLEGE AND THE STUDENT. Washington: American Council on Education, 1966. 137–140.

Lerner, R. S. and M. Martin. "What Happens to the College Student with a Physical Handicap? PERSONNEL AND GUIDANCE JOURNAL, 34 (October 1955), 80–85.

MacRae, James Bonner. "Responsibility of the College for the Welfare of the Student," CURRENT ISSUES IN HIGHER EDUCATION, 1 (1950), 51–56.

Moderator. "Just How Hygienic is the Campus Cuisine?" in Esther Lloyd-Jones and Herman Estrin, eds. THE AMERICAN STUDENT AND HIS COLLEGE. Boston: Houghton Mifflin, 1967. 101–106.

Tuobeville, G. "Smoking Behavior and Attitudes on a College Campus," SOCIOLOGICAL QUARTERLY, 6 (Spring, 1965), 147–156.

Turner, Ralph. "Pre-Occupation with Competitiveness and Social Acceptance Among American and English College Students," SOCIOMETRY, 23 (1960), 307–325.

F.1. Drugs on Campus

American Association for Health, Physical Education and Recreation. DRUG ABUSE. Washington, 1967.

Barten, James T. PATTERNS OF DRUG USE AMONG COLLEGE STUDENTS IN THE DENVER-BOULDER METROPOLITAN AREA: AN EPIDEMIOLOGICAL AND DEMOGRAPHIC SURVEY. Washington: Bureau of Narcotics and Dangerous Drugs, 1971.

Becker, Howard S. THE OUTSIDERS: STUDIES IN THE SOCIOLOGY OF DEVIANCE, Glencoe, Illinois: Free Press of Glencoe, 1963.

*Blum, Richard, *et al.* THE DREAM SELLERS: PERSPECTIVES ON DRUG DEALERS. San Francisco: Jossey-Bass, 1972.

Blum, Richard H., *et al.* HORATIO ALGER'S CHILDREN: THE ROLE OF THE FAMILY IN THE ORIGIN AND PREVENTION OF DRUG RISK. San Francisco: Jossey-Bass, 1972.

*Blum, Richard H., *et al.* STUDENTS AND DRUGS: COLLEGE AND HIGH SCHOOL OBSERVATIONS. San Francisco: Jossey-Bass, 1969.

Borgatta, Edgar F. SOME PROBLEMS IN THE STUDY OF DRUG USE AMONG COLLEGE STUDENTS. Detroit Michigan: National Association of Student Personnel Administrators, 1966.

Brenner, Joseph H., Robert Coles, and Dermot Meagher. DRUGS AND YOUTH: MEDICAL, PSYCHIATRIC AND LEGAL FACTS. New York: Liveright, 1970.

Carey, James. THE COLLEGE DRUG SCENE. Englewood Cliffs, New Jersey: Prentice Hall, 1968.

Cohen, Allan Y. LSD AND THE STUDENT: APPROACHES TO EDUCATIONAL STRATEGIES. Detroit, Michigan: National Association of Student Personnel Administrators, 1967.

Demos, George D., *et al.* DRUG ABUSE AND YOU. Moravia, New York: Chronicle Guidance Publications, 1968.

*Goldstein, Richard. 1 IN 7: DRUGS ON CAMPUS. New York: Walker, 1966.

Hogan, Robert, *et al.* PERSONALITY CORRELATES OF UNDERGRADUATE MARIJUANA USE. Baltimore, Maryland: Johns Hopkins University, 1969.

Hollander, C., ed. BACKGROUND PAPERS ON STUDENT DRUG INVOLVEMENT. Washington, D.C.: US National Student Association, 1967.

Kaplan, John. MARIJUANA—THE NEW PROHIBITION. New York: World Publishing, 1970.

McLean, Gordon R. and Haskel Bowen. HIGH ON CAMPUS: STUDENT DRUG ABUSE IS THERE AN ANSWER? Wheaton, Illinois: Tyndale House, 1970.

Maddox, G. L., ed. THE DOMESTICATED DRUG: DRINKING AMONG COLLEGIANS. New Haven, Connecticut: College and University Press, 1970.

Milbauer, Barbara and Gerald Leinwand. DRUGS. New York: Washington Square Press, 1970.

New York State Legislature. Joint Committee on Crime, its Causes, Control and Effect on Society. REPORT ON THE DRUG ABUSE PROBLEM AT THE STATE UNIVERSITY OF NEW YORK AT STONY BROOK. Albany: 1968.

*Nowlis, Helen. DRUGS ON THE COLLEGE CAMPUS. Garden City, New York: Doubleday, 1969.

Oursler, Will. MARIJUANA. New York: Hill and Wang, 1968.

Richards, Louise G. and John H. Langer. DRUG TAKING IN YOUTH: AN OVERVIEW OF SOCIAL, PSYCHOLOGICAL, AND EDUCATIONAL ASPECTS. Washington: Office of Scientific Support, U.S. Bureau of Narcotics and Dangerous Drugs, 1971.

Solomon, David, ed. LSD: THE CONSCIOUSNESS EXPANDING DRUG. New York: Putnam, 1964.

Straus, Robert and Selden D. Bacon. DRINKING IN COLLEGE. New Haven, Connecticut: Yale University Press, 1953.

Student Committee on Mental Health. PSYCHEDELICS AND THE COLLEGE STUDENT. Princeton, New Jersey: Princeton University Press, 1967.

U.S. Congress. House Committee of Education and Labor. Select Subcommittee on Education. DRUG ABUSE, HEARINGS. (91st Congress. 1st Session). Washington, D.C.: Government Printing Office, 1970.

Van Dyke, Henry Thomas. YOUTH AND THE DRUG PROBLEM. Boston: Ginn, 1970.

Wise, Francis H. YOUTH AND DRUGS: PREVENTION, DETECTION, AND CURE. New York: Association Press, 1971.

Young, Warren and J. R. Hixson. LSD ON CAMPUS. New York: Dell, 1966.

Atkinson, B. H. and A. T. Brugger. "Do College Students Drink Too Much? Two Deans Reply to this Perennial Question," JOURNAL OF HIGHER EDUCATION, 30 (June 1959), 305–312.

Becker, Howard S. "Ending Campus Drug Incidents," in H. Becker, ed. CAMPUS POWER STRUGGLE. Chicago: Aldine, 1970. 137–152.

Bently, Joseph. "Drink and Drugs on the Campus," in Charles Havice, ed. CAMPUS VALUES. New York: Charles Scribners Sons, 1968.

Booth, Jack. "Being Stoned—It's All in Your Mind," in Christopher Reaske and Robert Wilson jr., eds. STUDENT VOICES/ONE. New York: Random House, 1971.

Bottrill, John H. "Personality Change in LSD Users," THE JOURNAL OF GENERAL PSYCHOLOGY, 80 (April 1969), 157–161.

Bowers, William J. "Trends in College Campus Deviance," COLLEGE STUDENT SURVEY, 5 (Spring, 1971), 20–30.

Brehm, M. L. and K. W. Baek. "Self-Image and Attitudes Toward Drugs," JOURNAL OF PERSONALITY, 36 (June 1968), 299–314.

Bruyn, Henry B. "Control of Dangerous Drugs on University Campuses," JOURNAL OF THE AMERICAN COLLEGE HEALTH ASSOCIATION, 16 (October 1967), 13–19.

Burk, Margaret A. "Speed: the Use of Amphetamines on the Campus," JOURNAL OF THE NATIONAL ASSOCIATION OF WOMEN DEANS AND COUNSELORS, 32 (Spring 1969), 110–114.

502

Caliguri, J. P. "College Student Drug Abuse," CLEARING HOUSE, 44 (September 1969), 50–53.

Casse, Robert M. "Use of a 'Freakout' Control Center," JOURNAL OF COLLEGE STUDENT PERSONNEL, 11 (November 1970), 403–408.

Cohen, Allan. "Psychedelic Drugs and the Student: Educational Strategies," THE JOURNAL OF COLLEGE STUDENT PERSONNEL, 10 (March 1969), 96–101.

Cross, H. J. and G. L. Davis. "College Students' Adjustment and Frequency of Marijuana Use," JOURNAL OF COUNSELING PSYCHOLOGY, 19 (January 1972), 65–67.

Cross, H. J. and Richard G. Keir, "Drug Usage and Attitude Toward Drugs Among College Students," COLLEGE STUDENT SURVEY, 5 (Spring, 1971), 9–15.

Demos, G. D. "Drug Abuse and the New Generation," PHI DETA KAPPAN, 50 (December 1968), 214–217.

Dickenson, F. "Drugs on Campus: A Gallup Poll," READER'S DIGEST, 91 (November 1967), 114–115.

"Drugs," in D. Myrus, ed. THE YOUTH CULTURE. Chicago: Playboy Press, 1971. 56–84.

"Drugs and the Caltech Student," CHEMISTRY, 42 (November 1969), 4, 8–18.

"Drugs on Campus: Gallup Poll," NEWSWEEK, 77 (January 25, 1971), 52.

Druyn, Henry B. "Drugs on the College Campus," PROCEEDINGS, National Association of Student Personnel Administrators, Seattle, (June 1966), 226–236.

Eells, Kenneth. "Marijuana and LSD: a Survey of One College Campus," JOURNAL OF COUNSELING PSYCHOLOGY, 15 (September 1958), 459–467.

Freedman, Daniel X. "On the Use and Abuse of LSD," ARCHIVES OF GENERAL PSYCHIATRY, 18 (March 1968), 330–347.

*Freedman, Mervin and Harvey Powelson. "Drugs on Campus: Turned on and Tuned Out," NATION, 202 (January 31, 1966), 125–128.

Goldstein, R. "Drugs on the Campus," SATURDAY EVENING POST, 239 (May 21, 1966), 40–44+ and (June 4, 1966), 34–38+.

Goldstein, Richard. "The Question of Pot," in Esther Lloyd-Jones and Herman Estrin, eds. THE AMERICAN STUDENT AND HIS COLLEGE. Boston: Houghton Mifflin, 1967. 126–138.

Greenberg, D. S. "Pot and Politics: How They Busted Stony Brook," SCIENCE, 159 (February 9, 1968), 607–611.

Grenspoon, L. "Marijuana: Who Smokes It, and Why," MADEMOISELLE, 73 (May, 1971), 180–181+.

Gusfield, J. R. "The Structural Context of College Drinking," QUARTERLY JOURNAL OF STUDIES ON ALCOHOL, 22 (September 1961), 428–443.

Herr, M. "Drug Puzzle: Student Use of Drugs," MADEMOISELLE, 68 (August 1965), 246–247+.

Hogan, Robert, Donald Mankin, John Conway, and Sherman Fox. "Personality Correlates of Undergraduate Marijuana Use," JOURNAL OF CONSULTING AND CLINICAL PSYCHOLOGY, 35 (August 1970), 58–63.

Imperi, L. L., M. D. Kleber and J. S. Davie. "Use of Hallucinogenic Drugs on Campus," JOURNAL OF THE AMERICAN MEDICAL ASSOCIATION, 204 (June 17, 1968), 1021–1024.

Jessor, R. *et al.* "Expectations of Need Satisfaction and Drinking Patterns of College Students," QUARTERLY JOURNAL OF STUDIES ON ALCOHOL, 29 (March 1968), 101–116.

Kelley, Larry. "Drugs on Campus: Stoned out of Their Minds," TRENTON, 46 (March 1970), 14–21.

*Keniston, Kenneth. "Heads and Seekers: Drugs on Campus, Counter Cultures, and American Society," AMERICAN SCHOLAR, 38 (Winter, 1968–69), 97–112.

King, Francis W. "Marijuana and LSD Usage Among College Students: Prevalence Rate, Frequency and Self-Estimates of Future Use," PSYCHIATRY, 32 (August 1969), 265–276.

Kleber, Herbert D. "Student Use of Hallucinogens," JOURNAL OF THE AMERICAN COLLEGE HEALTH ASSOCIATION, 14 (December 1965), 109–117.

Koch, Stephen. "Busted," NEW REPUBLIC (March 23, 1968), 17–19.

Lake, A. "Drugs: A Student Report," SEVENTEEN, 25 (September 1966), 170–171+.

Larner, J. "College Drug Scene," ATLANTIC, 216 (November 1965), 127–130+.

Liebert, Robert. "Drug Use: Symptom, Disease or Adolescent Experimentation—the Task of Therapy," JOURNAL OF THE AMERICAN COLLEGE HEALTH ASSOCIATION, 16 (Number 1, 1967), 25–29.

Lipinski, E. and B. G. Lipinski. "Motivational Factors in Psycheledic Drug Use by Male College Students," JOURNAL OF THE AMERICAN COLLEGE HEALTH ASSOCIATION, 16 (December 1967), 145–149.

Masters, R. E. L. and Jean Houstan. "From the Varieties of Psychedelic Experience," in Harold Jaffe and John Tyted, eds. THE AMERICAN EXPERIENCE: A RADICAL READER. New York: Harper and Row, 1970. 222–240.

Murphy, B. W., A. M. Leventhal, and M. B. Balter. "Drug Use on the Campus: A Survey of University Health Services and Counseling Centers," JOURNAL OF THE AMERICAN COLLEGE HEALTH ASSOCIATION, 17 (June 1969), 389–402.

Nowlis, Helen H. "Student Drug Use," in F. F. Korten, S. W. Cook, and J. I. Lacey, eds. PSYCHOLOGY AND THE PROBLEMS OF SOCIETY. Washington: American Psychological Association, 1970. 408–419.

Olton, C. S. "Drugs and the Small College," NATIONAL ASSOCIATION OF STUDENT PERSONNEL ADMINISTRATORS JOURNAL, 8 (October 1970), 83–89.

Park, Peter. "Dimensions of Drinking Among Male College Students," SOCIAL PROBLEMS, 14 (Spring 1967), 473–482.

Pearlman, Samuel. "Drug Experiences and Attitudes Among Seniors in a Liberal Arts College," NATIONAL ASSOCIATION OF STUDENT PERSONNEL ADMINISTRATORS JOURNAL, 4 (January 1967), 121–126.

Philip, Anthony F. "The Campus Drug Problem," JOURNAL OF THE AMERICAN COLLEGE HEALTH ASSOCIATION, 161 (December 1967), 150–160.

Pollock, Marion B. "The Drug Abuse Problem: Some Implications for Health Education," JOURNAL OF THE AMERICAN HEALTH ASSOCIATION, 17 (June 1969), 403–411.

Robbins, Edwin S. et al. "College Student Drug Use," AMERICAN JOURNAL OF PSYCHIATRY, 126 (June 1970), 1743–1751.

Sanford, Nevitt and Susan Singer. "Drinking and Personality," in Joseph Katz et al. NO TIME FOR YOUTH. San Francisco: Jossey-Bass, 1968. 348–375.

Schwieder, R. M. and R. G. Koldan. "The Tranquil Society—or Why LSD?" THE RECORD, 70 (April 1968), 627–633.

"Students and Drug Abuse," TODAYS EDUCATION, 58 (March 1969), 35–50.

Suchman, Edward A. "The 'hang-loose' Ethic and the Spirit of Drug Use," JOURNAL OF HEALTH AND SOCIAL BEHAVIOR, 9 (June 1968), 146–155.

Toohey, J. V. "Analysis of Drug Use Behavior at Five American Universities," JOURNAL OF SCHOOL HEALTH, 41 (November 1971), 464–468.

"The Use of Marijuana and LSD on the College Campus," JOURNAL OF THE NATIONAL ASSOCIATION OF WOMEN DEANS AND COUNSELORS, 3 (Spring 1967), 124–128.

Walters, Paul A. "Therapist Bias and Student Use of Illegal Drugs," JOURNAL OF THE AMERICAN COLLEGE HEALTH ASSOCIATION, 16 (October 1967), 30–34.

Warner, Harry. "Alcohol Trends in College Life: Historical Perspective," in George Maddox, ed. THE DOMESTICATED DRUG: DRINKING AMONG COLLEGIANS. New Haven, Connecticut: College and University Press, 1970. 45–80.

Weil, A. T. "Strange Case of the Harvard Drug Scandal," LOOK, 27 (November 5, 1963), 38+.

Wilms, John H. "The Nature of the Mind and the Effect of Drugs Upon It," JOURNAL OF THE NATIONAL ASSOCIATION OF WOMEN DEANS AND COUNSELORS, 31 (Fall, 1967), 24–30.

Yolles, Stanley F. "Student Use of Drugs: Facts and Fables," TEACHING AND LEARNING, (1971), 3–14.

F.2. Dropping Out of the University

Allen, C. M. COMBATING THE DROPOUT PROBLEM. Chicago: Science Research Associates, 1956.

*Astin, Alexander W. COLLEGE DROPOUTS: A NATIONAL PROFILE. Washington, D.C.: Office of Research, American Council on Education, 1972.

Bayley, R. E., jr. "Student Retention and Withdrawal at the University of Nebraska." Unpublished Ph.D. dissertation, University of Nebraska.

Cervantes, L. F. THE DROPOUT. Ann Arbor, Michigan: University of Michigan Press, 1965.

Chase, Clinton I. WHO SHALL PERSIST? Bloomington, Indiana: Indiana University. Bureau of Educational Studies and Testing, 1966.

Cohen, Arthur and Florence Brawer. STUDENT CHARACTERISTICS: PERSONALITY AND DROPOUT PROPENSITY. Washington, D.C.: American Association of Junior Colleges, 1970.

Coker, David L. DIVERSITY OF INTELLECTIVE AND NON-INTELLECTIVE CHARACTERISTICS BETWEEN PERSISTING AND NON-PERSISTING STUDENTS AMONG CAMPUSES. Washington, D.C.: U.S. Office of Education, Bureau of Research, 1968.

Cope, R. G. "Differential Characteristics of Entering Freshman, Environmental Presses, and Attrition at a Liberal Arts College." Unpublished Ph.D. dissertation, University of Michigan, 1967.

Corley, Clifford Lee. "The Incidence of Certain Factors Relating to Drop-Outs from the 1948–1952 Class at the University of Missouri." Unpublished Ph.D. dissertation, University of Missouri, 1954.

Courter, J. F. "A Study of Student Mortality in Six Liberal Arts Colleges in Kansas." Unpublished M.A. thesis, Syracuse University, 1957.

Craven, C. J. "Why We Withdrew." Unpublished Ph.D. dissertation, Syracuse University, 1951.

*Demos, George D. ANALYSIS OF COLLEGE DROPOUTS—SOME MANIFEST AND COVERT REASONS. Washington, D.C.: ERIC Clearinghouse, 1967.

Edwards. T. W. "A Study of Attrition Rates of Students at Southern Illinois University over a Four Year Period of Time." Unpublished Ph.D. dissertation, Indiana University, 1954.

Engineering Manpower Commission. ENGINEERING STUDENT ATTRITION. New York: Engineers' Joint Council, 1963.

Faunce, L. D. "A Study of Within-Term Male Drop Outs at Michigan State College for the School Years 1947–1949." Unpublished Ed.D. thesis, Michigan State College, 1952.

Goble, R. I. "A Study of the Student Dropout Problem at Miami University. Unpublished Ph.D. dissertation, Indiana University, 1956.

Gurin, G., T. Newcomb, and R. Cope. CHARACTERISTICS OF ENTERING FRESHMEN RELATED TO ATTRITION IN THE LITERARY COLLEGE OF A LARGE STATE UNIVERSITY. Office of Education, U.S. Department of Health, Education and Welfare Project No. 1938. Ann Arbor, Michigan: Survey Research Center, Institute for Social Research, University of Michigan, 1968.

Hood, Albert Bullard. "Certain Non-Intellectual Factors Related to Student Attrition at Cornell University." Unpublished Ph.D. dissertation, Cornell University, 1957.

Horler, Frances L. "Factors Related to Withdrawal from the Four Year College of the University of Chicago." Unpublished Ph.D. dissertation, University of Chicago, 1950.

Howard, John. THE HIPPIE COLLEGE DROPOUT, FINAL REPORT. Office of Education, Department of Health, Education and Welfare. Washington, D.C.: Bureau of Research, 1969.

Hunnicutt, John Manley. "An Investigation of the Relation Between the Elements of the Social System and Withdrawals of Student Nurses." Unpublished Ph.D. dissertation, University of Nebraska, 1962.

Iffert, Robert E. RETENTION AND WITHDRAWAL OF COLLEGE STUDENTS. (U.S. Department of Health, Education and Welfare, Bulletin 1958, No. 1). Washington, D.C.: Government Printing Office, 1957.

Iffert, Robert E. and B. S. Clarke. COLLEGE APPLICANTS, ENTRANTS, DROPOUTS. (Bulletin No. 29). Washington, D.C.: U.S. Office of Education, 1965.

Kamens, David Hunt. "Institutional Stratification and Institutional Commitment: Contextual Effects on College Dropout." Unpublished Ph.D. dissertation, Columbia University, 1968.

Kamens, David H. SOCIAL CLASS, COLLEGE CONTEXTS, AND EDUCATIONAL ATTAINMENT: SOCIAL CLASS AND COLLEGE DROPOUT. Boston: Northeastern University, 1967.

Landskov, N. L. "A Survival Study of Three College of Education Classes, with Implications for Adjustment of Admissions Standards." Unpublished Ph.D. dissertation, University of Minnesota, 1946.

Lehr, Milton W. "A Statistical Description of Factors Related to Drop-Outs and Non-Dropouts at Northwestern State College." Unpublished Ph.D. dissertation, University of Oklahoma, 1956.

Lins, L. J. and A. P. Abell. SURVEY OF FALL, 1963, MADISON CAMPUS NEW FRESHMEN WHO LEFT THE MADISON CAMPUS PRIOR TO THE BEGINNING OF THE THIRD SEMESTER AFTER ENTRANCE. Madison, Wisconsin: Office of Institutional Studies, University of Wisconsin, 1966.

Lins, L. J. and A. P. Abell. FOLLOW-UP OF FALL 1958 MADISON CAMPUS NEW FRESHMEN WHO HAD LEFT THE MADISON CAMPUS. Madison, Wisconsin: Wisconsin University, Office of Institutional Studies, 1966.

Lloyd, C. E. "A Study of Scholastically Promising Students Who Withdraw from College Prior to Graduation." Unpublished M.A. thesis, University of Utah, 1955.

Luyten, B. Helene. "Mortality of the Student Body of New York University, 1923–1930." Unpublished Ph.D. dissertation, New York University, 1933.

Merigold, Frank A. THE DEVELOPMENT AND TESTING OF A SCALE TO IDENTIFY MALE DROPOUTS AT LIBERAL ARTS COLLEGES. Boston: Boston College, 1967.

Mock, Kathleen Ranlett and George Yonge. STUDENTS' INTELLECTUAL ATTITUDES, APTITUDE AND PERSISTENCE AT THE UNIVERSITY OF CALIFORNIA. Berkeley, California: Center for Research and Development in Higher Education, University of California, Berkeley, 1969.

Moore, Alice Joseph. CATHOLIC COLLEGE STUDENT RETENTION IN THE UNITED STATES. Washington, D.C.: Catholic University in America Press, 1957.

Nasatir, David. "Social Sources of Academic Failure: A Contextual Analysis." Unpublished Ph.D. dissertation, University of California, Berkeley, 1966.

Panos, R. J. and A. W. Astin. ATTRITION AMONG COLLEGE STU-

DENTS. (ACE Research Reports, No. 4). Washington, D.C.: Office of Research, American Council on Education, 1967.

Pervin, L. A. DISSATISFACTION WITH COLLEGE AND THE COLLEGE DROP-OUT: A TRANSACTIONAL APPROACH. (Office of Education, U.S. Department of Health, Education and Welfare Project No. 6–8421). Princeton, New Jersey: Princeton University, 1967.

Pervin, L. A. SOURCES OF STRAIN IN THE COLLEGE ENVIRONMENT AS RELATED TO STUDENT DISSATISFACTION AND THE DROPOUT. Princeton, New Jersey: Princeton University, 1967.

Pervin, L. A. *et al*, eds. THE COLLEGE DROPOUT AND THE UTILIZATION OF TALENT. Princeton, New Jersey: Princeton University Press, 1966.

Philip, W. A. "An Investigation of Undergraduate Student Withdrawals from the University of Mississippi." Unpublished Ph.D. dissertation, University of Mississippi, 1954.

Pitcher, Robert Walter and Babette Blaushild. WHY COLLEGE STUDENTS FAIL. New York: Funk & Wagnalls, 1970.

Russell, J. W. "A Comparison of Michigan State College First Term Freshman Drop-Outs and Non-Drop-Outs According to Certain Factors," Unpublished Ph.D. dissertation, Michigan State College, 1952.

Ryle, Anthony. STUDENT CASUALTIES. Baltimore, Maryland: Penguin Books, 1969.

Scoresby, J. E. "A Study to Determine the Relationship of Anticipated and Actual Perception of College Environment to Attrition and Persistance at Brigham Young University." Unpublished M.A. thesis, Brigham Young University, 1962.

Slocum, W. L. ACADEMIC MORTALITY AT THE STATE COLLEGE OF WASHINGTON. Pullman, Washington: State College of Washington, 1945.

Snyder, Fred A. and Clyde E. Blocker. A PROFILE OF NON-PERSISTING STUDENTS. Harrisburg, Pennsylvania: Harrisburg Area Community College, 1970.

Stucky, Milo O. and Kenneth E. Anderson. A STUDY OF PERSISTENCE IN COLLEGE ATTENDANCE IN RELATION TO PLACEMENT-TEST SCORES AND GRADE POINT AVERAGES. Lawrence, Kansas: University of Kansas, School of Education, 1959.

Suczek, R. F. and E. Alfert. PERSONALITY CHARACTERISTICS OF COLLEGE DROPOUTS: FINAL REPORT. (U.S. Department of Health, Education and Welfare Cooperative Research Project No. 5–8232.) Berkeley, California: University of California, Berkeley, 1966.

Van Erdewyk, Zeno M. VARIABLES RELATED TO PERSISTENCE, TRANSFER AND ATTRITION OF ENGINEERING STUDENTS. Grand Forks, North Dakota: North Dakota University, College of Education, 1967.

Warnecke, Richard B. "Dropouts from Collegiate Nursing: A Typological Study of Role Conflict." Unpublished Ph.D. dissertation, Duke University, 1966.

Astin, A. W. "Personal and Environmental Factors Associated with College

Dropouts Among High Aptitude Students," JOURNAL OF EDUCATIONAL PSYCHOLOGY, 55 (August, 1964), 219–227.

Bahn, Charles, Mary Cox, and Dorothy Lee. "Differential Failure Rates in College: Implicit Educational Concepts," in Galen Drewry, ed. THE INSTRUC-TIONAL PROCESS AND INSTITUTIONAL RESEARCH: PROCEEDINGS OF THE SEVENTH ANNUAL FORUM OF THE ASSOCIATION FOR INSTITU-TIONAL RESEARCH. N.p. Association for Institutional Research, 1967, 117–124.

Balaban, V. and H. F. French. "Preventing College Crack-ups," PARENTS MAGAZINE, 38 (February, 1963), 64+.

Banzet, E. M. "Some Drop Out," in P. L. Dressel, ed. EVALUATION IN THE BASIC COLLEGE AT MICHIGAN STATE UNIVERSITY, New York: Harper and Row, 1958, 65–75.

Bard, B. "College Students: Why They Drop Out," EDUCATION DIGEST, 34 (March, 1969), 18–21.

Bayer, A. E. "The College Drop-Out: Factors Affecting Senior College Com-pletion," SOCIOLOGY OF EDUCATION, 41 (Summer, 1968), 305–316.

Bragg, Emma W. "A Study of Student Withdrawal at 'W.U.,'" JOURNAL OF EDUCATIONAL PSYCHOLOGY, 47 (April, 1956), 199–202.

Brown, I. G. "Identifying College Dropouts with Minnesota Counseling Inventory," PERSONNEL AND GUIDANCE JOURNAL, 39 (December, 1960), 208–282.

Chamberlain, W. et al. "Why I Am Quitting College," LOOK, 22 (June 10, 1958), 91–94+.

Chambers, I. M. "College Admission Policy to Reduce Attrition," JUNIOR COLLEGE JOURNAL, 31 (January, 1961), 250–254.

Cope, R. G. "Limitations of Attrition Rates and Causes Given for Dropping Out of College," JOURNAL OF COLLEGE STUDENT PERSONNEL, 9 (Novem-ber, 1968), 386–392.

Cottle, Thomas. "Zero Man: Anatomy of an Academic Failure," CHANGE, 4 (November, 1972), 49–55.

Cowhig, J. D. "Why Do They Leave College?" SCHOOL REVIEW, 71 (Autumn, 1963), 330–336.

Doughan, R. P. "College Dropouts: Dismissed vs. Withdrew," PERSONNEL AND GUIDANCE JOURNAL, 46 (March, 1968), 685–690.

Dole, A. A. "Iffert Revisited: Persisters and Defaulters," JOURNAL OF COLLEGE STUDENT PERSONNEL, 10 (May, 1969), 185–192.

Dole, A. A. "Stability of Reasons for Going to College," JOURNAL OF EDUCATIONAL RESEARCH, 63 (April, 1970), 373–378.

Eckland, B. K. "A Source of Error in College Attrition Studies." SOCI-OLOGY OF EDUCATION, 38 (Fall, 1964), 60–72.

Eurich, A. "College Failure," SCHOOL AND SOCIETY, 37 (May 27, 1933), 692–696.

Edelston, H. "Educational Failure with High Intelligence Quotient: A Clinical Study," JOURNAL OF GENETIC PSYCHOLOGY, 77 (September, 1950), 85–116.

Ford. D. H. and H. B. Urban. "College Dropouts: Successes or Failures?" in L. A. Pervin, L. E. Reik, and W. Dalrymple, eds. THE COLLEGE DROPOUT AND THE UTILIZATION OF TALENT. Princeton, New Jersey: Princeton University Press, 1966, 83–106.

Fox, D. E. "Presentation of Attrition Study," in E. J. McGrath, ed. THE LIBERAL ARTS COLLEGE'S RESPONSIBILITY FOR THE INDIVIDUAL STUDENT. New York: Teachers College Press, 1966, 86–120.

Freeman, N. L. *et al.* "Engineering Student Dropouts: Report of the ASEE Sub-Committee on Dropouts of Engineering Students." JOURNAL OF ENGINEERING EDUCATION, 50 (April, 1960), 611–619.

Gadzella, B. M. "Factors Influencing Students to Withdraw from College," COLLEGE STUDENT SURVEY, 1 (No. 2, 1967), 55–60.

Gauss, Christian. "Why Students Fail," SATURDAY EVENING POST, 202 (September 20, 1930), 27, 117, 120–122.

Gekoski, N. and S. Schwartz. "Student Mortality and Related Factors," JOURNAL OF EDUCATIONAL RESEARCH, 54 (January, 1961), 192–194.

Gibbs, D. N. "Student Failure and Social Maladjustment," PERSONNEL AND GUIDANCE JOURNAL, 43 (February, 1965), 580–585.

Ginott, Haim. "The Affluent Drop-Out," in Alexander Klein, ed. NATURAL ENEMIES? YOUTH AND THE CLASH OF GENERATIONS, New York: Lippincott, 1969.

Gould, S. C. "How Can We Help the Failing College Student? HIGH POINTS, 45 (February, 1963), 8–18.

Grace, H. A. "Personality Factors and College Attrition," PEABODY JOURNAL OF EDUCATION, 35 (July, 1957), 36–40.

Hackman, J. R. and W. S. Dysinger. "Commitment to College as a Factor in Student Attrition," SOCIOLOGY OF EDUCATION, 43 (Summer, 1970), 311–324.

Harrison, R. "Leaving College Because of Emotional Problems," STUDENT MEDICINE, 4 (April, 1956), 49–60.

Heywood, J. "Report on Student Wastage," UNIVERSITIES QUARTERLY, 25 (Spring, 1971), 189–237.

Holmes, C. H. "Why They Left College: A Study of Voluntary Freshman Withdrawals from the College of Liberal Arts at Syracuse University," COLLEGE AND UNIVERSITY, 34 (Spring, 1959), 295–300.

Iffert, R. E. "Drop-outs: Nature and Causes: Effects on Student, Family and Society," CURRENT ISSUES IN HIGHER EDUCATION, 1956, 94–102.

Iffert, R. E. "Student Retention and Withdrawal Study," COLLEGE AND UNIVERSITY, 30 (July, 1955), 406–411.

Ikenberry, Stanley. "Factors in College Persistence," JOURNAL OF COUNSELING PSYCHOLOGY, 8 (Winter, 1961), 322–329.

Irvine, D. W. "Graduation and Withdrawal: an Eight-Year Follow-Up," COLLEGE AND UNIVERSITY, 41 (Fall, 1965), 32–40.

Jones, E. S. "Why Students Fail in College," ASSOCIATION OF AMERICAN COLLEGES BULLETIN, 39 (May, 1953), 282–287.

510

Keats, J. "College Majority: Dropouts," LIFE, 54 (June 21, 1963), 70–74+.

*Keniston, Kenneth. "Psychosocial Issues in Talented College Dropouts," PSYCHIATRY, 33 (No. 1, 1970), 1–20.

Knoell, D. M. "A Critical Review of Research on College Dropout," in L. A. Pervin, et al, eds. THE COLLEGE DROPOUT AND THE UTILIZATION OF TALENT. Princeton, New Jersey: Princeton University Press, 1966, 63–81.

Knoell, D. M. "Institutional Research on Retention and Withdrawal," in H. T. Sprague, ed. RESEARCH ON COLLEGE STUDENTS: INSTITUTE LECTURES CONSIDERING RECENT RESEARCH ON COLLEGE STUDENTS' MOTIVATION, VALUES AND ATTITUDES AND CAMPUS CULTURES. Boulder, Colorado: Western Interstate Commission for Higher Eduation and Berkeley, California: Center for Higher Education, 1960.

Knoell, D. M. "Needed Research on College Dropouts," in J. R. Montgomery, ed. PROCEEDINGS OF THE RESEARCH CONFERENCE ON COLLEGE DROPOUTS. U.S. Department of Health, Education and Welfare Cooperative Research Project No. F–065. Knoxville, Tennessee: University of Tennessee, 1964, 54–83.

Koelsche, C. L. "A Study of the Student Drop-Out Problem at Indiana University," JOURNAL OF EDUCATIONAL RESEARCH, 49 (January, 1956), 357–364.

Levenson, E., N. Stockhamer, and A. H. Feiner. "Family Transactions in the Etiology of Dropping Out of College," CONTEMPORARY PSYCHOANALYSIS, 3 (Spring, 1967), 134–152.

Love, R. A. "Call for Action: Shocking Mortality Rate of Evening Session Undergraduates," SCHOOL AND SOCIETY, 70 (October 8, 1949), 227–231.

McNeeley, J. H. "College Student Mortality Studies," JOURNAL OF AMERICAN ASSOCIATION OF COLLEGE REGISTRARS, 15 (1939),119–124.

Marsh, L. M. "College Dropouts: A Review," PERSONNEL AND GUIDANCE JOURNAL, 44 (January, 1966), 475–481.

Mayer, Tom. "So You Want to Be a Dropout," in ATLANTIC, ed. THE TROUBLED CAMPUS. Boston: Little, Brown, 1966.

Nasatir, David. "A Contextual Analysis of Academic Failure," SCHOOL REVIEW, 71 (Autumn, 1963), 290–298.

Newson, N. W. and M. W. Sturm. "Comparison of the College and High School Marks of Non-Graduating College Students," JOURNAL OF AMERICAN ASSOCIATION OF COLLEGE REGISTRARS, 12 (1937), 217–221.

Panos, R. J. and A. W. Astin. "Attrition Among College Students," AMERICAN EDUCATIONAL RESEARCH JOURNAL, 5 (January, 1968), 57–72.

Pervin, L. A. "The Later Academic, Vocational and Personal Success of College Dropouts," in L. A. Pervin, L. E. Reik, and W. Dalrymple, eds. THE COLLEGE DROPOUT AND THE UTILIZATION OF TALENT. Princeton, New Jersey: Princeton University Press, 1966, 37–62.

Pervin, L. A. and D. B. Rubin. "Student Dissatisfaction and the College Dropout: a Transactional Approach," JOURNAL OF SOCIAL PSYCHOLOGY, 72 (August, 1967), 285–295.

Pervin,.L. A. *et al.* "The Dropout in Conflict with Society," in L. B. Mayhew, ed. HIGHER EDUCATION IN THE REVOLUTIONARY DECADES. Berkeley, California: McCutchan, 1967, 265–279.

Phelps, M. O. and A. W. Astin. "Recent Findings from the ACE Research Program: Implications for College Choice and Admissions," COLLEGE AND UNIVERSITY JOURNAL, 44 (Summer, 1969), 341–356.

Quarles, B. "Student Separations from College: An Overview," ASSOCIATION OF AMERICAN COLLEGES BULLETIN, 35 (October, 1949), 404–409.

Remmers, H. H. "A Diagnostic and Remedial Study of Potentially and Actually Failing Students at Purdue University," PURDUE UNIVERSITY STUDIES IN HIGHER EDUCATION, 9 (1928).

Rossman, J. E. and B. A. Kirk. "Factors Related to Persistence and withdrawal Among University Students," JOURNAL OF COUNSELING PSYCHOLOGY, 17 (January, 1970), 56–62.

Sage, J. R. "Freshman Mortality," PROCEEDINGS OF AMERICAN ASSOCIATION OF COLLEGE REGISTRARS, (1927), 40–48.

Sanford, Nevitt. "Loss of Talent," in Fred F. Harcleroad, ed. ISSUES OF THE SEVENTIES. San Francisco: Jossey-Bass, 1970, 56–68.

Sexton, V. S. "Factors Contributing to Attrition in College Populations: Twenty-five Years of Research," JOURNAL OF GENERAL PSYCHOLOGY, 72 (1965), 301–326.

Shaeffer, Ruth G. "Campus Recruiting—More Dropouts?" CONFERENCE BOARD RECORD, 9 (March, 1972), 14–20.

Sherman, R. B. "College Drop-Outs: an Overview," JOURNAL OF EDUCATIONAL SOCIOLOGY, 29 (April, 1956), 347–350.

Slater, J. M. "Influences of Students' Perceptions and Persistence in the Undergraduate College," JOURNAL OF EDUCATIONAL RESEARCH, 54 (Summer, 1960), 3–8.

Slater, M. "Perception: a Context for the Consideration of Persistence and Attrition Among College Men," PERSONNEL AND GUIDANCE JOURNAL, 35 (March, 1957), 435–440.

Slocum, W. L. "Social Factors Involved in Academic Mortality," COLLEGE AND UNIVERSITY, 3 (No. 1, 1956), 53–64.

Snyder, L. M. "Why Do They Leave," JOURNAL OF HIGHER EDUCATION, 11 (January, 1940), 26–32.

Sorenson, David. "The Return of the College Dropout," in G. B. Blaine, jr. and C. C. McArthur, eds. EMOTIONAL PROBLEMS OF THE STUDENT. New York: Appleton-Century-Crofts, 1971, 255–267.

*Spady, W. G. "Dropouts from Higher Education: An Interdisciplinary Review and Synthesis," INTERCHANGE, 1 (April, 1970), 64–85.

*Spady, W. G. "Dropouts from Higher Education: Toward an Empirical Model," INTERCHANGE, 2 (No. 3, 1971), 38–62.

Stordahl, Kalmer, "Influences on Voluntary Withdrawal from College," COLLEGE AND UNIVERSITY, 45 (Winter, 1970), 163–171.

Summerskill, John. "Dropouts from College," in Nevitt Sanford, ed. THE AMERICAN COLLEGE. New York: Wiley, 1964, 627–665.

Vaughan, R. P. "College Dropouts: Dismissed vs. Withdrew," PERSONNEL AND GUIDANCE JOURNAL, 46 (March, 1968), 685–689.

Waller, C. "Research Related to College Persistence and Withdrawal," COLLEGE AND UNIVERSITY, 39 (Spring, 1964), 281–294.

Warman, R. E. "Study of Applicants for Readmission to College," PERSONNEL AND GUIDANCE JOURNAL, 34 (May, 1956), 553–558.

West, R. M. "Student Mortality, Student Survival and Student Accounting," in E. Hudelson, ed. PROBLEMS OF COLLEGE EDUCATION. Minneapolis, Minnesota: University of Minnesota Press, 1928, 199–209.

Whittaker, D. "Psychological Adjustment of Intellectual, Non-Conformist, Collegiate Dropouts," ADOLESCENCE, 6 (Winter, 1971), 415–424.

Williams, R. L. "Academic Records of Students Eliminated from the University of Michigan," SCHOOL AND SOCIETY, 47 (April 16, 1938), 515–520.

Williams, V. "The College Dropout: Qualities of His Environment," PERSONNEL AND GUIDANCE JOURNAL, 45 (May, 1967), 878–882.

F.3. Students Who Change Schools

ACADEMIC PERFORMANCE OF COLLEGE OF SAN MATEO TRANSFER STUDENTS AT THE UNIVERSITY OF CALIFORNIA AND STATE COLLEGES. San Mateo, California: San Mateo College, 1968.

Andrews, Hans A. EVALUATING THE FIRST SEMESTER SUCCESS OF JUNIOR COLLEGE TRANSFER TO THE UNIVERSITY OF MISSOURI. Washington, D.C.: ERIC Clearinghouse, 1968.

Barger, Ben, et al. TRANSFER STUDENTS SPEAK OUT. Gainesville, Florida: Florida University, 1968.

Cherniack, Saralee and Kathleen R. Mock. IMPRESSIONS FROM INTERVIEWS OF TRANSFER STUDENTS PARTICIPATING IN A STUDY OF SELECTED STUDENT TYPES ON THREE UNIVERSITY OF CALIFORNIA CAMPUSES. Berkeley, California: University of California Center for Research and Development in Higher Education, 1968.

Florida. Board of Control. THE ACADEMIC PERFORMANCE OF FLORIDA JUNIOR COLLEGE TRANSFER STUDENTS IN FLORIDA DEGREE-GRANTING INSTITUTIONS, FALL TERM 1959. Tallahassee, Florida: 1960.

Fulco, Jean. JUNIOR COLLEGE TRANSFER STUDENTS' NEEDS AND EVALUATION OF STUDENT PERSONNEL SERVICES. Washington, D.C.: ERIC Clearing House, 1968.

Gold, Ben K. INTERVIEW AND QUESTIONNAIRE FOLLOW-UP STUDY OF L.A.C.C. TRANSFERS ATTENDING UCLA, SPRING 1968. Los Angeles: Los Angeles City College, 1968.

Groesbeck, Edward G. "From Community College to University: Interrelations of Certain Selected Adjustment Factors." Unpublished Ph.D. dissertation, University of Michigan, 1954.

Hartman, Eugene L. A COMPARISON OF SELECTED TRANSFER STUDENTS WITH A MATCHED POPULATION OF NATIVE STUDENTS. Washington, D.C.: ERIC Clearing House, 1968.

Ihrig, James P. JUNIOR COLLEGE TRANSFERS AND THE ENVIRON-MENTAL ASSESSMENT TECHNIQUE. Washington, D.C.: ERIC Clearing House, 1968.

Johnson, Charles Eugene. A STUDY OF THE SCHOLASTIC ACHIEVE-MENT OF JUNIOR COLLEGE TRANSFER STUDENTS AT THE UNIVER-SITY OF MISSOURI. Columbia, Missouri: Missouri University, 1965.

*Knoell, Dorothy M. and Leland L. Medsker. FROM JUNIOR TO SENIOR COLLEGE—A NATIONAL STUDY OF THE TRANSFER STUDENT. Washington, D.C.: American Council on Education, 1965.

Lee, Donald C. and Sidney Suslow. A DIFFERENTIAL STUDY OF CALI-FORNIA JUNIOR COLLEGE TRANSFER STUDENTS AT THE UNIVERSITY OF CALIFORNIA, BERKELEY. Berkeley, California: California University, Office of Institutional Research, 1966.

Shoemaker, George K. "A Follow-Up of Certain College Transfer Students Who Were Scholastically Deficient on Admission to the University of Missouri." Unpublished Ph.D. dissertation, University of Missouri, 1951.

Thompson, Adoulphus P. "Factors Related to the Academic Achievement of Students Who Transferred to the College of Literature, Science and the Arts at the University of Michigan from Four Year Institutions in the State." Unpublished Ph.D. Dissertation, University of Michigan, 1959.

Tingey, Dale Thomas. "A Study of the Guidance Problems of Washington Junior College Students Transferring to the State Four Year Institutions in Washington." Unpublished Ph.D. dissertation, State College of Washington, 1958.

F.4. The Role of Counseling in Higher Education

Blaine, Graham B. and Charles C. McArthur, et al. EMOTIONAL PROB-LEMS OF THE STUDENT. New York: Appleton-Century-Crofts, 1961.

AN EXPERIMENTAL WORKSHOP IN THE EMOTIONAL PROBLEMS OF COLLEGE STUDENTS, REPORT OF THE ANNUAL WORKSHOP IN EMOTIONAL PROBLEMS OF COLLEGE STUDENTS. Greeley: Colorado State College, Counseling and Testing Center, 1967.

Farnsworth, Dana L. MENTAL HEALTH IN COLLEGE AND UNIVER-SITY. Cambridge: Harvard University Press, 1957.

Farnsworth, Dana. PSYCHIATRY, EDUCATION, AND THE YOUNG ADULT. Springfield, Illinois: Charles C. Thomas, 1966.

Gallagher, James J. "An Investigation Into Factors Differentiating College Students Who Discontinue Non-directive Counseling From College Students Who Continue Counseling." Unpublished Ph.D. dissertation, Pennsylvania State University, 1952.

Gehman, Winfield Scott, jr. "Analysis of a Program Involving Required Psychological Counseling and Other Services for a College Population Having Serious Scholastic Difficulties." Unpublished Ph.D. dissertation, Pennsylvania State University, 1951.

Ginsberg, Ethel L. THE COLLEGE AND STUDENT HEALTH. New York: National Tuberculosis Association, 1955.

Harvin, Ann Fredrina. "Social Factors in Student Counseling Needs: A Comparative Study of Student Counseling Clients and Non-clients Among College Freshmen." Unpublished Ph.D. dissertation, Washington State University, 1956.

Heston, Joseph E. and Frick, Willard B., eds. COUNSELING FOR THE LIBERAL ARTS CAMPUS: THE ALBION SYMPOSIUM. Yellow Springs, Ohio: Antioch Press, 1968.

International Conference on Student Mental Health (First Princeton, New Jersey, 1956), (ed. by Daniel H. Funkenstein). THE STUDENT MENTAL HEALTH AN INTERNATIONAL VIEW. London: World Federation for Mental Health, 1959.

Jesness, Carl Frandall. THE EFFECTS OF COUNSELING ON THE SELF-PERCEPTIONS OF COLLEGE MEN. University of Minnesota, 1955.

Kulick, William. "Personality Traits and Academic Standing of Probationary Engineering Students Before and After Counseling: An Evaluation of the Effectiveness of Non-directive Counseling by Means of the Rorschach Test." Unpublished Ph.D. dissertation, New York University, 1953.

Liebert, Roland, ed. STUDENTS, STRESS, AND THE COLLEGE EXPERIENCE. Washington, D.C.: U.S. National Student Association, 1965.

Long, Nicholas J. and Jody Long. CONFLICT AND COMFORT IN COLLEGE: MENTAL HEALTH OF THE COLLESCENT. Belmont, California: Wadsworth, 1970.

Mechanic, David. STUDENTS UNDER STRESS: A STUDY IN THE SOCIAL PSYCHOLOGY OF ADAPTATION. New York: Free Press, 1962.

Shoben, Edward J. STUDENTS, STRESS, AND THE COLLEGE EXPERIENCE. Washington, D.C.: Council Press, 1966.

Speegle, Philip Tenney. "The Effectiveness of Two Techniques of Counseling with Students on Academic Probation." Unpublished Ed.D. dissertation, North Texas State University, 1962.

Stroup, Herbert. THE COLLEGE STUDENT UNDER STRESS. St. Louis, Missouri: United Ministries in Higher Education, N.D.

Tolle, Donald J. IDENTIFICATION OF TROUBLESOME PROBLEMS AFFECTING ST. PETERSBURG JUNIOR COLLEGE STUDENTS, WITH IMPLICATIONS FOR GUIDANCE PROGRAM IMPROVEMENT. Tallahassee: Florida State University, 1957.

Webb, S. C. and D. G. Crowder. THE PSYCHOLOGICAL NEEDS OF EMORY COLLEGE STUDENTS. (Research Memorandum 861). Atlanta, Georgia: Testing and Counseling Service, Emory University, 1961.

Wedge, B. M., ed. THE PSYCHO-SOCIAL PROBLEMS OF COLLEGE MEN. New Haven: Yale University Press, 1958.

Williams, Jesse F. and Angela Kitzinger. HEALTH FOR COLLEGE STUDENTS. New York: Harper and Row, 1963.

Atkinson, J. M. "Suicide and the Student," UNIVERSITIES QUARTERLY, 23 (Spring, 1969), 213–224.

Baker, R. W. "Incidence of Psychological Disturbance in College Students," JOURNAL OF THE AMERICAN COLLEGE HEALTH ASSOCIATION, 13 (April, 1965), 532–540.

Blaine, Graham B., jr. "Stress and Distress and Identity Formation in College and High School," JOURNAL OF THE NATIONAL ASSOCIATION OF WOMEN DEANS AND COUNSELORS, 27 (October, 1963), 25–31.

Blos, Peter. "Psychological Counseling of College Students," in Theodore Newcomb, ed. THE ADOLESCENT. New York: Dryden Press, 1953, 670–682.

Brown, L. E. and A. Nemir. "Early Detection of Emotional Stress: Integration of Two Campus Resources," PERSONNEL AND GUIDANCE JOURNAL, 33 (April, 1955), 456–459.

Brown, O. H. and H. G. Richek. "Mental Health of Commuter College Students," MENTAL HYGIENE, 52 (July, 1968), 354–359.

Burman, A. C. "Emotional Adjustment of Junior College Students," JUNIOR COLLEGE JOURNAL, 24 (April, 1954), 491–496.

Carey, R. W. "Student Protest and the Counselor," PERSONNEL AND GUIDANCE JOURNAL, 48 (November, 1969), 185–191.

Carlson, H. B. "Characteristics of an Acute Confusional State in College Students," AMERICAN JOURNAL OF PSYCHIATRY, 114 (April, 1958), 900–909.

Carmen, L. R., et al. "Use of the Harvard Psychiatric Service by Athletes and Non-Athletes," MENTAL HEALTH, 52 (January, 1968), 134–137.

Conley, William. "The Role of the Individual Student in the Personnel Program," in George Donovan, ed. COLLEGE AND UNIVERSITY PERSONNEL SERVICES: PROCEEDINGS AS THE CATHOLIC UNIVERSITY OF AMERICA WORKSHOP ON ORGANIZATION AND ADMINISTRATION OF COLLEGE AND UNIVERSITY STUDENT PERSONNEL SERVICES, 1961. Washington, D.C: Catholic University of America Press, 1962.

Cross, K. P. "New Students and New Contours in Student Personnel Administration," NATIONAL ASSOCIATION OF WOMEN DEANS AND COUNSELORS JOURNAL, 35 (Winter, 1972), 49–58.

Darling, C. D. "One Year's Experience with Psychosis," STUDENT MEDICINE, 3 (April, 1955), 102–109.

De-Nour, A. K. and P. Noy. "Emotional Difficulties of Students at the Hebrew University," MENTAL HYGIENE, 52 (July, 1968), 360–366.

Elkins, D. "Students Face Their Problems," ENGLISH JOURNAL, 38 (November, 1949), 498–503.

Ellis, Ving. "Students who Seek Psychiatric Help," in Joseph Katz, et al, ed. NO TIME FOR YOUTH. San Francisco: Jossey-Bass, 1968, 318–346.

Etheridge, R. "Social Issues of the Day and Their Effect on Student Affairs Work," NATIONAL ASSOCIATION OF WOMEN DEANS AND COUNSELORS JOURNAL," 35 (Spring, 1972), 98–103.

Farnsworth, Dana L. "The Liberal Arts College's Responsibility For the Emotional Stability of Students," in E. J. McGrath, ed. THE LIBERAL ARTS COLLEGE'S RESPONSIBILITY FOR THE INDIVIDUAL STUDENT. New York: Teacher College Press, Columbia University, 1966, 1–21.

Farnsworth, D. L. "Maturity Through Student Counseling," PHI DELTA KAPPAN, 36 (February, 1955), 181–186+.

Farnsworth, Dana L. "Who Really Helps Our Students," in Robert L.

516

Sutherland, *et al*. PERSONALITY FACTORS ON THE COLLEGE CAMPUS. Austin: The Hogg Foundation for Mental Health, University of Texas, 1962, 93–106.

Foreman, Milton E. "Some Empirical Correlates of Psychological Health," JOURNAL OF COUNSELING PSYCHOLOGY, 13 (1966), 3–11.

Form, A. L. "Measurement of Student Attitudes toward Counseling Services," PERSONNEL AND GUIDANCE JOURNAL, 32 (October, 1953), 84–87.

Form, A. L. "Users and Non Users of Counseling Services: Michigan State College," PERSONNEL AND GUIDANCE JOURNAL, 32 (December, 1953), 209–213.

Frank, Alan. "Patterns of Student Stress," in Lawrence Dennis and Joseph Kauffman, eds. THE AMERICAN COLLEGE AND THE STUDENT. Washington: American Council on Education, 1966, 354–358.

Friedenberg, E. Z. "Measurement of Student Conceptions of the Role of a College Advisory System," EDUCATIONAL AND PSYCHOLOGICAL MEASUREMENT, 10 (Number 3, 1950), 545–568.

Good, J. E. and F. P. Robinson. "Feeling as a Criterion of Success in Different Types of Counseling Interviews," EDUCATIONAL AND PSYCHOLOGICAL MEASUREMENT, 11 (Number 4, 1951), 639–645.

Harford, E. J. "Counsel to Students Fresh from the Service," PEABODY JOURNAL OF EDUCATION, 34 (March, 1957), 284–289.

Harvey, William. "Identity and Depression in Students Who Fail," in L. A. Pervin, *et al.*, eds. THE COLLEGE DROPOUT AND THE UTILIZATION OF TALENT. Princeton, New Jersey: Princeton University Press, 1966, 223–236.

Hedquist, F. J. and B. K. Weinhold. "Behavioral Group Counseling with Socially Anxious and Unassertive College Students," JOURNAL OF COUNSELING PSYCHOLOGY,17 (May, 1970), 237–242.

Hiltner, Seward. "Religious Counseling," in Erich Walter, ed. RELIGION AND THE STATE UNIVERSITY. Ann Arbor: University of Michigan Press, 1958, 214–225.

Jackson, Donald. "Crack-Ups on the Campus," in Esther Lloyd-Jones and Herman Estrin, eds. THE AMERICAN STUDENT AND HIS COLLEGE. Boston: Houghton Mifflin, 1967, 139–141.

Kamm, R. B. "Inventory of Student Personnel Services," EDUCATIONAL AND PSYCHOLOGICAL MEASUREMENT, 10 (Number 3, 1950), 537–544.

King, P. T. and R. W. Matteson. "Student Perception of Counseling Center Services," PERSONNEL AND GUIDANCE JOURNAL, 37 (May, 1958) 358–364.

King, S. H. "Emotional Problems of College Students: Facts and Priorities," BULLETIN OF THE AMERICAN ASSOCIATION OF UNIVERSITY PROFESSORS, 50 (December, 1964), 327–332.

Kirkendall, Lester A. "An Emerging Morality and the College Counselor," in Joseph C. Heston and Willard Frick, eds. COUNSELING FOR THE LIBERAL ARTS CAMPUS. Yellow Springs, Ohio: Antioch Press, 1968, 45–71.

Klemer, R. H. "Student Attitudes toward Guidance in Sexual Morality," MARRIAGE AND FAMILY LIVING, 24 (August, 1962), 260–264.

Kysar, J. E. "Preventive Psychiatry on the College Campus," COMMUNITY MENTAL HEALTH JOURNAL, 2 (Spring, 1966), 27–34.

Lono, J. Mark. "Student Suicides," in Esther Lloyd-Jones and Herman Estrin, eds. THE AMERICAN STUDENT AND HIS COLLEGE. Boston: Houghton Mifflin, 1967, 142–148.

McKeachie, Wilbert. "Anxiety in the College Classroom," in Theodore Newcomb, ed. THE ADOLESCENT. New York: Dryden Press, 1953, 576–582.

McNeil, Elton B. "Is Counseling a Rat Fink Operation? PSYCHOLOGY IN THE SCHOOLS, 2 (January, 1965), 24–31.

Matteson, R. W. "Self-perceptions of Students Seeking Counseling," PERSONNEL AND GUIDANCE JOURNAL, 36 (April, 1958), 545–548.

Monks, J. and C. Heath. "A Classification of Academic, Social and Personal Problems for Use in a College Student Health Departments," STUDENT MEDICINE, 2 (April, 1954), 44–62.

Passow, A. H. "Identifying and Counseling the Gifted College Student," JOURNAL OF HIGHER EDUCATION, 28 (January, 1957), 21–29+.

Paulsen, J. A. "College Students in Trouble: Emotionally Disturbed Students," ATLANTIC, 214 (July, 1964), 96–101.

Peck, Robert F. "Student Mental Health: The Range of Personality Patterns in a College Population," in Robert L. Sutherland, et al. eds. PERSONALITY FACTORS ON THE COLLEGE CAMPUS. Austin: The Hogg Foundation for Mental Health, University of Texas, 1962, 161–199.

Pohlman, E. and F. P. Robinson. "Client Reaction to Some Aspects of the Counseling Situation," PERSONNEL AND GUIDANCE JOURNAL, 38 (March, 1960), 546–551.

Ptacek, Paul H. "A University's Attempts to Counsel Student Leaders," JOURNAL OF HIGHER EDUCATION, 28 (March, 1957), 137–142.

Reik, Louis. "Today's Student and the College Psychiatrist," in Charles Havice, ed. CAMPUS VALUES. New York: Scribner's, 1968, 175–181.

Rogers, William R. "Mental Health Issues in Liberal Arts Colleges and their Implications for Curricular Development," in Joseph C. Heston and Willard B. Frick, eds. COUNSELING FOR THE LIBERAL ARTS CAMPUS. Yellow Springs, Ohio: Antioch Press, 1968, 117–126.

Rutledge, Aaron, L. "A Systematic Approach to Pre-Marital Counseling," in Willard B. Frich and Joseph Heston, eds. COUNSELING FOR THE LIBERAL ARTS CAMPUS. Yellow Springs, Ohio: The Antioch Press, 1968, 158–171.

Seeley, J. R. "In Defense of the College Psychiatrist," TRANS-ACTION, 5 (June, 1968), 47–50.

Seiden, Richard H. "The Problem of Suicide on College Campuses," JOURNAL OF SCHOOL HEALTH, 41 (May, 1971), 243–248.

Sherburne, Philip. "Before the Doctor Comes: Conditions of Stress on the Campus," in Lawrence Dennis and Joseph Kauffman, eds. THE AMERICAN COLLEGE AND THE STUDENT. Washington: American Council on Education, 1966, 342–348.

Smith, W. G., N. Hansell, and J. English, et al. "Psychiatric Disorder in a College Population," ARCHIVES OF GENERAL PSYCHIATRY, 9 (October, 1963), 351–361.

518

Snyder, B. R. "Student Stress," in T. F. Lunsford, ed. THE STUDY OF CAMPUS CULTURES. Boulder, Colorado: Western Interstate Commission for Higher Education, 1963, 27–38.

Staton, W. M. and J. A. Rutledge. "Measurable Traits of Personality and Incidence of Somatic Illness among College Students," RESEARCH QUARTERLY, 26 (May, 1955), 197–204.

Stern, George G. "Congruence and Dissonance in the Ecology of College Students," STUDENT MEDICINE, 8 (April, 1940), 304–339.

Strang, R. "Guidance of the Gifted," PERSONNEL AND GUIDANCE JOURNAL, 31 (October, 1952), 26–30.

Stroup, Herbert. "Student Personnel Workers' Responsibility for Students' Expression on Social Issues," PERSONNEL AND GUIDANCE JOURNAL, 40 (October, 1961), 123–128.

*"Suicide and Student Stress," MODERATOR, 5 (October, 1966), 8–15.

Summerskill, J. and C. D. Darling. "A Progress Report on the Student Stability Studies," STUDENT MEDICINE, 3 (April, 1955), 85–91.

Sutton, W. C. "Appraisal of Health Attitudes and Practices of College Students," JOURNAL OF SCHOOL HEALTH, 26 (April, 1956), 125–130.

*Szasz, Thomas. "The Psychiatrist as Double Agent," in Howard Becker, ed. CAMPUS POWER STRUGGLE. Chicago: Aldine, 1970, 153-172.

Tucker, B. J., et al. "Anatomy of a Campus Crisis Center," PERSONNEL AND GUIDANCE JOURNAL, 48 (January, 1970), 343–348.

Walters, O. H. "Emotional Conflicts of University Students," CHRISTIANITY TODAY, 12 (February 16, 1968), 14–18.

Watson, G. H. "Emotional Problems of Gifted Students," PERSONNEL AND GUIDANCE JOURNAL, 39 (October, 1960), 98–105.

Wedge, B. M., et al. "Spontaneous Neurotic Clique Formation in University Students," PSYCHIATRIC QUARTERLY SUPPLEMENT, 35 (1961).

Whiteley, John M. "Student Stress, Suicide, and the Role of the University," JOURNAL OF THE NATIONAL ASSOCIATION OF WOMEN DEANS AND COUNSELORS, 30 (Spring, 1967), 120–123.

Williamson, E. G. "Preventive Aspects of Disciplinary Counseling," EDUCATIONAL AND PSYCHOLOGICAL MEASUREMENT, 16 (Spring, 1956), 68–81.

Williamson, E. G. "Student Personnel Workers' Responsibility for Students' Expression of Social Issues," PERSONNEL AND GUIDANCE JOURNAL, 40 (October, 1961), 123–128.

Williamson, E. G., et al. "What Kinds of College Students Become Discipline Cases?" EDUCATION AND PSYCHOLOGY, 4 (May 12, 1952), 608–619.

Wise, W. Max. "Counseling Individuals in Liberal Arts Colleges," in E. J. McGrath, ed. THE LIBERAL ARTS COLLEGE'S RESPONSIBILITY FOR THE INDIVIDUAL STUDENT. New York: Teachers College Press, 1966, 72–80.

F.5. Student Financial Problems and Employment

Baumback, Clifford M. A STUDY OF THE FINANCIAL RESOURCES OF STUDENTS AT PUBLIC INSTITUTIONS OF HIGHER EDUCATION IN IOWA.

Iowa City: Bureau of Business and Economic Research, State University of Iowa, 1959.

Berry, Charles A. STUDENT PART-TIME EMPLOYMENT POLICIES AND PRACTICES IN NEGRO LAND-GRANT COLLEGES. Ann Arbor: University Microfilms, 1954.

Crawford, Norman Crane, jr. "Effects of Offers of Financial Assistance On the On-going Decisions of Talented Students with Limited Financial Means." Unpublished Ph.D. Dissertation, Northwestern University, 1966.

Harris, S. E., et al., eds. HIGHER EDUCATION IN THE UNITED STATES: THE ECONOMIC PROBLEMS. Cambridge: Harvard University Press, 1960.

Lansing, John B., Thomas Lorimer, and Chikashi Moriguchi. HOW PEOPLE PAY FOR COLLEGE. Ann Arbor: Survey Research Center, Institute for Social Research, University of Michigan, 1960.

Mushkin, Selma J. and Eugene P. McLoone. STUDENT HIGHER EDUCATION, SOURCES OF INCOME. Washington: National Planning Association, 1960.

Schultz, Kenneth. A STUDY OF STUDENT FINANCIAL AID IN VIRGINIA. Richmond: State Council of Higher Education for Virginia, 1969.

Sherwood, Paul M. "Student and Family Attitudes toward Financing the College Experience." Unpublished Ph.D. dissertation, University of Pittsburgh, 1957.

West, Elmer D. FINANCIAL AID TO THE UNDERGRADUATE: ISSUES AND IMPLICATIONS. Washington: American Council on Education, 1963.

Baker, H. B. "The Working Student and His Grades," JOURNAL OF EDUCATIONAL RESEARCH, 35 (September, 1941), 28–35.

Brantley, E. J. "Study of Part-time Student Employment," JOURNAL OF HIGHER EDUCATION, 28 (March, 1957), 161–163.

Budd, W. C. "Effect of Outside Employment on Initial Academic Adjustment in College," COLLEGE AND UNIVERSITY, 31 (Number 2, 1956), 220–223.

Crandall, R. "College on the Installment Plan," AMERICAN MAGAZINE, (June, 1956).

D'Amico, L. A. and M. R. Raines. "Employment Characteristics of Flint Junior College Students," JUNIOR COLLEGE JOURNAL, 28 (December, 1957), 193–195.

Dickenson, C. and B. Newbegin. "Can Work and College Mix?" PERSONNEL AND GUIDANCE JOURNAL, 38 (December, 1959), 314–317.

Dykstra, J. W. "I Worked My Way Through College," PHI DELTA KAPPAN, 38 (June 1957), 379–380.

Eckelbury, J. "College Jobs for College Students," JOURNAL OF HIGHER EDUCATION, (March, 1956).

Eckstein, Otto. "The Problem of Higher College Tuition," in S. E. Harris, ed. HIGHER EDUCATION IN THE UNITED STATES: THE ECONOMIC PROBLEMS. Cambridge, Massachusetts: Harvard University Press, 1960, 61–72.

Johnson, Eldon. "Is the Low-Tuition Principle Outmoded? in S. E. Harris, ed. HIGHER EDUCATION IN THE UNITED STATES: THE ECONOMIC PROBLEMS. Cambridge, Massachusetts: Harvard University Press, 1960, 44–48.

Kaysen, Carl. "Some General Observations on the Pricing of Higher Education," in S. E. Harris, ed. HIGHER EDUCATION IN THE UNITED STATES: THE ECONOMIC PROBLEMS. Cambridge, Massachusetts: Harvard University Press, 1960, 55–60.

King, R. G. "Changing Picture in Student Support," EDUCATIONAL RECORD, 36 (July, 1955), 246–249.

Moon, Rexford. "Equalizing Opportunity under Higher Charges," in S. E. Harris, ed. HIGHER EDUCATION IN THE UNITED STATES: THE ECONOMIC PROBLEMS. Cambridge, Massachusetts: Harvard University Press, 52–54.

Moon, Rexford G., jr. "Student Aid in a Decade of Decision," in Gordon Klopf, ed. COLLEGE STUDENT PERSONNEL WORK IN THE YEARS AHEAD. Washington, D.C.: American Personnel and Guidance Association, 1966, 60–68

Silver, H. "Salaries for Students? UNIVERSITY QUARTERLY, 19 (September, 1965), 409–413.

Steckel, M. L. "Financial Insecurity as a Factor in Maladjustment of College Freshmen," JOURNAL OF SOCIAL PSYCHOLOGY, 25 (May, 1947), 247–251.

"Symposium: Student Aid and Orientation," COLLEGE AND UNIVERSITY, 30 (July, 1955), 476–482.

Trueblood, D. L. "Effects of Employment on Academic Achievement," PERSONNEL AND GUIDANCE JOURNAL, 36 (October, 1957), 112–116.

Warren, W. H. "Who Receives Our Scholarships? COLLEGE AND UNIVERSITY, 27 (April, 1952), 378–390.

West, Elmer, Robert Farrell and Martha Blakeslee. "Trends in College Costs—and in Family Income," COLLEGE AND UNIVERSITY JOURNAL, 3 (Summer, 1964), 37–42.

F.6. Job Market for College Graduates

Harris, S. E. THE MARKET PLACE FOR COLLEGE GRADUATES. Cambridge: Harvard University Press, 1949.

*Peterson, Richard E. AMERICAN COLLEGE AND UNIVERSITY ENROLLMENT TRENDS IN 1971. Berkeley, California: Carnegie Commission on Higher Education, 1972.

U.S. Bureau of Labor Statistics. OCCUPATIONAL OUTLOOK FOR COLLEGE GRADUATES, 1972–1973. Washington: Government Printing Office, 1972.

*Cartter, Allan M. "Scientific Manpower for 1970–1985," SCIENCE, 172 (April 9, 1971), 132–140.

"Fewer Jobs for the Class of '70," U.S.NEWS AND WORLD REPORT, 68 (March 9, 1970), 38–41.

Folger, John K. "The Job Market for College Graduates," JOURNAL OF HIGHER EDUCATION, 43 (March, 1972), 203–222.

Furlong, William B. "For the Class of '71 the Party's Over," NEW YORK TIMES MAGAZINE, (June 6, 1971), 34–35, 110–113.

"Graduates and Jobs: A Grave New World," TIME, 97 (May 24, 1971), 49–52.

*Harvey, James. "The Effects of the Ph.D. Glut," CHANGE, 4 (April, 1972), 13+.

"The Job Gap for College Graduates in the 1970's," BUSINESS WEEK, (September 23, 1972), 48–51+.

Radner, R., and L. S. Miller. "Demand and Supply in U.S. Higher Education: A Progress Report," AMERICAN ECONOMIC REVIEW, 60 (May, 1970), 326–334.

Wilson, L. "Will There Be Too Many College Graduates?" SCHOOL AND SOCIETY, 81 (April 2, 1955), 97–102.

*Wolfe, Dael and Charles V. Kidd. "The Future Market for Ph.Ds.", SCIENCE, 173 (August 27, 1971), 784–793.

G. GRADUATE STUDENTS: GENERAL MATERIAL

Alciatore, Robert T. and Ruth E. Eckert. MINNESOTA PH.D's EVALUATE THEIR TRAINING. Minneapolis: University of Minnesota, 1968.

Association of American Colleges. FELLOWSHIPS IN THE ARTS AND SCIENCES. Washington: American Council on Education, 1960–1961, 1961–1962, 1962–1063.

Atkinson, Carroll. TRUE CONFESSIONS OF A PH.D. AND RECOMMENDATIONS FOR REFORM. Boston: Meador, 1939.

Austin, C. G. THE IDENTIFICATION AND RECRUITMENT OF PROSPECTIVE COLLEGE TEACHERS. Ann Arbor, Michigan: Michigan Scholars in College Teaching Program, University of Michigan, 1966.

Axt, R. RESEARCH ON GRADUATE EDUCATION. Washington: Brookings Institute, 1959.

Baird, Leonard L. "Role Stress in Graduate Students." Unpublished Ph.D. dissertation, University of California at Los Angeles, 1966.

Barron, Frank X. PERSONAL SOUNDNESS IN UNIVERSITY GRADUATE STUDENTS: AN EXPERIMENTAL STUDY OF YOUNG MEN IN THE SCIENCES AND PROFESSIONS. Ann Arbor: University Microfilms, 1954.

*Berelson, Bernard. GRADUATE EDUCATION IN THE UNITED STATES. New York: McGraw-Hill, 1960.

Berger, Alan S. LONGITUDINAL STUDIES ON THE CLASS OF 1961: THE GRADUATE SCIENCE STUDENT. Chicago: National Opinion Research Center, 1967.

Besco, Robert Orin. "The Measurement and Prediction Of Success in Graduate School." Unpublished Ph.D. dissertation, Purdue University, 1960.

Boewe, Charles and Roy Nichols, eds. BOTH HUMAN AND HUMANE: THE HUMANITIES AND SOCIAL SCIENCES IN GRADUATE EDUCATION. Philadelphia: University of Pennsylvania Press, 1960.

Brown, Richard E. PROFESSIONAL ORIENTATIONS OF GRADUATE STUDENTS AND DETERMINANTS OF MEMBERSHIP IN THE GRADUATE STUDENTS UNION AT THE UNIVERSITY OF CALIFORNIA. Berkeley: University of California, Center for Research and Development in Higher Education, 1970.

Campbell, Rex R., *et al.* MISSOURI GRADUATE EDUCATION, ASSESSMENT NEEDS AND INSTITUTIONAL PLANS. Jefferson City: Missouri Commission on Higher Education, 1969.

Carmichael, Oliver C. GRADUATE EDUCATION. New York: Harper, 1961.

Cartter, Allen M. AN ASSESSMENT OF THE QUALITY OF GRADUATE EDUCATION. Washington: American Council on Education, 1966.

Clements, William H. "Relationships of Selected Characteristics of Graduate Students to Later Success." Unpublished Ph.D. dissertation, University of Wisconsin, 1956.

Corcoran, M. WHERE DOES COLLEGE TEACHING STAND IN THE CAREER PLANS OF SUPERIOR COLLEGE SENIORS? AN EXPLORATORY STUDY OF INTEREST IN ACADEMIC CAREERS. Minneapolis, Minnesota: Bureau of Institutional Research, University of Minnesota, 1961.

Creager, John A. THE AMERICAN GRADUATE STUDENT: A NORMATIVE DESCRIPTION. (ACE Research Reports). Washington: American Council on Education, 1971.

Davis, James A. GREAT ASPIRATIONS: THE GRADUATE SCHOOL PLANS OF AMERICA'S COLLEGE SENIORS. Chicago: Aldine, 1964.

Davis, James A. STIPENDS AND SPOUSES. Chicago: University of Chicago: University of Chicago Press, 1962.

Edmond, Vernon H. "Logical Error As A Function of Group Consensus: An Experimental Study of the Erroneous Group Consensus Upon Logical Judgments of Graduate Students." Unpublished Ph.D. dissertation, University of Missouri, 1962.

Florida, State University, (Tallahassee). Office of Educational Research and Service. A STUDY OF DOCTORAL GRADUATES AND THEIR REACTIONS TO THE DOCTORAL PROGRAM AT THE FLORIDA STATE UNIVERSITY. Tallahassee, 1957.

Friedenberg, Edgar Z. and Julius A. Roth. SELF-PERCEPTION IN THE UNIVERSITY: A STUDY OF SUCCESSFUL AND UNSUCCESSFUL GRADUATE STUDENTS. Chicago: University of Chicago Press, 1954.

Friedman, A., ed. CREATIVITY IN GRADUATE EDUCATION. Claremont, California: Clarement Graduate School, 1964.

Gustad, John W. THE CAREER DECISIONS OF COLLEGE TEACHERS. Atlanta: Southern Regional Education Board, 1960.

Goldblatt, Harold Solomon. "Controversial Teaching, Teachers, and Graduate Schools: A Continuity in the Study of the Academic Mind." Unpublished Ph.D. dissertation, Columbia University, 1964.

Gottlieb, David. "Processes of Socialization in the American Graduate School." Unpublished Ph.D. dissertation, University of Chicago, 1960.

Grigg, Charles M. GRADUATE EDUCATION. New York: Center for Applied Research in Education, 1965.

Grigg, C. M. RECRUITMENT TO GRADUATE STUDY: COLLEGE SENIORS' PLANS FOR POSTGRADUATE EDUCATION AND THEIR IMPLEMENTATION THE YEAR AFTER COMMENCEMENT. (SREB Research Monograph Number 10). Atlanta, Georgia: Southern Regional Education Board, 1965.

Gropper, George L. and Robert Fitzpatrick. WHO GOES TO GRADUATE SCHOOL? A STUDY OF THE DECISION TO ENTER GRADUATE TRAINING. Pittsburgh: American Institute for Research, 1959.

Hartung, E. W. SOME FACTORS IN THE CHOICE OF A CAREER IN COLLEGE TEACHING IN BIOLOGY. Winchester, Massachusetts: New England Board of Higher Education, 1961.

Harvey, James. THE STUDENT IN GRADUATE SCHOOL. Washington, D.C: American Association for Higher Education, 1972.

Hay, George Edward. A STUDY OF GRADUATE EDUCATION IN MASSACHUSETTS. Boston: Board of Higher Education, Commonwealth of Massachusetts, 1969.

Heard, Alexander. THE LOST YEARS IN GRADUATE EDUCATION. Atlanta, Georgia: Southern Regional Education Board, 1963.

*Heiss, Ann M. BERKELEY DOCTORAL STUDENTS APPRAISE THEIR ACADEMIC PROGRAMS. Berkeley: Center for Research and Development in Higher Education, University of California, 1968.

*Heiss, Ann M. CHALLENGES TO GRADUATE SCHOOLS. San Francisco: Jossey-Bass, 1970.

Hess, Dolph. "Prediction of Success in Casework Practice From Performance in the Graduate Program." Unpublished PH.D. dissertation, University of Minnesota, 1966.

Hunter, James Scott. THE ACADEMIC AND FINANCIAL STATUS OF GRADUATE STUDENTS. Washington: U.S. Department of Health, Education and Welfare, Office of Education, 1967.

Institute for Defense Analysis. TASK FORCE REPORT ON SCIENCE AND TECHNOLOGY. Washington: U.S. Government Printing Office, 1967.

Knapp, R. H. THE ORIGINS OF AMERICAN HUMANISTIC SCHOLARS. Englewood Cliffs, New Jersey: Prentice-Hall, 1964.

Knapp, R. H. and H. B. Goodrich. ORIGINS OF AMERICAN SCIENTISTS: A STUDY MADE UNDER THE DIRECTION OF A COMMITTEE OF THE FACULTY OF WESLEYAN UNIVERSITY. Chicago: University of Chicago Press, 1952.

*Knapp, Robert H. and Joseph J. Greenbaum. THE YOUNGER AMERICAN SCHOLAR: HIS COLLEGIATE ORIGINS. Chicago: University of Chicago Press, 1953.

Langlois, Eleanor. THE LENGTH OF TIME SPENT EARNING THE Ph.D. DEGREE AT THE UNIVERSITY OF CALIFORNIA. Berkeley: Office of Institutional Research, University of California, 1967.

Lyman, Howard B. A COMPARISON OF SELECTED BACKGROUND

VARIABLES AND GRADUATE ACHIEVEMENT IN EDUCATION AS MEASURED BY A GRADUATE EDUCATION BATTERY. Ann Arbor: University Microfilms, 1960.

McGrath, Earl J. THE GRADUATE SCHOOL AND THE DECLINE OF LIBERAL EDUCATION. New York: Teachers College, Columbia University, 1959.

McKinley, Richard, Peter H. Ross, and James A. Davis. STUDENTS AT THE MIDWAY: A SURVEY OF THE GRADUATE STUDENT PLANS OF THE UNIVERSITY OF CHICAGO CLASS OF JUNE, 1961. (National Opinion Research Center Report Number 86). Chicago: NORC, 1961.

Macrorie, Ken, ed. THE GRADUATE EXPERIENCE IN ENGLISH: TEN PERSONAL CASE HISTORIES. Champaign, Illinois: National Council of Teachers of English, 1964.

Martin, P. Y. "Selected Factors Which Influence the Pursuit of College Teaching as an Occupational Goal." Unpublished Ph.D. dissertation, Florida State University, 1964.

Matson, Margaret Hart Benson. "Selection of Academic Careers." Unpublished Ph.D. dissertation, Pennsylvania State University, 1954.

Mayhew, Lewis. REFORM IN GRADUATE EDUCATION. Atlanta, Georgia: Southern Regional Education Board, 1972.

Merz, Louise Elizabeth. "The Graduate School as a Socializing Agency: A Pilot Study of Sociological Aspects of Graduate Training in the Physical Sciences." Unpublished Ph.D. dissertation, Cornell University, 1961.

Metcalf, Homer Chandler. "Role Conflict in Married Graduate Students." Unpublished Ph.D. dissertation, Washington State University, 1968.

Moffett, M. SOCIAL BACKGROUND AND ACTIVITIES OF TEACHERS COLLEGE STUDENTS. Teachers College, Columbia University, 1929.

National Academy of Sciences, National Research Council. THE INVISIBLE EMPIRE: POST DOCTORAL EDUCATION IN THE UNITED STATES. Washington: National Academy of Sciences, 1969.

Newton, C. H. "Patterns of Career Decisions Within the Professions." Unpublished Ph.D. dissertation, Florida State University, 1962.

Office of Scientific Personnel. THE BACCALAUREATE ORIGINS OF SCIENCE DOCTORATES AWARDED IN THE UNITED STATES, 1936–1950. Washington: National Academy of Sciences, 1955.

Orth, C. D. III, SOCIAL STRUCTURE AND LEARNING CLIMATE: THE FIRST YEAR AT THE HARVARD BUSINESS SCHOOL. Boston, Massachusetts: Division of Research, Graduate School of Business, Harvard University, 1963.

Perkins, Dexter, John Snell, et al. THE EDUCATION OF HISTORIANS IN THE UNITED STATES. New York: McGraw-Hill, 1962.

Renetsky, Alvin. "All But the Dissertation: A Study of the Factors of Attrition in Graduate Education." Unpublished Ph.D. dissertation, University of Southern California, June, 1966.

Roe, Anne. THE MAKING OF A SCIENTIST. New York: Dodd, Mead, 1953.

Rogers, J. M. STAFFING AMERICAN COLLEGES, AND UNIVERSITIES. Washington, D.C.: Office of Education, U.S. Department of Health, Education and Welfare, 1967.

Rosenhaupt, Hans Wilhelm. GRADUATE STUDENTS: EXPERIENCE AT COLUMBIA UNIVERSITY, 1940–1956. New York: Columbia University Press, 1958.

Roth, Darlene. GRADUATE STUDENTS AND ACADEMIC AFFAIRS. Washington, D.C.: Council for Graduate Schools in the U.S., 1969.

Santos, Severino R. "Factors Associated with Successful Candidacy in Certain Fields of Graduate Study." Unpublished Ph.D. dissertation, Cornell University, 1964.

Sharp, Laure M. FIVE YEARS AFTER THE COLLEGE DEGREE. PART I: GRADUATE AND PROFESSIONAL EDUCATION. Washington: Bureau of Social Research, 1965.

Sibley, E. THE EDUCATION OF SOCIOLOGISTS: THE UNITED STATES. New York: Russell Sage Foundation, 1963.

Small, John Joseph. "Formative Influences in the Psycho-Educational Backgrounds of Superior Graduate Students." Unpublished Ph.D. dissertation, Ohio State University, 1957.

Spaeth, Joe L. GRADUATE STUDENTS IN HISTORY. Chicago: National Opinion Research Center, 1963.

Spaeth, Joe L. UNDERGRADUATE ORIGINS AND SUCCESS IN GRADUATE SCHOOL. Chicago: National Opinion Research Center, 1966.

Stark, Rodney. GRADUATE STUDY AT BERKELEY: AN ASSESSMENT OF ATTRITION AND DURATION. Berkeley: Survey Research Center, University of California, 1966.

Stewart, James W. A SURVEY OF ATTITUDE AND PERCEPTION OF THE GRADUATE STUDENT OF HIS ADVISOR OR COMMITTEE CHAIRMAN. Lincoln: Nebraska University, 1969.

Strom, Leonard Einar. FACTORS RELATED TO THE DROPOUT OF DOCTORAL CANDIDATES AT TEACHERS COLLEGE, COLUMBIA UNIVERSITY. New York: Teachers College, Columbia University, 1959.

Thistlethwaite, Donald L. THE EFFECTS OF COLLEGE ENVIRONMENTS ON STUDENTS' DECISIONS TO ATTEND GRADUATE SCHOOL. FINAL REPORT. Nashville: Vanderbilt University, 1968.

Tucker, A. FACTORS RELATING TO ATTRITION AMONG DOCTORAL STUDENTS. (Cooperative Research Project Number 1146. U.S. Office of Education) East Lansing: Michigan State University, 1964.

Tucker, Allan, David Gottlieb and John Pease, et al. ATTRITION OF GRADUATE STUDENTS AT THE Ph.D. LEVEL IN THE TRADITIONAL ARTS AND SCIENCES. Office of Research Development and the Graduate School, East Lansing: Michigan State University, 1964.

U.S. National Center for Educational Statistics. THE ACADEMIC AND FINANCIAL STATUS OF GRADUATE STUDENTS, SPRING 1965. Washington: U.S. Department of Health Education and Welfare, Office of Education, 1967.

526

U.S. National Science Foundation. GRADUATE STUDENT ENROLL-MENT AND SUPPORT IN AMERICAN UNIVERSITIES AND COLLEGES. Washington: Government Printing Office, 1954.

U.S. National Science Foundation. GRADUATE STUDENT SUPPORT AND MANPOWER RESOURCES IN GRADUATE SCIENCE EDUCATION, FALL 1969. Washington: Government Printing Office, 1971.

U.S. National Science Foundation. Office of Planning and Policy Studies. GRADUATE STUDENT SUPPORT AND MANPOWER RESOURCES IN GRADUATE SCIENCE EDUCATION: ANALYSIS OF STUDENT ENROLL-MENTS, SOURCE OF STUDENT SUPPORT, AND FACULTY AND POST-DOCTORALS IN GRADUATE-SCIENCE DEPARTMENTS: FALL 1965–FALL 1966. Washington: Government Printing Office, 1968.

U.S. Office of Education. EARNED DEGREES CONFERRED. Washington, D.C.: U.S. Government Printing Office, annual 1954–55 to 1963–64.

Warkov, Seymour, Bruce Frisbie and Alan S. Berger. GRADUATE STU-DENT FINANCES 1963. (Report Number 103) Chicago: National Opinion Research Center, 1965.

Western, John Stuart. "Some Aspects of the Socialization Process in Gradu-ate School." Unpublished Ph.D. dissertation, Columbia University, 1964.

Wilson, Kenneth M. OF TIME AND THE DOCTORATE. (SREB Research Monograph Number 9), Atlanta Southern Regional Education Board, 1965.

*Wilson, Logan. THE ACADEMIC MIND. New York: Oxford University Press, 1942.

Allison, David, ed. "The Graduate Student," INTERNATIONAL SCIENCE AND TECHNOLOGY, Number 49 (January, 1966), 24–35, 83–85.

Altbach, P. G. "Commitment and Powerlessness on the American Campus: The Case of the Graduate Student," LIBERAL EDUCATION, 56 (December, 1970), 562–582.

Anderson, J. R. "Honors Student Assesses Graduate Education," SUPERI-OR STUDENT, 7 (May, 1965), 14–18.

Astin, A. W. "Differential College Effects on the Motivation of Talented Students to Obtain Ph.D.," JOURNAL OF EDUCATIONAL PSYCHOLOGY, 54 (February, 1963), 63–71.

Astin, Alexander W. "Influences on the Student's Motivation to Seek Advanced Training: Another Look," JOURNAL OF EDUCATIONAL PSY-CHOLOGY, 53 (December, 1962), 303–309.

Astin, A. W. "Productivity of Undergraduate Institutions," SCIENCE, 136 (April 13, 1962), 129–135.

Astin, A. W. "A Re-examination of College Productivity," JOURNAL OF EDUCATIONAL PSYCHOLOGY, 52 (August, 1961), 173–178.

Astin, A. W. "Undergraduate Institutions and the Production of Scientists," SCIENCE, 141 (July 26, 1963), 334–338.

Arrowsmith, W. "Shame of the Graduate Schools," HARPER, 232 (March, 1966), 51–59.

Babcock, Henry. "Special Problems Encountered at the Graduate School of

Business Administration," in G. B. Blaine, jr. and C. C. McArthur, eds. EMOTIONAL PROBLEMS OF THE STUDENT. New York: Appleton-Century-Crofts, 1971, 334–350.

Baird, Leonard L. "A Study of the Role Relations in Graduate Students," JOURNAL OF EDUCATIONAL PSYCHOLOGY, 60 (Number 1, 1969), 15–21.

Barzun, J. "Where Are the Disciples?" ANTIOCH REVIEW, 20 (Spring, 1960), 5–14.

Boroff, D. "Graduate Limbo," MADEMOISELLE, 51 (October, 1960), 110–113+.

Carter, A. M. "After Effects of Blind Eye to Telescope: Lack of Academic Openings for Ph.D.," EDUCATION DIGEST, 36 (March, 1971), 15–18.

Carter, Allan. "Graduate Education and Research in the Decades Ahead," in Alvin Eurich, ed. CAMPUS 1980. New York: Delacorte Press, 1968, 254–278.

Cartter, A. M. "The Supply and Demand for College Teachers," JOURNAL OF HUMAN RESOURCES, 14 (Summer, 1966), 22–38.

Cikins, W. I. "Graduate Education, Public Service, and the Negro." PUBLIC ADMINISTRATION REVIEW, 26 (September, 1966), 183–191.

Clark, D. Cecil. "Competition for Grades and Graduate Student Performance," JOURNAL OF EDUCATIONAL RESEARCH, 62 (April, 1969), 351–354.

Crawford, Bryce L., jr. "The Graduate Student in the Natural Sciences," PROCEEDINGS OF THE COUNCIL OF GRADUATE SCHOOLS IN THE UNITED STATES, (1965), 12–20.

Cuzzort, R. P. "Superior Student in Graduate School: A Resumé of the Experience of 101 Honor Students," SUPERIOR STUDENT, 7 (May, 1965), 3–13.

Ellis, R. A., et al. "Collegiate Scholar: Education for Elite Status," SOCIOLOGY OF EDUCATION, 44 (Winter, 1971), 27–58.

Ellis, S. D. "Graduate Student: Where Does He Come From? Where Does He Go?" PHYSICS TODAY, 22 (March, 1969), 53–57.

Erbe, William. "Accessibility and Informal Social Relationships Among American Graduate Students," SOCIOMETRY, 29 (1966), 251–264.

Faia, Michael A. "College Grades As Graduate Admission Criterion," IMPROVING COLLEGE AND UNIVERSITY TEACHING, 17 (Summer, 1969), 187–190.

Feldman, Saul. "Marital Status and Graduate Education: Impediment or Stimulant," AMERICAN JOURNAL OF SOCIOLOGY, 78 (January, 1973).

Gottlieb, David. "American Graduate Students: Some Characteristics of Aspiring Teachers and Researchers," JOURNAL OF EDUCATIONAL PSYCHOLOGY, 52 (Number 5, 1961), 236–240.

*Gottlieb, David. "Processes of Socialization in American Graduate Schools," SOCIAL FORCES, 40 (December, 1961), 124–131.

"Graduate Student and the Modern University," GRADUATE JOURNAL, 7 (Spring, 1967), 301–346.

528

"Graduate Student: Symposium," PHYSICS TODAY, 22 (March, 1969), 23–33 +.

Graham, G. "Turmoil in the Grad Schools," NEW YORK TIMES MAGAZINE, (April 7, 1968), 46–47 +.

Greeley, A. M. "The Religious Behavior of Graduate Students," JOURNAL FOR THE SCIENTIFIC STUDY OF RELIGION, 5 (November 1, 1965), 34–40.

Green, A. E. S. "Post-doctoral Research Associate-Instructor," PHYSICS TODAY, 22 (June, 1969), 23–26.

Gregg, Wayne E. "Several Factors Affecting Graduate Student Satisfaction," JOURNAL OF HIGHER EDUCATION, 43 (June, 1972), 484–498.

Gruner, W. R. "Graduate Student Stipends," SCIENCE, 157 (September 29, 1967), 1530–1533.

Hall, Douglas. "Identity Changes During the Transition from Student To Professor," SCHOOL REVIEW, 76 (December, 1968), 445–469.

Harris, Richard N. "Intellectual Despotism in Graduate School," AMERICAN SOCIOLOGIST, 6 (February, 1971), 35–36.

Heard, Alexander. "The Lost Years in Graduate Education," in Kaoru Yamamoto, ed. THE COLLEGE STUDENT AND HIS CULTURE: AN ANALYSIS. Boston: Houghton Mifflin, 1968, 451–459.

Heiss, Ann. "Berkeley Doctoral Students Appraise Their Academic Programs," EDUCATIONAL RECORD, 48 (Winter, 1967), 30–44.

Heiss, Ann M. "Graduate Education Today: An Instrument for Change?" JOURNAL OF HIGHER EDUCATION, 39 (January, 1968), 1–10.

Heiss, Ann. "Preparing College Teachers," in G. K. Smith, ed. THE TROUBLED CAMPUS. San Francisco: Jossey-Bass, 1970, 165–178.

Hobbs, Walter C. and G. Lester Anderson. "Research Support for Graduate Students," COLLEGE AND UNIVERSITY, 44 (Winter, 1969), 154–157.

Holland, John L. "Undergraduate Origins of American Scientists," SCIENCE, 126 (September, 1957), 433–437.

Hurd, A. W. "Why Graduate and Professional Students Fail in College Courses," SCHOOL AND SOCIETY, 57 (May, 1949), 282–285.

Jacobson, Robert L. "Scholars Rank Graduate Study in 36 Fields," CHRONICLE OF HIGHER EDUCATION, 5 (January 4, 1971), 4–5.

James, W. "The Ph.D. Octopus," in W. James ed. MEMORIES AND STUDIES. New York: Longmans, Green, 1911.

*Jencks, C. and D. Riesman. "Where Graduate Schools Fail," ATLANTIC, 221 (February, 1968), 49–55.

Joanson, R. C. "Reflections on the Ph.D.," COLLEGE ENGLISH, 26 (January, 1965), 304–306.

Kostelanetz, R. "Graduate Student Blues," NATIONAL REVIEW, 20 (March 12, 1968), 237–241.

Lerner, M. "Death at an Early Age: Report from the Graduate School," THE NEW JOURNAL, 1 (1967), 3–5.

Levine, Edward and Joseph Weitz. "Job Satisfaction Among Graduate

Students: Intrinsic versus Extrinsic Variables," JOURNAL OF APPLIED PSYCHOLOGY, 54 (August, 1968), 263–271.

Loewenberg, Peter. "Emotional Problems of Graduate Education," JOURNAL OF HIGHER EDUCATION, 40 (November, 1969), 610–623.

Lynch, N. "Young American Graduate Student," MADEMOISELLE, 43 (September, 1956), 138–139+.

Macdonald, John. "The Topmost Layer: An Examination of the Purposes and Functions of American Graduate Schools," COMPARATIVE EDUCATION, 2 (June, 1966), 151–166.

McCarthy, John D., and Mayer N. Zald. "Toward a Permanent Revolution in the Graduate Curriculum," THE AMERICAN SOCIOLOGIST, 6 (February, 1971), 31–34.

McComas, J. D. and J. E. Uxer. "Graduates Perceptions of Research," IMPROVING COLLEGE AND UNIVERSITY TEACHING, 16 (Spring, 1968), 118–119.

Medalia, N. A. "On Becoming a College Teacher: A Review of Three Variables," SREB RESEARCH MONOGRAPH NUMBER 6. Atlanta, Georgia: Southern Regional Education Board, 1963.

Mehrens, William A. "Self-Concepts of Graduate Students," JOURNAL OF EDUCATIONAL RESEARCH, 61 (November, 1967), 112–113.

Miller, J. P. "Under the Tower: A Report on Graduate Education," VENTURE, 6 (Fall, 1966), 1–5.

Mooney, Joseph D. "Attrition among Ph.D. Candidates: an Analysis of a Cohort of Recent Woodrow Wilson Fellows," JOURNAL OF HUMAN RESOURCES, 3 (Winter, 1968), 47–62.

Nelson, R. L. "Psychiatric Needs of Graduate Students," SCHOOL REVIEW, 67 (Number 1, Spring, 1959), 93–105.

Nelson, Robert. "Special Problems of Graduate Students in the School of Arts and Sciences," in G. B. Blaine, jr. and C. C. McArthur, eds. EMOTIONAL PROBLEMS OF THE STUDENT. New York: Appleton-Century-Crofts, 1971, 320–334.

Nichols, R. T. "A Reconsideration of the Ph.D.," GRADUATE JOURNAL, 7 (Number 2, 1967), 325–335.

Nosal, W. S. "Five Year Comparison of Graduates in Two Professional Curricula," JOURNAL OF TEACHER EDUCATION, 7 (September, 1956), 238–243.

Osborn, M. O. and H. A. Stevens. "Characteristics of Graduates holding Advanced Degress with Majors in Home Economics and Nutrition, 1924–1966," JOURNAL OF HOME ECONOMICS, 60 (December, 1968), 777–783.

Packer, Herbert. "Piling Higher and Deeper: the Shame of the Ph.D.," CHANGE, 2 (November/December, 1970), 49–53.

Pease, J. "Faculty Influence and Professional Participation of Doctoral Students," SOCIOLOGICAL INQUIRY, 37 (Winter, 1967), 63–70.

Predmore, Richard L. "The Graduate Student in the Humanities," COUNCIL OF GRADUATE SCHOOLS OF THE UNITED STATES, (December 2, 1965), 5–12.

Reisman, A. "Higher Education: A Population Flow Feedback Model," SCIENCE, 153 (July 1, 1966), 89–91.

Riesman, David. "An Academic Great Depression?" UNIVERSITIES QUARTERLY, 26 (Winter, 1971), 15–27.

Rogers, C. R. "Graduate Education in Psychology: A Passionate Statement," in FREEDOM TO LEARN. La Jolla, California: Western Institute of Behavioral Science, 1964.

Roman, Paul. "The Future Professor: Function and Patterns of Drinking Among Graduate Students," in George Maddox, ed. THE DOMESTICATED DRUG: DRINKING AMONG COLLEGIANS. New Haven, Connecticut: College and University Press, 1970, 204–218.

Rose, A. M. "Graduate Training for the Culturally Deprived," SOCIOLOGY OF EDUCATION, 39 (Spring, 1966), 201–208.

Rosen, Bernard C. and Alan Bates. "The Structure of Socialization in Graduate Schools," in R. V. Pavalko, ed. SOCIOLOGY OF EDUCATION. Itaska, Illinois: Peacock, 1968, 244–257.

Rudd, Ernest. "The Troubles of Graduate Students," in D. Martin, ed. ANARCHY AND CULTURE. London: Rouletdge and Kegan Paul, 1969, 65–76.

Scarborough, B. and B. M. Harris. "Graduate Students' Perceptions of Leadership Roles," JOURNAL OF TEACHER EDUCATION, 13 (March, 1962), 60–64.

Sherlock, B. J. and R. T. Morris. "The Evolution of the Professional: A Paradigm," SOCIOLOGICAL INQUIRY, 37 (Winter, 1967), 27–46.

Shuck, E. "Cold War in the Graduate Schools," SCHOOL AND SOCIETY, 74 (September 29, 1951), 193–196.

Solotaroff, T. "Graduate Students: A Profile," COMMENTARY, 32 (December, 1961), 482–490.

Sorenson, G. and D. Kagan. "Conflicts between Doctoral Candidates and Their Sponsors," JOURNAL OF HIGHER EDUCATION, 38 (January, 1967), 17–24.

Stark, R. "On the Incompatibility of Religion and Science: A Survey of American Graduate Students," JOURNAL FOR THE SCIENTIFIC STUDY OF RELIGION, 3 (Fall, 1963), 3–20.

Steege, Ted, et al. "Radicals and the Professions," OUR GENERATION, 5 (Number 2, 1967), 48–102.

Strassenburg, A. A. and M. T. Ilano. "Graduate Student: What Does He Study?" PHYSICS TODAY, 22 (March, 1969), 45–51.

Suslow, Sidney. "The Graduate Student at Berkeley—A Profile," in Clarence H. Bagley, ed. RESEARCH ON ACADEMIC INPUT. Cortland, New York: Association for Institutional Research, 1966, 221–229.

Travers, R. M. W. and W. L. Wallace. "Assessment of the Academic Aptitude of the Graduate Student," EDUCATIONAL AND PSYCHOLOGICAL MEASUREMENT, 10 (Number 3, 1950), 371–379.

Trow, Martin A. "Recruitment to College Teaching," in A. H. Halsey, Jean Floud and C. Arnold Anderson, eds. EDUCATION, ECONOMY AND SOCIETY. New York: The Free Press of Glencoe, 1961, 602–620.

Trow, M. "Reflections on the Recruitment to College Teaching," in J. W. Gustad, ed. FACULTY SUPPLY, DEMAND AND RECRUITMENT. Winchester, Massachusetts: New England Board of Higher Education, 1959.

Trytten, M. H. "Science Graduate Students and Their Support," SCIENCE, 109 (May 20, 1949), 505–508.

Wegner, Eldon L. "Some Factors in Obtaining Postgraduate Education," SOCIOLOGY OF EDUCATION, 42 (Spring, 1969), 154–169.

West, P. S. "Materialism and the College Graduate," EDUCATIONAL RECORD, 34 (January, 1953), 32–37.

Wolfe, A. "Hard Times on Campus," NATION, 210 (May 25, 1970), 623–627.

Wright, C. R. "Changes in the Occupational Commitment of Graduate Sociology Students: A Research Note," SOCIOLOGICAL INQUIRY, 37 (Winter, 1967), 58–62.

G.1. Students in Professional Schools

*Becker, H. S., B. Geer, E. Hughes and A. Strauss, et al. BOYS IN WHITE: STUDENT CULTURE IN MEDICAL SCHOOL. Chicago: University of Chicago Press, 1961.

Caplovitz, David. "Student-Faculty Relations In Medical School: A Study of Professional Socialization." Unpublished Ph.D. dissertation, Columbia University, 1961.

Crowns, Arthur John, jr. "Attitude Differential and Professional Socialization of Successful and Unsuccessful Graduate Social Work Students Attending Florida State University." Unpublished Ph.D. dissertation, Florida State University, 1965.

Embree, Robert Arthur. "A Factor Analytic Investigation of Motivations and Attitudes of College Students With Intentions For the Ministry and A Comparison of the Performance of Persisters and Non-persisters on the Theological School Inventory." Unpublished Ph.D. dissertation, University of Denver, 1964.

Fasick, Frank Appleby. "The First Year Medical Student: Selected Factors Affecting His Expectations and Experiences." Unpublished Ph.D. dissertation, Columbia University, 1962.

*Feldman, David. "Social Class And Academic Achievement At Law School." Unpublished Ph.D. dissertation, Stanford University, 1960.

*Fredericks, Marcel Anthony. "The Professionalization of Medical Students: Social Class, Attitude, and Academic Achievement." Unpublished Ph.D. dissertation, Loyola University of Chicago, 1965.

*Goldstein, Marshall Nathan. "Political Involvement Among American Law Students." Unpublished Ph.D. dissertation, University of North Carolina at Chapel Hill, 1964.

Howard, Jan McDonald. "The Professionalization of Law Students: A Study In Facet Design." Unpublished Ph.D. dissertation, Stanford University, 1961.

Kandel, Denise Bystryn. "The Career Decisions Of Medical Students: A

532

Study in Occupational Recruitment and Occupational Choice." Unpublished Ph.D. dissertation, Columbia University, 1960.

Kubany, Albert J. "Evaluation of Medical Student Clinical Performance: A Criterion Study." Unpublished Ph.D. dissertation, University of Pittsburgh, 1957.

Meile, Richard Lawrence. "Performance and Adjustment of First Year Law Students." Unpublished Ph.D. dissertation, University of Washington, 1961.

Merton, R. K., Reader and Kendall, eds. THE STUDENT PHYSICIAN: INTRODUCTORY STUDIES IN THE SOCIOLOGY OF MEDICAL EDUCATION. Cambridge, Massachusetts: Harvard University Press, 1957.

Ontell, Robert. "Criterion Employed and the Reliability of Judgments in Making Decisions About the Acceptance of Applicants Into The Columbia University School of Social Work." Unpublished D.S.W., Columbia University, 1965.

O'Shea, Robert Michael. "Homophily and Friendship Choice in Dental School." Unpublished Ph.D. dissertation, The Catholic University of America, 1965.

Prince, Melvin. "The March Toward Doctorship: A Study of the Transition From Medical Student to Intern." Unpublished Ph.D. dissertation, Columbia University, 1962.

Pugh, Richard C., et al. AN ANALYSIS OF ACHIEVEMENT BEHAVIOR IN THE LAW SCHOOL. INDIANA STUDIES IN PREDICTION. NUMBER 9. Bloomington: Indiana University, 1967.

Quarantelle, E. L. THE DENTAL STUDENT: A SOCIAL PSYCHOLOGICAL STUDY. Unpublished Ph.D. dissertation, University of Chicago, 1959.

Snyder, Douglas Staley. "Selected Socialization Experiences of Medical Students and Their Conceptions of Professional Responsibility." Unpublished Ph.D. dissertation, University of Washington, 1966.

Taulbee, George C., sr. "Construction and Validation Of A Scale For Predicting Graduation From A College of Optometry." Unpublished Ph.D. dissertation, University of Houston, 1963.

Thielens, Wagner Perrin, jr. "The Socialization of Law Students: A Case Study in Three Parts." Unpublished Ph.D. dissertation, Columbia University, 1965.

Walther, Regis H. PERSONALITY VARIABLES AND CAREER DECISIONS, A PILOT STUDY OF LAW AND SOCIAL WORK STUDENTS. Washington: George Washington University, 1966.

Warkov, S. LAWYERS IN THE MAKING. Chicago: Aldine, 1965.

Becker, H. S. and B. Greer. "Fate of Idealism in Medical School," AMERICAN SOCIOLOGICAL REVIEW, 23 (February, 1958), 50–56.

Becker, Howard and Blanche Geer. "Student Culture in Medical School," HARVARD EDUCATIONAL REVIEW, 28 (Winter, 1958), 70–80.

Bloom, S. W. "The Process of Becoming a Physician," ANNALS OF THE AMERICAN ACADEMY OF POLITICAL AND SOCIAL SCIENCE, 346, (March, 1963), 77–87.

Bojar, Samuel. "Psychiatric Problems of Medical Students," in G. B. Blaine, jr. and C. C. McArthur, eds. EMOTIONAL PROBLEMS OF THE STUDENT. New York: Appleton-Century-Crofts, 1971, 350–364.

Christie, R. and R. R. Merton. "Procedures for the Sociological Study of the Values Climate of Medical Schools," in Helen H. Gee and Robert J. Glaser, eds. THE ECOLOGY OF THE MEDICAL STUDENT. A REPORT OF THE FIFTH TEACHING INSTITUTE. Evanston, Illinois: Association of American Colleges, 1958.

Coker, R. E., *et al.* "Patterns of Influence: Medical School Faculty Members and the Values and Specialty Interests of Medical Students." JOURNAL OF MEDICAL EDUCATION, 35 (June, 1960), 518–527.

Council on Dental Education. "Dental and Dental Hygiene Students: their Characteristics, Finances and Practice Plans, II: Characteristics of Dental Students," JOURNAL OF THE AMERICAN DENTAL ASSOCIATION, 52 (January, 1956), 72–80.

Eron, Leonard D. "Effect of Medical Educaton on Medical Students' Attitudes," JOURNAL OF MEDICAL EDUCATION, 30 (October, 1955), 559–566.

Gordon, L. and I. Mensch. "Values of Medical Students at Different Levels of Training," JOURNAL OF EDUCATIONAL PSYCHOLOGY, 53 (February, 1962), 48–51.

Heist, Paul. "Personality Characteristics of Dental Students," EDUCATIONAL RECORD, 41 (July, 1960), 240–252.

Hughes, Everett C. "Stresses and Strains in a Medical School: their Impact upon Students," PROCEEDINGS OF THE ASSOCIATION OF AMERICAN MEDICAL COLLEGES, 1957.

Hutchins, E. B. "The 1960 Medical School Graduate, His Perceptions of His Faculty, Peers, and Environment," JOURNAL OF MEDICAL EDUCATION, 36 (1961), 322–329.

Lortie, D. C. "Laymen to Lawmen: Law Schools, Careers, and Professional Socialization," HARVARD EDUCATIONAL REVIEW, 29 (Fall, 1959), 352–369.

Mann, William R. and Grace Perkin. "The Dental School Applicant," JOURNAL OF DENTAL EDUCATION, 24 (March, 1960), 16–37.

Maxmen, J. S. "Medical Student Radicals: Conflict and Resolution," AMERICAN JOURNAL OF PSYCHIATRY, 127 (March, 1971), 1211–1215.

Michaelson, Michael. "Medical Students: Healers Become Activists," SATURDAY REVIEW, 52 (August 16, 1969), 743–745, 755–756.

More, D. M. and Nathan Kohn, jr. "Some Motives for Entering Dentistry," AMERICAN JOURNAL OF SOCIOLOGY, 66 (July, 1960), 48–53.

Muntz, E. E., jr. "Opinions of Divinity and Law Students on Social Class," JOURNAL OF EDUCATIONAL SOCIOLOGY, 34 (January, 1961), 221–229.

Quarantelli, E. L., M. Heflich and D. Yutzy. "Faculty-Student Perceptions in a Professional School," SOCIOLOGY AND SOCIAL RESEARCH, 49 (October, 1964), 32–45.

Smith, Eugene L. "Is Education for Professional Responsibility Possible?" UNIVERSITY OF COLORADO LAW REVIEW, 40 (Summer, 1968), 509–535.

Stern, G. G. and J. S. Scanlon. "Pediatric Lions and Gynecological Lambs," JOURNAL OF MEDICAL EDUCATION, 33 (Part 2, October, 1958), 12–18.

Stevens, Robert. "Aging Mistress: The Law School in America," CHANGE, 2 (January/February, 1970), 32–42.

G.2. The Graduate Student as Teacher

Chase, John LeRoy. GRADUATE TEACHING ASSISTANTS IN AMERICAN UNIVERSITIES: A REVIEW OF RECENT TRENDS AND RECOMMENDATIONS. Washington, D.C.: U.S. Office of Education, 1970.

Hagiwara, Michio P. LEADERSHIP IN FOREIGN-LANGUAGE EDUCATION-TRENDS IN TRAINING AND SUPERVISION OF GRADUATE ASSISTANTS. New York: Modern Language Association, 1970.

*Harvey, James. THE STUDENT IN GRADUATE SCHOOL. Washington, D.C.: ERIC Clearing House on Higher Education, 1972.

*Nowlis, Victor, Kenneth E. Clark and Miriam Rock. THE GRADUATE STUDENT AS TEACHER. Washington: American Council on Education, 1968.

Teaching Assistant's Association of the University of Wisconsin. ANALYSIS OF THE STRIKE, OCTOBER 18–23. Madison: 1967.

U.S. Office of Education. GRADUATE TEACHING ASSISTANTS IN AMERICAN UNIVERSITIES. Washington: U.S. Government Printing Office.

*Bessie, Frederick and Robert Dubin. "The Assistant: Academic Subaltern," ADMINISTRATIVE SCIENCE QUARTERLY, 2 (Number 4, 1967), 521–547.

Hamilton, A. "Wisconsin: Teaching Assistant's Strike Ends in Contract Signing," SCIENCE, 168 (April 17, 1970), 345–349.

Heim, Peggy and Becky Bogard. "Compensation of Graduate Assistants 1968–1969," AMERICAN ASSOCIATION OF UNIVERSITY PROFESSORS BULLETIN, 53 (December, 1969) 483–490.

Heynes, R. W. "The Graduate Student: Teacher, Research Assistant, or Scholar?" GRADUATE JOURNAL, 7 (Number 2, 1967), 317–324.

Ingerman, Sidney. "Employed Graduate Students Organize at Berkeley," INDUSTRIAL RELATIONS, 5 (October, 1965), 141–150.

*Kruytbusch, Carlos E. and Sheldon L. Messinger. "Unequal Peers: the Situation of Researchers at Berkeley," AMERICAN BEHAVIORAL SCIENTIST, 11 (May–June, 1968), 33–43.

Mackertich, Alex. "Teaching Assistants," IMPROVING COLLEGE AND UNIVERSITY TEACHING, 18 (Summer, 1970), 223–226.

Nowlis, Vincent. "Graduate Students As Teachers," in G. K. Smith, ed. THE TROUBLED CAMPUS. San Francisco: Jossey-Bass, 1970, 179–183.

Otto, David. "A Study of Participative Management: the Teaching Assistant," in Cameron Fincher, ed. THE CHALLENGE AND RESPONSE OF INSTITUTIONAL RESEARCH. PROCEEDINGS OF THE NINTH ANNUAL FORUM ON INSTITUTIONAL RESEARCH. N.P. Association for Institutional Research, 1970, 63–72.

Overmyer, J. "In Defense of the Graduate Assistant," COLLEGE AND UNIVERSITY, 40 (Winter, 1965), 125–131.

4 Bibliographies

Altbach, Philip G. STUDENT POLITICS AND HIGHER EDUCATION IN THE UNITED STATES: A SELECT BIBLIOGRAPHY. Boston: Center for International Affairs, Harvard University, 1968.

Aptheker, Bettina. HIGHER EDUCATION AND THE STUDENT REBELLION IN THE UNITED STATES, 1960–1969: A BIBLIOGRAPHY. New York: American Institute of Marxist Studies, 1969, 1970.

Bienen, Henry. VIOLENCE AND SOCIAL CHANGE: A REVIEW OF CURRENT LITERATURE. Chicago: Adlai Stevenson Institute of International Affairs, 1968.

Blumberg, Herbert H. AN ANNOTATED BIBLIOGRAPHY OF SERIALS CONCERNED WITH THE NON-VIOLENT PROTEST MOVEMENT. New York: Essay Press, 1969.

Brooks, Gary and Bonnie Brooks. THE LITERATURE ON STUDENT UNREST. Englewood Cliffs, New Jersey: Educational Technology, 1971.

Division of Public Information. THE PEACE CORPS BIBLIOGRAPHY, MARCH 1961–MARCH 1965. Washington, D.C.: U.S. Peace Corps, 1965.

Fink, Ira Stephen. CAMPUS-COMMUNITY RELATIONSHIPS: AN ANNOTATED BIBLIOGRAPHY. Berkeley, California: Institute of Planning Librarians, 1971.

Gibbons, Carol. STUDENT POLITICAL AWARENESS: A SELECTIVE GUIDE TO RESEARCH MATERIALS IN THE UNIVERSITY OF CALIFORNIA (SANTA BARBARA) LIBRARY. Santa Barbara, California: University of California, 1972.

Harris, Evelyn J. GOVERNANCE OF THE UNIVERSITY: A SELECTED BIBLIOGRAPHY. San Diego, California: Malcolm A. Love Library, San Diego State College, 1971.

Heckman, Dale M., and Warren Bryan Martin. INVENTORY OF CURRENT RESEARCH ON HIGHER EDUCATION. New York: McGraw-Hill, 1968.

Hefferlin, J. B. Lon, *et al.* INVENTORY OF CURRENT RESEARCH ON POSTSECONDARY EDUCATION: 1972. Berkeley: Center for Research and Development in Higher Education, University of California, 1972.

Jacqueney, Mona G. RADICALISM ON CAMPUS: 1969–1971. New York: Philosophical Library, 1971.

Kelsey, Roger R. A.A.H.E. BIBLIOGRAPHY ON HIGHER EDUCATION. Washington, D.C.: American Association for Higher Education, 1970.

Keniston, Kenneth. RADICALS AND MILITANTS: AN ANNOTATED BIBLIOGRAPHY OF EMPIRICAL RESEARCH ON CAMPUS UNREST. Lexington, Mass.: Heath-Lexington, 1973.

Leslie, David W. STUDENT UNREST ON THE AMERICAN UNIVERSITY

CAMPUS: A BIBLIOGRAPHY. University Park, Pa. Pennsylvania State University, Center for the Study of Higher Education, 1969.

Meeth, L. Richard, ed. SELECTED ISSUES IN HIGHER EDUCATION: AN ANNOTATED BIBLIOGRAPHY. New York: Institute of Higher Education, Teachers College, Columbia University, 1965.

Moore, Laurence. MARIJUANA (CANNABIS): BIBLIOGRAPHY, 1960–1968. Los Angeles, California: Bruin Humanist Forum, 1969.

Muller, Robert H., Theodore Jurgen Spahn and Janet M. Spahn. FROM RADICAL LEFT TO EXTREME RIGHT: A BIBLIOGRAPHY OF PROTEST, CONTROVERSY, ADVOCACY OR DISSENT. Ann Arbor, Michigan: Campus, 1970.

*Newcombe, Theodore and Kenneth Feldman, THE IMPACT OF COLLEGE ON STUDENTS, San Francisco: Jossey-Bass, 1968. (2 volumes).

Research Committee of Sociologists for Women in Society. BIBLIOGRAPHY OF CURRENT RESEARCH ON SEX ROLES. Berkeley: Research Committee of Sociologists for Women in Society, 1971.

Robinson, Lora H. and Janet Shoenfeld. STUDENT PARTICIPATION IN ACADEMIC GOVERNANCE. Washington, D.C.: ERIC Clearinghouse on Higher Education, 1970.

Schramm, W. THE RESEARCH ON PROGRAMMED INSTRUCTION. AN ANNOTATED BIBLIOGRAPHY. U.S. OFFICE OF EDUCATION BULLETIN NUMBER 35 (OE–34034). Washington, D.C.: U.S. Government Printing Office, 1962.

Shulman, Carol H. LEGAL ISSUES AND STUDENT RIGHTS. Washington, D.C.: ERIC Clearinghouse on Higher Education, 1971.

Suljak, Nedjelko. CAMPUS DISORDER AND CULTURAL COUNTER-REVOLUTION. Davis, California: Institute of Governmental Affairs, University of California, 1970.

Szekely, Kalmans and James L. Jones. HIGHER EDUCATION: ITS MISSION, GOALS, AND PROBLEMS: A SELECTIVE BIBLIOGRAPHY. Bowling Green, Ohio: Bowling Green State University Libraries, Bibliographic Research Center, 1969.

U.S. National Clearinghouse for Mental Health Information. BIBLIOGRAPHY ON DRUG DEPENDENCE AND ABUSE, 1928–1966. Chevy Chase, Maryland: 1969.

U.S. Office of Education. RESEARCH IN SCHOOL AND COLLEGE PERSONNEL SERVICES: SUMMARIES OF UNPUBLISHED STUDIES. September, 1956/September 1958. Washington, D.C.: Government Printing Office.

Westervelt, Esther and Deborah Fixter. WOMEN'S HIGHER AND CONTINUING EDUCATION: AN ANNOTATED BIBLIOGRAPHY. New York: College Entrance Examination Board, 1971.

Williams, Daniel T. THE SOUTHERN STUDENTS' PROTEST MOVEMENT: A BIBLIOGRAPHY. New York: Kraus Reprint, 1970.

Williams, Marguerita P. YOUTH MOVEMENTS HERE AND ABROAD: A SELECTED BIBLIOGRAPHY WITH A DIRECTORY OF LEADING AMERICAN MOVEMENTS. New York: Bulletin of the Russell Sage Foundation, 1936.

Bostick, C. "Individual and War Resistance: A Media List for High School Libraries," LIBRARY JOURNAL, 97 (March 15, 1972), 1140–1145.

"College Student Uprisings," SPECTRUM, 45 (January, 1969), 19–22.

Constance, C. L. "Greeks of the Campus," SCHOOL AND SOCIETY, 30 (September 21, 1929), 409–414.

DiBona, Joseph. "No One Over 30: Books Toward an Understanding of Student Protest," CHOICE, 5 (July–August, 1968), 593–598.

Fairchild, R. P. "Student Challenge and Establishment Response," SOCIAL EDUCATION, 34 (January, 1970), 109–116.

Farrell, E. and L. Ruth. "The Scene," ENGLISH JOURNAL, 58 (December, 1969), 1382–1390.

Foster, Julian. "Student Protest: What Is Known, What Is Said," in J. Foster and D. Long, eds., PROTEST! New York: Morrow, 1970, 27–58.

Hanson, A. H. "Some Literature on Student Revolt," in Bernard Crick and William Robson, eds. PROTEST AND DISCONTENT, 131–150. Baltimore, Maryland: Penguin Books, 1970.

Hull, W. F. IV. "Black Student in Higher Education: A Bibliography," JOURNAL OF COLLEGE STUDENT PERSONNEL, 11 (November, 1970), 423–425.

Hunter, Allen and James O'Brien. "Reading About the New Left," RADICAL AMERICA, 6 (July–August, 1972), 73–94.

Keniston, K. and M. Lerner. "Selected References on Student Protest," ANNALS OF THE AMERICAN ACADEMY OF POLITICAL AND SOCIAL SCIENCE, 395 (May, 1971), 184–194.

Rubin, Isador. "Sex and the College Student: A Bibliography of New Findings and Insights," JOURNAL OF THE NATIONAL ASSOCIATION OF WOMEN DEANS AND COUNSELORS, 26 (1963), 34–39.

Korn, Harold. "Recent Research: A Brief Review," in E. Sampson and H. Korn, eds. STUDENT ACTIVISM AND PROTEST. San Francisco: Jossey-Bass, 1970, 236–256.

·Thomas, Walter L. "A Selected Bibliography on Student Dissent," COLLEGE STUDENT SURVEY, 3 (Spring, 1969), 6–7.

Bostick, C. "Individual and War Resistance: A Media List for High School Libraries," LIBRARY JOURNAL, 97 (March 15, 1972), 1140–1145.

"College Student Uprisings," SPECTRUM, 45 (January, 1969), 19–22.

Constance, C. L. "Greeks of the Campus," SCHOOL AND SOCIETY, 30 (September 21, 1929), 409–414.

DiBona, Joseph. "No One Over 30: Books Toward an Understanding of Student Protest," CHOICE, 5 (July–August, 1968), 593–598.

Fairchild, R. P. "Student Challenge and Establishment Response," SOCIAL EDUCATION, 34 (January, 1970), 109–116.

Farrell, E. and L. Ruth. "The Scene," ENGLISH JOURNAL, 58 (December, 1969), 1382–1390.

Foster, Julian. "Student Protest: What Is Known, What Is Said," in J. Foster and D. Long, eds., PROTEST! New York: Morrow, 1970, 27–58.

Hanson, A. H. "Some Literature on Student Revolt," in Bernard Crick and William Robson, eds. PROTEST AND DISCONTENT, 131–150. Baltimore, Maryland: Penguin Books, 1970.

Hull, W. F. IV. "Black Student in Higher Education: A Bibliography," JOURNAL OF COLLEGE STUDENT PERSONNEL, 11 (November, 1970), 423–425.

Hunter, Allen and James O'Brien. "Reading About the New Left," RADICAL AMERICA, 6 (July–August, 1972), 73–94.

Keniston, K. and M. Lerner. "Selected References on Student Protest," ANNALS OF THE AMERICAN ACADEMY OF POLITICAL AND SOCIAL SCIENCE, 395 (May, 1971), 184–194.

Rubin, Isador. "Sex and the College Student: A Bibliography of New Findings and Insights," JOURNAL OF THE NATIONAL ASSOCIATION OF WOMEN DEANS AND COUNSELORS, 26 (1963), 34–39.

Korn, Harold. "Recent Research: A Brief Review," in E. Sampson and H. Korn, eds. STUDENT ACTIVISM AND PROTEST. San Francisco: Jossey-Bass, 1970, 236–256.

· Thomas, Walter L. "A Selected Bibliography on Student Dissent," COLLEGE STUDENT SURVEY, 3 (Spring, 1969), 6–7.

About the Authors

Philip G. Altbach is Associate Professor of Educational Policy Studies and South Asian Studies at the University of Wisconsin-Madison. He has been Lecturer on Education and Research Associate at the Center for International Affairs at Harvard University. He is author of *Student Politics in America* (1973), *University in Transition: An Indian Case Study* (1972), *Student Politics in Bombay* (1968), and editor of *Academic Supermarkets* (with R. Laufer and S. McVey, 1971), *The New Pilgrims* (with R. Laufer, 1971), and *Students in Revolt* (with S.M. Lipset, 1970). Dr. Altbach is also Associate Editor of the *Comparative Education Review.*

David H. Kelly is a Ph.D. candidate in American history at Indiana University.